THE ILLUSTRATOR 6 BOOK

Deke McClelland

LightSpeed Publishing
Glen Ellen, California

Peachpit Press
Berkeley, California

THE ILLUSTRATOR 6 BOOK

Deke McClelland

PEACHPIT PRESS

2414 Sixth Street
Berkeley, CA 94710
510/548-4393
800/283-9444
510/548-5991 (fax)

Find us on the World Wide Web at:
http://www.peachpit.com

Peachpit Press is a division of Addison Wesley Longman

Editor: Scott Calamar, LightSpeed Publishing
Cover design: TMA Ted Mader Associates
Part opener art: Ron Chan
Interior design and production: Michele Cuneo

ISBN 0-201-88610-3

9 8 7 6 5 4 3 2 1

Printed and bound in the United States of America

DEDICATION

*This book is dedicated to my cool blue Lava Lite,
which captures primordial ooze in perpetual
motion. It says so right here on the box.*

ACKNOWLEDGMENTS

The creation of this book has generally been a modest affair, involving myself and a few friends sniffing processing chemicals as we ground out the pages. But I needed the help of some earnest and capable professionals to wrench the book apart and reassemble the pieces to create this most recent edition. I owe a sincere debt of gratitude to these wonderful folks.

Thanks first to Roslyn Bullas and Ted Nace at Peachpit Press, who gave me the time and support I needed to produce the best book that my finite capabilities will permit. The net result would have been a sprawling mess of gook without the considerable help and talents of the crew at LightSpeed Publishing, including production supervisor Joel Fugazzotto, designer Michele Cuneo, and my most-excellent editor Scott Calamar.

Thanks to the invaluable encouragement and advice of super-agent Matt Wagner. Thanks also to Ron Chan, the singularly gifted artist who created the parts pages. Rarely have I encountered such a pleasant blend of killer aptitude and affable modesty.

Finally, thanks to the folks I conned into quotes, including David Pogue, Sandee Cohen, and newly christened international correspondent Jeanette Borzo. Thanks also to the many readers and user group reviewers who have contributed comments and valuable insights over the years.

Elizabeth Pheasant is in a class all by herself, which is why I married her. Life is a dream, sweetheart.

CONTENTS AT A GLANCE

TABLE OF CONTENTS

Chapter 2
Witness the Splendor That Is Illustrator 13

Chapter 3
Objects, Images, and the File Formats that Love Them 57

PART TWO
CREATING

Chapter 4
Drawing the Simple Stuff

Chapter 5
Exact Points and Precision Curves 135

Chapter 6
How to Handle Typical Type 179

Chapter 7
Some of Your Wackier Text Effects 217

Chapter 8
This Is Your Brain on Graphs 273

PART THREE
CHANGING 325

Chapter 9
Modifying and Combining Paths 327

Chapter 10
Developing a Flair for the Schematic 375

Chapter 11
Traditional Homespun Transformations 415

Chapter 12
Hog-Wild Special Effects 449

Chapter 13
Becoming Master of the Raster 481

PART FOUR
COLORING 513

Chapter 14
The Slippery Science of Color 515

Chapter 15
Gradations and Other Fab Fills 551

Chapter 16
Stroking Your Curves 597

Chapter 17
Blends, Masks, and Special Inks 641

Chapter 18
Printing Your Illustrations 687

Index 725

INTRODUCTION

Although I'm still in my early thirties, a phase that's sadly unlikely to last too much longer, I sometimes feel like a crusty old codger who's witnessed more than anyone cares to hear recounted. For instance, I might venture that where computer graphics are concerned, you are spoiled rotten. Adobe Illustrator is a prime example of a professional-quality application that—despite any problems you may or may not have with it—performs without crashing and prints like a champ. You can get up in the morning, start working in the program, and expect to make substantial progress. The darn thing works.

It's quite a different story than when I was a boy. I don't think I could have endured desktop publishing back in 1986—before Illustrator hit the market—if I hadn't been a kid. When I began working as artistic director for a small service bureau, our world consisted of a laughably inept collection of software and hardware. We had PageMaker 1.2 to lay out pages. Sure, the files corrupted regularly and the program took an extra 15 minutes to print a page with a downloadable font on it, but it was better than facing the customer and admitting that desktop publishing was a cruel joke.

We used a program called FullPaint to create black-and-white bitmapped graphics, because it could rotate a selection (an operation that MacPaint couldn't handle). We scanned images using a ThunderScanner, which boasted photocopier quality when it wasn't stretching and slanting photos as it curled them around its roller. There were less than 100 fonts in all the world, most of which were clumsily executed by folks still learning their trade. For printing, we had a Linotronic 100 imagesetter—the number of which coincidentally corresponded to the thousands of dollars it cost—and a film processor that looked and acted like it had fallen off the back of a truck. And our best computer was a supercharged Macintosh 512Ke with a whopping 2MB of RAM and two 400K floppy drives. There wasn't such a thing as a hard drive.

The following year, we purchased better machines, we upgraded PageMaker, and we continued to pour expensive chemicals into our increasingly frightening processor. But the event that most changed how *I* worked was the arrival of Illustrator 1.0. It was the first drawing program that worked worth a hill of beans. MacDraw was nearly unusable; you couldn't get two lines to properly match up with each other. And though CricketDraw permitted gradations and type along a curve—both missing from Illustrator at the time—it crashed on the hour and absolutely refused to print to our imagesetter. Frankly, that program went a long way toward loosening my fragile grasp on reality.

But Illustrator was an entirely different kind of program, quite unlike anything that I had used before. Although other programs supplied more features, Illustrator provided exactly what I needed, implemented in the most logical fashion I could imagine. But most importantly, I could actually depend on the program. Call me a sentimental fool, but I have no memory of it ever once crashing or failing to print. It always came through.

The new Illustrator is far more capable than its distant ancestor. And though nostalgia may cloud my judgment, it's frequently less logical and less streamlined. But it remains the most reliable application for printing computer-generated graphics that I've ever used. After eight years of writing, designing, and reworking this book, I have yet to conceive of a graphic that I couldn't manage one way or other. I can still open every illustration just as I originally created it, with no line, shape, or character of text missing or moving on the page. (I'd love to see *any* version of PageMaker do that.) And I know that everything I draw will eventually print, even if it requires some minor modifications. Mind you, I don't like everything about Illustrator—in fact, there are quite a few features I would change—but this is an important program that has *never* been absent from any of my hard drives. Heck, I'd still be using Illustrator 1.0 if Adobe hadn't upgraded the program.

Now, tell me honestly. I sound like I'm at least 86, don't I?

Illustrator and You

Adobe Illustrator 6 is a drawing program that exists only for the Macintosh computer. (The Windows version is currently lagging behind at Version 4.1.) You can draw high-contrast graphics with perfectly smooth edges. You can also edit the outline of any shape long after you create it. You see Illustrator graphics every day in newspapers, magazines, and other print media; they're even turning up in large numbers on the World Wide Web. Artists use Illustrator to create diagrams, info-art, maps, logos, posters, photo-realistic renderings, and all sorts of other illustrations that defy categorization. You can even integrate photographs corrected and enhanced in Adobe Photoshop or a similar application.

Illustrator is a graphics workshop; as expansive, elaborate, and perplexing as any traditional workshop on earth. Like any powerful collection of tools, Illustrator demands your attention and rewards your understanding. That's why this book guides you through every feature of the program as if you've never seen a drawing application in your life. Regardless of your level of experience, you'll find yourself easily graduating into the advanced topics that consume most of the pages in this book. Every section explains not only how to perform a technique, but also provides enough background so you know why you'd want to. And most importantly, there isn't a single detail in any of the several hundreds illustrations that I don't tell you how to create yourself. Though I hope they're pleasing to look at, my figures aren't meant to amaze; they're included to educate. I want you to amaze yourself.

The Long and Painful History of a Bestseller

This book is as old as the hills. It's not the longest running book on Illustrator, but it is the second oldest, originally distributed by a different publisher in 1988. Counting an edition for an early Windows version of the product—which sold abysmally poorly—you are now holding the sixth edition of this book.

This edition's predecessor, *The Illustrator 5.0/5.5 Book*, was the bestselling title on Illustrator. Naturally, I find this fact highly gratifying. But whenever I look at the book, I see only problems. Not the smattering of typos and the occasional factual errors—unpleasant as such mistakes are, they are virtually impossible to avoid. The more significant problem was the quality of the writing, the appearance of the figures, and the general organization. None of these factors measured up to its full potential. (What can I say? I'm older and more experienced than I was back in 1986.)

Over the years, I have consistently upgraded text and figures from previous editions. But while I always added new material, some old stuff continued to linger. The new writing was lively, the old writing was stiff; the new voice was active, the old voice was passive; the new figures were insightful, the old ones inane. Part of the difficulty was that I was trying to do too many jobs at once. In addition to the writing and artwork chores, I had been in charge of design, layout, typesetting, and even overseeing the editing. As a result, I was working inside documents that had their origins in PageMaker 2.0. The fact that most of the files opened year after year without text and figures altogether corrupting qualified as a minor miracle. In this atmosphere, compromise was inevitable.

Predictably, this changes with *The Illustrator 6 Book*. (I wouldn't tell you this story if the punchline were, "Guess what? *The Illustrator 6 Book* is more of the same!") This edition is altogether reorganized, rewritten, and redesigned. I turned over design, layout, editing, and typesetting responsibilities to the capable people at LightSpeed Publishing, leaving me free to concentrate on the text and figures. And concentrate I have. I spent four times as long creating this edition as the last one, and I hope you'll agree, the quality of the results are well worth the effort.

The Structure of This Book

If you're familiar with previous editions of this book, don't expect to find much of anything where it was before. I've pretty much dumped the old book on the floor, sorted out and thrown away 95 percent of it, and reassembled the remaining 5 percent with a tremendous amount of new stuff.

The Illustrator 6 Book contains a total of 18 chapters organized into four distinct parts. Each part explores a simple concept in exhaustive and engaging detail. My hope is that at the end of every part, you feel sufficiently confident with the material that you begin to see the gaps in my explanations. "Oh, sure, you can do *that*, but how about *this*, and *this*, and *this*?" Once you understand the topics, you can invent techniques on your own without the slightest hesitation.

Part One, Starting: The first part contains three chapters that introduce the fundamental issues in Illustrator 6. I explain how Illustrator differs from other graphics programs. I introduce you to Illustrator's network of tools and palettes. And I tell you everything there is to know about the new file formats included with Illustrator 6. If you're familiar with previous editions of Illustrator, this part will get you up and running in no time at all.

 Part Two, Creating: These five chapters tell you how to create the basic type and graphic elements in Illustrator. I explain all the tricks you need to know to get the most out of the new polygon, star, and spiral tools. I make sense out of the pen tool and Bézier curves. Chapters 6 and 7 devote close to 100 pages to the topic of creating and editing text. And I close the part with a look at one of Illustrator's most overlooked features, charts and graphs.

 Part Three, Changing: In sculpture, a substance like clay is considered "forgiving" by comparison to, say, marble because it permits you to modify your mistakes. By this standard, Illustrator provides the most forgiving environment possible. Nothing in Illustrator is permanent; everything you create is subject to adjustment. In Chapters 9 through 13, I tell you how to cut apart lines and shapes, and how to put them back together again. I spend more pages discussing such essential features as compound paths and Pathfinder filters than any other book. I also make sense of Illustrator's transformation and special effects capabilities. And this book alone spends an entire chapter showing you how to exploit the new relationship between Illustrator 6 and Photoshop.

 Part Four, Coloring: To keep the cover price as low as possible, there is no color in this book. And yet, I devote more than 200 pages showing you how color works, how to use color, and how to print grayscale and color illustrations. If you want to see color, there are books more colorful. But if you want to master and manage color, this book contains everything there is to know. Chapter 14 simplifies the science of color and shows how it applies to Illustrator 6. Later chapters cover gradations, tile patterns, strokes, blends, masks, and the new Ink Pen patterns. I wrap up with printing in Chapter 18. Though you certainly don't need to know everything in this perhaps overly thorough chapter, I can't be accused of leaving anything out.

I've written the chapters so you can read them from beginning to end without finding the information either repetitive or overwhelming. If you prefer to read when you're stumped, you can look up a confusing topic in the index. Or you can simply browse through the pictures until you come to something that looks interesting. But no matter how you approach the text, I hope that it snags you and teaches you more than you bargained for. If you look up from the book at your watch and think, "Dang, I've got to get back to work!" then I've done my job.

Meet the Margin Icons

Throughout this book, we've designed two kinds of special text elements to attract your attention and convey fast information. The first are the figure captions. A caption is worthless unless it tells you something about the figure that you don't already know. Between the graphic and the caption text, an experienced user should be able to glean enough information to perform a similar effect in Illustrator. If you need to know more, the text contains the full story, including additional hints and details. But you shouldn't *have* to read if you don't want to.

The second special text element is the icon text. If a paragraph contains very important information or an offhand aside that you can feel free to skip, I include an icon next to the paragraph to distinguish it from the surrounding text. If you already know Illustrator, you can get up to speed in Illustrator 6 by just reading these paragraphs.

Here are the four icons that you can expect to jockey for your attention:

This icon points out features that are new to Illustrator 6. Sometimes, the paragraph tells you everything you need to know about the new feature. Other times, the icon introduces several pages of text. Either way, you'll know it's something you didn't have in Illustrator 5.5 or earlier.

It seems like every book offers a tip icon. So I try to steer clear of the boring old tips that every Illustrator user hears a million times, and concentrate on the juicy stuff that most folks don't know. But keep in mind, these are fast tips. For the more involved killer techniques, you have to read the text.

This icon explains an action to avoid. Few operations are hazardous in Illustrator, but many are time wasters. And you can bet that after I tell you what not to do, I include a preferable alternative as well.

I've been using Illustrator and other Macintosh programs for as long as they've been out, so I occasionally feel compelled to share my thoughts on a variety of subjects. Sometimes it's a bit of history, other times it's a thoughtful observation, and every once in a while it's just me complaining. Whatever it is, you can skip it if it gets on your nerves.

Contacting the Guy Who's Responsible for All This Gibberish

I have close to ten books on the market at any one time. These plus my magazine and speaking commitments keep me busier than I care to admit. With one thing and another, I regret that I can't talk to every reader. But I do invite you to submit your comments, questions, and general observations to either one of two electronic mail accounts:

- If you're on America Online, write me at DekeMc. Or if you're on the Internet, try DekeMc@AOL.com.
- My CompuServe address is 70640,670.

I'm not very regular about checking and responding to my e-mail, so you can expect a delay of a week to a month, depending on what the current deadline situation is like. But you have my word. One day, when you least expect it, you'll hear back from me.

PART ONE
STARTING

ILLUSTRATOR 6: WHAT IT IS

Illustrator: what is it? Illustrator 6: what's new? That's the stuff of Chapter 1. This chapter is a general overview of Illustrator, specifically the most recent Version 6.

For those of you who have never used Illustrator before, I'll tell you what it is and why you've probably heard its name bandied about. I'll show you where it fits into the world of computer graphics. Along the way you'll see Illustrator's relation to its more popular sibling, Photoshop—a graphics program with an entirely different purpose.

3

If you're a long-time Illustrator enthusiast, this chapter provides some amusing—if not terribly insightful—analysis, along with a practical assessment of Illustrator 6's new capabilities. I even tell you which chapter to turn to for more information on the new features.

Adobe, the Microsoft of Graphics

To understand Illustrator, you have to know the company behind it. Adobe Systems is among of the five largest software companies in this quadrant of the galaxy. It is widely considered to be the one software developer that Microsoft cannot destroy. Adobe knows electronic graphics and design; Microsoft never will. It's that simple.

Case in point: Photoshop, Adobe's phenomenally successful image-editing program. Regarded as the most powerful personal computer application for mucking around with computerized photographs, Photoshop is equally revered by expert and novice, young and old, educated and self-taught, sophisticate and bottom-feeding slimefish. Photoshop isn't altogether perfect, but it has universal appeal.

Microsoft, meanwhile, has squat: no image editor now, none planned for the future.

Adobe also sells Premiere, the number one program for editing computerized video sequences. Premiere needs a fast computer and an awfully big hard disk, and you need special hardware to capture the movies and then send them back out to videotape. But there's absolutely nothing like it for messing around with moving images and creating simple animated effects.

Microsoft is currently unaware of any need for a video editing package among the populace at large.

Are you beginning to see the trend? Adobe is absolutely steeped in the world of professional artistry and business graphics, and Microsoft hasn't even begun to compete. And perhaps they never will.

In the mind of your everyday industry analyst, Adobe is the Microsoft of graphics. Like Microsoft, Adobe is the dominant force, not only lording it over an entire discipline of computing with an iron fist but also managing to consistently churn out quality software. Lesser companies regard Adobe with a combination of envy, respect, and fear. For better or worse, Adobe is currently where the artwork is.

Where Illustrator Fits in

Illustrator is important because it set current events in motion. Prior to Illustrator—back in the mid-1980s, when the world was learning to pronounce

Mikhail Gorbachev and Scritti Politti—Adobe was the small company that had invented the PostScript printing language. PostScript revolutionized the world of typesetting and jump-started the career of at least one computer author, but it didn't exactly make Adobe a household word (except in New Mexico, where adobe households are quite common).

The problem with PostScript was its inaccessibility. In theory, PostScript let you design incredibly ornate, twisty curvy lines and fill them with any of several millions of colors. But unless you wanted to resort to PostScript programming—the equivalent of instructing a friend to draw an object by reciting numerical coordinates over the phone—your options were limited to text surrounded by a few straight lines and rectangles.

Illustrator single-handedly changed all this. One of the few programs designed from start to finish by Adobe employees—Photoshop, Premiere, PageMaker, and other top titles started out as non-Adobe products—Illustrator was so far-and-away better than anything that had previously blessed the Macintosh computer that artists started moving to the Mac strictly to use this one program. Before Illustrator, Macintosh graphics looked blocky and turgid; after Illustrator, most folks couldn't tell Mac graphics from those drawn with pen and ink. The transition couldn't have been more abrupt, or more welcome.

Close, But Not Kin: Illustrator Versus Photoshop

Now in its tenth year, many artists see Illustrator as a kind of support program for Photoshop, thanks to the latter's dramatic and overshadowing success. Mind you, Illustrator's growth has been consistent and commendable over the years, and to this day it remains the world's most popular PostScript drawing program. But Photoshop manages to sell roughly twice as well, despite being nearly three years younger.

Truth be told, Adobe tries to piggyback Illustrator on Photoshop's success. Since Photoshop came out, Illustrator's popularity has mushroomed, and the two programs have become more and more closely related. But they remain highly independent creatures, and both belong on your computer at all times.

Illustrator Does Smooth Lines; Photoshop Does Pixels

The easiest way to explain how Illustrator works is to start off explaining how it does *not* work, and that is precisely how Photoshop *does* work. As its name implies, Photoshop's primary purpose is to edit photographs. When you scan a photograph into a computer, the software converts it to a collection of tiny colored *pixels*. Each pixel is perfectly square, and one is perfectly adjacent to the next with no wiggle room between them. The only purpose of Photoshop's hundred or so functions is to adjust the colors of these pixels.

Although you can force Illustrator to edit pixels in a comparatively crude fashion, its main purpose is to create line art. Each line, shape, and character of text is altogether independent of its neighbors. These independent elements are known collectively as *objects*, which is why Illustrator is sometimes called an *object-oriented* application. Illustrator keeps track of each object by assigning it a separate mathematical equation. (Don't worry, there is no math in this book. Well, none that's important, anyway.) Illustrator later prints the lines, shapes, and text by sending the equations to the printer and letting the printer figure it out. The result is uniformly smooth artwork, with high-contrast edges and crisp detail.

The Right Tool for the Right Job

As you might imagine, this difference in purpose leads to a difference in approach. Pixels are great for representing continuous color transitions, in which one color gradually changes into another. Such color transitions are the norm in real life, which is why pixels are so well suited to photographs. (Experienced/pretentious computer artists have even been known to call photographs *continuous-tone images*, but for our purposes, just plain *image* will suffice.)

Illustrator, though, is perfect for high-contrast artwork, which can vary from schematic, or cartoonish to just barely stylized. This kind of computer art is known as a *drawing* or *illustration*.

Take as examples the two graphics in Figure 1-1. Both depict a sea lion in an attitude of aquatic grace, to be sure. But while the first is a photograph snapped by Marty Snyderman and distributed on CD-ROM by Digital Stock Professional, the second is a line drawing created in Illustrator. To achieve the left-hand image, I converted the color image to grayscale, corrected the brightness and contrast, and sharpened the focus, all in Photoshop. To achieve the right-hand illustration, I had to meticulously trace the photograph in Illustrator and fill each shape with a different shade of gray.

The first image looks like a photo. But while the second is a recognizable member of the wildlife community, it is obviously executed by human hands, not snapped with a camera. This is the most significant difference between Photoshop and Illustrator.

Flexible Resizing

Another difference is in the details. Photoshop's details can be grainy, but Illustrator's are forever smooth.

Figure 1-1: A photographic image enhanced in Photoshop (left) compared with a line drawing created in Illustrator (right).

As you increase the size of a Photoshop image, the square pixels likewise grow and become more obvious. On the left side of Figure 1-2, for example, I've enlarged the sea lion image to 200, 400, and 800 percent. At each level of magnification of the photograph, your eye is better able to separate the pixels as individual colored squares. As a result, a photograph looks great when printed at high *resolutions*, that is, when a lot of pixels are packed into a small space. But it begins to look coarse, jagged, and out of focus when printed at low resolutions, with fewer pixels per inch.

Illustrator art isn't like that at all. As shown on the right side of Figure 1-2, the drawing looks great no matter how much you enlarge it. Every line is mathematically accurate regardless of size. The downside, of course, is that it took me about five minutes to adjust the sea lion photo in Photoshop, but almost three hours to draw the sea lion in Illustrator. Apart from the photography process itself, illustrations typically require a more sizable time investment than photographic images.

Objects and Pixels Together

The final difference between Photoshop and Illustrator is that Photoshop can handle only pixels, while Illustrator accommodates both. Don't get me wrong, Photoshop is several times more capable than Illustrator where pixels are concerned,

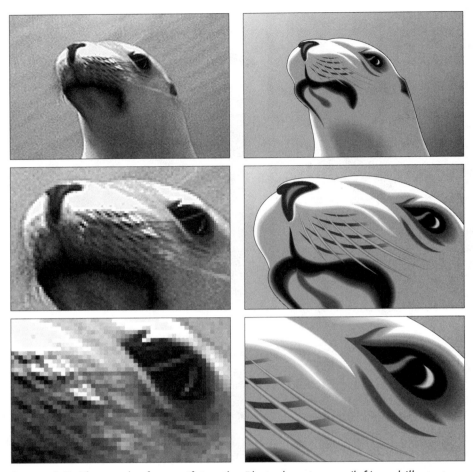

Figure 1-2: The result of magnifying the Photoshop image (left) and Illustrator drawing (right) to 200, 400, and 800 percent.

but Photoshop doesn't do anything except pixels. With Illustrator, you can draw objects as well as import images from Photoshop or some other pixel editor. Figure 1-3 shows the object-oriented sea lion layered in front of the original Photoshop image, so that the image serves as a background.

But to interpret Illustrator's acceptance of pixels as an advantage over Photoshop's ignorance of objects misses the point. Illustrator and Photoshop are designed to work together, more now than ever before. There may even be times when you prefer to convert an entire illustration to pixels inside Photoshop to apply special effects that only Photoshop can handle, or merely to simplify the

Figure 1-3:
This inspiring
creature is the
product of Photoshop
and Illustrator
working together.

printing process since the printer has to solve fewer equations. Illustrator and Photoshop are two halves of the artistic process, each taking up where the other one leaves off, each making up for the other one's weaknesses. It's the perfect marriage, and you're the happy beneficiary.

The Lowdown on Illustrator 6

 If you're familiar with previous versions of Illustrator, then you probably already know the stuff I've told you so far (although it never hurts to revisit the basics every now and then). What you may not know is what the new Illustrator 6 has to offer that its predecessors did not. For you, I provide the following quick but riveting list, designed to get you up and running with little pain and lots of potential. Note that I also indicate which corresponding chapter spells out the new feature in detail, so you know where to turn when you need more information.

- **Support for more formats (Chapter 3)**: Illustrator 5.5 and older versions supported the EPS and PDF (Adobe Acrobat) formats, and that's about it. It was very sad and the programmers were thoroughly ashamed of themselves. But now, Version 6 has redeemed itself by supporting such popular and essential file formats as TIFF (yes, TIFF!), JPEG, Windows formats BMP and PCX, Kodak Photo CD, and more. You can even colorize black-and-white TIFF images, just as you've been able to do in rival program FreeHand since 1988. Honestly, it's about time!

- **Improved compatibility with Photoshop (Chapter 13)**: Illustrator 6 and Photoshop 3.0.5 now trade low-resolution images and objects as effortlessly as sisters trade culottes. You drag objects into Photoshop and convert them to pixels on the fly, or drag images from Photoshop directly into Illustrator. Though System 7.5 has permitted dragging and dropping between applications for some time, Illustrator and Photoshop are two of the earliest programs to put the technique into practice.

- **Lift colors from imported images (Chapter 14)**: You can lift colors from an image imported into Illustrator—or from a background image opened inside Photoshop!—by clicking on the color with the eyedropper tool. Illustrator automatically converts the color to CMYK (Cyan, Magenta, Yellow, Black; the four process colors), even if the image is grayscale.

- **Change objects into pixels (Chapter 13)**: In the past, if you wanted to convert a handful of objects into pixels, a technique known as *rasterizing,* you had to save the illustration as an EPS file and open the file in Photoshop. No more. Now you can rasterize objects inside Illustrator. Nothing earth-shattering, just a convenient feature, but useful nonetheless.

- **Photoshop filters (Chapter 13)**: After selecting an imported or rasterized image inside Illustrator 6, you can apply a Photoshop-compatible filter to it. Now, Photoshop isn't the only program that does Radial Blur. Adobe has even gone so far as to throw in twelve filters from its three-volume Gallery Effects collection.

- **Dialog box previews (Chapter 3)**: Not to be outdone by Photoshop, you can now add previews to your Illustrator files, visible inside the standard Open dialog box. So if the name of a file doesn't ring a bell,

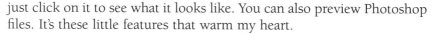

just click on it to see what it looks like. You can also preview Photoshop files. It's these little features that warm my heart.

More logical plug-in organization (various chapters): As in Illustrator 5.5, *plug-ins* are little miniprograms that enhance Illustrator's core capabilities. One plug-in lets you align objects, for example, while another draws stars. In the past, all plug-ins manifested themselves as commands under the Filter menu—even though most of them were completely unrelated. But life is more logical with Illustrator 6. A plug-in can appear under any menu, or it can even be a palette or a tool, as in the case of the new Align palette and the star tool. There are still too many miscellaneous plug-ins in the Filter menu, but at least we're headed in the right direction.

The Control palette (Chapter 10): Illustrator now includes a Control palette, like the one in PageMaker, which lets you position objects numerically and scale and rotate them without using tools. Frankly, the implementation could be a lot better—for example, you can't specify the position of individual points or even determine how many points are in a shape—but no doubt it satisfies one of Adobe's cross-application compatibility rules.

The knife tool (Chapter 9): In addition to the standard scissors tool, which lets you sever a line at a point, Illustrator 6 provides a knife tool. Drag to slice an object apart in an irregular, knifelike fashion.

Improved special-effects filters (Chapter 12): In Illustrator 5.5, you could distort objects using a series of special-effects filters similar to those found in Photoshop. But to make them work, you had to add anchor points to your objects, increasing their complexity and ensuring some downright ugly results. Illustrator 6 includes new curve-fitting technology that makes distortion filters smarter. This enables them to change the curvature of segments and add anchor points where needed. Although this may sound somewhat esoteric, you'll see that it's a very practical enhancement.

Stroke lines with custom path patterns (Chapter 16): Just as you can fill objects with custom tile patterns, you can now create patterns that follow the outline of a line or shape. You design a base pattern and then create variations for the inner and outer corners. Illustrator 6 stretches and rotates pattern elements to fit the object.

Create cross-hatch patterns (Chapter 17): The so-called Ink Pen has got to be Illustrator 6's strangest and most complicated feature. Simply put, it fills a selected shape with a crosshatch pattern that you design using the scariest set of controls you've ever seen in your life. Most folks won't have the patience for it—Adobe doesn't even acknowledge Ink Pen's existence in its marketing material—but it is certainly interesting.

- **Expand gradients to blends (Chapter 17)**: Ever wished you could make slight adjustments to an automated gradation? Well, now you can. Choose the Expand command to convert a gradation into a blend with as many steps as you want. You can also convert tile patterns to objects, a great way to avoid printing errors.

- **Find and eliminate stray gunkage (Chapter 10)**: A new Cleanup filter finds all stray points, transparent objects, and empty text blocks and deletes them.

- **Let Illustrator do the math (Chapter 10)**: If you want to adjust a value, but you can't do the math in your head, have Illustrator do it for you. To add a smidgen or subtract a mite, just enter the math—say, 4–1 or 3+2—into an option box, hit the Return key, and Illustrator will perform the calculation.

- **Print color separations from inside Illustrator (Chapter 18)**: For reasons that no one quite understands, Illustrator has long required you to use a separate utility to print color separations. No more. Illustrator 6 offers a single command, Separation Setup, that provides access to the revised color printing operations. This is the way it should have been all along.

The Illustrator 6 package also includes a few hundred fonts, lots of clip-art and stock photography, and a collection of path patterns to help get you started. In addition you also get Dimensions 2, Adobe's 3-D drawing utility. You can design 3-D objects in Dimensions, copy them, and paste them into Illustrator without any loss in quality, thanks to Adobe's new PostScript-on-Clipboard feature.

Well, as you can see, there's a lot here to learn. So let's get started.

CHAPTER 2

WITNESS THE SPLENDOR THAT IS ILLUSTRATOR

Whenever I hear folks speak about Illustrator, someone always seems to drop the word *elegant* into the conversation. And truly, it fits. Despite its occasional flaws, Illustrator has always delivered a rare combination of logical interface and extremely reliable performance. What, I ask you, could be more elegant than that?

But even an elegant application can bewilder and vex the user it has sworn to serve. The biggest strike against Illustrator is that it doesn't always work like other programs. You can't resize an object by dragging a corner handle, as you can in every other drawing program on the planet. Illustrator provides three different arrow tools, whereas all other programs manage to make do with one. You change the performance of many tools by clicking *with* them, rather than double-clicking *on* them. The program lacks a regular grid (although Illustrator 4.1 for Windows has one), the pen tool takes some getting used to, and many of the keyboard equivalents are just plain weird.

The end result is that the elegant Illustrator is hard to learn. Once you come to terms with it, you'll never go back. But coming to terms with it takes some concentrated and patient effort.

This chapter is my way of introducing Illustrator to new users, reminding casual users how it works, and bringing long-time users up to speed. I explain the interface, briefly introduce the tools and palettes, and examine every single one of the preference settings in excruciating detail. I round out the chapter with a comprehensive list of keyboard equivalents and other shortcuts that should save you a lot of time over the long run.

None of this stuff is meant to be read sequentially. Feel free to skip around, read bits and pieces over the course of several weeks, or cut out the pages and fold them into paper airplanes. Follow whatever learning style makes you smart in the shortest amount of time.

Getting Illustrator Up and Running

Most folks are pretty clear on how you start up a program on the Mac, and Illustrator is no exception. For example, you can double-click on the Adobe Illustrator icon, which looks like a face with a triangle covering one of the eyes. Or you can double-click on any Illustrator file. Or you can drag some other suitable file onto the Illustrator application icon. Some folks call this technique *launching* a program, or *running* a program. But whatever you call it, you have to do it before you can use Illustrator.

Setting Aside Memory

Prior to starting up Illustrator, you may want to adjust the amount of memory (called *RAM*, like the goat) that your Mac assigns to the application. To do this, first select the Adobe Illustrator application icon and choose the Get Info command from the File menu (or press ⌘-I while the icon is highlighted).

This brings up the dialog box shown in Figure 2-1. Change the Preferred Size value to assign more or less RAM to Illustrator. (Even though you can also change the Minimum Size value, don't do it! Lowering this value can wreak havoc on Illustrator's performance and may even prevent the program from running.)

Not sure how much RAM to assign to Illustrator? First of all, don't lower the value to less than the Minimum Size value. Illustrator absolutely needs a certain amount of memory, and the Minimum Size value is it.

You can raise the Preferred Size value to as high as 90 percent of the free RAM available to your Mac. (You need to leave the other 10 percent free so the Macintosh system has enough wiggle room to expand and contract.) To check how much RAM is free, choose About This Macintosh from the Apple ( ) menu and check out the Largest Unused Block value. Generally speaking, you don't need to assign more than 14,000K to Illustrator, unless you plan on importing a lot of images or applying path operations to lots of complex objects.

The Splash Screen

After you launch Illustrator, the splash screen shows you that your computer is indeed obeying your instructions. Little messages come up telling you that

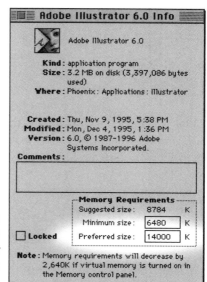

Figure 2-1:
You can change the
Preferred Size value, but
it's best to leave
Minimum Size alone.

Illustrator is loading fonts or reading plug-ins. This is a perfect time to get a cup of coffee.

If you ever want to look at the splash screen again, choose About Illustrator from the Apple menu. Of course, there's no practical reason you'd ever want to do this, but there are a couple of silly features that you might find mildly amusing, depending on how desperate you are for entertainment:

 Click on the Adobe icon to watch a silly animated sequence that features little colored dots turning into the words Adobe Illustrator and some pictures of the programmers. Click again to make the silly animation go away. There are actually many sequences, so you can click on the logo over and over again if you can't think of anything better to do.

● Wait a while to see a list of credits. Whoopee.

● Press the Option key while choosing the About Illustrator command to see the programmers' silly nicknames, followed by something about a short-lived creature named Popeye (which is actually the code name for the alpha version of Illustrator 6).

● Click or press a key to make the splash screen go away.

There you have it, a bunch of silly information that won't do you a lick of good, except to clog your mind when you're in your dotage. I wouldn't blame you if you tore this page out of the book, ripped it up, and used the fragments to pick your teeth.

 Well, except for one other thing. You know all that silly animation? It takes up a fair amount of room in Illustrator's RAM partition. Around 200K to 300K. To streamline Illustrator, you can delete the animation file from memory. Just take the About Box Extension file from the Extensions folder inside the Plug-ins folder and throw it in the trash. This saves room on disk and in memory. If you're serious about getting work done in Illustrator, the animation has got to go.

The Illustrator Desktop

After the splash screen goes away, the Illustrator desktop takes over the screen, as in Figure 2-2. Illustrator automatically creates a new illustration window so you can start right in drawing, without wasting another fraction of a second.

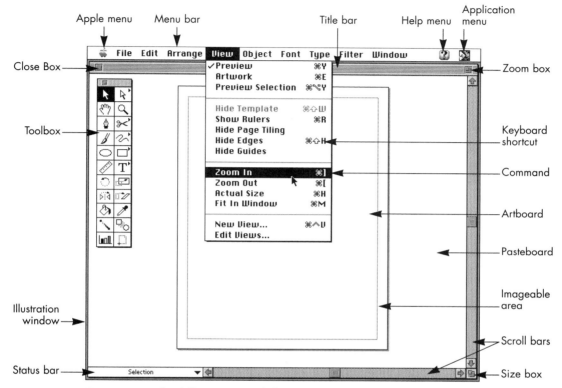

Figure 2-2: The fully annotated Illustrator 6 desktop.

If you've been working on the Mac for any amount of time, you're probably familiar with the basic desktop elements labeled in Figure 2-2. If you're new to the Mac, however, or new to Illustrator, go ahead and read over the following descriptions. (Labeled items from the figure appear in italic type.)

● The *menu bar* provides access to Illustrator 6's nine menus, as well as the universal *Apple, Help,* and *Application* menus, all identified by icons. Drag on a menu name to display a list of *commands* that perform various operations. To choose a command, drag on top of it so it becomes highlighted, then release. *Keyboard shortcuts* are listed to the right of commands. If a command is dimmed (like Hide Template in Figure 2-2), it isn't applicable to the current situation. You can't choose a dimmed command.

If a right-pointing arrowhead follows a command name, choosing the command displays a submenu of additional commands. To choose

Object » Graphs » Style you drag from the Object menu down to the Graphs command, then drag over to the submenu and down to the Style command.

The *toolbox* includes 22 default tools and 8 alternate tools. Illustrator 6 also offers 5 plug-in tools, which you display by choosing Window » Show Plug-in Tools. I introduce all 35 tools in the "Using Tools" section later in this chapter.

Both toolboxes are known generically as *palettes*. In addition to the tool-boxes, Illustrator 6 provides nine palettes, which I detail in the "Using Palettes" section of this chapter.

The *illustration window* is the large window in the middle of the desktop. A window appears for every open illustration. The illustration window is topped off by a *title bar* that gives the name of the drawing. If the illustration has not been saved, the name appears as "Untitled art" followed by a number.

You can move the illustration window by dragging the title bar. Close the illustration by clicking in the *close box* in the upper left-hand corner. Drag the *size box* in the bottom right corner of the window to manually enlarge or reduce the size of the window. Click in the *zoom box* on the right side of the title bar to expand the window to fill the entire screen. Click in the zoom box again to reduce the window to its previous size.

The page with the drop shadow in the middle of the window is the *art-board*. This represents the size of the drawing you want to create. Surrounding the artboard is the *pasteboard*. You can move objects out into the pasteboard if you like; these objects will be saved with your illustration, but they will not print. (Experienced artists typically use the pasteboard as a storage area for objects they can't quite bear to delete.) The dotted line around the *imageable area* shows the portion of the art-board that your printer can actually print. Most printers can't print all the way to the extreme edges of a page.

Together, the artboard and pasteboard are known as the *drawing area*.

The *scroll bars* appear along the right and bottom edges of the illustration window, as they do in most Mac applications. They allow you to move your drawing with respect to the window to better see various portions of your illustration. Click one of the arrows on either end of a scroll bar to nudge the drawing a small distance; click in the gray area of a scroll bar to move the drawing a greater distance. Drag the tab in either scroll bar to manually determine how far you move the drawing.

The *status bar* in the lower left corner of the illustration window lists all kinds of moderately useful information about the program. Click on the status bar to display a pop-up menu of status bar options, as shown in the top example of Figure 2-3. You can have the status bar list the active tool, the date and time, the amount of RAM that's going unused inside Illustrator, and the number of available undos and redos.

Press the Option key as you click on the status bar to access the additional options shown in the bottom example of Figure 2-3. Most of these options are very silly—Random Number and Shopping Days 'til Christmas—but two are actually useful. If you use Illustrator on a PowerBook, you might appreciate the Eyes option, which brings up a pair of eyes that follow your cursor around the screen. No more lost cursor! And if you can't get Illustrator to work correctly, Option-choose DougO's Home Number. You won't really get Doug Olson, Illustrator engineer and product manager; you'll get Adobe's technical support line.

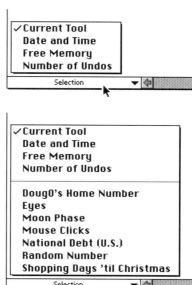

Figure 2-3:
The pop-up menus that appear when you click (top) and Option-click (bottom) on the status bar.

Using Tools

The toolbox is entirely independent of all other desktop elements. So if you reduce the size of a drawing window, the toolbox remains unchanged, with 22 tools visible and easily accessible. The toolbox serves, and is positioned in front of, any and all open illustrations. You can move the toolbox by dragging its title bar, or hide the toolbox by clicking its close box. To redisplay the toolbox, choose Window » Show Toolbox or press ⌘-Control-T.

 You can also hide the toolbox and all other palettes by pressing the Tab key. Press Tab again to bring all the palettes back. To get rid of all palettes except the toolbox, press Tab and then press ⌘-Control-T.

As with other graphics and publishing programs, you select a tool in Illustrator by clicking on its icon in the toolbox. Illustrator highlights the active tool so it stands out prominently. Even folks in the next cubicle can't help but know which tool you're using.

The toolbox contains 22 tool *slots*. In addition to the default tools that occupy these slots, Illustrator offers 8 alternate tools that are initially hidden. For example, of the four path-alteration tools provided by Illustrator, only one, the scissors tool, appears in the toolbox by default. To use one of the other three, you have to drag on the scissors icon to display a pop-up menu of alternates, as demonstrated in Figure 2-4. Select the desired tool as you would a command, that is, by highlighting the tool and releasing the mouse button. Slots that offer alternate tools have tiny right-facing arrowheads in their upper right corners.

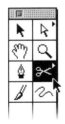 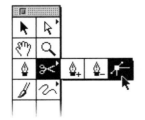

Figure 2-4:
Drag at a slot that features
a small arrowhead to select
an alternate tool.

 All 30 default and alternate tools appear in the composite screen shot in Figure 2-5. These tools work just like their counterparts in Illustrator 5.5. But Illustrator 6 adds to the list the five plug-in tools shown in Figure 2-6. These tools appear in a separate toolbox, which you can display by choosing Window » Show Plug-in Tools. Since there are only five tools, the sixth slot is empty.

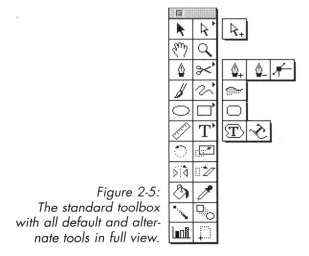

*Figure 2-5:
The standard toolbox
with all default and alternate tools in full view.*

 You can reshape the plug-in toolbox by dragging on the
empty slot, as Figure 2-6 illustrates. Also, if you don't like the
order of the tools, you can move any one of them by Control-
dragging its icon.

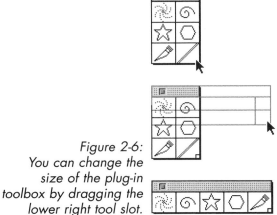

*Figure 2-6:
You can change the
size of the plug-in
toolbox by dragging the
lower right tool slot.*

The following paragraphs explain how to use each of Illustrator's 35 tools in the
illustration window. For example, if an item says *drag*, you click on the tool's icon to
select it and then drag inside the drawing area; you don't drag on the tool icon itself.

These are intended as introductory descriptions only. Subsequent chapters contain more info, which is why I include chapter numbers in my descriptions.

Selection (Chapter 5): The selection tool—which I usually call the *arrow tool* in deference to its appearance—is active when you first start Illustrator. Use this tool to select objects that you've created so you can manipulate them. Click on an object to select the entire object. Drag an object to move it. You can also use the selection tool to select text blocks.

Direct selection (Chapters 5 and 10): Click with this hollow arrow to select individual anchor points and segments in a line or shape. This is also the perfect tool for editing the Bézier control handles that govern the curvature of segments.

Group selection (Chapters 5 and 10): Click with this tool (or just Option-click with the direct selection tool) to select whole objects at a time. Though it frequently acts the same as the standard arrow tool, the group selection tool lets you select individual objects inside groups, whereas the arrow tool selects *all* objects in a group.

Hand (Chapter 3): Drag with the hand tool to scroll the drawing inside the illustration window. It is much more convenient than the scroll bars. You can also double-click on the hand tool icon in the toolbox to fit the entire artboard into the illustration window.

Zoom (Chapter 3): Click with this tool to magnify the size of the illustration. (This doesn't affect the printed size of the drawing, just how it looks on screen.) Option-click to zoom out. You can also drag with the tool to surround the exact portion of the illustration you want to magnify. Double-click on the zoom tool icon to view your drawing at the very same size it will print.

Pen (Chapter 5): This is Illustrator's most powerful drawing tool, the one that's most responsible for Illustrator's success. Use the pen tool to draw a line as a series of individual points. Click to add corners to a line, drag to add arcs. You can also Option-drag on an arc to change it to a cusp. Illustrator automatically connects your points with straight or curved segments.

Scissors (Chapter 9): Click on a line to cut it into two. Illustrator inserts two points at the spot where you click, one for each line.

Add anchor point (Chapter 5): Click on a segment with the add point tool to insert a new point into a line.

Delete anchor point (Chapter 5): Click on a point with this tool to remove the point while leaving the line intact. That's why I prefer to call this tool the *remove point tool*: "deleting" a point would create a hole.

Convert direction point (Chapter 5): Use this tool to change a corner in a line to an arc or vice versa. Click on an arc to make it a corner; drag on a corner to make it an arc.

Brush (Chapter 4): Drag with the brush tool to create a closed shape that resembles a brushstroke. If you own a pressure-sensitive tablet, you can use the brush tool to draw shapes that vary in thickness depending on how hard you press.

Freehand (Chapter 4): Drag with the freehand tool to draw a free-form line, much as if you were drawing with a pencil. Press the ⌘ key while the mouse button is down and drag back over part of your path to erase it.

Autotrace (Chapter 4): Click within six screen pixels of an imported black and white template to trace a line around the image. This tool is easily Illustrator's worst; you're almost always better off tracing images by hand.

Oval (Chapter 4): Drag with this tool to draw an ellipse. You can also Shift-drag to draw a circle or Option-drag to draw outward from the center. Click with the tool to enter numerical dimensions for your ellipse.

Rectangle (Chapter 4): This tools works just like the oval tool, except it makes rectangles and squares.

Rounded rectangle (Chapter 4): If you want your rectangles to have rounded corners, use this tool. To adjust the roundness of the corners of future shapes, click in the drawing area.

Measure (Chapter 10): Drag with this tool to measure the distance between two points. Alternatively, you can click in one spot and then click in another. Illustrator displays the measurements in the Info palette.

Type (Chapter 6): Click with this tool and then enter text from the keyboard to create a line of type. To create a text block with type that automatically wraps from one line to the next, drag with the type tool and then start banging away at the keyboard. You can also use this tool (or one of the other two type tools) to highlight characters inside a text block in order to edit or format them.

Area type (Chapter 7): Click on a line or shape to create text that wraps inside an irregular boundary.

Path type (Chapter 7): Click on a line or shape to create text that follows the contours of the object. This process is better known as text on a curve.

Rotate (Chapter 11): This tool lets you rotate selected objects. Click with the tool to determine the center of the rotation, and then drag to rotate the objects around this center. Or just drag right off the bat to center the rotation smack dab in the middle of the selected objects. You can also Option-click with the tool or double-click on the tool icon in the toolbox to specify a rotation numerically.

Scale (Chapter 11): This tool and the two that follow work just like the rotate tool. The only difference is that the scale tool enlarges and reduces selected objects.

Reflect (Chapter 11): Use this tool to flip objects across an axis. Usually, it's easiest to just drag with this tool, or Option-click to flip horizontally or vertically.

Shear (Chapter 11): Drag with the oddly named shear tool to slant selected objects. The effects of shift-dragging are generally easier to predict; when the shift key is down, the shear tool slants the objects horizontally or vertically.

Paint bucket (Chapter 14): Click on an object using the paint bucket tool to apply the fill and stroke from the Paint Style palette to the object.

Eyedropper (Chapter 14): Click on an object to copy its fill-and-stroke attributes to the Paint Style palette. You can also double-click on an object to copy the colors from that object to all selected objects.

Gradient vector (Chapter 15): Drag inside a selected object that's filled with a gradation to change the angle of the gradations, as well as the locations of the first and last colors. Shift-drag to create perfectly horizontal or vertical color transitions.

Blend (Chapter 17): The blend tool allows you to create custom gradations. After selecting two objects with one of the arrow tools, use the blend tool to click on a point in one object, then click on a point in the other object. Illustrator automatically creates a collection of intermediate shapes between the two objects, which are filled with intermediate colors.

Graph (Chapter 8): Drag with the graph tool to specify the boundaries of a bar chart, pie chart, or other graph. Illustrator then presents you with a spreadsheet in which you can enter your data. Double-click on the graph tool icon in the toolbox to specify the kind of graph you want to create.

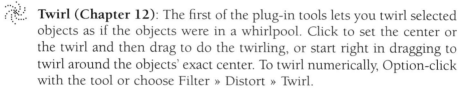 **Page (Chapter 3)**: Drag with the page tool to move the imageable area within the artboard. Unless the artboard is larger than the printed page size, you don't have to worry about this tool.

The following five tools are new to Illustrator 6:

Twirl (Chapter 12): The first of the plug-in tools lets you twirl selected objects as if the objects were in a whirlpool. Click to set the center or the twirl and then drag to do the twirling, or start right in dragging to twirl around the objects' exact center. To twirl numerically, Option-click with the tool or choose Filter » Distort » Twirl.

Spiral (Chapter 4): Drag to draw a spiraling line, like a stylized pig's tail. To change the number of times the line twists inside itself, click with the tool in the drawing area.

Star (Chapter 4): Drag with this plug-in tool to draw a star with symmetrical points. Option-drag to constrain the star so opposite "arms" are perfectly aligned, as with a five-pointed American star or a Star of David. Click with the tool to change the number of points.

Regular polygon (Chapter 4): When you drag with this tool, you draw a regular polygon, like a triangle or pentagon. Click with the tool to change the number of sides.

Knife (Chapter 9): Drag with the knife tool to slice shapes into new shapes, just as if you had dragged though them with a real knife. This tool cuts through any objects in its path, whether selected or not.

Recognizing Cursors

One item I didn't label back in Figure 2-2 is the arrow-shaped cursor, which moves around on screen in response to the way you move your mouse. But the arrow isn't the only cursor that Illustrator offers. In fact, Illustrator 6 is downright cursor-happy. The program provides nearly 60 unique cursors. Illustrator uses these cursors to communicate with you. Sometimes a cursor merely tells you what tool you're using, but more often, it tells you what kind of operation you're about to perform. Recognizing the meaning of various cursors helps to reduce the confusion and frustration that sometimes comes with using a complex program like Illustrator.

Arrow: The arrow cursor appears when the cursor moves outside the illustration window, as well as when you use the arrow tool to select objects.

Direct select: This cursor appears when selecting points and segments with the direct selection tool.

Group select: When using the group selection tool, or when pressing the Option key with the direct selection tool, you see this cursor. It means you are about to select whole objects.

Drag: This cursors appears whenever you move a point, control handle, or object, with either the pen tool or one of the arrow tools. It also appears when using the rotate, scale, reflect, or shear tools.

Clone: You can create a copy of an object by pressing the Option key anytime you're dragging an object. Such a copy is called a *clone* because it occurs independently of the Copy command or Macintosh Clipboard. When cloning, you see this cursor.

Snap: This is one of Illustrator's most important cursors. It shows you that the point or object you're dragging has snapped into exact alignment with a stationary point or guideline in the drawing area. If you don't see this cursor, things are not precisely aligned.

Snap and clone: When in the midst of cloning an object (by Option-dragging) and snapping to a stationary point or guide, the cursor looks like this.

Convert point: Here's the cursor you see when using the convert anchor point tool. If it comes up while using some other tool, you must have keys pressed (Control, and possibly others) that access this tool.

Hand: When the hand tool is active, this cursor appears.

Fist: When dragging the drawing area with the hand tool, the hand cursor clenches into a fist. A similar cursor appears when dragging layer names in the Layers palette.

Zoom in: Click with this cursor to magnify the drawing on screen.

Zoom out: This cursor shows that Illustrator is poised to reduce the view size of the drawing.

Zoom limit: If you have zoomed in or out as far as you can, this cursor tells you that you've reached a dead end.

New path: When no line or shape is active, the pen tool cursor has an X next to it so you know you'll be creating a new path. Keep an eye out for this cursor, since it's very easy to deactivate paths.

Pen: While you are drawing a path, the cursor looks like the pen tool without any little doodads next to it. Each time you click or drag, Illustrator adds another segment to your path.

Cusp point: When you position the pen cursor over the point you just finished creating, you see a pen with a tiny convert point icon next to it. Illustrator's telling you that if you click or drag, you might change the recent point from a corner or an arc to a cusp.

Close path: You close an active path by clicking or dragging with the pen tool on the very first point in the shape. As your cursor hovers over the first point, the little O shows that a close is about to occur.

Activate path: If you want to extend an inactive line, you can click or drag on one of the endpoints with the pen tool. This cursor shows that reactivation is imminent.

Connect paths: When a path is active, you can click or drag on an endpoint in an inactive line to connect the two lines into one. This cursor lets you know you're ready to connect.

Add point: A little plus sign next to the pen cursor means that you're about to insert a new point into a path using the add anchor point tool.

Remove point: The pen with minus sign shows that the remove anchor point tool is about to send a point to meet its maker.

Brush: When using the brush tool, you get this cursor.

Freehand: The cursor for the freehand tool looks like a little pencil. Drag away to draw a line.

Connect freehand: You can extend any line—whether drawn with the freehand tool, pen tool, or any other tool—by dragging from one of its endpoints with the freehand tool. When you do, you get this cursor.

Close freehand: Dragging back to the first point in a line with the freehand tool closes the shape, and you get this cursor.

Erase freehand: This cursor shows you are erasing a freehand line by ⌘-dragging back over it.

Type edit: The familiar I-beam cursor appears when any one of the three type tools is selected and the cursor is positioned over some text. It means Illustrator is prepared to edit text, but not create a new text block. If you want to create a new text block, you need to move the cursor off the type.

New block: If you position the type tool over a portion of the drawing area that does not contain type, you get this cursor, which shows you that Illustrator expects you to create a new text block.

Area type: This cursor appears any time the area type tool is active, or when the standard type tool is positioned over the outline of a shape. If you click on something other than a path with this cursor, Illustrator complains.

Path type: This cursor accompanies the path type tool. It also appears when you move the standard type tool over a line. As with the preceding cursor, Illustrator is happy only if you click on a path.

Data edit: This I-beam without a cross is a very rare and frankly unnecessary cursor that you can feel free to ignore. It only appears when editing data in the Graph Data dialog box.

Column width: When adjusting the width of spreadsheet columns in the Graph Data dialog box, Illustrator blesses the screen with this cursor.

Eyedropper: This cursor appears anytime the eyedropper tool is active. More importantly, you see this cursor when clicking outside an object with the eyedropper, which means Illustrator is copying no color or just the color of a stroke to the Paint Style palette.

Lift color: By contrast, this cursor appears when you click inside an object or imported image with the eyedropper. It means that Illustrator is copying both the fill and stroke colors to the Paint Style palette.

Paint bucket: This cursor appears when using the paint bucket tool.

Delete color: You'd think the scissors cursor would appear when using the scissors tool, but you would be terribly mistaken. Illustrator just doesn't work that way. When you least expect it, the program turns the tables on you and completely messes up your world. The scissors cursor actually appears when ⌘-clicking on a color to delete it from the Paint Style palette.

Move layer: When dragging a layer name to a new position in the Layers palette, you see this cursor.

Clone layer: If you Option-drag a layer name in the Layers palette, this cursor shows you Illustrator is set to clone all contents of that layer onto a new layer.

Locked layer: This cursor can be irritating, because it prevents you from doing a doggone thing. What it means is that the layer on which you're trying to create or edit objects is locked. To make this cursor go away, switch to a different layer in the Layers palette, or just unlock the layer.

Crosshair: This is one of Illustrator's most generic cursors. It appears when using the scissors, autotrace, oval, rectangle, rounded rectangle, measure, gradient vector, blend, graph, or page tools; when the rotate, scale, reflect, shear, or twirl tool is active but not in operation; when using the pen, brush, freehand, paint bucket, or knife tool; or when the Caps Lock key is down. (The Caps Lock key results in so-called precise cursors that aren't quite so intrusive.)

Center oval: If you press the Option key while the oval tool is active, you see this short-lived cursor, which tells you that you're about to draw an ellipse from the center out.

Center rectangle: This cursor is just like the last one, except it applies to the rectangles and rounded rectangles.

Numerical transformation: If you press the Option key while the rotate, scale, reflect, shear, or twirl tool is active, you see this cursor. It foretells that Illustrator is ready to display a dialog box of numerical transformation options.

Precise new path: These next few cursors only appear when using the pen tool while the Caps Lock key is down. This first one shows that no path is active, so any clicking or dragging will create a new path. (When a path is active and the Caps Lock key is down, you see the plain crosshair cursor.)

Precise cusp point: The pen tool is active, the Caps Lock key is down, and the cursor is positioned over the point you just created.

Precise close path: You are about to close the active path with the pen tool while the Caps Lock key is down.

Precise activate path: When you position the path tool (with Caps Lock down) over the endpoint in an inactive path, you see this cursor.

Precise connect paths: Caps Lock is down, pen tool is active, and you are about to connect the active path to an inactive one.

Precise add point: If the Caps Lock key is down and the add anchor point tool is selected, here's the cursor you see.

Precise remove point: Same thing, but for the remove anchor point tool.

Precise connect freehand: If you position the freehand tool over the endpoint in a line while the Caps Lock key is down, you see this cursor, which indicates you're ready to extend the line.

Precise close freehand: This cursor shows you that you've successfully dragged back to the first point in a freehand line (with Caps Lock down, and frankly, a little depressed).

Precise erase freehand: Finally, the last Caps Lock cursor! This special dotted cursor shows that you are ⌘-dragging with the freehand tool and thus erasing some portion of the line in progress.

Mini crosshair: This smaller crosshair cursor is used by the new spiral, star, and regular polygon tools.

Knife: Gad, is this cursor ugly or what? It goes with Illustrator 6's new knife tool.

Precise eyedropper: Did I say we were done with the Caps Lock cursors? Oops, what a lie. This is what the eyedropper cursor looks like when the dreaded locking key is down.

Precise lift color: Here is your optical reward for pressing the Caps Lock key and clicking with the eyedropper tool.

Watch: When Illustrator gets busy, it displays this cursor. You can't do anything but sit there and wait. It's the Mac's way of saying, "Go soak your head."

My, wasn't that entertaining? Personally, I was having a rollicking time until we came to the precise cursors, at which point my brain started to erode. I think we should all try to avoid the words Caps Lock for a while, especially when children are in the room.

Using Dialog Boxes

When you choose any command whose name includes an ellipsis (…), such as File » New… or Arrange » Move…, Illustrator has to ask you some questions before it can complete the operation. It asks you these questions by displaying a palette or dialog box. I'll explain palettes in the next section, but I'll start with dialog boxes because they're more common.

A *dialog box* is a window that comes up on screen and demands your immediate attention. You can sometimes switch to a different application while a dialog box is on screen, but you can't do any more work in Illustrator until you address it, either by filling out a few options and clicking on the OK button, or by clicking on the Cancel button.

Options naturally vary from one dialog box to the next, but there are eight basic kinds of options in all. Figure 2-7 shows examples of these option types as they

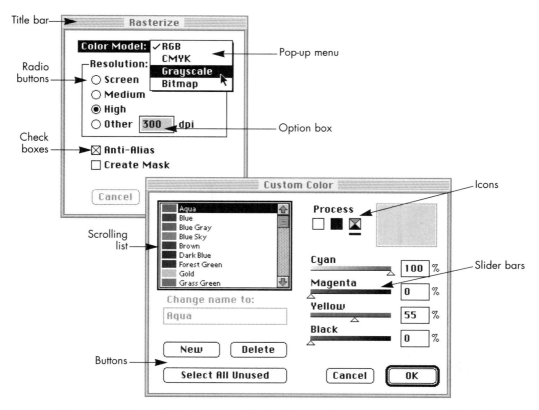

Figure 2-7: Two dialog boxes with the basic elements and options labeled.

appear in two of Illustrator's dialog boxes. Also labeled is the title bar, which tops off just about every Macintosh dialog box these days. If the dialog box is blocking some important portion of your illustration, just drag the title bar to move it to a more satisfactory location.

Here's a quick run-down of the eight kinds of dialog box options:

- **Radio buttons**: When you can select just one option from a group of options, a round radio button precedes each option name. To select a radio button, click either on the button itself or on the name of the option following the button. This deselects all other radio buttons in the group. A radio button filled with a black dot is selected; a hollow radio button is not.

- **Check boxes**: When you can select several options in a group, square check boxes come before the option names. To turn a check box on or off, click either on the box itself or on the option name. An X indicates a selected check box; a deselected check box is empty.

- **Pop-up menus**: A pop-up menu looks like a word in a box. Click on the word to display a menu of options, as shown in Figure 2-7. Select the desired option from the menu just as you would a command from a menu.

- **Option boxes**: If a dialog box were a test, then radio buttons, check boxes, and pop-up menus would be multiple-choice questions; while option boxes (also called *numerical fields* by the nerd faction) are fill-in-the-blank questions. Option boxes are typically reserved for numbers, like dimensions or color percentages. To select the current value in an option box, double-click on it. Then enter a new value from the keyboard.

If a dialog box contains lots of option boxes, you can advance from one box to the next by pressing the Tab key. To go in the other direction, press Shift-Tab.

- **Scrolling lists**: When Illustrator really wants to pack in a lot of options, it presents them inside a scrolling list. Use the scroll bar on the right side of the list to check out more options. Then click on the option you want to use. You can only select one option from a scrolling list.

In most cases, you can select a specific option from a scrolling list by typing in the first few letters of its name. For example, pressing the P key selects the first option whose name begins with a P. You may want to first make sure the list is active by clicking on it. (When active, the list has a second border around it, as in Figure 2-7.) If an option box value is active, typing replaces the value instead.

- **Icons**: Every once in a while, Illustrator just doesn't feel like being locked into all the other options it has at its disposal, so it resorts to small graphic icons. These icons are like radio buttons in that you can select just one icon from a group. Illustrator either highlights or underlines the selected icon.

- **Slider bars**: If you come across a horizontal line or colored bar with one or more triangles underneath it, you've encountered a slider bar. Drag the slider triangle back and forth to lower or raise the value, which is usually displayed in an option box. (You can also enter a different option box value if you prefer.)

- **Buttons**: Not to be confused with radio buttons, standard dialog box buttons look like words inside rounded rectangles. Click on a button to make something happen. Two of the most common buttons are OK, which closes the dialog box and applies your settings, and Cancel, which closes the dialog box and cancels the command. Some dialog boxes offer Copy buttons, which apply settings to a copy of a selected object. And there are Apply buttons, which let you apply your settings without closing the dialog box.

 Instead of clicking on the OK button, you can press the Return or Enter key. Press Option-Return or Option-Enter to activate a Copy or Apply button. And press Escape or ⌘-Period (that's ⌘ plus the . key) to cancel the operation.

A dialog box that conveys information rather than requests it is called an *alert box*. As its name implies, the purpose of an alert box is to call your attention to an important bit of news. Some alert boxes warn you about the consequences of an action so you can abort the action before these hideous consequences occur. Others are just Illustrator's way of whining at you. "I can't do that," "You're using me wrong," and "Don't you think I have feelings, too?" are common alert box messages. (Okay, that's an exaggeration, but it's not far from the truth.)

Using Palettes

A palette is nothing more than a dialog box that can remain open while you fiddle about inside the software. You can gain access to every one of Illustrator's 11 palettes (which include the two toolboxes) by choosing commands from the

Window menu. In many cases, commands in other menus bring up these same palettes. For example, you can display the Character palette by choosing any one of five commands.

 To hide all palettes, including the toolbox, press Tab. To redisplay them, press Tab again. Illustrator only displays those palettes that were up on screen prior to the first time you pressed Tab.

Figure 2-8 shows a couple of typical palettes from Illustrator 6. As you can see, palettes offer many of the same kinds of options that you find inside dialog boxes, including check boxes, scrolling lists, and the like. Each palette is likewise topped off by a title bar. Drag the title bar to move the palette on screen. Illustrator's palettes snap into alignment with other palettes; they also snap into alignment with the edges of the screen.

Options vary more widely in palettes than they do in dialog boxes. Some are so unusual there's no point in explaining them here. For now, I'll just cover the ones that you see quite a bit in Illustrator and other applications (including Photoshop).

- **Close box**: Click in the close box in the left corner of the title bar to close the palette.

- **Zoom box**: A few palettes offer zoom boxes on the right side of their title bars. When you click in the zoom box, Illustrator changes the size of the palette, either making it larger to show off more options or reducing its size to show fewer options. In the case of the Tabs palette, clicking in the zoom box aligns the palette with the active text block.

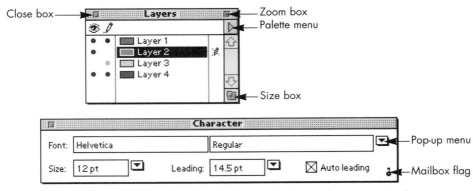

Figure 2-8: Two palettes with their strange little options labeled.

If you have Apple's WindowShade control panel running, you can collapse a palette so only its title bar is visible. In most cases, you do this by double-clicking on the title bar. (If double-clicking doesn't work, choose Apple » Control Panels » WindowShade to see how many clicks are required. You may also have to press ⌘, Option, or Control.) Double-click (or whatever) the title bar again to display the palette in full.

- **Palette menu**: Though quite prevalent in Photoshop and other programs, only one of Illustrator's palettes, Layers, offers a palette menu. Click on the right-pointing arrowhead to display the menu, then drag to choose the desired command.

- **Size box**: Drag the size box to change the size of the palette. (Only the Tabs and Layers palettes offer this element.)

- **Pop-up menu**: If you see a little down-pointing arrowhead in a box, this indicates a pop-up menu. Drag from the arrowhead to display the menu and select your favorite option.

- **Mailbox flag**: This peculiar screen element is found in the Character, Paragraph, and Gradient palettes. When the tiny mailbox flag is up, many secondary options are hidden to save screen space. If you click on the flag, it snaps down and the palette expands to reveal a whole mess of additional options. Some commands cause the flag to go up or down on its own.

 After you enter a value into a palette's option box, you can press the Return or Enter key to make the value take effect and to return control to the drawing area. You can also hide a palette when an option box is active by pressing ⌘-Return.

Accommodating Your Personal Style

No two folks draw alike. It's a cliché, but it happens to be true (except in the case of very close twins). For those who draw to a different drummer—in other words, all of us—Illustrator provides the File » Preferences submenu, which provides four commands that allow you to edit a variety of attributes that control Illustrator's performance. All of these commands affect Illustrator *global* preferences, that is, preferences affecting every single illustration you create or edit in the future. (I discuss Document Setup and other commands that affect one illustration at a time in the next chapter.)

General Preferences

Choosing File » Preferences » General or pressing ⌘-K displays the General Preferences dialog box, shown in Figure 2-9. Here you can control the way objects look on screen, how elements react to transformations, the distance a selected object moves when you press an arrow key, the sensitivity of the freehand and

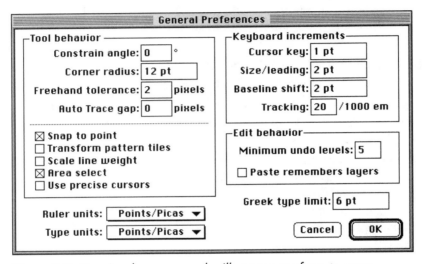

Figure 2-9: Here's where you make Illustrator conform to your idiosyncratic whims.

autotrace tools, whether dialog boxes display information in points or inches, plus much, much more.

The following list describes each option available in this dialog box. Naturally, I haven't provided the background you need to understand many of these options by this early page in the book. But have no fear, I cover each option in context in one or more chapters, as the descriptions indicate. For now, content yourself with the certain knowledge that these pages contain an invaluable resource that you can refer to over and over throughout your happy and productive illustrating years.

Here are the options, in the order they appear in the General Preferences dialog box:

- **Constrain Angle (Chapters 4, 11, and others):** If you press the Shift key while dragging an object, you constrain the direction of its movement to a multiple of 45 degrees; that is, straight up, straight down, left, right, or one of the four diagonal directions. These eight angles make up an invisible… er… thingamabob called the *constraint axes*. You can rotate the entire constraint axes by entering a value (measured in degrees) in the Constrain Angle option box. This value affects the creation of rectangles, ellipses, and text blocks, as well as the performance of transformation tools.

- **Corner Radius (Chapter 4):** This option lets you round off the corners on shapes drawn with the rounded rectangle tool. A value of 0 indicates perpendicular corners; larger values make for progressively more rounded rectangles. This value does not affect regular rectangles drawn with the rectangle tool.

- **Freehand Tolerance (Chapter 4):** This complex little option controls the sensitivity of *both* the freehand and the autotrace tools. Any value between 0 and 10 is permitted, and it is measured in screen pixels. Low values make the tools very sensitive, so that a freehand path closely matches your cursor movements or an autotrace path closely matches the form of the imported template. Higher values give Illustrator license to ignore small jags and other imperfections when creating the path. Quite contrary to any semblance of logic, this value has no effect on the performance of the brush tool.

- **Auto Trace Gap (Chapter 4):** Black-and-white tracing templates frequently contain loose pixels and rough edges. Using the Auto Trace Gap option, you can instruct Illustrator to trace over these gaps. A value of 0 turns the option off, so that the autotrace tool traces rough edges as they appear in the template. A value of 1 allows paths to jump over single-pixel gaps; a value of 2 (the highest value allowed) allows paths to hurdle two-pixel gaps.

- **Snap to Point (Chapter 5):** By selecting this option, you ensure that an object moves sharply toward a stationary point or guideline when you move the object within two pixels of it. (When a snap occurs, the cursor becomes hollow, as mentioned in the "Recognizing Cursors" section above.) If you're tired of all that incessant snapping, turn the check box off.

- **Transform Pattern Tiles (Chapters 11 and 15):** When an object is filled or stroked with a tile pattern, you can specify whether or not the pattern moves, grows, shrinks, or rotates as you move, scale, or rotate the object. By default, the tile patterns remain impervious to transformations; but you have only to turn on this check box to make the patterns a little more flexible.

- **Scale Line Weight (Chapters 11 and 16)**: When you scale an object proportionally—so that both height and width grow or shrink by the same amount—Illustrator can likewise change the thickness of the stroke assigned to the object. Check the box to scale the stroke; turn it off to leave the line weight unchanged.

- **Area Select (Chapter 5)**: This option controls how you go about selecting filled objects in the preview mode. When checked, you can click anywhere inside an object to select the object, so long as the object is filled. When the option is off, you can select an object only by clicking on its points and segments. I recommend experienced users leave this option off, thereby permitting easy selection of objects behind other objects without the fills getting in the way.

- **Use Precise Cursors (Chapter 2)**: Aaagh, I thought we agreed to have no more talk about precise cursors in this chapter! Well, what can you do? The option's here, so we'd better discuss it. When this option is checked, Illustrator displays crosshair cursors in place of the standard cursors for all drawing and editing tools. These special cursors let you better see what you're doing, but they're not as much fun to look at.

In truth, there's no reason on earth to select this check box. Just press the Caps Lock key (the mere mention of which causes me to break out in hives) to access the precise cursors when the check box is off. If the check box has been mysteriously turned on, pressing Caps Lock (scratch, scratch) displays the standard cursor.

- **Ruler Units (Chapter 10)**: Select Points/Picas, Inches, or Millimeters from this pop-up menu to specify the system of measurement used throughout all dialog boxes (including this one) as well as the horizontal and vertical rulers. Unlike the similar option in the Document Setup dialog box—which affects just the one drawing you're working on—this option applies to *all* future illustrations in addition to the one you're working on.

To change the system of measurement without bringing up the General Preferences dialog box, just press ⌘-Control-U (for "units"). Each time you press ⌘-Control-U, Illustrator cycles to the next unit, that is, from Points/Picas to Inches, Inches to Millimeters, or Millimeters to Points/Picas. (This shortcut does not work when a dialog box is open.)

- **Type Units (Chapter 6):** You *could* select an option from this pop-up menu to specify the measurement system used specifically for type. But no one in their right mind *would* do this, since points are the standard for measuring type in nearly every corner of the globe. Honestly, leave this option set to Points/Picas, as by default. (Incidentally, this option controls the units used by three options in the General Preferences dialog box: Size/Leading, Baseline Shift, and Greek Type Limit.)

- **Cursor Key (Chapter 10):** Illustrator allows you to move selected objects from the keyboard by pressing one of the four arrow keys (↑, ↓, ←, →). Each keystroke moves the selection the distance entered into this option box. The default value is one point, equivalent to one screen pixel at the 100 percent view size. That's a subtle nudge.

- **Size/Leading (Chapter 6):** Just as you can nudge objects from the keyboard, you can likewise adjust the size and leading of selected text with keystrokes. To define the increment of each keystroke, enter a value into this option box.

- **Baseline Shift (Chapter 6):** Baseline shift raises and lower characters relative to the baseline, ideal for creating superscript and subscript type. To define the increment by which selected type will be raised and lowered, type a new value into this option box.

- **Tracking (Chapter 6):** To keep large text looking good, you may want to adjust the amount of space between neighboring characters, called *kerning* or *tracking*. You can modify the kerning from the keyboard by the increment entered into this option box. This value is always measured in 0.001 em space. (An em space is as wide as the current type size is tall.

- **Minimum Undo Levels (Chapter 5):** Here you enter the minimum number of undos and redos that Illustrator can perform in a row. If you set the value to 7, you can backstep through the last seven consecutive operations, or possibly more, depending on the complexity of the operations. (Note that changing the value to a higher number will not allow you to undo operations that you couldn't undo prior to changing the value.)

- **Paste Remembers Layers (Chapter 10):** Select this check box if you want to paste objects back onto the layers from which they were originally copied. When this option is turned off, Illustrator pastes all objects onto the current layer, regardless of where they were copied from.

- **Greek Text Limit (Chapter 3):** If text size gets smaller than this value, Illustrator shows the text blocks as gray bars, an operation called *greeking*. Both type size and view size figure into the equation, so that 6-point type greeks at 100 percent view size and 12-point text greeks at 50 percent. Greeking speeds up the screen display because gray bars are easier to draw than individual characters of type.

Color Matching

Next in the File » Preferences submenu is the Color Matching command, which lets you *calibrate* your monitor so that the colors you see on screen match your printed output. But before I go any farther, I should mention two things:

- First, calibrating consumer monitors is virtually impossible. Monitors project color as a combination of red, green, and blue light. (Your eyes similarly read colors using red-drag, green-drag, and blue-sensitive cones in the retina.) Printed colors, for the most part, are made up of a combination of cyan (light blue with a hint of green), magenta (hot pink), yellow, and black inks. These two very different color models (RGB versus CMYK) are exceedingly difficult to reconcile.

- Second, Illustrator's brand of color matching is not nearly as well implemented or (thankfully) as essential as Photoshop's. Photoshop uses monitor and printer information to convert colors in images from the RGB world of scanners through the RGB world of monitors to the CMYK world of printers. In Illustrator, you define *all* colors in terms of CMYK; therefore, no color space conversion is necessary.

In fact, the only reason Illustrator provides the Color Matching command is to accommodate Photoshop images and to ensure that you see your drawing on screen in roughly its true colors. But even given these limited goals, the command doesn't work particularly well.

If you're serious about producing predictable colors—some folks are more concerned about this than others—here are some better solutions than File » Preferences » Color Matching:

- Spend a few thousand bucks on a calibrated monitor. The only professional-quality Macintosh monitors currently out there are the PressView SR series from Radius (408/434-1010). Available in 17- and 21-inch sizes for roughly $1,500 and $3,000 respectively, these excellent screens ensure the closest thing to an exact color-for-color match. I'm using one right now, and I can't stress enough how much I value it. If you don't already own a video board that can handle 24-bit color at large screen sizes, add another $1,000 to the expense.

Obviously, the previous suggestion is reserved for those relative few who are sufficiently interested in good color to invest until it hurts. If the mere idea of saving $3,000 makes you feel better already about your crummy color, then you can at least predict what you're going to get by purchasing an $85 Colorfinder swatch book from Trumatch (212/302-9100). This essential collection of colors demonstrates hundreds of CMYK color combinations in smooth, logical progressions, and every one of them is printed from a personal computer just like yours. There simply is not a better guide to color. (Incidentally, Illustrator includes the entire Trumatch color library on disk, as described in Chapter 14, but you really need to buy the swatch book to accurately gauge the printed results.)

Where imported images are concerned, Photoshop offers better color conversion controls. So be sure to convert all images to the CMYK color space inside Photoshop before importing them into Illustrator. If an image looks different in Illustrator than it did in Photoshop, trust Photoshop. (Not that Photoshop is altogether accurate; it's simply more likely to be close to the truth than Illustrator.)

If, after all my warnings, you still want to use the Color Matching command, then I suppose I should explain how it works. The following steps explain how to use every one of Illustrator's color matching options. Steps 2 through 4 merely change how colors look on screen. Steps 5 through 8 expressly affect the printing of imported Photoshop images.

1. Choose File » Preferences » Color Matching to display the dialog box shown in Figure 2-10.

2. Compare the color swatches at the top of the dialog box to printed versions of these colors. Ideally, you'll want to acquire a set of color swatches directly from your commercial printer. But if you don't work with the same printer regularly, you can find these colors in absolutely any color swatch book, whether from Trumatch, Pantone, or some fly-by-night company.

3. If you see a color that doesn't exactly match—which you will—click on it to display the standard Apple Color Picker dialog box. Drag inside the central color wheel to change the color; use the slider bar to change the brightness. You will *never* get it exactly right—in fact, the better your color perception, the more alarming the color disparity will seem—so just pretend you're working for NASA and try to get it as close as possible. Then press Return.

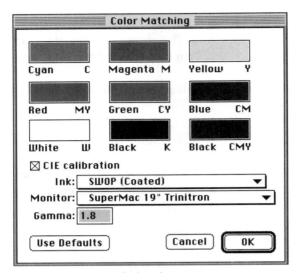

Figure 2-10: This dialog box contains some options that are marginally useful for matching screen colors to printed output.

4. Keep repeating this pointless ritual for each color swatch that doesn't look right on.

5. Select the CIE Calibration check box. CIE is a scientific color model that describes colors as your eye sees them, not as a monitor or printer creates them. (The initials CIE stand for the unpronounceable French name of an international color conference that started back in 1931.)

6. Select the kind of printing process and paper stock you plan to use from the Ink pop-up menu. If you can't find an exact match, select something similar. If you really become desperate, call your commercial printing house and ask them which setting they recommend.

7. Select your model of monitor from the Monitor pop-up menu. Many models are not listed, so you may have to select a close equivalent.

8. If you're feeling daring, enter a Gamma value. Gamma indicates the brightness of medium gray displayed by your monitor. This should match the setting you've assigned to Photoshop using that program's File » Preferences » Monitor Setup command. Most computer monitors have a Gamma of 1.8. The television standard is 2.2. My PressView monitor is calibrated at 2.55, far too high for most screens.

None of this is a condemnation of Illustrator. It's just that most Macs are incapable of displaying accurate color, and Illustrator's methods of correcting this problem aren't very substantial. When in doubt, keep a Trumatch swatch book close at hand.

Hyphenation Options

Moving right along, you can choose File » Preferences » Hyphenation Options to exclude words from Illustrator's automatic hyphenating capabilities (covered in Chapter 7). Although most Illustrator users go their entire working careers without ever giving a second though to automatic hyphenation, you may feel compelled to rule out the occasional proper noun, so that Johnson never appears as John-son. Here's how:

1. Choose File » Preferences » Hyphenation Options to display the dialog box captured for time immemorial in Figure 2-11.

2. Select a language from the Default Language pop-up menu to determine which set of rules Illustrator uses to hyphenate your words. For example, you wouldn't want Hungarian hyphenation if you were writing in Finnish.

Figure 2-11:
The Hyphenation
Option dialog box
lets you specify words
that Illustrator should
never hyphenate.

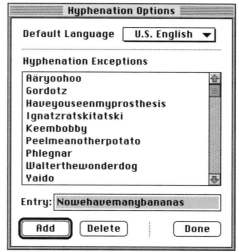

3. Enter the word you want to protect from hyphenation harm into the Entry option box.

4. Click on the Add button. The word appears in the scrolling list of Hyphenation Exceptions.

5. If you decide you've added a word in error, select it from the scrolling list and click on the Delete button.

6. Click on the Done button to exit the dialog box.

Plug-ins

The final item in the File » Preferences submenu is the Plug-ins command, which allows you to tell Illustrator the location of the folder that contains the plug-ins you want to use. By default, all Illustrator plug-ins are installed in the Plug-ins folder, inside the same folder that contains the Illustrator application. But because plug-ins consume a large amount of RAM, you may want to organize your plug-ins into a series of separate folders. This may make Illustrator perform faster or get it to work better on Macs with little memory. Then you can use the File » Preferences » Plug-ins command to tell Illustrator which set of filters you want to use the next time you start the program.

1. Choose File » Preferences » Plug-ins.

2. Locate the folder that contains the set of plug-ins you want to use next. Then click on that folder so its name appears inside the Select button.

3. Click on the Select button.

4. Quit Illustrator by pressing ⌘-Q.

5. Launch Illustrator again to load the program as well as the new set of plug-ins.

The Prefs File

All global preference settings—including those specified in the General Preferences, Color Matching, Hyphenation Options, and Plug-ins dialog boxes—are saved to a file called Adobe Illustrator 6.0 Prefs. It's located in the Preferences folder inside the System folder. Illustrator also saves a list of open palettes, as well as the physical location of the palettes on screen, in the preferences file. These settings affect every file that you create or modify from this moment on (until you next change your preferences).

To reset all preferences and related dialog boxes to their original settings, quit Illustrator and drag the Adobe Illustrator 6.0 Prefs file into the Trash. Then choose Special » Empty Trash to get rid of it for all time. This can be a particularly good thing to do when Illustrator starts flaking out on you. In fact, I recommend that you throw away your preferences file once every three months or so to avoid long-term problems. This goes for other Adobe programs such as Photoshop as well.

Keep in mind: Illustrator updates the Adobe Illustrator 6.0 Prefs file *every* time you quit the program, and *only* when you quit the program. If you crash or force quit Illustrator (by pressing ⌘-Option-Escape), Illustrator leaves the Prefs file untouched. Therefore, if you want to force Illustrator to save your preferences, quit the program by pressing ⌘-Q.

 If you're the adventurous type, you may want to try your hand at editing the Adobe Illustrator 6.0 Prefs file in a word processor, such as Apple's SimpleText utility. After quitting Illustrator, double-click on the Adobe Illustrator 6.0 Prefs to open it in SimpleText. You'll see a list of items in code. There's an item to turn off the splash screen (/showSplashScreen); you can even change the default typeface and size (/faceName and /faceSize). Limit your changes to numerical values and items within parentheses. In most cases, 0 means off and 1 means on. (If you totally muck things up, you can always throw away the Prefs file and let Illustrator create a fresh one.)

The Startup File

The other method for changing Illustrator's global preferences is to edit the Adobe Illustrator Startup file, contained in the Plug-ins folder. You can change the custom colors, gradients, tile patterns, and path patterns available to every illustration. But perhaps more alluring, you can change the window size, the view size, and the position of the artboard inside the window. These are minor adjustments, of course. But if you hate the way Illustrator always fills your screen with the illustration window or the way it zooms the artboard out so it fits inside the window, minor adjustments can go a long way toward creating a more comfortable environment.

1. Open the Adobe Illustrator Startup file.

2. The file contains all kinds of patterns, gradients, and colors. Read Chapters 14 through 16 for information about editing these or creating your own. Placement is not important; just fill a shape with whatever color, pattern, or gradation you want to add.

3. Size the illustration window as desired by dragging the size box.

4. Magnify the window to the desired view size using the zoom tool, as explained in Chapter 3.

5. Use the hand tool to scroll the artboard to the desired position (also described in the next chapter).

6. Use File » Document Setup and File » Page Setup to make any desired changes to the size and shape of the artboard and imageable area. (For the third time, see Chapter 3.)

7. Choose View » Show Rulers or press ⌘-R if you want the rulers to come up every time you start Illustrator.

8. Close the file (⌘-W) and press the Return key to save it to disk.

From now on, every new illustration you create will subscribe to these adjusted settings.

Shortcuts

As with any drawing program, you spend much of your time interacting with Adobe Illustrator by clicking and dragging with your mouse or some other input device. However, a number of commands, options, and other operations can also be executed by way of the keyboard or via keyboard and mouse combinations. The charts in this section contain all keyboard equivalents applicable to Illustrator, categorized by function.

For each keyboard equivalent listed in the chart, I separate key names by hyphens. You should press all keys simultaneously. For example, the keyboard equivalent for Edit » Select All is ⌘-A. This means that you should press both the ⌘ key and the A key *at the same time* to perform the Select All command.

Mouse actions are a little more complicated. If one or more key names precede a mouse action, you should press the keys, perform the action, *and then release the keys.* For example, *Shift-click* means to press and hold the Shift key, click on the item, and release the Shift key; the shift key is down throughout the mouse operation.

These aren't all the weird little tricks you can perform in Illustrator, just the hottest little doodads that I can communicate in the shortest order. I don't include drawing tricks here—like the myriad pen tool tricks and cloning options—because they require more detailed descriptions and are better explained in proper context later in the book.

By the way, you can also look up shortcuts inside Illustrator 6 by choosing Show Shortcuts from the Help menu (the icon in the upper right corner of the screen).

A company called Key Finder (314/997-3667) creates a series of Mouse pad inserts that include shortcuts for Illustrator, Photoshop, and other major Macintosh programs. They're especially useful if you're new to the program—you can just look at the mousepad to see how to perform an operation more quickly. Key Finder also offers inserts that show how to access special text characters including the weird stuff in the Symbol and Zapf Dingbats fonts.

Menu Commands

The following list shows how to access most of the menu commands included in Adobe Illustrator 6.0 using keystrokes and simple mouse operations. (When a command involves a palette, you have to press a shortcut twice: once to activate the palette, and again to hide it.) Commands that are not listed here cannot be accessed from the keyboard and must be chosen from a menu.

Command or option	Keystroke and/or mouse action
Actual Size	⌘-H or double-click on zoom tool icon in toolbox
Average	⌘-L
Average (and Join)	⌘-Option-J or ⌘-Option-L
Artwork	⌘-E
Attributes	⌘-Control-A
Bring To Front	⌘-equal (=)
Centered (alignment)	⌘-Shift-C
Character	⌘-T
Clear	Delete or Clear
Close	⌘-W or click in close box
Copy	⌘-C
Custom Color	double-click on custom color name in Paint Style palette
Cut	⌘-X
Document Setup	⌘-Shift-D
Fit In Window	⌘-M or double-click on hand tool icon in toolbox

continued on next page

continued from previous page

Command or option	Keystroke and/or mouse action
General Preferences	⌘-K
Group	⌘-G
Hide (selected objects)	⌘-3
Hide (deselected objects)	⌘-Option-3
Hide Character palette	⌘-T twice
Hide Edges (of selections)	⌘-Shift-H
Hide Info palette	⌘-Control-I
Hide Layers palette	⌘-Control-L
Hide Paint Style palette	⌘-I twice
Hide Paragraph palette	⌘-Shift-P twice
Hide Rulers	⌘-R
Hide Tab Ruler	⌘-Shift-T
Hide Template	⌘-Shift-W
Hide Toolbox	⌘-Control-T
Join	⌘-J
Join (first Average)	⌘-Option-J or ⌘-Option-L
Justify (alignment)	⌘-Shift-J
Justify Last Line (alignment)	⌘-Shift-B
Kern (characters)	⌘-Shift-K
Last Filter (repeat)	⌘-Shift-E
Last Filter (bring up dialog box)	⌘-Shift-Option-E
Left (alignment)	⌘-Shift-L
Link Blocks	⌘-Shift-G
Lock (selected objects)	⌘-1
Lock (deselected objects)	⌘-Option-1
Lock Guides	⌘-7
Make Compound Paths	⌘-8
Make Guides	⌘-5
Move	⌘-Shift-M or Option-click on arrow tool icon in toolbox
New (with template)	⌘-Option-N
New (without template)	⌘-N
New View	⌘-Control-N
Open	⌘-O

Command or option	Keystroke and/or mouse action
Other Type Size	⌘-Shift-S
Paint Style	⌘-I
Paragraph	⌘-Shift-T
Paste	⌘-V
Paste In Back	⌘-B
Paste In Front	⌘-F
Pattern	Double-click on pattern name in Paint Style palette
Preview Illustration	⌘-Y
Preview Selection	⌘-Option-Y
Print	⌘-P
Quit	⌘-Q
Redo	⌘-Shift-Z
Release Compound Paths	⌘-9
Release Guides	⌘-6 or Shift-Control-double-click on guide with selection tool
Reset Toolbox (all slots)	⌘-Shift-double-click any slot in toolbox
Reset Toolbox (single slot)	Shift-double-click specific slot in toolbox
Right (alignment)	⌘-Shift-R
Save	⌘-S
Select All	⌘-A
Select None	⌘-Shift-A
Send To Back	⌘-hyphen (-)
Show All (hidden objects)	⌘-4
Show Character palette	⌘-T
Show Edges (of selections)	⌘-Shift-H
Show Gradient palette	Double-click on gradient name in Paint Style palette
Show Info palette	⌘-Control-I
Show Layers palette	⌘-Control-L
Show Paint Style palette	⌘-I
Show Paragraph palette	⌘-Shift-P
Show Rulers	⌘-R
Show Tab Ruler	⌘-Shift-T
Show Template	⌘-Shift-W

continued on next page

continued from previous page

Command or option	Keystroke and/or mouse action
Show Toolbox	⌘-Control-T
Spacing	⌘-Shift-O
Transform Again	⌘-D
Tracking	⌘-Shift-K
Undo	⌘-Z
Ungroup	⌘-U
Unlink Blocks	⌘-Shift-U
Unlock All (locked objects)	⌘-2
Unlock Guides	⌘-7
Zoom In	⌘-Right bracket (])
Zoom Out	⌘-Left bracket ([)

Activating Tools

This list shows how to access many of Illustrator's tools. In most cases, you can access a tool temporarily by holding a key down. Releasing the key returns you to the previously selected tool. Such equivalents are distinguished by the word *hold*. Any tool that is not listed cannot be accessed from the keyboard and must be selected normally.

Tool	Keystroke
Last selection tool used	Hold ⌘ key when any tool is active
Selection tool	⌘-Tab when direct selection or group selection tool is active
Direct selection tool	⌘-Tab when selection tool is active
Group selection tool	Hold Option key when direct selection tool is active; Hold ⌘-Option when any other tool is active (assuming direct selection tool was last tool used)
Zoom tool	Hold ⌘-spacebar when any tool is active
Zoom out tool	Hold Option key when zoom tool is active; hold ⌘-Option-spacebar when any other tool is active
Hand tool	Hold spacebar when any tool is active; hold ⌘-spacebar when type tool is active, then release ⌘ key

Tool	Keystroke
Type tool	Hold Control key when area type tool or path type tool is selected
Area type tool	Click on closed path or Option-click on open path with type tool
Path type tool	Click on open path or Option-click on closed path with type tool
Paint bucket tool	Hold the Option key when eyedropper tool is active
Eyedropper tool	Hold the Option key when paint bucket tool is active
Pen tool	Hold Control when freehand tool is active
Add anchor point tool	Hold Control when pen tool is active; hold the Option key when scissors or delete anchor point tool is active; hold ⌘-Control when freehand tool is active
Delete anchor point tool	Hold Option when add anchor point tool is active
Convert point tool	Hold Control key when selection tool is active; hold Control-Option when pen tool is active; hold ⌘-Control-Option when freehand tool is active; ⌘-Control when any other tool is active

Creating and Manipulating Type

This list explains how to create, select, flow, and reposition type. Unless otherwise indicated, you perform all techniques using any of the three type tools.

Type manipulation	Mouse action
Create single line of type	Click with type tool
Create new text block	Drag with type tool
Create type inside path	Click on shape with type tool or area type tool
Create type on path	Click on line with type tool or path type tool
Insert type in text block	Click inside block
Select type in text block	Drag across characters
Select word	Double-click on word

continued on next page

continued from previous page

Type manipulation	Mouse action
Select paragraph	Triple-click in paragraph
Flow text into new column	Option-drag outline of column with direct selection tool
Move text along path	Drag I-beam with selection tool
Flip direction of text on path	Double-click on I-beam with selection tool

Formatting Type

This next list spells out the formatting functions that you can access from the keyboard along with those that include special mouse shortcuts. Many keyboard formatting controls rely on increments set using the Size/Leading, Baseline Shift, and Tracking options in the General Preferences dialog box. All shortcuts assume text is selected using either a selection or a type tool.

Formatting function	Keystroke and/or mouse action
Insert line break	Enter
Highlight Font option	⌘-T; ⌘-Shift-F; or ⌘-Shift-Option-M
Increase type size	⌘-Shift-greater than (>)
Decrease type size	⌘-Shift-less than (<)
Highlight Size option	⌘-Shift-S
Increase leading	Option-down arrow
Decrease leading	Option-up arrow
Solid leading	Click on the word *Leading* in Character palette
Kern together by increment	Option-left arrow
Kern apart by increment	Option-right arrow
Kern together by five times increment	⌘-Option-left arrow
Kern apart by five times increment	⌘-Option-right arrow
Reset kerning to 0	Click on the word *Kerning* in Character palette
Highlight Kerning option	⌘-Shift-K
Increase tracking	Option-right arrow
Decrease tracking	Option-left arrow
Increase track by five times increment	⌘-Option-right arrow
Decrease track by five times increment	⌘-Option-left arrow
Reset tracking to 0	Click on the word Tracking in Character palette

Formatting function	Keystroke and/or mouse action
Highlight Tracking option	⌘-Shift-K
Raise baseline shift	Shift-Option-up arrow
Lower baseline shift	Shift-Option-down arrow
Reset baseline shift to 0	Click on the words Baseline Shift in Character palette
Reset horizontal scale to 0	Click on the words *Horizontal Scale* in Character palette
Force-hyphenate word	⌘Shift-Hyphen (-)
Left-align paragraph	⌘-Shift-L
Center-align paragraph	⌘-Shift-C
Right-align paragraph	⌘-Shift-R
Justify paragraph	⌘-Shift-J
Justify all, including last line	⌘-Shift-B
Move multiple tab stops at a time	Shift-drag tab stop in Tabs palette
Change type of tab stop	Option-click on tab stop in Tabs palette
Change tab measurement	Click on measurement in Tabs palette

Working with Colors

FreeHand users boast that their program lets you drag and drop colors onto objects. But Illustrator provides far more hidden shortcuts for trading colors between objects and palettes. The only trick is to remember them all.

Color function	Keystroke and/or mouse action
Copy colors to selected objects	Double-click on deselected objects with eye-dropper
Tint color	Shift-drag slider triangle in any color palette or dialog box
Advance color value 1%	Option-click on slider in any color palette or dialog box
Advance color value 5%	Shift-Option-click on slider in any color palette or dialog box
Replace Paint Style color swatch	Option-click on swatch
Delete Paint Style color swatch	⌘-click on swatch
Delete swatch without warning	⌘-Option-click on swatch
Delete range of Paint Style swatches	⌘-drag across swatches
Delete range of swatches without warning	⌘-Option-drag across swatches

continued on next page

continued from previous page

Color function	Keystroke and/or mouse action
Reset all Paint Style swatches	⌘-Shift-click on any swatch
Clone color in Gradients palette	Option-drag slider triangle
Replace color in Gradients palette	Control-click with eyedropper tool in drawing area
Select multiple contiguous colors	Click on one, Shift-click on another in any palette or dialog box but Paint Style
Select multiple independent colors	Click on one, ⌘-click on another in any palette or dialog box but Paint Style

Using Dialog Boxes

Keyboard equivalents can also be used to select options and activate buttons inside dialog boxes. Most of the keystrokes listed below work inside all dialog boxes. The only exceptions are the Copy button, which only exists in transformation dialog boxes, and Don't Save, which appears when closing a drawing that hasn't been saved.

Dialog box function	Keystroke
Advance to next option box	Tab
Return to previous option box	Shift-Tab
Cancel button	⌘-Period or Escape
OK button	Return or Enter
Copy button	Option-Return or Option-Enter
Don't Save button	D
Select contents of option box	Double-click on option box; ⌘-A when option is active

Entering Graph Data

The Graph Data dialog box operates differently from all other dialog boxes in Adobe Illustrator. It provides additional and alternate keyboard equivalents, as listed below.

Dialog box function	Keystroke
Select cell data	Click in cell
Select multiple cells	Drag over cells
Select all cells with values	⌘-A

Dialog box function	Keystroke
Clear selected cells	Clear
Return character in cell data	Shift-\ (the vertical line character, |)
Use numerical value as label	Straight quotes (") around numbers
Move one cell right	Right arrow or Tab
Move one cell left	Left arrow
Move one cell up	Up arrow
Move one cell down	Down arrow or Return
Change width of cell	Drag column handle
OK button	Enter
Cancel change to cell data	⌘-Z
Cancel all changes	Click close box, D

OBJECTS, IMAGES, AND THE FILE FORMATS THAT LOVE THEM

When you first start Illustrator, the program rewards you with an empty illustration window. It's Illustrator's way of saying, "Come on, Champ. Don't just sit there, get drawing!" Like any ultra-powerful graphics software, Illustrator is anxious for you to get the show on the road. This chapter shows you how.

At this juncture, you have the following options:

- Modify the artboard to meet your needs, then start drawing your new masterpiece.
- Close the empty illustration (⌘-W) and create a new one with a tracing template (⌘-Option-N).
- Open an illustration that you've previously saved to disk (⌘-O).
- Just sit there and stare with mute horror at the empty window.

I explain all but the last option in this chapter. (After all, every person must deal with artist's block in his or her own fashion.) I also tell you everything you need to know about importing graphics, magnifying your drawing and otherwise changing the way it looks on screen, and saving your artwork so you can come back to it later. And as if that's not enough, I describe how computer graphics are stored on disk and examine why in the world you should care.

By the time you finish this chapter, you'll be saying to yourself, "Whelp, looks like that's it for Chapter 3." It's that kind of incredibly meaningful chapter.

Preparing a New Illustration

Some programs require you to address a dialog box full of options before you create a new document. What size are your pages? Do you want to create tall pages or wide ones? How big are the margins? And on and on.

To its credit, Illustrator doesn't makes such a big deal about new document settings. As I mentioned in Chapter 2, the program simply assumes you want to use the settings stored in the Adobe Illustrator Startup file. This doesn't mean you have to accept the settings—you can modify the page size and orientation for an illustration any time you want—it's just that you don't have to worry about it up front.

The reason Illustrator soft-pedals page setup is that it isn't necessarily important. Sometimes you care about page setup; sometimes you don't. It depends on what kind of document you want to create:

- If you're creating a drawing, logo, or other graphic that you intend to place into a layout program such as PageMaker or QuarkXPress, then you aren't interested what the page looks like in Illustrator. When you import an Illustrator drawing into PageMaker or XPress, all empty portions of the artboard are cropped away, leaving just the graphic itself. Heck, you can create the entire graphic in the pasteboard if you like. Therefore, the graphic is all that matters.

But issues like page size, orientation, and placement become very important when building a small document or slide. Although touted as an illustration program, Illustrator is well suited to full-page fliers, double-sided mailers, and even 8-page newsletters. After all, what's the point of using a page-layout program that lacks drawing tools when you have all the tools you need for small-document production right here inside Illustrator?

For you page-conscious folks, Illustrator provides two commands—File » Document Setup and File » Page Setup—as well as one tool—the page tool. The following sections explain how these features work.

The Artboard Versus the Printed Page

In Illustrator, you specify the size and orientation of the printed page in one step, and the size and orientation of the artboard in another. This may seem flat-out bizarre—aren't the artboard and printed page the same thing?—but it makes sense given Illustrator's flexible approach to pages. See, in Illustrator, you can create humongous pages, up to 10 feet by 10 feet—larger than many bedrooms. Since very few printers can handle this extreme page size, Illustrator lets you divide your artwork onto several printed pages if you so desire.

Now, I know you aren't looking to print 10-foot by 10-foot artwork, but you might still find a use for an artboard that's larger than the printed page.

Say you want to create a 17 by 22-inch poster in Illustrator. Although this size is rather small for a poster—most are twice that large—it's awfully large for a printer. Office printers, for example, top out at 11 by 17 inches. This means you'll probably have to print your poster onto several pages and paste the pages together by hand (at least in the proofing stage).

Illustrator gives you one artboard—no more, no less. So if you want to create a multiple-page document like a newsletter, you have to compose the entire document on a large artboard and subdivide the artboard into pages. For example, to create an 8-page newsletter, you'd want to set the artboard to 34 inches wide by 22 inches deep, big enough to hold four pages horizontally and two pages vertically.

In most cases, you'll want to specify the size of the printed pages first and then adjust the size of the artboard. You don't have to work in this order—you can keep adjusting the two back and forth until the dogs come home—but this is frequently the most logical order. It's also the order that I discuss the commands in the following sections.

Setting up the Printed Page

To specify the size of the pages Illustrator prints, you first need to make sure you have selected the proper printer. Select the Chooser command from the Apple menu. On the left side of the Chooser dialog box you'll see a scrolling list of icons. These icons are *printer drivers*.

Select the proper driver for your printer:

● If you're using a PostScript-compatible printer, select the PSPrinter icon. If PSPrinter is not available, select LaserWriter 8. (The two are virtually identical. PSPrinter comes from Adobe and is therefore probably more recent; LaserWriter 8 comes from Apple.)

● If you own a non-PostScript printer, select the icon named after your printer. It may even look like your printer.

After you select the proper driver, click in the close box or press ⌘-W to close the Chooser dialog box.

Next, choose File » Page Setup. Assuming that you're using a PostScript printer, this displays the standard PSPrinter (or LaserWriter) Page Setup dialog box pictured in Figure 3-1. If you're using a non-PostScript printer, the dialog box will look a little different, but the important options are the same.

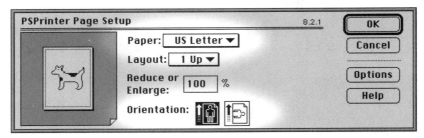

Figure 3-1: Your everyday average Page Setup dialog box with important options spotlighted.

For the time being, only two options in this dialog box matter. These are Paper and Orientation. (For descriptions of the others, read Chapter 18.)

● **Paper:** Select the paper size you want to print on from this pop-up menu. As you might imagine, it's important to make sure your printer can handle the paper size you select. Don't select Tabloid (11 by 17 inches), for example, if your printer maxes out at Legal (8.5 by 14 inches). A4, B5, and others are European page sizes.

● **Orientation**: You can create an upright page (portrait) or turn it over on its side (landscape). It just depends whether you want a page that's taller than it is wide, as by default, or one that's wider than it is tall.

After you respond to these two options, click on the OK button or press the Return key. Illustrator automatically redraws the dotted outlines inside the artboard. One outline represents the border of the printed page, the other represents the size of the imageable area (the portion of the page Illustrator can print).

Configuring the Artboard

To change the size of solid-bordered artboard in the drawing area, choose File » Document Setup, or press the magic key combination ⌘-Shift-D. Most of the options in the Document Setup dialog box (shown in Figure 3-2) control the size and orientation of the artboard, as well as the relationship between the artboard and the printed page. But a few are simply preference settings that Adobe saw fit to put in a dopey location. The difference between these preferences and those available from the File » Preferences submenu are that these affect the single foreground drawing while those affect *all* open drawings.

Whatever their purpose, here is how the Document Setup options work (in the order the options appear in the dialog box):

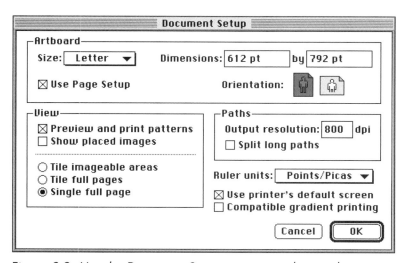

Figure 3-2: Use the Document Setup options to change the size and orientation of the artboard.

- **Size**: This pop-up menu lets you choose from a bunch of predefined artboard sizes.

- **Use Page Setup**: If you want to match the artboard to the printed page size, select this check box.

- **Dimensions**: If you don't want to use one of the predefined settings, specify the height and width of the artboard by entering values into these option boxes. It doesn't matter which value you enter first and which second—by default, the smallest value is treated as the width and the largest as the height. To change this, you have to select a different Orientation icon.

Unless you've changed the measurement systems in the General Preferences dialog box (using the Ruler Units pop-up menu), the Dimensions values are probably listed in points. While a good unit for precise measurements, few of us think in terms of points for larger measurements. To enter values in inches, just enter the value, followed by *in*. Illustrator automatically converts the measurement to points. You can also enter values in millimeters (*mm*) or picas (*p*). For example, *55p6* stands for 55 picas plus 6 points, which is 666 points or 9.25 inches. When working in inches or millimeters, you can enter *pt* for points.

- **Orientation**: Here you specify whether your artboard is taller than it is wide or vice versa. Be sure to select an option. Regardless of how you enter values in the Dimensions option boxes, Illustrator conforms to the selected orientation.

- **Preview and Print Patterns**: This is the first of Illustrator's misplaced preference settings. It determines whether tile patterns applied to the fills and strokes of objects are accurately previewed and printed, or whether they simply preview and print as gray. Turn this option off to speed up previewing and printing operations. (Chapter 15 explains tile patterns in detail.)

- **Show Placed Images**: When this preference setting is turned off, an imported Illustrator-type EPS image is not displayed properly in the artwork mode. Instead, it appears as a rectangle bisected by diagonal lines. When the check box is selected, Illustrator shows a monochrome version of the image in the artwork mode.

  Placed images of all varieties—EPS or otherwise—*always* show up in the preview mode—not to mention print—regardless of the Show Placed

Images check box. Also worth remembering, TIFF, PCX, and other types of images *never* display properly in the artwork mode. (I cover EPS, TIFF, and other formats as well as the artwork and preview modes later in this chapter.)

 Tile Imageable Areas: The three radio buttons below the Show Placed Images check box determine how Illustrator prints oversized artboards. By selecting the Tile Imageable Areas radio button, you tell Illustrator to chop up the artboard into as many imageable areas as will fit, thus ensuring no gap between an object printed half on one page and half on another.

 In other words, select this option when subdividing poster-sized artwork onto many printed pages.

 Tile Full Pages: Select this option to display as many whole pages as will fit in the drawing area. No partial pages are allowed.

 This is the option to select when creating a multi-paged document like a newsletter. Illustrator numbers the page boundaries inside the artboard so you know the order in which the pages will print.

 Single Full Page: This is the default setting. It instructs Illustrator to display just one set of dotted lines and print just one page, regardless of the size of the artboard. Some artists like to use this option with a slightly oversized artboard so they can adjust the way the illustration fits on the page using the page tool.

 Output Resolution: Set this value to reflect the resolution of the printer you want to use to produce your finished illustration or small document. This option affects Illustrator's automatic path-splitting function (described next) and the accuracy at which curves print.

 This is one of two options inside the Document Setup dialog box that affect all artwork created in Illustrator, whether printed from Illustrator or some other application. (The other is the Split Long Paths check box.) Do *not* lower this value below the default 800 unless you are encountering printing problems! And then, be sure to first consult the "Flatness and Path Splitting" section of Chapter 18!

● **Split Long Paths**: This check box automatically breaks up complex paths with gobs of points into smaller paths, in an attempt to eliminate printing errors. Illustrator determines which paths are split and to what degree based on the Output Resolution value.

 Illustrator automatically splits paths whenever you save or print a file! Do *not* select the this check box unless you are experiencing printing problems and you have read the "Flatness and Path Splitting" section of Chapter 18! There is no automatic way to reassemble paths that have been split apart; you have to join paths manually, which is a major pain in the butt.

● **Ruler Units**: Select an option from this pop-up menu to change the measurement system for the current drawing only (compared with the identically named option in the General Preferences dialog box, which affects all drawings from now on).

● **Use Printer's Default Screen**: With few exceptions, a printer has to convert the various colors and shades of gray in your illustration to small dots called *halftone cells*. If you turn this check box off, Illustrator automatically optimizes the halftone cells to print the best possible illustration. Leave the check box on to use your printer's built-in halftone scheme, which generally works faster. See Chapter 18 for more info.

● **Compatible Gradient Printing**: When Illustrator 5 introduced its automatic multi-color gradients, many folks had problems printing them. Adobe claims the culprits were out-of-date or non-standard PostScript interpreters—the code readers built into the printers—but whatever the scapegoat, this option is the solution. If gradations give you fits, just select this check box. Illustrator automatically converts gradations to blends on the fly, greatly slowing the printing process but also avoiding irritating printing errors.

Once you exit the Document Setup dialog box (by pressing Return, naturally), you'll see the altered page boundaries against the altered artboard. To adjust the position of the page boundaries, read on.

Positioning the Pages on the Artboard

You can't move the artboard. (That is, you can scroll it around inside the illustration window, but you can't actually change its location.) The artboard is always positioned smack dab in the center of the 10 by 10-foot pasteboard. However, you can move the page boundaries with respect to the artboard using the page tool.

The page tool is the last tool on the right side of the toolbox. Select this tool and then click or drag inside the artboard to set the location of the lower left corner of the imageable area of a printed page. If you selected the Tile Imageable Areas or Tile Full Pages option in the Document Setup dialog box, a network of page boundaries emanate from the point at which you release the mouse button.

(If just one page boundary appears, even though you selected the Tile Full Pages radio button, it's because this is the only whole page that fits at this location. Drag again with the page tool or increase the size of the artboard to see more pages.)

 Always use the page tool to change the placement of an illustration on a page. It's easier and always faster than trying to move a huge squad of graphic objects and text blocks with the arrow tool. If you need more wiggle room, increase the size of the artboard one or more inches all around.

Hiding the Page Boundaries

If the dotted page boundaries get in your face, choose View » Hide Page Tiling to make them go away. This is, of course, merely a temporary measure. You can make the page boundaries reappear at any time by choosing View » Show Page Tiling.

Adding a Tracing Template

Drawing from scratch in Illustrator is fairly difficult for experienced computer artists—and especially so for folks accustomed to traditional tools. The plain fact of the matter is that Illustrator's tools are well suited to line construction but poorly suited to sketching and establishing composition.

This is why so many Illustrator artists first sketch their artwork either the old-fashioned pencil-and-paper way or inside a program that provides decent sketching tools, such as Photoshop. You can then introduce the sketch into Illustrator as something called a *tracing template*.

Here's what you do:

1. **Sketch away**.

   If you own a scanner, you can sketch the graphic on a piece of paper and then scan it into Photoshop. Be sure to go over the sketch with heavy, bold lines prior to scanning so you can easily distinguish the important compositional elements inside Illustrator.

   If you don't own a scanner, sketch directly inside Photoshop or some comparable program using the brush and pencil tools. Keep it clean and simple; work in the grayscale mode, not in color; and don't go nuts with shading and airbrushing since you can't easily trace these elements in Illustrator.

You can also use a photographic image as a template. Open it in Photoshop and convert it to grayscale by choosing Mode » Grayscale.

2. Convert the image to black-and-white.

Illustrator's method for handling tracing templates is—to put it politely—a cruel joke. The first painful constraint is that the program can accommodate black-and-white templates only. If you save your sketch as a grayscale or color image, Illustrator converts it to black-and-white for you, and does a very cruddy job of it. Therefore, you should convert the image to black-and-white directly inside your sketching program.

 If you're sketching in Photoshop, the best command for converting a grayscale sketch to a black-and-white template is Image » Map » Threshold (⌘-T). Be sure the Preview check box is selected inside the Threshold dialog box. Then adjust the slider triangle at the bottom of the dialog box and gauge the effect it has on the sketch (which you can see in the background). When you get the nice, strong lines you need, press the Return key. Finally, choose Mode » Bitmap and immediately press Return. (Thanks to your use of the Threshold command, the settings inside the Bitmap dialog box are irrelevant.)

If you're working from a photograph, you may find it helpful to apply Filter » Other » High Pass to your grayscale image. Set the Radius value to 10 to draw out the clearest detail. (It'll look like a mess, but it works, take my word for it.) Then use the Threshold and Bitmap commands as directed above. Finally, use the eraser tool to erase the unnecessary detail. Figure 3-3 shows how I boiled down the image of a lobster to its skeletal essentials.

3. Set the resolution of the image to 72 pixels per inch (ppi).

Second among Illustrator's list of irritating tracing flaws it that it displays a template at 72 ppi regardless of its original resolution. So if you save the template at a higher resolution, it merely appears smaller and with fewer pixels. You can anticipate this problem by setting the resolution to 72 ppi before saving it to disk. (In Photoshop, choose Image » Image Size, select the File Size check box, and enter 72 into the Resolution option box.)

Figure 3-3:
After converting this Digital Stock photograph to grayscale (top), I applied the High Pass filter (middle), converted the image to black-and-white, and erased away the garbage (bottom).

4. Save the image in the MacPaint or PICT format.

Weirdness number three: Despite Illustrator 6's support for TIFF and other common image formats, it recognizes templates in just two formats: MacPaint, from the now historic—i.e., dead gone dead—painting program that started it all, and PICT, which is the vanilla Macintosh graphics format. (In Photoshop, press ⌘-S, select MacPaint or PICT from the Format pop-up menu, enter a name for your file, and press Return.)

5. Open the template in Illustrator.

You can't drag a template from Photoshop and drop it into Illustrator, nor can you import it into an open illustration window. You have to open the template using File » New or File » Open.

To create a new illustration with a template, choose File »
Open and open the MacPaint or PICT template file directly.
When Illustrator asks you how you want to open the image,
select the Illustrator Template radio button and press Return.

Or, if you prefer, you can press the Option key while choosing the
New command (or press ⌘-Option-N). Pressing Option causes
Illustrator to ask you to select a template file on disk.

To add a template to an illustration you've already begun, first close the
illustration if it's open, then press the Option key while choosing File »
Open (or press ⌘-Option-O). Select the illustration file you want to
open and press Return. Illustrator then displays another dialog box
asking you which template you want to open.

No matter how you introduce the template, it appears in the center of the artboard. The template appears on screen in a uniform gray tone, so you can easily
distinguish it from the lines and shapes in the illustration, as in Figure 3-4. Only

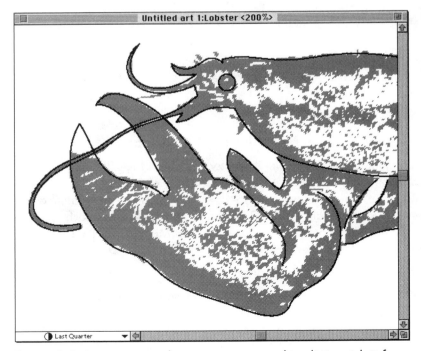

*Figure 3-4: A tracing template appears grayed to distinguish it from
the lines used to trace it.*

one template can exist within an illustration at a time, and you can't move or manipulate the template in any manner. And naturally, templates don't print. In Illustrator, a template is useful for tracing, and nothing more.

 Periodically, someone accuses me of being biased in favor of Illustrator or its arch-rival FreeHand. In truth, I'm neither; I'm just very free and easy with my criticism of each. In this spirit, I feel obligated to mention that FreeHand's template capabilities are substantially better than Illustrator's. You can save color templates in any format and at any resolution. You can import multiple templates and move and scale them as you please. For those of us sworn to Illustrator, Adobe will probably improve its handling of templates in Version 7, which is slated to be rewritten from the ground up. If this happens, it will be the first enhancement to the worn-out template feature since 1988.

In the meantime, this book is here to smooth out the rough spots. Chapter 10 provides a tip for isolating an imported image on a separate layer, permitting you to trace it with any tool *except* the autotrace tool. If you have Photoshop, Chapter 13 shows you how to automatically trace a sketch in that program and copy the resulting paths into Illustrator. These are some bang-up techniques, guaranteed to put a smile on the grumpiest artist's face.

Opening and Importing

Illustrator lets you have multiple illustration windows open at a time. To create another empty illustration window, you can choose File » New or press ⌘-N. You can also open an illustration saved to disk by choosing File » Open or pressing ⌘-O, all without closing a window that's already open.

You can open four kinds of files in Illustrator:

- Drawings previously created in Illustrator.

- Drawings created in FreeHand or some other drawing program and saved in the Illustrator file format. (You cannot open a drawing saved in FreeHand's native format.)

- Documents created in PageMaker, QuarkXPress, or Microsoft Word, and converted to the Acrobat PDF format.

- Images saved as TIFF, JPEG, or some other compatible format.

If you open an Illustrator file or an Illustrator-compatible FreeHand file, the illustration pops up on screen in a new illustration window. You can edit any line, shape, or word of text as explained throughout the myriad chapters that follow.

You can also edit graphic objects and text inside opened PDF files, although it is possible that some objects may be lost in the PDF conversion.

When you open a TIFF file or other image, Il'ustrator displays the images in a new illustration window. You can move or transform (scale, rotate, flip, or skew) images, as well as apply Photoshop filters (as described in Chapter 13). But you can't edit them in the same way that you edit object-oriented illustrations.

If you want to add an illustration or image to the illustration you're working on, choose File » Place. Rather than creating a separate illustration window, Illustrator imports the graphic to the foreground window. The graphic appears selected so you can begin working on it immediately. You can move or transform an imported graphic, but you can't edit it, even if the graphic was created using Illustrator. You can also apply Photoshop filters to imported images (unless you import the image as Illustrator EPS, as I discuss later in this chapter).

 You can replace one imported illustration or image with another using the Place command. Just click on the previously imported graphic with the arrow tool prior to choosing File » Place. After you select the file you want to import, Illustrator asks you if you want to replace the selected graphic with the new one. Click on the Replace button to make it so; click on the Ignore button to import the graphic as a new object.

I discuss individual file formats and the special ways to deal with them in the section "Those Crazy, Kooky File Formats" later on in this chapter. But first, I want to briefly go over the basics of opening or placing a file from disk. If you already know all about opening files, feel free to skip this section.

Using the Open Dialog Box

When you choose File » Open or File » Place, Illustrator displays the Open dialog box (shown in Figure 3-5), which requests you to locate and select the

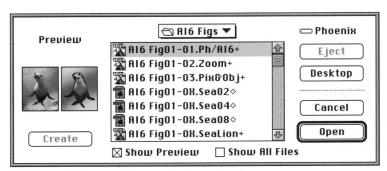

Figure 3-5: The Open dialog box is nothing more than a tool for locating graphics stored on disk.

drawing you want to open. The dialog box lets you search through all folders on all available hard drives, CD-ROMs, and floppy disks. Sometimes, you can even preview what the file looks like before you open it.

The Folder Bar

The top of the Open dialog box sports a *folder bar,* which tells you where you are inside the folder hierarchy. The name that appears in the bar matches the current folder. Drag from the folder bar to switch to a *parent folder;* that is, one of the folders that contains the current folder.

The Scrolling List

Below the folder bar is a scrolling list that contains the names of all folders inside the current folder as well as all graphics that you can open inside Illustrator. You can use the scrolling list as follows:

- **Select a document or folder**: Select a document or folder by clicking on its name.

- **Select by key entry**: To quickly locate a specific document or folder name, enter the first few letters of its name from the keyboard. The first item in alphabetical order whose name begins with these letters becomes selected.

- **Scroll through the list**: Press the up arrow or down arrow key to advance one name at a time through the scrolling list. On an extended keyboard, press the Page Up or Page Down key to scroll up or down several names at a time. Press the Home key to scroll all the way to the top of the list; press the End key to scroll all the way to the bottom.

- **Open an item**: Open a file or folder by double-clicking on its name, or by selecting it and pressing the Return key.

- **Open a folder**: If a folder name is selected, press ⌘-⌥ to open that folder and display its contents.

- **Exit a folder**: To exit the current folder and display the contents of its parent folder, press ⌘-⌃. You also can close the current folder by clicking on the disk icon above the Eject button.

The Navigation Buttons

To the right of the scrolling list is the name of the current disk. Below the disk name are four buttons. Each button has a keyboard equivalent, indicated in parentheses in the following list:

- **Eject (⌘-E)**: Ejects the current disk from the disk drive. The disk remains mounted, enabling you to access it later. If the current disk is a hard drive, the Eject button appears dimmed.

- **Desktop (⌘-D)**: Exits the current folder and displays all documents and folders located at the Finder desktop.

- **Cancel (⌘-period or Escape)**: Cancels the Open command and returns to the application desktop.

- **Open (⌘-O or Return)**: Opens the selected document or folder. When the Open button is surrounded by a heavy outline, you also can activate it by pressing the Return or Enter key.

 You can switch from one drive to another from the keyboard. Press ⌘-→ to display the contents of the next disk; press ⌘-← to display the contents of the previous disk.

The Preview Options

 The Open dialog box has been revised slightly under Illustrator 6. It includes a thumbnail preview of the selected illustration or image on the left side of the scrolling list, as well as a couple of check boxes under the scrolling list.

The beauty of the preview is that you don't have to open the graphic in order to remember what it looks like. But in order to see a preview, QuickTime (the popular Macintosh multimedia extension) has to be loaded, *and* you have to have specifically saved a thumbnail along with the file inside either Illustrator 6 (previous versions didn't support previews) or Photoshop 2.5.1 or later. Illustrator can also display the PICT previews included with some EPS files.

I'll explain how to save thumbnail previews later in this chapter. In the meantime, here's how the new Open dialog box options work:

- **Create**: Let me start by saying this button is darn near useless inside Illustrator. It theoretically allows you to create a preview of a selected graphic on the fly. However, QuickTime must be running for this button to function, and even then, the button only applies to PICT graphics. All other files—even Illustrator drawings—are inapplicable.

- **Show Preview**: When selected, this check box instructs Illustrator to display the thumbnail preview image on the left side of the dialog box.

If you turn the option off, the preview disappears and the Open dialog box collapses to save screen space.

Keep in mind, the preview depends on QuickTime. So if the preview is missing and the Show Preview check box is dimmed, chances are QuickTime did not load when you started up your Mac.

Show All Files: Select this check box to see all files in the current folder, whether Illustrator can open them or not. It lets you force Illustrator to at least attempt to open a graphic that it doesn't recognize as being compatible.

Those Crazy, Kooky File Formats

 Prior to Version 6, Illustrator was a program in a bubble. It relied on PostScript file formats and expected every other graphics application to support PostScript in kind. Thankfully, Illustrator 6 has broadened its horizons and joined the real world. It has gone from supporting three graphic file formats to supporting five times that many.

For the record, *file formats* are different ways to save a file to disk. Just as Betamax and VHS are different videotape formats, TIFF and PCX are different image formats. By supporting a wider variety of formats, Illustrator can accept graphics from all kinds of Macintosh and Windows applications.

The following sections explain all the formats supported by Illustrator 6, starting with the native Illustrator format and continuing through the others in alphabetical order. I tell you how the format works, what good it is, and offer additional instructions where needed.

Native Illustrator

The native Illustrator format—the one Illustrator likes to use the most—is a pure PostScript file. If you know how to program in PostScript, you can even open the file in a word processor and edit it line by line.

The great thing about an Illustrator file is that you can import it into just about any program that supports PostScript. If you import a PostScript file into PageMaker, for example, you won't be able to view the illustration accurately on screen—it just looks like a gray box—but you can print it to any PostScript printer. Many other drawing programs, including FreeHand and CorelDraw, can open Illustrator files and even save them.

There are six variations on the basic Illustrator format, each corresponding to a different version of the software:

- **Illustrator 6.0**: This format saves every little thing you can do in Illustrator 6.

- **Illustrator 5.0/5.5**: The Illustrator 5 format does not support imported image files or thumbnail previews. Otherwise, it is identical to the Illustrator 6 format.

- **Illustrator 4.0 (for Windows)**: From a Macintosh user's perspective, this Windows-only version of the Illustrator format is identical to the Illustrator 3 format. Illustrator 4 also supported grids and TIFF templates—neither of which Illustrator 6 has managed to integrate—but it hardly matters format-wise. The only thing to remember is, if you get an Illustrator 4 file, it comes from the Windows platform.

- **Illustrator 3.0/3.2**: This format doesn't support gradients, layers, large artboard sizes, tabs, and columns or rows. Gradient fills are converted to blends and all objects are combined onto a single layer. Objects in the pasteboard may be lost.

- **Illustrator 88**: This format does not support compound paths, area and path text, text blocks with more than 256 characters, custom guides, and charts. All paths remain intact, but they may not serve their original function. Text blocks are divided into pieces; area and path text may be broken up into individual letters.

- **Illustrator 1.0/1.1**: This only things this format supports are paths and small text blocks. What it doesn't support could fill a book: Tile patterns, masks, imported EPS images, and colors—that's right, colors—are just a few examples.

Acrobat PDF

Adobe's Acrobat is a paperless office program that lets you print to the screen instead of wasting precious scraps of Oregon forest. The suite of Acrobat utilities acts as a PostScript interpreter, much like the one built into your printer. You can trade PDF (*Portable Document Format*) files with other Mac and Windows users, and regardless of which program you used to create the original file or which fonts you used to format the text, all anyone needs to view the file is Acrobat. Illustrator goes one better, letting you edit text and graphic objects as well.

Taken to its logical extreme, this means you can create a document in just about any program that supports PostScript printing and open and edit the file in Illustrator. Here's how it works:

1. **Create your document in whatever program you want**.

   For the best results, you should use a program that offers proven support for PostScript, such as PageMaker or XPress.

2. **Rather than printing your document to the printer, print it to disk**.

   Assuming you're using the PSPrinter driver, you print to disk by choosing File » Print, selecting the File radio button from the Destination options, and then pressing the Return key.

3. **Save font definitions with your file**.

   Another dialog box appears, asking where you want to save the file. Name the file and select a destination. Then select the All But Standard 13 option from the Font Inclusion pop-up menu. This ensures that all but the most common fonts are included with your document. Press Return to save the pure-PostScript file.

4. **Launch the Acrobat Distiller program**.

   Illustrator opens and reads a limited set of PostScript commands, but it can't read the full gamut of PostScript generated by a program like PageMaker or XPress. But a program called Acrobat Distiller can do this. If you installed Acrobat along with Illustrator, you should be able to locate this program somewhere on your hard drive.

5. **Open the PostScript file**.

   Don't be put off if the cursor remains a revolving beachball after you've launched Acrobat Distiller. Forge right ahead by pressing ⌘-O and opening the file that you printed to disk. Distiller will ask where you want to save the file. Then it will begin converting the rambling PostScript file to the smaller subset of commands permitted by PDF.

7. **Open the PDF file in Illustrator**.

   After the conversion is completed—it may take a while—quit Distiller, switch to Illustrator, and open the PDF file. A dialog box will appear, asking you which pages you want to open. Illustrator can only open one page per document. You can have two pages open at once, but you have to open them in separate passes and as separate documents.

That's all there is to it. The process isn't foolproof, but it hums along surprisingly well. After printing a five-page PageMaker document to disk, I converted it using Distiller and opened the PDF file inside Illustrator. Every element was there, mostly intact and altogether editable. I could even access original objects inside an EPS illustration created back in Illustrator 3 and imported into PageMaker.

The only oddity was the text. Rather than interpreting text in continuous blocks, each line of type was independent and some lines were even broken into multiple objects. These breaks seemed to occur at points where I had kerned letters. This made editing the text tricky, but the fact remains that not a single letter was lost.

Of course, your experience, depending on which program you use to create the original file, may be more or less successful.

By the way, you'll notice there's another program in the Acrobat folder called Acrobat Exchange. This program lets you look at PDF file without editing it. If you want to free up some disk space, trash it. You don't need Exchange when you have Illustrator.

Amiga IFF

The Amiga is a variety of personal computer that offers a graphical operating system similar to the Mac's and is popular among a small number of multimedia folks. The original creator of the Amiga, Commodore, keeled over dead a little while ago, and the last I heard, the Amiga was in limbo. But dead or alive, the computer still has its fans, many of whom like to write me and urge me to stop making fun of the darn thing.

If you have an Amiga buddy, you can import images saved in IFF (*Interchange File Format*), which is the Amiga's all-around graphics format and serves much the same function as PICT on the Mac. Illustrator can save to the IFF format as well, but it converts the illustration to pixels with a fixed resolution of 72 ppi. Your Amiga pal better be a good friend for you to go through that.

Encapsulated PostScript (EPS)

The EPS (*Encapsulated PostScript*) format combines a pure PostScript description of an illustration with a PICT preview so you can see what the image looks like on screen. It is far and away the best format for saving Illustrator drawings so that you can import them into PageMaker or XPress.

Illustrator has been able to save EPS files since its first version in 1987. In fact, it was the first program I ever saw that produced reliable EPS files. And it has been able to open its own EPS files, no matter how long ago (i.e., in which version) they were produced.

Up until Illustrator 6, the program didn't stand a chance in heck of opening EPS files created in other programs such as FreeHand. Now it can. Illustrator 6 includes a new EPS *parser*, which is a program that reads code and converts it to editable objects and text. Personally, I've been able to open every single FreeHand EPS file I've tried, including illustrations that contain gradations and special PostScript fill patterns.

If you use FreeHand, or you know someone who does, you have two ways to swap files. On one hand, you can save in the Illustrator format from inside FreeHand, but you may lose imported TIFF images, special text effects, custom halftone dots, and other fill patterns. To avoid these oversights, save the illustration as an EPS file inside FreeHand and open the file in Illustrator 6.

You can also store images in the EPS format. Though generally an inefficient format for images (EPS offers no compression plus a lot of header info), the benefit of EPS is that you can save special PostScript routines such a halftoning information. EPS images also print faster, which is why the format is a favorite of high-end service bureaus.

When you import an EPS image into Illustrator, an alert box comes up offering you two strange options:

- **Parsed EPS**: This option imports all EPS code into the Illustrator file and converts the image to its internal image format. The image will look like a blank box in the artwork mode, without bisecting diagonal lines. Illustrator also lets you apply Photoshop-compatible filters to an image imported with this option (as I explain in Chapter 13).

- **Placed EPS**: Select this option to tag the EPS file on disk without loading all the code into your drawing. The advantage of this is that it doesn't increase the size of your file or force Illustrator to rasterize the image to its internal image format. You can also view such an image in the artwork mode if the Show Placed Images check box is highlighted in the Document Setup dialog box, or dim the image on a layer in order to trace it (as discussed in Chapter 10). However, you can't apply a Photoshop-compatible filter.

Select the Parsed EPS radio button if the image is very large and you have included special halftoning or color adjustment information that you want

Illustrator to send directly to the printer. Select the Placed EPS option if you're more concerned with how the image looks on screen, and you want to be able to apply filters to it inside Illustrator.

FilmStrip

Adobe Premiere is the foremost QuickTime movie-editing application for the Mac. The program is a wonder when it comes to fades, frame merges, and special effects, but it lacks frame-by-frame editing capabilities.

If you want frame-by-frame editing, you can export the movie to the FilmStrip format and modify the frames inside Photoshop or Illustrator. FilmStrip organizes frames into a long vertical strip. A gray bar separates each frame. The number of each frame appears on the right; time codes appear on left. Though Photoshop is a far more useful program for editing FilmStrip files, you can open and add to these files in Illustrator.

JPEG

Named after the folks who designed it—the Joint Photographic Experts Group—JPEG is the most efficient file format available to image editors. An image saved in JPEG almost always takes up less room on disk than if it were saved in any other format. To achieve these savings, JPEG uses a "lossy" compression scheme, which means that it sacrifices image quality to conserve space on disk. You control how much data is lost when savng the image.

JPEG is best used when compressing photographs and other *continuous-tone* images, in which the distinction between immediately neighboring pixels is slight. Any image that includes gradual color transitions qualifies for JPEG compression. JPEG is not well suited to screen shots, line drawings, and other high-contrast images. Therefore, you should avoid saving an illustration to the JPEG format at all costs. Illustrator supports JPEG so it can import images, not export them.

Kodak Photo CD

Photo CD is the affordable photographic scanning technology that leaves flatbed scanners in the dust. You can take a roll of undeveloped film, color negatives, or slides into your local Photo CD dealer and have the photos scanned onto CD-ROM at 2,048 by 3,072 pixels for about $1 to $2 per photo. Each CD holds 100 images, allowing you to acquire a library of images without taking up a lot of room in your home or office. Better yet, Photo CDs are designed to resist the ravages of time and last well into the 22nd century (longer than any of the people that use them).

The only problem is, Kodak's software is a nightmare. If you installed the Kodak Photo CD software when installing Illustrator, you added about 20 files to your hard drives, none of which are named logically and all of which have to be left absolutely alone. Rename a file, move it, or turn it off with an extensions manager, and you may very well crash your computer when trying to open a Photo CD image.

When you open or place a Photo CD image—found inside the Images folder in the Photo_CD folder on the CD—Illustrator displays the dialog box shown in Figure 3-6. Here you can select the resolution of the image you want to import and specify options so that Kodak's software can adjust the colors of the image to suit your screen.

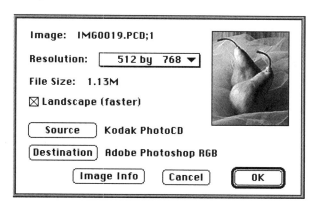

Figure 3-6: When you open a Photo CD image, Illustrator follows up the standard Open dialog box with this one.

Here's how the Photo CD options work:

- **Resolution**: Select from five resolution options, from a dinky 128 by 192 pixels to 2,048 by 3,072 pixels. A sixth option, 4,096 by 6,144 pixels, is dimmed unless you are working with a super-deluxe Pro Photo CD. The larger image you open, the longer it will take, but the better the image will look when printed.

- **Landscape**: Leave this check box selected. When turned on, it opens a vertically oriented image on its side. That's okay, because you can rotate the image with the rotate tool (as described in Chapter 11) in far less time than it would take Kodak's software to make those calculations.

- **Source**: Click on this button to specify the kind of film from which the original photographs were scanned. You can select from two specific Kodak brands—Ektachrome and Kodachrome—or settle for the generic Color Negative Film option. Your selection determines how the Kodak software transforms the colors in the image.

- **Destination**: After clicking on this button, select an option from the Device pop-up menu to specify the color model you want to use. The Adobe Photoshop RGB option is the most compatible with Illustrator.

 You can also open images from the folders inside the Photos folder on a Photo CD. But these images are converted to the PICT format by the Macintosh system software, which involves a middle man and doesn't permit you to take advantage of Kodak's automatic color corrections.

MacPaint

MacPaint was the earliest program for the Macintosh computer. In its day, MacPaint was wonderful, but having been last updated in 1987, it is severely lacking by today's standards. The MacPaint format accommodates a black-and-white image on a vertically-oriented, 7.5 by 10.5-inch page. This is why MacPaint is such a good format for Illustrator's lame templates, but darn near worthless for anything else.

PC Paintbrush (PCX)

PCX doesn't stand for anything. Rather, it's the extension that PC Paintbrush assigns to images saved in its native file format. By all accounts, PCX is one of the most popular image file formats in use today, largely due to the fact that PC Paintbrush is the oldest painting program for DOS. PCX images can include up to 16 million colors.

Photoshop 3

Illustrator can open and place images stored in Photoshop 3's native format, but this is largely a waste of time. Photoshop already supports every image format under the sun—more than Illustrator 6 supports—so why bother with the native format? After all, the only advantage to the Photoshop 3 format is that it supports multiple layers, and Illustrator 6 doesn't support Photoshop 3 layers. In fact, Illustrator won't properly display a Photoshop image that contains layers unless you have the 2.5 Format Compatibility check box selected in the More Preferences dialog box inside Photoshop. Instead, it displays a weird little error message in several different languages. This is a lesson in what happens when you violate the old adage: Do it right or don't do it at all.

PICT

The PICT (*Macintosh Picture*) format is a graphics exchange format Apple designed more than ten years ago and has updated irregularly over time. You can save both object-oriented illustrations and photographic images in the PICT format, but the format isn't ideally suited to either. Frankly, TIFF is better for images and EPS is better for illustrations.

In any case, you can open PICT illustrations—from MacDraw, Canvas, and the like—and edit the graphic objects and text blocks as if they were created inside Illustrator. Illustrator's PICT conversion isn't perfect—bitmapped patterns and other oddities may get lost in the translation—but you'll probably find it preferable to redrawing the objects and reinputting the text from scratch.

You can also introduce black-and-white PICT images as templates (as I described earlier) and open color PICT images inside new illustration windows. As I write this, a bug in the program prevents Illustrator 6 from importing a PICT image using File » Place. If you're bound and determined to include a PICT image in an existing illustration, open it (⌘-O), copy it (⌘-C), and then paste it (⌘-V) into the existing file.

Pixar

Pixar recently became a household word when the company went public shortly after the release of its monumentally popular movie *Toy Story*. But the company has been creating terrific computer animation for some time, from the father and son desk lamps in *Luxo, Jr.* to the run-amok toddler in the Oscar-winning *Tin Toy* to the commercial adventures of a Listerine bottle that boxes Gingivitis one day and swings Tarzan-like through a spearmint forest the next.

In its spare time, Pixar managed to create a few 3-D graphics applications for the Mac, including MacRenderMan, ShowPlace, and Typestry. But the company works its 3-D magic using mondo-expensive Pixar workstations. Illustrator can now open a still image created on a Pixar machine.

PixelPaint

PixelPaint from Pixel Resources was the first color painting application for the Mac. PixelPaint Pro 3 is still around today, and by all accounts, it's a very good application. But Illustrator's support for PixelPaint is limited to the old 8-bit format, the native format for the PixelPaint 2.0 and earlier. To trade an image with PixelPaint Pro, use the TIFF format.

Targa

TrueVision's Targa and NuVista video boards let you overlay computer graphics and animation onto live video. The effect is called *chroma keying* because typically, a key color is set aside to let the live video show through. TrueVision designed the Targa format to support 32-bit images that include so-called *alpha channels* capable of displaying the live video. Illustrator doesn't know a video from a rodeo, but it can import a still Targa image.

Tag Image File Format (TIFF)

Developed by Aldus to standardize electronic images so you could easily import them into PageMaker, TIFF (*Tag Image File Format*) is one of the most widely supported formats across both the Macintosh and Windows platforms. Unlike PICT, it can't handle object-oriented artwork, but it is otherwise unrestricted, supporting 16 million colors and virtually infinite resolutions.

Photoshop lets you apply so-called LZW (Lempel-Ziv-Welch) compression to a TIFF image, which substitutes frequently used strings of code with shorter equivalents. This makes the files smaller on disk without altering so much as a single pixel. Imaging professionals call this kind of compression *lossless*, because it preserves the integrity of each and every scanned color.

Illustrator 6 likewise supports LZW compression. It also opens both the Mac and Windows varieties of TIFF, so you never have to worry about your Photoshop images being compatible with Illustrator.

Windows BMP

BMP (*Windows Bitmap*) is the native format for the cheesy little Paint utility that ships with Windows. When Microsoft says, "Jump," software vendors respond, "How high?" so naturally BMP has become something of a standard over the years. BMP is the equal of PCX, supporting 16 millions colors and high resolutions. If you get a BMP image, rest assured you can import it into your illustration.

Getting Around in Illustrator

Illustrator works a lot like other graphics programs. You can zoom in and out to alternatively take a closer look at a detail or view your illustration in its entirety. You also scroll the illustration to bring different bits and pieces into view. And if you own an older, slower, machine—such as a IIci or an early model PowerBook—you can view objects in a special wireframe mode that speeds up screen display.

The next few sections explain how to get around quickly and expertly. If you don't know them already, pay special attention to the keyboard shortcuts. Using navigational shortcuts rather than selecting tools and commands expedites the artistic process more than any single factor.

Fit-in-Window and Actual Sizes

Illustrator provides 17 *view sizes*, which are the magnification levels that Illustrator uses to display your drawing in the illustration window. Magnified view sizes provide great detail but permit you to see small portions of the illustration at a time. Reduced view sizes show you a larger portion of the drawing area, but may provide insufficient detail for creating and manipulating objects. Because Illustrator makes it easy to quickly switch between view sizes, you can accurately edit your artwork and still maintain compositional consistency.

Assuming that you haven't altered the Adobe Illustrator Startup file, Illustrator displays every new illustration at *fit-in-window size*, which reduces the artboard so its fits inside the illustration window. The specific magnification level required to produce the fit-in-window size depends on the size of your monitor and the size of the artboard. In Figure 3-7, for example, the artboard fits in the window at 50 percent magnification.

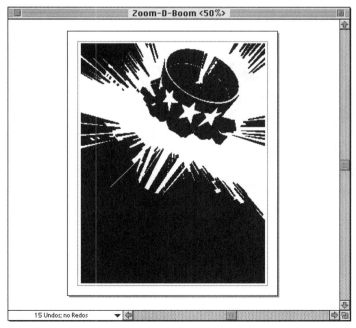

Figure 3-7: A typical illustration viewed from far away at fit-in-window size.

You can return to fit-in-window size at any time by choosing View » Fit In Window or pressing ⌘-M. But because this key equivalent makes absolutely no sense, most folks just double-click on the hand tool icon in the toolbox. (To help you remember, think about using that hand tool to push back the illustration.)

Another useful view size is *actual size*—or 100 percent view—at which the visible details of your illustration appear on screen more or less as they will print. Figure 3-8 shows an example.

 Actual size is not an *exact* representation of your illustration, and even approximate accuracy assumes your monitor displays 72 pixels per inch. Many monitors can pack in more pixels, causing an illustration viewed at actual size to appear quite a bit smaller than it prints. If you want to get a truly accurate feel for how your illustration will print, then print it (as described in Chapter 18).

Figure 3-8: Switch to actual size to see your illustration as it will print.

You can switch to actual size by choosing the View » Actual Size command or pressing ⌘-H (for "Where in Holy Heck did that shortcut come from?") But your intelligent, right-minded artist is more likely to double-click on the zoom tool icon in the toolbox (the one that looks like a magnifying glass). Just remember this handy poem:

Two clicks on the glass shows you blades of grass;
Two clicks on the hand gives you lay of land.

 You can zoom out to the smallest view size (6.25 percent) by Option-double-clicking on the zoom tool. On 17-inch and larger screens, this allows you to see all 100 square feet of the pasteboard.

Magnifying as the Mood Hits You

You can access each of Illustrator's 17 view sizes using the zoom tool. Select the zoom tool—second tool on the right—and click in the illustration window to magnify your drawing to the next higher view size. For example, when viewing an illustration at actual size, clicking with the zoom tool takes you to 150 percent size. Clicking again takes you to 200 percent. Each view affords you greater detail but shows off less of your artwork.

Drag with the zoom tool to surround the portion of the illustration that you want to magnify with a dotted rectangle called a *marquee*. Illustrator zooms in until the surrounded area fills the entire screen, as demonstrated in Figure 3-9.

 Once you get a feel for marqueeing, try out these techniques in mid-drag to make your zooms more precise:

- Press the Control key while dragging to create your marquee from the center outward. (Most other tools require you to Option-drag to draw out from the center; but with the zoom tool, the Option key is reserved for zooming out.)

- Press the spacebar as you drag to move the marquee. To again change the shape of the marquee, just release the spacebar.

- If you decide in mid-drag that you don't want to magnify the illustration after all, drag back to the spot where you started so the dotted marquee disappears, then release. Illustrator knows you chickened out and leaves the view size unchanged.

Figure 3-9: Drag with the zoom tool to surround an area with a marquee (top). Illustrator then magnifies that area to fill the window (bottom).

When you press the Option key, the cursor displays an inset minus sign, showing you that it's all set to zoom out. Option-clicking with the zoom tool reduces the view size to the next lower view size. You can see more of your artwork, but less detail.

As you zoom out, you may notice text blocks turning into gray bars. This is the greeking phenomenon I alluded to in Chapter 2, which is designed to speed up screen redraw. So far as Illustrator is concerned, you can't see such small text anyway, so why bother drawing it? If you disagree, you can instruct Illustrator to display the text as tiny letters by pressing ⌘-K and lowering the Greek Type Limit value.

The zoom tool cursor is empty when your current view size is at either the maximum (1600 percent) or minimum (6.25 percent) level of magnification possible. At that point, you can zoom in or out no further.

 You can also zoom in and out using a whole mess of keyboard shortcuts:

- To temporarily access the zoom tool when some other tool is selected, press and hold the ⌘ key and spacebar. I know, it's a weird shortcut, but very common—PageMaker, Photoshop, and FreeHand all use it. Releasing the two keys returns the cursor to its previous appearance.

- You can also zoom in one level by pressing ⌘-⌐ (right bracket), the shortcut for View » Zoom In.

- Press ⌘-Option-spacebar to get the zoom out cursor. Again, all the best applications use this shortcut.

- Or zoom out by pressing ⌘-⌐ (left bracket), which selects View » Zoom Out.

Dragging the Drawing

Since most screens aren't as large as a full page, you probably won't be able to see your entire illustration at actual size or larger. Therefore, Illustrator lets you move the artboard inside the illustration window, a technique known as *scrolling*. It's like looking through a pair of binoculars, in a way. You can see the action more clearly, but you can see only part of the action at a time. To look at something different, you have to move the binoculars (and your head) to adjust your view. This is the same thing that happens when you scroll in Illustrator.

One method for scrolling the drawing area is to use the two scroll bars, which are located at the bottom and right sides of the window. But only saps use the scroll bars, because Illustrator provides a better tool, the hand tool.

Second tool on the left side of the toolbox, the hand tool allows you to drag the drawing area inside the window. As you drag, the hand cursor changes to a fist to show you that you have the illustration in your vise-like grip.

 To temporarily access the hand tool when some other tool is selected, press and hold the spacebar. Then drag as desired. Release the spacebar to return the cursor to its previous appearance.

When a text block is active, pressing the spacebar results in a bunch of spaces. You can get around this by pressing the ⌘ key, pressing the spacebar, and then releasing the ⌘ key. So long as you keep the spacebar down, the hand tool is yours and the text block remains active.

Changing the Display Mode

Another way to control what you see on screen is to change the *display mode*— that is, how you see individual objects on screen. You can select from two basic modes in Illustrator:

- In the *preview mode,* you see objects and text in full color, more or less as they will print. (Again, Illustrator does its best with this what-you-see-is-what-you-get stuff. It's only software, after all.) Illustrator displays your drawing in the preview mode by default, and you can return to it at any time by choosing View » Preview or pressing ⌘-Y.

- If you own a slower Mac, you may grow impatient with the lethargic speed at which Illustrator draws objects on screen. To speed things up, choose View » Artwork or press ⌘-E (for "Excellerate!" a variation on accelerate that's Extra fast). Illustrator's *artwork mode* is what other programs call a *wireframe* or *keyline* mode: Text appears black, graphic objects have thin outlines and transparent interiors, and there's not a color in sight. Figure 3-10 shows how artwork and preview modes compare.

The artwork mode is very fast, because Illustrator doesn't have to spend time displaying complicated visual effects. However, it also takes some time to get used to. You basically have to imagine how the colors, strokes, gradations, and other effects are going to look. That's why most experienced artists switch back and forth between the artwork and preview modes by pressing ⌘-E one moment and ⌘-Y the next.

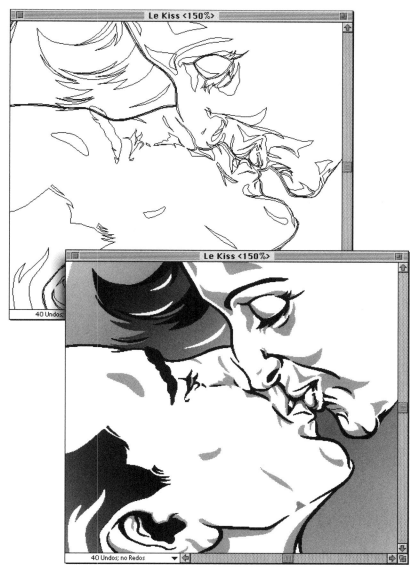

Figure 3-10: A relatively complicated illustration displayed in the out-lines-only artwork mode (top) and the preview mode (bottom).

Illustrator also lets you preview some objects while viewing others as wireframes. This can be useful for gauging how objects will print without dramatically slowing down screen redraw, or for examining a few objects out of context. For example, you might want to see through a few objects to some other objects in the background.

To do this, select the objects you want to view accurately with the arrow tool, then choose View » Preview Selection or press ⌘-Option-Y. Objects that are not selected appear as wireframes whether you start out in the artwork or preview mode. (To learn how to select objects, read the beginning of Chapter 5.)

Whether instigated using the Preview or Preview Selection command, you can cancel a screen preview that's taking too long by pressing ⌘-period. Illustrator immediately returns you to the artwork mode.

Creating a View You Can Come Back To

Do you find yourself switching back and forth between two or three views over and over again? First you zoom in on an individual leaf in a tree, then you scroll down and zoom out a little to examine the trunk, and next you zoom two or three increments to take in the whole tree. Then you magnify the leaf again and start the process again. This kind of zooming and scrolling back and forth between key locations in your illustration can eat up a lot of valuable drawing time.

Luckily, Illustrator has a solution. You can save specific views of your illustration and return to them at the press of a key. When you choose View » New View (or press ⌘-Control-V), Illustrator asks you to name the current view of your illustration. Enter a name and press the Return key. Illustrator saves the view size, the relative location of the page to the illustration window, and even the display mode.

Illustrator appends the view name to the bottom of the View menu. From now on, you can return to this exact view size, page position, and display mode just by choosing the view name, or by pressing ⌘-Control along with a number. (Illustrator numbers views in the order you create them.)

You can create more than ten views, but only the first ten get keyboard shortcuts. All views are saved with the illustration; they change from one illustration to the next.

To change the name of a view, or delete one or more views, choose View » Edit Views. Then select a view from the scrolling list in the Edit Views dialog box and enter a new name, or press the Delete key to get rid of it. If you want to delete many views at a time, you can Shift-click on a view name to select consecutive views, or ⌘-click to select a view here and another there.

Two Windows into the Same Illustration

You can create multiple views into a single illustration by choosing Window » New Window. Illustrator doesn't create a copy of the artwork, but rather a second illustration window to track your changes. Here are a couple of ways in which this seemingly strange technique might come in handy:

- Set one window to fit-in-window size and zoom in on the other so you can see some really tiny detail. Now edit the detail. It changes in both window. It's like looking at your illustration both normally and through a microscope.

- You can look at two different portions of your artwork by scrolling to one location in one window and another location in the other window. This way, you can edit one object so it looks like another or make other comparative decisions without scrolling back and forth like a madman.

Once the additional window outgrows its usefulness, close it. Illustrator doesn't ask you to save changes because the illustration is still open; it's just a view that you closed.

Saving Your Work to Disk

Whenever the topic of saving files comes up, I'm always tempted to jump on a soapbox and recite broken-down slogans:

- Save your illustration early and often!

- The only safe illustration is a saved illustration!

- An untitled illustration is a recipe for disaster!

- If you're thinking of switching applications, hit ⌘-S! If you hear thunder, hit ⌘-S! If a child enters your room, hit ⌘-S!

If you see a man running down the streets screaming "⌘-S! ⌘-S! ⌘-S!" at the top of his lungs and shaking his hands in the air, you'll know that I've come to visit. I'm absolutely despotic about saving, and with good reason. In my many years of writing and creating artwork on computers, I've lost more work than I can measure, and all because I didn't save in time.

So save, for crying in a bucket. The file you lose might be your own!

Using the Save Dialog Box

If the foreground image is untitled, as it is when you work on a new image, choosing File » Save or pressing ⌘-S displays the Save dialog box, shown in Figure 3-11. This is Illustrator's way of encouraging you to name the illustration, specify its location on disk, and select a file format. After you save the illustration once, choosing the Save command updates the file on disk without bringing up the Save dialog box.

Choose File » Save As to change the name, location, or format of the illustration. The Save As command always brings up the Save dialog box.

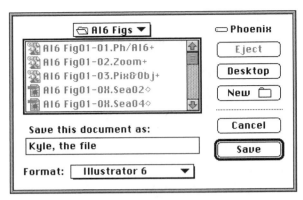

Figure 3-11: The Save dialog box lets you save a document from the current application.

The Save dialog box is much like the Open dialog box, with only a few exceptions. For example, when you first display the Save dialog box, the option box in the lower left corner is active. Here's where you enter a name for the drawing, up to 31 characters long.

If you click on the scrolling list or press the Tab key, you activate the scrolling list and deactivate the option box. A heavy line surrounds the scrolling list when it is active, as in Figure 3-11. You then can scroll through document and folder names by pressing keys from the keyboard. To reactivate the file name, press Tab again.

The navigation buttons—Eject, Desktop, and Cancel—work just like their counterparts in the Open dialog box. But two buttons are unique to the Save dialog box:

- **New Folder (⌘-N):** Clicking on this button creates a new folder inside the current folder. The system software displays an alert box that asks you to name the prospective folder.

- **Save (⌘-S):** This button saves the drawing to disk. If you haven't entered a file name, the Save button is dimmed. If you activate the scrolling list and select a folder, the Save button temporarily changes to an Open button (which is why the button also reacts to pressing ⌘-O, even when labeled Save). To again access the Save button, press Tab to deactivate the scrolling list. You can also select the Save button by pressing the Return or Enter key.

Selecting a File Format

The last option in the Save dialog box is the Format pop-up menu. This option lets you specify the file format you want to use to save your illustration. These are the same formats I discussed earlier in the section "Those Crazy, Kooky File Formats," but there are a few tidbits of wisdom I feel compelled to pass along:

- The only safe formats—the only ones that save every shred of information in your illustration—are Illustrator 6 and Illustrator EPS. These formats even save the window size, magnification level, scrolling, and display mode, and they include thumbnails so that you can preview the file inside Illustrator's Open dialog box. All the other formats sacrifice or reorganize objects in ways that make them more difficult or even impossible to edit.

- Use one of the older Illustrator formats to make an illustration compatible with a previous version of Illustrator, or a drawing program that only supports old Illustrator formats. FreeHand 5, for example, supports the Illustrator 5 format but not Illustrator 6. FreeHand 4 supports Illustrator 3, but nothing later.

- Adobe is trying like crazy to promote the Acrobat PDF format, so it's only natural that Illustrator permits you to save your drawing in this format. Theoretically, it allows you to share the drawing with other folks, who could view it on their screens without owning Illustrator or some other graphics application. But Acrobat isn't quite as pervasive as Adobe would like you to believe, so it's unlikely you'll ever want to use PDF.

- In most cases, you won't want to save your illustration to one of the image formats—Amiga IFF, BMP, PCX, Pixar, Targa, and especially not JPEG. In fact, if you try to do this, Illustrator warns you sternly that you're about to save your illustration as a mess of pixels, which will totally ruin everything.

  The only time an image format is useful is when you want to trace something. For example, suppose you open a FreeHand EPS illustration that contains an imported image, and you want to convert the image to objects with the autotrace tool. You could copy the image to a new illustration, save the illustration in the PCX format, open it in Photoshop, convert it to black-and-white, and save it to the PICT format. (Alas, Illustrator can't save to the PICT format directly.) Then you could open the PICT image as a template inside Illustrator and trace it. Sure, it's not the kind of activity you're going to want to engage in every day, but it's there if you need it.

 If you save an illustration in any format other than Illustrator 6 or Illustrator EPS, make sure you have created a backup version of the illustration in the Illustrator 6 format! (You can do this by choosing File » Save As.) Otherwise, you are needlessly and deliberately throwing away some amount of your hard work.

Saving an EPS Illustration

To use an illustration in PageMaker or XPress, select Illustrator EPS from the Format pop-up menu. After you click on the Save button or press Return, Illustrator displays the EPS Format dialog box depicted in life-like detail in Figure 3-12. You

```
┌──────────────────── EPS Format ────────────────────┐
│  ┌─ Compatibility ──────────┐   ┌─ Preview ──────┐  │
│  │ ○ Illustrator 1.1   ○ Illustrator 3/4 │  ○ None        │
│  │ ○ Illustrator 88    ● Illustrator 5/6 │  ○ 1-bit IBM PC│
│                                     ○ 1-bit Macintosh   │
│  ┌─ Options ──────────────────┐     ● 8-bit Macintosh   │
│  │ ⊠ Include Placed EPS Files       │                   │
│  │ ⊠ Include Document Thumbnails     │                   │
│                                                           │
│  ┌─ Fetch™ Information ──────────────────────────┐        │
│  │  Author:     │ Deke McClelland │               │        │
│  │  Keywords:   │ Bugs, critters, larva, yummy, │ │        │
│  │              │ scrumptious                   │ │        │
│  │  Description:│ This illustration shows a fancy dinner │
│  │              │ plate piled high with maggots. Too bad │  ┌────────┐
│  │              │ you can't see it. I guess you'll just  │  │ Cancel │
│  │              │ have to use your imagination.          │  └────────┘
│  │                                                │        ┌────────┐
│  │                                                │        │   OK   │
│  └────────────────────────────────────────────────┘        └────────┘
└─────────────────────────────────────────────────────────────────────┘
```

Figure 3-12: Illustrator presents you with a world of options when saving an EPS file.

can probably figure out the majority of these options on your own, but I might as well run through them if only to eliminate all possible traces of confusion:

- **Compatibility**: These radio buttons are identical to the different Illustrator formats I discussed earlier. The basic deal is this: Previous versions of Illustrator can't read an EPS file created by Illustrator 6 unless you select the option that corresponds to its version number. If you don't care about previous versions of Illustrator, leave the 6.0 option selected so you don't lose anything.

- **Preview**: These options control the PICT screen preview that Illustrator attaches to an EPS file. Unless the program that you want to import the illustration into doesn't support color, leave the 8-Bit Macintosh option selected. If you want to import the illustration into a Windows program, select 1-Bit IBM PC.

- **Include Placed EPS Files**: This check box is usually dimmed. It's available only if you imported an EPS image or illustration, as discussed back in the "Encapsulated PostScript (EPS)" section. When checked, this option includes imported EPS code into the new EPS file. To bag the code, turn this check box off. (Frankly, I can think of no reason on earth why you'd want to do this.)

- **Include Document Thumbnails**: Always select this check box. It creates a thumbnail of the illustration so you can preview it from the Open dialog box inside Illustrator, Photoshop, and an increasing number of other programs.

- **Fetch Information**: Fetch is a wonderful program that lets you catalog graphics, either for archival purposes or for collections that you intend to sell. Adobe purchased Fetch along with PageMaker and the rest of Aldus a couple of years ago, so it's not a surprise to see Illustrator 6 integrate a little bit of support for the program. If you intend to integrate this particular EPS illustration into a Fetch catalog, go ahead a fill out a few keywords (for searches) and a description into these option boxes. Illustrator automatically grabs the Author info from the name you've assigned to your system (using the Sharing Setup control panel), but you can replace the author name if you like.

In most cases, you can ignore this dialog box and just press the Return key to tell Illustrator to do its stuff. The default settings ensure no loss of illustration integrity on the off chance that you aren't paying a lick of attention to what you're doing. It's the kind of service any decent program is all too happy to perform.

PART TWO
CREATING

CHAN

CHAPTER 4

DRAWING THE SIMPLE STUFF

Heaven help the experienced artist who encounters Illustrator for the first time. If you've drawn with pencil and paper, or sketched inside a painting program like Photoshop, but you've never used Illustrator before, now is a good time to open your skull, remove your brain, and replace it upside down. Drawing with an illustration program is a very different adventure, and although it pains me to say it, your previous experience is as likely to impede your progress as to expedite it.

Drawing in Illustrator is actually a three-part process: You draw lines and shapes, you manipulate these objects and apply special effects, and you stack the objects one in front of another like pieces of paper in a collage.

This means the lines and shapes remain forever flexible. You can select any object and edit, duplicate, or delete it, regardless of its age or location in the illustration. I'm still playing around with drawings I created 10 years ago, and every object responds exactly as it did the day I drew it. Pencil and paper do not give you this degree of control.

But Illustrator's flexibility comes at a price. It takes a lot of time and a fair amount of object-oriented savvy to create even basic compositions. There are no two ways about it—Illustrator is harder to learn and more cumbersome to use than conventional artist's tools.

In this chapter, I explain how to use Illustrator's most straightforward drawing tools. If you're feeling a little timid—particularly after my pessimistic introduction—have no fear. With this chapter in front of you, you'll be up and running within the hour. If you're the type who prefers to dive right in and investigate basic functions on your own, you can discover how these tools work largely without my help. For you, I explain options, suggest keyboard tricks, and point out small performance details that many novice and intermediate users overlook.

But before I start, I want to take a few brief paragraphs to explain how lines and shapes work inside Illustrator. You'll better understand how drawing tools work if you first understand what you're drawing.

Everything You Need to Know About Paths

Any line or shape you create in Illustrator is called a *path*. (That way, you don't have to say "lines or shapes" all the time; the one word comprises both.) Conceptually, a path is the same as a line drawn with a pencil. A path may start at one location and end at another, as in the case of an open line. Or it may meet back up with itself to form a closed shape. Paths can range in length and complexity from tiny scratch marks to elaborate curlicues that loop around and intersect like tracks on a roller coaster.

The cartoon face in Figure 4-1 contains 12 paths. Ten of the paths are open (lines) and two are closed (shapes). So that you can clearly distinguish open from closed, I've given thick outlines to the lines and thin outlines to the shapes. The closed paths surround the face, with the white shape mostly covering the gray one. The open paths represent the features.

Figure 4-1: A simple cartoon composed of open paths (thick outlines) and closed ones (thin).

All paths—whether open or closed—are made up of basic building blocks called *anchor points* (or just plain *points*). The simplest line is a connection between two anchor points— one at each end. (Anyone familiar with a little geometry will recognize this principle: Two points make a line.) But Illustrator can just as easily accommodate paths with hundreds of points, each connected to another like dots in a dot-to-dot puzzle.

Points and Segments

Figure 4-2 shows the points required to create the cartoon face. I've applied thinner outlines to the lines and made the shapes transparent so you can better see the square points. The most complicated path contains 11 points; the least complicated contains two.

The bits of line between points are called *segments*. A segment can be straight, as if it were drawn against the edge of a ruler. A straight segment flows directly from one point to another in any direction. A segment may also curve, like the outline of an oval. Curved segments connect two points in an indirect manner, bending inward or outward along the way.

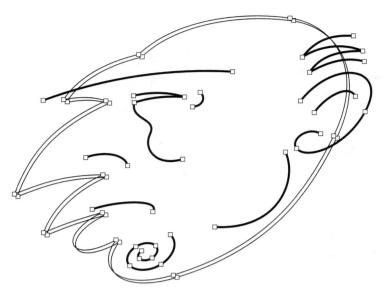

Figure 4-2: The small white squares represent the points needed to represent the cartoon in Illustrator.

Strokes and Fills

Although a line drawn with a dull pencil is heavier than a line drawn with a sharpened one, the thickness of any line fluctuates depending on how hard you press the pencil tip to the page. In Illustrator, the thickness (or *weight*) of an outline is absolutely consistent throughout the course of a path. In other words, different paths can have different weights, but the weight of each path is constant (as Figure 4-1 shows).

The thickness of an outline is called the *stroke*. In addition to changing the weight of the stroke, you can change its color. Strokes can be black, white, gray, or any of several million colorful variations.

You can also color the interior of a path by assigning it a *fill*. Like a stroke, a fill may be black, white, or any color. In Figure 4-1, the shapes that encircle the face are filled with white and gray. You can even assign a transparent fill, as in the case of the shapes in Figure 4-2.

Seeing What You Draw

I explore strokes and fills in amazing detail (if I do say so myself) in Chapters 15 through 18. But because these two attributes are so important to the way you see paths on screen, I need to impart a bit of basic info in the meantime. Here's the problem: By default, Illustrator applies black fills and transparent strokes to each path you draw. This means you can't see the outline of a path as you're drawing it, and the black fills cover each other and make the shapes look like they're globbing together. The default stroke and fill are particularly ill-suited to learning and experimentation.

There are two solutions, either of which is acceptable:

- Switch to the artwork mode by pressing ⌘-E (or choosing View » Artwork). The fills disappear and the strokes become black hairlines.

- Change the fill to transparent and the stroke to black in the Paint Style palette.

To change the fill and stroke, follow these steps:

1. Choose Object » Paint Style, or press ⌘-I. This brings up the Paint Style palette, as shown in Figure 4-3.

2. Click on the Fill icon in the upper left corner of the palette. Then click on the None icon—the one with the gray diagonal line—in the row of icons on the right side of the palette. This makes the fill transparent.

3. To assign a black stroke, click on the Stroke icon in the upper left corner of the palette, then click on the Black icon in the row of icons on right.

Figure 4-3 shows how the Paint Style palette should look when you've finished modifying the fill and stroke settings. These settings will affect every path you draw until the next time you change the fill or stroke.

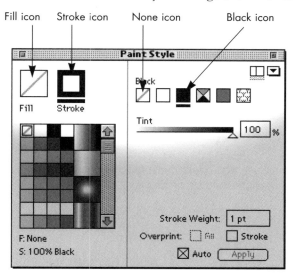

Figure 4-3: Change the fill to transparent and the stroke to black to best experiment inside Illustrator.

The Simplest of Simple Shapes

Illustrator offers a total of six tools for creating rectangles and ovals. The standard rectangle and oval tools appear by default in the middle of the toolbox. You can also select the rounded rectangle tool from a pop-up menu by clicking and holding on the rectangle tool slot, as shown on the left side of Figure 4-4.

 As if that's not enough, Illustrator offers a variation on each of these tools that draws a shape from the center outward. To access one of these tools, double-click on either the oval or rectangle tool icon in the toolbox. Small crosses appear inside the icons (as in the right example in Figure 4-4) to show that they will now draw from the center outward. To return to the corner-to-corner tools, double-click on one of the icons again.

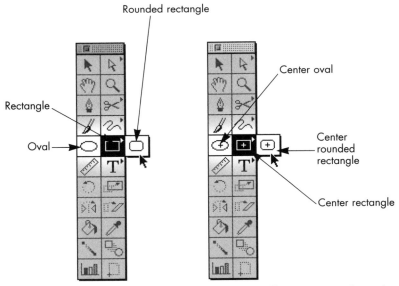

Figure 4-4: Ironically, Illustrator offers more tools to draw ovals and rectangles than any other kinds of shapes.

Drawing a Rectangle

To draw a rectangle, select the rectangle tool (fifth tool on the right side of the toolbox) and drag inside the drawing area. The point at which you start dragging sets one corner of the rectangle; the point at which you release sets the opposite

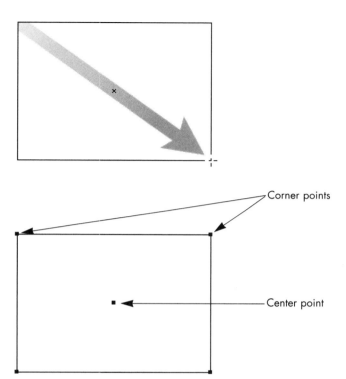

Figure 4-5: Drag from one corner to the opposite corner to draw a rectangle.

corner, as shown in Figure 4-5. The two remaining corners line up vertically or horizontally with their neighbors.

Illustrator creates a fifth point called the *center point* in the center of the shape. This special point floats free of the shape; it is not connected to any other point by a segment. If you move the rectangle, change its size, or completely mess it up, Illustrator repositions the center point so it remains in the center of the shape. You can use the center point to align the rectangle to another shape. I explain how to take advantage of this feature in Chapter 10.

 In the preview mode, you can only see the center point when the rectangle is selected. To see the center point of a deselected rectangle, switch to the artwork mode by pressing ⌘-E.

You can also use the rectangle tool as follows:

 If you press the Option key while drawing with the rectangle tool, the beginning of your drag marks the center of the rectangle. As before, the release point becomes a corner point.

> **TIP** You can press and release Option in mid-drag to switch between dragging from corner-to-corner and center-to-corner. Give it a try.

 If the center rectangle tool is active (as when you double-click on the rectangle or oval tool), Option-dragging creates a rectangle normally, from corner to opposite corner.

 Shift-drag with the rectangle tool to draw a perfect square. You can press and release the Shift key in mid-drag to switch between drawing a rectangle or a square. Isn't it great how Illustrator lets you change your mind?

 Shift-Option-dragging with the rectangle tool creates a square from center to corner.

Drawing by the Numbers

You can also enter the dimensions of a rectangle numerically. Click with the rectangle tool—that's right, just click inside the drawing area—to display the dialog box shown in Figure 4-6. Here, you can enter values for the Width and Height options. You can also round off the corners by changing the Corner Radius value (as I explain in the next section). After pressing Return, Illustrator creates a rectangle to your exact specifications.

> **TIP** Since no placement options are given in the Rectangle dialog box, the point at which you clicked with the tool serves as the upper left corner point of the shape. If you want the click point to be the center of the shape, Option-click (or click with the center rectangle tool).

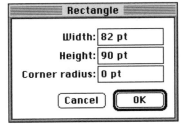

Figure 4-6:
Click with any
rectangle tool to
enter the exact
width and height of
your rectangle.

Notice that each option box in Figure 4-6 includes the letters *pt*, an abbreviation for points (1/72 inch). This refers to the unit of measure you set using the Ruler Units option in the General Preferences dialog box. The unit of measure can alternatively be inches (*in*) or millimeters (*mm*).

 If you don't like the current unit of measure, enter your own abbreviation. For example, by entering *2in* into the Width option box, you create a rectangle 2 inches wide, regardless of the active unit of measure. Illustrator automatically converts the measurement to the unit of measure (2 inches converts to 144 points) when you tab to the next option box. To enter a value in picas, enter the value followed by *p* and then the points. For example, *2p3* means 2 picas and 3 points, or 27 points.

You can enter spaces between the number and the measurement abbreviation, but you don't have to. If you enter a value without an abbreviation, Illustrator assumes the active unit of measurement (points by default).

 Want to create a square? You could enter the same value in both option boxes, but that's frankly too much effort. Just enter the desired size into the Width option box, then click on the word Height to duplicate the value. You can likewise duplicate the Height value by clicking on the word Width.

 You can only use the Rectangle dialog box to create new shapes. If you want to change the size of a rectangle you've already drawn, use Illustrator 6's new Control palette (shown in Figure 4-7). Make sure the rectangle is selected, so its points are visible. (Use the arrow tool to click on the shape if it is not selected.) Then choose Window » Show Control Palette. Then enter new values in the W and H option boxes.

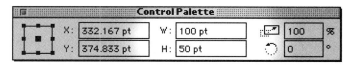

Figure 4-7: You can now change the dimensions of an existing rectangle by modifying the W and H values in the Control palette.

Rounding off a Rectangle's Corners

To draw a rectangle with rounded corners, select the rounded rectangle tool from the rectangle tool slot and drag away. Illustrator creates a shape with eight

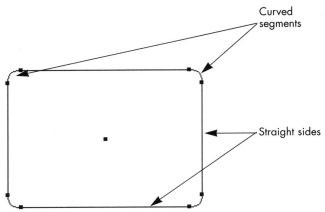

Figure 4-8: *Illustrator uses curved segments to join straight sides in a rounded rectangle.*

points—two along each side, with a curved segment around each corner—as in Figure 4-8.

You can change the roundness of the corners of a rectangle in two ways:

- Change the Corner Radius value in the General Preferences dialog box.

- Click with the rectangle or rounded rectangle tool and enter a value into the Corner Radius option box.

In each case above, you change the roundness of all future rectangles. There is presently no way to change the round-ness of an existing rectangle, except to edit it by hand. (Honestly, in its nine years, you'd think Illustrator would have resolved this problem!)

Just how does the Corner Radius value work? Well, as you may recall from your school days, the *radius* is the distance from the center of a circle to any point on its outline. You can think of a rounded corner as being one quarter of a circle, as shown in the first example of Figure 4-9.

The size of the circle increases as the radius increases, so a large Corner Radius value rounds off the corners of a rectangle more dramatically than a smaller value. To demonstrate this idea, the second example in Figure 4-9 shows the result of increasing the radius. I've included a grayed version of the radius from the first example for comparison.

A corner radius of 0 indicates a sharp, perpendicular corner. If you click with the rounded rectangle tool and enter a Corner Radius of 0, Illustrator automatically switches you back to the standard rectangle tool.

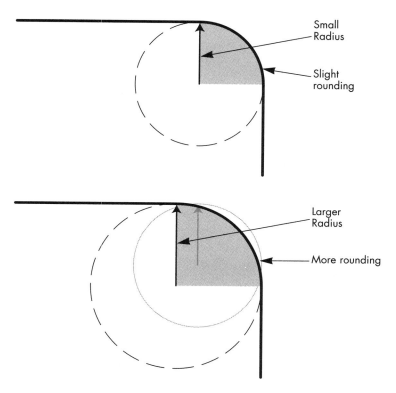

Small Radius

Slight rounding

Larger Radius

More rounding

Figure 4-9: A small corner radius (top) results in a less pronounced rounding effect than a larger radius (bottom).

Drawing an Ellipse

The oval tool—the fifth tool on the left of the toolbox—works much like the rectangle tool. The main difference, of course, is that the oval tool draws ellipses and circles rather than rectangles and squares. But there is also another difference. Rather than representing corners (the bounding rectangle outside shape as in most programs), the points at which you begin dragging and releasing represent opposite points along the arc of the shape.

As you drag with the oval tool, imagine that a dotted rectangle forms inside your drag, as shown in Figure 4-10. This rectangle exists entirely within the ellipse. (By contrast, when you draw an ellipse in FreeHand, PageMaker, or another Macintosh application, the shape fits inside the rectangular boundary of your drag.)

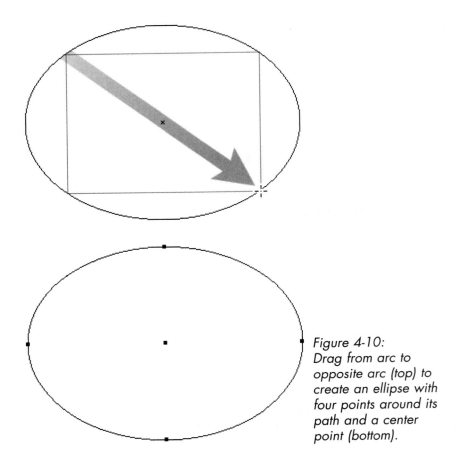

*Figure 4-10:
Drag from arc to
opposite arc (top) to
create an ellipse with
four points around its
path and a center
point (bottom).*

This unusual approach to ellipses mystifies many users, but in fact, Illustrator's oval tool makes a more efficient tracing tool. You trace an oval or circular template shape simply by dragging from the middle of one arc to the middle of the opposite arc. There is no guesswork, since you begin and end your drag on portions of the template shape. (In other programs, you must begin and end your drag well outside the template shape, estimating the points where the vertical and horizontal extremes of the ellipse intersect.)

Otherwise, the oval tool works much like the rectangle tool:

- Option-drag with the oval tool to create an ellipse outward from the center. As always, the release point becomes the middle of an arc, determining the size and shape of the ellipse.

- You can also double-click on the oval tool icon in the toolbox to select the center oval tool. Option-drag with this tool to draw an ellipse normally, from arc to opposite arc.

- Shift-drag to draw a perfect circle. Shift-Option-drag to draw a circle from the center point outward.

- Click in the drawing area to bring up the Oval dialog box. It contains Width and Height options for specifying the width and height of the shape. The shape aligns to your click point by the middle of the upper left arc. If you Option-click with the oval tool, the ellipse aligns by its center. And remember, you can click on the Height option name to copy the Width value—or vice versa—thus ensuring a perfect circle.

- Use the W and H values in the Control palette to change the width and height of an ellipse that you've already drawn.

Simple Shapes at an Angle

When drawing a shape with the rectangle or oval tool, you may find that your path rotates at an odd angle, as demonstrated in Figure 4-11. Don't worry, you aren't misusing the tool and Illustrator isn't broken. Someone has gone and changed the Constrain Angle value in the General Preferences dialog box.

The *constraint axes* control the angles at which you move and transform objects when pressing the Shift key. But they also control the creation of rectangles, ellipses, and text blocks. If the Constrain Angle value is set to anything besides 0, Illustrator rotates a rectangle or ellipse to that angle as you draw.

If someone has indeed reset your Constrain Angle, press ⌘-K (or choose File » Preferences » General). Then enter 0 into the Constrain Angle option box and press Return.

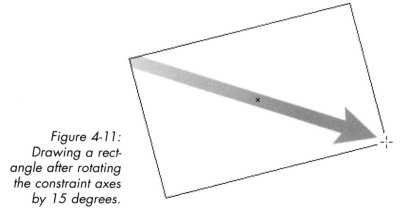

Figure 4-11:
Drawing a rect-
angle after rotating
the constraint axes
by 15 degrees.

Polygons, Stars, and Spirals

If you wanted to create a polygon, star, or spiral in Illustrator 5, you had to choose a command and enter numerical size and shape info. It wasn't drawing, it was shape creation by data entry.

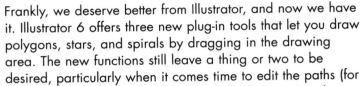 Frankly, we deserve better from Illustrator, and now we have it. Illustrator 6 offers three new plug-in tools that let you draw polygons, stars, and spirals by dragging in the drawing area. The new functions still leave a thing or two to be desired, particularly when it comes time to edit the paths (for example, you can't automatically change the number of points assigned to a star after you create it). But they're much more capable and empowering than they were in the past.

To display the plug-in tools, choose Window » Show Plug-in Tools. Figure 4-12 shows the plug-in tools palette with shape-creation tools labeled.

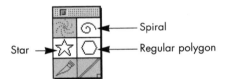

Figure 4-12: Illustrator 6 offers new tools for drawing polygons, stars, and spirals.

Drawing a Regular Polygon

A regular polygon is a shape with multiple straight sides—each side is identical in length and meets with its neighbors at a constant angle. An equilateral triangle is a regular polygon, as is a square. Other examples include pentagons, hexagons, octagons, and just about any other shape with a *gon* in its name. Figure 4-13 shows a few regular polygons for your visual edification.

To draw a polygon, select the regular polygon tool—second tool on the right-hand side of the palette—and drag in the drawing area. You always draw a polygon from the middle outward, whether you press the Option key or not (i.e., there's no point in pressing Option). The direction of your drag determines the orientation of the shape.

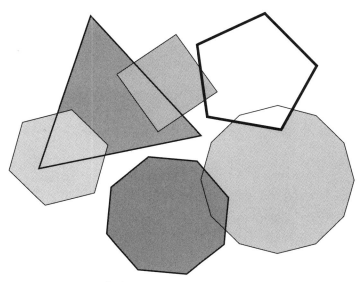

Figure 4-13: A whole mess of regular polygons, ranging from 3 to 12 sides.

 By default, Illustrator draws octagons (8-sided shapes). You can change the number of sides while dragging with regular polygon tool by pressing the up and down arrow keys. The up arrow key adds a side; the down arrow key deletes one. You can also add or delete many sides at a time by holding down the arrow key.

Another way to change the number of sides is to click in the drawing area with the regular polygon tool. Illustrator displays the Polygon dialog box, which lets you specify a Radius value and the number of sides.

- The Radius value is the distance from the center of the shape to any corner point in the shape. Therefore, a regular polygon with a radius of 100 points would fit entirely inside a circle with a radius of 100 points.

- You can enter any number of sides from 3 to 999. Shapes with more than 20 sides tend to looks like circles with bumps.

As always, the values you enter into this dialog box affect all future polygons you create. You cannot make changes to an existing polygon using the Polygon dialog box. If you want to change the size of a polygon, use the scale tool, as discussed in Chapter 11. To change the orientation of a polygon, use the rotate tool, also covered in Chapter 11. But if you want to change the number of sides, you have to delete the polygon and redraw it.

Here are a few more (marginally useful) things you can do with the regular polygon tool:

- Shift-drag with the tool to constrain a polygon's orientation so the bottom side is horizontal. (This is the same way Illustrator draws a shape when you click with the regular polygon tool.)

- Press the spacebar while dragging to move the shape rather than change its size. When you get the polygon positioned properly, release the spacebar and continue dragging or release.

- Press the W key while dragging to create a series of concentric polygons. Whatever the W stands for—Weird, Wacky, or possibly What in the world is going on here?—this is a singularly bizarre technique. It's great for getting ooohs and aaahs from your friends but it's rarely practical.

Drawing a Star

Illustrator lets you draw regular stars, in which each spike looks just like its neighbors. To draw a star, drag with the star tool, which is the second tool down on the left side of the plug-in tools palette. Illustrator draws the shape from the center outward.

You can modify the performance of the star tool by pressing the Control and Option keys. But to adequately explain what you're doing, I need to conduct another small geometry lesson. A star is made up of two sets of points, one at the points where the spikes meet and one at the tips of the spikes. These points revolve around one of two circles, which form the inner and outer radiuses of the star, as pictured in Figure 4-14.

Radius is one of those darn *us* words that doesn't sound right when you make it plural. Scholarly folks who wear mortar boards prefer the Latin *radii*, in which you pronounce one *i* as *ee* and the next as *ai*. Most editors go with *radiuses*, which sounds vaguely pejorative. I'd just as soon avoid talking about more than one radius at a time, but this inner and outer thing really forces my hand.

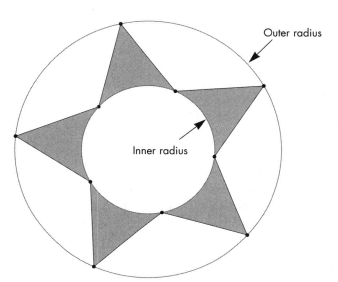

Figure 4-14: The inner and outer points in a
star revolve around two imaginary circles.

 When you drag with the star tool, Illustrator scales the two
radiuses proportionately, so that the inner radius is exactly
half the outer radius (as it is in Figure 4-14). If you don't like
this particular arrangement, you can gain more control by
pressing the following keys:

Press Control while dragging to scale the outer radius independently of
the inner radius. So long as the Control key is down, the inner radius
remains fixed. You can even drag inside the inner radius to make the
outer radius the inner radius. Then you can adjust the inner radius
while the outer one is fixed. To again resize both radiuses proportionally, release Control and keep dragging.

Option-drag to snap the inner radius into precise alignment so that
opposite spikes align with each other. The top sides of the left and right
sides of a five-sided star, for example, form a straight line.

Because Control and Option have mutually exclusive effects on a star,
they cannot be in effect at the same time. If you do hold down both the
Control and Option keys, Option takes precedent.

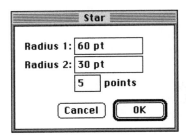

Figure 4-15:
*You can specify the
precise inner and outer
radius values by clicking
with the star tool.*

Just as when drawing with the polygon tool, you can add or
delete spikes from a star by pressing the up and down arrow
keys in mid-drag. You can also move a star in progress by
pressing the spacebar, or orient the star upright by pressing
Shift. And—lest I forget the least important tip of all—you
can press the W key to create concentric stars.

Click in the drawing area with the star tool to bring up the Star dialog box. As
shown in Figure 4-15, this dialog box permits two Radius values, one for the outer
radius and one for the inner. You can also specify the number of spikes (which
Illustrator calls "points," not to be confused with the points between segments,
which number twice the number of spikes—for example, a path with five spikes
has 10 points).

Drawing a Spiral

Most folks look at spirals and think, "Why in Tarnation would I want to draw
that?" Spirals don't exactly lend themselves to a wide range of drawing situations,
but I must admit, I've become something of a enthusiastic spiralist over the last
year. You can create text on a spiral (Chapter 7) or use a spiral as a guideline
(Chapter 10). And naturally, a spiral is the perfect ornament for a pig's rump. But
I find myself adding spirals to all kinds of illustrations, the most recent example
being the chin dimple in Figure 4-1.

But wouldn't you know it, spirals are one of the most difficult things to create
in Illustrator. Oh sure, you can draw them easily enough; Just drag with the spiral
tool (top right tool in the plug-ins palette) and the spiral grows outward from its
center. But controlling the number of times the spiral wraps around itself requires
a fair amount of dexterity and reasoning.

Let's start with the Spiral dialog box, shown in Figure 4-16. To access this dialog
box, click with the spiral tool inside the drawing area. The Spiral dialog box contains
these options:

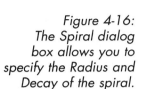

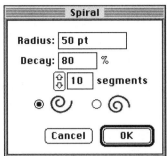

Figure 4-16:
The Spiral dialog
box allows you to
specify the Radius and
Decay of the spiral.

- **Radius**: Enter a Radius value to specify the size of the spiral. This represents the distance from the center of the shape to the last point on the spiral.

- **Decay**: The Decay value determines how quickly the spiral loops in on itself. Figure 4-17 demonstrates the effects of several decays. As you can see, small values result in short loops. Larger values—up to 99.99 percent—result in more tightly packed spirals.

  So far so good; but here's where things get weird. If you enter a value of 100 into the Decay option box, the spiral coils on top of itself, creating a circle. Values above 100 (up to 150 percent) turn the spiral inside out, looping it in the opposite direction and outside the radius, as in the bottom two examples of Figure 4-17.

- **Segments**: Enter the number of curved segments between points into the Segments option box. Each segment represents a quarter coil in the spiral. Figure 4-18 shows the results of six Segments values.

- **Direction**: Select a radio button to coil the spiral counterclockwise or clockwise. (As I said earlier, this assumes the Decay value is less than 100 percent. If the Decay is higher than 100, the spiral coils the opposite direction.)

By itself, an increased Segments value may not result in more coils. Strange, but it's true. You have to raise both the Decay and Segments values to wind the coils more tightly. This is because Illustrator drops segments if the decay is too low to accommodate them.

For example, the Segments value is set to a constant 100 in Figure 4-19. But as you can see, by upping the Decay value, I give Illustrator more room to draw segments, and thus increase the number of coils in the path.

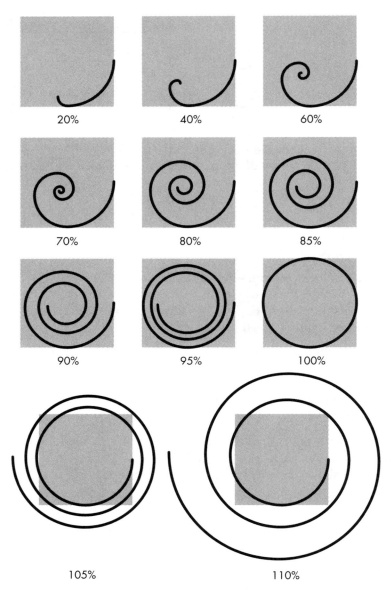

Figure 4-17: The results of changing the Decay values while the radius is set to 35 points and the number of segments set to 10.

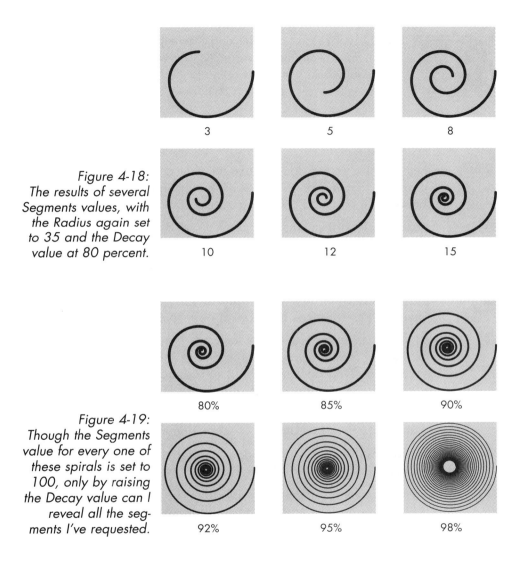

Figure 4-18:
The results of several
Segments values, with
the Radius again set
to 35 and the Decay
value at 80 percent.

Figure 4-19:
Though the Segments
value for every one of
these spirals is set to
100, only by raising
the Decay value can I
reveal all the seg-
ments I've requested.

If the decay is set higher than 100 percent, Illustrator adds segments to the outside of the spiral. This means the spiral actually gets larger as you increase the Segments value. Beware, however. A Decay value as small as 105 combined with a high Segments value can completely take over your artwork. I prefer to play it safe and keep decay set to less than 100.

By now you're probably thinking, "Whelp, that's it for spirals." But wait, there's more. As luck would have it, you can modify coils without resorting to the Spiral dialog box. It takes a little getting used to, but it works. Here's how:

- When you drag with the spiral tool, you're changing the radius and rotating the spiral around. I just want to get that straight before I go any farther.

- Press the Control key while dragging to modify the decay. Drag outward to lower the decay, drag inward to raise it. If you drag inward past one of the coils, the spiral flips on itself, indicating a decay of more than 100 percent.

- Don't press the Control key the moment you start dragging or you'll pop the Decay value to some ridiculously low number like 7 percent. Start dragging, then press Control in mid-drag. Release the key to again modify the radius.

- Press the up and down arrow keys while dragging with the spiral tool to alternatively raise or lower the number of segments in a spiral.

- You can also change the number of segments by pressing the Option key. Option-drag toward the center of the spiral to delete segments and reduce the radius. Drag outward to both add segments and increase the radius, thus better accommodating the new coils.

- If you press both Control and Option simultaneously, Control takes precedent (unlike with the star tool, where Option is dominant).

- You can also press the spacebar while dragging with the spiral tool to reposition the path. Shift-drag to constrain the spiral to some 45-degree angle.

- And, as if it's not goofy enough to be able to create concentric polygons and stars, you can create a series of sprials by pressing the W key as you drag. Just the thing to embellish the next annual report

If you're at all familiar with how spirals used to work in Illustrator 5, you'll notice something right off the bat about Illustrator 6's spirals: They look better. As you can see in Figure 4-17 through 4-19, the spirals curve smoothly. In Illustrator 5, spirals were blocky, almost as if they were made of rounded rectangles. This is a result of Illustrator's new and improved curve fitting, a largely invisible but wonderful enhancement to the program.

Drawing Free-Form Paths

The tools I've discussed so far are all well and good. But Illustrator's true drawing power is based in its ability to define free-form lines and shapes. Such paths may be simple shapes like zigzags or crescents. Or they may be intricate polygons and naturalistic forms. It all depends on how well you can draw.

The equivalent of a pencil in Illustrator is the freehand tool (the squiggly line icon, fourth down on the right side of the toolbox). It lets you draw anything you want. Heck, the freehand cursor even looks like a pencil.

As you drag with the tool, Illustrator tracks the motion of the cursor with a dotted line. After you release the mouse button, Illustrator automatically assigns and positions the points and segments needed to create your freehand path.

Adjusting the Tolerance

Alas, automation is rarely perfect. (If it were, what need would these machines have for us?) Try as it might, Illustrator doesn't always do such a hot job of drawing freehand paths. When the program finishes its calculations, a path may appear riddled with far too many points, or equipped with too few.

Fortunately, you can adjust the performance of the freehand tool to accommodate your personal drawing style with the Freehand Tolerance option in the General Preferences dialog box. Press ⌘-K to display the option. You can enter any value between 0 and 10 into the Freehand Tolerance option box. Illustrator measures the value in screen pixels. A value of 2, for example, instructs the program to ignore any jags in your cursor movements that do not exceed 2 pixels in length or width. Setting the value to 0 makes the freehand tool extremely sensitive; setting the value to 10 smoothes the roughest of gestures.

A Freehand Tolerance value of 2 or 3 is generally adequate for most folks, but you should experiment to determine the best setting. Keep in mind, Illustrator saves the Freehand Tolerance value with the other preferences settings, so it remains in force until you enter a new value.

You can't alter the Freehand Tolerance value for a path after you've drawn it because Illustrator calculates the points for a path only once, after your release the mouse button.

 Want to draw smoother freehand paths? Swap your mouse for a drawing tablet. They're inexpensive and they work great. My favorite is the ArtPad II from Wacom Technology (360/750-8882). Available for under $150, this diminutive 7 by 7.5-inch tablet is no bigger than a mouse pad, but provides sufficient resolution to register the most subtle gestures. The wireless stylus (the name for the electronic pen) is lighter than many mechanical pencils, and it even includes an eraser that you can use with Photoshop and other image editors. (Okay, so it's a gimmick, but sometimes it comes in handy.) Your drawing can't help but improve.

Using the Command Key

Normally, when you drag with the freehand tool, a continuous dotted line tracks your every movement . If you press the ⌘ key while drawing, however, the cursor changes from a pencil to an eraser, indicating that something new is happening. You can ⌘-drag to produce one of two results:

● Press the ⌘ key to erase a mistake. While drawing with the freehand tool, press ⌘ and trace back over a portion of a path that you've just drawn. As you drag, the dotted line disappears to show that it's being erased. After you finish erasing the undesirable section, release ⌘ and continue drawing.

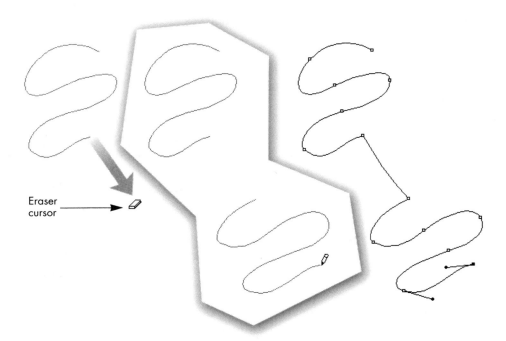

Eraser
cursor

Figure 4-20: After ⌘-dragging away from my path (left), I released ⌘ and continued drawing (middle). Illustrator automatically connected the two squiggles with a single segment (right).

Rather than ⌘-dragging back over your path, try ⌘-dragging away from it. Then release the ⌘ key and continue to draw. At the end of your drag, Illustrator connects the points at which you pressed and released the ⌘ key with a single segment, as demonstrated in Figure 4-20. It's all part of the same drag, so Illustrator treats it as one path.

Extending and Closing a Path

You can use the freehand tool to extend any open path. First position the pencil cursor over either end of the line. You'll know you're ready to go when you get the connect cursor, shown on the left side of Figure 4-21. Then drag away. Illustrator treats your cursor movements as an extension of the existing path.

Normally, Illustrator tries to connect the old path to its extension with a continuous arc, called a *smooth point*. Even if you drag in the opposite direction of the last segment in the path, Illustrator uses a smooth point, but it uses it in a highly undesirable fashion. (It locks both control handles into alignment on the same side of the point. If you don't know what I'm talking about, all will be revealed in Chapter 5.)

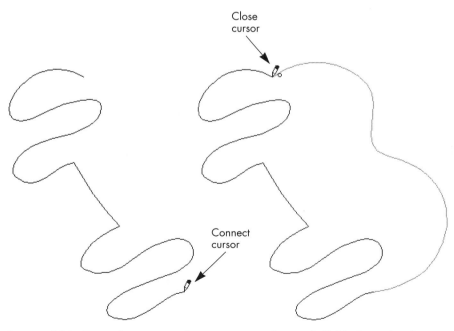

Figure 4-21: Drag from an endpoint to extend a path (left). Drag back to the other endpoint to close it (right).

If you want to create a corner at the connection between old path and new, be sure to Option-drag from the endpoint with the freehand tool. Make a special note to remember this tip; even experienced folks tend to forget it.

To close a path, drag from one endpoint in a path all the way back to the other. In the right example of Figure 4-21, I've dragged up to the first point in the path. Notice that Illustrator displays a pencil cursor with a little O to show that closure has been made.

As when extending a path, Illustrator tries to close the path with a smooth point. If you want to close with a corner, remember to press the Option key and hold it down until after you release the mouse button.

Painting Closed Shapes

The brush tool (fourth tool down on the left) is the other free-form path creation tool. The brush tool lets you draw lines with substance, like strokes laid down with a conventional paintbrush. As you drag with the brush tool, a line flows from the end of the cursor. As with the freehand tool, Illustrator automatically assigns and positions points and segments after you release the mouse button.

At first glance, a brush path may look like a thicker version of a line drawn with the freehand tool. But unlike the freehand tool, the brush tool always produces a closed path. Illustrator draws a path all the way around your cursor movements, as demonstrated in Figure 4-22. The result is typically an extremely complicated path with lots of overlapping segments.

To simplify a path you've just finished drawing with the brush tool, choose Filter » Pathfinder » Unite while the path is still selected. All overlapping segments disappear. I explain how this command works in Chapter 9, but for now, suffice it to say, it works wonders.

Changing Thickness and Shape

By default, Illustrator draws brush paths 9-points thick. However, you can vary this thickness from 0 to 1296 points (0 to 18 inches). To do so, display the Brush dialog box (seen in Figure 4-23) by double-clicking on the brush tool icon in the toolbox. Then change the Width value in the top half of the dialog box.

The options at the bottom of the Brush dialog box influence the shape of a brush-tool path. You can select between two Caps options, which shape the ends

Figure 4-22: After drawing a line with the brush tool (top), Illustrator converts it to a closed paths with lots of overlapping segments (bottom).

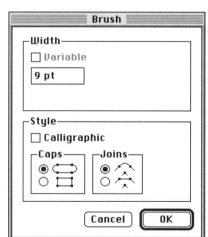

Figure 4-23: You can adjust the way the brush tool works by double-clicking on its icon in the toolbox.

of the shape. The first option rounds off the end, the second flattens it. You can also select between two Joins options, which affect the appearance of corners. The first option permits round corners, the second bevels the corners for a straight edge.

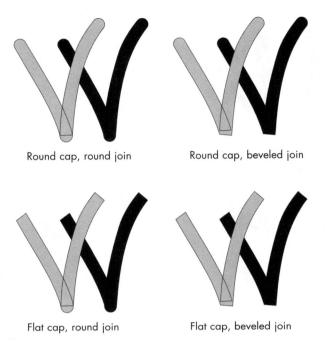

Round cap, round join   Round cap, beveled join

Flat cap, round join   Flat cap, beveled join

Figure 4-24: Each of the four possible Caps and Joins combinations.

Figure 4-24 demonstrates all four Caps and Joins permutations. In each case, I've included stroked and filled examples so you can judge how the paths look either way.

As always, the options in the Brush palette affect future paths. You cannot edit an existing path using any of these options.

Using the Calligraphic Brush

Another advantage to the brush tool is that you can create shapes that look like calligraphic pen strokes. Click on the Calligraphic check box in the Brush dialog box to dim the Caps and Joins radio buttons and reveal a new option box named Calligraphic Angle. The angle you enter here indicates the slant of the brush tool—the angle of the pen tip against the page.

Figure 4-25 shows two sets of letters created with different Calligraphic Angle settings. As the letters themselves suggest, I drew the top paths with the value set to 120 degrees and the bottom paths with an angle of 200 degrees.

A calligraphic path varies from as thin as 1 point to as thick as the Width value in the Brush dialog box. In Figure 4-25, the Width value was set to 18 points. The

Figure 4-25: A few paths created with the Calligraphic check box selected and the Calligraphic Angle value set to 120 (top) and 200 (bottom).

top letters look heavier, however, because the angle of the brush and the angle of my drawing more frequently synced to produce the highest thickness.

Drawing with a Pressure-Sensitive Tablet

The brush tool is the only tool in Illustrator that supports *pressure-sensitivity*. Provided that you have a pressure-sensitive drawing tablet hooked up to your Mac (such as the ArtPad II that I mentioned earlier), you can have the brush tool respond to the amount of pressure you apply to the stylus. It's just like real life. Press harder, and the path gets thicker; let up on the stylus and the path thins down.

Once the drawing tablet is connected and its driver software is properly loaded into your System Folder, the Brush dialog box offers access to the otherwise dimmed Variable check box. When the option is checked, the Width disappears and two Minimum and Maximum options appear in its place. The first value defines the width that Illustrator assigns to the lightest stylus pressure; the second value does the same for the strongest pressure.

Using the brush tool and a pressure-sensitive tablet together can greatly reduce the time and effort it takes to create complicated paths. For example, it took me approximately seven seconds to draw the two lines of paths in Figure 4-26. The Variable check box was turned on for all paths; I also turned on the Calligraphic check box to create the second line. Admittedly, the results aren't exactly super-smooth—I expect most experienced illustrators could readily identify it as computer art—but if you need quick results with a dash of spontaneity, brush tool and pressure-sensitive tablet make a wonderful pair.

Figure 4-26: Two Wows drawn with a pressure-sensitive tablet, one with the Calligraphic check box turned off (top) and the other with the option on (bottom).

Tracing a Black-and-White Template

An illustration program should make it easy to convert black-and-white images into paths. You should be able to scan in some line art and make it into an illustration in a matter of minutes. Sure, you'd have to go in and clean up the paths after the fact—you can't expect automation to completely eliminate artistic effort—but the majority of the grunt work should be done for you.

If this were FreeHand, I could assure you that you are in possession of an adequate tracing function that creates multiple paths at a time and accommodates TIFF images without a whimper. But alas, this is not FreeHand, this is Illustrator. And Illustrator's tracing tool is about as up-to-date as a pair of platform shoes and as capable as a hammer without a handle.

 To some Illustrator users, the suggestion that FreeHand might in some way be superior to Illustrator amounts to fighting words. Naturally, I don't have any desire to raise the dander of hard-core Illustrator fans. No, I prefer to irritate Adobe. My hope is that some programmer or product manager will turn to this page and become sufficiently embarrassed by my caustic critique to fix this feature. After all, Illustrator's tracing capabilities haven't changed one iota since they were introduced more than eight years ago.

Using the Autotrace Tool

After importing a template into your illustration (as described in the "Adding a Tracing Template" section of Chapter 3), you can trace the edges manually using any of Illustrator's drawing tools. But if you want Illustrator to do the work for you, your only choice is the autotrace tool (and it makes me gnash my teeth just to think of it).

 Chapter 13 explains how to trace paths around a scanned image—black-and-white or grayscale—inside Photoshop and then copy the paths into Illustrator. Photoshop's tracing capabilities are superior to Illustrator's, and they're really easy to use. So if you have Photoshop 3, you can skip the rest of the chapter. If you don't, read on.

 The autotrace tool traces one path at a time and is entirely incapable of matching the black or white areas of the template. This means if the fill is set to black, Illustrator will trace interior and exterior spaces alike with black, resulting in a lot of overlapping black shapes. For the best results, switch to the artwork mode by pressing ⌘-E. After you trace your paths, select them and color them using options in the Paint Style palette. Then switch back to the preview mode (⌘-Y) and fine-tune the paths. This will help to make Illustrator's automatic tracing a little less confusing.

Select the autotrace tool by dragging from the freehand tool slot in the toolbox. Figure 4-27 shows me doing just that, with a tracing template all ready to go in the background.

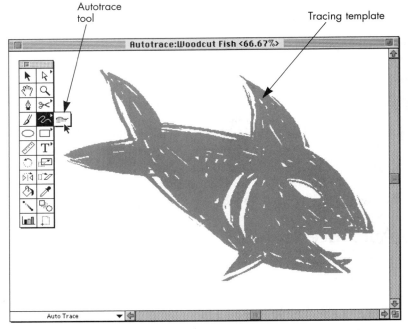

Figure 4-27: Select the autotrace tool, then click or drag within six pixels of the template.

You can use the autotrace tool is one of two ways:

- Click within six pixels of an edge in the tracing template. Illustrator automatically encircles that edge with a closed path.

- Drag from within six pixels of an edge to within six pixels of some other portion of that same edge. Illustrator traces an open path between the point at which you clicked and the point at which you released.

For example, to trace around the outside of the fish, I clicked at the top of the fin, as in the top example of Figure 4-28. (Illustrator always creates a point at the

Figure 4-28: I clicked above the fin to trace the outside of the fish (top). Then I clicked beside the eye to trace inside its edge (bottom).

spot on the template nearest your click, so it's best to click near a corner.) To trace the eye, I clicked just to the right of its edge, as shown in the lower example.

Dragging is a less common way to trace shapes, but it can be useful if you want to automatically trace one portion of the template and manually trace the rest. After you complete your drag, Illustrator traces to the left. This means that it traces clockwise around exterior edges, as demonstrated in Figure 4-29, and counterclockwise

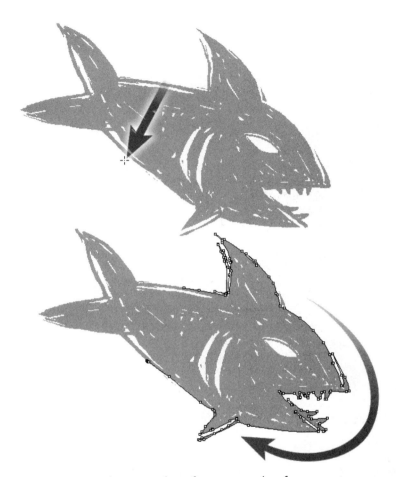

Figure 4-29: When you drag from one side of an exterior surface to another (top), Illustrator traces between the two points in a clockwise direction (bottom).

around interior edges. This is true even if it's the longer of the two distances between where you started your drag and where you released.

 Remember, you can temporarily hide the template and get a better view of your artwork by pressing ⌘-Shift-W (or choosing View » Hide Template). Press these keys again to bring the template back into view.

Adjusting Autotracing Sensitivity

If you are dissatisfied with Illustrator's tracing accuracy, you can adjust the autotrace tool's sensitivity by changing the Freehand Tolerance value in the General Preferences dialog box. Yes, this is the very same value that affects the freehand tool. A Freehand Tolerance value of 0 instructs Illustrator to trace every single pixel of a bitmapped template. If you raise the value to 10, the software ignores large jags in the outline of a template and smoothes out all kinds of details.

Generally speaking, it's better to have too many points than too few. After all, you can always delete points later, as discussed in the next chapter. So for the most reliable autotracing, set the Freehand Tolerance value no higher than 2.

Tracing Across Gaps

The autotrace tool is most effective in tracing the borders between the black and white areas in a template. But it can also trace gray areas and areas with broken or inconsistent outlines. To accommodate such rough spots, Illustrator provides an Auto Trace Gap option in the General Preferences dialog box.

You can set this value to any value from 0 to 2 in 0.01 pixel increments (though it's hardly worth the effort to enter a decimal point value).

- The default value 0 instructs Illustrator to trace around a template image from one black pixel to the next. If even a single white pixel separates one black area from another, the traced path does not pass over the gap.

- A Gap value of 1 permits Illustrator to jump one pixel gaps in order to incorporate more areas from the template into a single path.

- If you raise the value to 2, Illustrator can jump 2 pixels gap. This is an especially useful setting when tracing photographic images and other templates with loose pixels.

Adding to a Traced Line

Illustrator lets you extend an open path with the autotrace tool. The rules are a little more strict than they are with the freehand tool; you can't extend just any old line. A template image must exist within six pixels of the line's endpoint to qualify for autotrace extension. (This makes the feature practically useless, of course, but a feature is a feature, and I'm sworn to leave no stone unturned.)

Drag from the endpoint to another point along an edge of the template to extend a path. (Unlike with the freehand tool, Illustrator doesn't offer any special cursor icon to show you when you have the cursor positioned correctly.) To close the path, drag from one endpoint to another. In a small show of flexibility, the second endpoint does not have to be anywhere near the template.

Like the freehand tool, the autotrace tool conr ects and closes paths by default with smooth points. This is true even when the point appears to be a corner. To create a true corner point (which is much easier to edit), Option-drag from the first endpoint and press Option when releasing onto the second endpoint.

Yet One Tool Beats Them All

Before I close this chapter, I want to leave you with one parting bit of wisdom. We've tackled all but one of Illustrator's drawing tools, and that one remaining tool—the pen tool—is by far and away the best. If is infinitely more flexible than the rectangle, oval, and plug-in tools, and equally more precise than the freehand, brush, and autotrace tools. (The pen tool is also mightier than the sword tool, but that's another story.) It is, in fact, the only tool you really need. In fact, there was a time when the pen, rectangle, and oval tools were all Illustrator offered. Yet there wasn't a thing you couldn't draw.

That's why the next chapter is so important. It shows you how to edit the paths that you create with the tools in this chapter, and how to create more exacting shapes with the pen. These features require more work, but they pay back several times over.

EXACT POINTS AND PRECISION CURVE

Much as the $695 Illustrator tries, it just can't live up to the 25¢ pencil when it comes to smooth, real-time drawing. Whether you use the freehand, brush, or autotrace tool, you still get the same thing—clunky paths. A drawing tablet helps, but only to communicate smoother lines to Illustrator; it doesn't help Illustrator to better interpret your beautiful work.

There is hope for the future, of course. Illustrator 6 does a way better job of interpreting freehand paths than did Illustrator 88 (the first Illustrator to offer the tool). So one might expect Illustrator 2001 to perform even better, and Illustrator 2525 to be right on the money. But in the meantime, we can either suffer with clunky paths, or we can fix them.

With that said, it would be a sin if fixing paths wasn't what this chapter is all about. We'll explore a whole mess of path-editing theory—you'll see how to move anchor points and bend segments to get lines that are as smooth as water droplets and as organic as flower petals. I'll also cover the pen tool, the only tool in all of Illustrator that lets you draw paths correctly the first time out. And just when you think Illustrator couldn't be any dreamier, I'll throw in some pointers for adding, deleting, and converting points.

If Illustrator is nothing else, it's the most excellent path creation and manipulation tool the world has ever enjoyed. This chapter tells why.

 By the way, you can now reshape any kind of path, whether it was created using the flexible freehand tool or the rigid rectangle tool. Illustrator used to lock rectangles and ellipses so you couldn't get to their points without first ungrouping them. But no more! Rectangle, ellipse, regular polygon, star, spiral, or whatever—you manipulate them all in the same way. Once you lay a path down on the page, Illustrator cares not how it originated. All paths are equal in its eyes (bless its equal-opportunity heart).

Selecting like a House on Fire

The job of sprucing up paths rests on the shoulders of three very sturdy tools. These are the selection tools, available from the top two slots in the toolbox, as shown in Figure 5-1. Clicking on a point or segment with one of these suckers selects all or part of a path. The tools differ only in the extent of the selection they make.

You can't create a darned thing with a selection tool. But you can do all kinds of stuff to objects that you've already created using one of the tools from the previous chapter. Just click on a path and start dragging at its points and segments.

The Plain Black Arrow Tool

The selection tool—which I call the arrow tool to better distinguish it from its selection pals—is the first tool on the left side of the toolbox and the most straightforward of the bunch. When the arrow tool is active, you can click anywhere along the outline of a path to select the path in its entirety. If the path is filled and the

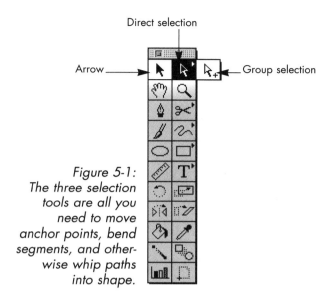

Direct selection

Arrow

Group selection

*Figure 5-1:
The three selection
tools are all you
need to move
anchor points, bend
segments, and other-
wise whip paths
into shape.*

*Figure 5-2: Click on any part of a path with the arrow tool
(left) to select the entire path (right).*

Area Select check box is turned on inside the General Preferences dialog box, you
can also click inside the shape to select it. All points become visible as filled
squares, as demonstrated in Figure 5-2.

After selecting a path, you can move it, apply a transformation, or perform any
other manipulation that affects the path as a whole. You cannot move points or

bend segments. If the path has been grouped with other paths (as explained in Chapter 10), the arrow tool selects the entire group, prohibiting you from altering one grouped path independently of another.

Here are a few other ways to select paths with the arrow tool:

● When you click on a path, you not only select the path on which you click, you also deselect any previously selected path. To select multiple paths, click on the first path, then Shift-click on each additional path you want to select. The Shift key prevents Illustrator from deselecting paths as you click on new ones.

● Another way to select multiple paths is to *marquee* them. Drag from an empty portion of your drawing area to create a dotted rectangular outline, called a marquee. All paths that fall even slightly inside this outline become selected when you release the mouse button. In Figure 5-3, for example, I drag midway inside the apple and leaf to select both shapes.

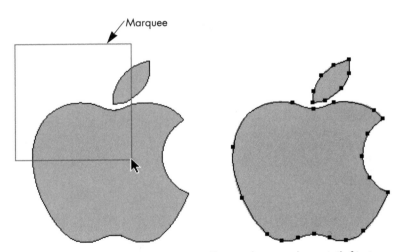

Figure 5-3: By marqueeing partially inside two shapes (left), I select them both (right).

● You can combine marqueeing with Shift-clicking to select multiple paths. You can also drag a marquee while pressing Shift, which adds the surrounded objects to the present selection.

● If you Shift-click on an object that is already selected, Illustrator deselects it, as I discuss in the upcoming "Deselecting Stuff that You Don't Want to Mess Up" section.

To temporarily access the arrow tool when some other tool is active, press and hold the ⌘ key. Release the key to return to the last tool used. If pressing ⌘ gets you one of the hollow selection cursors instead, press ⌘-Tab and then press ⌘ again.

The Hollow Direct Selection Tool

The direct selection tool is the hollow arrow in the upper right corner of the toolbox. Click with the direct selection tool to select an individual point or segment in a path. If you click on a point, you select the point; if you click on a segment, you select the segment. This works even if the path that contains the point or segment is part of a group.

Different elements have different ways of showing that they are selected. For example, when you select a point, it appears as a small filled square, as shown in the first example of Figure 5-4. If the point borders a curved segment, you can also see a round Bézier control handle connected to the point by a thin lever.

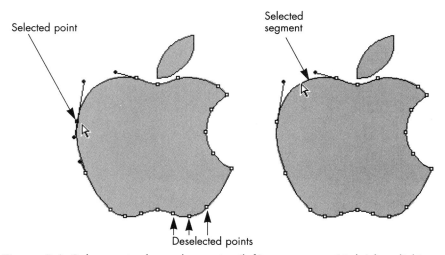

Selected point

Selected segment

Deselected points

Figure 5-4: Select a single anchor point (left) or segment (right) by clicking with the direct selection tool.

 For those of you reading aloud to loved ones, Bézier is pronounced *bay-zee-ay*. Named after Pierre Bézier—the French fellow who designed this particular drawing model to expedite the manufacturing of car bodies, of all things—Bézier curve theory lies at the heart of both Illustrator and the PostScript printing language. I would be unforgivably remiss if I didn't tell you how Bézier control handles work later in this chapter.

When you select a path, Illustrator shows you selected and deselected points alike. The deselected points appear as hollow squares, showing that they are part of a partially selected path, but these points are not selected.

When you click on a segment with the direct selection tool, Illustrator shows you the Bézier control handles for that segment—if there are any—as in the right example of Figure 5-4. Unless some point in the path is also selected, all points appear hollow. Illustrator shows you the control handles only, so you may find it a little confusing when selecting straight segments, which lack handles. You just have to click on the segment and have faith that it's selected. (Frankly, I wish Illustrator thickened the segment to provide a little visual feedback.)

You can also drag with the direct selection tool to marquee elements. All points and segments that lie inside the marquee become selected, even if they belong to different paths, as Figure 5-5 shows.

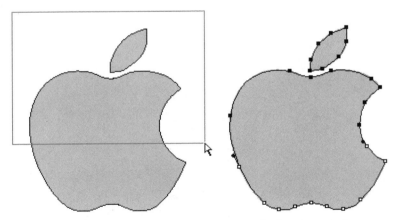

Figure 5-5: When dragging a marquee with the direct selection tool (left), all points and segments that fall inside the marquee become selected (right).

These and other ways to select elements with the direct selection tool are summarized in the following list:

● If the Area Select check box in the General Preferences dialog box is turned on (as it is by default), you can click inside a filled shape to select the entire path.

● Frankly, I'm not a big fan of the Area Select option. If you don't click dead on a point or segment, you can easily select the entire path. Also, if a path is mostly hidden by a filled shape, it can be difficult to select the path in back. I much prefer to click on an outline when I want to select a path. If you want to give my recommended approach a try, press ⌘-K, turn off the Area Select check box, and press Return.

● Shift-click on a point or segment to add it to the current selection. You can also Shift-marquee around elements. (If you Shift-click on a point or segment that's already selected, it becomes deselected. The same goes for Shift-marqueeing.)

● Option-click on a point or segment to select an entire path. This is a great way to select paths inside groups.

● Option-marquee or Shift-Option-click on paths to select multiple paths at a time.

 To switch back and forth between the arrow tool and the direct selection tool, press ⌘-Tab. If you last used the direct selection tool (as opposed to the arrow tool), you can access it while any other tool is active by pressing ⌘. If you last used the arrow tool, press ⌘-Tab, then press ⌘.

The Sad Little Group Selection Tool

Adobe added the group selection tool to Illustrator so folks who were afraid to press the Option key could select paths inside groups. In other words, you can either Option-click on a path to select it with the direct selection tool, or click on the path with the group selection tool. If you're not afraid of the occasional Option-click, feel free to ignore the group selection tool. I, for one, never touch it. Honestly, it's useless.

If you don't believe me, and you'd prefer to know everything about everything, you can select the group selection tool by dragging from the upper right slot in the toolbox. Then do any of the following:

● Click on a point or segment to select a whole path in a group. You can also select groups within groups by clicking multiple times on a path, but you can do this as well with the direct-selection tool if you keep the

Option key down. I don't even know why I mentioned it. I cover all this grouping stuff in Chapter 10.

- Marquee paths with the group selection tool to select the paths, whether they fall entirely or partially inside the marquee.

- Shift-click on a path to add it to the selection. You can also Shift-marquee if you get the urge.

- Option-click on a point or segment to select it independently of its path. The Option key converts the group selection to direct selection.

See, what did I tell you? Dumb tool. Steer clear of it.

Selecting Everything

If you want to select all paths in your drawing, choose Edit » Select All or press ⌘-A. This causes Illustrator to select every last point, segment, and other element throughout the illustration, even if it's on the pasteboard. (An exception occurs if you've selected a letter inside a text block, in which case Select All highlights all text in the story.)

Inversing the Selection

To select everything that's not selected and deselect what is, choose Filter » Select » Inverse. It's Illustrator's way of letting you reverse a selection.

Both the Select All and Inverse commands make it easier to select most of the objects in a complicated drawing. You can either choose Select All and then Shift-click on the objects you don't want to select. Or start off by clicking and Shift-clicking on the stuff you don't want to select, and choose Filter » Select » Inverse. Either way works fine; it's entirely a matter of personal preference.

Hiding the Points and Handles

All those points, handles, and colored outlines that Illustrator uses to show you an object is selected can occasionally get in your face. If you're aware of your selection but you want to see the selected objects unadorned against their deselected settings, choose View » Hide Edges or press ⌘-Shift-H. (This is based on the Hide Edges command in Photoshop; its shortcut is ⌘-H.)

From that point on, no selection outline appears on screen, even if you select a different object. To again see the selection outlines, you have to choose View » Show Edges or again press ⌘-Shift-H.

Deselecting Stuff that You Want to Leave As Is

Selecting is your way of telling Illustrator, "This thing is messed up, and now I'm going to hurt it," or fix it, or whatever. If you don't want to hurt an object, you need to deselect it. (Folks also say "unselect," and I suppose one or two might even say "antiselect" or "get it out of the selection loop," but I think the unremarkable "deselect" sounds the least yichy.)

To deselect all objects—regardless of form or gender—press ⌘-Shift-A (Edit » Select None) or just click with one of the selection tools on an empty portion of the drawing area.

You can make more discrete deselections using the Shift key:

- To deselect an entire path or group, Shift-click on the object with the arrow tool.

- To deselect a single point or segment, Shift-click on it with the direct selection tool.

- To deselect a single path inside a group, Shift-Option-click on it with the direct selection tool.

- You can also deselect elements and objects by Shift-marqueeing around them. Selected element become deselected, deselected elements become selected. A simple marquee becomes a blanket of opposites when the Shift key is down.

Dragging Stuff Around

Once you've selected a point or segment, you can move it around, changing its location and stretching its path. In fact, dragging with the direct selection tool is the single most common method for reshaping a path inside Illustrator. You can move selected points independently of deselected points. And you can stretch segments or move Bézier control handles to alter the curvature of a path. The next few pages explain all aspects of dragging.

Dragging Points

To move one or more points in a path:

1. Select the points you want to move with the direct selection tool.

2. Drag any one of them.

3. Squeal with delight.

When you drag a selected point, all other selected points move the same distance and direction. When you move a point while a neighboring point remains stationary (not selected), the segment between the two points shrinks or stretches in length to accommodate the change in distance, as demonstrated in Figure 5-6.

Figure 5-6: When you drag a selected point bordered by deselected points (left), Illustrator stretches the segments between the points (right).

When you move a point, any accompanying control handles move with it. As a result, the curved segments on either side of the point must not only shrink or stretch, but also bend to accommodate the movement. Meanwhile, segments located between two deselected points—or two selected points—remain unchanged during

Figure 5-7: When you drag more than one selected point at a time (left), the segments between the select points remain unchanged (right).

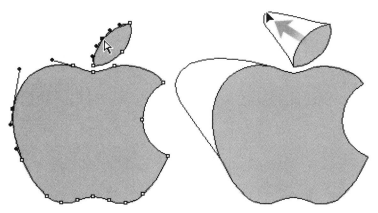

Figure 5-8: You can move multiple points even when selected points reside in different paths.

a move, as demonstrated in Figure 5-7. Illustrator lets you move multiple points within a single path, as in Figure 5-7, or in separate paths, as in Figure 5-8. This means you can reshape multiple paths at a time.

While you move a point, Illustrator displays both the previous and current locations of the point and its surrounding segments. This useful feature permits you to gauge the full effect of a move as it progresses. Also worth noting: When you drag a single selected point, Illustrator displays the point, any Bézier control handles associated with the two neighboring segments, and the neighboring deselected points, as shown back in Figure 5-6. When dragging multiple points, Illustrator hides the points and handles, as in Figures 5-7 and 5-8. I, for one, wish we could see the points and handles, but Adobe reasons that all that screen clutter might prove a mite confusing.

Keeping Your Movements in Line

You can constrain your cursor movements horizontally, vertically, or diagonally by pressing the Shift key. For example, if you want to move a point horizontally, without moving it so much as a smidgen up or down, press the Shift key while dragging the point with the direct selection tool.

 Almost every Macintosh program assigns the Shift key to constrain cursor movements. The weird thing about Illustrator is that you press Shift *after* you begin dragging. If you press Shift before you drag, you deselect the selected point on which you click, which causes Illustrator to ignore your drag. Then hold down the Shift key until after you release the mouse button.

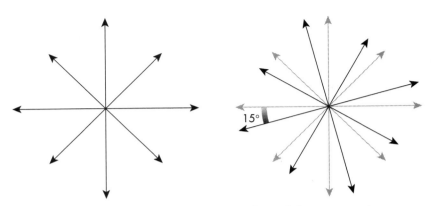

Figure 5-9: The default constraint axes (left) and the axes as they appear when rotated 15 degrees (right).

You can adjust the effects of pressing Shift by changing the Constrain Angle value in the General Preferences dialog box. This rotates the constraint axes. Figure 5-9 shows what happens when you rotate the axes 15 degrees. So a horizontal (0-degree) move becomes a 15-degree move; a 45-degree move becomes a 60-degree move, and so on.

Why would you ever want to do this? Because you might want to move a point along an angled object without the point and object drifting apart. For example, the top segment along the tent thing in Figure 5-10 is oriented at a 15-degree angle. To move the ball forward along the segment, I first rotate the constraint axes to 15 degrees and the drag the object while pressing Shift.

How do you know the segment is angled to 15 degrees? You mean you can't just tell by looking at it? Then I guess it's a good thing you can measure it using the measure tool, which I discuss in Chapter 10.

Remember, the constraint axes also affects the creation of rectangles, ellipses, and text blocks. So you'll generally want to reset it to 0 degrees when you finish making your moves.

Snapping Point to Point

When dragging a point, you may find that it has a tendency to move sharply toward a stationary point in your illustration. This effect is called *snapping*, and it's Illustrator's way of ensuring that points that belong together are flush against each other to form a perfect fit.

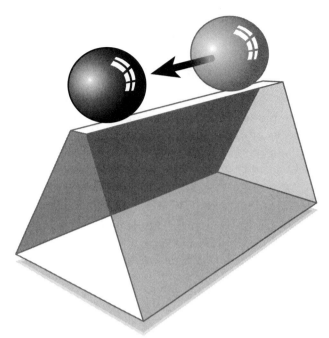

Figure 5-10:
Rotating the constraint
axes to 15 degrees
allows me to precisely
move the ball along a
15-degree segment.

When you drag a point within two pixels of any deselected point on your drawing area, your cursor snaps to the stationary point, so that both point and cursor occupy the very same spot on the page. At the moment the snap occurs, your cursor changes from a filled arrowhead to a hollow arrowhead, as shown in Figure 5-11. (This is particularly useful after a long day in the office when your snap-perception capabilities have all but vanished.)

Snap cursor

Figure 5-11: Your cursor changes to a hollow arrowhead when snapping a point to a stationary point.

For example, you might drag the center point of a rectangle until it snaps to the center point of a stationary ellipse. In this way, both shapes are centered at exactly the same point.

Your cursor snaps to stationary points as well as to the previous locations of points that are currently being moved. (This last item is more useful than it sounds. You'll see, one day it'll come in handy.) Your cursor also snaps to text blocks and to guides (covered in Chapters 6 and 10 respectively).

You can turn Illustrator's snapping feature on and off by clicking on the Snap to Point check box in the General Preferences dialog box. When this option is turned off, dragged points don't snap to jack.

Dragging Segments

You can also reshape a path by dragging its segments. When you drag a straight segment, its neighboring segments stretch or shrink to accommodate the change in distance, as shown in the first example in Figure 5-12. However, when you drag a curved segment, you stretch only that segment. The effect is rather like pulling on a rubber band extended between two nails, as the second example illustrates.

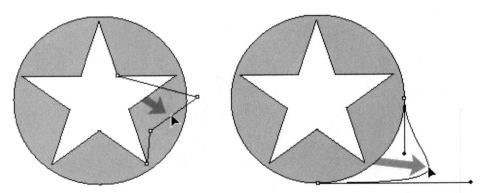

Figure 5-12: The difference between dragging a straight segment (left) and a curved segment (right).

Figure 5-13 is a detailed examination of what happens when you drag on a curved segment. The longer the drag, the more the segment has to bend. But more important is how the segment bends. Notice the two Bézier control handles on either side of the segment. The handles automatically extend and retract as you drag. Each handle moves along an imaginary line consistent with the

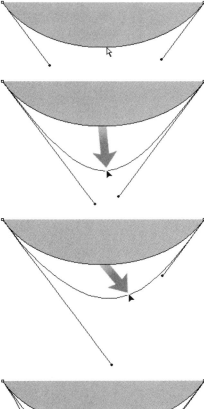

Figure 5-13:
When you drag at a curved
segment, each Bézier control
handle moves back and forth
along a constant axis.

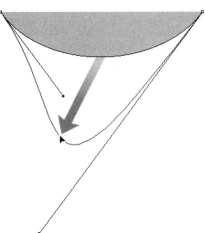

handle's original inclination. The angle of a control handle does change one whit when dragging a segment, thus guaranteeing that the curved segment moves in alignment with neighboring stationary segments.

When dragging a segment, drag on the middle of the segment, approximately equidistant from both of its points, as I have done in Figure 5-13. This provides the best leverage and keeps you from losing control over the segment. (Believe it or not, these things can spring away from you if you're not careful.)

If you want to move a control handle in a different direction, you have to drag the handle itself, as I describe in the "Dragging Control Handles" section, later in this chapter.

Nudging Points and Segments

Another way to move a selected element is to press one of the four arrow keys at the bottom of your keyboard (⬅, ➡, ⬆, ⬇) Not surprisingly, each arrow key nudges a selection in the direction of the arrow.

You can change the distance that a single keystroke moves a selected element by adjusting the Cursor Key value in the General Preferences dialog box (⌘-K). By default, the value is set to 1 point, which is equivalent to one screen pixel when viewing the illustration at actual size. However, you can set the value anywhere from 0.001 point up to 18 inches. I usually keep it somewhere between 0.1 point and 10 points, depending on the situation. (In fact, I must admit, I'm constantly changing the value, usually setting it smaller and smaller as my illustration becomes more detailed.)

You can use arrow keys to move points as well as straight and curved segments. (Sadly, you can't move a single control handle with an arrow key; to do this, you must drag the handle with the direct selection tool.) This is very handy for stretching two segments the exact same distance. Just click on one segment, Shift-click on the other, and whack away at the arrow keys.

The arrow keys move a selection with respect to the constraint axes. If you rotate the axes, you affect the direction in which a selected element moves. For example, if you enter 15 degrees for the Constrain Angle value in the General Preferences dialog box, pressing the right arrow key moves the selection slightly upward, pressing the up arrow moves it slightly to the left, and so on, just as I demonstrated back in Figure 5-9.

If pressing an arrow key doesn't seem to produce any noticeable result, one of two things could be wrong. First, you may have the Cursor Key value in the General Preferences dialog box set so low that you simply can't see the effect of the movement at your particular view size.

Second, a palette might be active. For example, if you just got through applying a fill from the Paint Style palette, Illustrator may be forwarding the arrow key signal to the palette, even if no option appears to be active. To remedy this situation, press Return to deactivate the palette. Then press the arrow keys to nudge without hindrance.

Dragging Control Handles

The only element that we've so far neglected to move is the Bézier control handle. I've saved it for last because it's the most difficult and the most powerful element you can manipulate.

After referencing control handles several times in this chapter, I suppose it's high time I defined my terminology. The *Bézier control handle* (*control handle* or *handle* for short) is the element that defines the arc of a segment as it exits or enters an anchor point. It tugs at a segment like an invisible thread. You increase the curvature of a segment when you drag the handle away from its point, and decrease the curvature when you drag a handle toward its point.

To display a control handle, you can either select the point to which the handle belongs or select the segment it controls. You then drag the handle with the direct selection tool, just as you drag a point.

Figure 5-14 shows three paths composed of five points each. I drew the first path—the one that looks like a 2—with the freehand tool and assigned it a thick gray stroke. The second and third paths in are based on the 2; the only differences

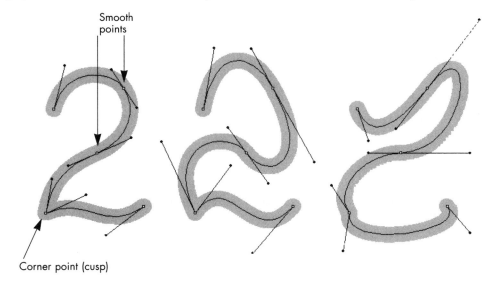

Smooth
points

Corner point (cusp)

Figure 5-14: Three paths comprising five points apiece. The points remain stationary, only the control handles move.

are the positions of the control handles and the curvatures of the segments. The points remain unmoved from one path to the next. And yet, the results are unique. The third path in particular bears little resemblance to a 2.

The 2 comprises two smooth points around its loop and a special kind of corner point called a *cusp* where the loop and base meet. A cusp forms a corner between two curved segments. (We don't really care what kinds of points the endpoints are, because no segments follow them.)

The other two paths contain these same points in the same order. So not only has no point been moved, no point has been converted to a different kind of point. As a result, the bottom left point in each path remains a corner, permitting me to move the two control handles on either side of the point independently of each other. This is the very nature of a corner point.

Likewise, the points in the middle and upper right portions of the path remain smooth points. When I move one control handle, the other moves in the opposite direction, making for a sort of fulcrum effect. This ensures a continuous arc through each point. Not only is there no corner at either location, there's no hint of even the slightest crease. The path continues through the points as smooth as a bend in the road.

 Dragging a control handle can turn ugly when working inside a very complex illustration. If the handle rests near a point or segment from a different path, Illustrator may think you're trying to drag the point or segment rather than the handle. To bring the handle out of the fray where you can get to it more easily, drag the curved segment that the handle controls. Stretching the segment will lengthen the handle; then you can drag the handle without busybody points and segments horning in.

Bézier Rules

The paths in Figure 5-14 demonstrate how control handles work, but they aren't exactly attractive. In fact, one reason I assigned such heavy strokes was to cover up how very ugly these paths are.

Figure 5-14 is proof of the old Bézier adage that just because you *can* drag control handles all over the place doesn't mean you *should*. Manipulating handles is not so much a question of what is possible as what is proper. Several handle-handling rules have been developed over the years, but the best are the *All-or-Nothing rule* and the *33-Percent rule*:

- The All-or-Nothing rule states that every segment in your path should be associated with either two control handles or none at all. In other words, no segment should rely on only one control handle to determine its curvature.

The 33-Percent rule tells us that the distance from any control handle to its point should equal approximately one third the length of the segment. This means that one third of the segment is covered by one handle, the opposite third is covered by other handle, and the middle third is handle free.

The top path in Figure 5-15 violates the All-or-Nothing rule. Its two curved segments are controlled by only one handle apiece, resulting in weak, shallow arcs. Such puny curves are sure to inspire snorts and guffaws from discriminating viewers.

The second example in Figure 5-15 obeys the All-or-Nothing rule. As the rule states, its straight segment is associated with no handle and the two curved segments have two handles apiece. The result is a full-figured, properly rendered path that is a credit to any illustration.

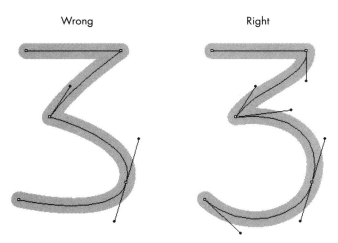

Figure 5-15: The All-or-Nothing rule says that every curved segment should be controlled by two handles, one for each of its points.

The first path in Figure 5-16 violates the 33-Percent rule. The handles are either much too short or much too long to fit their segments. The result is an ugly, misshapen mess. In the second example, each handle is about one-third of the length of its segment. The top segment is shorter than the other two, so its handles are shorter as well. This path is smooth and consistent in curvature, giving it a naturalistic appearance.

Goofus   Gallant

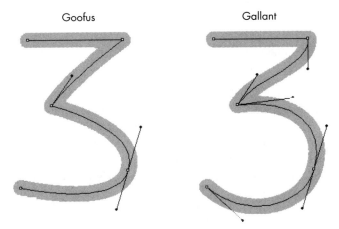

*Figure 5-16: According to the 33-Percent rule, every
control handle should extend about one third the
length of its segment.*

The Great and Powerful Pen Tool

Now that you've had a taste of Bézier theory, it's time for full immersion. The pen tool is the absolute Bézier champ, capable of creating anything from schematic newspaper charts to detailed scenes of heightened reality. Though nearly a decade old, no software can touch Illustrator's pen tool—not FreeHand (which has redesigned its core Bézier drawing tools three times), not any of the 3-D drawing programs, not even Photoshop (which has cloned bits and pieces of Illustrator's pen tool over the years).

 You can access the pen tool when the freehand tool is selected by pressing the Control key. Releasing Control returns you to the freehand tool. It's a pretty limited shortcut, but it can be useful if you find yourself switching back and forth between the freehand and pen tools a lot.

Pen Tool Basics

When drawing with the pen tool—third tool down on the left side of the toolbox—you build a path by creating individual points. Illustrator automatically connects the points with *segments*. The following list summarizes how you can use the pen tool to build paths in Illustrator. I describe each of these methods in more detail later in this chapter.

- Path building: To build a path, create one point after another inside the drawing area until the path is the desired length and shape. You create and position a point by either clicking or dragging with the pen tool. (Clicking creates a corner, dragging creates a smooth point.) Illustrator automatically draws a segment between each new point and its predecessor.

- Adjusting a point: Midway into creating a path, you can reposition points or change the curvature of segments that you've already drawn. Just press the ⌘ key to access the direct-selection tool (press ⌘-Tab if the arrow tool comes up instead) and drag the points, segments, and control handles as desired. When you've finished, release ⌘ and continue adding points.

 Be sure not to ⌘-click in an empty portion of the drawing area or on a different path. Clicking off the active path deactivates it, which means you can't add any more points to it without first reactivating the path (as described in the "Extending an open path" item, coming right up).

- Closing the path: To create a closed shape, click or drag on the first point in the path. Every point will then have one segment coming into it and another segment exiting it.

- Leaving the path open: To leave a path open, so it has a specific beginning and ending, deactivate the path by pressing ⌘-Shift-A (Edit » Select None). Or you can press ⌘ to get the arrow or direct selection tool and click on an empty portion of the drawing area. Either way, you deactivate the path so you can move on and create a new one.

- Extending an open path: To reactivate an open path, click or drag on one of its endpoints. Illustrator is then ready draw a segment between the endpoint and the next point you create.

- Joining two open paths: To join one open path with another open path, click or drag on an endpoint in the first path, then click or drag on an endpoint in the second. Illustrator draws a segment between the two, bringing them together in everlasting peace and brotherhood.

That's basically all there is to using the pen tool. A click here, a drag there, and you have yourself a path. But to achieve decent results, you need to know exactly what clicking and dragging do, and how to use these techniques to your best advantage. If the devil is in the details, the pen tool is Illustrator's most fiendish tool. I probe the pits of pen one level at a time in the following sections.

Defining Points and Segments

Points in a Bézier path act as little road signs. Each point steers the path by specifying how a segment enters it and how another segment exits it. You specify the identity of each little road sign by clicking or dragging, sometimes with the Option key gently but firmly pressed.

The following items explain the specific kinds of points and segments you can create in Illustrator. Look to Figure 5-17 for examples.

- Corner point: Click with the pen tool to create a corner point, which represents the corner between two segments in a path.

- Straight segment: Click at two different locations to create a straight segment between two corner points, like the first example in Figure 5-17.

 After positioning one corner point, you can Shift-click to create a perfectly horizontal, vertical, or 45-degree segment between that point and the new one. As discussed in the "Keeping Your Movements in Line" section earlier in this chapter, you can modify the angle of constraint by entering a value into the Constrain Angle option box in the General Preferences dialog box.

- Smooth point: Drag with the pen tool to create a smooth point with two symmetrical Bézier control handles. A smooth point ensures that one segment fuses into another to form a continuous arc.

- Curved segment: Drag at two different locations to create a curved segment between two smooth points, as illustrated by the second example in Figure 5-17.

- Straight segment followed by curved: After drawing a straight segment, drag from the corner point you just created to add a control handle. Then drag again at a different location to append a curved segment to the end of the straight segment.

- Curved segment followed by straight: After drawing a curved segment, click on the smooth point you just created to delete the forward control handle. This converts the smooth point to a corner point with one handle. Then click again at a different location to append a straight segment to the end of the curved segment.

- Cusp point: After drawing a curved segment, Option-drag from the smooth point you just created to redirect the forward control handle. This converts the smooth point to a corner point with two independent handles, sometimes known as a *cusp point*. Then drag again at a new location to append a curved segment that sprouts off in a different direction. The last example in Figure 5-17 shows the cusp point in action.

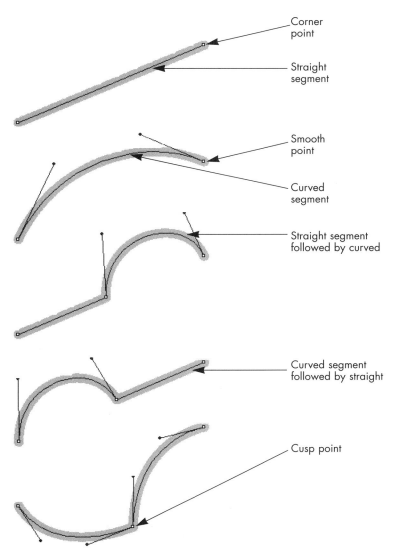

Figure 5-17: The complete annotated guide to the different kinds of points and segments you can draw with the pen tool.

Modifying the Closing Point

When you close a shape, you click, drag, and Option-drag, just as you do when creating other points. But because you modify and close in one gesture, it seems a good idea to revisit these techniques within this slightly different context:

- Click on the first point in a path to clip off any control handle that may have been threatening to affect the closing segment and close with a corner point.

- If the first point in the path is a smooth point, drag on the point to make sure it remains a smooth point, thus closing the path with an arc.

- If the first point is a corner point, drag to add a control handle that curves the closing segment.

- To convert a smooth point to a cusp on closing, Option-drag on the first point in the path.

Putting the Pen Tool to Work

Well now, that was a whole lot of information crammed into a small amount of type. Perhaps too much. To make things a little clearer for those of you who are still struggling with this amazing tool, I give you the chance to try out the pen tool in the next three sections. I first show you how to use corner points, then smooth points, and finally cusps.

Drawing Free-Form Polygons

Clicking with the pen tool is a wonderful way to create straight-sided polygons. Unlike the shapes you draw with the regular polygon tool, pen tool polygons may be any shape or size. These are pistol packin' polygons of the Wild West, with no customs to guide their behavior or laws to govern their physical form. I'm talking outlaw polygons, so be sure to take cover as you click:

1. **Click to create a corner point.**

   Select the pen tool and click at some location in the drawing area to create a corner point. The X next to the pen cursor disappears to show you that a path is now in progress. The new corner point appears as a filled square to show that it's selected. It is also *open-ended*, meaning that it doesn't have both a segment coming into it and a segment going out from it. In fact, this new corner point—I'll call it point A—is associated with no segment whatsoever. It's a lone point, open-ended in two directions.

2. **Click to add another corner point**.

Click at a new location in the illustration to create a new corner point—point B. Illustrator automatically draws a straight segment from point A to point B, as demonstrated in Figure 5-18. Notice that point A now appears hollow rather than filled. This shows that point A is the member of a selected path, but the point is deselected. Point B is selected and open-ended. Illustrator automatically selects a point immediately after you create it and deselects all other points.

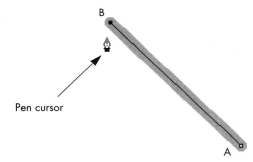

Figure 5-18:
Draw a straight segment by clicking at each of two separate locations with the pen tool.

3. **Click to add yet another corner point**.

Click a third time with the pen tool to create a third corner point—point C. Since a point may be associated with no more than two segments, point B is no longer open-ended, as verified by Figure 5-19. Such a point is called an *interior point*.

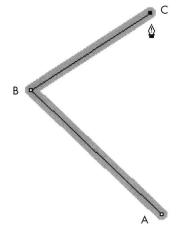

Figure 5-19:
Point B is now an interior point, incapable of receiving additional segments.

4. Click on the first point in the path.

You can keep adding points to a path one at a time for a long as you like. When finished, you can *close* the path by again clicking on point A, as demonstrated in Figure 5-20. Illustrator displays the close cursor to show you that it's ready to draw the last segment. (If you don't see the little O with the pen cursor, you don't have it positioned properly.) Since point A is open-ended, it willingly accepts the segment drawn between it and the previous point in the path.

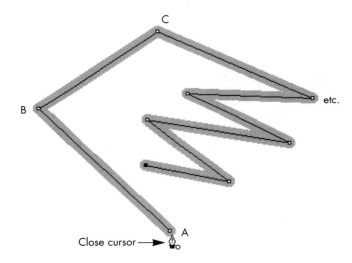

Close cursor ⟶

Figure 5-20: Clicking on the first point in a path closes the path and deactivates it. The next point you create will begin a new path.

5. Click to start a new path.

All points in a closed path are interior points. Therefore, the path you just drew is no longer active. Illustrator displays the new path cursor, as in Figure 5-21, to show it will draw no segment between the next point you create and any point in the closed path. To verify this, click again with the pen tool. You create a new independent point, which is selected and open-ended in two directions, just like point A. Meanwhile, the closed path becomes deselected. The path-creation process is begun anew.

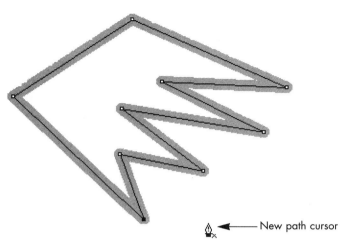

New path cursor

Figure 5-21: After you close a path, Illustrator adds a little X to the pen tool cursor to show that the next point you create starts a new path.

Drawing Supple Curves

Free-form polygons are great, but you can create them in any drawing program, even something old and remedial like MacDraw. The real advantage to the pen tool is that it lets you draw very precise curves.

When you drag with the pen tool to create a smooth point, you specify the location of two control handles. Each of these handles appears as a tiny circle perched at the end of a thin line that connects the handle to its point (see Figure 5-22). These handles act as levers, bending segments relative to the smooth point itself.

The point at which you begin dragging with the pen tool determines the location of the smooth point; the point at which you release becomes a control handle that affects the *next* segment you create. A second handle appears symmetrically from the first handle, on the opposite side of the smooth point. This handle determines the curvature of the most recent segment, as demonstrated in Figure 5-22. You might think of a smooth point as if it were the center of a small seesaw, with the control handles acting as opposite ends. If you push down on one handle, the opposite handle goes up, and vice versa.

Smooth points act no differently than corner points when it comes to building paths. You can easily combine smooth and corner points in the same path by alternatively clicking and dragging. However, if the first point in a path is a smooth

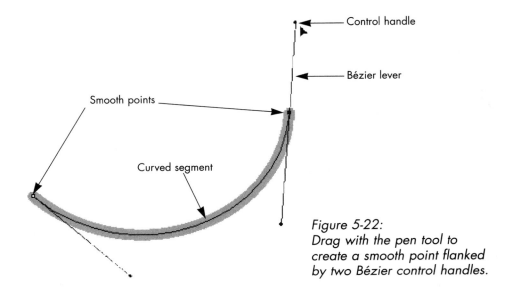

Figure 5-22:
Drag with the pen tool to
create a smooth point flanked
by two Bézier control handles.

point, you should drag rather than click on the point when closing the path. Otherwise, you run the risk of changing the point to a cusp, as discussed in the next section.

Creating Corners Between Curves

A smooth point must *always* have two Bézier control handles, each positioned in an imaginary straight line with the point itself. A corner point, however, is much more versatile. It can have zero, one, or two handles. To create a corner point that has one or two control handles (sometimes called a cusp), you must manipulate an existing corner or smooth point while in the process of creating a path. I'll demonstrate three examples of how this technique can work.

Deleting Handles from Smooth Points

These steps explain how to add a flat edge to a path composed of smooth points:

1. **Draw some smooth points**.

    Begin by drawing the path shown in Figure 5-23. You do this by dragging three times with the pen tool: First drag downward from point A, then drag leftward from point B, and finally drag up from point C (which is selected in the figure). The result is an active path composed of three smooth points.

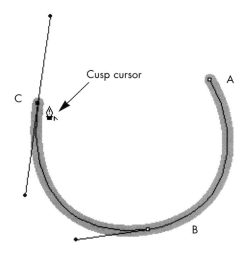

Cusp cursor

C

A

B

Figure 5-23:
An active semicircular
path with a selected,
open-ended smooth point.

2. Click on the last point created.

Illustrator lets you alter the most recent point while in the process of creating a path. Suppose that you want to flatten off the top of the path to create a sort of tilted bowl, like the one in Figure 5-24. Since smooth points can be associated only with curved segments, you must convert the top two smooth points to corner points.

To convert the most recent point—the one on right—position the pen tool over point C so the pen changes to the cusp cursor (as in Figure 5-23). Then click to amputate the forward handle, which does not yet control a segment.

3. Click on the first point in the path.

You now have an open path composed of two smooth points (A and B) and a cusp (C). You still need to close the path and to amputate a handle belonging to point A. Both maneuvers are accomplished in a single operation, that of clicking on the first smooth point. It's that simple. With one click, you close the path and amputate the control handle that would have otherwise curved the closing segment. Hence, the new segment is straight, bordered on both sides by corner points with one handle each, as in Figure 5-24.

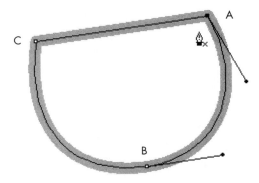

Figure 5-24:
By clicking with the pen tool on the two top points, you change the existing smooth points to corner points with one Bézier control handle apiece.

Converting Smooth Points to Cusps

These steps show you how to close the path from Figure 5-23 with a concave top, resulting in a crescent shape:

1. **Draw some smooth points.**

   Begin again by drawing the path shown in Figure 5-23, as described in the first step of the previous section.

2. **Option-drag down from the last point created.**

   All segments in a crescent are curved, but the upper and lower segments meet to form two cusps. This means that you need to change the two top smooth points to cusps with two control handles apiece—one controlling the upper segment and one controlling a lower segment.

   To subtract a handle from a smooth point and add a new handle to the resulting corner point in one operation, press the Option key and drag from point C. The moment you begin to Option-drag, the point's identity changes from smooth to corner and a new handle emerges, as shown in Figure 5-25. This handle will control the next segment you create.

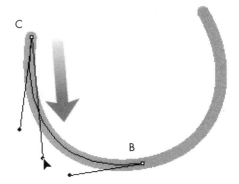

Figure 5-25:
Press the Option key and drag from the selected smooth point to convert the point to a cusp.

3. Option-drag up from the first point in the path.

Close the path in a similar manner, by Option-dragging upward from
point A. Notice the location of the cursor as you drag, as demonstrated
by Figure 5-26. You drag in one direction, but the handle emerges in the
opposite direction. This is because, when dragging with the pen tool,
you always drag in the direction of the forward segment—that is, the one
that *exits* the current point. Illustrator positions the handle that controls the
closing segment symmetrically to your drag, even if it is the only handle
being manipulated. It's kind of weird, but it's Illustrator's way.

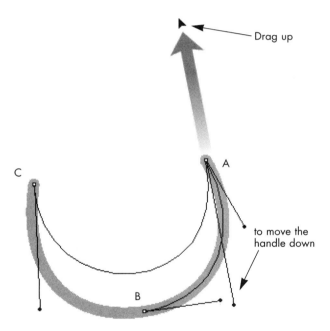

*Figure 5-26:
Close the path by
Option-dragging
up from the first
point in the path.*

Adding Handles to Corner Points

Last but not least, the next steps tell you how to add a curved segment to a path
composed of straight segments:

1. Draw some corner points.

Begin by creating the straight-sided path shown in Figure 5-27. Well,
create something like it, anyway. Actually, it doesn't matter how many
points are in the path, just so long as they're all corner points.

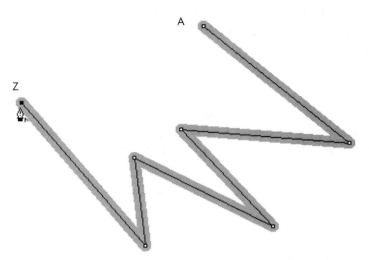

Figure 5-27: An active path composed entirely of straight
segments with a selected, open-ended corner point.

2. Drag from the last corner point created.

Drag from the most recent corner point you've created (point Z in
the figure) to extract a single control handle, as shown in Figure 5-28.

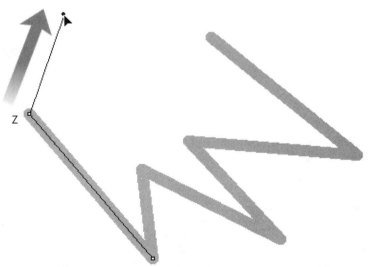

Figure 5-28: Drag from the selected corner point to add a
Bézier control handle.

Note that you don't convert the corner point to a smooth point by dragging from it. The fact is, you can't change a corner point to a smooth point using the pen tool.

3. Drag from the first point in the path.

To close the path, drag at the first corner point in the path, as demonstrated in Figure 5-29. Once again, you drag in the opposite direction of the emerging Bézier control handle.

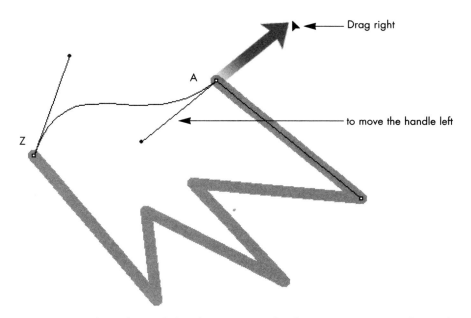

Figure 5-29: Close the path by dragging on the first corner point in the path.

Operating on Points Long After the Path Is Done

Right about now, you're probably figuring Illustrator's path-editing capabilities have completely revealed themselves to you like a lotus blossom unfurling its petals. Armed with the direct selection and pen tools, you are more or less master of all you survey.

Well, that's almost true. But there are still a few questions left unanswered. For example, how do you insert a point into a path? For that matter, how do you remove a point without breaking the path in half? And what do you do if you want to change a corner point in an existing path to a smooth point, or a smooth point to a corner?

Illustrator provides three tools that let you operate on existing paths, whether drawn with the pen tool or one of the tools covered in Chapter 4. These are the add anchor point tool, the delete anchor point tool, and the convert anchor point tool. (All those anchors weigh down my lucid prose, so I just dump them over-board, leaving the shorter tool names listed in Figure 5-30.) To select one of these tools, drag from the scissors tool icon in the toolbox and select the tool from the pop-up menu.

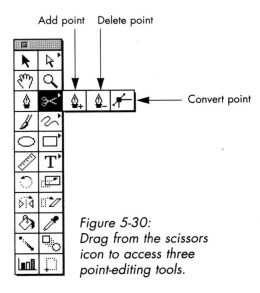

Figure 5-30:
Drag from the scissors
icon to access three
point-editing tools.

The following sections explain how to use these three tools. But you can also add points with the pen and freehand tools and delete points and segments with the direct selection tool, so I discuss these techniques as well. If it has anything to do with adding, deleting, or converting, it's covered in the next pages.

Adding Points to a Path

A path is nothing more than an illusion your computer creates to make you think you're accomplishing something. Like an imaginary creature, it is constantly subject to revision and enhancement. It is not, in other words, in any way permanent, even if you created it years ago in a different version of Illustrator or even a different program. What I'm trying to say here is: If a path doesn't have enough points to get the job done, don't hesitate to add some:

- Appending a point to the end of an open path: If an existing path is open, you can add points to either end of it. First, activate one of its endpoints by clicking or dragging on it with the pen tool. When you position the pen tool over an inactive endpoint, you get the activate cursor, which looks like a pen with a little slash next to it. Drag from the point if you want to retain or add a control handle; click if you want to trim off a control handle or avoid adding one; and Option-drag if you want to change the direction of a handle. Then click and drag to add more points to the path.

  You can also lengthen an open path by dragging from one of its endpoints with the freehand tool. In the unlikely event the path touches a portion of a tracing template, you can even use the autotrace tool.

- Closing an open path: Once the path is active, you can close it in any of the ways discussed in the "Putting the Pen Tool to Work" section earlier in this chapter. Just click, drag, or Option-drag on the opposite endpoint with the pen tool. You can also close a path by dragging from one endpoint to the other with the freehand tool. In either case, Illustrator adds a little O to the cursor to show a closing is in the making.

- Insert a point into a segment: To insert a new interior point into a path, select the add point tool and click anywhere along a segment (except on an existing point). Illustrator inserts the point and divides the segment in two. Illustrator automatically inserts a corner or smooth point depending on its reading of your path. If the point does not exactly meet your need, you can modify it with the convert point tool, as I explain a few paragraphs from now.

The add point tool is great for filling out a path that just isn't making the grade. If a path isn't curving correctly, it may be that you're trying to make the existing points in the path do too much work. For example, the first path in Figure 5-31 obeys both the All-or-Nothing and 33-Percent rules, but it still looks overly squarish. That's because it violates a lesser rule that says handles shouldn't point wildly away from each other. To smooth things out, I clicked on the path midway between the two points with the add point tool. In this case, Illustrator inserted a smooth point, because the segment is ultimately smooth at the point where I clicked. I then used the direct selection tool to adjust the control handles and get the more rounded curve shown here.

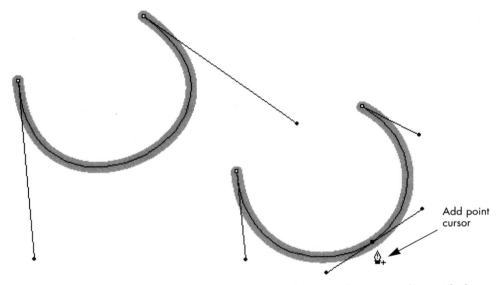

Add point
cursor

Figure 5-31: If a curve looks squarish no matter how much you monkey with the control handles (left), insert a point with the add point tool (right).

 Illustrator lets you access the add point tool from the keyboard when certain tools are active:

● Press the Option key to temporarily access the add point tool when either the delete point or scissors tool is selected.

● When the pen tool is selected, press the Control key to get the add point tool.

● If the freehand tool is active, press ⌘ and Control together.

In any case, the add point tool remains available only so long as the keys are down.

Removing Points from a Path

To delete an entire path, you just select it with the arrow tool and press the Delete key. (If you're using an old keyboard, press Backspace.) If you love to use your mouse, you can choose Edit » Clear (although I must admit, I've never seen anyone choose that command in my life).

To delete a point or segment, try out one of the following techniques:

- Delete a point and break the path: To delete a point, select it with the direct selection tool and press the Delete key. When you delete an interior point, you delete both segments associated with that point, resulting in a break in the path. If you delete an endpoint from an open path, you delete the single segment associated with the point.

- Delete a segment: You can delete a single interior segment from a path without removing a point. To do so, click on the segment you want to delete with the direct selection tool and press Delete. Deleting a segment always creates a break in a path.

- Deleting the rest of the path: After you delete a point or segment, Illustrator selects the remainder of the path. To delete the whole path, just press Delete a second time. This can be a handy technique if you don't want to switch to the arrow tool. Just click on some portion of the path and press Delete twice in a row to delete the whole path.

- Removing a point without breaking the path: If you want to get rid of a point but you don't want to create a break in the path, select the delete point tool and click on the point you want to disappear. Illustrator draws a new segment between the two points that neighbor the deleted point.

 You can press keys to get the delete point tool when the add point, pen, or freehand tool is selected:

- Press Option to access the delete point tool when the add point is active. (Have you noticed Option is a toggle between the add and delete point tools? When one is active, Option gets you the other.)

- If the pen tool is selected, press the Control key and move the cursor over a point. A little minus sign appears to show you Illustrator is ready to delete.

● When using the freehand tool, press ⌘ and Control and move the cursor over a point.

Releasing any of these key combinations returns you to the selected tool.

 Beware of deleting a point from a line that consists of only two points, or deleting a point or segment that neighbors an endpoint. This will leave a single-point path, which is completely useless unless you intend to build on it immediately. Lone points clutter up the drawing area and make editing that much more confusing. (If your illustration does have lots of lone points—someone else's fault I'm sure—choose Filter » Objects » Cleanup and select the Delete Stray Points check box.)

Converting Points Between Corner and Smooth

Of the tools discussed in this chapter, I would probably rank the direct selection tool as most important, the pen tool as number two, and this next tool—the convert point tool—as number three. The convert point tool lets you change a point in the middle of a path from corner to smooth or smooth to corner. When a path is shaped wrong, this tool is absolutely essential.

You can change the identity of an interior point in any of the following ways:

● Smooth to corner: Using the convert point tool, click on a smooth point to convert it to a corner point without a control handle.

● Smooth to cusp: Drag a control handle belonging to a smooth point to move it independently of the other control handle, thus converting the smooth point to a cusp.

● Corner to smooth: Drag from a corner point to convert it to a smooth point with two symmetrical control handles.

● Cusp to smooth: Drag one of the control handles belonging to a cusp point to lock both handles back into alignment, resulting in a smooth point.

Figure 5-32 shows a path created with the star tool. Like any star, it's made up entirely of corner points and straight segments. But with the help of the convert point tool, you can put some curve on that puppy, as the following steps make clear:

1. Drag from one of the points along the inner radius.

Select the convert point tool and drag from one of the inner radius of points, as demonstrated in Figure 5-33. The corner point changes to a smooth point with symmetrical control handles, bending both neighboring segments.

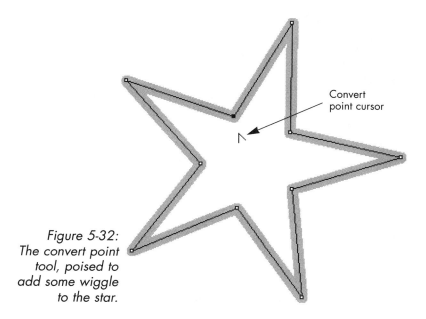

Convert
point cursor

Figure 5-32:
The convert point
tool, poised to
add some wiggle
to the star.

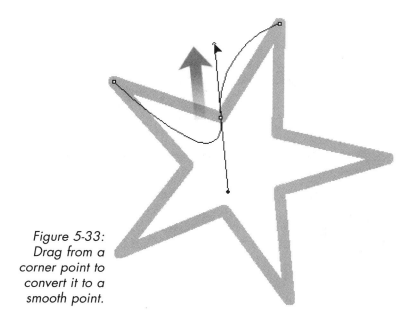

Figure 5-33:
Drag from a
corner point to
convert it to a
smooth point.

2. Drag the inside control handle outside the star.

Drag the control handle that moved inside the star to a position outside the star, so that the two spikes form mirror images of each other, as demonstrated in Figure 5-34. This converts the smooth point to a cusp, permitting the control handles to move independently.

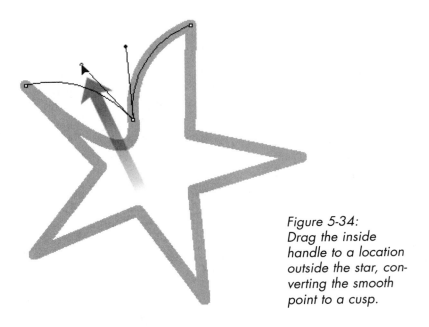

Figure 5-34: Drag the inside handle to a location outside the star, converting the smooth point to a cusp.

3. Repeat Steps 1 and 2 on all the inner radius points.

By dragging control handles from all the points and converting them to cusp points, you can create the flower shape shown in Figure 5-35. Oh, sure, it violates the All-or-Nothing rule; each segment gets just one control handle. But after all, that's why we have rules—so we can occasionally ignore them and feel like we're getting away with something.

In between converting points, it's very tempting to adjust the placement of control handles using the convert point tool. If you do so, however, you will most certainly convert the point. To move a point or adjust a handle without converting a point, be sure to press the ⌘ key to temporarily access a direct selection tool before beginning your drag. Of course, if you forget to heed this advice and inadvertently convert a point, you can immediately choose Edit » Undo (⌘-Z) to convert the point back again.

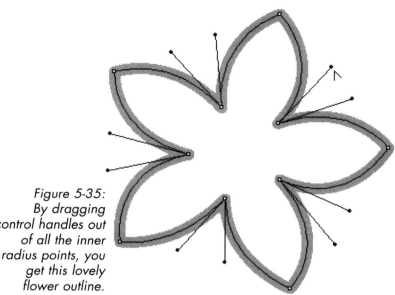

Figure 5-35:
By dragging
control handles out
of all the inner
radius points, you
get this lovely
flower outline.

 If you thought it was complicated to select the add point or delete point tool from the keyboard, it's nothing compared with the 90 ways to get the convert point tool. The one advantage is that you can access the convert point tool when just about any tool is selected:

- Press the Control key to temporarily access the convert point tool when a selection tool is active.

- Press Control and Option together when the pen tool is selected.

- If the freehand tool is active, press ⌘, Control, and Option.

- When any other tool is selected—except the scissors, add point, or delete point tools—press ⌘ and Control to get to that most excellent of point conversion tools.

Reliving the Past

Because we all make mistakes, especially when drawing and tracing complicated paths, Illustrator provides you with the ability to nullify the results of previous operations. In fact, Illustrator lets you retract several operations in a row. So when drawing anxiety sets in, remember this simple credo: *Undo, redo, relaxum.* That's Latin for "Chill, it's just a computer."

Undoing Consecutive Operations

Edit » Undo—and its universal shortcut ⌘-Z—let you negate the last action performed. For example, if you move a point and decide you don't like how it looks, choose Edit » Undo Move and the new point disappears. More to the point, Illustrator returns you to the exact moment before you moved the point. Better yet, you can *always* undo the last action, even if you have since clicked on screen or performed some minor action that the command does not recognize.

Get this: You can even undo an operation performed prior to the most recent Save operation (although you cannot undo the Save command itself). For example, you can delete an element, save the illustration, then choose Undo Clear to make the element reappear. It's a real life saver.

Illustrator lets you undo up to 200 consecutive operations. This powerful feature takes a great deal of the worry out of using Illustrator. You can even reverse major blunders one step at a time.

To change the number of possible consecutive undos, press ⌘-K to display the General Preferences dialog box and enter a new value in the Minimum Undo Levels option box. The word *minimum* appears in the option name because Illustrator permits you to undo as many operations as it can store in its undo buffer, regardless of the option value. The value merely sets aside space in your computer's memory so Illustrator can undo at least that many operations. As a result, you may be able to undo 200 path operations even if the Minimum Undo Levels value is set to 5.

To monitor how many undo levels are available at any given time, select the Number of Undos option from the status bar pop-up menu in the lower left corner of the illustration window.

After you exhaust the maximum number of undos, the Undo command appears dimmed in the Edit menu. Pressing ⌘-Z will produce no effect until you perform a new operation. And remember, Illustrator can undo operations performed in the current session only. You can't undo something you did back before the most recent time you started Illustrator.

Redoing Undo Operations

Just as you can undo as many as 200 consecutive actions, you can redo up to 200 consecutive undos by choosing Edit » Redo or pressing ⌘-Shift-Z. You can choose Redo only if the Undo command was the most recent operation performed; otherwise, Redo is dimmed. Also, if you undo a series of actions, perform a new series of actions, and then undo the new series of actions to the point where you had stopped undoing previously, you can't go back and redo the first series of undos. Instead, you can simply continue to undo from where you left off.

Returning to the Last-Saved File

If your modifications to an illustration are a total botch, you can revert to the last-saved version of the file by choosing File » Revert. It's like closing a file, clicking on the Don't Save button, and reopening the file in one step. You probably won't need this command very often, but keep in mind that's it's here when things go terribly wrong.

If you haven't done anything to an illustration since you last saved it, or if you've never saved the drawing, File » Revert is dimmed.

CHAPTER 6

HOW TO HANDLE TYPICAL TYPE

If a picture is worth a thousand words, Illustrator must be worth a thousand Microsoft Words. (Even as I write this in Word 6, I'm hard pressed to think of anything that's *not* worth a thousand Words.) But however powerful pictures may be, and although they admittedly bridge the boundaries of culture and language (heck, I bet extraterrestrials living in Roswell could understand them) Illustrator knows that every once in a while, text comes in handy. As a result, the program has assembled some of the most flexible and uniquely capable tools for creating and formatting type of any Macintosh program.

179

Illustrator's type capabilities are so amazing that I'll explore them over the course of two chapters. This chapter examines the relatively basic stuff—how to create text blocks and apply formatting attributes such as typeface and style. I close out the chapter with a generous description of tabs, one of Illustrator's more recent features. Even if you know type, this chapter imparts lots of useful tips and keyboard shortcuts that you'll most assuredly want to learn.

Chapter 7 looks at type effects that are virtually unknown outside Illustrator. You can fix type to a curve, set text inside free-form text blocks, apply effects to Adobe's specialized Multiple Master fonts, and convert letter outlines to fully-editable paths. Look for this and more in the next chapter.

Establishing Text Objects

Altogether, Illustrator provides three tools for creating text. But for now, we're concerned with only one: the type tool, sixth tool down on the right side of the toolbox (the one that looks like a T). Armed with the type tool, you can create a text object—which is any object that contains type—in one of two ways:

- Click with the type tool in the drawing area and enter a few words of type for a logo or headline. This kind of text block is called *point text,* because Illustrator aligns the text to the point at which you click.

- Drag with the type tool to draw a rectangular *text block.* Then enter your text from the keyboard. Illustrator fits the text to the rectangular text block, automatically shifting text that doesn't fit on one line down to the next. Create a text block when you want to enter a full sentence or more.

I explain point text and text blocks in more detail in the following sections.

Creating Point Text

Figure 6-1 shows the three steps involved in creating point text. (Incidentally, this figure and several that follow sport default Helvetica, 12-point text magnified to 400 percent on screen.) The three steps go something like this:

1. Select the type tool, and click in some empty portion of the drawing area with the new block cursor, labeled in Figure 6-1. The new block cursor shows you that you are about to create a new text object.

After you click with the type tool, Illustrator creates an *alignment point,* which appears as an X in the artwork mode. (In the preview mode, you see the alignment point only if the point text is selected.) Not surprisingly, Illustrator aligns the text to this point.

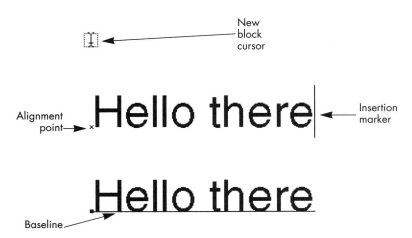

Figure 6-1: Click with the type tool (top), enter your text (middle), and select a different tool to complete the text object (bottom).

2. Enter the desired text from your keyboard. By default, the text appears to the right of the alignment point. (I explain how to change the alignment later in this chapter.) As you type, a blinking *insertion marker* flashes to the right of the last character. The insertion marker shows you where the next letter you enter will appear.

With point text, Illustrator keeps all characters on a single line unless you tell it to do otherwise. This is why point text is better suited to a few words or less. If you want to move the insertion marker down to create a new line of type, press the Return or Enter key.

3. When you have finished entering your text, click on any tool in the toolbox except the hand, zoom, or measure tool. The text block appears selected, as shown in the bottom example of Figure 6-1. The alignment point now looks like a filled square, just like a selected anchor point.

You can drag the alignment point with any of the three selection tools to reposition the text in the drawing area. You can also drag point text by its *baseline*, which is the line that runs under each line of type. The baseline is the imaginary line on which letters sit. Only a few lowercase characters—g, j, p, q, and y— descend below the baseline.

Creating Text Blocks

Point text is easy to create, but because Illustrator forces all text onto a single line unless told to do otherwise, point text is not well suited to whole paragraphs and longer text. To accommodate lengthy text, you need to create a text block:

1. **Drag with the type tool.** This creates a rectangle, as shown in the first example in Figure 6-2, just as if you were dragging with the rectangle tool. This rectangle represents the height and width of the new text block.

   When you release, Illustrator shows you a box with a blinking insertion marker inside it. If you are working inside the artwork mode, you also see a center point, just as in a standard rectangle.

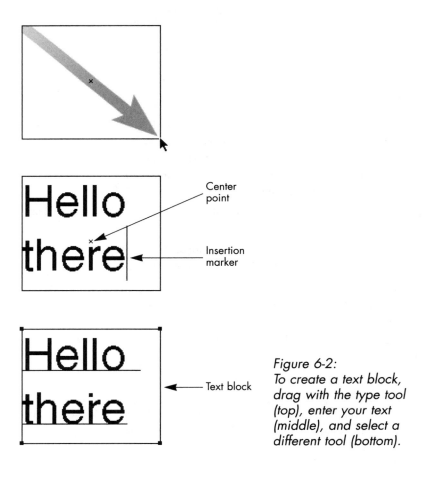

Center point

Insertion marker

Text block

Figure 6-2:
To create a text block, drag with the type tool (top), enter your text (middle), and select a different tool (bottom).

2. Enter type from the keyboard. If a letter extends beyond the right edge of the text block, Illustrator sends the word down to start a new line of type. Known as *automatic wrapping*, this is precisely the capability that point text lacks.

3. Click on any tool (other than hand, zoom, or measure) to stop entering text. The text block appears selected, showing off four corner points connected by straight segments and a center point hovering in the middle. Baselines underscore the type to indicate that the letters themselves are selected.

Resizing Text Blocks

As with point text, you can reposition a text block by dragging either the rectangular boundary or one of the baselines with the arrow tool. You can also change the size and shape of a text block with the direct selection tool.

For example, say that the text you entered from the keyboard doesn't entirely fit inside the text block. Or worse yet, the text block isn't wide enough to accommodate a particularly long word. Both of these problems are illustrated in Figure 6-3. The little square with a minus sign in it shows that Illustrator had to break the word *everybody* onto two lines. The square with a plus sign shows that there is more text that does fit inside the text block and is temporarily hidden. This text is called *overflow text*.

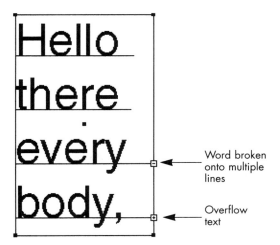

Figure 6-3: Illustrator shows you when a word doesn't fit on a line, or when text extends outside the text block.

By reshaping a text block, you can fit long words on a single line, reveal overflow text, or simply change how words wrap from one line to the next. To reshape a text block, you have to use the direct-selection tool to select and modify the rectangular boundary independently of the text inside it. Here's how it works:

1. **Create your text block**.

   After creating the text block, select the direct-selection tool.

2. **Deselect the text block**.

   Unlike nearly every other program on earth, you can't resize a text block just by dragging a corner point. You have to select one of the segments and drag it, just as if you were reshaping a standard path. And—just to make things as painful as possible—you can't select a segment until you deselect the path. So choose Edit » Select None or press ⌘-Shift-A to deselect the text block.

3. **Select the right or bottom edge of the text block**.

   If you're working in the preview mode, the text block outline disappears. This makes selecting one of the edges of the text block rather difficult. That's why I recommend you drag a tiny marquee around the portion of the outline you want to move. If you want to make the text block wider, drag a marquee around the right side, as in the first example of Figure 6-4. If you want to make the text block taller, marquee the bottom side. In either case, the desired edge becomes selected. (Because it's a straight segment, you can't see that it's selected. But have faith, it is.)

    Make sure you don't select a baseline. If you select a baseline, you select the entire text block, which prevents you from resizing it. So if a baseline appears, press ⌘-Shift-A and try again.

    If you can't seem to get the darn segment selected, switch to the artwork mode by pressing ⌘-E. In the artwork mode, you can see the text block outline even when it's not selected. This makes it easier to click on the segment you want to select.

4. **Shift-drag the edge**.

   To maintain the rectangular shape of the text block, Shift-drag the right segment to the right, as in Figure 6-4. Or Shift-drag the bottom segment downward. (You can also drag without pressing Shift to create diamond-shape text blocks.)

When you release the mouse button, Illustrator rewraps the text and displays as much overflow text as will fit. If there is still more overflow text, the little plus icon remains in the lower right corner of the text block.

 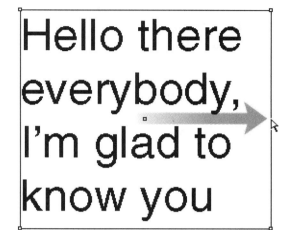

Figure 6-4: Use the direct selection tool to marquee around the edge of the text block you want to expand (left), then Shift-drag the edge (right).

 To resize the height and width of a text block at the same time, select the entire block outline by Option-clicking on it with the direct selection tool. (Make sure the baselines remain invisible.) Then drag with the scale tool. For more info on the scale tool, turn to Chapter 11.

You can reshape the outline of a text block using any of the techniques discussed in Chapter 5. In addition to dragging points and segments, you can do any of the following:

- Change the corner points to smooth points with the convert point tool.
- Drag the control handles to bend the segments.
- Insert or remove points with the add point and delete point tools.
- Select a segment with the direct selection tool and press Delete to open up the path.
- Extend the open path using the pen or freehand tools.

If this kind of thing interests you—and why shouldn't it?—Chapter 7 explains how to create text inside any old wacky shape, as well as pour overflow text from one text block into another.

Selecting and Editing Text

Before you can change a character of type or change the way the text looks on the page, you have to select the type using the arrow or type tool.

- Clicking along the baseline of a line of type with any selection tool selects all type in the object. If you change the font, type size, style, or some other formatting attribute, you change all characters in the selected text object.

- With the arrow tool, click on one text object and Shift-click on another to format multiple text objects at a time. (Illustrator doesn't let you format a text block if you select just a portion of the outline with the direct selection tool.)

- If you select text with a type tool, you can edit that text by entering new text from the keyboard or format the selected text independently of other text in the object.

Selecting with the Type Tool

Though the selection tools are certainly useful, the type tool is the most common instrument for editing type in Illustrator because it affords the most control. The following items explain how to select type with the type tool:

- Drag over the characters that you want to select. Drag to the left or to the right to select characters on a single line; drag upward or downward to select characters on multiple lines. The selected text becomes highlighted—inverted colors against a black background—as shown in Figure 6-5.

- Double-click on a word to select that word. Hold down the mouse button on the second click and drag to select more words.

- Triple-click to select an entire paragraph, from one Return character to the next. Triple-clicking in point text selects an entire line, since you have to press Return to go from one line to the next (i.e., a line of point text is the equivalent of a paragraph). Hold down the mouse button on the third click and drag to select additional paragraphs.

Figure 6-5:
Drag across charac-
ters with the type tool
to highlight them.

- Click to set the insertion marker at one end of the text you want to select, then Shift-click at the opposite end of the desired selection. Illustrator highlights all characters between the first click and the Shift-click.

- Click anywhere in a text block and press ⌘-A (or choose Edit » Select All) to select all text in the object.

 After you click with the type tool to set the insertion marker inside a text object, you can use the arrow keys to move the insertion marker around or select text:

- Press the left or right arrow key to move the insertion marker to the left or right one character.

- Press the up or down arrow key to move the insertion marker up or down one line.

- Press ⌘-→ to move the insertion marker one whole word to the right. Press ⌘-← to move back a word.

- Press ⌘-↑ to move the insertion marker to the beginning of the paragraph. Press ⌘-↓ to move to the end of the paragraph.

- Press Shift along with any of these keystrokes to select text as you move the insertion marker. For example, press Shift-right arrow to select the character after the insertion marker. Press ⌘-Shift-up arrow to select everything from the insertion marker to the beginning of the paragraph.

Replacing, Deleting, and Adding Text

After you highlight some text, you can format it (as I begin explaining in the next section) or replace it by entering new text from the keyboard.

- To delete selected text, press the Delete key.

- You can remove the selected text and send it to the Macintosh Clipboard by choosing Edit » Cut (⌘-X).

- To leave the selected text intact and send a copy to the Clipboard choose Edit » Copy command (⌘-C).

- You can even replace the selected text with text that you cut or copied earlier by choosing Edit » Paste (⌘-V). The pasted text retains its original formatting.

The only way to convert a line of point text to a text block— or vice versa—is via the Clipboard. Select the text you want to convert with either the arrow or type tool, cut or copy it, then drag with the type tool to create the text block (or click for the point text) and paste.

If you want to add text rather than replace it, just click with the type tool inside a text block to position the insertion marker. Then bang away at the keyboard and let the mouse take you where it will.

If Illustrator seems to ignore you when you enter text or press the Delete key, press the Return key. The problem is Illustrator thinks a palette is active and is trying desperately to apply your typing to that palette; pressing Return deactivates the palette and returns control to the illustration window.

Formatting Type

Where type is concerned, *formatting* means nothing more than changing the way characters and lines of text look. Illustrator provides an exhaustive supply of formatting functions which let you modify far more than you'll ever want to. Alas, if I had owned Illustrator 6 back when I ran a service bureau, I would never have had an unfulfilled typographic desire.

You can divide formatting attributes into two categories—those that apply to individual characters of type, and those that apply to entire paragraphs.

Character-level formatting includes options such as typeface, size, leading, kerning and tracking, baseline shift, and horizontal scaling. To change the formatting of one or more characters, you select the characters with the type tool and apply the desired options. Illustrator changes the highlighted characters and leaves surrounding characters unaltered.

 Paragraph-level formatting includes indents, alignment, paragraph spacing, letter spacing, and word spacing. To change the formatting of a single paragraph, you need only position the blinking insertion marker inside that paragraph; Illustrator changes the entire paragraph no matter how little of it is selected. To change the formatting of multiple paragraphs, select at least one character in each of the paragraphs you want to modify.

 If you want Illustrator to consider two different lines of type as part of the same paragraph, press the Enter key (instead of Return) to separate them. The Enter key inserts a line break as opposed to a carriage return. All paragraph formatting applied to one line becomes applicable to the other as well.

Illustrator adopts the most recently applied formatting attributes as the default settings throughout the rest of the session (or until you further modify the settings). But the next time you quit Illustrator and start it up again, the program restores the original default settings (though you can alter some defaults permanently by editing the Adobe Illustrator 6.0 Prefs file, as mentioned in the "The Prefs File" section of Chapter 2).

Character-Level Formatting

To format characters, you can either choose commands from the Font and Type menus or avail yourself of the options in the Character palette. The latter is the more convenient.

 The one character formatting attribute that I don't discuss in this chapter is color. To change the color of selected text, you merely change the fill color in the Paint Style palette, as I explain in Chapter 15. You can even stroke text, as you'll learn in Chapter 16.

To display the character palette, choose Type » Character, or press ⌘-T, the universal shortcut for character-level formatting (except in Microsoft Word, but I've already mentioned what I think of that program). By default, the Character palette shows only five options, as in the top example of Figure 6-6. But if you click on the flag icon in the lower right corner, you expand the palette to display several more options, as in the bottom example of the figure.

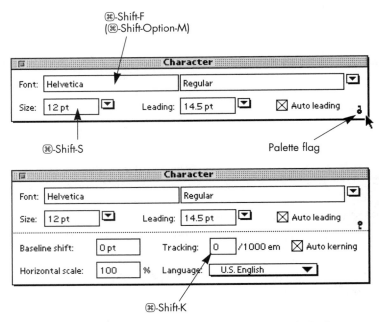

Figure 6-6: The Character palette, collapsed (top) and expanded (bottom), with the keyboard shortcuts used to activate various options.

 You can also display the Character palette by choosing Window » Show Character. Or you can press one of the following keystrokes:

- ⌘-Shift-F (or ⌘-Shift-Option-M, as in QuarkXPress) displays the Character palette and activates the Font option box.

- ⌘-Shift-S displays the palette and highlights the Size option box.

- ⌘-Shift-K highlights the Tracking or Kerning option box. (The option box changes names depending on how the type is selected.) If the palette is collapsed, pressing ⌘-Shift-K expands it.

You can also hide the Character palette by pressing ⌘-T. If that doesn't work, press ⌘-T twice, once to activate the palette and a second time to hide it.

Selecting a Typeface

The Font menu lists all typefaces installed into the Fonts folder inside the System Folder on your computer's hard drive, as well as those mounted with a utility like Master Juggler or Suitcase. This is the way it is and has always been inside all Macintosh programs. In fact, the Mac was the first personal computer to integrate typefaces into the operating system.

But where most programs let you assign typeface and style separately—you might select Helvetica in one step and Bold in another—typeface and style are inseparable inside Illustrator. Illustrator lacks the ability to embellish plain typefaces with bold, italic, underline, and other fabricated styles. Instead, Illustrator relies strictly on *stylized fonts*, which provide separate design characteristics for each type style. Therefore, Helvetica Regular and Helvetica Bold are completely separate entities in Illustrator's mind, as independent as Cooper Black is from Poppl-Residenz Light. (Typefaces have notoriously odd names; it's part of the union credo.) This is much more in keeping with the historic conception of a *font*, in which characters cast from metal were housed in separate containers according to style.

This setup is ideal for fonts with extensive collections of designer styles. The complete Helvetica font, for example, includes not only Bold and Oblique (slanted), but also Light and Black (heavier than bold). By adhering strictly to styled fonts, Illustrator simplifies the application of any font, regardless of how idiosyncratic the family may be.

You can select a font from the Font menu or from the Font pop-up menu in the Character palette. (To access the pop-up menu, drag from the down-pointing arrowhead in the upper right corner of the palette.) Assuming Type Reunion is running—you have the option of installing this system extension when you install Illustrator—styles appear in submenus next to their parent typefaces. For example, to assign Times Italic, you would choose Font » Times » Italic.

 If you know the name of the font you want to apply, just enter the first few letters of its name into the Font option box in the Character palette. Each time you enter a character, Illustrator tries to guess which font you want. For example, if both American Typewriter and Avant Garde are available to your system, entering *a* gets you American Typewriter—the first font in alphabetical order—while entering *av* gets you Avant Garde. To change the style, press the Tab key and enter the first few letters of the style, such as *b* for Bold or *i* for Italic.

TrueType Incompatibilities

Sadly, Illustrator's inability to assign software styles inhibits its compatibility with TrueType fonts, because no submenu of stylized fonts appears next to the name of a TrueType typeface. This means you can choose the TrueType font New York—included with all Macs—but you can't make it bold or italic.

 Illustrator has a few other TrueType compatibility problems as well. It occasionally misinterprets TrueType font metrics (such as character width), and it has a habit of complaining when you open illustrations created with TrueType fonts. You'll likewise encounter these problems if you have both TrueType and PostScript versions of the same font installed (as is required by QuickDraw GX, for example).

To help prevent these problems, the Adobe Type Manager 3.9 installer (included with Illustrator 6) trashes all TrueType versions of common fonts like Helvetica and Times and replaces them with their PostScript Type 1 equivalents. It's a rather extreme solution, but most artists can get along just fine without TrueType. Let's face it, PostScript fonts offer better character outlines and are more universally compatible with commercial printers and service bureaus.

Adobe Type Manager Issues

 If the bottoms of descenders appear prematurely cut off, as in Figure 6-7, it's not a problem with your font, it's a problem with your font administrator, Adobe Type Manager (or ATM). To fix the problem, open the ATM control panel (Apple » Control Panels » ~ATM) and select the Character Shapes radio button. (This option controls how ATM deals with documents created without ATM, but since most Illustrator users have been using ATM most of their lives, Character Shapes is the more appropriate setting.) The next time you restart your Mac, ATM will redraw characters in their entirety, with bottoms intact.

Note that the ATM setting doesn't affect how fonts are printed to PostScript printers, nor does it affect characters converted to path outlines. Regardless of which ATM option you select, these operations work just fine. However, the Character Shapes setting does affect fonts printed to non-PostScript printers, since ATM is responsible for drawing font outlines when a PostScript interpreter is not present.

 Oh, and one more item: Recent versions of ATM let you add fonts to the Fonts folder inside the System Folder while Illustrator is running. The added fonts immediately become available in the Character palette and Font menu; you don't have to quit Illustrator and restart as in the old days.

Figure 6-7: The bottoms of descenders frequently appear cut off if you have ATM set to preserve lines spacing instead of character shapes.

Reducing and Enlarging Type

To change the size of any selected type, choose a command from the Type » Size submenu, or enter a value into the Size option box in the Character palette. *Type size*, as it is called, is measured in points from the top of an ascender (such as a *d* or *f*) to the bottom of a descender (like *g* or *p*). You can enter any value between 0.1 (1/10 the size of the smallest character in Figure 6-8) and 1296 (four times the size of the largest character) in 0.01-point increments.

Figure 6-8:
A character set in three type sizes—324-point, 48-point, and 1-point.

If you dramatically reduce the size of a line of type, it appears as a gray bar. Illustrator figures it's too small to be readable on screen, so why waste the time trying to draw it accurately? If you want to see text at smaller sizes, press ⌘-K to display the General Preferences dialog box and enter a smaller Greek Type Limit value. As long as the type appears smaller on screen than this value, Illustrator "greeks" it, replacing the type with a gray bar.

To quickly change the type size of some selected characters, press ⌘-Shift-S to activate the Size option box, then enter a new size value and press Return. You can also adjust the type size incrementally from the keyboard. Press ⌘-Shift-> to enlarge the characters or ⌘-Shift-< to reduce them. You can adjust the increment by changing the Size/Leading value in the General Preferences dialog box. By default, the increment is set to 2 points.

Specifying the Distance Between Lines

Some programs call the distance between lines of type *line spacing*, and let you adjust line spacing by applying options like Single Space and Double Space. These programs model themselves after the typewriter, one of the most outdated pieces of technology on the planet. Steam engines, record players, and dolls that wet themselves all offer more practical benefits for modern living than the typewriter. Though I know many typewriter-loving technophobes and hold a special place for them in my heart, typewriters are nonetheless obsolete and so are the programs that emulate them.

Illustrator derives its approach to line spacing from hot-metal typesetting, which—though it predates the typewriter by several hundred years—is more relevant to modern typographic trends. Printer operators of yore inserted thin strips of lead between lines of type, hence the term *leading* (pronounced *ledding*). Leading specifies the distance between a selected line of type and the line below it, as measured in points from one baseline to the next. Therefore, 14-point leading leaves a couple of points of extra room between two lines of 12-point type.

You can change the leading by choosing a command from the Type » Leading submenu. But it's much simpler to enter a value into the Leading option box in the Character palette. To speed things up, press ⌘-Shift-S to highlight the Size option box, press Tab to advance to Leading, enter a new value, and press Return. Then sit back and experience the warm glow that comes when friends and family members look over your shoulder and say, "Gosh, you're fast. I can't even insert a page into my typewriter that quickly."

Select the Auto Leading check box in the Character palette (or choose Type »
Leading » Auto) to make the leading equal to 120 percent of the current type size
(rounded off to the nearest half-point).

 To set the leading to exactly match the type size—an
arrangement known as *solid leading*—click on the word
Leading in the Character palette. Then press the Return key to
deactivate the palette and return control to the drawing area.

 As with type size, you can adjust the leading incrementally
(according to the Size/Leading value in the General
Preferences dialog box). Press Option-up arrow to reduce the
leading; press Option-down arrow to increase it.

If a line of text contains characters with two different leading specifications, the
larger leading prevails. If you begin a paragraph with a large capital letter, for
example, you might combine a 24-point character on the same line as 12-point characters. If both the 24-point character and the 12-point character use auto leading,
then the entire line will be set at 29-point leading (120% the 24-point type size).

Raising and Lowering Characters

The Baseline Shift option in the lower half of the Character palette determines
the distance between the selected type and its baseline. A positive value raises the
characters; a negative value lowers them. The default value of 0 leaves them sitting on the baseline where they typically belong.

You can modify the baseline shift to create superscripts and subscripts, or to
adjust type along a path (as I discuss in the next chapter). To access the Baseline
Shift value from the keyboard, press ⌘-Shift-K to activate the Tracking option, and
press Shift-Tab twice to back up two option boxes. Then enter any value between
–1296 and 1296 points.

 Baseline shift is instrumental in creating fractions. First enter
the fraction, using the real fraction symbol (Shift-Option-1)
rather than the standard slash. Then select the numerator (the
top number), make it about half the current type size, and
enter a baseline shift value equal to about one-third the original type size. Then select the denominator (bottom number) and match its
type size to that of the numerator, but leave the Baseline Shift value set to 0.
The result is a fraction like the one shown in Figure 6-9.

22/531

Figure 6-9: In this fraction, the type size of the slash is 160-point while the numerator and denominator are set to 80-point. The numerator is shifted 53 points above the baseline.

 You can adjust the baseline shift incrementally from the keyboard (according to the Baseline Shift value in the General Preferences dialog box, 2 points by default). Press Shift-Option-up arrow to raise the selected text above its baseline; press Shift-Option-down arrow to lower the text. You can restore the original baseline shift of 0 by clicking on the words Baseline Shift.

Changing the Width of Characters

The next option in the Character palette, Horizontal Scale, modifies the width of selected characters. You can expand or condense type to any extent between 1 and 10,000 percent (1/100 to 100 times its normal width) by entering a new Horizontal Scale value and pressing Return.

Changing the width of a character distorts it. The Horizontal Scale option does not create the same effect of designer condensed or expanded fonts. For example, Figure 6-10 shows two variations on Helvetica. In the first example, I took 200-point Helvetica Bold and scaled it 45 percent horizontally. Notice how the horizontal bars of the *A* and *B* are much thicker than the vertical stems. This is because Horizontal Scale affects vertical proportions and leaves horizontal proportions untouched.

While the bars and stems in a designer font may not be identical, they are proportional. The second example in Figure 6-10 shows a specially condensed font called Helvetica Compressed Ultra. The strokes vary, but there is an overall consistency that the skinny Helvetica Bold type lacks. The designer has also taken the time to square off some of the curves, making Helvetica Compressed Ultra more legible in small type sizes.

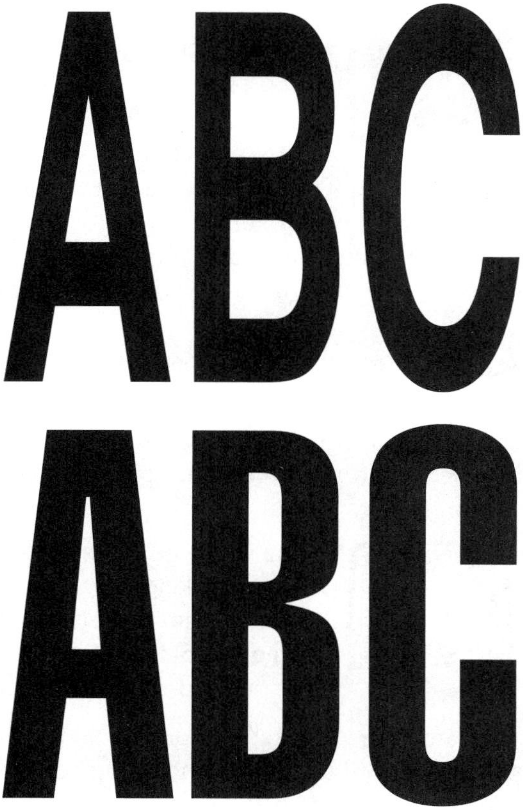

ABC

ABC

Figure 6-10:
Helvetica Bold scaled
45 percent (top) compared
with a specially designed
font called Helvetica
Compressed Ultra.

With this in mind, there are two basic reasons to use the Horizontal Scale option:

- If you *want* the type to appear distorted, go for broke. There are no hard and fast rules in page design; type that specifically calls attention to itself can be just as effective as type that doesn't, given a bold design and an open-minded audience.

- If slightly widening or narrowing a few lines of type will make them better fit on the page, you can get away with Horizontal Scale values between 95 and 105 percent without anyone being the wiser.

To select the Horizontal Scale value, press ⌘-Shift-K and then press Shift-Tab once. To reset the value to 0, click on the words Horizontal Scale in the palette.

Incidentally, if you've scaled a text block disproportionately using the scale tool (as described in Chapter 11), the Horizontal Scale value reflects the discrepancy between the current width and the normal width of the selected type. You can reset the type to its normal width by clicking on the option name.

Adjusting the Space Between Characters

Illustrator lets you adjust the amount of horizontal space between characters of text. When you adjust the space between a pair of characters, Illustrator calls it *kerning*. When you adjust the space between three or more characters, Illustrator calls it *tracking*.

 If you're a type savant, you'll soon notice that Illustrator's idea of tracking is not the real thing. There's no automatic spacing variation between large and small type sizes, which is what proper tracking is all about. Illustrator's tracking is uniform, and should therefore be called *range kerning*.

In any case, Illustrator alternatively calls the sixth option box in the Character palette (as well as the fourth command in the Type menu) Kerning or Tracking. When you click with the type tool to position the insertion marker between two characters, the option is Kerning. When you select so much as a single character, Illustrator calls it Tracking. It may sound confusing, but the name is irrelevant. Whatever you call it, the option controls the amount of space between each selected character and the character directly to its right.

Normally, Illustrator accepts the dimensions of each character stored in the screen font file on disk and places the character flush against its neighbors. The screen font defines the width of the character as well as the amount of space that is placed before and after the character width. As demonstrated in the top example of Figure 6-11, these bits of before and after space are called *side bearings*. Illustrator arrives at its normal letter spacing by adding the right side bearing of the first character to the left side bearing of the second.

However, font designers can specify that certain pairs of letters, called *kerning pairs*, should be positioned more closely together than the standard letter normal allows. Whenever the two characters of a kerning pair appear next to each other, as in the case of the *W* and *A* in Figure 6-11, Illustrator can space them according to the special kerning information contained in the font.

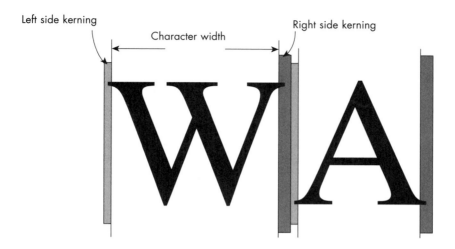

Left side kerning

Character width

Right side kerning

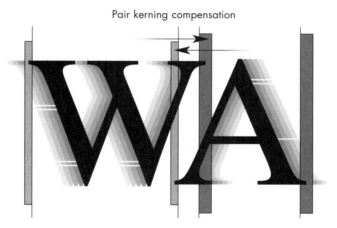

Pair kerning compensation

Figure 6-11: A kerning pair is a set of two letters that look weird when set shoulder to shoulder (top). Spacing them closer together (bottom) draws less attention to the letters and makes them more legible.

   To instruct Illustrator to apply special kerning information, make sure the Auto Kerning check box in the lower half of the Character palette is turned on. In Illustrator 6, this option is active by default. (For rather boring and convoluted reasons, it used to be off by default in Illustrator 5.) Unless you want ugly type, there is no reason on earth to turn off Auto Kerning.

If you aren't satisfied with the default kerning between two characters, click with the type tool to position the insertion marker between the characters and enter a value into the Kerning option box in the Character palette. If you want to change the kerning between multiple characters, select those characters and enter a value into the Tracking option box. Then press the Return key. A negative value squeezes letters together; a positive value spreads them apart.

Illustrator measures both the Kerning and Tracking values in 1/1000ths of an em space. An *em space* is a character as wide as the type size is tall. So if the type size is set to 12-point, an em space is 12 points wide. This ensures that the kerning remains proportionally constant as you increase or decrease the type size.

A Kerning or Tracking value of 25 is roughly equivalent to a standard space character. But you can enter any value between −1,000 and 10,000 in 0.01 increments.

If you don't know what kerning value to use, you can adjust the kerning incrementally from the keyboard. Press Option-⍇ or ⌘-Shift-[to squeeze letters together; press Option-⍈ or ⌘-Shift-] to spread them apart. By default, each keystroke changes the kerning by 0.02 (20/1000) em space, but you can change the increment by entering a new value into the Tracking option box in the General Preferences dialog box.

For more dramatic changes, press ⌘-Option-⍇ or ⌘-Option-⍈ to decrease or increase the kerning by five times the Tracking value in the General Preferences dialog box.

To highlight the Kerning or Tracking value in the Character palette (and automatically expand the palette if necessary), press ⌘-Shift-K. To restore the Kerning or Tracking value to 0, click on the option name.

When kerning small type, you may not be able to see a visible difference as you add or delete space because the display is not accurate enough. In such a case, use the zoom tool to magnify the drawing area while kerning or tracking characters from the keyboard. Assuming you've installed the Adobe Type Manager, magnified view sizes show spacing adjustments more accurately than reduced views.

Changing the Hyphenation Language

The last option in the Character palette is the Language pop-up menu. New to Illustrator 6, it controls how Illustrator hyphenates words when the Auto Hyphenate check box is selected in the Paragraph palette. Frankly, it'd make more sense if Adobe had put all the hyphenation options in the same place. Instead, Illustrator requires you to turn automatic hyphenation on and off for an entire paragraph, while you can change the dictionary from one word to the next. Granted, this is useful for combining words from different languages into the same sentence, but it's rather confusing.

Assuming you own the U.S. version of Illustrator 6, the Language option is set to U.S. English. (In a land where a friend is a mate and a buck is a quid, I reckon it's safe to assume that a different language is active by default.) If you want Illustrator to hyphenate a word according to some other language, select that word and choose another option from the language pop-up menu.

 According to the most recent survey, 99.9999999999963 percent of all Illustrator users don't give a tinker's darn about the Language option. But I can't bear the thought of leaving anything out.

Paragraph-Level Formatting

Illustrator's paragraph formatting controls are found in the Paragraph palette. To display the palette, choose Type » Paragraph or press ⌘-Shift-P. By default, the Paragraph palette is collapsed, as in the top example of Figure 6-12. Click on the flag icon to expand the palette and display the options shown in the bottom example of the figure.

 You can also display the Paragraph palette by choosing Window » Show Paragraph. Or you can press ⌘-Shift-O to display the palette and activate the Desired value from the Word Spacing options. If the Paragraph palette is collapsed, pressing ⌘-Shift-O expands it. You can also hide the Paragraph palette by pressing ⌘-Shift-P once or twice in a row.

Changing the Alignment

So far as I know, every computer program that lets you create type lets you change how the rows of type line up:

- To align a paragraph so that all the left edges line up (*flush left, ragged right*), press ⌘-Shift-L, choose Type » Alignment » Left, or select the first Alignment icon in the Paragraph palette.

- To center all lines in a paragraph, press ⌘-Shift-C, choose Type » Alignment » Center, or select the second Alignment icon in the Paragraph palette.

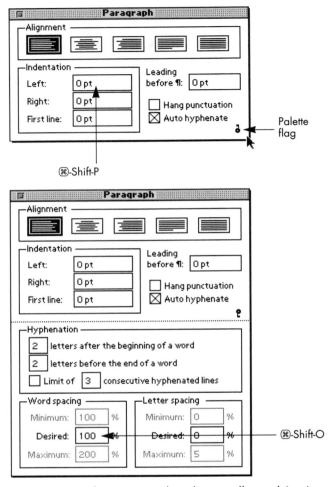

Figure 6-12: The Paragraph palette, collapsed (top) and expanded (bottom), with the keyboard shortcuts used to activate various options.

● To make the right edges of a paragraph line up (*flush right, ragged left*), press ⌘-Shift-R, choose Type » Alignment » Right, or select the third Alignment icon.

● You can also *justify* a paragraph, which stretches all lines except the last line of a paragraph so they entirely fill the width of the text block. (The last line in a justified paragraph remains flush left.) To justify a paragraph, press ⌘-Shift-J, choose Type » Alignment » Justify, or select the fourth Alignment icon.

If you want to *force justify* the last line in a paragraph, press ⌘-Shift-B. (⌘-Shift-F would make more sense, but this highlights the Font option in the Character palette. In most programs, ⌘-Shift-B makes text bold, so I guess you could think of force justification as a bold action in Illustrator.) If you prefer to click and drag, you can choose Type » Alignment » Justify Last Line or click on the last Alignment icon in the Paragraph palette.

Examples of all five alignment settings appear in Figure 6-13. As you can see, I've applied all settings to text blocks. When you align point text, Illustrator moves

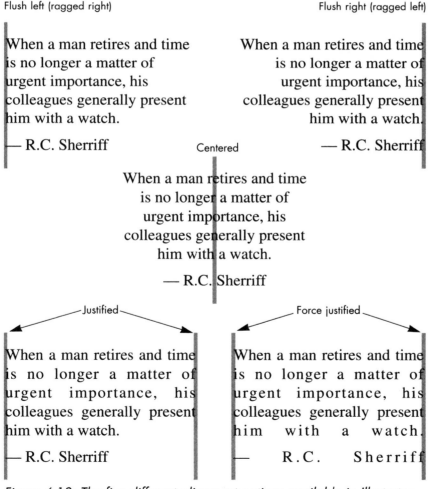

Figure 6-13: The five different alignment options available in Illustrator.

selected lines relative to the alignment point. The Justify and Justify Last Line commands result in flush left text, because each line of point text is a separate paragraph.

Indenting Paragraphs

Figure 6-14 demonstrates the two basic ways to indent a paragraph. You can indent the first line to distinguish one paragraph from another, or you can create a *hanging indent*, in which all lines *but* the first line are indented. A hanging indent is great for creating bulleted or numbered lists.

Sixty years ago I knew everything; now I know nothing; education is a progressive discovery of your own ignorance.

—Will Durant

• Sixty years ago I knew everything; now I know nothing; education is a progressive discovery of your own ignorance.

— Will Durant

Figure 6-14: A paragraph with a first-line indent (top) and a hanging indent (bottom).

To create a standard paragraph indent, enter a value into the First Line option box in the Paragraph palette and press Return. I created the first example in Figure 6-14 with a First Line value of 20 points.

If you assign a first line indent to a paragraph, remember that you can break a word onto the next line of type without indenting it by pressing the Enter key. Two words divided by Enter appear on different lines, but are part of the same paragraph.

- To create a hanging indent, enter a positive value into the Left option box and the inverse of that value in the First Line option box. For example, to create the second example in Figure 6-14, I set the Left value to 20 points and the First Line value to –20 points.

  You also have to set the tab so the first line lines up with the others. In the figure, I pressed the Tab key after the bullet to insert a tab character. Then I pressed ⌘-Shift-T to display the Tabs palette and created a left tab at the 20 point mark, even with the left indent. For complete information about tabs, read "The Amazing World of Tabs" section near the end of this chapter.

You can enter any value between –1296 and 1296 points into any of the Indentation option boxes. The Left value indents all text on the left side of a paragraph, creating a gap between the left edge of the text block and the affected paragraph. The Right value indents all text on the right side of a paragraph. And First Line indents the first line of a paragraph without affecting any others.

 You can highlight the Left value by pressing ⌘-Shift-P, the very same key combination that brings up the Paragraph palette. Then Tab from one indentation option box to the next.

There's really no reason to apply Indentation values to point text (except to make it wrap around an object, as discussed in the "Adjusting the Standoff" section of Chapter 7). To reset any of the Indentation values to 0, click on the option name in the Paragraph palette.

Adding Paragraph Leading

Enter a value into the Leading before ¶ option box to insert some extra space before a selected paragraph. This so-called *paragraph leading* helps separate one paragraph from another, much like a first-line indent. Most designers use first-line indents *or* paragraph leading to distinguish paragraphs, but not both. The two together are generally considered design overkill (though I must admit I've done it and been rather pleased with the results).

 Click on the Leading before ¶ option name to reset the value to 0.

Dangling a Quotation Mark

Select the Hanging Punctuation check box to make punctuation such as quotation marks, commas, hyphens, and so on, hang outside one of the edges of a text block:

- In a flush left or justified paragraph, punctuation is most likely to hang outside the left side of the text block.

- In a flush right paragraph, the punctuation hangs outside the right side.

- If the paragraph is centered, Hanging Punctuation typically has no effect, since the punctuation can manage its way over to the left or right side.

- And if you force justify the paragraph, the punctuation hangs off both sides.

I force justified the paragraph in Figure 6-15 so that all lines were both flush left and flush right. This way, Illustrator forced the quotation marks outside both sides of the text block. I also increased the type size of the quotation marks, kerned them slightly, and used baseline shift to lower them 4 points each. You can't expect a single option like Hanging Punctuation to do everything for you.

"Nothing is so ignorant as the ignorance of certainty."

— Aldous Huxley

*Figure 6-15:
Here I,ve applied the Hanging Punctuation option and force justi-fication to move the quote marks outside of the text block.*

Activating Automatic Hyphenation

There are three ways to hyphenate text in Illustrator:

- If a long word wraps onto a new line, you can enter a standard hyphen character (-) to break the word onto two lines and better fill the text block. But inserting a standard hyphen can cause problems. If you edit the text later on, you may end up with stray hyphens between words that no longer break at the ends of lines.

- A better idea is to insert a *discretionary hyphen,* which disappears any time it is not needed. You can enter a discretionary hyphen character by pressing ⌘-Shift-hyphen (-). If no hyphen appears when you enter this character, it simply means that the addition of the hyphen does not help Illustrator to break the word. You can try inserting the character at a different location or expand the width of the text block to permit the word to break.

- The third option is to let Illustrator do the hyphenating for you by selecting the Auto Hyphenate check box in the Paragraph palette. (This option has no effect on point text, just text blocks.)

Of all the options, I like the last one the least. It's the easiest, to be sure, but some of its suggestions are goofy—as in hyphenating *everyone* as *eve-ryone*—and Illustrator may open old illustrations and apply new hyphenation. Unless you're creating newsletters or other small documents with lots of type, it's usually safer to manually enter discretionary hyphens where needed.

Still, if you do decide automatic hyphenation is for you, here's how it works:

1. **Turn Auto Hyphenate on**.

   Select the text block you want to hyphenate with the arrow tool and turn on the Auto Hyphenate check box in the Paragraph palette. Without further ado, Illustrator adds hyphens where it deems necessary.

2. **Expand the Paragraph palette**.

   If you want to limit where and how hyphenation occurs, expand the Paragraph palette by clicking on the palette flag.

3. **Specify how many letters must appear before and after a hyphen**.

   Enter a value into the first Hyphenation option box (Letters After the Beginning of a Word) to specify the minimum number of letters that can come between a hyphen and the beginning of a word. Enter a value into the next option box to determine minimum number of letters between a hyphen and the end of a word. For example, with both values set to 2, Illustrator could split the word *apple* as *ap-ple* since both the first and last syllables are at least 2 letters long.

4. Specify the possible number of consecutive hyphens.

If you want to limit the numbers of consecutive lines of type Illustrator can hyphenate, select the Limit check box and enter the maximum limit in the option box. By default, the value is set to 3, so that Illustrator can hyphenate no more than three consecutive lines before it has to permit one line to go without hyphenation. But as far as I'm concerned, any more than two hyphenated lines in a row looks amateurish and interferes with legibility.

In addition to the Hyphenation options in the Paragraph palette, you can prohibit Illustrator from hyphenating certain words by choosing File » Preferences » Hyphenation Options. Simply type the word you want never to hyphenate into the Entry option box and click on the Add button. To remove a word and permit Illustrator to hyphenate it in the future, select it from the scrolling list and click on the Delete button. Click on the Done button when you're all through.

If you add a word in the Hyphenation Options dialog box that already exists in a text block, it won't unhyphenate without a little help from you. Select the text block, then deselect and immediately reselect the Auto Hyphenate check box in the Paragraph palette to make Illustrator reapply its automatic hyphenation.

Spacing Letters and Words in a Justified Paragraph

The final options in the Paragraph palette let you control the amount of space that Illustrator places between words and characters in a text block. As you might imagine, *word spacing* controls the amount of space between words; *letter spacing* controls the amount of space between letters.

Now, a few of you quick-minded types are probably thinking to yourselves, "How is letter spacing, which controls the amount of space between individual characters, different from kerning, which controls the amount of space between individual characters? Call me stupid, but it sounds like the same thing to me." Well, for one, kerning applies to selected characters and letter spacing affects entire paragraphs. Also, the two are measured differently. Kerning is measured in fractions of an em space; letter spacing is measured as a percentage of the standard space character. But most importantly, kerning is fixed, letter spacing is flexible. As we'll soon see, Illustrator can automatically vary letter spacing inside justified paragraphs between two extremes.

There are two primary reasons for manipulating spacing:

- To give a paragraph a generally tighter or looser appearance. You control this general spacing using the Desired options.

- To determine the range of spacing manipulations Illustrator can use when justifying a paragraph. Illustrator tightens up some lines and loosens others to make them fit the exact width of your text block. You specify limits using the Minimum and Maximum options.

When spacing flush left, right, or centered, paragraphs, Illustrator relies entirely on the two Desired values. In fact, the other options are dimmed. All values are measured as a percentage of a standard space, as determined by the information contained in the current font. For example, a Desired Word Spacing value of 100 percent inserts the width of one space character between each pair of words in a paragraph. Reducing or enlarging this percentage makes the space between words bigger or smaller. A Desired Letter Spacing of 10 percent inserts 10 percent of the width of a space character between each pair of letters. Negative percentages squeeze letters together, a value of 0 percent spaces letters normally.

If one or more justified paragraphs are selected, the Minimum and Maximum options become available. (These options appear dimmed if so much as one flush left, centered, or flush right paragraph is even partially selected.) These values give Illustrator some wiggle room when tightening and spreading lines of type. You're basically saying to Illustrator, "I'd prefer you used the Desired spacing, but if you can't manage that, you can go as low as Minimum and as high as Maximum. But that's where I cut you off."

The Word Spacing and Letter Spacing values must fall inside the following ranges:

- The Minimum Word Spacing value must be at least 0 percent; the Minimum Letter Spacing must be at least –50 percent. Both must be less than their respective Desired values.

- The Maximum Word Spacing value can be no higher than 1,000 percent; Maximum Letter Spacing can be no more than 500 percent. Neither can be less than its respective Desired value.

- Each Desired value can be no less than its corresponding Minimum value and no higher than the corresponding Maximum value.

Figure 6-16 shows a justified paragraph subjected to various word spacing and letter spacing combinations. In the first column of paragraphs, only the word spacing changes; all letter spacing values are set to a constant 0 percent. In the second column, only the letter spacing changes; all word spacing values are set to

100 percent. Above each paragraph is a headline stating the values that have been changed. The percentages represent the values for the Minimum, Desired, and Maximum options respectively.

Word: 100%, 100%, 200%

Neither can I believe that the individual survives the death of his body, although feeble souls harbor such thoughts through fear or ridiculous egotism.

—Albert Einstein

Letter: 0%, 0%, 5%

Neither can I believe that the individual survives the death of his body, although feeble souls harbor such thoughts through fear or ridiculous egotism.

—Albert Einstein

Word: 0%, 25%, 50%

Neither can I believe that the individual survives the death of his body, although feeble souls harbor such thoughts through fear or ridiculous egotism.

—Albert Einstein

Letter: –15%, –10%, –5%

Neither can I believe that the individual survives the death of his body, although feeble souls harbor such thoughts through fear or ridiculous egotism.

—Albert Einstein

Word: 200%, 225%, 250%

Neither can I believe that the individual survives the death of his body, although feeble souls harbor such thoughts through fear or ridiculous egotism.

—Albert Einstein

Letter: 25%, 35%, 50%

Neither can I believe that the individual survives the death of his body, although feeble souls harbor such thoughts through fear or ridiculous egotism.

—Albert Einstein

Figure 6-16: Examples of several different word and letter spacing combinations. Letter spacing is constant in the left column and word spacing is constant in the right.

To highlight the Desired Word Spacing value in the Paragraph palette (and automatically expand the palette if necessary), press ⌘-Shift-O.

To restore the Desired Word Spacing value to 100 or the Desired Letter Spacing to 0, click on the option name. Click on the word Minimum to match the Minimum value to the Desired value. Click on Maximum Word Spacing to make it half again larger than the Desired Word Spacing value. Click on Maximum Letter Spacing to make it 5 percent larger than Desired Letter Spacing. I wouldn't worry about trying to remember all this; just click on an option name when you want Illustrator to give you some spacing advice.

The Amazing World of Tabs

Prior to Version 5.5, Illustrator didn't know a tab from a tackle box. Now Illustrator offers some of the best tab capabilities of any program. You can create lists and tables with tremendous ease, and even throw in artistic flourishes that are absent from page layout programs such as PageMaker and QuarkXPress.

For those unfamiliar with the subject, *tabs* are little more than variable width spaces. By pressing the Tab key after entering a bullet or number, you can create hanging indents, as I showed you back in Figure 6-14. By entering tabs between items in a list, you can create columns that align with each other precisely. Whenever you're tempted to use multiple spaces, press the Tab key instead.

There are really only two rules to using tabs:

- Never enter two tab characters in a row.
- To specify the width of a tab character, adjust the tab stop settings in the Tabs palette.

To this day, I see more folks misuse tabs than I see use them correctly. If you never touch a tab stop and merely rely on multiple tabs or—gad!—spaces to do the work for you, you limit your formatting freedom and you make future editing more cumbersome and confusing. Whereas, if you simply follow the two rules mentioned above and never, *never* stray, you'll be fine.

Using the Tabs Palette

Choose Window » Show Tab Ruler (⌘-Shift-T) to display the Tabs palette, shown in Figure 6-17. Known by the less formal moniker *tab ruler*, this palette lets you position tab stops and align tabbed text.

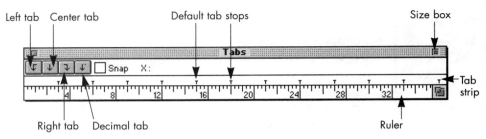

Figure 6-17: Use the tab ruler to position tab stops and align tabbed text.

Like the Paragraph palette, the tab ruler affects entire paragraphs, whether entirely or only partially selected. The following items explain how the tab ruler works and offer a few guidelines for using it.

- When you first bring up the Tabs palette, Illustrator automatically aligns it to the selected paragraph. To align the palette to a different paragraph, select the paragraph and click in the size box on the far right side of the title bar.

- To create a tab stop, click in the ruler along the bottom of the palette, or click inside the tab strip just above the ruler. If you drag the tab stop, Illustrator projects a vertical alignment guide from the Tabs palette, as labeled in Figure 6-18. The line moves with the tab stop, permitting you to more accurately predict the results of your adjustment. The Tabs palette also tracks the numerical position of the tab stop—with respect to the left edge of the text block—just below the title bar.

- When you create a new tab stop, all default tab stops (those little *T*s) to the left of the new stop disappear. The default stops merely tell Illustrator to space tabbed text every one-half inch.

- A question mark in the tab ruler means that at least one line of selected text does *not* align to that tab stop. Just click on the tab stop to make all selected lines align.

 To move more than one tab stop at a time, Shift-drag a stop. All tab stops to the right of the dragged stop move in kind; tab stops to the left remain stationary.

- Select the Snap check box to align new and moved tab stops to the nearest increment on the ruler. I heartily recommend this option.

Tab stop

Tab stop position

```
┌─────────────────────────── Tabs ───────────────────────────┐
│ [↲][↓][↑][↓] ⊠ Snap    X: 96 pt.                            │
│ ‖‖‖‖‖‖‖‖‖‖‖‖‖‖‖‖‖‖‖‖‖‖‖‖‖‖‖‖‖‖‖‖‖‖‖‖‖‖‖‖‖‖‖‖‖‖‖‖‖‖‖‖‖‖‖‖    │
│       4       8      12      16      20      24      28      32        │
```

Annual earnings of a few fictional characters:

Name	Primary occupation	Salary	Additional income	Source
Santa Claus	toy distributor	none	$12,000	Macy's
Rudolf	bad-weather beacon	none	$266,370	Duracell spokesman
Peter Cottontail	egg distributor	none	$56,050	stuntman for Bugs Bunny
Tooth Fairy	tooth purchaser	none	$23,920	gold wholesaler
Superman	vigilante	none	$42,500	Daily Planet
Batman	vigilante	none	$21,354,350	CEO, Wayne Enterprises
Robin	vigilante's buddy	none	$6,250	Gotham City Malt Shop
The Wizard of Oz	wish granter	none	$765,130	owner, Kansas City Slots
Cinderella	princess	none	$8,700	housecleaning
Sleeping Beauty	princess	none	$216,500	No-Doz spokesperson
Pooh Bear	stuffed animal	none	$1.50	found in hollow tree
Piglet	stuffed animal	none	$0.75	stole from Owl
Lochness Monster	fresh-water dweller	none	$128,900	sighting fees
Big Foot	forest dweller	none	$0.75	stole from Piglet
E.T.	illegal alien	none	$89,450	pediatrician
Big Bad Wolf	pig chaser	none	$120,360	demolitions expert
Little Bo Peep	sheepherder	none	$35,000	animal reconnaissance
Gilligan	little buddy	none	$47.13	Mrs. Howell's concubine
Scooby Doo	crime-solving pet	none	-$152	loans to Shaggy

Alignment guide

Figure 6-18: When you drag a tab stop, a vertical line drops down from the palette, showing how the adjusted text will align.

 You can also snap a single tab stop on the fly when the Snap check box is turned off. To do this, press Control while dragging the tab stop. You can likewise Control-drag to move a tab stop freely when the Snap option is active.

To change the identity of a tab stop, select the tab stop by clicking on it, then select a different identity from the four buttons on the left side of the palette. From left to right, these buttons make tabbed text align along the left side, center, right side, or decimal point. In Figure 6-18, for example, I centered the *Salary* column by assigning a center tab stop. The *Additional income* column was aligned with a right tab stop. Decimal tab stops are ideal for aligning numbers, such as prices.

Another way to change the identity of a tab stop is to Option-click on it. Each Option-click switches the stop to the next variety, from left to center to right to decimal and back to left.

To delete a tab stop, drag it upward, off the tab strip and out of the palette. The X: item reads *delete*. To delete all tab stops, Shift-drag upward on the leftmost tab stop in the ruler.

 By default, the unit of measure used by the tab ruler conforms to the unit used by Illustrator's standard rulers (as set using the Ruler Units option in the General Preferences dialog box). But you can cycle through other units—without affecting the standard rulers—by clicking on the tab stop position listed just to the right of the Snap check box.

(Note that a tab stop must be selected for this last tip to work. If you click too far to the right of the tab stop position, you may end up deselecting the tab stop, which prevents you from further changing the unit of measure. Until you select another tab stop, that is.)

You can also change the unit of measure used by the Tab palette by pressing ⌘-Control-U, but this changes the Illustrator's other dialog box and ruler measurements as well.

Taking Tabs to a New Level

What if you don't want to align text tabbed text in straight up-and-down columns? What if you want to create something a little more graphic, something worthier of Illustrator's attention, such as the table in Figure 6-19? Can you do this in Illustrator?

Well, of course you can. In fact, you've been able to do something like this since Illustrator 3.0. It involves wrapping the text block around several open paths, as explained in the following steps:

1. **Create your text block**.

   Enter one tab—and only one tab—between each entry, just as you would normally. In the figure, for example, there is one tab between *Santa Claus* and *toy distributor*.

2. **Use the direct-selection tool to reshape the boundaries of the text block**.

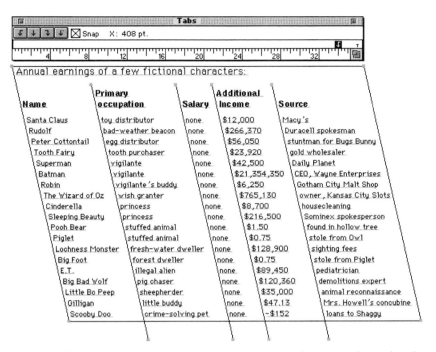

Figure 6-19: I created this slanted table—seen in the artwork mode—by wrapping tabbed text around a series of straight lines.

For example, to create the slanted block shown in Figure 6-19, I clicked on the bottom segment of the text block and dragged it to the right. You may want to work in the artwork mode, where you can see the text block outline when it's not selected.

3. Add a tab stop to the far right side of the tab ruler.

Your text should now be a total mess. But no matter. Click in the size box in the Tabs palette to align it to your text, then create a left tab stop on the far right side of the palette. If any other tab stops exist, delete them. In Figure 6-19, for example, I positioned a single tab stop at the 34-pica mark. The purpose of this step is to eliminate all of the default tabs, thereby ensuring that each tab carries the entry that follows it to the next open path.

4. Draw a few open paths to serve as guides.

Ugh, your text is worse than ever. But don't try to fix it. Instead, it's time to add graphic tab stops in the form of a few open paths. In Figure 6-19,

I drew a straight line with the pen tool by clicking on each of the two points on the left side of the slanted text block. This way, the angle of the line matched the angle of the block. Then I used the arrow tool to drag the line into position, just to the right of *Santa Claus*, so it could serve as the tab stop for the *Primary occupation* column. I then cloned the line by Option-dragging it three times, thus creating three additional tab stops. (I discuss cloning in Chapter 9.)

5. **Apply the Make Wrap command**.

To convert the lines into tab stops, select both the lines and the text block and choose Type » Make Wrap (covered in Chapter 7). Illustrator automatically aligns each tabbed entry with the nearest line.

6. **Drag the lines into proper position with the direct selection tool**.

It's unlikely the text will wrap exactly the way you hoped right off the bat. But now that the text is roughly in place, the lines act just like normal tab stops. To reposition one of these graphic tab stops, use the direct-selection tool to move the line to the left or right.

7. **Make the lines transparent so they don't interfere with the table**.

Once you have all the lines in place, select the lines and make their fills and strokes transparent (using the options in the Paint Style palette).

Graphic tabs are generally every bit as versatile as regular tabs, except for one thing: Each tab stop is the same. In other words, you can't mix left tabs and right tabs inside the same text block, and there are no decimal tabs. Rather, each entry is aligned the same way the paragraph is aligned. If the paragraph is flush left, each entry is flush left; if the paragraph is centered, each entry is centered between the graphic tabs; and so on.

Graphic tabs bridge the border between the world of sedate formatting options that every publishing program provides and the more wild text effects Illustrator is so rightly famous for. To cross all the way over to the other side of the border, read the next chapter.

SOME OF YOUR WACKIER TEXT EFFECTS

Creating and formatting text is all very well and good, but where Illustrator excels is in the creation of specialized—dare I say wacky?—type. You can attach text to a curve, wrap text inside an irregular outline, flow text from one text block to another, and wrap text around graphics.

If you plan to use Illustrator to create pages with a fair amount of text on them, you can import text from a word processor, then check the spelling, perform complex search and replace operations, and even export the text back out to disk. And just to show you there are no limits, you can convert one of more letters to paths, and then edit the character outlines as discussed back in Chapter 5.

Illustrator is clearly one of the most proficient text-manipulation programs on the planet, superior to either QuarkXPress or PageMaker when relatively small chunks of text are concerned. In fact, only arch-rival FreeHand is more adept. But where FreeHand requires you to navigate through palette after palette of cryptic options—many of which are more trouble than they're worth—Illustrator provides a more hands-on approach, allowing you to drag elements around and rewarding you with immediate feedback.

Topsy-Turvy Type on a Curve

As demonstrated in Figure 7-1, Illustrator lets you bind a line of text to a freeform path. Adobe calls such a text object *path text*, but folks call it *type on a curve* as well.

To create type along the outline of a path, follow these simple steps:

1. **Draw a path**.

   Curved paths work better than those with sharp corners, so you'll probably want to avoid corner points and cusps, and stick with smooth points. Ovals, spirals, and softly sloping paths work best.

2. **Select the path type tool**.

   To get to the path type tool, drag from the type tool in the toolbox to display a pop-up menu. The path type tool looks like a T on a wiggly line, as labeled in Figure 7-2.

3. **Click on the path and start typing**.

   The point at which you click determines the position of the blinking insertion marker. As you enter text from the keyboard, the characters follow the contours of the path.

    If your text appears on the underside of the path, or if no text appears and all you see is a plus sign inside a little box, you need to flip the text to the other side of the path. Select the arrow tool and double-click on the alignment handle, which looks like an I-beam attached to the path. Then select the type tool and click on the path to continue adding text.

Figure 7-1: Path text as it appears when selected on screen (top) and when printed (bottom).

You can't attach more than one line of text to a path. This means Illustrator never drops the insertion marker down to the next line, even if you press the Return or Enter key. Instead, it just inserts what looks like a space. The same goes for pressing the Tab key.

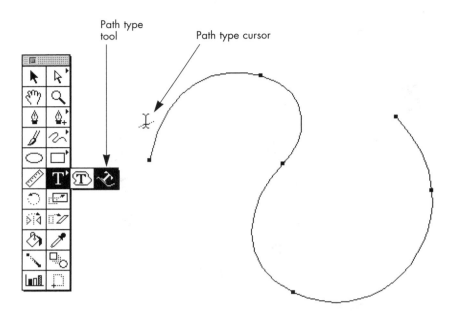

Figure 7-2: Select the path type tool and click on a path.

4. **Complete the path text**.

When you finish entering text, select another tool in the toolbox to finish the text object. The path text appears selected, as in the first example back in Figure 7-1.

 You don't have to use the path type tool to create path text. In fact, it's generally easier to use the standard type tool. To attach text to an open path, just click on it with the type tool. The cursor changes to the path type cursor (as in Figure 7-2) the moment you move the cursor over the path. To attach type to a closed path, Option-click on the path. (Without Option pressed, clicking on a closed path with the type tool creates area text, which I discuss later in this chapter.)

Like point text (covered in the previous chapter), path text is ill-suited to anything longer than a sentence. When a word extends past the end of an open path, it disappears from view like a ship sailing off the edge of the world. Long text simply wraps around and around a closed path, forcing words to overlap.

Press the Control key to temporarily access the standard type tool when the path-type tool is selected. Release Control to return to the path type tool.

Converting Point Text to Path Text

Illustrator does not provide a command for binding text to a path. So if you want to bind an existing line of point text to a path, you have to copy and paste it:

1. Select the point text with the arrow tool.

2. Press ⌘-C to copy it (or choose Edit » Copy).

3. Click on an open path with the type tool, or Option-click on a close path.

4. Press ⌘-V to paste the copied text (or choose Edit » Paste).

You can also attach words from a text block to a path. Just select the words with the type tool and follow Steps 2 through 4.

Moving Type Along Its Path

When you click on path text with the standard arrow tool, you select both path and type at the same time. A special *alignment handle* displays, as labeled in Figure 7-3. This handle allows you to adjust the placement of the text on the path in any of the following ways:

- Drag the handle to slide the text back and forth along the path, as in the second example in the figure.

- Double-click on the handle to flip the text to the other side of the path, as in the third example in Figure 7-3.

- Drag the handle to the other side of the path to move the text as you flip it in the opposite direction.

In addition to clicking with the arrow tool, you can also select both path and type by Option-clicking twice on the path with the direct selection tool. Be sure to click on the path. Don't try to click at the location where you expect the handle to be; it won't do you any good. However, you can marquee around the handle if you want.

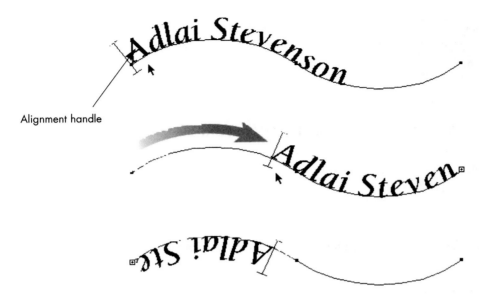

Alignment handle

Figure 7-3: The alignment handle appears when the both path and type are selected (top). You can drag the handle to move text (middle) or double-click on it to flip the text (bottom).

Reshaping a Path Right Under Its Text

When creating path text, you typically run into the same problems you encounter when entering words into a text block. If the path is too short to accommodate all the text, for example, a plus sign appears in a small box located on the last point in the path, as shown in Figure 7-4. In path text, Illustrator makes no distinction between a single word that can't fit or a sentence. Since path type can't wrap to a second line, it either fits on the path or it doesn't.

You can't flow path text into another text object, so you have only three choices for fixing type along an inadequate path:

- Reduce the size of the type.

- Delete a few words or characters until the text fits on the path.

- Lengthen the path by reshaping it until all text is visible.

To lengthen a path with text on it, you can drag both segments and points with the direct selection tool in any direction that you want. After each drag, the text will refit the path, so you can see your progress. Suppose, for example, that you

Figure 7-4: Any amount of overflow text prompts the boxed plus sign, whether the text breaks in the middle of a word or sentence.

want to lengthen the lower line shown in Figure 7-4. The following steps explain a few ways to do it:

1. First press ⌘-Shift-A (or choose Edit » Select None) to deselect the type. You have to deselect the path *text* before you can select the path by itself. But before you can do this, you have to deselect both.

2. Using the direct selection tool, click on the path. This selects the path without selecting the type on the path. (Notice that the alignment handle I-beam isn't visible. This shows you that the text is not selected.)

3. Drag one of the endpoints to stretch the path, as shown at the top of Figure 7-5. The type immediately refits to the path, as in the bottom example.

Figure 7-5: By dragging the endpoint of an open path with the direct selection tool (top), you stretch the path to accommodate more text (bottom).

4. Notice that the line no longer curves as gracefully as it used to. To correct this, you can drag down on the segment or adjust the control handles as shown in Figure 7-6.

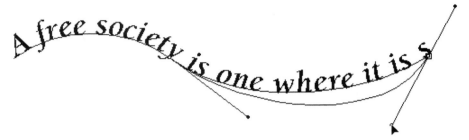

Figure 7-6: You can also move the Bézier control handles using the direct selection tool.

5. If your path needs to be lengthened dramatically, you might prefer to add points to the path using the freehand or pen tool. In Figure 7-7, for example, I've used the pen tool to add segments to the path. With each additional segment, more text becomes visible until eventually no overflow text remains. When the path is long enough to accommodate its text, the boxed plus sign disappears, as Figure 7-7 shows.

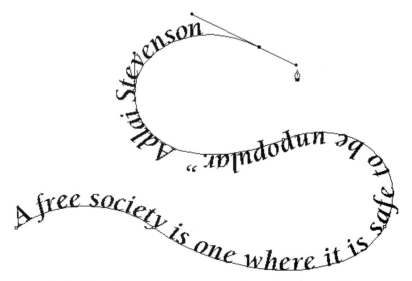

Figure 7-7: The plus sign goes away when all text is visible on screen.

In addition to editing a path with the direct selection tool, you can use the add point, delete point, and convert point tools (as described in the "Operating on Points Long After the Path Is Done" section of Chapter 5). In fact, all of the editing techniques discussed in Chapter 5 are applicable to a path with text on it. The next section explores one way to use the add point tool.

Trimming away Excess Path

What if, instead of being too short, your path is too long? Certainly you can enlarge the type size, add words, or move points around to make the path shorter. But what if you want to simply trim a little slack off the end of the path?

No, you can't split it off with the scissors tool (covered in Chapter 9), because Illustrator won't let you split an open path with text on it into two pieces. Instead, follow these steps:

1. Click with the add point tool at the spot where you want the path to end, as shown in Figure 7-8. (Remember, if the pen tool is selected, you can press the Control key to get to the add point tool.)

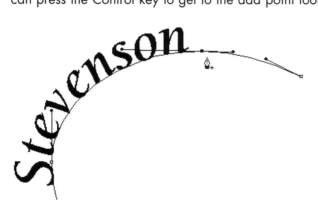

Figure 7-8: Use the add point tool to insert a point at the location where you want the path to end.

2. Select all points beyond the newly inserted point with the direct selection tool, as in Figure 7-9. (Don't select the new point itself.)

3. Press the Delete key. The selected points and their segments disappear, making the inserted point the new endpoint.

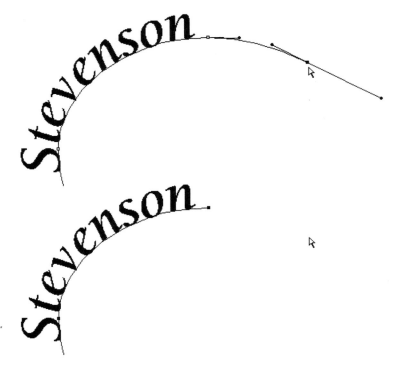

*Figure 7-9: Select all points to the right of the inserted point
(top) and delete them (bottom).*

Normally, you don't need to worry about excess path. The path is hidden by default when previewing or printing an illustration. Only if you want to stroke the path separately of its text—as explained in Chapter 16—does shortening a path become an issue.

Shifting Type in Relation to Its Path

Illustrator lets you raise and lower type with respect to its path using baseline shift (introduced in the last chapter). With path text, the baseline is the path itself, so moving type away from the baseline also moves it away from the path.

As you may recall, you can change the baseline shift by entering a value into the Baseline Shift option box in the Character palette, or by pressing Shift and Option with the up and down arrow keys. The keyboard shortcuts are generally the preferred method.

The following steps demonstrate why baseline shift is so useful. They show you how to create text along the top and bottom halves of a circle, a job for baseline shift if there ever was one.

1. **Draw a circle.**

   You know, Shift-drag with the oval tool.

2. **Option-click with the type tool at the top of the circle.**

   Illustrator snaps the alignment handle to the top of the shape.

3. **Enter the text you want to appear along the top of the path.**

   I wanted to create the William Allen White quote "Peace without justice is tyranny." So I decided to enter "Peace without justice" across the top.

    Incidentally, in case you think I'm this amazingly learned guy who goes around spouting off quotes from history's movers and shakers, nothing could be farther from the truth. The quotes throughout the figures in this chapter and the previous one come from *Peter's Quotations* (Bantam Books). Kind of makes me seem a little more human, huh?

4. **Center the text.**

   Press ⌘-Shift-C or choose Type » Alignment » Center. Just as you can move text along a path by dragging the alignment handle, you can also use Illustrator's alignment formatting functions to position text. It comes in handy when you want to get things exactly right.

5. **Format the text as desired.**

   Press ⌘-A to highlight the text. Then format at will. I used the font Herculanum, which offers a collection of exclusively capital letters. Quite frankly, text on a circle usually looks best in all caps.

6. **Clone your text.**

   This is the most important step, and one of the trickiest to pull off. First, select the path text with the arrow tool. Then drag the alignment handle around the path to the bottom of the circle. Without releasing—don't release till I tell you to—drag upward so the type flips to the other side of the path. Then drag down ever so carefully until your cursor snaps onto the bottom point in the circle. Finally, press the Option key, release the mouse button, and then release the Option key. A clone of the type moves and flips to the interior of a cloned circle, as illustrated in Figure 7-10.

Snap and clone cursor

Figure 7-10: Option-drag the type to the inside bottom portion of the circle. The hollow double cursor shows that you have snapped to a point and cloned both type and circle.

7. Edit the bottom type as desired.

Click inside the cloned text with the type tool, and press ⌘-A to select it. Then enter the words that you want to appear along the bottom of the circle. I entered "is tyranny," because that's the way old Willy White would have wanted it.

8. Shift the bottom text downward.

With your keen mind, you've undoubtedly noticed that the upper and lower text blocks don't align properly. You need to move the lower text outward without flipping it. While the text is still active, press ⌘-A to highlight the lower text block. Since you want to lower the type with respect to its path, press Shift-Option-⬇ to move the type downward 2 points (assuming you haven't changed the Baseline Shift value in the General Preference dialog box). I pressed Shift-Option-⬇ seven times in a row to get the effect shown in Figure 7-11.

9. Similarly lower the text along the top of the circle.

Press ⌘-Shift-A to deselect the text. Then click in the upper text block with the type tool and press ⌘-A to highlight the first words you created.

*Figure 7-11:
Press Shift-Option-⊕
several times to lower
the text along the
bottom of the circle.*

*Figure 7-12:
Highlight the upper
text block and press
Shift-Option-⊕ several
times to lower this
text as well.*

Press Shift-Option-⊕ several times to lower the top text so it aligns with
the bottom text. I pressed these keys eight times to arrive at Figure 7-12.

Figure 7-13: The finished text on a circle, repeated several times to create a tunnel-of-type effect.

Just for laughs, Figure 7-13 shows the final illustration as it appears when printed. I selected both circles by marqueeing around a segment with the arrow tool. Then I cloned the circle, reduced it to 70 percent, and rotated it 30 degrees. I did this over and over again.

Getting that Irritating Alignment Handle off a Path

Once you click on a path with the type tool, Illustrator thinks you want to use the path to hold text for all time. Even if you delete all text from the path at some later date, the alignment handle will hang in there, showing you that this is path text.

Illustrator 5.5 shipped with a little plug-in that removed the alignment handle. I don't know what happened to it, but you don't need it. Here's how to remove the alignment handle all by yourself:

1. Select the path by Option-clicking on it with the direct selection tool. Do not use the arrow tool.

2. Press ⌘-C or choose Edit » Copy to copy the path to the Clipboard.

3. Option-click on the path again. This selects the text and displays the alignment handle.

4. Press the Delete key to destroy the path text for all time. (Don't worry, you've copied the path to the Clipboard, so it's safe.)

5. Press ⌘-F or choose Edit » Paste In Front. The path is reborn on screen with no alignment handle. Stroke the path or fill it at will.

Filling a Shape with Text

If the Adobe engineers were a typical lot, they would have added type on a curve to Illustrator, slapped it onto a features list, and sold the product. But Adobe folks are frequently (though not always) more thoughtful than that. So when they added type on a curve to Version 3 back in 1991, they thought, "Gosh, if artists want text *on* a curve, maybe they want text *inside* a curve as well." And after much sage nodding of heads, *area text* was born.

In area text, type exists inside a path. A standard text block is a variety of area text—text inside a rectangle. But you can create text inside polygons, stars, or free-form shapes. Heck, you can even create text inside an open path if you want to.

To create type inside a path, goest thou thusly:

1. **Draw a path.**

   Unlike with path text, corner points work just as well as smooth points where area text is concerned. But keep the corners obtuse—wide rather than sharp. It's very difficult, and in many cases impossible, to fill sharp corners with text.

2. **Select the area type tool.**

   Select the area type tool from the type tool pop-up menu in the toolbox. The area type tool looks like a T trapped in Jell-O, as labeled in Figure 7-14.

3. **Click along the outline of the path and enter some text.**

   You have to click on the outline of the path; you can't click inside the path (even if the path is filled and the Area Select check box is active in the General Preferences dialog box). A blinking insertion marker appears at the top of the path.

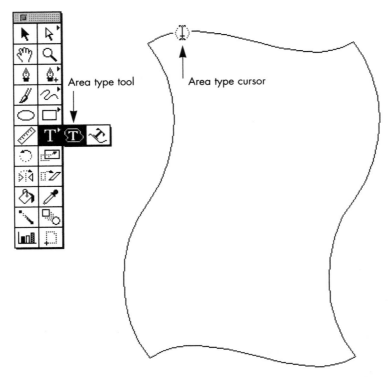

Figure 7-14: Click on the outline of a path with the area type tool.

As you enter text, it fills the path. Words that would otherwise exceed the edge of the shape wrap to the next line.

4. Complete the path text.

Select the type tool, arrow tool, or some other tool to finish off the text block. You'll get something like the area text shown in Figure 7-15.

You can also create area text with the standard type tool. Just click on a closed path to create area text, or Option-click on an open path. When the area type tool is active, press Control to access the standard type tool.

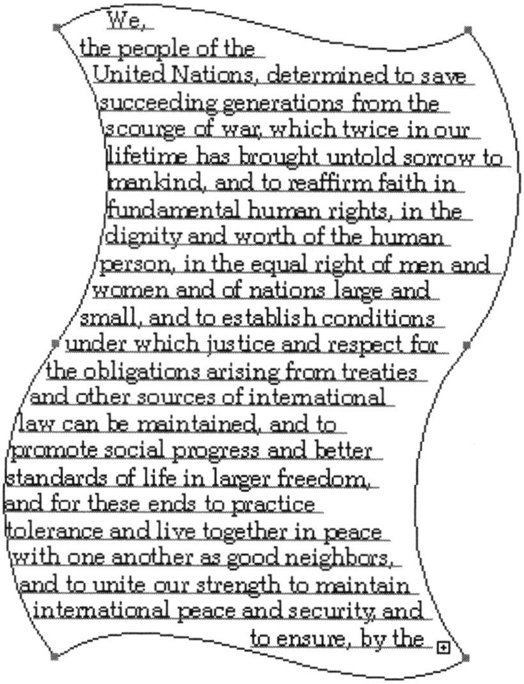

Figure 7-15:
Behold area text—
a free-form shape
filled with type.

Flowing Text from One Shape to Another

If your text overflows the path or you simply don't like the way it wraps, you can edit the path with the direct selection tool. Press ⌘-Shift-A to deselect the text block, then click on the path with the direct selection tool and reshape at will. (Be careful not to click on any of the baselines; that selects the entire area text.) As you reshape the path with the direct selection, add point, delete point, and convert point tools, Illustrator rewraps the text to fit inside the revised path outline.

You can also *flow* text from one area text block into another (something you can't do with point text or path text). This allows you to create multiple columns or even multiple pages of text. Figure 7-16 shows a several lines of text flowed between two paths. A single collection of paragraphs flowed over many text blocks is called a *story*.

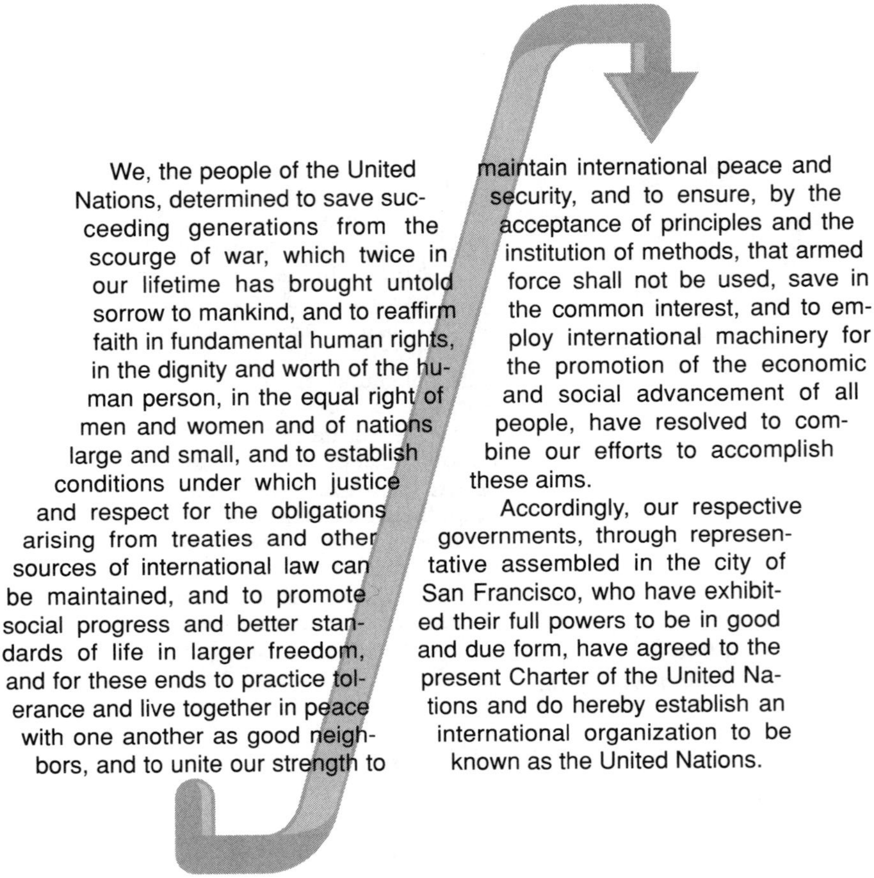

We, the people of the United Nations, determined to save succeeding generations from the scourge of war, which twice in our lifetime has brought untold sorrow to mankind, and to reaffirm faith in fundamental human rights, in the dignity and worth of the human person, in the equal right of men and women and of nations large and small, and to establish conditions under which justice and respect for the obligations arising from treaties and other sources of international law can be maintained, and to promote social progress and better standards of life in larger freedom, and for these ends to practice tolerance and live together in peace with one another as good neighbors, and to unite our strength to maintain international peace and security, and to ensure, by the acceptance of principles and the institution of methods, that armed force shall not be used, save in the common interest, and to employ international machinery for the promotion of the economic and social advancement of all people, have resolved to combine our efforts to accomplish these aims.

Accordingly, our respective governments, through representative assembled in the city of San Francisco, who have exhibited their full powers to be in good and due form, have agreed to the present Charter of the United Nations and do hereby establish an international organization to be known as the United Nations.

Figure 7-16: A single story flowed between two area text blocks.

To flow text from one block to another, you need to link them. You can link text blocks in one of two ways. These techniques are equally applicable to area text and rectangular text blocks:

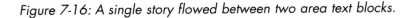 **Use the Link Blocks command**: With the arrow tool, select the path that contains the overflow text. Then select one or more other paths (by Shift-clicking on them) and choose Type » Link Blocks (⌘-Shift-G). All selected paths fill with as much overflow type as will fit, as demonstrated in Figure 7-17.

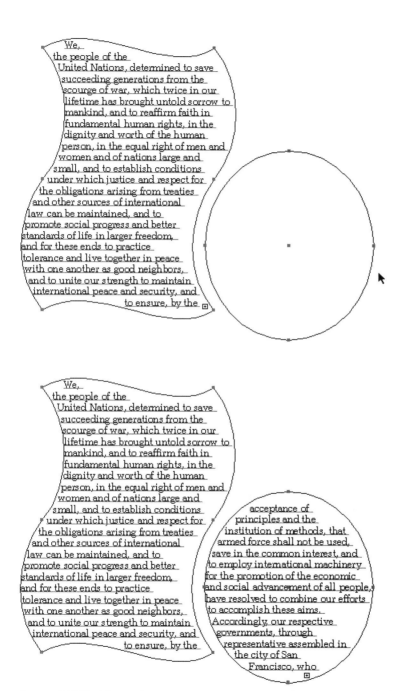

Figure 7-17: After selecting some area text and an empty path (top), choose Edit » Link Blocks to fill all selected paths with a single story (bottom).

Illustrator fills the paths in the order they are stacked. This means if you select a path that lies behind the area text and choose Link Blocks, the beginning of the story shifts to the rear path and then continues in the forward one. If you don't like the order in which the text flows, read the section "Reflowing a Story" coming up shortly in this chapter.

- **Clone the path that contains the text**: The second method for flowing text is by far the simplest. After pressing ⌘-Shift-A to deselect everything, Option-click on the text block outline with the direct selection tool. This selects the path without selecting the text inside. Next, drag the path to a new location, press the Option key, and release the mouse button. When you press the Option key, you get the clone cursor, as labeled in Figure 7-18, which shows that Illustrator is prepared to duplicate the path. The cloned path automatically fills with the overflow type from the first path, as in the bottom example of Figure 7-18.

 If this new path also displays a boxed plus sign, more overflow text exists. Choose Arrange » Repeat Transform or press ⌘-D to automatically create another clone. Illustrator creates a third path the same distance and direction from the second path as the second path is from the first. Continue choosing this command to add more columns.

The advantage to cloning a path to flow area text is that each block of text is the same size and shape. Also, you never have to worry about text flowing in the wrong order. It always flows from the first path to the clone.

 After selecting a path with the direct selection tool, there are many ways to clone it. You can choose Arrange » Move (⌘-Shift-M) and click on the Copy button inside the Move dialog box. Or you choose Edit » Copy (⌘-C) followed by Edit » Paste In Front (⌘-F) to create a duplicate directly in front of the original path; then use the direct selection tool to move the path to a new location. (I cover cloning in more detail in Chapter 9. Arrange » Move and Edit » Paste In Front are the subjects of Chapter 10.)

Selecting Linked Text Blocks

A collection of linked text blocks is a cohesive object, much like a group. You can select the entire story—all text and all paths—by merely clicking on any one

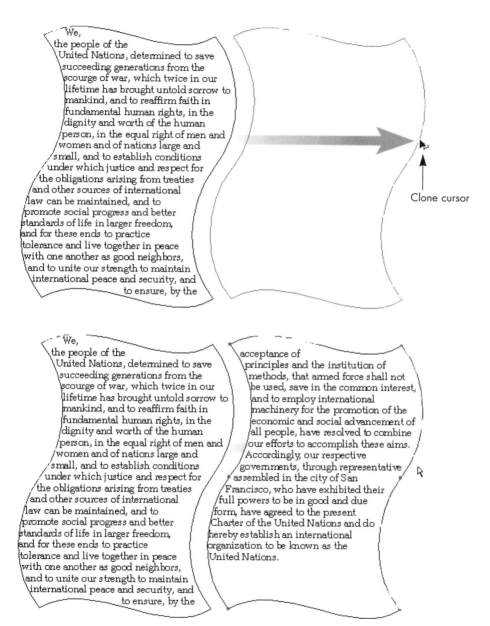

Figure 7-18: Option-drag a path containing text with the direct selection tool (top) to clone it and fill the clone with overflow text (bottom).

of the paths with the arrow tool. But you can still access individual paths and text blocks with the direct selection tool as follows:

- Click on a path with the direct selection tool to select a point or segment. Then reshape the path as desired.

- Option-click on a path to select the entire path without selecting the text inside it. This is useful if you want to clone the path or change its stacking order (as I explain in the next section).

- Option-click on the path a second time to select the entire text block—both path and text—independently of other text blocks in the story. (Or you can click on the baseline of any line of text with the direct selection tool.) Then you can drag the text block to move it.

- Option-click on the path a third time with the direct selection tool to select the entire story, just as if you had clicked on it with the arrow tool.

You can also add and subtract elements from the selection by pressing the Shift key. For example, if you've selected an entire text block but you only want to select the path, Shift-click with the direct selection tool on a baseline in the text to deselect the text.

Note that while you can select paths without the text, you cannot select text without also selecting the path. Just one of life's little inequities.

Reflowing a Story

A story flows from one text block to the next in the order that the paths are stacked, starting with the rearmost path and working its way forward. This phenomenon is known as the *linking order*. In Figure 7-19, for example, the right path is the rear path, the middle path is the front path, and the left path is in between. Therefore, the story starts in the right path, flows into the left path, and ends in the middle path; despite the fact that the story started in the left path before I chose Type » Link Blocks.

To rearrange the order in which a story flows, you can changing the stacking order of the paths by following these steps:

Next to back
Front
Back

promote social progress and better standards of life in larger freedom, and for these ends to practice tolerance and live together in peace with one another as good neighbors, and to unite our strength to maintain international peace and security, and to ensure, by the acceptance of principles and the institution of methods, that armed force shall not be used, save in the common interest, and to employ international machinery for the promotion of the economic and social advancement of all people, have resolved to

combine our efforts to accomplish these aims. Accordingly, our respective governments, through representative assembled in the city of San Francisco, who have exhibited their full powers to be in good and due form, have agreed to the present Charter of the United Nations and do hereby establish an international organization to be known as the United Nations.

We, the people of the United Nations, determined to save succeeding generations from the scourge of war, which twice in our lifetime has brought untold sorrow to mankind, and to reaffirm faith in fundamental human rights, in the dignity and worth of the human person, in the equal right of men and women and of nations large and small, and to establish conditions under which justice and respect for the obligations arising from treaties and other sources of international law can be maintained, and to

Figure 7-19: This story flows in the stacking order, from the rear shape on right to the front shape in the middle.

1. **Deselect the story**.

   By pressing ⌘-Shift-A, naturally.

2. **Send the desired starting path to back**.

   Using the direct selection tool, select the path that's supposed to be the first text block in the story. Then choose Arrange » Send To Back (⌘-hyphen). Illustrator automatically reflows the story so it starts in the selected path.

3. **Send the starting path and the next path to back**.

   Press the Shift key and click on the path that you want to represent the second text block. Then choose Arrange » Send To Back (or press ⌘-hyphen) again. This sends both selected paths to back, with the first path the rearmost path and the second path just in front of the first.

 In case you're thinking, "Why do I have to send that path to back again after I already sent it to back?"—as my editor was—it's because you're trying to establish a stacking sequence. Illustrator doesn't have any single command that juggles multiple paths into a specific order, so you have to do it a little bit at a time.

4. Send the starting path, the next path, and the one after that to back.

Keep adding one path after another to the selection in sequential order and choose Arrange » Send To Back after selecting each path.

Obviously, you don't have to work in exactly the order I suggest above. You can select the last text block and choose Arrange » Bring To Front (⌘-equal) if you prefer. Here are a few other ways to reflow text inside a story:

- Reduce the size of any path to flow text out of that path and into the next path in the linking order.

- Enlarge the size of a path to flow text into that path and out of the next path in the linking order.

- To merge two stories into one, select both stories with the arrow tool, then press ⌘-Shift-G (or choose Type » Link Blocks). Illustrator combines the selected area text into one story, flowing the text between the selected paths in the order the paths are stacked.

- Delete a path in the linked object by Option-clicking on the path with the direct selection tool and pressing the Delete key. Illustrator flows all text out of that path and into the next path.

Figure 7-20 demonstrates the effect of deleting the middle path from a story. Notice that Illustrator automatically flows the text from the middle path into the last path, while the text that used to be in the last path becomes overflow text. Therefore, deleting a path does not delete the text inside it; the text merely reflows. (This is why you can't delete a path if it's the only path in the story—there's no place for the overflow text to go.)

If you want to delete both path and text from the story, you have to select both path and text before pressing Delete. As I mentioned earlier, you can select a text block independently of others in a story by Option-clicking on it twice with the direct selection tool.

Unlinking Text Blocks

To unlink text blocks in a linked object, choose the Type » Unlink Blocks (⌘-Shift-U). This command isolates the paths so that each text block is its own story. Use the Unlink Blocks command only when you are happy with the way text appears in each column of type and you want to prevent it from reflowing under any circumstance.

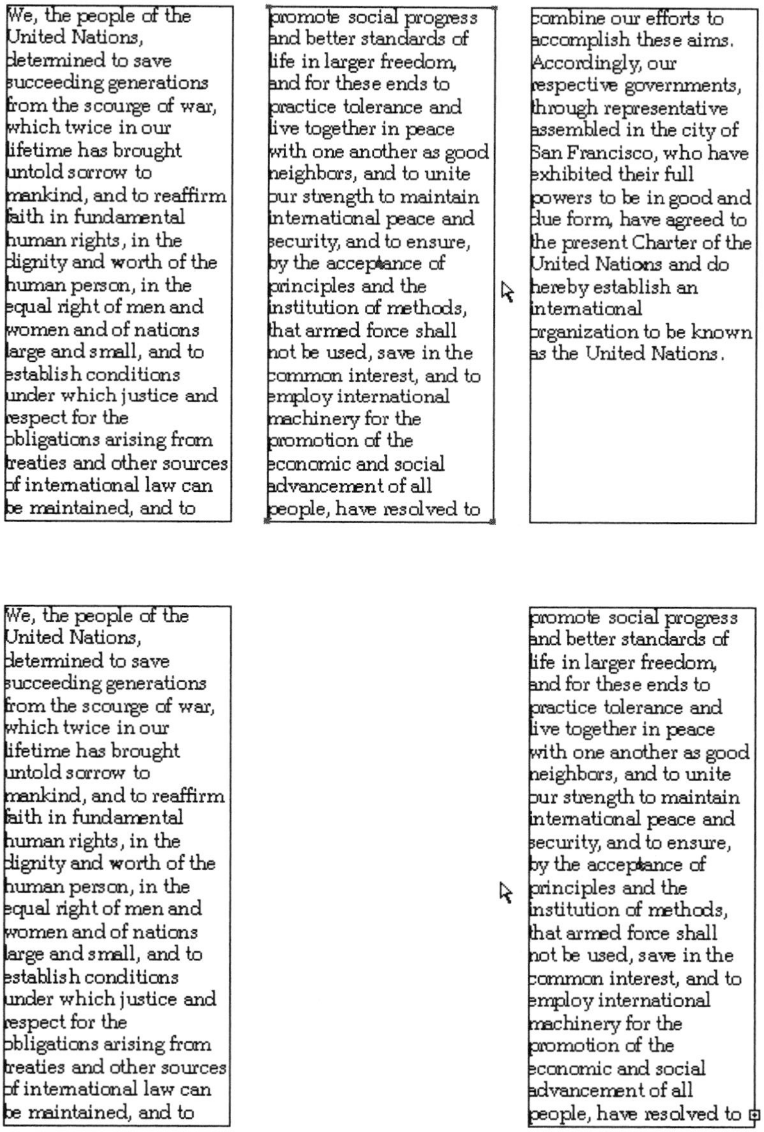

We, the people of the United Nations, determined to save succeeding generations from the scourge of war, which twice in our lifetime has brought untold sorrow to mankind, and to reaffirm faith in fundamental human rights, in the dignity and worth of the human person, in the equal right of men and women and of nations large and small, and to establish conditions under which justice and respect for the obligations arising from treaties and other sources of international law can be maintained, and to

promote social progress and better standards of life in larger freedom, and for these ends to practice tolerance and live together in peace with one another as good neighbors, and to unite our strength to maintain international peace and security, and to ensure, by the acceptance of principles and the institution of methods, that armed force shall not be used, save in the common interest, and to employ international machinery for the promotion of the economic and social advancement of all people, have resolved to

combine our efforts to accomplish these aims. Accordingly, our respective governments, through representative assembled in the city of San Francisco, who have exhibited their full powers to be in good and due form, have agreed to the present Charter of the United Nations and do hereby establish an international organization to be known as the United Nations.

We, the people of the United Nations, determined to save succeeding generations from the scourge of war, which twice in our lifetime has brought untold sorrow to mankind, and to reaffirm faith in fundamental human rights, in the dignity and worth of the human person, in the equal right of men and women and of nations large and small, and to establish conditions under which justice and respect for the obligations arising from treaties and other sources of international law can be maintained, and to

promote social progress and better standards of life in larger freedom, and for these ends to practice tolerance and live together in peace with one another as good neighbors, and to unite our strength to maintain international peace and security, and to ensure, by the acceptance of principles and the institution of methods, that armed force shall not be used, save in the common interest, and to employ international machinery for the promotion of the economic and social advancement of all people, have resolved to

Figure 7-20: Deleting the middle path (top) reflows the text into the last path (bottom).

If you're goal is to reflow type, do *not* start things off by choosing Unlink Blocks, since this busts the text apart. Simply make your changes with the direct selection tool and the Send To Back command, as explained in the "Reflowing a Story" section.

If you want to relink a story so it bypasses one path and flows into another one, delete the path that you no longer need, then select the new path and press ⌘-Shift-G (or choose Type » Link Blocks) to redirect the flow. Again, do *not* choose the Unlink Blocks command. (I know, I keep repeating myself, but you watch— you'll mess up and choose Unlink Blocks one day, only to be mystified that it doesn't work the way you thought it would.)

Wrapping Type Around Graphics

For the history buffs in the audience, Illustrator was the first drawing program to permit you to wrap text around graphics, previously the exclusive domain of page-layout programs such as PageMaker and XPress. This feature instructs Illustrator to automatically wrap type around the boundaries of one or more graphic objects, as illustrated in Figure 7-21.

Wrapping text around a graphic is a four-step process:

1. **Select the paths that you want to wrap the text around**.

   After selecting the paths with the arrow tool, choose Arrange » Group (⌘-G) to keep the paths together.

2. **Position the paths with respect to the text**.

   Drag the group into position, then choose Arrange » Bring To Front (⌘-equal). The paths must be in front of the text block to wrap properly.

3. **Select the text block that you want to wrap**.

   Shift-click on the text block with the arrow tool to add it to the selection. Illustrator can wrap text blocks and area text around graphics, but it cannot wrap point text or path text.

4. **Choose Type » Make Wrap**.

   Illustrator wraps the text around the graphics and fuses text and paths into a single *wrapped object*.

After this point, you can select the entire wrapped object by clicking on it with the arrow tool, or by Option-clicking two or three times on one of the paths with

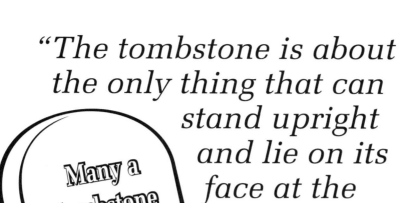

Figure 7-21: Illustrator lets you wrap type around the boundaries of graphic objects, as in the case of the text above and to the right of the tombstone.

the direct selection tool (depending on whether you wrap the text around a single path or multiple grouped paths). You can also reshape the paths with the direct selection tool. Illustrator constantly rewraps the text to compensate for your edits.

You can also modify the formatting for wrapped text by clicking or dragging inside the text with the type tool—or Option-clicking on the text blocks a few times with the direct selection tool—and adjusting the settings in the Character and Paragraph palettes. The two formatting attributes that you'll want to pay the most attention to are alignment and indentation:

* Select a different Alignment option from the Paragraph palette to change the way words align between the sides of the column and the boundaries of the paths. For example, the quote in Figure 7-21 is flush left, but the name is centered.

● The Indentation values in the Paragraph palette determine the amount of room between the graphic and the text. The following section explores how you can use these options to their best advantage.

Adjusting the Standoff

In publishing circles, the *standoff* is the amount of space between a graphic and the text wrapped around it. In Illustrator, there are two ways to adjust the amount of standoff around a graphic object.

● **Increase the Indentation values**: Adjust the Left and Right Indentation values in the Paragraph palette. Illustrator treats the outlines of the graphics as additional sides to the text block. Therefore, the Left value increases the space along the right sides of the graphic objects, and the Right value adds space along the left edges. (It might sound like the opposite of how it should work, but it makes sense if you sit down and ponder it a while. After all, the Left value moves text to the right and the Right value moves text to the left.)

The first example of Figure 7-22 shows justified text wrapped around a circle with all Indentation values set to 0. As a result, the text touches the circle, an effect that is best summed up as ugly. In the second example, I selected the text blocks by Option-clicking on them three times with the direct selection tool. Then I raised the Left value to 18 points and the Right value to 9.

● **Create a special standoff dummy**: You can also establish a standoff by creating a special path to act as a dummy for the actual graphic. If you make both the fill and stroke transparent, the standoff dummy is invisible and the text appears to wrap around thin air.

The following steps explain how to create your very own standoff dummy. These steps assume that you've already wrapped your text around a few graphics, and that you aren't altogether pleased with the appearance.

1. **Draw the dummy path**.

   I drew the path shown in Figure 7-23 with the regular polygon tool. I was able to exactly position the polygon by occasionally pressing the spacebar while drawing the shape. (As you may recall, the spacebar lets you move the shape while in the process of drawing it.)

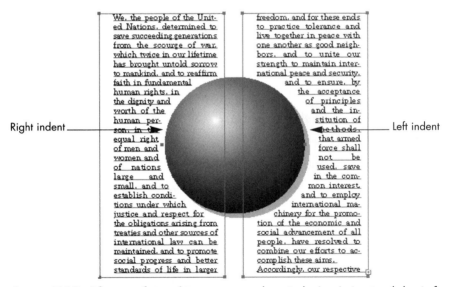

We, the people of the United Nations, determined to save succeeding generations from the scourge of war, which twice in our lifetime has brought untold sorrow to mankind, and to reaffirm faith in fundamental human rights, in the dignity and worth of the human person, in the equal right of men and women and of nations large and small, and to establish conditions under which justice and respect for the obligations arising from treaties and other sources of international law can be maintained, and to promote social progress and better standards of life in larger freedom, and for these ends to practice tolerance and live together in peace with one another as good neighbors, and to unite our strength to maintain international peace and security, and to ensure, by the acceptance of principles and the institution of methods, that armed force shall not be used, save in the common interest, and to employ international machinery for the promotion of the economic and social advancement of all people, have resolved to combine our efforts to accomplish these aims. Accordingly, our respective governments, through representative assembled in the city of San Francisco, who have exhibited their full powers to be in good and due form, have agreed to the present Charter of the United Nations and do hereby establish an international organization to be known as the United Nations.

Right indent _____   _____ Left indent

Figure 7-22: After justifying this text around a circle (top), I raised the Left and Right Indentation values to 18 and 9 points respectively (bottom).

2. Make the fill and stroke transparent.

Inside the Paint Style palette (which you can display by pressing ⌘-I), select the Fill icon, then select the None icon. If necessary, also select the Stroke icon and select the None icon. (Part IV covers the Paint Style palette in extreme depth.)

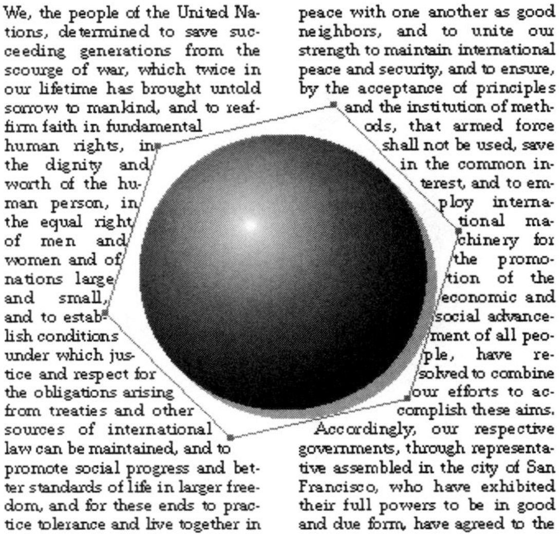

We, the people of the United Nations, determined to save succeeding generations from the scourge of war, which twice in our lifetime has brought untold sorrow to mankind, and to reaffirm faith in fundamental human rights, in the dignity and worth of the human person, in the equal right of men and women and of nations large and small, and to establish conditions under which justice and respect for the obligations arising from treaties and other sources of international law can be maintained, and to promote social progress and better standards of life in larger freedom, and for these ends to practice tolerance and live together in peace with one another as good neighbors, and to unite our strength to maintain international peace and security, and to ensure, by the acceptance of principles and the institution of methods, that armed force shall not be used, save in the common interest, and to employ international machinery for the promotion of the economic and social advancement of all people, have resolved to combine our efforts to accomplish these aims. Accordingly, our respective governments, through representative assembled in the city of San Francisco, who have exhibited their full powers to be in good and due form, have agreed to the

Figure 7-23:
This unfilled, unstroked polygon serves as a dummy path, creating a standoff that is not only larger than the circle but differently shaped as well.

3. Cut the path to the Clipboard.

Choose Edit » Cut or press ⌘-X.

4. Select one of the graphic objects.

Do this by Option-clicking on a path inside the wrapped object with the direct-selection tool.

5. Choose Edit » Paste In Back.

Or press ⌘-B. Because you used the direct selection tool to select the graphic object, Illustrator pastes the dummy path between the object and the text block, making the dummy path part of the wrapped object.

6. Press the up arrow key, then press the down arrow key.

Illustrator is a little slow to recognize the new dummy path, so you have to give it a little nudge to get the program's attention. When you press the up arrow key, Illustrator suddenly wraps the text around the dummy path. Pressing the down arrow key just puts the path back where it was.

I followed these steps to create the standoff shown in Figure 7-23. The polygon is selected in the figure. If it were not selected, it would be invisible. (To see the dummy path, switch to the artwork mode by pressing ⌘-E.)

Using Tabs with Wrapped Objects

You can force text in a wrapped object to jump to the other side of a path by pressing the Tab key. It's a weird little function left over from the old days, back when Illustrator didn't really support tabs. But it still comes in handy every blue moon.

In order for it to work, the graphic has to fall entirely inside the text block, so that words inside the block flank both sides of the graphic. (This is not the case in Figure 7-23, for example, in which the graphic falls to the right of one text block and the left of the other.)

If Illustrator just nudges the word when you press Tab, try pressing the key a few more times. Eventually, the word will go to the other side of the graphic. I know, I know, I told you not to press Tab more than once in a row in the last chapter. But what can you do? Screwy situations call for screwy measures.

 If the graphic merely falls to one side or the other of the text, you can force a word to the next line by pressing the Enter key. As you may recall from Chapter 6, Enter inserts a line break character but keeps all lines in the same paragraph.

Importing and Exporting Text

My guess is that most of the time, you'll enter your text directly inside Illustrator. But with free-flowing text, multiple pages, and excellent drawing tools at your disposal, Illustrator is quite the program for creating graphic-rich layouts.

That's why Illustrator lets you import text documents created in major word-processing programs. After all, word processors are faster for text entry and permit luxuries such as style sheets, thesauruses, and glossary and revision capabilities. And despite Illustrator's crack text capabilities, it's frankly easier to edit text and apply formatting attributes inside a word processor.

You can also export text from Illustrator to the same word processing file formats. This allows you to recover text that you've laid out inside Illustrator and even transfer it to a mightier layout program like QuarkXPress.

Preparing Your Text for Import

When importing a text file, Illustrator reads the file from disk and copies it to the illustration window. As this copy is being made, the text file passes through a filter that converts the file's formatting commands into formatting commands recognized by Illustrator.

 In order to import text, you need to have installed the so-called Claris XTND System, a translation utility that lives inside a folder called Claris within your System Folder. (You can install Claris XTND at any time by running the Illustrator installer program.) Illustrator's text filters reside inside the Claris Translators folder in a file called XTND for Illustrator. The great thing about the Claris XTND System is that multiple programs can use it at a time. (Claris, incidentally, is Apple's software publishing subsidiary.)

Assuming everything is installed correctly, Illustrator 6 lets you import the following formats:

- Microsoft Word, Versions 3.0, 4.0, 5.0, and 5.1 (no Word 6, but nobody besides me and my editor seems to use that program anyway)

- RTF (Rich Text Format), Microsoft's coded file format

- MacWrite, Versions 4.5 and 5.0

- MacWrite II, Versions 1.0 and 1.1

- WriteNow 3.0

- WordPerfect for the Mac, Versions 2.0 and 2.1

- WordPerfect for the PC, Versions 5.0 and 5.1

- plain text with no formatting whatsoever, also known as ASCII (pronounced *ask-ee*)

Though I've never met a Macintosh user who has a kind word for Microsoft, most folks use Word 5. If this is your program of choice, just save the file normally and import it into Illustrator. If you use Word 6, be sure to save the file in the Word 5 format. For those few but proud WordPerfect 3 users in the audience, be sure to save your files in the WordPerfect 2.1 format. Almost no one uses MacWrite or WriteNow anymore, but if you do, be sure to save in one of the formats listed above. And finally, if you're that rarest of all living creatures, the Nisus user, I recommend the Word 5 or RTF format.

PageMaker and QuarkXPress also let you export text in many of the formats listed above. Again, Word 5 or RTF are your best bets. (These are the most common formats and therefore the ones Illustrator is likely to support most consistently.)

The absolute last alternative is the plain text format, which sacrifices all formatting and leaves you with nothing but a string of characters, spaces, tabs, and carriage returns. You'll have to reformat the text in Illustrator.

Import filters may not be able to convert all formatting attributes correctly from a word processor file. The following list describes how Illustrator handles a few prevailing formatting attributes and offers a few suggestions for preparing each:

- **Typeface**: Illustrator is supposed to use the typeface specified in the word processor, but sometimes it gets mixed up. If Illustrator can't find the typeface in your system—if the document was created on another machine, for example—it substitutes Helvetica. But even when the typeface is available, Illustrator may flip out and substitute Chicago. Adobe blames Claris for this occasional weirdness, but there are a sufficient number of other bugs in Illustrator 6 to make me think Adobe itself is not above suspicion.

- **Type style**: Illustrator does not apply styles the way word processors do. As I dutifully explained in the previous chapter, Illustrator requires that you specify typeface and style together by selecting a stylized font. As a result, bold and italic styles convert successfully, but most others do not. If Illustrator comes across a style for which a stylized font does not exist—underline, outline, strikethru, small caps, and so on—the program simply ignores the style. The happy exceptions are superscript and subscript styles, which transfer intact thanks to Illustrator's baseline shift function.

- **Type size and leading**: All text retains the same size and leading specified in the word processor. If you assign automatic leading or "single spacing" inside the word processor, Illustrator substitutes its own automatic leading, which is 120 percent of the type size.

- **Alignment**: Illustrator recognizes paragraphs that are aligned left, center, and right, as well as justified.

- **Carriage returns**: Illustrator successfully reads carriage return characters (which you create by pressing the Return key); each carriage return indicates the end of a paragraph. Some word processors also offer line break characters, which knock words to the next line without adding paragraph spacing. Though Illustrator offers a line break character of its own, the program converts line breaks from imported text into carriage returns. Therefore, you're well advised to steer clear of line breaks and use carriage returns only to distinguish the ends of paragraphs (not the ends of lines).

- **Indents**: All paragraph indents, including first-line, left, and right indents remain intact. (Hanging indents won't look quite right, since

Illustrator doesn't import tab stops.) Adjusting the margins in your word processor may also affect indentation. To clear the indents, just click on the individual Indentation option names in Illustrator's Paragraph palette.

- **Paragraph spacing**: Some word processors divide paragraph spacing into two categories: "before spacing," which precedes the paragraph, and "after spacing," which follows the paragraph. Illustrator combines them into the Leading before ¶ value in the Paragraph palette, essentially retaining the same effect. (Separate before and after spacing are only useful when a program offers styles sheets, which Illustrator does not.)

- **Tabs, tab stops, and tab leaders**: Illustrator imports tab characters successfully. But it ignores the placement of tab stops, and tab leaders (such as dots and dashes) are a complete mystery to the program. Use the Tabs palette (⌘-Shift-T) to reset the tab stops as desired.

- **Special characters**: Many word processors provide access to special characters that are not part of the standard Apple-defined character set. These include em spaces, nonbreaking hyphens, automatic page numbers, date and time stamps, and so on. Of these, only the discretionary hyphen character (⌘-Shift-hyphen in Illustrator) transfers successfully.

- **Page markings**: Illustrator ignores page breaks in imported text, as well as headers, footers, and footnotes.

If you can't find a formatting option in this list, chances are Illustrator simply ignores it.

Importing Text into Columns

You can import text into any kind of text object. But because point text and path text are so badly suited to long stories—path text doesn't even support carriage returns or tabs—you'll most likely want to import stories into area text blocks.

To import a story into a bunch of text blocks, grab your partner and follow these steps:

1. **Create your first text block**.

   Select the type tool and click on the outline of a closed path. Or drag with the type tool to create a new text block. If you want to append an imported story inside a text block that you've already started, click at the point inside the text where you want to insert the story.

2. **Choose File » Import Text**.

This displays the Import File dialog box, which looks just like a standard Open dialog box.

(Note that the Import Text command is dimmed if no text block is active. If your command is dimmed, go back and perform Step 1.)

3. **Locate the text file on disk and open it**.

If you can't find the file, but you know it's there, select the All Available from the Show pop-up menu in the lower left corner of the dialog box. This allows you to see all formats that Illustrator supports. If that doesn't work, Illustrator doesn't recognize the file; go back to your word processor and try saving it in a different format.

Once you locate your file in the scrolling list, double-click on it or select the file name and press Return. After a few moments, Illustrator displays the imported text inside the text block.

4. **Flow the text into additional paths**.

Unless your text file contains less than a paragraph of text, Illustrator probably won't be able to fit all the text into a single block. You can enlarge the path by reshaping it with the direct selection tool. But more likely, you'll want to flow the text into additional paths as explained in the "Flowing Text from One Shape to Another" section.

Exporting Text to a Text File

Illustrator's Export plug-in allows you to export text from Illustrator to disk using one of the common word processing formats that I mentioned earlier. Keep in mind that when you export text from Illustrator, you save only the type and its formatting attributes. No path information is included.

For example, if you export a line of path type that surrounds a circle and then open the text file in a word processor, the type looks like any other line of type, oriented from left to right along a straight line. You won't see so much as a trace of a circle. Therefore, the purpose of Type » Export is to save text that you want to arrange differently in another program.

 To export fancy type including paths and everything, export the illustration in the EPS format, as described in the "Saving an EPS Illustration" section of Chapter 3. You won't be able to edit the type, but it will look great.

Here's how to export text from Illustrator:

1. **Select the text you want to export**.

   Use the type tool to select one or more characters of from any kind of text object. You can export a single letter or any entire story. But you have to use the type tool; you can't select the text with the arrow tool. (To select the entire story—even if you can't see all of it on screen—click inside the block with the type tool and press ⌘-A.)

2. **Choose Type » Export**.

   Illustrator 6 puts the Import Text command under the File menu, but the Export command under the Type menu. Go figure. Choosing Type » Export displays a standard save dialog box.

3. **Select a file format from the Export File pop-up menu**.

   You can select from any of the formats that Illustrator imports. Use the format that your word processor supports best. (The default ought to be set to MS Word 5, but it's always set to the first format alphabetically, DOS WordPerfect 5.0. Sheesh!)

4. **Name the file and specify a destination on disk**.

   It's just like saving an illustration. Press Return when everything's ready to go. Illustrator exports the selected text to disk as instructed.

Checking Your Spelling

Imagine what it must be like to be a kid today. (Unless you *are* a kid, in which case, you must have a fair grasp on the topic already.) Ah, to have grown up in a time of calculators and spell checkers. These two devices automated everything we learned in grade school, with the possible exceptions of social studies and P.E. Here I am in my 30's, and I already feel like saying, "Back in my day, we had to add numbers by hand—with pencils!—and we had to know how to spell *squirrel* and stuff! And, by thunder, we liked it! You kids nowadays can add and spell any daggum way you please and let the machines clean up after you! It's a disgrace, I tell you, a complete disgrace!"

Spell checkers are so prevalent, in fact, that even Illustrator offers one. Without the help of an outside application, Illustrator can transform the sentence, "Teh

couw rann awai wyth theh sponn," to something that English-speaking humans
might find recognizable.

1. **Choose the Type » Check Spelling**.

   You don't have to select any text; Illustrator automatically checks the
   spelling of all text, hidden or visible, in your drawing.

   After you choose the Check Spelling command, Illustrator immediately
   sets about revealing your mistakes. (No need to click on any Start
   button, as in some programs.) If Illustrator doesn't find any word that is
   missing from its dictionary, it displays an ego-stroking message about
   how excellent your spelling is. If the program does find mistakes—the
   more likely scenario—it lists *all* mistakes throughout the entire document
   in the Misspelled Words list at the top of the Check Spelling dialog
   box, as in Figure 7-24.

Figure 7-24:
Illustrator finds all
spelling mistakes in
one pass, so that you
can examine and
correct them in any
order you please.

2. **Select all words that are spelled properly**.

   Scroll through the Misspelled Words list to see which words are truly
   misspelled and which words Illustrator is simply too inexperienced in
   the ways of the world to know. If a word is spelled to your satisfaction,

you can either add it to Illustrator's dictionary or simply skip the word
for the time being.

Go ahead and select all the words that are fine as is. Press
the Shift key and click on a word to select many words in a
row; ⌘-click to add one word at a time to the selection. You
can also ⌘-click to deselect a word.

3. Click on the Learn button.

This adds the words to Illustrator's auxiliary dictionary, so that the program will never again bug you about the spelling. (Don't worry if you
add a word that you didn't mean to; you can always delete it later by
clicking on the Edit List button.)

If you just want to ignore the words for the time being, click on the Skip
button. Click on Skip All to ignore all other occurrences of these particular misspellings at the same time.

4. Select a word that's misspelled.

To correct a word that is indeed misspelled, select it from the Misspelled
Words list. (You can only correct one misspelling at a time.) Illustrator
highlights the first occurrence of the word in the illustration window and
displays a few alternative spellings in the Suggested Corrections list.

5. Select the proper spelling.

If one of the alternates in the Suggested Corrections list is correct, click
on it. If none of the spellings are correct, enter the new spelling in the
option box below the list.

It's unfortunate that you can't transfer the wrong spelling to
the option box as a jumping off point for your manual correction. Also irritating, the Suggested Corrections list constantly updates as you enter the correct spelling, which
greatly slows down the reaction speed.

6. Click on the Change button.

Or you can press the Return key or double-click on the proper spelling
in the Suggested Corrections list. If you know that many words are misspelled in the same way, click on the Change All button to correct all
misspellings at once. Illustrator corrects the spelling of the words in the
illustration window and moves on to the next misspelling.

7. End the spell checking.

After you tell Illustrator to either learn, skip, or change every word in the Misspelled Words list, an alert box comes up to tell you it's finished. If you want to cut things off early, click on the Done button or press the Escape key or ⌘-period.

After you enter your own proper spelling into the option box above the Change button, you may wonder how you can add the new spelling into Illustrator's auxiliary dictionary? (If you click on the Learn button, Illustrator adds the word from the Misspelled Words list, not the word from the option box.) The answer is that you have to apply the new spelling to the illustration window, close the dialog box, and again choose Type » Check Spelling or press ⌘-Shift-E.

 That's right. Even though the Check Spelling command is now under the Type menu, you can repeat the command by choosing it from the top of the Filter menu, or by pressing ⌘-Shift-E.

To edit the auxiliary dictionary—whether during this or some other session—choose Type » Check Spelling and click on the Edit List button. Illustrator displays the dialog box shown in Figure 7-25. Here you can select a word and delete it by clicking on the Remove button; change the spelling of the word by replacing a few characters and clicking on Change; or create a variation on a spelling by clicking on Add. Note that Illustrator is smart enough to know that an 's on the end of a word doesn't constitute a misspelling, something Microsoft just figured out with Word 6. So you don't have to create variations like *Eeyore's* and *Tigger's* to cover your bases. However, if you want to prepare for plurals, such as *Kangas* or *Roos*, you have to add those.

Figure 7-25: You can view the words that you've added to the dictionary by clicking on the Edit List button.

Illustrator saves the auxiliary dictionary to disk as AI User Dictionary in the Plug-Ins folder inside a folder called Text. This means you can take the dictionary from one machine and copy it to another to maintain a consistent auxiliary dictionary. (You can open the dictionary in SimpleText—the mini word processor that comes with all Macs—but don't do it. Illustrator uses a bunch of special characters in the file; mess them up, and you can damage your dictionary for good.)

Let's see, what have I missed? Oh yeah:

- The Case Sensitive check box lets you correct words depending on whether they're capitalized or not. For example, you might want to change *wol* to *owl*, but add *Wol* to the dictionary (since that's Owl's proper name).

- The Language button lets you add a dictionary for a different language, such as U.K. English. You have to open the language file from disk. Look for the language files in the Plug-Ins folder inside the Text folder.

The Check Spelling command is a wonderful feature. Even if your illustration doesn't contain much text, you'd be surprised how few words it takes to make a wrong spelling. Choosing Type » Check Spelling only takes a moment and is always worth the time.

Searching and Replacing Stuff

Another amazing feature of Illustrator is its ability to automatically search for bits of text and replace them with other bits of text. For example, you can search and replace words, search and replace fonts, and even search and replace special design characters. No program—not Word, not XPress, not FreeHand—provides such sophisticated searching capabilities.

The following features are absolute gems. Don't forget they're here; they can save you a lot of time.

Replacing Words and Phrases

The Find filter lets you locate all occurrences of a particular collection of characters and replace them with a different collection of characters. You can search for as many characters as you like, including spaces.

1. **Click with the type tool at the location where you want to begin the search process**.

   You don't have to perform this step. If you have the arrow tool selected, for example, Illustrator searches all stories throughout the entire drawing, from beginning to end. But if you want to limit your search to a specific area of a story, click in the story with the type tool. By default, Illustrator searches forward from the insertion marker; it does not search the text before the insertion marker. (You can reverse the direction of the search by selecting the Search Backward check box, as we'll soon see.)

2. **Choose Type » Find**.

   Illustrator brings up the Text Find dialog box, pictured in Figure 7-26.

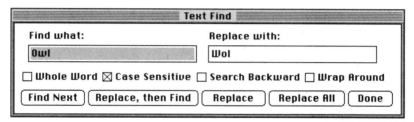

Figure 7-26: Use the Text Find dialog box to search for some text and replace that text with some other text.

3. **Enter the text you want to search for, and the text you want to replace it with**.

   Enter the search text in the Find What option box, press Tab, and enter the replacement text in the Replace With option box. If you don't want to replace the text—you're just trying to figure out where it went—don't enter anything into the Replace With option box.

4. **Click on the Find Next button**.

   Or just press Return. Illustrator highlights the first occurrence of the word in the illustration window.

 If Illustrator beeps at you, it can't find the text anywhere. Try selecting the arrow tool or deselecting a few option boxes to broaden your search.

5. Replace the word and move on.

Click on the Replace button to simply replace the selected text. Click on the Replace Then Find button to replace the text and then look for the next occurrence of the Find What text. (If there is no more to be found, Illustrator callously beeps at you.) Or click on Replace All to replace all Find What text with the contents of the Replace With option box.

6. When you're finished, click on the Done button.

Or press ⌘-period or Escape.

You can modify your search by turning on and off the check boxes in the middle of the dialog box:

- **Whole Word**: This option limits the search to whole words that exactly match the Find What text. With this option turned off, searching for *owl* would find the characters inside *growl* and *cowlick*. With Whole Word turn on, *owl* must appear by itself.

- **Case Sensitive**: Select this check box to search for characters that exactly match the uppercase and lowercase characters in the Find What text. Searching for *Owl* would find neither *owl* nor *OWL* when this option is on.

- **Search Backward**: This option begins the search at the insertion marker and proceeds backward towards the beginning of the story.

- **Wrap Around**: To search the entire illustration, no matter where the insertion marker is set, select Wrap Around. This option begins the search at the insertion marker and proceeds to the end of the story, starts over at the next story, continues through to the beginning of the first story, and back to the insertion marker.

Neither Search Backward or Wrap Around is of any use when the arrow tool is selected, since Illustrator automatically searches all text in the illustration.

Type » Find can search and replace text inside locked and even hidden text blocks. So if you click on the Find Next button, only to be greeted by neither a beep nor any highlighted text inside the illustration window, the text block is probably hidden. Press ⌘-period to close the Text Find dialog box, then choose Arrange » Show All (⌘-4).

Replacing One Font with Another

Type » Find Font is another of Illustrator's amazing searching functions. But instead of replacing words, it lets you search for one font and replace it with another.

Why would you want to do that? Well, imagine that an associate of yours created an illustration a couple of years back using Geneva. You think Geneva is pretty smelly, as far as fonts go, so you want to replace all occurrences of this font with a different one. Here's how you proceed:

1. Choose Type » Find Font.

In response, the Find Font dialog box bounds into view, as shown in Figure 7-27.

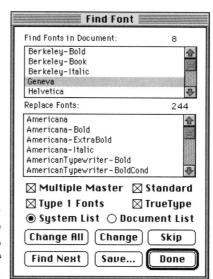

Figure 7-27:
This dialog box lets you
replace one or more
occurrences of one font
with a different font.

2. Select the font that you want to get rid of from the first list.

In this case, you'd select Geneva. Illustrator highlights the font in the illustration window.

3. Select the substitute font from the second list.

Initially, the second list contains only the names of those fonts that are used in the current illustration. If you want to choose from a wider variety, select the System List radio button, which instructs Illustrator to list every font loaded into your system, a potentially time consuming task.

 You can pause font listing by clicking on an empty portion of the dialog box. To start up the listing again, turn on and off one of the check boxes, or switch between the radio buttons.

4. Click on Change or one of the other buttons.

The Change button replaces the first occurrence of the bad font and searches for the next. To change all occurrences of the font, click on the Change All button. If you're feeling a little more selective—maybe you like Geneva this one time—you can click on the Find Next button (or just click on the font name again) to ignore one occurrence of a font and find the next.

Then there's the Skip button, which does the exact same thing as the Find Next button. Sloppy sloppy.

5. Click on the Done button when you're finished.

Or press Return, Escape, or ⌘-period. (So many shortcuts for Done, but none for the other buttons. What gives, Adobe?)

Use the check boxes to decide which kinds of fonts you can see inside the two lists. Click on the Save button to save a list of the fonts used in your document to a text file. You can then submit that file to a service bureau or commercial printer when it comes time to output the file. (If this kind of thing interests you, check out the description of File » Document Info in Chapter 18.)

Automatic Character Changes

And if you still aren't convinced that Illustrator's going nuts in the desktop-publishing department, there are two more commands that prove it beyond a shadow of a doubt. These are Change Case and Smart Punctuation, both located under the Type menu (where else?).

Type » Change Case lets you change lowercase text to initial caps or all caps, or all caps to lowercase or initial caps, or some other variation.

1. Select the text you want to change. For example, perhaps you want to change some text you accidentally entered with the Caps Lock key down.

2. Choose Type » Change Case.

3. Select the desired option. In this case, select the Lower Case radio button, which ought really to be one word.

4. Press Return.

The Change Case command is so simple, a sightless tree frog could use it. Type » Smart Punctuation is only slightly more complicated. This filter searches for all "dumb" punctuation in your document—straight quotes, double hyphens, double spaces after periods—and replaces them with their more acceptable and better looking equivalents—curly quotes, en dashes, and single spaces after periods.

Select the type you want to change with the type tool, then choose Type » Smart Punctuation to display the dialog box shown in Figure 7-28. Next select the check boxes representing the kinds of punctuation you want to change and press the Return key.

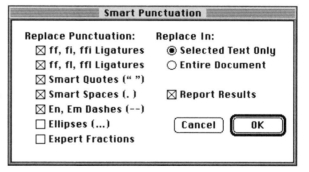

Figure 7-28:
Use these options to
automatically convert
various characters in
your illustration to
more design-accept-
able characters.

 Unfortunately, the check boxes themselves are a little convoluted. Three of them—ff, fi, ffi Ligatures; ff, fl, ffl Ligatures; and Expert Fractions—require that a so-called Expert Collection font be on hand. This is an Adobe typeface that contains a second alphabet of special typographic symbols, including small caps, ligatures (two characters joined into one), and fractions. Additionally, the Expert Collection has to correspond to the base font. For example, in order to take advantage of Utopia Expert Collection, the text in question has to be set in Utopia. Text set in Univers will not change. Lots of great Expert Collection fonts exist—including variations for Bembo, Bodoni, and Caslon, among others—but most fonts don't offer them.

Very quickly, let's look at each option:

- **ff, fi, ffi Ligatures**: If a font comes with an expert collection, this option replaces *ff, fi,* and *ffi* with their respective ligatures. In Figure 7-29, for example, I've set several words in Adobe Caslon. I also had Adobe Caslon Expert Collection loaded into my system. When I selected this check box, Illustrator replaced the black letters in *affable, fickle,* and *difficult* with their equivalent, single-character ligatures from the Expert Collection. If I had used a standard font, Illustrator would have replaced the *fi* in *fickle* and *difficult* with the common *fi* ligature (Shift-Option-5), but that's it.

affable, fickle,
difficult,
flowery, afflicted

affable, fickle,
difficult,
flowery, afflicted

Figure 7-29:
After setting a few words in Adobe Caslon (top), I applied the Smart Punctuation command to convert the ligatures (black) to their single-character equivalents from the Expert Collection font (bottom).

- **ff, fl, ffl Ligatures**: Tell me what's wrong here. That's right, the *ff* ligature is repeated unnecessarily in this option. But whatever the name of the option, it was responsible for replacing the black letters in *flowery* and *afflicted* in Figure 7-29. (It would have also taken care of the *ff* in *affable,* but the previous option got to it first.) If no Expert Collection font is available, Illustrator replaces the *fl* in *flowery* and *afflicted* with the *fl* ligature (Shift-Option-6), available to most Macintosh fonts.

- **Smart Quotes**: This option turns straight quotes (") into curly ones (" and ") and straight apostrophes (') into curly ones ('). Of course, you don't need this option; you already enter your quotes correctly in the first place using Option-[, Shift-Option-[, and Shift-Option -], right?

- **Smart Spaces**: If you learned to type on a typewriter, someone somewhere may have taught you to enter two spaces after a period. This is a cardinal sin when typesetting. In typesetting, you enter only one space after a period. Why? Because two spaces looks like garbage. See, spaces on a computer can be any width the program wants to make them, particularly when justifying text. If Illustrator has to stretch one space to justify a line, it has to stretch two spaces twice as far, which interrupts the readability of the paragraph. Bad typewriter habits must die!

- **En, Em Dashes**: This option is a little off. It replaces two hyphens in a row with an en dash (–, which you can access by pressing Option-hyphen), and three hyphens with an em dash (—, Shift-Option-hyphen). The problem is, most folks who don't use real em dashes in the first place use double-hyphens as a substitute. I've never heard of anyone using triple hyphens. Furthermore, en dashes are equivalent to minus signs, so few folks think to use them at all. My suggestion is to ignore this option and learn the proper keyboard equivalents, Option-hyphen and Shift-Option-hyphen.

- **Ellipses**: This option replaces three periods with the special ellipsis symbol, accessed by pressing Option-semicolon. The only real reason to use this character is to prevent the periods from breaking across a line.

- **Expert Fractions**: Every Adobe typeface includes three fraction characters, 1/4, 1/2, and 3/4. But thanks to the way Apple structured the extended character set, none are available when using the Mac. No way, no how. You can access them easily in Microsoft Windows, but not on the Mac. Forget it. So Adobe smartly built fractions into the Expert Collections, which include fractions in 1/8 increments. Figure 7-30 shows three fractions, created with the standard slash symbol, set in the font Apollo, and the single-character versions from the Apollo Expert

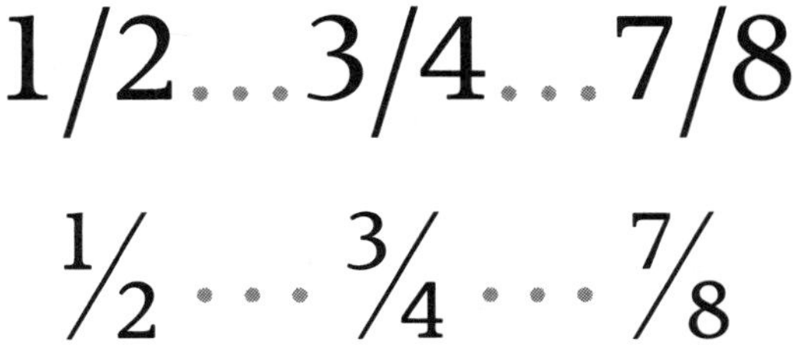

Figure 7-30: I created three fractions using standard slash symbols (top) and used the Smart Punctuation command to replace them with designer fractions from the Expert Collection font (bottom).

1/2...3/4...7/8

½ ... ¾ ... ⅞

Collection. If you don't have access to an Expert Collection font, build your own fractions as explained in the "Raising and Lowering Characters" section of Chapter 6.

Select the Report Results check box if you want Illustrator to present you with an alert box after it's smartened up your document. The alert box lists the variety and quantity of each dumb punctuation that has been replaced.

Select the Entire Document radio button to search and replace characters throughout the entire illustration, whether selected with the type tool or not. I prefer to keep this option set to Selected Text Only—which requires you to have text selected with the type tool—since this way I know exactly what Illustrator is up to.

Dividing Tables into Rows and Columns

Back in Chapter 6, I explained how to set up tables using the Tabs palette. But while tabs have many advantages, they have one irritating limitation—they can't accommodate multiple lines of type per entry. If you want to wrap a heading or table entry onto two lines, you wrap and tab the text manually.

For example, Figure 7-31 shows a detail from Figure 6-18 just to jog your memory (assuming there is any memory there to jog). To create the two-line headings *Primary occupation* and *Additional income*, I had to enter the text on two separate lines and tab the text into position—as in Tab, *Primary*, Tab, Tab, *Additional*, Return, *Name*, Tab, *occupation*, and so on.

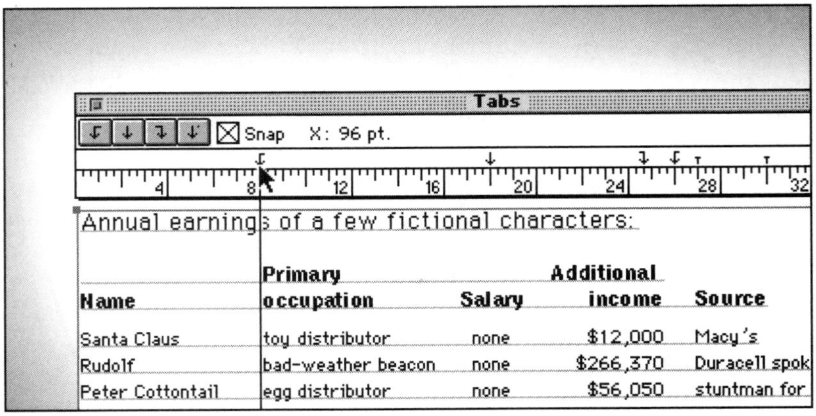

Figure 7-31: A detail from Figure 6-18, showing a two-line heading created manually using tabs.

The Rows & Columns Command

Thank golly, it doesn't have to be this way. You can create complex tables that permit multiple lines per entry using the Rows & Columns command. After selecting a text block or other area text with the arrow tool—not with the type tool—choose Type » Rows & Columns. This displays the Rows & Columns dialog box shown in Figure 7-32. Here you can specify the number of columns and rows in the text block, the width and height of each column and row, the amount of space (called the *gutter*) between each pair of columns and rows, and the width and height of the entire text block. (Incidentally, in case you get confused by over this kind of thing, columns are vertical and rows are horizontal.)

You can click on the arrow icons to incrementally change the values in the option boxes. Because changing any value affects at least one other, the arrows come in handy. Whenever possible, Illustrator tries to maintain consistent values in the Columns, Rows, Total Width, and Total Height option boxes. This means if you make a change to the Column Width value, Illustrator adjusts the Gutter value—rather than the Columns or Total Width value—to compensate. Bigger column width, smaller gutter, and vice versa.

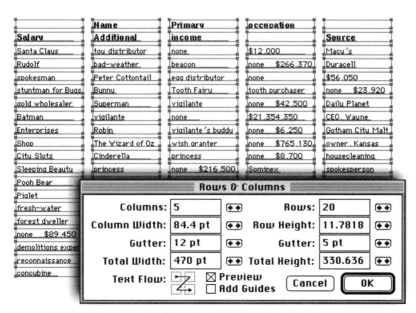

Figure 7-32: You can divide a text block into multiple rows and columns using the options inside this dialog box.

Click on the Text Flow option to change the order in which text flows through the columns and rows—that is, from left to right and then top to bottom, or from top to bottom and then left to right. The Add Guides check box creates horizontal and vertical lines which are the entire width and height of your page—this can be useful for establishing grids. (For more on this topic, check out Chapter 10.)

As long as the Preview option is checked, Illustrator continually updates the selected text block as you make changes. Unfortunately, this goes a long way toward slowing down the program, particularly on Quadras and older machines. I prefer to deselect the Preview check box when making changes, then reselect it when I want to view the results.

In Illustrator 5.5, the Preview check box actually applied your changes to the selected text block. Clicking on the Cancel button, therefore, did not cancel the operation, but instead left the most recent preview in effect. This problem has been eliminated in Illustrator 6. The Cancel button cancels, just as it should.

Modifying Rows and Columns Manually

After you create the desired number of rows and columns, you may have to edit the rows and columns by hand a bit, and you'll certainly have to edit the text to fit. Notice that all this filter does is break a text block into multiple text blocks that are linked together. Therefore, you can resize the text blocks in an way you like.

For example, in Figure 7-33, I used the direct selection tool to select the top segments in the first row, then I dragged the segments upward to allow room for both lines of text in the table heads. I also adjusted the width of the rows to better fit the text.

To force a word into the next text block—whether to the right or down from the current block—enter a carriage return by pressing the Return key. (Don't use the tab key, since the width of each tab may vary depending on the location of the tab stops in the Tabs palette.) To set up the table head, therefore, I entered Return, *Name*, Return, *Primary occupation*, Return, Return, *Salary*, Return, *Additional income*, and so on. The Return before *Name* and the double Return before *Salary* ensure that each of these entries appears on the second line. It may sound as cumbersome as entering all those tabs back in Figure 7-31, but it has one important advantage—you can enter words in order, rather than having to cut and paste them into different positions to make them line up properly.

If you want to later go back and add more rows and columns, just select all of your text and rechoose Type » Rows & Columns again. Keep in mind, however, that Illustrator resizes and respaces the selected text blocks to make them absolutely identical, which may necessitate some additional reshaping on your part.

Name	Primary occupation	Salary	Additional income	Source
Santa Claus	toy distributor	none	$12,000	Macy's
Rudolf	bad-weatherbeacon	none	$266,370	Duracell spokesman
Peter Cottontail	egg distributor	none	$56,050	stuntman for Bugs Bunny
Tooth Fairy	tooth purchaser	none	$23,920	gold wholesaler
Superman	vigilante	none	$42,500	Daily Planet
Batman	vigilante	none	$21,354,350	CEO, Wayne Enterprises
Robin	vigilante's buddy	none	$6,250	Gotham City Malt Shop
The Wizard of Oz	wish granter	none	$765,130	owner, Kansas City Slots
Cinderella	princess	none	$8,700	housecleaning
Sleeping Beauty	princess	none	$216,500	Sominex spokesperson
Pooh Bear	stuffed animal	none	$1.50	found in hollow tree
Piglet	stuffed animal	none	$0.75	stole from Owl
Lochness Monster	fresh-water dweller	none	$128,900	sighting fees
Big Foot	forest dweller	none	$0.75	stole from Piglet
E.T.	illegal alien	none	$89,450	pediatrician
Big Bad Wolf	pig chaser	none	$120,360	demolitions expert
Little Bo Peep	sheepherder	none	$35,000	animal reconnaissance
Gilligan	little buddy	none	$47.13	Mrs. Howell's concubine
Scooby Doo	crime-solving pet	none	-$152	loans to Shaggy

Figure 7-33: After dividing a text block using the Rows & Columns command, you can edit the divided text blocks independently with the direct selection tool.

Fitting Multiple Master Fonts on the Fly

Only two more commands left in the Type menu—Fit Headline and Create Outlines. The first shrinks or stretches a line of type to fit the width of a column; the second converts character outlines to paths, as I discuss in the next section.

The purpose of the Fit Headline command is to modify a line of text so it fills the entire width of a text block. The command takes an entire paragraph, from one carriage return to the next, and puts it all on one line. Therefore, you'll want to apply it to headlines no more than a few words long, like *Monkey Brains* in Figure 7-34.

To use this feature, click in the paragraph you want to shrink or stretch with the type tool and choose Type » Fit Headline. You can apply the command only after selecting the text with the type tool—clicking inside the paragraph is enough—and the paragraph must be set inside a text block or area text.

The top two examples in Figure 7-34 show what happens when you apply the Fit Headline command to line of type. In the first example, the single word *Monkey* is too narrow to fit the width of the column. When I chose Type » Fit Headline, Illustrator added sufficient kerning to the letters to stretch them across the column. In the second example, the two-word paragraph is too wide to fit. Fit Headline reduced the kerning of these characters to fit.

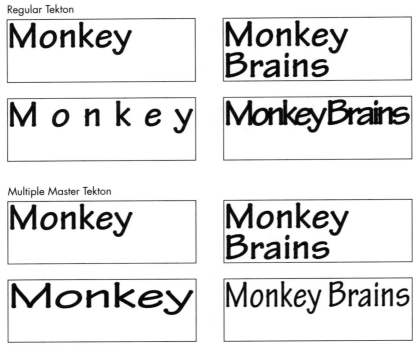

Regular Tekton

Multiple Master Tekton

Figure 7-34: The results of applying the Fit Headline command to lines of type that are too narrow (left) and too wide (right) for their text blocks.

But let's be honest. You could have kerned the text yourself by pressing Option with the left and right arrow keys. And you wouldn't have kerned Monkey Brains to the points that the characters overlapped, as in the second example in the figure. That's just plain ugly.

In fact, Fit Headline is actually designed to work with Multiple Master fonts, which are special PostScript fonts designed by Adobe. Unlike the Expert Collection fonts, which are just extra sets of characters, Multiple Master fonts are entirely different creatures. These fonts permit an application to consult pairs of opposing *master designs*, each of which represent extremes in formatting attributes. For example, one master design might be very bold, while its opposite is very light. Or one might include fat characters, while its opposite includes thin ones. The program then blends the two master designs to arrive at a unique variations, called *instances*. Each Multiple Master typeface permits literally thousands of variations in weight, width, size, and slant. Though it's been rather slow to catch on, Multiple Master technology is absolutely amazing stuff.

If a paragraph is formatted with a Multiple Master font, Type » Fit Headline adjusts the weight and width of the font on the fly to fit the text across the length of the column. The lower two examples of Figure 7-34 feature a Multiple Master version of the font Tekton. Notice how Illustrator stretches the word Monkey to fit the line, exaggerating the weight and expanding the width of each character. There is none of the distortion that you get with the Horizontal Scale option; the proportions of the characters appear uniform and even. The kerning remains unchanged as well. The condensed *Monkey Brains* text is likewise proportional. Though significantly reduced in weight and width, it is just as legible and unremarkable as the original text. Illustrator adjusts all characters according to designer-approved specifications, which is the inherent beauty of Multiple Master fonts.

 If you have a Multiple Master typeface loaded into your system, you can use Adobe Type Manager 3.9 to generate stylistic variations that you can then use in Illustrator and other applications. After choosing Apple » Control Panels » ~ATM, click on the Create MM Instances button. ATM displays the dialog box shown in Figure 7-35. Select the font that you want to adjust from the pop-up menu on the left side of the dialog box (TektoMMObl in the figure). Then adjust the slider bars to modify the weight, width, and other attributes. (The specific sliders available depend on the selected font.) Once you get an effect you like, click on the Create button. ATM adds the variation to the font menu of every application you run from now on.

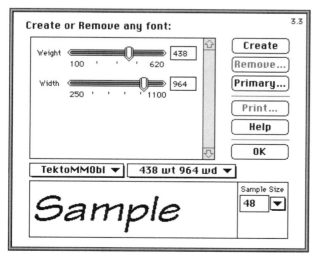

Figure 7-35: You can now create variations on Multiple Master fonts inside the ATM 3.9 control panel.

Converting Character Outlines to Paths

The final type ability in Illustrator is both the most essential and more straightforward. By choosing Type » Create Outlines, you can convert any selected text block into a collection of editable paths. The only catch is that the type must be selected with the arrow tool—you can't highlight it with the type tool. But this will seem like a small inconvenience when you see how quickly and powerfully the command performs.

The left example in Figure 7-36 shows a three-character text block selected using the arrow tool. The second example shows the characters after choosing the Create Outlines command. The characters are now standard paths, composed of points and segments, just like those created with the freehand or pen tool.

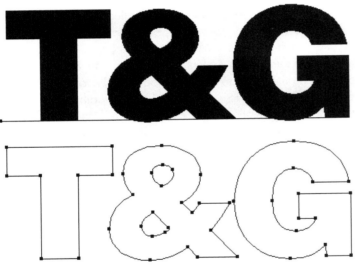

Figure 7-36: Select a text block (top) and choose Type » Create Outlines to produce a collection of fully editable points and segments (bottom).

Of the three characters in the figure, notice that Illustrator has converted the *T* and *G* into a single path apiece, while it converted the ampersand into three paths. To make interior paths transparent, like those in the ampersand, Illustrator converts each character into a *compound path*. In this way, it lets you see through the holes in the character to the objects behind it (as discussed in Chapter 9).

Compound paths are all very well and good, but they can also get in your way. If you later try to join part of a path in the ampersand to another path, for example, Illustrator will refuse to participate, whining that the two paths have to be part of the same group. If you encounter something along these lines, select the character with the arrow tool and choose Object » Compound Paths » Release (⌘-9). The transparent areas will fill with color, but you'll be able to edit the paths with absolute freedom.

After you choose the Create Outlines and Release commands, you can reshape, transform, duplicate, and otherwise manipulate converted type in any manner, as demonstrated by the fantastic example in Figure 7-37. It may not be art, but by golly, it's possible.

Figure 7-37: And to think, this was once Helvetica.

 It frequently a good idea to convert logos and headline text to paths, even if you don't plan on editing them. This way, there's no chance the text will shift or the font won't print correctly. For example, I don't know if the designers I'm working with have Tekton loaded on their machines—I assume they don't—so I converted the characters back in Figure 7-34 (and half a billion other figures in this book) to paths to ensure that they print correctly. It increases the size of the file on disk significantly, but insurance has its price.

If you want to reserve the right to edit the text from the keyboard, save one copy of the illustration prior to choosing Type » Create Outlines, and another copy afterward.

THIS IS YOUR BRAIN ON GRAPHS

This seems to me as good a time as any to take a moment out of our busy Illustrator learning schedules and look back on the knowledge we've amassed so far. Since Chapter 4, we've learned how to create just about every kind of graphic and text object on the planet, including geometric shapes, free-form paths, text blocks, path text, and hundreds of infinitesimal variations too tedious to mention.

That leaves just one more item that you can create in Illustrator—a combination of paths and text known as the graph. Yes, few folks know it (and even fewer folks seem to care), but Illustrator lets you create a graph from an everyday average spreadsheet of numbers. And it does a very good job of it.

"Illustrator for graphs?" I hear you arguing, "Surely there are better products for this purpose." Granted—I argue back (tastefully sidestepping the obvious "stop calling me Shirley" joke)—Microsoft Excel provides better number-crunching capabilities, PowerPoint and Persuasion let you build presentations around graphs, and no program competes with DeltaGraph Professional when it comes to scientific and highfalutin' business graphs guaranteed to please long hairs and think tankers in roughly equal portions. But if you're looking to create simple graphs with a designer appeal—like those picture charts that are forever popping up in *USA Today*—then Illustrator is far and away the best program on the market.

But before I go any further, there are some important questions to answer:

- What is the difference between a graph and a chart?
- Are these two terms interchangeable?
- Will snooty power graphers look down their noses at me if I say "chart" when I mean "graph," or vice versa?

The answers are: Nada, yes, and who gives a flying fish? The term *chart* is a little more inclusive than *graph*. Weather folks use charts (not graphs) to show cold fronts and navigators use charts (not graphs) to make sure your plane doesn't plow into a mountainside, but everything that can be called a graph can also be called a chart. So for the purposes of this chapter, they are one and the same.

What I personally rail against is the use of the term *graphic* to mean *graph*, as in Harvard Graphics and Freelance Graphics, two PC charting programs that are altogether useless for drawing. A graphic is a brilliant illustration that sparks the interest, enthusiasm, and imagination of the viewer; a graph is a bunch of lines and rectangles that bores folks silly.

Only in Illustrator can a graph be a graphic.

Creating a Graph

Though you wouldn't know it to look at it, Illustrator offers a lot of graphing options. In fact, it's very easy to get mired down by these options—there are so many of them, they each make such a tiny difference in the outcome of your graph, and they are just plain hard to use.

This is why I've provided the following handy-dandy chart-making steps. Illustrator's many minute graphing variations are likely to make more sense after you've had a chance to create a few graphs of your own.

1. Decide what kind of graph you want to create.

Illustrator offers six kinds of graphs—two kinds of bar graphs (which it calls column graphs), as well as a line graph, pie, area graph (filled lines), and scatter graph (a line graph variation). Never fear, I explore each of these graphs in excrutiating detail later in this chapter.

To specify the kind of graph you want to create, double-click on the graph tool—bottom icon on the left side of the toolbox—to display the Graph Style dialog box. (Or you can choose Object » Graphs » Style.) Then select an option from the Graph Type radio buttons and press Return. (Figure 8-1 demonstrates this step for visual thinkers.) Illustrator even changes the appearance of the graph tool icon to show you that you have switched to a different kind of chart.

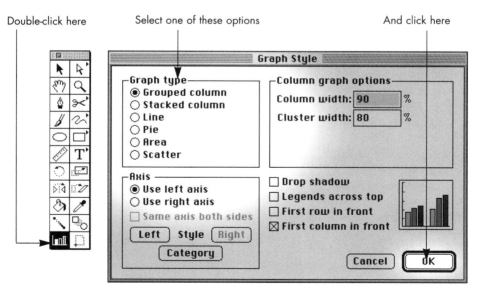

Figure 8-1: Double-click on the graph tool and select a Graph Type option to decide which kind of graph you want to create.

2. **Drag with the graph tool**.

   The dimensions of your drag determine the size of the graph. After you release the mouse button, Illustrator displays the Graph Data window, which is where you enter the numbers you want to graph.

3. **Enter or import your data**.

   You can either enter numbers directly into the Graph Data window, or import them from a spreadsheet program. If you hate math, make a coworker give you the numbers. You're an artist, darn it, not an accountant!

4. **Press the Enter key**.

   Illustrator closes the Graph Data window and generates a chart from your numbers. You just have to sit there and admire the wonderful world of automation.

5. **Change the Graph Style attributes**.

   With the graph selected, double-click on the graph tool icon in the toolbox to again display the Graph Style dialog box. Here you can monkey around with a bunch of weird options until Illustrator creates a graph more or less to your liking. You can even change the kind of graph, if you want.

6. **Edit the graph manually with the direct selection tool**.

   Ultimately, a graph is just a collection of paths and point text. This means you can move graph elements and text with the direct selection tool, edit the text with the type tool, and fill and stroke the paths with different colors.

You can revisit Steps 3 through 6 as many times as you want to modify the graph again and again. To modify the data for a selected chart, for example, choose Object » Graphs » Data and edit the numbers in the spreadsheet. You can even import an entirely new set of numbers.

There are just two points to keep in mind:

● Applying options from the Graph Style dialog box or Graph Data window may negate manual changes that you've made with the direct selection and type tools. Illustrator tries to retain your manual changes when possible, but be prepared to reapply your modifications. Or better yet, try to get the automated stuff in Steps 3 through 5 out of the way before making your manual changes in Step 6.

In Illustrator, a graph is a special kind of grouped object. Some path operations—particularly the Join and Pathfinder commands that I discuss in Chapter 9—won't work on paths inside a group. You also can't convert type to outlines inside a graph. If you need access to these functions, you have to first ungroup the graph by choosing Arrange » Ungroup (or pressing ⌘-U).

WARNING While the Ungroup command expands your range of creative adjustments, it also terminates the graph, eliminating any link between the one-time chart and its data. After you press ⌘-U, you forfeit your ability to apply options from either the Graph Style dialog box or Graph Data window. Therefore, don't ungroup until you are absolutely 100 percent satisfied with the numerical data represented in the graph.

You can of course backstep an operation by pressing ⌘-Z (Edit » Undo). If you apply a few Graph Style options and upset a manual adjustment, or if you ungroup the graph and think better of it, the Undo command is always at the ready to bring things back to their previous state.

Defining the Graph Size with the Graph Tool

The main purpose of any graphing tool is to determine the rectangular dimensions of a chart. You draw with a graphing tool just as if you were drawing with the rectangle tool. In other words, you can avail yourself of any of the following techniques:

- Drag to draw the chart boundary from corner to corner.

- Option-drag to draw the boundary from center to corner.

- Shift-drag or Shift-Option-drag to draw a square boundary.

- Click to display the tiny Graph dialog box, which contains Width and Height option boxes. Enter the horizontal and vertical dimensions of the desired chart and press Return. The click point becomes the upper left corner of the chart boundary.

- Option-click with the graph tool and enter the numerical dimensions if you want the click point to serve as the center of the graph.

Regardless of how you define the boundary of the graph, this area encloses only the graphic elements of the chart. The labels and the legend extend outside the boundary. In Figure 8-2, for example, the dotted outline shows the dimensions of the drag with the graph tool. The gray area represents portions of the graph that lie outside the boundary. You can change the size of the labels and you can move the legend if you need to, but they do take up space.

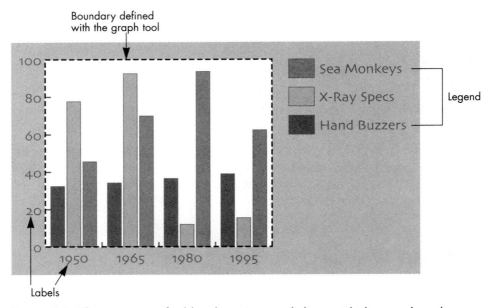

Figure 8-2: The area specified by dragging or clicking with the graph tool (represented by the dotted outline) holds just the graphic elements.

Don't worry too much if you don't know exactly how large or small you want the graph to be when you first create it. You can always enlarge or reduce it with the scale tool later. (The scale tool is a prominent topic of Chapter 11.) The only thing is, if you resize the graph disproportionately, you'll likewise disproportionately stretch (or shrink) text and other elements.

Figure 8-3 demonstrates what happens when you scale two kinds of graphs—bar and pie—disproportionately. The top two examples were created by clicking with the graph tool and entering 14p and 12p (14 and 12 picas) into the Width and Height options. To create the bottom two examples, I entered 8p and 10p for the Width and Height values, resulting in graphs that were taller than they were wide. I then enlarged the graphs disproportionately with the scale tool.

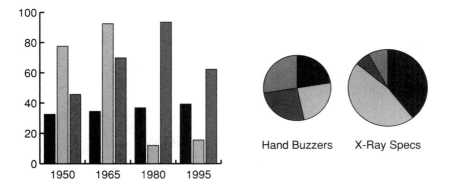

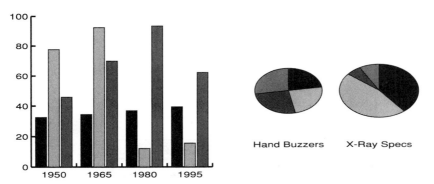

Figure 8-3: I created the top two graphs at the size you see them, but I drew the bottom graphs at smaller sizes and enlarged them disproportionately.

The scaled bar graph generally looks fine; only the text appears stretched. The pie graph, however, does not fare so well. Because each pie is a perfect circle, the shapes suffer when you scale them disproportionately. So my advice is, go ahead and scale bar, line, and area graphs any old way you want; but be careful to scale pie charts and scatter graphs (which have square points in them) by the same percentage vertically and horizontally.

 Scaling is a necessary part of the graphing process. But that's no excuse for stretched or squished text. After you scale, return your text to the proper proportions using the Horizontal Scale option in the Character palette. Assuming the graph is still selected, display the Horizontal Scale option by pressing ⌘-Shift-K (which makes sure the palette is expanded) and click on the words Horizontal Scale. Illustrator restores the Horizontal Scale value to 100 percent.

If this makes the text too small or too large, press ⌘-Shift-S and enter a new Size value, or press ⌘-Shift-⊙ or ⌘-Shift-⊙ to adjust the type size incrementally.

Using the Graph Data Window

After you drag with the graph tool (or click and enter the graph dimensions), the Graph Data window pops up on screen, as in Figure 8-4. This is a window, not a dialog box, which contains its own size box and scroll bars. It is also more functional than a dialog box. You can click outside the Graph Data window to bring the illustration window to the front of the desktop. Although the Graph Data window may disappear from view, it remains open behind the illustration window, so you don't lose any changes you may have made. To bring the Graph Data

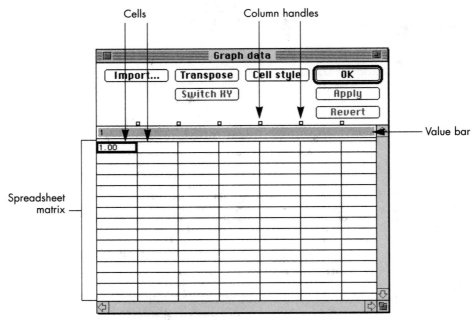

Figure 8-4: The Graph Data window contains a spreadsheet made up of rows and columns of cells.

window back to the front of the desktop, click on its title bar or choose the Object » Graphs » Data command from the Graph menu. (Alas, while this is for all intents and purposes an open window, Illustrator does not list it as an option under the Window menu.)

The *spreadsheet matrix* that occupies the lower two-thirds of the Graph Data window is similar to the matrix provided inside a standard spreadsheet program like Excel. The spreadsheet contains rows and columns of individual containers, called *cells*. Numbers entered into the cells can represent dollars, times, dates, or percentages (though you should avoid symbols, such as $, %, and others). You can even enter words for labels and legends.

However, unlike a true spreadsheet, you cannot enter formulas, since Illustrator lacks a calculation feature. (You can't even take advantage of Illustrator 6's adding function, which works in many palettes and dialog boxes, including the little dialog box that comes up when you click with the graph tool.)

Data entered from the keyboard appears in the value bar at the top of the spreadsheet (labeled in Figure 8-4). Press Return or Tab to transfer the data from the value bar into the current cell and advance to another cell.

As you type, most keys insert the standard characters that appear on the key. Some keys and characters, however, perform special functions:

- **Tab or right arrow**: Accepts the data in the value bar and moves one cell to the right (to the next cell in the row).

- **Left arrow**: Accepts the data in the value bar and moves one cell to the left.

- **Return or down arrow**: Accepts the data in the value bar and moves one cell down (to the next cell in the column).

- **Up arrow**: Accepts the data in the value bar and moves one cell up.

- **Quote marks** ("): Enter quotes around numeric data to use a number as a label, such as a product number or year. If a cell consists entirely of numbers without quote marks, Illustrator interprets the data as a value and graphs it.

 If you want Illustrator to display your quotes in the graph, use the curly opening and closing quotes, " and " (Option-Ⓣ and Shift-Option-Ⓣ), rather than the straight quote.

- **Vertical line character** (|) . If you want a label to contain multiple lines of text, enter the vertical line (Shift-\) to represent a line break character.

⬤   **Enter**. Accepts the data in the value bar and selects the OK button, exiting the Graph Data window.

For most kinds of charts, you can enter legend text into the top row, and labels into the left-hand column of cells. (Legend text explains what the different colors in the graph mean; labels typically appear along the bottom of the graph). To create such graph text, delete the data from the very first cell (at the intersection of the first row and column) and leave it empty. All other cells in the top row and left column should contain at least one non-numeric character or quote marks around the numbers, as in Figure 8-5.

	Hand Buzzers	X-Ray Specs	Sea Monkeys	
"1950"	32.57	77.60	45.70	
"1965"	34.44	92.50	69.90	
"1980"	36.84	12.04	93.60	
"1995"	39.34	15.55	62.34	

Figure 8-5: As long as the first cell is empty, you can use the top row and the left column to hold labels.

If you don't want Illustrator to create a legend, enter a label or value into the first cell and fill the top row of cells with values. If I just deleted the first line of items from the matrix in Figure 8-5, for example, and scooted up the other rows, I would get labels but no legend.

If after entering a label or legend text, you can't see the full text inside the cell, it isn't because the text is lost, the cell is just too narrow to display it. You can widen the cell by dragging a column handle (labeled in Figure 8-4) as described in the "Adjusting the Way Cells Look" section later in this chapter.

Importing Data from Disk

Because the Graph Data window provides no calculation capabilities and its cell-editing functions are limited—you can't insert, delete, or sort cells—you may prefer to import values created in another program. You can create your data in any spreadsheet program capable of saving a *tab-delineated* file, which is a plain text file with tabs between values and carriage returns between rows. Virtually every spreadsheet program supports this format, including Microsoft Excel, Claris Resolve, the age-old MacCalc, and Lotus 1-2-3. The file can originate on a PC just as easily as on a Mac.

 You can even create your data in a word processor such as Microsoft Word or WordPerfect. When entering the data, insert tabs between values and insert carriage returns between rows of values. Then save the finished file as a plain text document.

   To import data from disk, open the Graph Data window and click on the cell where you want the imported data to start. Click on the Import button to display a standard Open dialog box. Locate the file you want to import and double-click on its name in the scrolling list, or select the file and press Return. The imported data appears in the spreadsheet in rows and columns starting in the selected cell.

 If any of the cells below or to the right of the selected cell already contain data, Illustrator replaces the old data with the new.

Subscribing to Published Data

   If you create graphs with any degree of regularity, you'll appreciate the Graph Data window's support for your system software's *publish and subscribe* function. In a nutshell, you can use Excel, Word, or some other program to publish a spreadsheet to disk, and then subscribe to it inside Illustrator. From this point on, whenever you modify the published spreadsheet from Excel or Word, the graph inside Illustrator will automatically update.

 This little-known technique (discovered, I must confess, not by myself, but by Thunder Lizards cofounder and crack trainer Steve "Magic Fingers" Broback) involves a tiny bit more work than simply importing a spreadsheet from disk. But it's one of those classic situations where a little effort expended now ensures far less effort in the future. Here's what you do:

1. **Inside Excel or Word, select the numbers that you want to graph inside Illustrator**.

   Just drag over the numbers with the cursor to highlight them.

2. Choose Edit » Publishing » Create Publisher.

This command takes the data and publishes it inside something called an *edition file*. (Don't you just love all this newspaper lingo? You publish a late-breaking edition from one program, and another program scurries to subscribe to it.) The Create Publisher command brings up a modified Save dialog box.

3. Enter a name for the edition and press Return.

That's it. You don't have to select any special options when you're working inside either Excel or Word. (The same holds true for most other applications, although I can't vouch for all of them.)

4. Switch to Illustrator.

If the sacred program is not running, by all means, fire it up.

5. Create a new graph with the graph tool.

Or select an existing graph with the arrow tool and choose Object » Graphs » Data. You can just as easily apply published data to a graph you created eons ago as to a new one.

6. Click on the cell where you want the published data to start.

Any cells to the right and down will be overwritten.

7. Choose Edit » Publishing » Subscribe To.

You can access this command from inside the Graph Data window.

8. Locate the edition file, select it, and press Return.

Illustrator loads the published numbers into the Graph Data spreadsheet. A heavy border surrounds the published data, as in Figure 8-6. Though you can select cells inside this heavy outline, you cannot modify their contents.

The border always appears when you click inside a subscribed cell. If you don't want to see the border when some other cell is selected, choose Edit » Publishing » Hide Border.

9. Press the Enter key.

Illustrator closes the Graph Data window and updates the graph in the illustration window.

	Hand Buzzers	X-Ray Specs	Sea Monkeys	
"1950"	32.57	77.60	45.70	
"1965"	34.44	92.50	69.90	
"1980"	36.84	12.04	93.60	
"1995"	39.34	15.55	62.34	

Figure 8-6: The heavy border shows that the data inside comes from an edition file on disk.

That's it for establishing a link between data saved to disk and a graph created inside Illustrator. To update the graph in the future, all you have to do is update the data inside the original Excel or Word document—you never open the edition file—then save the modified document as you normally do by pressing ⌘-S. Excel or Word automatically saves both the original document and the published data at once.

When you switch back to Illustrator, this program automatically updates the graph, whether or not the Graph Data window is open, entirely without any help or encouragement from you.

 If the graph doesn't appear to change, the default publish and subscribe setting may be messed up. Inside Excel 5, choose Edit » Links and make sure the Automatic radio button is selected. Inside Word, choose Edit » Publishing » Publisher Options and make sure the On Save radio button is selected. And last but clearly not least, open up the Graph Data window inside Illustrator, click on the subscribed data, choose Edit » Publishing » Subscriber Options, and select Automatic from the Get Editions radio buttons.

If you ever want to break the link between the Illustrator graph and the edition file on disk, choose Edit » Publishing » Subscriber Options from inside the Graph Data window, and click on the Cancel Subscriber button. Then click on the Yes button inside the meddlesome alert box.

Selecting and Modifying Cells

You select cells in the spreadsheet by dragging across them. Or you can press the Shift key while pressing one of the arrow keys to add to a range of selected cells, or delete from them. All selected cells become highlighted—white against black—except the cell that you're entering data into, which has a big, fat border around it.

Though you can't perform fancy tricks like inserting or deleting cells inside the Graph Data window, you can move data around within cells using one of the following techniques:

- Cut or copy data from one location and paste it into another. You can either use the keyboard shortcuts ⌘-X, ⌘-C, or ⌘-V, or choose commands from the Edit menu.

 For example, to nudge all cells upward one row (the effect achieved by deleting a row inside Excel), select the cells, press ⌘-X, click on the first cell in the row you want to replace, and press ⌘-V.

- Click on the Transpose button to swap rows and columns of data in the spreadsheet matrix. The data in the top row goes to the left column, and vice versa. This button affects all data in the spreadsheet, regardless of which cells, if any, are selected.

- Click on the Switch XY button to swap columns of data in a scatter chart. The data in the first column moves to the second, the data in the second column moves to the first, the data in the third column moves to the fourth, and so on. This button is dimmed when you're creating or editing any kind of chart except a scatter chart, and it applies to all data in the spreadsheet.

- You can delete the contents of multiple selected cells by choosing Edit » Clear or by pressing the Clear key. (Pressing the Delete key deletes the contents of the active cell only.)

- Press ⌘-Z or choose Edit » Undo to undo the last operation. If you just finished changing a cell value, for example, ⌘-Z restores the previous data in the value bar. As in the rest of Illustrator, you have multiple undos inside the Graph Data window, so edit with impunity. You can even undo large operations like importing, transposing, or pasting data.

Copying Data from a Different Graph

The fact that the Graph Data window stays up on screen makes it easy to copy data from one graph and paste it into another. For example, suppose that you just dragged with the graph tool to start a new graph, and Illustrator has displayed the Graph Data window. Suddenly, you remember that you want to create this new chart based on a chart you created a few days ago. But you don't have that old chart open right now. No problem. You can access the data without even closing the Graph Data window:

1. Click in the illustration window to bring it to front. This gives you access to Illustrator's standard menu commands.

2. Press ⌘-O and open the illustration that contains the chart that you want to copy.

3. Select the chart with the arrow tool.

4. If you can see a smidgen of the Graph Data window, click on its title bar to bring it to front. Otherwise, choose Object » Graphs » Data. The Graph Data window shows the data for the selected graph.

5. Drag over the data that you want to copy from the previous chart and press ⌘-C (or choose Edit » Copy).

6. Click on the title bar for the illustration window that contains the new chart in progress. If necessary, select the chart with the arrow tool.

7. Click on the Graph Data window again. When you bring the Graph Data window to front, it automatically shows the data for the selected chart.

8. Click the first cell and press ⌘-V (or choose Edit » Paste). There's your data. Now you can edit it in any manner you deem appropriate.

You can copy as much data or as little data as you wish. To highlight the cells you want to copy, just drag over them. And click on a cell before pressing ⌘-V to decide where you want the pasted data to start.

 Illustrator lets you paste any type into the Graph Data window. You can copy words or paragraphs from a block of text in the illustration window and paste them into a graph. You can also copy data from the spreadsheet and paste it into a text block.

Changing the Way Cells Look

The final adjustment that you can make to cells in the Graph Data window is purely cosmetic. The Cell Style button allows you to adjust both the width of the columns in the spreadsheet and the number of digits that follow a decimal point. These controls affect only the appearance of data in the spreadsheet; they do not affect the appearance of the chart in the illustration window.

Click on the Cell Style button to display a dialog box that contains the following two option boxes:

- **Number of Decimals**: Enter any value between 0 and 10 into the Number of Decimals option box. This option determines the number of *significant digits*; that is, the number of characters that can appear after a decimal point in a cell.

- **Column Width**: This value controls the default width of each cell in the Graph Data window, measured in digits. Enter any value between 3 and 20.

 To adjust the width of a single column of cells, drag the corresponding column handle above the value bar, as demonstrated in Figure 8-7. The column is widened or narrowed by the nearest whole-digit increment.

	Hand	X-Ray	Sea			
"1950"	12.57	77.60	45.70			
"1965"	14.44	92.50	69.90			
"1980"	16.84	12.04	93.60			
"1995"	19.34	15.55	62.34			

	Hand	X-Ray Specs	Sea	
"1950"	12.57	77.60	45.70	
"1965"	14.44	92.50	69.90	
"1980"	16.84	12.04	93.60	
"1995"	19.34	15.55	62.34	

Figure 8-7: Drag the column handle above the value bar (top) to change the width of a column of cells (bottom).

Transforming Your Data into a Graph

So far, I've instructed you to press the Enter key to update the graph in the illustration window. But this isn't the only way to go. The Graph Data window provides many ways to update the graph; or you can exit the window without updating.

The following is a brief explanation of the update, exit, and reversion elements in the Graph Data window:

- **The OK button** (Enter key): Click on the OK button or press Enter (not Return) to exit the Graph Data window and apply your changes.

- **The Apply button** (Option-Enter): Click on the Apply button or press Option-Enter to update the graph in the illustration window without leaving the Graph Data window. If you can't see the graph because the Graph Data window is in the way, drag the Graph Data title bar to move the window partially off screen. By keeping the Graph Data window up on screen, you can quickly make changes if the data doesn't graph the way you hoped it would.

- **The Revert button**: Click on Revert to restore the data that were in force the last time you clicked on the OK or Apply button.

- **Close box**: If you want to exit the Graph Data window without implementing your changes, click in the close box in the upper left corner of the window, then click on the Don't Save button in the alert box (or press the D key).

 You can also cancel your modifications to a graph by simply selecting a different object in the illustration window or in a different drawing altogether. Illustrator displays an alert box, asking if you want to save your changes to the last graph. Press D if you don't want to, Return if you do.

You can undo the creation or alteration of a chart after clicking on the OK or Apply button by pressing ⌘-Z.

Organizing Your Data for Different Kinds of Graphs

You might hope that you could enter your data in any old way and have Illustrator graph it in the precise manner you've envisioned in your head. But the program isn't quite so gifted at reading your mind. Therefore, you have to organize your data in a manner that Illustrator—mildly dictatorial program that it is—deems appropriate.

Just to keep you on your toes, Illustrator requires you to organize your data differently for different kinds of graphs. The following sections explore each of the six kinds of graphs and tell you how to set up your data for each.

Bar Chart Data

When creating a plain old everyday bar graph—called a grouped column chart for reasons that will become apparent as our graphing journey progresses—Illustrator expects you to organize your data in what I will henceforth call "standard form." But before I tell you what that standard form is, a word or two about this classic kind of chart.

Bar charts are most commonly used to demonstrate a change in data over a period of time. The horizontal axis (*X-axis*) may be divided into time units, measured in days, months, or years. The vertical axis (*Y-axis*) tracks values, which may be measured in units sold, dollars or other currency, or whatever your favorite commodity may be.

As shown in Figure 8-8, bars rise up from the X-axis equivalent in height to a value on the Y-axis. The taller the bar, the greater the value it represents. Illustrator's bar are always vertical—there's no way to change this except by rotating the graph. (In fact, this is the reason Illustrator uses the term *columns* instead of *bars*. Graphing pros call vertical rectangles *columns*, horizontal ones *bars*, and never the twain shall meet. But I'm not a graphing pro, so I can say *bar* whenever I feel like it.)

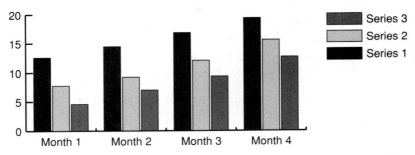

Figure 8-8: An example of a standard bar chart, in which series of bars are clustered together to show change in multiple items over time.

You can graph multiple collections of data in the chart. Each collection is called a *series*. Back in Figure 8-2, for example, Sea Monkeys, X-ray Specs, and Hand Buzzers are each separate series. Corresponding bars from each series are clustered together for the sake of visual comparison. Hence, this type of chart is known in some circles as a *cluster bar chart* or—according to Illustrator—a *grouped column chart* (although these clusters aren't groups according to Illustrator's usual interpretation of the word).

By default, bars from different series are filled with different gray values (though you can apply your own colors using the direct selection tool, as I explain later in the chapter). The colors representing the series are defined in the legend, which appears in the upper right portion of Figure 8-8.

To create a bar chart, arrange your data as shown in Figure 8-9. Here are a few details to keep in mind:

◉ Delete the contents of the first cell, and leave it empty.

◉ Enter series labels in the top row of cells. This text will appear in the legend.

Figure 8-9: Organize bar chart data into columns under series labels. This data corresponds to the bar chart shown in Figure 8-3.

	Series 1	Series 2	Series 3	
Month 1	12.57	77.60	45.70	
Month 2	14.44	92.50	69.90	
Month 3	16.84	12.04	93.60	
Month 4	19.34	15.55	12.63	

◉ Enter X-axis labels in the left column. They will appear underneath the chart along the horizontal axis.

◉ Organize each series of data into a column under the appropriate series label. Do not enter characters other than numbers. If you use a currency symbol, such as $, £, or ¥, Illustrator won't graph the value.

◉ Illustrator generates the Y-axis labels automatically, in accordance with the data. You can customize the Y-axis labels using options in the Graph Style dialog box, which I naturally explain later.

Stacked Bar Chart Data

Stacked bar charts (which Illustrator calls *stacked column charts*) are much like cluster bar charts, except that bars from each series are stacked on top of each other, rather than positioned side by side. A stacked bar chart shows the sum of every series.

You can create a *percentage chart* like the one shown in Figure 8-10 by organizing your data so that all values for each series add up to 100. Percentage charts demonstrate relative performance. If Department A is trouncing Department B, you can broadcast the news with a percentage chart.

Arrange data for a stacked bar chart in the standard form, with series labels in the top row, and X-axis labels in the left column, as in Figure 8-11. Organize series

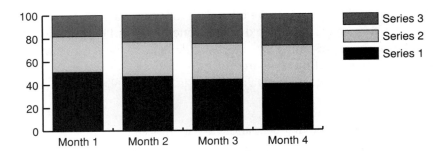

Figure 8-10: This percentage chart is a variety of stacked bar chart in which each column of series values adds up to 100.

of data into columns under the series labels. Whatever you do, don't enter a percentage symbol or any other non-number characters. If you do, Illustrator won't graph the value.

	Series 1	Series 2	Series 3	
Month 1	51.00	31.00	18.00	
Month 2	47.00	30.00	23.00	
Month 3	44.00	31.00	25.00	
Month 4	40.00	33.00	27.00	

Figure 8-11: This data corresponds to the percentage chart shown in Figure 8-10. Notice that the values along each row add up to 100.

Illustrator can't automatically convert sales values to percentages, so you can either enter the percentages manually or make a program like Excel do the work. To accomplish the latter in Excel 5, follow these steps:

1. Enter the sales values in Excel in standard form.

Don't even think about percentages. Just enter normal values.

2. Select each row of values one at a time, and click on the AutoSum button.

Labeled in Figure 8-12, the AutoSum button looks like a sigma (Σ) in the ribbon bar. Excel creates a sum total for each row in the column after the selection (the bold items in the figure).

3. Create a new cell in which you divide the first sales number by the first sum and multiply the result by 100.

Make sure to fix the column letter using the dollar sign character. For example, if the first cell were B2, and the sum cell were E2—as they are in Figure 8-12—you'd enter *B2/$E2*100* (where / is the division symbol and * is multiply).

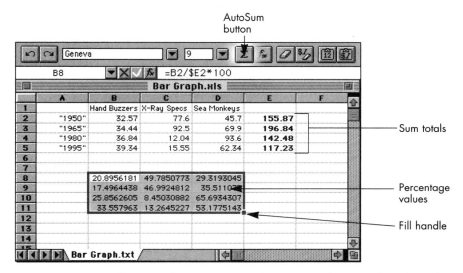

Figure 8-12: A collection of percentage values created in Excel and ready to publish for use in Illustrator.

 I know, you're thinking, "But, Deke, how do you know so much about creating formulas in Excel?" The truth is, while my first major in college was art, my second was math. The one thing I *never* studied was writing (which I demonstrate daily in my peculiar abuse of the English language).

4. Duplicate the formulas to the right and then down by dragging the fill handle.

The fill handle is that little square in the lower right corner of the selected cell (labeled in Figure 8-12). You have to drag it right and then drag down in two separate movements. This creates a matrix of new percentage values. They may not look like percentages—just a bunch of long numbers like the selected cells in Figure 8-12. But they'll work fine. And don't change the number formatting—remember, Illustrator can't read percentage signs.

5. **Select the new percentage values and publish them**.

   Follow the same steps I outlined back in the "Subscribing to Published Data" section earlier in this chapter.

6. **Switch to Illustrator and subscribe to the data**.

   Create a new stacked bar chart, enter your own labels in the top row and left column, and subscribe to the Excel data starting in the second-to-top, second-to-left cell.

7. **Press the Enter key**.

   You now have a percentage chart.

To update the chart in the future, just edit your sales values in Excel. The program will automatically calculate the totals and percentage numbers and ship them off to Illustrator every time you press ⌘-S.

Line Chart Data

Like bar charts, line charts are generally used to show changes in items over a period of time. Straight segments connect points which represent values, as shown in Figure 8-13. Several straight segments combine to form a line, which represents a complete series. The inclination of a segment clearly demonstrates the performance of a series from one point in time to the next. Because large changes result in steep inclinations, line charts clearly demonstrate dramatic fluctuations.

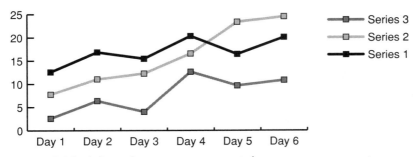

Figure 8-13: A line chart comprises straight segments connecting square value points.

Figure 8-14 shows the data used to create Figure 8-13. As with bar charts, you organize the data into the standard form, with series labels at top, X-axis labels on the left, and columns of series data.

Figure 8-14:
Here's the data for the
line chart in Figure 8-13.
Each column of numbers
results in a single line.

	Series 1	Series 2	Series 3	
Day 1	12.57	7.76	2.57	
Day 2	16.84	11.04	6.36	
Day 3	15.44	12.25	3.99	
Day 4	20.34	16.55	12.63	
Day 5	16.42	23.35	9.65	
Day 6	20.08	24.49	10.82	

Although line chart data may fluctuate dramatically, you don't want series to cross each other more than one or twice in the entire chart. If the series cross too often, the result is what snooty graphing pros derisively call a "spaghetti chart," which is difficult to read and can prove more confusing than instructive.

Pie Chart Data

A pie chart is the easiest kind of chart to create. However, pie charts are not nearly as versatile as the bar and line varieties. Only one series can be expressed per pie. If you want to show more than one series for comparative purposes, each series gets a pie of its own, as in Figure 8-15.

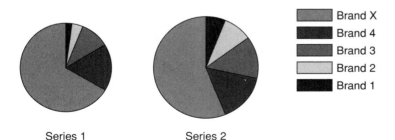

Series 1   Series 2

Figure 8-15: Two pie charts, each representing a single series. The first pie is smaller than the second because the second series includes larger values.

The advantage of a pie chart is that it always displays a series of values in relation to the whole. The entire series inhabits a 360-degree circle and each value within the series occupies a percentage of that circle.

Figure 8-16 shows the data for the pies in Figure 8-15. You organize data for a pie chart in virtually the opposite manner you organize it for a bar or line chart, with the series running across the rows instead of down the columns. Here are a few guidelines:

- Delete the contents of the first cell, and leave it empty, just like always.
- Enter value labels in the top row of cells. These labels appear in the legend.
- Enter series labels in the left column. The labels appear as titles below the pies, as in Figure 8-15. (If you plan on graphing more than two series, I recommend you use a different kind of chart.)
- Organize each series of data into a row to the right of the series label.

	Brand 1	Brand 2	Brand 3	Brand 4	Brand X	
Series 1	0.98	1.56	4.07	6.76	26.57	
Series 2	3.24	4.67	6.99	8.25	29.34	

Figure 8-16: Organize pie chart data into rows. Each row represents a different pie.

If you want to take a couple of series from a bar chart and represent them inside pie charts, copy them from the spreadsheet for the bar chart, paste them into the pie chart spreadsheet, and click on the Transpose button to switch the rows and columns.

Area Chart Data

An area chart is little more than a filled-in line chart. However, the series of an area chart are stacked one on top of another—just as in a stacked bar chart—to display the sum of all series, as shown in Figure 8-17.

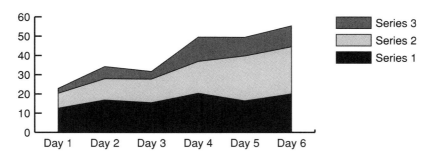

Figure 8-17: In an area chart, series are stacked on top of each other and filled in with colors or gray values.

 If you encounter the spaghetti effect (overlapping lines) when creating a line chart, the easiest solution is to convert the line chart into an area chart.

When creating an area chart, arrange your data in the standard form. In fact, Figure 8-17 uses the same data as the line chart from Figure 8-13. The data appears in Figure 8-14.

Scatter Chart Data

Like a line chart, a scatter chart plots points again the horizontal and vertical axes and connects these points with straight segments. However, rather than merely aligning series of values along a set of X-axis labels, the scatter graph pairs up columns of values. The first column of data represents Y-axis (series) coordinates; the second column represents X-axis coordinates. This setup permits you to map scientific data or to graph multiple series that occur over different time patterns.

For example, in Figure 8-18, the black line (Series 1) connects 13 points, while the gray line (Series 2) connects 10. And yet, both lines run the entire width of the graph. You tell Illustrator which X-axis and Y-axis coordinates to plot; Illustrator just connects them with segments. This is both the most versatile and most complex graph you can create.

Figure 8-19 shows the data for the scatter chart in Figure 8-18. The data is arranged into pairs of columns, each pair representing a separate series.

● Enter series labels into the top row of cells, one label for each odd column (first, third, fifth, and so on). Leave even-numbered cells empty.

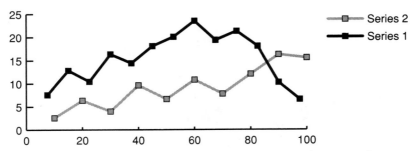

Figure 8-18: Illustrator plots points in a scatter graph at specific X, Y-coordinates and connects the points with straight segments.

As with line charts, the series labels appear in the legend.

● Enter Y-axis (series) data in the odd-numbered columns.

● Enter X-axis data in the even-numbered columns. Illustrator plots side-by-side columns of data as paired points. In other words, each pair of values in the first and second columns is plotted as a point in the first series, each pair in the third and fourth columns is plotted as a point in the second series, and so on.

● Illustrator automatically generates Y-axis and X-axis labels that correspond to the data.

Series 1		Series 2		
7.57	7.50	2.57	10.00	
12.84	15.00	6.36	20.00	
10.44	22.50	3.99	30.00	
16.34	30.00	9.63	40.00	
14.42	37.50	6.65	50.00	
18.08	45.00	10.82	60.00	
20.06	52.50	7.76	70.00	
23.49	60.00	12.04	80.00	
19.35	67.50	16.25	90.00	
21.26	75.00	15.55	100.00	
18.05	82.50			
10.24	90.00			
6.56	97.50			

Figure 8-19: Each series of scatter chart data takes up two columns, with the Y-axis values first and the X-axis values second.

Applying Automated Changes to a Graph

Remember the six basic steps required to create a graph in Illustrator? (If not, you can refresh your memory by peeking at the "Creating a Graph" section at the beginning of this chapter.) As of this moment in time, we've exhausted the first four. Step 5 encouraged you to apply automated changes using the Graph Style dialog box. That's what these next sections are all about.

To access these options, select the graph you want to edit and double-click on the graph tool icon in the toolbox (or choose Object » Graphs » Style). Illustrator displays the Graph Style dialog box, shown in Figure 8-20. This dialog box is quite complicated, providing access to a bunch of options that you don't see on first perusal, including a whole other dialog box.

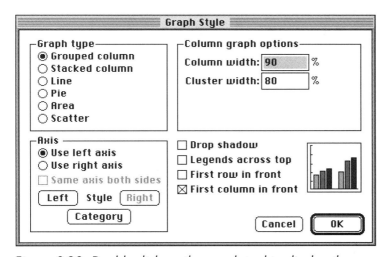

Figure 8-20: Double-click on the graph tool to display the Graph Style dialog box, which lets you apply automated adjustments to a selected graph.

 You can apply options from the Graph Style dialog box to an entire graph selected with the arrow tool, or to a partial graph selected with the direct selection tool. For example, Option-click three times with the direct selection tool on a straight segment in a previously deselected line graph to select the entire series, including the color swatch in the legend. You can then modify that one line independently of the others inside the Graph Style dialog box.

Converting and Tweaking a Graph

You can convert a selected graph from one variety to another—say, from a bar chart to a line chart—by selecting a radio button from the list of Graph Type options in the upper left portion of the dialog box. Just select an option, press Return, and whamo, the chart is changed.

Most likely, you could've figured out that little bit of information without my help. So I mention it by way of introducing an additional set of options in the upper right portion of the Graph Style dialog box. These specialized options change depending on which kind of graph you've selected.

The following items list the type of chart selected from the Graph Type radio buttons, and explain the options associated with each:

- **Grouped Column**: When you select this radio button, two options appear in the Column Graph Options area on the right, as pictured in Figure 8-21. The Column Width value controls the width of each bar in the chart. A value of 100 percent causes bars to touch each other, rubbing shoulders, as it were. The default value of 90 percent allows slight gutters between bars, and values greater than 100 percent cause bars to overlap.

  The second option, Cluster Width, controls the width of each cluster of bars, again measured as a percentage value. The last bar from Series 1 touches the first bar of Series 2 at 100 percent. The default value of 80 percent allows a gutter between clusters. (I don't recommend values greater than 100 percent since it causes clusters to not only overlap each other, but to overlap the vertical axis as well. Frankly, it can be mighty ugly.)

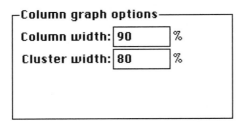

Figure 8-21:
Use these options to change the width of bars and clusters of bars in a chart.

- **Stacked Column**: The Column Graph Options area contains the same options whether a grouped or stacked column chart is selected (see Figure 8-21).

Line: When you select Line from the Graph Type options, four check boxes appear in the Line Graph Options area on right, as shown in Figure 8-22. When selected, the Mark Data Points check box creates square markers at the data points in each line. Turn the check box off to make the square markers disappear. The Connect Data Points check box draws straight segments between points. If this option is deselected, stray markers appear without lines. (Turning off both check boxes makes the series disappear entirely.)

Figure 8-22: These options let you change the square points and straight segments associated with line graphs (and scatter charts).

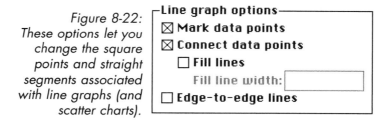

When Connect Data Points is selected, the Fill Lines check box becomes available, permitting you to create thick paths filled with different gray values or colors. Enter the desired thickness into the Fill Line Width option box. Figure 8-23 shows a line graph with paths 12 points thick. Generally, you don't need data points when using fat paths, so you can turn the Mark Data Points check box off.

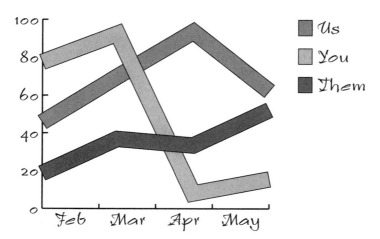

Figure 8-23: A line graph with the Fill Lines check box turned on, the Width value set to 12 points, and Mark Data Points turned off.

Select Edge-to-Edge Lines to draw lines that extend the entire width of the chart, starting at the Y-axis and continuing to the end of the X axis. This option is turned on in Figure 8-23. (By default, it is off.)

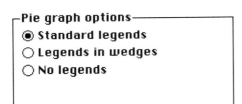 **Pie**: The Pie Graph Area grants you three radio buttons when editing a pie chart. Pictured in Figure 8-24, these options let you change the placement of the pie labels. By default, the Standard Legends radio button is selected, which results in a typical legend that identifies the gray values and colors in the graph. If you instead select Legends in Wedges, Illustrator omits the legend and labels the pie slices directly, as in Figure 8-25. (You'll have to modify the colors of the slices to see the labels, as in the figure—the first slice is always black by default.) Select No Legends to trash the legend altogether.

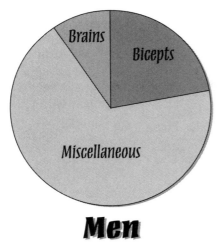

Figure 8-24:
You can change the way slices are labeled when editing a pie chart.

Figure 8-25:
Select the Legends in Wedges to apply labels to the pie slices.

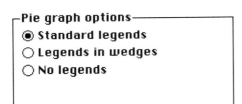 **Area**: I don't know why, but there are no special options associated with an area chart. I wish Illustrator provided at least the Edge-to-Edge check

box to eliminate the gaps between the data lines and the Y-axis, but alas, no such option exists.

- **Scatter**: When you select Scatter from the Graph Type options, you get three check boxes in the Scatter Graph Options area. These are the same options that appear for a line graph, as shown in Figure 8-22, with the exception of the Edge-to-Edge check box, which does not appear.

Adjusting Axes and Labels

The Axis area in the lower left corner of the Graph Style dialog box allows you to control the appearance and positions of the vertical and horizontal axes in a selected chart. All options are dimmed when working on a pie chart, since there is no such thing as a pie chart axis, and the first two radio buttons are dimmed when editing a scatter chart. All other charts have access to the same collection of options.

The first three options control the placement of the vertical Y-axis:

- **Use Left Axis**: Select this radio button to make the Y-axis appear on the left-hand side of the chart, as it does by default. You can then modify the axis by clicking on the Left button. (The Right button is dimmed.)

- **Use Right Axis**: Select this radio button to send the Y-axis to the right side of the chart. Now the Right button is available and the Left button is dimmed.

- **Same Axis Both Sides**: Select this check box to make the Y-axis appear on both sides of the chart. If you have specified different attributes for the left and right axes using the Left and Right buttons, select the Use Left Axis or Use Right Axis radio option to determine which set of attributes is used. (Unfortunately, you can't create a chart with two different Y-axes, as you can in more sophisticated graphing programs.)

Three Style buttons appear at the bottom of the Axis area; only two of the buttons are available at any time. The Left and Right buttons control the Y-axis, and the Category button (called the Bottom button when a scatter chart is selected) controls the horizontal X-axis.

Clicking on any of these buttons displays the Graph Axis Style dialog box shown in Figure 8-26. Here you can specify the location of tick marks and labels on the current axis. The options in the Axis Label and Tick Line Values area affect the labels for the vertical axis, while the options in the Axis Tick Lines and Marks area control the size of *tick marks*, those little lines that indicate numbers along the axes.

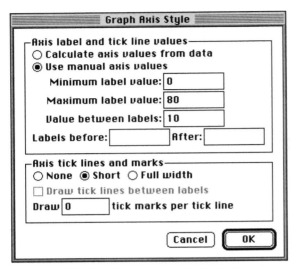

Figure 8-26: The Graph Axis Style dialog box lets you modify the labels on the Y-axis, and the tick marks on both the X- and Y-axes.

The Axis Label and Tick Line Values options are available only when you are setting attributes for the Y-axis of a chart, or the X-axis for a scatter chart. These options are dimmed when editing the X-axis of a bar, line, or area chart (which is any time you entered the dialog box by clicking on the Category button). The options work as follows:

- **Calculate Axis Values from Data**: By default, this radio button is selected. Illustrator automatically determines the number of tick marks and labels that appear on the axis without worrying your pretty head.

- **Use Manual Axis Values**: If you want to specify a range of labels in an axis to enhance the appearance of a chart, select this radio button and enter values in the three option boxes that follow. The Minimum Label Value determines the lowest number on the axis; the Maximum Label Value determines the highest number; and the Value between Labels determines the increment between labels.

  In Figure 8-27, I've raised the Minimum Label Value to 50 and changed the Value between Labels to 10. Illustrator now graphs any data values under 50 below the X-axis. This way, I can track poor performance. For example, this chart tells me I can take Them off probation, but I'm afraid I'm going to have to fire You.

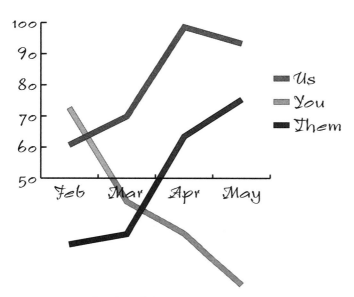

Figure 8-27: If values fall below the Minimum Label Value, Illustrator plots them on the south side of the X-axis.

To turn a chart upside down, so that the highest number is at the bottom of the axis and the lowest number is at the top (as in Figure 8-28), enter a negative number into the Value between Labels option box. To create an axis without labels, enter 0 into this option box.

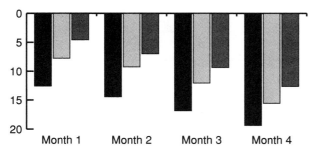

Figure 8-28: Flip a chart upside-down by entering a negative value in the Value between Labels option box.

● **Labels Before/After**: These option boxes permit you to enter symbols or words up to nine characters long to precede or follow each label in a chart. For example, enter $ into the Before option box to precede every label with a dollar sign, as in Figure 8-29. Enter g in the After option box to indicate that each value is in thousands of dollars.

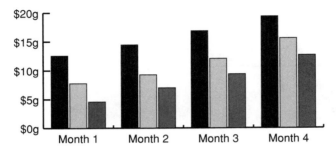

Figure 8-29: Enter characters to precede and follow the labels, such as the $ and g shown here, using the Labels Before/After options.

Most of the options in the Axis Tick Lines and Marks area are available when setting attributes for either the horizontal or vertical axis. These options include:

● **None**: Select this radio button to display no tick marks on the current axis. This option does not affect the placement or appearance of labels.

● **Short**: This option displays short tick marks that extend from the axis toward the chart, as by default.

● **Full Width**: Select this radio button to create tick lines that extend the full width or height of the chart. In Figure 8-30, I've selected this option

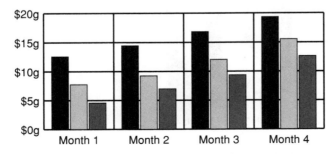

Figure 8-30: Select the Full width option to extend the tick marks across the entire chart. Here, I've applied the option to both axes.

for both the X- and Y-axes. As you can see, Illustrator transforms the tick marks into grid lines, permitting you to easily see how the bars in the chart measure up.

- **Draw Tick Lines between Labels**: This check box is available only when modifying the X-axis. (If you displayed the Graph Axis Style dialog box by clicking on the Left or Right button, the check box is dimmed.) When the check box is selected—as it is by default—tick marks appear centered between labels, as demonstrated by the vertical lines in Figure 8-30. If you turn off the option, each tick mark is centered above its label, as shown in Figure 8-31.

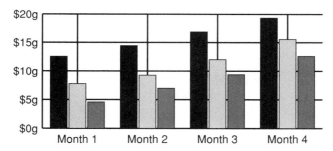

Figure 8-31: When working on a bar, line, or area chart, deselect the Draw Tick Lines between Labels check box to create tick marks directly above the labels along the horizontal axis.

- **Draw __ Tick Marks per Tick Line**: This option should read Tick Marks per Label, because it allows you to control the number of tick marks per labeled increment. In Figure 8-32, I've applied a value of 4 to the vertical axis, creating a total of four tick marks per each label.

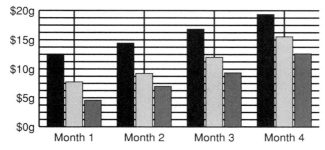

Figure 8-32: The same chart after entering 4 into the Draw __ Tick Marks per Tick Line option box.

Other Weird Graph Style Options

Now that we've polished off the Graph Axis Style dialog box, we return to the Graph Style dialog box to explore four remaining options, all of which are more or less useless. I speak, of course, of the check boxes in the lower right portion of the dialog box—Drop Shadow, Legends across Top, First Row in Front, and First Column in Front. These dorky options work as follows:

- **Drop Shadow**: Select this check box to create drop shadows behind the bars, lines, pie slices, or areas in a chart. This option is easily one of the dopiest in all of Illustrator. The drop shadow is always black, and you can't modify the distance between the shadow and the graph elements. You can more easily create your own drop shadow by selecting a few elements, copying them (⌘-C), pasting them in back (⌘-B), nudging them into the desired position with the arrow keys, and applying a fill color.

- **Legends across Top**: This option moves the legend from the right side of the chart to the top of the chart. The text is listed horizontally instead of vertically. Unfortunately, Illustrator has a nasty habit of overlapping text when you select this option, particularly when more than three series are involved. You're better off moving the legend manually.

- **First Row in Front**: Select this check box to layer elements representing rows of data in the selected chart in descending order, with the first row in front and the last row in back. This option is only useful when modifying a cluster bar chart in which the Cluster Width is set to greater than 100 percent. Because each row of data equates to a cluster, you can modify which cluster appears in front and which in back.

- **First Column in Front**: Finally, a halfway useful option! Select this option to layer elements representing columns of data (we're talking series, here) in descending order, with the first series in front and the last series in back. This option works with any chart except a pie chart. But it is most useful when editing a line or scatter chart, since it allows you prioritize the manner in which lines overlap.

 Do not turn off the First Column in Front check box when editing an area chart. If you do, the last series will completely cover up all other series in the chart.

Manually Customizing a Graph

If you've been reading this chapter sequentially, your brain is undoubtedly a little numb by now. Either that, or you've been reading the book in bed in lieu of a sedative. I mean, let's face it, taking in Illustrator's half million graphing options is a daunting—not to mention boring—task.

That's why it may come as a welcome shock that one tool—the direct selection tool—is more capable than every option in the Graph Style and Graph Axis Style dialog boxes combined. Armed with the direct selector, you can move elements around, apply different colors, edit the size of text and legend swatches, and just plain customize the heck out of your graph.

Selecting Elements inside Graphs

But in order to get anywhere with the direct selection tool, you have to understand how to select elements inside a graph. A graph is actually an extensive collection of grouped objects inside grouped objects, inside other grouped objects, which are—needless to say—grouped. This means a lot of Option-clicking with the direct selection tool.

The following list demonstrates a few of the different kinds of selections you can make with the direct selection tool:

- Click on a point or segment in the graph to select that specific element. You can then move the point or segment. However, you cannot delete it by pressing the Delete key, since this would leave a gap in the path, and Illustrator does not permit gaps in graphs.

- Click on a text object to select it. All text in a graph is point text, so be sure to click along the baseline of the text (not on one of the letters). You can then change the font, type size, alignment, and half a dozen other formatting attributes without affecting any deselected text in the graph.

- Option-click to select a whole object in the chart, such as an axis or column.

- Option-click a second time to select an entire axis, including tick marks and labels, or an entire series. If you Option-click a second time on some text, you select all text belonging to that subgroup in the graph. For example, Option-clicking twice on some legend text selects all legend text.

- Option-click a third time on a bar to select an entire series as well as its color swatch in the legend. Now you can apply a different color from the Paint Style palette to modify the fill or stroke of the series.

- ● Option-click a fourth time to select all series and legend swatches in the chart.
- ● Option-click a fifth time to select the entire chart.

This is a rather imprecise science, and different kinds of charts require a different number of Option-clicks, depending on how many series are involved and other factors. For example, you may find you only need to Option-click twice to select a series and its legend swatch in a line chart, where you had to Option-click three times in a bar chart. Keep an eye on the screen as you Option-click to monitor your progress.

Selecting Multiple Series Inside a Graph

Another handy key to keep in mind when selecting graph elements is Shift. As you know, this key permits you to select multiple objects, but it just as easily deselects objects. Therefore, you have to be deliberate in your actions, particularly when the Option key is involved.

For example, suppose you want to select two series of bars in a bar chart, including their swatches in the legend. Here's how you'd do it:

1. **Using the direct selection tool, Option-click on a bar in the chart.**

   This selects the bar.

2. **Option-click on the bar again.**

   This second click selects all other bars in the series.

3. **Option-click on the bar a third time.**

   Now the legend swatch becomes selected.

4. **Shift-Option-click on a bar in a different series.**

   Illustrator adds this new bar to the growing collection of selected objects.

5. **Option-click on that same bar again.**

   This is the important step, the one that baffles thousands of users on a daily basis. If you Shift-Option-click again, you deselect the bar; but without the Shift key, you can't add to the selection, right?

   Wrong. As long as the item on which you Option-click is selected, Illustrator broadens the selection to include the next group up. Therefore, this Option-click selects the other bars in this series.

6. **Option-click a third time on this bar**.

   This selects the swatch for the series in the legend. You now have two entire series of bars selected independently of any other series in the graph.

It's operations like this that make users of other programs, including FreeHand, roll their eyes and utter nasty comments. Not that FreeHand has a better method for dealing with this situation—FreeHand doesn't even offer a graphing function—it's just that Illustrator's methods seem so complicated.

But the truth is, this operation makes absolute sense once you understand the order of the Illustrator universe. These steps may be cumbersome, but they are impeccably logical. Come to terms with these steps, and you'll never have problems selecting objects inside Illustrator again. The good news is, it simply doesn't get more complicated than this.

 What good is selecting a couple of series in a chart? Well, I'll tell you. You can switch selected series to a different chart type, as in Figure 8-33. This chart started off as a bar chart, but I wanted to highlight my client's product, hand buzzers. Therefore, I decide to convert the sea monkey and x-ray specs series to line graphs. I first selected both series, as outlined in the previous steps, and double-clicked on the graph tool to display the Graph Style dialog box. I then selected the Line radio button from the Graph Type options, modified the Line Graph Options, and pressed Return to implement the change.

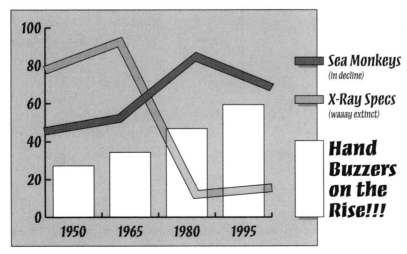

Figure 8-33: Starting from a bar chart, I converted two of the series to line graphs.

Obviously, I didn't stop there. In fact, I ended up ungrouping the graph to achieve some of the effects. To create the faded intersection between the x-ray specs line and the hand buzzer bars, I cloned the shapes and combined them using Filter » Pathfinder » Intersect, as explained in Chapter 9. I also added drop shadows behind the legend swatches, another technique covered in Chapter 9. Like any other kind of art you can create in Illustrator, graphs are limited only by your creativity, ingenuity, and patience.

More Custom Modification Options

Once you figure out how to select graphs of items with some degree of predictability, you'll discover hundreds of methods for altering them. Rather than wasting reams of paper stepping you through every possible variation, I offer a few parting tidbits of wisdom to whisk you on your way:

- One of the first things I edit when creating a graph is the legend. I hate where Illustrator puts this thing, and I hate how big it is. The text and swatches in the legend are parts of several different subgroups, but because they are physically separated from other graph elements, you can easily select them by marqueeing then with the direct selection tool. Then drag them anywhere you want, or use the scale tool to reduce their size.

- You can edit text inside a graph with the type tool, as I did in Figure 8-33. But be careful; if you have to go back later and edit the data, Illustrator restores the text entered into the Graph Data window. (Unfortunately, Illustrator is not smart enough to implement your text changes into the spreadsheet automatically.)

- You can edit paths inside a graph with the add point, delete point, and convert point tools without first ungrouping the path. Again, changes made inside the Graph Data window or Graph Style dialog box may override these adjustments.

Graphing with Graphics

What kind of illustration program would Illustrator be if it didn't allow you to create graphs with pictures? In a valiant effort to satisfy you, the customer, Illustrator lets you create *pictographs*, which are graphs in which series are represented by graphic objects. The graphics can form columns in a bar chart, like the cent symbols in Figure 8-34, or they can appear as markers in a line or scatter chart. The following sections describe how pictographs work.

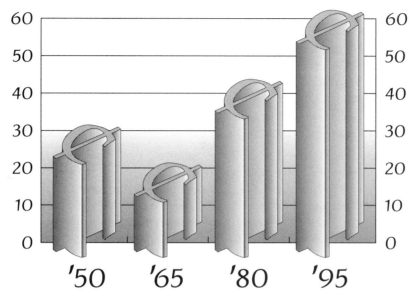

Figure 8-34: Using Illustrator's pictograph feature, you can create graph designs and apply them to bar, line, and scatter graphs.

Creating a Graph Design

You create pictographs by establishing *graph designs*—collections of graphic objects that can be applied to a chart. The following steps describe how to transform a few common, everyday objects into a graph design inside Illustrator:

1. **Draw your objects and fill them as desired**.

   Figure 8-35 shows how I constructed the objects in the cent sign. Many of the tools and commands I used are covered in later chapters.

   I started with a large Palatino character (Option-4 for ¢) and converted it to paths (example 1 in the figure). Then I rotated and slanted it with the rotate and shear tools (2). Next I selected several points and segments along the outline of the shape by clicking and Shift-clicking at the spots indicated by the arrowheads in the figure (3). I copied the selected elements to the Clipboard (⌘-C), pressed ⌘-Shift-A to deselect the elements, and chose Edit » Paste in Front (⌘-F).

   I dragged the selected items down to a point where I could more easily work on them. Then I Shift-Option-dragged them downward to clone them (4). These open paths represent the tops and bottoms of the sides coming down from the cent sign back in Figure 8-34; all I have to do is connect them with straight segments. To do this, I used the direct selection tool to select the endpoints of corresponding paths (like the selected points in example 4 in the figure) and chose Object » Join (⌘-J). Then I Option-clicked on the newly joined path with the direct selection tool to select the whole path, and pressed ⌘-J again. I repeated this for each pair of paths.

Finally, I selected all the paths (except the cent itself) and filled them with gradations from the Paint Style palette (5). I also had to fill the interior of the cent sign with a gradation, but because the path is serving as a hole in the cent sign, I have to make a duplicate. I selected it, copied it (⌘-C), pressed ⌘-Shift-A to deselect everything, and pasted the path in front (⌘-F). Then I filled it with the same gradation as the other paths. To finish it off, I dragged the sides up to the cent outline so sides and cent snapped into alignment.

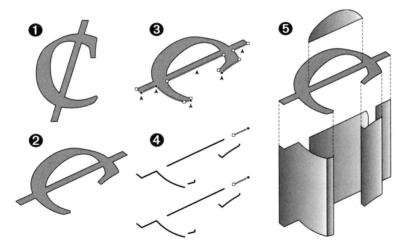

Figure 8-35: The steps involved in creating a cent symbol with mock 3-D sides.

2. **Draw a straight, horizontal line across the middle of the portion of the graph you want Illustrator to elongate when applying the design to a bar chart.**

If you're designing a marker for a line graph, you don't need to add this horizontal line, and you can skip to Step 4.

Use the pen tool to draw a horizontal line slightly wider than the graph design by clicking at one point and Shift-clicking at another. Then position the line along the spot where any stretching should occur. For example, I created the line approximately in the middle of the sides of the cent symbol, as indicated by the dotted line in Figure 8-36. This tells Illustrator to stretch the sides, not the cent symbol itself.

3. **Select the horizontal line and choose Object » Guides » Make**.

Or press the memorable shortcut ⌘-5. (That's, I say, that's sarcasm, my boy.) The line becomes dotted, as pictured in Figure 8-36. Also, make sure Object » Guides » Lock is turned off. If the Lock command has a check mark next to it, choose the command to unlock the guide. Illustrator requires you to convert the line to a guide for the stretching function to work. (For more about guides, turn to Chapter 10.)

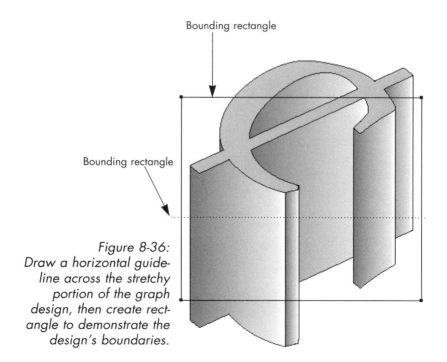

Bounding rectangle

Bounding rectangle

Figure 8-36: Draw a horizontal guide-line across the stretchy portion of the graph design, then create rect-angle to demonstrate the design's boundaries.

4. **Draw a rectangle to specify the boundaries of the graph design**.

Where graphs are concerned, Illustrator thinks largely in terms of rectangles. Bars are rectangles, for example, and line graph markers are squares. When creating a graph design, you have to tell Illustrator how the design fits onto the standard rectangle.

Use the rectangle tool to draw a boundary around the graph design as I have done in Figure 8-36. If the rectangle doesn't completely enclose the design, the design may overlap graph elements. For example, my design extends below the rectangle, therefore it will overlap the X-axis, as it does back in Figure 8-34. The design also extends over the top of the rectangle, so it will rise slightly higher than the data value. (If you're feeling very strict about your data, make sure the top of the rectangle exactly touches the top of the graph design.) The fact that the rectangle is wider than the design, however, keeps the design slightly slimmer than a standard bar.

5. **Send the rectangle to the back of the illustration**.

Choose Arrange » Send To Back (⌘-equal). This may sound like an inconsequential step, but it's very important. Illustrator insists that the boundary rectangle is in back.

6. **Make the fill and stroke transparent**.

Select the None icon in the Paint Style palette.

7. **Select all graph objects and choose Object » Graphs » Design**.

Select the graph design, horizontal guide, and rectangle. (If these are the only objects in the illustration, press ⌘-A.) Then choose Object » Graphs » Design to display the Design dialog box shown in Figure 8-37.

8. **Click on the New button**.

Illustrator shows you a preview of the graph design cropped inside your bounding rectangle, as in Figure 8-37. (Don't worry, the actual graph design is not cropped.) The program also adds an item to the scrolling list called *New Design* followed by a number.

If Illustrator complains when you click on New, it's because the rectangle is not the backmost object you've selected. It may be because you didn't properly follow Step 5, or it may be that you accidentally selected other objects even farther back. In any case, press Escape to close the dialog

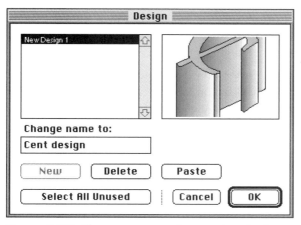

Figure 8-37: Illustrator crops the preview in the upper right corner of the Design dialog box to reflect the top and bottom edges of the bounding rectangle.

box, press ⌘-Shift-A to deselect everything, select the rectangle, cut it to the Clipboard (⌘-X), make sure the arrow tool is active, and paste the rectangle in back (⌘-B). Now try Steps 7 and 8 again.

9. Enter a name for the design and press Return.

The graph design is now ready to apply to any bar, line, or scatter graph.

 Your new graph design is available to all other open illustrations. But if you close the illustration in which you created the graph design before applying it to a chart, the design is no longer available. If you want to make a graph design available to all future illustrations whether this particular document is open or not, open the Adobe Illustrator Startup file in the Plug-ins folder. Then choose Object » Graphs » Design to display the Design dialog box and click on the Paste button. This creates a copy of the design inside the Startup file. Press Return to leave the dialog box, move the design to a suitable spot in the illustration window (but don't delete it!), and save the Startup file to disk.

Organizing Graph Designs

In addition to allowing you to create new graph designs, the Design dialog box provides the following options for organizing and editing existing graph designs:

- **Delete**: Click on this button to delete a selected design from the scrolling list. Illustrator removes the design from *all* open illustrations! Therefore, do not delete a design when a graph that uses the design is open.

 If you delete a design you didn't mean to, press Escape or click on the Cancel button to cancel the operation. If you realize your mistake only after pressing Return or clicking on the OK button, you can still restore the graph design by pressing ⌘-Z.

- **Paste**: Even if you throw away the original copy of your graph design, it may not be lost for good. As long as the design has been applied to a graph, you can retrieve the original objects. Inside the Design dialog box, select the design name from the list and click on the Paste button. Illustrator pastes the original objects into the illustration window. Then press Return to close the dialog box and edit the objects as desired. (If you leave the dialog box by pressing the Escape key, Illustrator cancels the paste operation.)

 After you edit the pasted objects, you can redefine the graph design and all open graphs that use the design. Select the objects and choose Object » Graphs » Design. Then select the design name from the list and press Return or click on the OK button. (That's it; no special buttons to press.) Illustrator displays an alert box asking if you want to redraw all graphs or just redefine the graph design for future graphs. Press Return to do both.

- **Select All Unused**: This button selects all designs that are not applied to graphs in any open illustration. Then you can click on the Delete button to get rid of them.

You can rename a pattern by clicking on its name in the scrolling list and entering a new name into the Change Name To option box.

Applying a Design to a Bar Chart

To apply a design to a bar chart or stacked bar chart, select the bar chart with the arrow tool, or select the single series that you want to convert to a pictograph with the direct selection tool. Then choose Object » Graphs » Column to display the Graph Column Design dialog box shown in Figure 8-38.

Select a graph design from the scrolling Column Design Name list, select a radio button from the Column Design Type options, and press the Return key. Illustrator applies the design to all selected series.

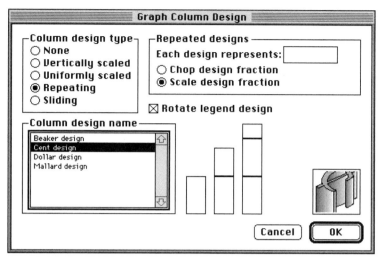

Figure 8-38: The Graph Column Design dialog box lets you apply a graph design to a bar chart.

The Column Design Type options allow you to change the way Illustrator stretches or repeats the graph design from one bar to the next. Figure 8-39 demonstrates the effect of the four options (except None) in the order they appear in the dialog box. Here's how each option works:

- **None**: Select this option only when you want to remove a graph design from the selected series. The Column Design Name list becomes dimmed.

- **Vertically Scaled**: This option stretches the graph design vertically to represent different values, as demonstrated at the top of Figure 8-39. Notice that in the case of the cent symbol, Illustrator stretches both the sides and the outline of the cent. This is sometimes useful, though it's not the best match for my cent design.

- **Uniformly Scaled**: Select this radio button to scale the graph design proportionally according to the size of the data, as in the second example in Figure 8-39. Large values have a tendency to take over the graph; this option is useful primarily when your data has little variation.

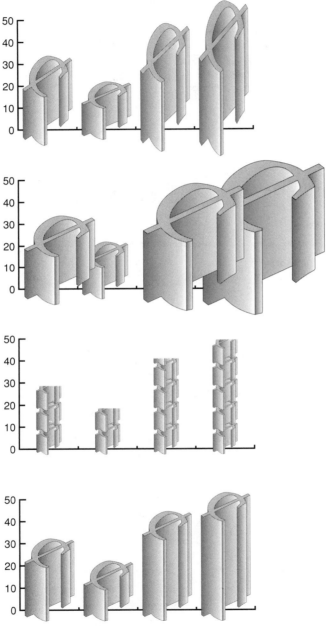

Figure 8-39: The Vertically Scaled (top), Uniformly Scaled (second), Repeating (third), and Sliding (bottom) options change the way Illustrator applies a graph design to a bar chart.

- **Repeated**: If you want to repeat the graph design over and over again, select this option. Illustrator creates stacks of the object, as in the third example in Figure 8-39. This style of pictograph is very popular—you can stack coins, dollar bills, cars, footballs, computer monitors, little disembodied Newt Gingrich heads . . . in short, anything you want.

When the Repeated radio button is selected, the otherwise-dimmed Repeated Designs options become available. Enter a value in the Each Design Represents option box to determine the data increment represented by each repetition of the graph design. For example, if a value in the selected series is 49, and you enter 10 for the Each Design Represents value, the design repeats four full times and a fifth partial time, just like the last bar in the figure.

The two radio buttons determine how Illustrator slices or scales the last graph design to accommodate remainder data that doesn't divide evenly into the Each Design Represents value. Select the Chop Design Fraction radio button to lop off the extraneous top design, as in Figure 8-39; select Scale Design Fraction to vertically scale the top design to fit its fractional value.

- **Sliding**; Select this option to elongate the graph design at the spot indicated by the horizontal guideline, as in the final example in Figure 8-39. This is usually the most desirable option, and it certainly looks the best when combined with the cent design. Illustrator stretches the sides of the design, but leaves the cent symbol itself unmolested.

Select the Rotate Legend Design check box to display the graph design on its side in the legend. (I omitted the legend in Figure 8-39 by neglecting to enter any column headings in the Graph Data window.) If you deselect the Rotate Legend Design check box, the design appears upright in the legend.

Applying a Design to a Line Chart

To apply a design to a line or scatter chart, select the graph with the arrow tool or select the specific markers you want to change with the direct selection tool. (Do not select the line segments.) Then choose the Object » Graphs » Marker, which brings to life the Graph Marker Design dialog box in Figure 8-40.

Select the On Data Point radio button, select a graph design from the scrolling Marker Design Name list, and press Return. Illustrator applies the graph design to the individual markers in the chart.

To create Figure 8-41, I Option-clicked twice on one selection of markers with the direct selection tool to select all the markers in one series, and I applied the

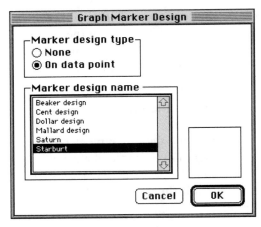

*Figure 8-40:
The Graph Marker Design
dialog box lets you apply a
graph design to the markers
in a line or scatter chart.*

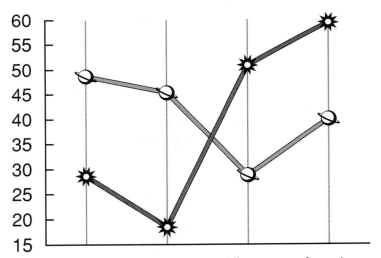

*Figure 8-41: Here I've applied two different sets of graph
designs to the markers of a line graph.*

starburst graph design. I then Option-clicked twice on the other set of markers
and applied the Saturn design.

Illustrator determines the size of a graph design based on the size of the
bounding rectangle that you drew when defining the original graph design. The
bounding rectangle is reduced to match the size of the square marker that normally appears in a line or scatter chart. Therefore, to create a design that scales to

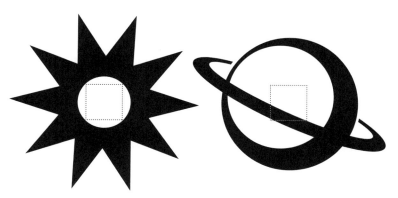

Figure 8-42: I created small bounding rectangles to make the graph designs appear large in the line graph in Figure 8-41.

a reasonable size, draw a relatively small bounding rectangle. Figure 8-42 shows the bounding rectangles for the starburst and Saturn patterns as dotted outlines.

 If you don't like how large Illustrator draws the markers and you don't feel like going back and messing around with the original graph designs, you can scale them on the fly with Arrange » Transform Each. Option-click on one of the markers three times to select the entire series—or four times to select all markers—and choose Arrange » Transform Each. Then enter values larger than 100 percent into the Horizontal and Vertical option boxes and press Return. (To scale the markers proportionally, make sure the Horizontal and Vertical values are identical.

PART THREE
CHANGING

MODIFYING AND COMBINING PATHS

Now that you've had the opportunity to create every kind of object available to Illustrator, it's time to talk in earnest about messing up these objects. This chapter specifically discusses how to edit paths created with the drawing tools covered in Chapters 4 and 5. You can clone paths to create copies, join paths together and hack them apart, and carve transparent holes in otherwise filled paths.

As the *pièce de résistance*, you can combine simple paths into highly intricate ones using an assortment of so-called Pathfinder filters. Though indisputably some of Illustrator's most enigmatic capabilities—many artists I've talked to are only vaguely aware that they exist—the Pathfinder filters can easily cut your drawing time in half, if you'll only invest the time to learn them.

With the exception of cloning, you can't apply the operations covered in this chapter to text, unless you first convert the characters to paths using Type » Create Outlines. And you can edit elements inside graphs only if you first ungroup the graphs by pressing ⌘-U or choosing Arrange » Ungroup.

In fact, you'll have to ungroup portions of the graph more than once to break apart the nested groups. To be sure, press ⌘-U four times to ungroup every single object in the graph. Or you can simply wait and see if Illustrator complains when you try to perform an operation; if it does, press ⌘-U and try again.

One Million Ways to Replicate

When creating a pencil sketch on paper, you have to draw each pencil stroke from scratch. Then you have to trace pen strokes, add colors, and otherwise embellish the artwork—again, one stroke at a time—to convert the sketch into a useable illustration. Not so in Illustrator. Certainly, you have to draw many paths from scratch, but you can also duplicate paths and reshape or combine them to create different lines and shapes. It's like having an artistic replicator within easy reach. Each path that you create or reshape becomes fresh grist for the mill.

Adobe understands the benefits of duplicating paths, which is why it has blessed Illustrator with so many techniques for cloning and copying. Each of these are useful in different situations, as I explain in the following sections. If you aren't already familiar with these techniques, study these sections carefully and commit the techniques to memory. Those poor souls who don't understand duplication miss out on one of the keys factors that gives Illustrator the edge over the common household pencil.

If you think you know pretty much everything about duplication already, at least skim the next few sections. I'm confident that you'll pick up a handful of techniques that you never heard of, had forgotten, or hadn't considered in quite this context. I'm equally confident you'll find a way to put these new techniques to work in the very near future. Simply put, duplication is one of those areas with which you can't be too familiar.

Plain Old Copying and Pasting

Most folks are familiar with the Clipboard, which is a portion of memory set aside to hold objects that you want to duplicate or transfer to another program. It's kind of like the Mem button on a calculator. You store something one minute and retrieve it the next.

I've discussed a few Clipboard techniques in previous chapters, and I'll continue to sprinkle in more later on. But now's a good time for an overview of the three most fundamental Clipboard commands— Cut, Copy, and Paste:

- You can copy selected objects to the Clipboard by pressing ⌘-C (or choosing Edit » Copy). To remove the selected objects from the illustration and send them to the Clipboard, press ⌘-X (Edit » Cut).

- Press ⌘-V (Edit » Paste) to retrieve the objects from the Clipboard. Illustrator pastes the objects in the center of the illustration window and selects them so that you can immediately manipulate them.

- After pasting, the objects remain in the Clipboard until the next time you press ⌘-C or ⌘-X. Both commands shove out the old contents of the Clipboard and bring in the new.

You might be thinking, "I understand ⌘-C for Copy, but why ⌘-X for Cut and ⌘-V for Paste?" You've no doubt heard colleagues speculate that the X looks like a pair of scissors or that the V stands for *vomit*, but these suggestions lack the ring of truth. It's very simple, really. The first few commands in the Edit menu are assigned the first few keys along the bottom row of the keyboard. ⌘-Z, X, C, and V activate Undo, Cut, Copy, and Paste, respectively. It's like this for all Mac applications (and most Windows programs as well).

 Illustrator also adds neighboring keys D, F, and B to the duplication family—⌘-D for Repeat Transform, ⌘-F for Paste In Front, and ⌘-B for Paste In Back, as in Figure 9-1. I explain these commands in an upcoming section, but for now, just keep in mind that the lower left corner of the keyboard is where the duplication action is.

Figure 9-1: Ever notice that all of Illustrator's duplication shortcut keys are clustered in one corner of the keyboard? Coincidence or alien intervention? You decide.

Pasting Paths into Other Programs

You can also use the Clipboard to hold objects that you want to transport to another program. For example, you can copy paths from Illustrator and place them inside, say, a PageMaker document using the standard Copy and Paste commands.

 Illustrator 6 always adds a PostScript description of its paths to the Clipboard. This is why you get the message "Converting Clipboard to EPS (AICB) format" when you switch out of Illustrator. Adobe calls this feature *PostScript on the Clipboard*, and most of Adobe's other products support it, including the most recent versions of Photoshop, PageMaker, and PageMill (the Worldwide Web page-layout utility).

If a program does not support PostScript on the Clipboard (Microsoft Word, for example, is completely ignorant of this and many other subjects), pasting an Illustrator graphic produces the placeholder shown in Figure 9-2. The graphic *may* print correctly to a PostScript printer—though I wouldn't place money on it—but it sure as heck won't look right on screen.

Figure 9-2:
If you see this after pasting
paths inside another pro-
gram, you'll know that the
program you're using
doesn't fully support
PostScript on the Clipboard.

Adobe Illustrator artwork:
one object in one layer

To transfer Illustrator objects to a PostScript-stupid program like Word, press the Option key when choosing Edit » Copy inside Illustrator (or pressing ⌘-Option-C). This instructs Illustrator to copy PICT versions of the paths to the Clipboard. Then you can paste them inside Word or any other program that supports PICT by pressing ⌘-V as usual. (You can also press ⌘-Option-C to avoid Clipboard errors when transferring paths between Illustrator and Photoshop, as I discuss in Chapter 13.)

Creating Clones

The Clipboard isn't the only means for copying paths and segments inside Illustrator. In fact, you can completely bypass the Clipboard—and leave the contents of the Clipboard intact—by dragging a path and pressing the Option key. This technique is called *cloning.*

To clone a path, select it with the arrow or direct selection tool, drag the path, press and hold the Option key in mid drag, release the mouse button, and release Option. It's very important to press the Option key *after* you start to drag, since Option-clicking with the direct selection tool selects whole paths and groups. And you have to keep Option pressed until after you release the mouse button to create the clone. So again, drag, press Option, release the mouse button, and release Option.

Illustrator positions the clone just in front of the original path. If you clone multiple shapes, Illustrator positions the clones in front of the foremost original. If the original paths lie behind other paths—which were not cloned—the clones lie in back of these paths as well. No big deal, of course; there are merely nuances of cloning that I think you should be aware of.

You can also use the Option key with the scale, rotate, reflect, and shear tools to clone a path while transforming it. Chapter 11 tells all there is to know on the subject.

Nudge and Clone

You might think that you could clone and nudge a path by pressing Option with an arrow key. But noooo. The Option-arrow keystrokes change the Leading or Tracking values in the Character palette, even when a path with no text is selected. (You adjust the default Leading and Tracking values that will affect the next text object you create.)

 If you want to nudge and clone, you have to press ⌘, Shift, and Option, plus one of the arrow keys. That's right, press your nose, ear, and eyebrow against the keyboard while tapping an arrow key with a spare finger. While hardly the most convenient keystroke in the world, ⌘-Shift-Option-arrowing is a useful way to create clones evenly spaced from their originals. Press ⌘-Shift-Option-arrow key to establish the clone, then release the modifier keys and continue pressing the arrow key to nudge the clone into position.

Cloning Partial Paths

If you Option-drag or ⌘-Shift-Option-arrow a path in which all points are selected, Illustrator clones the entire path. But you also can clone individual points and segments that you've selected with the direct selection tool. In fact, Illustrator was the first drawing program on the Mac that let you duplicate bits and pieces of a path. This precise control over partial paths is one of the primary ingredients that distinguishes a professional-level program like Illustrator from the greater midrange morass.

Figure 9-3 shows what happens when you clone a single segment independent of the rest of the path. If you Option-drag a straight segment (or press ⌘-Shift-Option-arrow when the segment is selected), you clone the segment at a new location, as demonstrated in the two left-hand examples in the figure. If you clone a curved segment, you stretch the segment and leave its points at their original positions, as in the right-hand examples.

When dragging or nudging one or more selected points, you clone the points as well as any segments connected to those points. Whether straight or curved, each segment between a selected point and a deselected point stretches to keep up with the drag, as Figure 9-4 illustrates.

Copying in Place

The problem with Option-dragging partial paths, therefore, is that it almost always results in distortions. You can Option-drag a straight segment without

Figure 9-3: Option-drag a straight segment (top left) to move and clone the segment (bottom left). Option-drag a curved segment (top right) to stretch and clone the segment (bottom right).

changing it, but when you clone curved segments or selected points, you stretch segments.

This is why so many experienced Illustrator artists duplicate partial paths using the Copy and Paste In Front commands. By simply pressing ⌘-C followed by ⌘-F (Edit » Paste In Front), you can copy one or more selected points and segments to the Clipboard and then paste them directly in front of their originals. No stretching, no distortion; Illustrator pastes the paths just as they were copied.

Also worth noting, the Paste In Front command positions the pasted paths at the same spot where they were copied. (By contrast, Edit » Paste positions the paths in the middle of the illustration window, regardless of the placement of the originals.) Therefore, ⌘-C, ⌘-F creates a copy in place.

 Edit » Paste In Back (⌘-B) works just like the Paste In Front command, except that it pastes the copied paths in back of the selected elements. Unless you specifically want to change the stacking order of objects (as explained in Chapter 10), Paste In Front is usually preferable, since it permits you to

Figure 9-4: Option-drag selected points (top examples) to clone all segments connected to those points (bottom).

easily select and edit paths after you paste them. With Paste In Back, some path undoubtedly covers the pasted paths, making them difficult to access.

Cloning in Place

You can also create a quick duplicate directly on top of the original by pressing ⌘-Shift-Option-↑ followed by the ↓ key. This creates a clone and then nudges it back into place.

Perhaps this wonderful technique strikes a few of you as odd, even dopey. I've demonstrated it at several conferences lately, only to be met with puzzled stares and not a few derisive guffaws. "Surely you aren't suggesting we devote both hands to this bizarre keyboard medley," mock the boldest hooligans in the front rows, "When we can just press ⌘-C, ⌘-F?"

But, of course, this is precisely what I'm suggesting, and I'll tell you why. ⌘-C, ⌘-F replaces the contents of the Clipboard; ⌘-Shift-Option-⊤, ⊥ does not. If you don't mind replacing the Clipboard, ⌘-C, ⌘-F is great. If you'd rather leave the sleeping Clipboard lie in peace, ⌘-Shift-Option-⊤, ⊥ is just the ticket.

Naturally, you can exploit or ignore this clever trick as you see fit. I mention a few specific reasons for cloning in place in later chapters, but it's ultimately up to you to decide its merit. If you do choose to add ⌘-Shift-Option-⊤, ⊥ to your regular repertoire, remember this: When used with partial paths, it results in the same distortion as Option-dragging. ⌘-Shift-Option-⊤ distorts the path and clones it, and because Illustrator selects the entire clone, pressing the ⊥ key moves all points and leaves the distortion intact.

You can anticipate the distortion and fix it as follows:

1. With the direct selection tool, select the points that you want to clone.

2. Press ⌘-Shift-Option-⊤. This clones the points and surrounding segments and selects the cloned path in its entirety.

3. Shift-click on two endpoints in the cloned path to deselect them. These points weren't selected when you cloned the path, so they shouldn't be selected now.

4. Press the ⊥ key. The distortion goes away, making all segments in the clone identical to their counterparts in the original path.

Needless to say, these steps require an additional level of effort that may prompt clone-in-place obstructionists to roll their eyes even more emphatically. But I maintain that all good things have their price. More importantly, if you want to avoid the Clipboard, there isn't a better method to duplicate in place.

Creating a Series of Clones

After Option-dragging or ⌘-Shift-Option-arrowing, you can repeat the distance and direction that a clone has moved by choosing Arrange » Repeat Transform or pressing ⌘-D. This command creates series of clones, as in Figure 9-5.

If you clone an entire path, the Repeat Transform command duplicates the path over and over again, as shown at the top of Figure 9-5. This is a standard series duplication—hence the keyboard shortcut ⌘-D—dating back to the first MacDraw more than a decade ago.

You can also apply Arrange » Repeat Transform to a partially cloned path. But rather than further distorting the path each time it's repeated, Illustrator moves all selected points the same distance and direction, as the bottom examples in Figure 9-5 show.

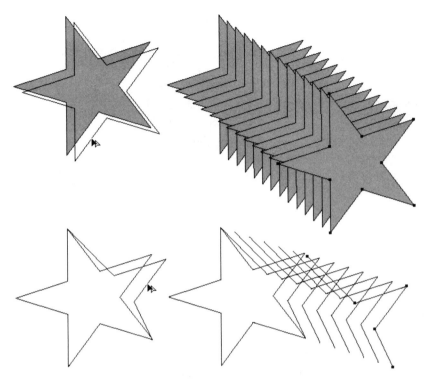

Figure 9-5: After cloning a path (top left), press ⌘-D to create a strings of equally spaced clones (top right). If you create a series of partial clones (bottom), Illustrator applies the same movement to all points.

In addition to creating a linear series of paths, you can use the Repeat Transformation in one of the following two ways:

- After dragging one path, you can move another the same distance and direction by selecting the path and pressing ⌘-D. No cloning occurs. This is why Illustrator calls the command Repeat Transform; it's frequently more useful for repeating a simple movement or other transformation than for cloning.

- You can also repeat a resizing, rotation, or other transformation, whether or not the transformation involves cloning. For more on this topic, check out Chapter 11.

Expanding the Clone

A little-known technique for cloning paths is the Offset Path command. Buried in the Filter menu, this command clones a selected path and expands the outline of the clone an equal distance in all directions.

Select a path and choose Filter » Objects » Offset Path. The dialog box shown in Figure 9-6 appears. Enter the numerical distance of the expansion into the Offset option box. If you want to create a slimmer, smaller path, enter a negative value. Then press Return.

Figure 9-6:
Enter a value into the
Offset option box to
specify how far Illustrator
should expand a
selected path.

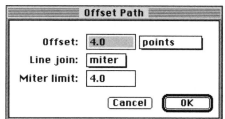

In the first example of Figure 9-7, I applied an Offset value of 4 points to a letter set in the Linotype font Notre Dame and converted to paths. The original letter appears as white; I filled the cloned path with light gray. I want you to notice three things about the clone in the figure, all of which are indicative of the Offset clone command:

- Offset Path is the one cloning operation that positions clones in back of their originals, so that all paths are plainly visible.

- The outline of the clone has lots of overlapping folds at the corners of the shape. To remove these, choose Filter » Pathfinder » Unite, as I did to create the second example in Figure 9-7.

- Expanding a path is not the same as scaling it. Filter » Objects » Offset Path dilates the path inward and outward, as the light gray shape shows. By contrast, the scale tool enlarges the interior areas so that they no longer align with the original.

 To create the final example in Figure 9-7, I reapplied the Filter » Objects » Offset Path to the first clone, followed by Filter » Pathfinder » Unite to remove the corner folds. I then copied each path (⌘-C)—one at a time—pasted the copy behind the original (⌘-B), and nudged the copy a few fractions of a point down and to the right. I also added a thicker stroke to each

Figure 9-7: The results of applying an Offset value of 4 points (left), removing the corner folds with the Unite command (middle), and repeating the Offset Path and Unite commands (right).

copy, creating the impression of depth (a technique I explore in Chapter 16). To top things off, I filled the three front paths with gradations.

In addition to the Offset option box, the Offset Path dialog box (Figure 9-6) offers the Line Join and Miter Limit options, both of which affect how Illustrator draws the corners of the cloned paths. The default Line Join setting, Miter, creates pointed corners, but you can also round off the corners (Round) or cut them short (Bevel). The Miter Limit value chops the corner short if the path threatens to grow too long. For more information on these basic stroking concepts, consult Chapter 16.

Dragging and Dropping

The one remaining method for duplicating objects is new to Illustrator 6. You can drag an object from one illustration window and drop it into another.

Naturally, you have to be able to see at least a little bit of the illustration window you're dragging from and the one that you're dragging into on your computer screen at the same time. Then, armed with the arrow or direct selection tool, simply drag one or more selected objects out of one window and onto a background window. As illustrated in Figure 9-8, a dotted outline shows the position of the dragged objects, while a heavy gray border skirts the inside of the background window to show that this window is poised to receive. As soon as you get the heavy border, you can release the mouse button to drop the selection.

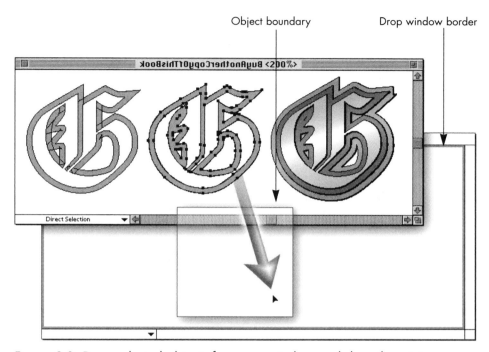

Figure 9-8: Drag selected objects from one window and drop them into another to clone objects between illustrations.

There's no need to press the Option key when dragging and dropping. Illustrator automatically clones the object, leaving the original in one window and adding a duplicate to the second. (As with other cloning techniques, the Clipboard contents remain unchanged.) After you drop, Illustrator brings the receiving window to front, so that you can position the object and edit it if need be.

You can also drag and drop objects from Illustrator into other applications. I discuss how to drag and drop paths into Photoshop, for example, in Chapter 13.

Dragging Scraps and Clips

If you've been using the Mac for any period of time, you undoubtedly know about the Scrapbook. Made available by choosing the Scrapbook command from the Apple menu, you can paste items into the Scrapbook window to create a sort of rolodex of Clipboard stuff. Later, when you need to use an item, you just copy it from the Scrapbook and paste it into your favorite program.

What you didn't know—what nobody seems to know—is that you don't have to copy objects from Illustrator 6 to paste them into the Scrapbook. You can drag and drop objects directly into the Scrapbook, as shown in Figure 9-9. Again, the Clipboard is totally out of the picture. Illustrator creates both a PostScript and PICT representation on the fly, so that you can copy the objects from the Scrapbook and paste them into Word if you get the fancy.

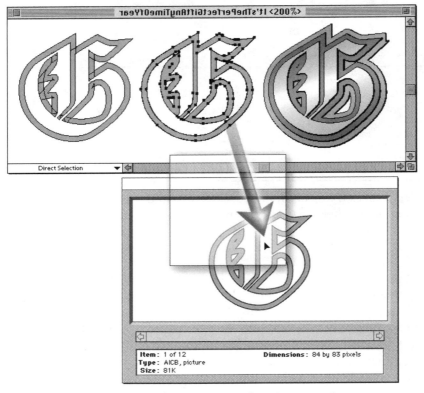

Figure 9-9: Don't copy and paste to transfer objects to the Scrapbook; just drag and drop!

You can also create so-called *picture clippings* by dragging objects from Illustrator and dropping them onto the Finder desktop. Picture clippings are little holding cells that keep objects until you need them later. When you drag and drop objects onto the desktop, Illustrator works with the system software to create a picture clipping file, which looks like a frayed page with a bent corner. You can

Figure 9-10: Double-click on a picture clipping file icon (left) to view its contents (right).

double-click on the file icon at the Finder level to view its contents, as in Figure 9-10. (Illustrator doesn't have to be running to view the picture.)

Any time in the future, you can add the objects from the picture clipping to an illustration by dragging the picture clipping file and dropping it into an open illustration. You can likewise drop the file into the Scrapbook, Photoshop, or some other application that supports the Illustrator format.

 Illustrator 6's drag-and-drop functions takes advantage of code built into the Macintosh system software. You need to be using System 7.5 with two extensions, Macintosh Drag and Drop and Clipping Extension, in your Extensions folder. (Macintosh Drag and Drop is not needed in System 7.5.1 or later.) If you can't get any of the drag-and-drop operations detailed in this book to work, chances are you're running the wrong system, or one of the extensions is missing from your Extensions folder. (These files are included with all Macs sold since late 1994.)

What About Auto-Scrolling?

Now that Illustrator 6 offers drag and drop, it's easy to accidentally drag objects out of the illustration window when you simply mean to invoke the auto-scroll function. See, in the old days, Illustrator scrolled the window when you dragged an object outside the window. This way, you could make big movements without zooming away from the page. Typically, the farther you dragged, the faster it scrolled. But no more. Any time you drag outside the window in Illustrator 6, the program tries to do a drag and drop, even if there's no receiving window in the background.

These days, to make Illustrator automatically scroll the window as you drag an object, you need to hover your cursor over a scroll bar or title bar. For example, after grabbing a selected object, drag it onto the right scroll bar and hold it there; Illustrator scrolls to the right. If you drag onto the title bar, Illustrator scrolls upward. But what if you want to scroll to the left, where there is no scroll or title bar? In this case, drag onto the left edge of the window. It's tricky, but it works. When you've scrolled far enough, drag back into the window and drop the object into place.

Joining Points and Paths

Enough duplicating already. It's time to do something different with all these paths we're making, starting with joining. Illustrator's Join command lets you join two open paths to create one longer open path. Or you can connect two endpoints in a single open path to form a closed path.

Here's the scoop on using Object » Join:

● Drag one endpoint onto another with the direct-selection tool so that it snaps into alignment. Then select the two endpoints (by marqueeing around them with the direct selection tool) and choose Object » Join or press ⌘-J. This fuses the two endpoints into a single interior point. Illustrator displays the Join dialog box, which lets you select whether you want to fuse the points into a corner point or smooth point. Make your selection and press Return.

 If you don't see the Join dialog box after pressing ⌘-J, your points aren't coincident—that is, one point isn't exactly, precisely snapped into alignment with the other. Press ⌘-Z to undo the join, then try again to drag one point into alignment with the other, or just press ⌘-Option-J. The latter averages and fuses the points, as I explain shortly.

● If so much as 0.001 point stands between two selected points, Object » Join bypasses the Join dialog box and simply connects the points with a straight segment. (To put things in perspective, 0.001 point is roughly 0.3 micron, the size of one of your tinier bacteria—no joke—hence the insightful Figure 9-11.) Though one might argue Illustrator is a little *too* ready to join points in this way, it's a terrific method for quickly closing off a shape. So if you need a straight segment in a hurry, select two endpoints and press ⌘-J.

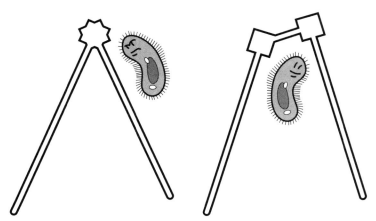

Figure 9-11: Object » Join fuses two exactly aligned points into a single point (left). But if a bacterium can fit between the points (right), it connects the points with a straight segment.

 If you aren't particularly concerned with the placement of your points, and you want to join the points into one, press ⌘-Option-J (or press the Option key while choosing Object » Join). This brings the points together by averaging their locations and then fuses them into a corner point. (You can also press ⌘-Option-L or Option-choose Object » Average.)

To undo the effects of ⌘-Option-J, you have to press ⌘-Z twice in a row—once to undo the joining, and again to undo the averaging. Weird but true.

To close an open path, you can select the entire path with the arrow tool and press ⌘-J. If the endpoints are coincident, a dialog box comes up, asking you how you want to fuse the points. Otherwise, Illustrator connects the points with a straight segment.

 Whatever you do, don't press ⌘-Option-J when an entire path is selected. Illustrator averages all points in the path into a single location, creating a very ugly effect. If you mess up and do what I told you not to do, press ⌘-Z twice to make it better.

The Join command is a great way to join similarly shaped open paths to create a shape that looks like a variable-width line. Figure 9-12 shows a plethora of spirals created by taking two spiral paths and joining them together. Here's how I created each variation:

To create the first (labeled 1 in Figure 9-12), I drew two paths of different sizes with the spiral tool. Both paths had the same decay and an equal number of segments. I then dragged one path by its inner endpoint so it snapped onto the inner endpoint of the other path. I marqueed these inner points with the direct selection tool and pressed ⌘-J to fuse them. Next, I Option-clicked on the path with the direct selection tool to select the entire thing and pressed ⌘-J again to connect the outer endpoints with a straight segment.

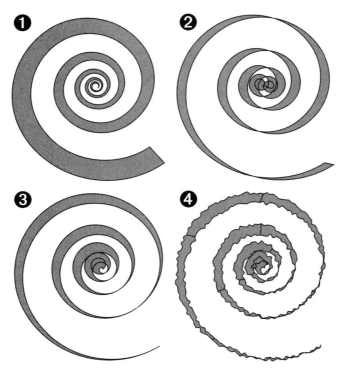

Figure 9-12: Four shapes created by taking two open spiral paths and joining them together.

To create the second shape (2) in the figure, I drew a spiral and cloned it to create two identical paths. I moved the two spirals a few points away from each other and joined the corresponding endpoints in either path with straight segments.

The bottom left*si!* shape (3) is the result of cloning a spiral with Filter » Objects » Offset Path. I then selected the entire clone, dragged it by its inner endpoint so it snapped into alignment with the original, and fused the inner endpoints into one. Finally, I selected the two outer endpoints with the direct selection tool and pressed ⌘-Option-J to average and fuse them.

The last shape (4) is a bit of a cheat, but it shows you where joining can ultimately take you. All I did was take the third path (3) and apply Filter » Distort » Roughen. Inside the Roughen dialog box, I set the Size value to 1, the Detail value to 30, and selected the Smooth radio button. See Chapter 12 for more info on Roughen and other automated special effects filters.

> **NOTE** Those little lines across the last spiral are the points at which I had to split the sucker because it was too complicated to print. I clicked with the scissors tool where I wanted to assign breaks and connected opposite sides with straight segments using the Join command. (The scissors tool is the topic of the very next section.)

Splitting Paths into Pieces

The opposite of joining is splitting, and Illustrator provides three basic ways to split paths apart. I touched on the first method in Chapter 5: You can select a segment or interior point with the direct selection tool and press the Delete key. This deletes one or two segments and leaves a gaping rift in the path. You either split an open path into two paths, or open a closed path.

But what if you want to break a path apart without creating a rift? Or what if you want to break a path in the middle of a segment? The answer to either question is to use the scissors tool, knife tool, or Object » Apply Knife. The scissors tool creates a break at a specific point, the knife tool creates a free-form slice, and the Apply Knife command uses a selected path to slice through all other paths that it comes in contact with. The only things lacking are a nail file and a toothpick. (Er, that was a pocket knife joke, in case you missed it.)

Snipping with the Scissors

The scissors tool is one of Illustrator's earliest tools, predating just about every path-editing tool but the arrow tool. The third tool on the right side of the toolbox, its operation hasn't changed since the old days. You click anywhere along the out-

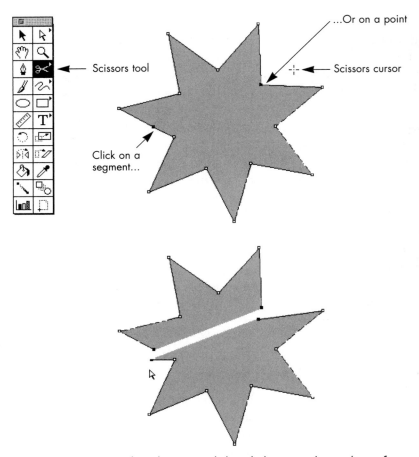

...Or on a point

Scissors tool

Scissors cursor

Click on a
segment...

Figure 9-13: Snip a break in a path by clicking on the outline of a
path with the scissors tool.

line of a path to snip the path at that point. As Figure 9-13 shows, you can click
on either a segment or a point.

Whenever you click with the scissors tool, Illustrator inserts two endpoints. As
the second example in Figure 9-13 illustrates, you can drag one endpoint away
from the other with the direct selection tool. The problem is, one endpoint is necessarily in front of the other. Why a problem? Every so often, you'll want to drag
the point that's in back, and you won't be able to get to it because the front point
is in the way.

Naturally, you can drag the front point out of the way, and then drag the rear point. But that means moving both points. What if you want the front point to stay exactly where it is, and just move the rear one?

  The solution is to select both points, deselect the top one, and nudge the bottom point clear with the arrow keys. To select both points, marquee around them with the direct selection tool. Then Shift-click on the point to deselect the top point. Now just the bottom point is selected. Press an arrow key three or four times to nudge the bottom point so you can easily select it, then drag it to the desired location.

Inserting a Point with the Scissors

Incidentally, Illustrator didn't offer an add point tool (discussed in Chapter 5) until Version 3, and yet, you always had this capability with the scissors tool. Just Option-click. Clicking with the scissors tool inserts two endpoints, Option-clicking inserts a single interior point. Makes sense, right?

  Which brings me to an interesting tip. As Chapter 5 explained, the add point tool automatically determines the identity of a new point—corner or smooth—based on the shape of the segment on which you click. But what if you don't like the point Illustrator creates? What if it creates a corner point when you want a smooth point? Well, just undo the point insertion (⌘-Z), select the scissors tool, and click at that same point. Next press ⌘-J to join the points. (Both points are already selected after you click with the scissors.) Select the kind of point you want to create from the Join dialog box, and press Return.

Illustrator always gives you control; you just need to know how to find it.

Wielding the Knife

  The other path-splitting tool is located in the plug-in tools palette. (If the palette is hidden, choose Window » Show Plug-In Tools.) The last tool in the palette, it looks like a little X-acto blade.

The knife tool slices multiple paths at a time. First assemble the objects that you want to cut through. The knife tool splits filled paths only; it doesn't matter whether they're open or closed, just that they have fills. And it doesn't affect text, unless the text is first converted to paths with Type » Create Outlines.

To operate the knife tool, just drag with it, much as you would with the free-hand tool. (Illustrator tracks your knife gestures a little differently than the free-hand tool—with a more accurate solid line that adjusts slightly as you drag—but this is a minor point. You probably don't care. Sorry to bother you.) As demonstrated in Figure 9-14, Illustrator slices through all filled paths that the knife tool comes into contact with. (I changed the fills of the left and right halves of the slashed objects to better demonstrate the effects of the knife.) It also deletes any strokes associated with those paths. Only the unfilled open path and text object come out unharmed.

 The knife tool is in need of sharpening in Illustrator 6.0. If you drag over a closed path with no fill, the knife tool deletes it. If you drag back and forth over an open path with no fill, the knife tool trashes it, too. (In Figure 9-14, I just dragged over the path once, so Illustrator ignored it.) And to make matters worse, a tip in the manual doesn't work! It tells you to double-click on the knife tool to access a check box so that you can clone paths as you cut them—which would preserve filled and unfilled paths alike. But Adobe decided to deactivcate this feature at the last minute. What a confusing, chaotic mess!

 You can thank your lucky stars that I discovered an undocumented tip to help you. If you Control-drag with the knife tool—yes, *Control*-drag—Illustrator cuts through both filled and unfilled paths, without deleting either. As always, the knife tool gets rid of the strokes, so that the unfilled paths become invisible in the preview mode. But you can always reassign the strokes from the Paint Style palette. Better to lose a few strokes than a bunch of paths any day.

 Another tip you may hear bandied about involves the Option key. If you Option-drag with the knife tool, the tool ostensibly clones the path and then slices it. But for the present, this technique is flawed. It works okay when knifing a single path, in which case it cuts a sliver from the clone while leaving the original unharmed. But do *not* Option-drag over two or more paths. It goes absolutely haywire, tracing the knife path, creating multiple clones of some shapes, and altogether ignoring others. Dang, this tool is buggy!

 Regardless of how you use the knife tool, it slashes or deletes *all* closed paths over which you drag. In other words, it doesn't matter if the paths were selected or not. If you want to protect a path from being cut or destroyed, select it and choose Arrange » Lock (⌘-1). When you finish knifing,

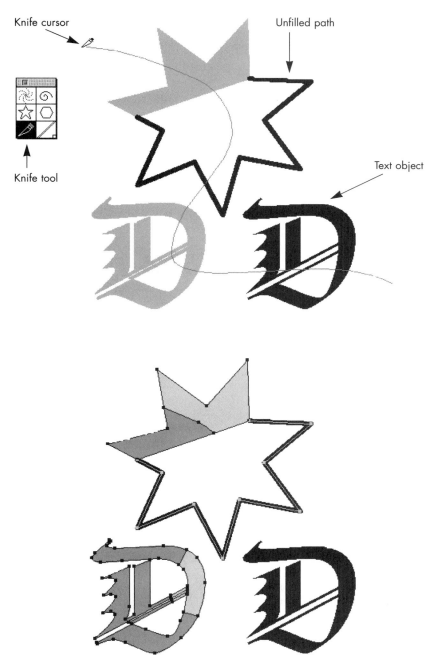

Figure 9-14: Drag with the knife tool (top) to cut through filled paths (bottom). Open paths with transparent fills and text are not affected.

choose Arrange » Unlock All (⌘-2) to unlock the paths. I explain both of these commands in Chapter 10.

One of my favorite uses for the knife tool is indiscriminate slashing. (What better way to use such a twisted tool?) For example, in Figure 9-15, I start with a star and then scribble back and forth over it with the knife tool. This busts up the path into a hundred or so pieces, as on the right side of the figure. You can then fill each sliced path with a different color. In Figure 9-16, I've applied one of three gradations to each of the shards, creating a sort of stained glass effect.

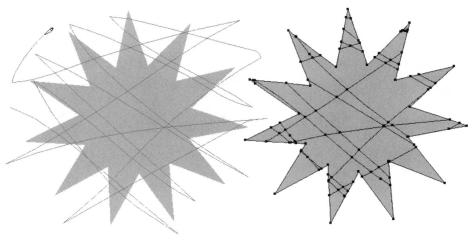

Figure 9-15: Drag willy nilly with the knife tool (left) to hack a path into a hundred or more shards (right).

Slicing with a Path

The bad news about the knife tool is that is doesn't offer much control. You can't carefully position points and control handles to specify the exact directions of your slice; you can't edit the slice after drawing it; heck, you can't even create a series of straight slices.

 That's why Illustrator 6 gives you the Apply Knife command. After drawing a path with any of Illustrator's precision drawing tools, you can use the path to cut through filled objects in your drawing. Here's how it works:

1. Assemble the filled objects that you want to hack to pieces.

Figure 9-16: This lovely star is the product of haphazard knife handling and meticulously filling the paths with radial gradations.

2. Draw the path that you want to use to slice the objects. You can use the pen tool, star tool, spiral tool, or any other drawing tool.

3. Position the path over the objects. Then choose Object » Apply Knife. Illustrator slices through all objects that the selected path overlaps. Even objects in front of the path feel the blade.

In Figure 9-17, I used a spiral to slice through a star. After cutting with the spiral, I also drew a short straight line into the center of the shape with the pen tool (as noted in the figure) and chose the Apply Knife command again. The permitted me to fill different loops of the spiral with different colors. Note that I had to apply these two slices in two different passes. You can't use the Apply Knife command on more than one cutting path at a time.

 Like the knife tool, the Apply Knife command has a habit of deleting unfilled paths. To cut the paths instead of deleting them, press the Control key as you choose Object » Apply Knife. Again, you'll need to reinstate the strokes.

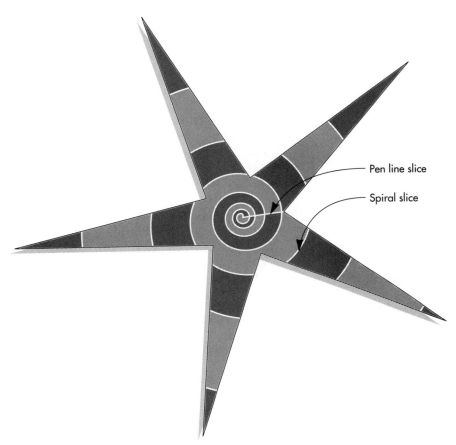

Figure 9-17: Using Object » Apply Knife, I twice sliced into a star, first with a spiral and then with a small straight line created with the pen tool.

Carving Holes into Compound Paths

Illustrator lets you carve holes inside a path. You can see through these holes to objects and colors that lie behind the path. A path with holes in it is called a *compound path*, which is what this section is about.

The most common kind of compound path is converted text. Consider the baroque character in Figure 9-18. This character is actually the combination of three paths—the serrated ruffles on the left side, the main body of the *B*, and the hole inside the *B* (filled with white in the figure). Illustrator automatically

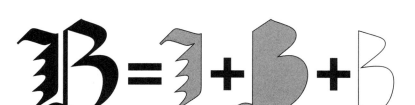

Figure 9-18: This character of type comprises three paths all combined into a single compound path.

combined these three paths into a single compound path when I chose Type » Create Outlines.

At this point you might say, "Why do you need a path with a hole in it? Why not just stick the smaller path in front of the bigger path and fill the smaller path with the background color?" Two reasons:

- First, the background may contain lots of different colors, as in Figure 9-19. To create the first *B* in the figure, I filled the interior shape with light gray in an attempt to vaguely match the background, but it doesn't look right at all. The second *B* is a proper compound path, allowing us to see through the *B* to anything behind it.

Figure 9-19: Three filled paths set in front of a multi-colored background (left) compared with a compound path with a transparent hole carved into it (right).

Second, working with opaque paths limits your flexibility. Even if you can get away with filling an interior path with a flat color, you'll have to change that color any time you change the background or move the objects against a new background. But with a compound path, you can move the object against any background without changing a thing. You can even add elements like drop shadows without modifying the compound path one iota. It's flexibility at its finest.

Creating a Compound Path

Now as I said, Illustrator automatically turns letters into compound paths. But you may want to create additional compound paths of your own. Doughnuts, eyeglasses, windows, ski masks, and guys shot full of bullet holes are just a few of the many real-world items that lend themselves to compound paths.

To make a compound path, do the following:

1. Draw two shapes.

Make one smaller than the other. You can use any tool to draw either shape. The paths can be open or closed, though you'll probably want to stick with closed paths to ensure even curves and continuous strokes. (You can fill open paths, but the fills get flattened off at the open edge.)

2. Select both shapes and choose Object » Compound Paths » Make.

Or press the memorable keyboard equivalent ⌘-8. (Actually, an 8 has two holes in it—more than any other numeral—so it's moderately memorable.) Where the two shapes overlap, the compound path is transparent; where the shapes don't overlap, the path is filled.

For example, I've combined a circle and a star in Figure 9-20. The center of the compound path is transparent, because that's where the two shapes overlap. The outer areas are opaque because the shapes don't overlap. Couldn't be simpler.

If you combined two shapes without getting any holes at all, you must have drawn the shapes in different directions. The solution is to select one of the shapes with the direct selection tool, choose Object » Attributes, and turn the Reverse Path Direction check box on or off. (If it's on, turn it off; if it's off, turn it on.) Then press the Enter key. For a detailed explanation of this weird phenomenon, read the "Reversing Subpath Direction" section a few short pages from now.

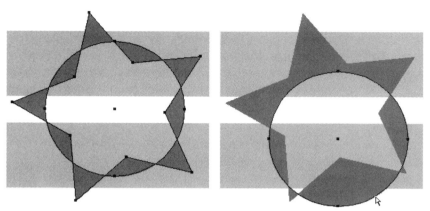

Figure 9-20: After combining a circle and a star into a compound path (left), I can move the circle independently of the star to shift the transparent area (right).

3. Edit the individual shapes in the compound path with the direct selection tool.

After you combine two or more shapes into a compound path, select the entire path by clicking on it with the arrow tool. If you want to select a point or segment belonging to one of the *subpaths*—that's the official name for the shapes inside a compound path—press ⌘-Shift-A to deselect the path and click on an element with the direct selection tool. You can then manipulate points, segments, and control handles as usual.

Option-click with the direct selection tool to select an entire subpath. The second example of Figure 9-20 finds me dragging the circle independently of the star. Notice how Illustrator automatically alters the opaque and transparent areas to account for this movement. You can actually move a hole with respect to the rest of the object. (Wouldn't it be great if you could do that in real life? Think how many favorite old shirts and socks you could recover.)

With the direct selection tool, Option-click a second time on a subpath to select the entire compound path. If you decide later to restore the compound path back to its original independent parts, select the entire path and choose Object » Compound Paths » Release, or press ⌘-9. (How do you remember ⌘-9? Well now, it's the number after 8, isn't it?)

Working with Compound Paths

Compound paths are very special and wonderful things that you can screw up very easily. If you know what you're doing, you can juggle tens or hundreds of subpaths, and even add holes to existing compound paths. But by the same token, you can accidentally add a hole when you don't mean to, or you may encounter a perplexing error message when editing a subpath in a manner that Illustrator doesn't allow.

The following tidbits of information are designed to help eliminate as much confusion as possible:

- You can edit subpaths with the direct selection tool, and even use the add point, delete point, and convert point tools. You can even apply the scissors and knife tools to compound paths.

- What you *can't* do is connect a subpath from one compound path to a subpath from a different compound path, or a different group, whether with the Join command or the pen or freehand tool. This may sound like something you'll never want to do, but believe me. One day, you'll try to connect points from two different compound paths or groups, and you'll go absolutely nuts trying to figure out why Illustrator won't let you do it. It happens to everybody.

  When (not if) it happens to you, you have two options. Give it up, or break the compound paths and groups apart. If you decide on the latter, select two paths you want to connect with the arrow tool. This selects all other subpaths associated with these paths. Then press ⌘-9 once and press ⌘-U about four times in a row. It's overkill, but it's preferable to wasting a lot of time with trial and error. Who knows how many nested groups are involved? Then join the paths and recreate the compound path as desired.

- Another wonderful constraint is that you can't combine shapes from different groups or compound paths into a compound path. If Illustrator complains when you press ⌘-8 that the selected objects are from different groups, press ⌘-9 and ⌘-U a few times to free the chains that bind the objects, and then press ⌘-8 again.

- You can combine as many shapes inside a compound path as you like. You can likewise add subpaths without releasing the compound path. There are two ways to do this. One way is to select the compound path with the arrow tool, Shift-click on the shapes you want to add, and press

⌘-8 again. That's what I did to add the smaller circle to the mix in Figure 9-21. (This doesn't create a compound path inside a compound path or anything weird like that. It just adds the new shapes as a subpaths.)

 Alternatively, you can select the shapes that you want to add to the compound path and cut them by pressing ⌘-X. Then select any subpath in the compound path with the direct selection tool—*not* the arrow tool!—and press either ⌘-F or ⌘-B to paste the cut shapes in front or in back of the selection. This automatically makes the pasted shapes part of the compound path.

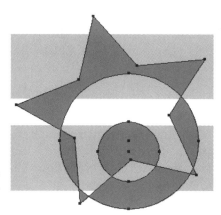

Figure 9-21:
Here I added the smaller circle to the existing compound path by selecting all paths and again pressing ⌘-8.

⦿ Because you can paste a shape into a compound path, you may find yourself doing it accidentally when you don't want to. To avoid pasting inside a compound path, select the entire compound path with the arrow tool and press ⌘-F or ⌘-B. Or deselect all objects in the illustration (⌘-Shift-A) and paste away. In either case, Illustrator understands that the pasted path and compound path are to be treated as two separate entities.

⦿ As far as Illustrator is concerned, a compound path is a single path. Therefore, changing the fill or stroke of one subpath in the compound path changes all other subpaths as well. So if you ever change the color of one shape, and another shape changes as well, you can rest assured both shapes are part of the same compound path.

Reversing Subpath Direction

By this time, you've probably created a compound path or added a new sub-path, only to find that you're not getting any holes. You think you did something wrong, or perhaps I failed to convey a step or two. Neither is the case. It's just that Illustrator needs a little kick in the rear end to make it shape up and fly right.

See, Illustrator calculates opaque and transparent areas in a compound path based on the directions in which the subpaths flow. This may be news to you, but each segment in a path actually goes from one point into another point. This implies a clockwise or counterclockwise flow.

In order for one subpath to create a hole in another, the two paths have to flow in opposite directions. Alternately clockwise and counterclockwise paths do the trick.

At this point you might think, "Oh, great, now I have to pay attention to how I draw my shapes." Luckily, you don't. When you combine two or more shapes into a compound path, Illustrator automatically changes the backmost shape to a clockwise flow and all others to counterclockwise. It does this *regardless of how you drew the shapes!* I emphasize this because I have heard experts expound on stage and in print that the original draw directions matter, and this simply is not true. The back shape is clockwise, others are counterclockwise—it's that cut and dry.

Illustrator's default approach works well when the rear shape in the selection is also the largest shape. The first example in Figure 9-22 shows precisely this setup. The large backmost circle flows clockwise, and the two smaller squares flow coun-

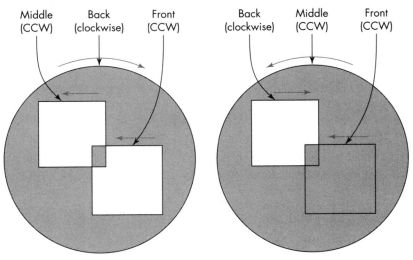

Figure 9-22: Compound paths created when the large circle is in back (left) and one of the squares is in back (right).

terclockwise. Therefore, the counterclockwise squares cut holes in the clockwise circle. But things go awry in the second example, in which one of the squares is in back. The circle and square do not cut holes into the rear square, which leaves the forward square opaque.

But Illustrator wouldn't be Illustrator if it didn't give you the power to correct the situation. You can change the direction of any path by selecting it with the direct selection tool and modifying the setting of a special option in the Attributes dialog box. Here's how to correct a problem like the second example in Figure 9-22:

1. Press ⌘-Shift-A to deselect everything.

2. Select the largest subpath in the compound path with the direct selection tool.

3. Choose Object » Attributes or press ⌘-Control-A. Up comes the Attributes dialog box shown in Figure 9-23.

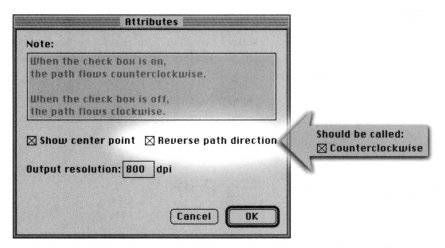

Figure 9-23: The Reverse Path Direction check box just changes the selected subpath from clockwise to counterclockwise.

4. Turn the Reverse Path Direction check box off. This changes the flow of the path from counterclockwise to clockwise. (If the check box is already off, leave it off.)

5. Press the Enter key to close the Attributes dialog box. (Pressing Return inserts carriage returns in the big Note option box.)

6. Now select one of the smaller subpaths that doesn't seem to be behaving correctly with the direct selection tool.

7. Press ⌘-Control-A to bring up the Attributes dialog box again, and turn on the Reverse Path Direction check box to switch the flow of the subpath to counterclockwise.

8. Press Enter to close the dialog box and change the selected subpath.

Keep selecting paths and fiddling with the Reverse Path Direction option as much as you want until you get things the way you want them. Keep in mind you can only achieve transparency in areas where an even number of subpaths overlap. If an odd number of subpaths overlap, the area is always opaque. For example, back in Figure 9-22, the small center space where the circle and both squares overlap is filled with gray regardless of the directions of the subpaths.

 Oh, and one last bit of explanation about the Reverse Path Direction check box: You might think this option would change the direction of the path from the way you drew it to the opposite direction. But no. This option is actually a very simple toggle. It should be called Counterclockwise. Because when it's on, the subpath flows in a counterclockwise direction; and when it off, the subpath flows clockwise.

The Reverse Path Direction check box is dimmed unless a subpath inside a compound path is selected. You cannot change the direction of standard paths for the simple reason that there's no point in doing so.

Use a Path to Clip a Path

The last items on my list of things to discuss—and then I'll let you poor people go home to your families—are the Pathfinder filters. Illustrator 6 provides a total of 14 commands under the Filter » Pathfinder submenu, all of which permit you to combine simple paths into more complex ones. You can merge paths together, subtract one path from another, break paths into bits, and so on.

As you become more adept at using the Pathfinder filters, you'll find them very helpful for assembling primitive shapes—such as rectangles, ovals, polygons, and stars—into more elaborate paths, rather than drawing the elaborate paths from scratch with the pen tool. You can also use the filters to generate translucent color overlays and drop shadows.

In the following sections, I explain every one of the Pathfinder filters except Trap. (Filter » Pathfinder » Trap lets you generate so-called "traps" to eliminate gaps in color printing. I cover this particular filter with the other printing functions in Chapter 18.)

Rather than merely discussing the filters in the order they appear in the Filter » Pathfinder submenu, I examine them in logical order to help you make sense of the commands and determine when and if they might prove beneficial. I also step you through a few specific techniques so you can get a feel for using the filters.

I don't know anyone who uses all 14 of the Pathfinder filters. So don't feel too frustrated if you walk away from this chapter thinking, "I'll be hog-tied if I know what to do with Filter » Pathfinder » Outline," because that's the exact same thing the experts think. Some filters are great, some are fairly lame. The next few sections will make it clear which—according to at least one artist—are which.

Adding Shapes Together

Filter » Pathfinder » Unite combines all selected shapes into a single path. Illustrator removes all the overlapping stuff and turns the selected paths into a single, amalgamated object. It fills and strokes this new object with the fill and stroke from the foremost of the selected paths.

In Figure 9-24, for example, I selected the star, circle, and stripes at top and applied the Unite filter. The result is the single combined path in the middle of the figure.

You can use the Unite filter to combine simple objects to create more complex ones. You can also use the filter to create drop shadows, as in the bottom example of Figure 9-24. Here's what you do:

1. Select the objects that you want to cast the shadow.

2. Copy the objects (⌘-C) and paste them in back of the selection (⌘-B). The Unite filter replaces the selected objects with the united path, so if you want to keep your objects, you need to first duplicate them.

3. Choose Filter » Pathfinder » Unite. Illustrator combines the selected paths into one.

4. Use the arrow keys to nudge the united path down and to the left or right a little. In Figure 9-24, I nudged the path down 4 points and right 3 points.

5. Use the options in the Paint Style palette to delete the stroke and change the fill as desired.

By duplicating and uniting the selected objects, you can create a drop shadow behind multiple objects at a time. Of course, this technique is designed to work with a flat background. In Figure 9-24, for example, I've created a gray shadow against solid white. How do you cast a shadow against a multicolor background?

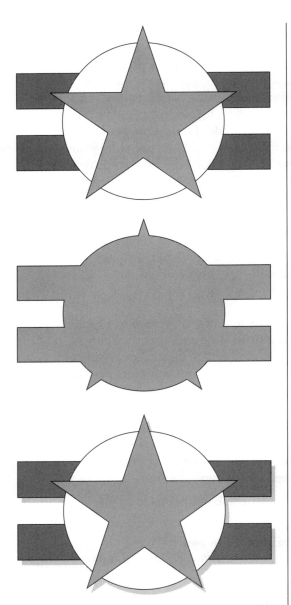

Figure 9-24: Four shapes before (top) and after (middle) applying Filter » Pathfinder » Unite. I then used the united path as a drop shadow behind the original shapes (bottom).

Figure 9-25: After assembling five shapes (top), I applied Filter » Pathfinder » Merge (middle) and deleted the central star shape (bottom).

Well, I still have a few a Pathfinder filters left to discuss, and when I do, you can be sure this technique will be among them.

Illustrator provides one other filter for combining paths, Filter » Pathfinder » Merge. This filter unites paths with the same fill color. It also clips surrounding shapes so there are no overlaps, and (for reasons I can't imagine) deletes the stroke.

Figure 9-25 starts out with a dark gray border around the star that matches the dark gray of the stripes. When I select all five shapes and choose the Merge command, Illustrator combines the dark gray paths into one, as in the middle example of the figure. Because the Merge filter also removes overlaps, I was able to delete the star path to create a "negative space" effect, in which the surrounding objects maintain the shape of the star. I also assigned new strokes to create the last item in Figure 9-25.

Subtracting Shapes from Each Other

Illustrator provides three Pathfinder filters—Exclude, Minus Front, and Minus Back—that subtract shapes from each other:

- Filter » Pathfinder » Exclude is a kind of poor man's compound path function. It removes all overlapping sections of the selected shapes. As shown at the top of Figure 9-26, this leaves a series of holes, much like those in a compound path. The difference is that each filled area is actually a separate shape. In the figure, the Exclude filter has converted my four original paths into 16 new shapes filled with gray.

  The downside is that you can't transform one of the original paths to reposition a hole, as you can inside a compound path. The advantage is that you can fill the individual excluded paths with different colors, as I have in the bottom example of Figure 9-26.

  An exception occurs if one of the selected shapes falls entirely inside another when you apply the Exclude filter. In this case, Illustrator has no choice but to convert the shapes into a compound path.

- The Minus Front filter clips all selected paths out of the rear path in the selection. In Figure 9-27, for example, I selected the star and the circle and chose Filter » Pathfinder » Minus Front. The result is a circle with a star cut out of it.

- Minus Back is exactly the opposite of Minus Front, clipping all selected paths out of the front path in the selection. In Figure 9-28, I selected the circle and stripes and chose Filter » Pathfinder » Minus Back. This left the circle with a two stripes cut out of it.

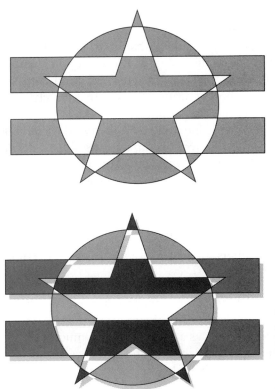

Figure 9-26:
After applying the Exclude filter
to the star, circle, and stripes
(top), I filled the paths with different shades of gray and
added a drop shadow (bottom).

Figure 9-27:
The result of clipping the
star out of the circle with the
Minus Front filter. Again, I
added a drop shadow using
the Unite filter.

Both Minus Front and Minus Back are capable of clipping multiple paths out of a single path. In Figure 9-28, for example, I cut two stripes out of one circle. But what if I want to do it the other way around? What if I want to cut the circle out

Figure 9-28:
Here I used the Minus
Back filter to clip the
stripes out of the circle.

of the two stripes? If I merely select all three paths and choose Filter » Pathfinder » Minus Front, Illustrator clips both the circle and one of the stripes out of the backmost stripe. No matter how I rearrange the shapes, I get scraps from one stripe or the other, but not both.

 The solution is to bring our old friend the compound path into the picture. When you combine shapes into a compound path, Illustrator is fooled into thinking that they're all part of one path. In Figure 9-29, I selected the two stripes and pressed ⌘-8 to combine them together. They don't overlap, so there aren't any holes, but they're all one path as far as Illustrator is concerned. Then I select the circle and choose the Minus Front filter. Illustrator clips the circle from the compound stripes, resulting in what you see in the figure.

Figure 9-29:
After combining the
stripes into a compound
path, I selected stripes
and circle and applied
the Minus Front filter.

Finding Overlap and Intersection

The rest of the Pathfinder filters are devoted to the task of finding and separating the intersecting portions of selected shapes. Foremost among these is Filter » Pathfinder » Intersect, which merely retains the overlapping sections of a bunch of selected shapes and throws away the areas where the shapes don't overlap. Illustrator fills and strokes the resulting shapes with the colors from the frontmost shape in the selection.

 If every one of the selected paths does not overlap at some location, the Intersect command delivers an error message, telling you that the filter would delete everything if Illustrator were dumb enough to let it finish.

The following steps explain how I used the Intersect filter to create the sequence of objects shown in Figure 9-30:

1. I started by selecting the familiar star and circle shapes and copying them to the Clipboard (⌘-C).

2. Next I chose Filter » Pathfinder » Intersect to retain the overlapping portions of the selected star and circle. This resulted in the rounded off star shown at the top of the figure.

3. I pasted the star and circle behind the rounded star (⌘-B). Then I deleted the pasted pointy star for the moment, because, frankly, it was in my face. (It wasn't gone forever, as you'll see when I retrieve it in Step 7.)

4. I next selected the dark stripes and combined them into a single compound path by pressing ⌘-8.

5. I pressed ⌘-Shift-Option-↑, ↓ to create a quick clone of the stripes. Why didn't I simply copy them? Had I done that, I would have replaced the star and circle in the Clipboard, which I needed later (in Step 7). See, I told you that clone-in-place trick would come in handy.

6. I Shift-clicked on the circle to add it to the selection and chose the Intersect command again. (I could have alternatively pressed ⌘-Shift-E, since Intersect was the last filter applied, as I explain at the end of this chapter.)

 Because the stripes were a single compound path, Illustrator found the intersection of each stripe and the circle, as verified by the rounded white stripes in the middle example in Figure 9-30. Had I neglected to combine the stripes in Step 4, Illustrator would have given me an error message, since

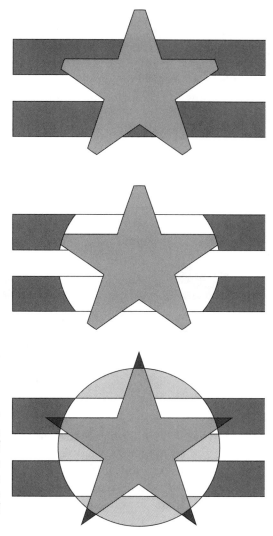

Figure 9-30:
The results of applying the
Intersect filter to the star and
circle (top) and to the circle
and compound stripes
(middle). Then I restored the
original star and circle and
changed their fills (bottom).

the stripes don't overlap with each other. All paths have to overlap to produce an intersection, but Illustrator gives special dispensation to the subpaths in a compound path.

7. Finally, with the newly intersected shapes selected, I pressed ⌘-B to paste the original star and circle in back of the rounded stripes. I then filled the circle with light gray and the star with dark gray to get the effect shown at the bottom of Figure 9-30.

In addition to Intersect, Illustrator provides six Pathfinder filters that split paths into pieces based on the way the paths overlap. All of these commands group the resulting paths together, and all except Outline remove the strokes from the paths. So be prepared to ungroup paths or edit them with the direct selection tool. And you'll have to reapply the strokes, as I've done throughout the figures.

Here's how the six remaining filters work:

- **Crop**: The Crop filter uses the front selected path to crop all other paths in the selection. In Figure 9-31, I selected the circle and stripes, copied them to the Clipboard, and chose Filter » Pathfinder » Crop. The results were the two rounded dark gray stripes. Then I pasted the original circle and stripes behind the cropped shapes, and changed the stripes to black.

*Figure 9-31:
The result of cropping a copy of the stripes inside a copy of the circle and changing the original stripes to black.*

- **Divide**: This filter subdivides all paths according to how they overlap. As shown in the top example of Figure 9-32, the paths don't look much different after you apply the filter, but they are in fact separated into many more shapes than before. In the second example, I've nudged the shapes apart, so you can see how the filter has divvied up the paths and deleted hidden areas.

 Divide is a wonderful filter for creating shadows against a multicolor background. The top example in Figure 9-33 shows the united path (created back in Figure 9-24) positioned against three differently colored shapes. I selected all shapes and applied Filter » Pathfinder » Divide. Then I adjusted the colors of the shadow shapes to get the subtle darkening effect shown in the second example in Figure 9-33. And finally, I pasted the original star, circle, and stripes in front of the shadow to create completed artwork at

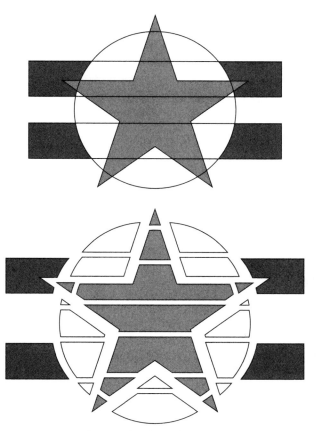

Figure 9-32: The result of applying the Divide filter to all shapes (top) and then nudging them apart (bottom).

the bottom of the figure. (To see a similar technique applied to gradient shadows, check out Chapter 15.)

● **Trim**: This filter is just like Divide, except that it only clips rear shapes, while leaving front shapes intact. Or if you prefer, it's just like Merge, except that it doesn't unite shapes that have the same fill. If you find that Divide breaks up your shapes too much, try Trim instead. I must say, however, that I've never used it in my life and am absolutely bereft of ideas for your using it.

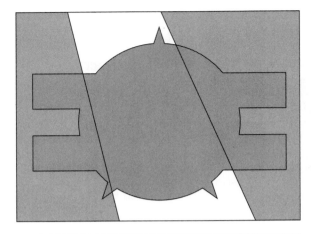

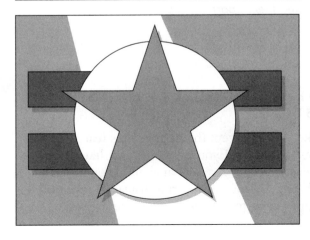

Figure 9-33:
Starting with the united
shadow shape, I divide the
shadow against three dif-
ferently colored shapes
(top), adjust the gray
values (middle), and paste
in the objects casting the
shadow (bottom).

Hard and Soft: The Hard and Soft filters break up objects just like the Divide filter. But they also change the fills of the new paths to represent a mix of the colors in the overlapping objects. The Hard filter mixes the colors in the objects at their highest percentages—that is, the highest amounts of cyan, magenta, yellow, and black ink from all overlapping objects. The Soft filter lets you specify what percentage of the inks you want to blend, thus resulting in lighter colors than the Hard command.

As Figure 9-34 illustrates, both filters are wonderful for blending colors from different shapes. Unfortunately, Figure 9-34 doesn't quite do it justice. See, both Hard and Soft are meant to be used with color illustrations, and here I am faking the effect in grayscale. In fact, if you try to mix two gray shapes with Hard, you'll always get the darkest of the gray values, not a darker blend as shown in the figure. Still, the figure gives you a rough idea of what you can expect.

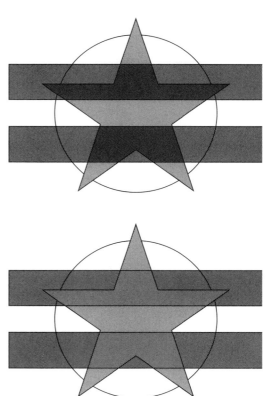

Figure 9-34:
The star, circle, and stripe
shapes mixed using the
Hard (top) and Soft
(bottom) filters, the latter
set to 50 percent.

Outline: Identical to the Divide Stroke from Illustrator 5.0, Outline draws open paths around overlapping areas of selected shapes and strokes these paths with the old fill colors. Figure 9-35 shows this filter applied to the star, circle, and stripes. I've thickened up the strokes (the filter applies 0-point strokes, which is utterly stupid) and added a black rectangle in back so you can see the white outlines around the circle.

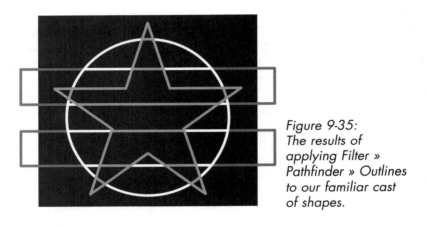

Figure 9-35: The results of applying Filter » Pathfinder » Outlines to our familiar cast of shapes.

Pathfinder Options

Filter » Pathfinder » Options lets you set the parameters for all Pathfinder operations, and does so in an incredibly complicated way. When you choose Filter » Pathfinder » Options, Illustrator displays the dialog box shown in Figure 9-36. Though small, it will melt your brain if you look at it too long.

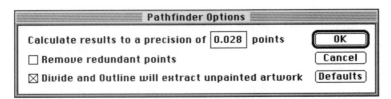

Figure 9-36: My guess is that whoever designed this dialog box has since moved on to a successful career at Microsoft.

The first option lets you control the accuracy of the Pathfinder operations. This value has to be bigger than 0.001 point (0.3 micron, remember?),which means that no path will stray farther than one bacterium off its true course. Larger values are less accurate, but they also speed up the performance of the filters. The maximum value is 999 points, but you probably don't want to go much higher than 4 or 5. I don't recommend changing this value, except for adjusting the Trap filter, as I discuss in Chapter 18. And then be sure to change it back when you're done.

The two check boxes in the Pathfinder Options dialog box delete points that overlap each other and objects created by the Divide and Outline commands that have transparent fills and strokes. I recommend you select both these options and leave them selected, unless you have some special reason for retaining overlapping points and invisible objects.

 To change the performance of the Hard, Soft, or Trap filter before applying it, press the Option key when choosing the filter. The Pathfinder Options dialog box appears, just as if you had chosen the Options command. After you change the settings, press the Return key to initiate the filter. It's an obscure little tip, and you may never find yourself needing to take advantage of it, but there it is just the same.

Reapplying a Pathfinder Filter

Oh, and one more thing: Assuming the last command you chose from the Filter menu was a Pathfinder filter, you can reapply the filter by either choosing the first command in the Filter menu or pressing ⌘-Shift-E. To change the settings for the command (as with the Hard or Soft filters), press ⌘-Shift-Option-E. This is a common function that applies to all commands under the Filter menu, including Filter » Objects » Offset Path.

DEVELOPING A FLAIR FOR THE SCHEMATIC

Every so often, I run into artists who tell me that they use FreeHand because it offers better precision drawing controls—rulers, guides, grids, and so on. Others tell me they use Illustrator because they don't need all those precision controls. The irony is that Illustrator offers some very capable schematic tools—frequently outperforming FreeHand, and pretty thoroughly making mincemeat of CorelDraw and other illustration programs.

FreeHand's notable schematic advantage over Illustrator is that it offers a grid, which helps to keep basic illustrations in alignment. (Strangely, Illustrator 4.1 for Windows provides a grid, which remains absent from Illustrator 6. Are we to assume Windows users like grids more than Mac folks, or that grids are easier to pull off on the Windows side? Go figure.) FreeHand also lets you move points and objects to exact numerical coordinates, while the new Control palette in Illustrator 6 lets you position objects only.

But Illustrator provides a more flexible system of guidelines, a superior measuring function, center points for all shapes, and the ability to align both objects and individual points. (FreeHand aligns objects only.) I wouldn't go so far as to say that Illustrator is better than FreeHand in the precision department, but I would argue that the two programs run neck-and-neck—each has its own strengths and weaknesses.

So if you're the type who values a structured drawing environment, keep your chin up and continue reading. This chapter explains everything, from distance to distribution, groups to guidelines, and locks to layers. If it helps you toe the line, it's front and center in the following pages.

Measuring and Positioning with Microscopic Precision

One of my favorite things about Illustrator is that you can measure dimensions and distances right inside the program. There's no need to print the illustration and measure the output, which is dreadfully inconvenient. And you sure as heck wouldn't want to take a pica pole to the screen, which is horribly inaccurate. Fortunately, Illustrator's built-in capabilities are both more convenient and more accurate than either of those alternatives. Where else can you click on screen to measure discrepancies as slight as 0.0001 point, roughly the length of bacteria razor stubble?

Okay, bacteria don't actually shave—they'd get caught in the blades. But if an average-sized bacterium had eyes, its pupils would be about 0.0001 point across. Infectious diseases have a hard time measuring distances as small as 0.0001 point, and at your relatively gargantuan height of 4,000 to 5,000 points tall, you can't get anything close to that kind of accuracy without a powerful microscope.

Illustrator provides three sets of measuring and positioning devices:

- The horizontal and vertical rulers are handy for tracking the cursor. They're about as accurate as real-life rulers, meaning that they're good enough for simple alignment but you can't quite measure bacteria with them.

- The measure tool records scrupulously precise dimensions and distances into the Info palette. When the palette is up on screen, you can measure an object simply by selecting it. You can even record values with the measure tool, then turn around and move an object that precise distance and direction.

- The Control palette lets you position objects according to numerical coordinates. You can move objects or clone them by merely entering a value and pressing Return. The palette has its disadvantages, but it can be useful for quick adjustments.

The following sections explain these items, as well as Arrange » Move, which captures all the pertinent statistics recorded with the measure tool. Together, the rulers, measure tool, Info palette, Move command, and Control palette form a powerful collection of measuring and positioning gadgets. I doubt you'll find their equal in any program this side of a Cray supercomputer.

Adding Rulers to the Illustration Window

Illustrator gives you two rulers—one vertical and one horizontal—that track the movement of your cursor. To bring them up on screen, press ⌘-R or choose View » Show Rulers. The horizontal ruler appears along the bottom of the illustration window, and the vertical ruler appears on the right side, as in Figure 10-1.

 You control the unit of measure used by both rulers by pressing ⌘-K and selecting an option from the Ruler Units pop-up menu in the General Preferences dialog box. Alternatively, you can cycle through the units—from picas to inches to millimeters and back to picas—by pressing ⌘-U. U know, U for units.

As on traditional rulers, whole picas, inches, and centimeters are indicated by long tick marks; individual points and millimeters appear as short tick marks. If you magnify the view size, the units on the rulers become more detailed; as you zoom out, some of the tick marks drop away.

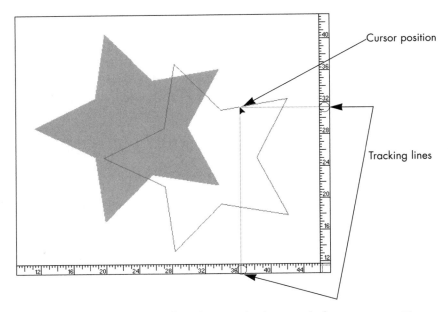

Figure 10-1: The horizontal and vertical rulers track the cursor position.

The rulers constantly track the position of the cursor, as long as the cursor is inside the illustration window. Figure 10-1 labels the dotted tracking line in each ruler. As you can see, the rulers track the tip of the cursor, known as the *hot spot*. In the figure, the hot spot measures 31 picas, 6 points above and 36 picas, 3 points to the right of the absolute zero point where the rulers begin (as explained in the next section).

Illustrator displays rulers independently for each open drawing, so you can have one illustration window with the rulers visible and another with the rulers hidden. Illustrator saves the ruler status along with the illustration file; if the rulers are up when you save the file, they'll be up again next time you open it.

 To make the rulers come up for all new illustrations, open the Adobe Illustrator Startup file in the Plug-ins folder, press ⌘-R to display the rulers, draw a rectangle (or something simple) and then delete it to get the Save command's attention, and press ⌘-S. From now on, each new illustration window will come with rulers.

To get the rulers the heck out of the way, press ⌘-R or choose View » Hide Rulers. Oh sure, you already knew that, but we don't leave any stone unturned around here.

Setting the Point Where All Things Are Zero

The point at which both rulers show 0 is called the *zero point* or *ruler origin*. By default, the ruler origin is located at the bottom left corner of the artboard. If you change the size of the artboard or the location of the page boundary, the ruler origin may get jostled around a bit.

You can relocate the ruler origin at any time by dragging from the ruler origin box, which is that little square where the rulers intersect. In Figure 10-2, I've dragged the ruler origin onto a point in the star, allowing me to measure all distances from that point. The ruler values update after you release the mouse button. The new ruler origin affects not only the rulers, but also the coordinate positioning values in the Info and Control palettes.

 You can save a revised ruler origin with the Adobe Illustrator Startup file. For example, you might prefer to have the zero point in the upper left corner of the illustration. Your change will affect all future illustrations.

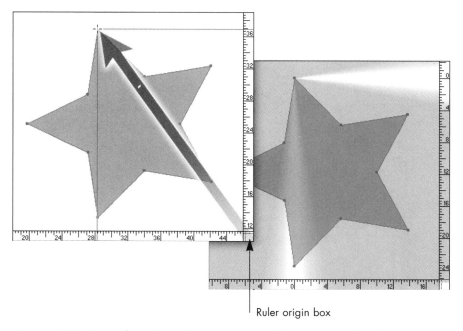

Ruler origin box

Figure 10-2: Drag from the ruler origin box (left) to reposition the zero point (right).

Measuring the Minutia

The measure tool and its sidekick, the Info palette, are Illustrator's dynamic duo of precision positioning features . Both items allow you to measure distances and objects. There are three ways to measure in Illustrator:

- Select the measure tool, the sixth tool on the left side of the toolbox. Then drag from one location in the illustration window to another. Illustrator displays the Info palette, which lists the distance and direction between the beginning and end of your drag. You can also click with the measure tool. When you do, the Info palette lists the distance and angle between the new click point and the previous one.

- Press ⌘-Control-I to display the Info palette, or choose Window » Show Info. Then use the arrow tool to select the object that you want to measure. The width and height of the segment appear automatically in the palette.

- With the Info palette up on screen, drag with one of the tools in the main toolbox. When you move the pen tool cursor, the Info palette tells you the distance and direction of the cursor from the last point. When

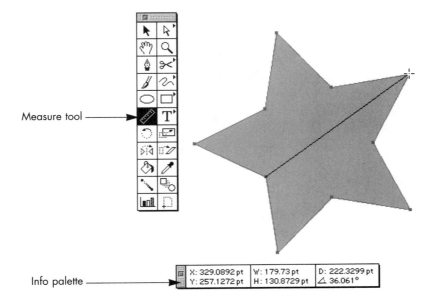

Measure tool

Info palette

Figure 10-3: Drag with the measure tool to display the distance and direction between two points in the Info palette.

dragging an object with the arrow tool, the palette tells you the distance and direction of the drag. When using the scale or rotate tool, the palette lists the percentage of the scaling or the angle of rotation. The palette is constantly trying to tell you something when you create and edit objects. Only when using a plug-in tool does the Info palette fail to provide feedback.

Assuming the Snap to Point check box in the General Preferences dialog box is selected, the measure tool snaps to an anchor point when you click within 2 screen pixels of it. In Figure 10-3, for example, I dragged from one anchor point to another to measure the precise distance between the two. Sadly, Illustrator doesn't give you any snap cursors to show that you've hit the points, but you can see the cursor snap into place if you watch carefully. Or just trust The Force.

The Info palette includes as many as six numerical values. Here's what they mean:

- **X, Y**: When using a drawing tool, the X and Y values in the Info palette represent the coordinate position of your cursor, as measured from the ruler origin.

  When using the measure tool, the values tell the last place you clicked with the tool (or released when dragging). This way, you know what Illustrator is measuring from the next time you click—providing you are proficient at reading coordinates.

  If the direct selection or arrow tool is active, X and Y indicate the top left corner of the selection.

  And when using a transformation tool, X and Y tell the center of the scaling, rotation, reflection, or skew. More on this topic in Chapter 11.

- **W, H**: The W and H values list the width and height of a selected object. They also tell you the dimensions of a rectangle, ellipse, text block, or graph as you draw it.

  When moving an object, or when dragging with the measure, pen, convert point, or gradient vector tool, the W and H values tell you the horizontal and vertical components of your drag, as demonstrated by the W and H values in Figure 10-4.

- **D**: This item tells the direct distance between one point and another, as the crow flies. When dragging with the pen or convert point tool, this value tells the length of the Bézier lever, which is the distance between the anchor point and control handle. With other tools, it simply tells you the distance of your drag.

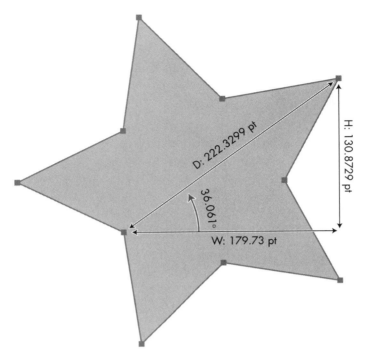

Figure 10-4: The values from the Info palette in Figure 10-3 diagrammed onto the star shape.

 Angle: The ∠ item indicates the angle of your drag, as measured from the mean horizontal. Figure 10-4 shows how Illustrator measures counterclockwise starting at 3 o'clock. 90 degrees is a quarter circle, 360 degrees is a full circle.

> If you want to exactly match the angle of a measured line, you can write down the angle value in the Info palette and then enter it into the Constrain Angle option box in the General Preferences dialog box. This rotates the constraint axes, permitting you to Shift-drag objects relative to the angled line, as I discussed back in the "Keeping Your Movements in Line" section of Chapter 5.

However, keep in mind that rotating the contraint axes also affects the angle value in the Info palette. For example, if the Constrain Angle value in the General Preferences dialog box is set to 40 degrees and you measure a horizontal line, the Info palette tells you the line is set to –40 degrees. In other words, don't trust the angle value in the Info palette except when the Constrain Angle value is 0 degrees.

When using the rotate tool, this value tells you the angle of rotation. The reflect tool uses the angle value to impart the angle of the reflection axis. When using the shear tool, you get two angle values, one for the axis, and the other for the skew. I cover all these wacky terms in Chapter 11 when I explore transformations in earnest.

- **W%, H%**: These values appear when scaling an object. They tell you the change in width and height, measured as percentages of the original dimensions.

When using the zoom tool, the Info palette tells you the current view size (which is redundant, since Illustrator tells you this in the title bar). When editing text, the Info palette lists the type size, font, and tracking. When kerning, the second item lists the general tracking values minus the kerning value to give you an overall kerning total.

Translating Measurement to Movement

After you measure a distance with the move tool, Illustrator automatically stores those W, H, D, and angle values in a tiny buffer in memory. Use the tool again, and the previous measurements are tossed by the wayside to make room for the new ones. Illustrator also uses this buffer to track movements made by dragging with the arrow or direct selection tool, or nudging with the arrow keys. Again, whatever action is most recent replaces the previous contents of the buffer.

You can translate these buffered measurements into movements by selecting an object or two and choosing Arrange » Move. Or try one of the following shortcuts:

- Press ⌘-Shift-M, the keyboard equivalent for Arrange » Move.

- Option-clicking on the arrow tool icon in the toolbox also displays the Move dialog box. This is a weird way to go, admittedly, but a lot of Illustrator folks use it by pure force of habit. It's a leftover from Illustrator 1.0, when Option-clicking on the arrow tool was the *only* way access the Move feature. (Sigh.) Those were the days—back when Illustrator didn't support color and you had to ungroup a circle to edit it. Makes me kind of misty just thinking about it.

Whatever method you use, you get the Move dialog box shown in Figure 10-5. As you can see, the option boxes contain the same values I recorded in the Info palette back in Figure 10-3. The Move dialog box always supplies you with the buffered distance and angle values, permitting you to quickly move objects a measured distance or to repeat a move made by dragging with the arrow tool. You can likewise negate a move by changing positive values to negative and vice versa. Or you can retain just the horizontal portion of a move by changing the Horizontal value to 0 and inverting the Vertical value. Then again . . . well, you get the idea. There are all kinds of ways to rehash old measurement and movement information.

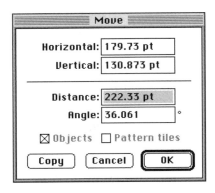

Figure 10-5:
The Move dialog box
always presents you
with the results of the last
measurement or movement.

If you feel the urge, you can even enter totally new values into the various option boxes. You can express your move by entering values into the Horizontal and Vertical option boxes, *or* the Distance or Angle option boxes. Since these are two different ways to express the same information, changing one set of values automatically changes the other.

 You can also do math inside the option boxes. Simple arithmetic, but math nonetheless. Enter + to add, – to subtract, * to multiply, and / to divide. For example, if you know you want to move a select object 3 points farther than your last measurement, you can enter *+3* after the value in the Distance option box. Then press Tab and watch Illustrator do the math for you. This technique works inside a smattering of other palettes and dialog boxes as well, including the Control palette.

The two check boxes, Objects and Pattern Tiles, affect objects with tiled fills exclusively. For the lowdown on these—and a wonderful shortcut involving the P key—consult the authoritative Chapter 15.

You can move the selected objects the specified distance and direction by pressing the Return key. To clone the objects before moving them, click on the Copy button, or press Option-Return.

 One regrettable difference between Move dialog box and Info palette is that the former is slightly less accurate. The Move dialog box accepts no more than three digits after the decimal point, so measured values get rounded off. For example, the H: 130.8729 value from Figure 10-3 becomes a Vertical value of 130.873 in Figure 10-5. And D: 222.3299 loses two digits on its way to a Distance value of 222.33. In most cases, such small difference won't make a lick of difference in your printed output. But if it does, you may want to resort to Illustrator's automatic alignment options, which I discuss later in this chapter.

Coordinate Positioning

 The last item on the precision position parade is the Control palette, pictured in Figure 10-6. You bring the palette up on screen by choosing Window » Show Control Palette. (Sorry, no keyboard shortcut.) You can then enter values into one of the six option boxes and press Return to apply them to one or more selected objects.

The first item in the Control palette is the reference point icon. Labeled in the figure, this items lets you specify whether the coordinates in the X and Y option boxes represent the upper left corner of the selection, the middle of the selection, or one of seven other locations. Click on one of the little points in the icon to relocate the reference point. Illustrator updates the X and Y values automatically.

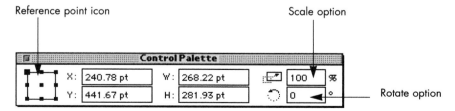

Figure 10-6: The new Control palette included with Illustrator 6.

Illustrator positions the reference points around an object with respect to its imaginary bounding box, as illustrated in Figure 10-7. Therefore, the center indicated by the reference point icon in the Control palette is almost never the true center of the object (except with very simple shapes like rectangles and ellipses). In Figure 10-7, I've marked the true center of the star with a gray X, which lies several points to the right of the bounding box center. In fact, *anytime* Illustrator calculates the center of an object—a theme I will revisit several times in this chapter and the next—it uses the bounding box center. It's something to keep in mind as you use Illustrator's automated tools.

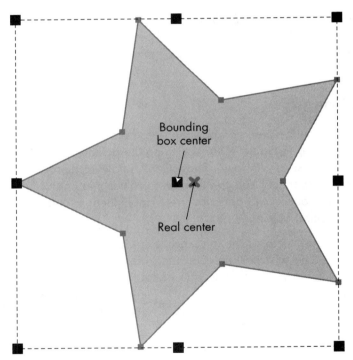

Figure 10-7: The center of the bounding box is rarely equivalent to the true center of an object.

You can enter new values into the X and Y option boxes to change the location of the object on the artboard. You can also adjust the W and H values to change the width and height of the bounding box, which in turn stretches or shrinks the selected objects. The scale and rotate options on the right side of the palette let you resize and rotate selections. Chapter 11 covers these transformations in depth.

As in the Move dialog box, you can perform arithmetic calculations in the X, Y, W, and H options using the standard +, −, *, and / operators. Unfortunately, you can't do math inside the scale or rotate option boxes.

 Amazing as it may seem, you can clone objects directly from the Control palette. Just enter a value into one of the option boxes, press Option-Return if you want to clone the selection, and exit the Control palette. Or press Option-Tab—that's right, Option-Tab—to clone and tab to the next option box. Very cool implementation, I must say.

Aligning and Distributing Objects

 Adobe has slightly reworked the alignment options in Illustrator 6. First, the options are now presented in a floating palette instead of a dialog box. And second, Illustrator 6 offers a few additional distribution options for evening out the distance between selected objects.

To display the Align palette, choose Window » Show Align. (Again, there is no shortcut.) Shown in Figure 10-8, this dainty little palette contains six Align icons and six Distribute icons. The first row of each aligns or distributes objects horizontally; the second row works vertically. For example, click on the first icon in the top row to align the selected objects along their left edges, click on the second icon to center the objects, and click on the right icon to align the right edges. Select the objects that you want to align or distribute and click on an icon. Illustrator adjusts the objects immediately.

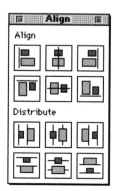

Figure 10-8:
Select the objects that
you want to align or
distribute and click on an
icon in the Align palette.

When aligning objects, Illustrator aligns to the most extreme object in the group. For example, if you align selected objects along their left-hand sides, the leftmost object remains stationary and the other objects line up to meet it.

 As with the Control palette, the options in the Align palette work from the bounding boxes of selected objects. This means that centered objects in particular may not look properly centered. If you encounter this problem, try the workaround I suggest in the upcoming "Adding a Center Point" section.

To use one of Illustrator's Distribute options, you have to select three or more objects. This is because Illustrator compares the space between objects when distributing them; you have to select three objects to have two spaces to compare.

Rather than evening out the amount of space between objects—which is what you might expect—the Distribute options even out the space between the edges or centers of the bounding boxes. Figure 10-9 shows the effects of the first row of Distribute icons on three objects. The figure depicts the bounding box for each object as a gray rectangle; I've also used dotted lines to show which portion of the object gets distributed. As you can see, it's the dotted lines—not the objects themselves—that are evenly spaced.

 To align or distribute multiple objects together, first group the objects by choosing Arrange » Group (⌘-G). For example, I grouped each of the simple paths with its bounding box before applying settings from the Align palette.

Aligning Individual Points

The options in the Align palette affect whole objects at a time. But Illustrator also lets you align selected points independently of their objects by choosing Object » Average (⌘-L). You can arrange two or more points into horizontal or vertical alignment, or you can snap the points together to make them coincident. In each case, Illustrator averages the locations of the points, so all points move.

First select the points you want to align with the direct selection tool. Then press ⌘-L to display the Average dialog box, which provides three radio buttons. You can either make all points coincident (Both), arrange them in a horizontal line (Horizontal Only), or arrange them vertically (Vertical Only).

In top example of Figure 10-10, I selected the bottom three points in each of two star shapes. Then I applied the Average command and selected the Horizontal

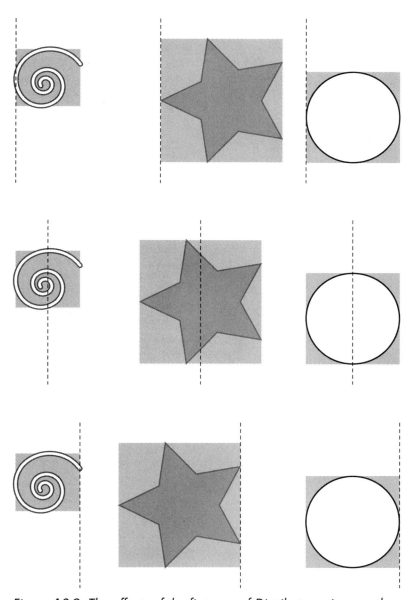

Figure 10-9: The effects of the first row of Distribute options on three objects. The gray rectangles represent bounding boxes; the dotted lines show which portions of the bounding boxes get distributed.

Figure 10-10: After selecting a few points in a couple of shapes with the direct selection tool (top), I aligned the points into horizontal formation (bottom).

Only radio button. Illustrator responded by flattening off the bottoms of both stars, as in the second example. Kinda makes it look like they're comin' out of the earth, don't it?

NOTE Lots of folks use the Average command to move two points together before fusing them with Object » Join. If that's all you want to do, just press ⌘-Option-J and have done with it (as I advised in Chapter 9). You're better off using the Average command when you want to align points in formation or bring points together from different shapes *without* joining them.

 You can even average the alignment points in point text, which is a great way to arrange bits of point text into columns, or align labels with callout lines. The hyper-realistic medical illustrations in Figures 10-11 and 10-12 show what I mean. After creating the series of labels and callout lines along the right side of the figures, I selected a label and the rightmost point in its line. Then I averaged their locations by pressing ⌘-L and selecting the Both radio button. (This option is the default setting, so I could press ⌘-L and immediately whack the Return key if I wanted to.) I repeated this for each label to get the results in Figure 10-11.

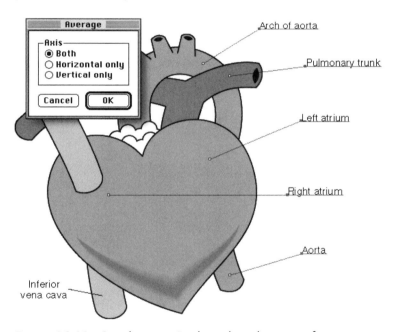

Figure 10-11: One by one, I selected each piece of point text and the right point in its callout line and averaged their locations.

Then I selected all labels and the right points in their callout lines and pressed ⌘-L again, this time selecting the Vertical Only radio button. Illustrator arranged the labels into one column, as in Figure 10-12.

Labels don't look so hot stuck to their callout lines, so I would next select the point text and nudge it to the right and down a few points with the arrow keys. And finally, I would ship the illustration to John Hopkins where it would be used to train the surgeons of tomorrow.

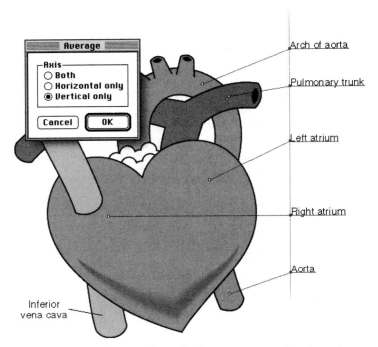

Figure 10-12: Then I selected all point text and right points in all callout lines and arranged them into a vertical column.

Adding a Center Point

Illustrator lets you assign any object a center point. You do so by selecting the object, choosing Object Attributes (⌘-Control-A), selecting the Show Center Point check box, and pressing Enter. This center point acts just like the ones Illustrator automatically includes with rectangles and ellipses. You can view the center point in the artwork mode or when the object is selected in the preview mode. You can also drag the object by its center point.

This should be a great feature. For example, you should be able to drag the center point from one point onto the center point of another shape and have Illustrator align them exactly. Unfortunately, just like the Control and Align palettes, Illustrator positions the center point with respect to the bounding box, which is rarely the true center of the shape except in the case of rectangles (which are the same shape as their bounding boxes) and ellipses (which are uniformly round).

For example, suppose that you want to center a star inside a circle. If you first draw the circle, and then draw the star from the circle's center point, you'd end up with two precisely aligned shapes, as demonstrated in Figure 10-13. This is because Illustrator knows where the real center of a star is when you're drawing it. But if you add a center point to the star, and then drag the center point until it snaps onto the center point of the circle, you get the weird effect shown in Figure 10-14. (The same thing happens if you select the two shapes and click on the two center icons in the Align palette.) Illustrator hasn't centered the shapes; it's centered the bounding boxes.

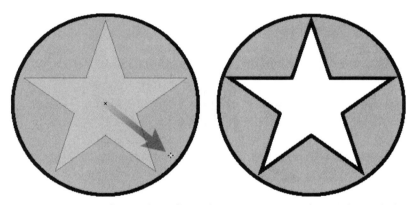

Figure 10-13: When I drag from the center point of a circle with the star tool (left), Illustrator precisely aligns both star and circle by their true centers (right).

*Figure 10-14:
If I add a center point to the star and then drag the star by that point until it snaps to the circle's center point, the shapes align like this.*

Luckily, there's a workaround that's as old as the first version of Illustrator. To create your own accurate center point, follow these steps:

1. **Delete any center point you've already added with the Attributes command**.

   Press ⌘-Control-A, turn off the Show Center Point check box, and press the Enter key.

2. **Duplicate the shape in place**.

   Press ⌘-C, ⌘-F to go the copy-in-place route. Or press ⌘-Shift-Option-⬆, ⬇ to clone.

3. **Choose Filter » Objects » Add Anchor Points**.

   This technique accounts for the locations of points only, which means that curved segments can throw it off. If there are any curved segments in the shape, apply the Add Anchor Points filter to double the number of anchor points in the shape. If there are lots of curved segments, choose the filter and press ⌘-Shift-E a couple of times to reapply it.

4. **Average all points in the shape**.

   Press ⌘-L to bring up the Average dialog box. Immediately press Return to accept the default Both setting. This causes Illustrator to average all points in the path. If the path is composed entirely of straight segments—as with a star—you'll see what looks like a single point in the middle of the shape. If the path includes curved segments, you'll see a point with a bunch of squiggles coming out of it. In both cases, you're actually seeing a bunch of points clustered into a single location.

5. **Shift-click on the point with the direct selection tool and press Delete**.

   Now you have a gob of points, but you want to keep just one of them. Shift-click on the selected center point with the direct selection tool to deselect the single frontmost point. The point turns hollow to show that it's still part of a selected path. Then press Delete to clear all points except the one you just deselected. This leaves one true center point.

6. **Change the fill and stroke to transparent**.

   Some printers will try to print the fill or stroke of a single, disconnected point. To avoid this, it's a good precaution to make the point transparent.

7. Group the center point with the shape.

Shift-click on the path with the arrow tool (or Shift-Option-click with the direct selection tool) and press ⌘-G to group the selection.

Now if you drag the center point with the arrow tool, you can snap it to the center point of another path to precisely align the two.

 There is one downside, however: Unlike automatic center points, custom center points don't automatically reposition themselves when you reshape a path. That is to say, the custom centers remain on target when you move or transform the entire grouped shape, but if you alter individual points and segments, the center becomes inaccurate.

Creating and Using Custom Guides

Another way to align objects is to establish a system of *guidelines* (or just plain *guides*). These are special kinds of paths that appear dotted on screen but never print. Assuming the Snap to Point option is turned on in the General Preferences dialog box, your cursor aligns to the guideline any time you drag within two pixels of it. Unlike standard paths, your cursor snaps to *any* position along the outline of a guide, regardless of the placement of anchor points.

You can create a guide in one of the following ways:

• Drag from one of the rulers to create a perpendicular guide the entire width or height of the 10-foot by 10-foot pasteboard. In Figure 10-15, for example, I dragged from the horizontal ruler to create a horizontal guide. The guideline appears in the illustration window as a dotted line, clearly distinguishing it from printing objects.

 If you change your mind while dragging a guide from one of the rulers, press the Option key to rotate it 90 degrees. So Option-dragging from the horizontal ruler creates a vertical guide. The guides remains rotated only so long as the Option key is down.

• To create a custom guideline in the shape of a circle, star, or even a character of type, select a path that you've drawn in the illustration window and choose Object » Guides » Make. Or you can use the shortcut ⌘-5. (I might suggest that you can remember ⌘-5 because guides are right in the middle of things and 5 is the middle number. But that would be a stretch.)

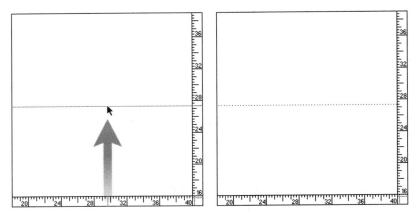

Figure 10-15: Dragging from the bottom ruler (left) creates a horizontal guideline that stretches the entire width of the pasteboard (right).

You can convert all varieties of paths to guidelines, including compound paths. You can even convert groups, selections inside groups, and the bars or lines inside graphs. The one thing you can't turn into a guide is text (unless you first convert the text to paths with Type » Create Outlines, like the big R in Figure 10-16). So if you get an error message when pressing ⌘-5, you can be sure your selection includes some text. Deselect the text and try again.

To create a guideline without sacrificing the original path, copy the path (⌘-C), paste it in back (⌘-B), and then choose Object » Guides » Make (⌘-5) to convert the duplicate to a guideline.

If you convert a single path within a group to a guideline, without converting other paths in the group, the guideline remains a member of that group. Drag the group with the arrow tool, the guide moves as well. It's a very handy way to keep certain guides and objects together.

Unlocking and Editing Guides

By default, Illustrator locks guides so they don't get too tangled up with your printed paths. You can't select a locked guide by clicking on it, which prevents you from messing it up. To unlock all guides in an illustration, choose the Object » Guides » Lock, or press ⌘-7. The check mark in front of the Lock command disappears, showing that the lock is off.

Once the guides are unlocked, you can select and manipulate them as you can any other graphic object. When you click on a guide with the arrow or direct

Figure 10-16: Press ⌘-5 to convert selected paths—including converted text and compound paths (top)—to custom snap-to guidelines (bottom).

selection tool, Illustrator shows you the guide's anchor points (see Figure 10-17) to let you know it's selected. Use the direct selection tool to reshape the guide. Shift-click or marquee to select multiple guides at a time. Press the Delete key to delete a selected guide. You can also move guides or transform them. You can even use the add point, delete point, and convert point tools on a guideline.

Once you've gotten the guides the way that you want them, press ⌘-7 again to relock them. This locks *all* guides, not just those that were selected.

Manipulating Locked Guides

As fortune would have it, it's not absolutely necessary to unlock a guide in order to select it. You can select a locked guide by Shift-Control-clicking on it with the arrow or direct selection tool. The points momentarily appear and then disappear again, showing that Illustrator acknowledges your click.

The following items describe ways to manipulate a locked guide:

- To move a locked guide with the arrow or direct selection tool, Shift-Control-drag it to a new location. After beginning the drag, release the keys to move the guide without constraint.

- If any other tool is selected, ⌘-Shift-Control-drag the guide.

- Press Option along with the other keys to clone a locked guide. Be sure to keep the Option key pressed until after you release the mouse button.

You can't reshape a locked guide, since you can't select a point or segment independently of any others. And you can't select or manipulate multiple locked guides at a time unless they are members of the same group or compound path.

Want to hear a weird one? If a guide is part of a group or compound path, it and its pals remain selected after you Shift-Control-drag them. This is true even if the other paths in the group or compound path are also guides. This means that after you move the guides, you can then scale or rotate them from the Control palette, even though they're still locked. To take advantage of this peculiarity, I group each and every path—by itself—before I make it a guide. This way, I have a wider range of editing options when the guides are locked.

Converting Guides to Objects

If your eyes grow tired from editing sparsely dotted guidelines, or if you simply want to turn a guide into a printing object, you can convert a guide back to a path. To do so, unlock the guide by pressing ⌘-7, select it, and then choose Object » Guides » Release (or press ⌘-6). Illustrator converts custom guides back to paths, even remembering their original fill and stroke colors. Ruler guides convert into lines that extend the entire width or length of the pasteboard.

To convert a locked guide back into a path, Shift-Control-double-click on the guide with one of the selection tools. If some other tool is selected, Press ⌘-Shift-Control-double-click.

Assembling Paths into Groups

Most of the time, you'll apply transformations to whole paths rather than to individual points or segments. You may even want to transform multiple objects at a time. So imagine that instead of working with paths and objects, you can manipulate whole pieces of artwork. A boy here, a dog there, a great white shark preparing to eat the both of them a few meters away. This is the beauty of grouping, which allows you to assemble throngs of elements into a single object.

Suppose, for example, that you've created a graphic made up of several paths. You want to rotate the graphic, but you're afraid of upsetting the fragile relationship between the paths during the transformation. To safeguard the basic appearance of the graphic, select the objects and choose Arrange » Group. Or press the common-as-dirt keyboard equivalent, ⌘-G.

Illustrator always groups entire objects. Even if you select a single point in one object and a segment in another, the two objects join the group in their entirety. There's no way to group a couple of points or segments independently of others in a path.

You can group paths, compound paths, text objects, imported images, or any other kind of artwork. You can even group other groups. Illustrator permits infinite hierarchies of groups, so that one group may contain two groups which each contain six others, and so on. It's like a giant family tree of object protection.

Selecting Objects within Groups

Paths and text blocks inside groups remain autonomous objects. You can apply different fills and strokes, reshape the paths, move and transform them, and do most of the same things that you can do to ungrouped paths and text blocks. There are a few limitations, but Illustrator does a good job of beeping at you and telling you where you've gone wrong if you step over the line.

In order to edit objects inside groups, you have to first select them:

- Click on any object in a group with the arrow tool to select the entire group.

- To edit text inside a group, drag across the characters with the type tool, as you normally would.

- If you use the direct selection tool to click on a point or segment inside a group, you select that one element independently of all other points and segments in the group. You can also Shift-click and marquee elements with the direct selection tool, just as when working with non-groups.

- Option-click on a path twice in a row—it's not necessary to double-click—to select the entire path and the group that contains that path.

- Option-click a third time to select the group that contains the selected group. Each successive Option-click selects the next group up.

There's no limit to the number of ways you can select paths inside extensive, multi-story groups. To select two groups inside a larger group, for example, Option-click twice on one group, the Shift-Option-click on a path in the other group and Option-click a second time on that same path.

🌑   If you find Option-clicking with the direct selection tool too confusing, you can use the group selection tool—that hollow arrow with the plus sign in the direct selection tool slot. It works just like the direct selection tool with the Option key down, but some folks find it easier to work with.

If you clone an object within a group by Option-dragging it, the clone becomes part of the group as well. Or you can copy a path inside a group and paste it in front or in back to make it part of the group. Illustrator also lets you use the Clipboard to transfer outside objects into a group. To do this, select the object you want to insert into the group, cut it (⌘-X), select any path inside the group with the direct selection tool, and choose Paste In Front or Paste In Back (⌘-F or ⌘-B).

If you want to duplicate an object separately of its group, be sure to deselect the group before pasting it. That is, select the object with the direct selection tool, copy it (⌘-C), press ⌘-Shift-A to deselect the group, and choose any of the Paste commands (⌘-V, ⌘-F, or ⌘-B). I know, it sounds like a lot of nit-picky mumbo jumbo, but once you try it out a few times, you'll quickly get the hang of it.

Ungrouping

You can ungroup any group by choosing Arrange » Ungroup or pressing ⌘-U. You have to ungroup each group one level at a time. So if a group contains three other groups, you'd have to press ⌘-U four times in a row to disassociate all of them.

Ungrouping is occasionally an essential part of the reshaping process. Most notably, you can't combine two paths from different groups, whether by joining their endpoints or making them into a compound path. So if you want to join two open paths from different groups into a single longer path, for example, you have to first ungroup the paths and then apply the Join command.

Distinguishing Groups from Non-Groups

What if ungrouping a path doesn't produce the desired effect? It may be that the object wasn't grouped in the first place. Illustrator permits you to create various kinds of collective objects, including compound paths, linked text blocks, and wrapped objects. You can determine exactly what kind of object you've selected by displaying the commands in the menu. If Arrange » Ungroup is black, you have a group on your hands; if the command is dimmed, the selection is not a group. The same goes for Object » Compound Paths » Release, Type » Unlike Blocks, and Type » Release Wrap. A black command means you've found your culprit.

When Grouping Isn't Protection Enough

Grouping helps to protect the relative placement of objects. But it doesn't get objects out of your way when you're trying to edit a complex illustration, nor does it protect your artwork from the unpredictable motor skills of less adept artists who may come after you.

For those of us who have learned a little something about what we're doing, Illustrator provides a laundry list of protection alternatives. You can lock objects, preventing you or anyone else from accidentally selecting and altering them. You can temporarily hide an object if it impairs your view of other objects. And you can relegate entire collections of objects to independent layers, which you can in turn lock and hide as you choose.

I explain locking and hiding in the next few pages. Because layers are a more involved topic, I discuss them toward the end of the chapter, after a smidgen of transitional information.

Putting an Object Under Lock and Key

Locking an object prevents you from selecting it. This means you won't be able to delete the object, edit it in any manner, or change its fill or stroke. Once an object is locked, it immediately becomes deselected. If you attempt to click on a locked object with a selection tool, you will instead select some nearby unlocked object or select no object at all. Likewise, neither marqueeing nor choosing the Select All command selects a locked object. Until you unlock the object, it remains off limits.

You lock objects by selecting them and choosing Arrange » Lock command (or pressing ⌘-1). You can't lock a single point or segment independently of other elements in a path. If you specifically select one point in a path and choose the Lock command, Illustrator locks the entire path.

You can, however, lock a single path inside a group or other collective object (graph, compound path, etc.). Unfortunately, this doesn't afford much protection, since Illustrator allows you to continue editing that path as long as you click on some other object in the group.

When working on a very specific detail in an illustration, you may find it helpful to lock every object *not* included in the detail. There may be hundreds of objects, possibly making it difficult and time consuming to select every one of them. So instead, you can simply select the objects that you *don't* want to lock and press the Option key while choosing Arrange » Lock command, or press ⌘-Option-1.

 Here's another weird aside that you might find helpful if you remember it long enough to put it to use. When the guides are unlocked (Object » Guides » Lock is off), you can lock individual guides by selecting them and choosing Arrange » Lock. In other words, Object » Guides » Lock and Arrange » Lock work completely independently of each other. They can even be in force at the same time.

Locking is saved when you save an illustration. Therefore, when you open a file, all objects that were locked during the previous session are still locked. This is a great way to protect special objects so they don't get messed up by mischievous hands. Of course, there's always the risk a clever user will find and choose Arrange » Unlock; but you're not trying to protect the file from clever users, are you?

Unlocking Everything that Was Ever Locked

Because you can't select a locked object, there's no way to indicate which objects you'd like to unlock and which you'd like to leave locked. So you have to unlock all locked objects at the same time.

To do so, choose Arrange » Unlock All (⌘-2). Illustrator unlocks all locked objects and selects them, so that you can see which objects they are and manipulate them if necessary. Or Shift-click with the arrow tool on the few objects you want to leave unlocked and press ⌘-1 to relock the others.

Sending Objects into Temporary Hiding

If an object is really in your way, you can do more than just lock it; you can totally hide it from view. You can't see a hidden object in any display mode, nor does it appear when the illustration is printed. Since a hidden object is always invisible, you can't select or manipulate it.

You hide objects by selecting them and choosing Arrange » Hide (⌘-3). You can't hide a single point or segment; Illustrator always hides entire paths at a time. But you can hide objects inside groups, compound paths, and other collective objects. The path disappears, but it still moves and otherwise keeps up with the group when you select the entire group with the arrow tool.

 To hide all objects that are not selected and leave the selected ones visible, Option-choose Arrange » Hide or press ⌘-Option-3.

Unlike locking, hiding is not saved with the illustration. Adobe's afraid that you'll forget the hidden objects were ever there. Therefore, when you open an illustration, all objects in the file are in full view.

Hiding Unpainted Objects

Illustrator 3 provided a command that hid only transparent objects. Since you couldn't work in the preview mode, the idea was that you might want to see only those objects that are stroked and filled in the artwork mode. Of course, nowadays, you can work in the preview mode, where such objects are automatically invisible. But if you prefer to work in the artwork mode, you can still hide just the unpainted objects by selecting one of them, choosing Filter » Select » Same Paint Style, and then pressing ⌘-3. For more on selecting shapes by their colors, see Chapter 14.

Revealing Everything that Was Hidden

You can't select a hidden object any better than a locked one, so there's no way to show a specific object. Instead, you have to display all hidden objects at the same time by choosing the Arrange » Show All or pressing ⌘-4. Illustrator shows all previously hidden objects and selects them. This way, the objects are called to your attention, allowing you to easily send them back into hiding if you want.

The Celebrated Stacking Order

When you preview or print an illustration, Illustrator describes it one object at a time, starting with the first object in the illustration window and working up to the last. The order in which the objects are described is called the *stacking order*. The first object described lies behind all other objects in the illustration window. The last object sits in front of its cohorts. All other objects exist on some unique tier between the first object and the last.

Left to its own device, stacking order would be a function of the order in which you draw. The oldest object would be in back; the most recent object would be in front. But Illustrator provides a number of commands that allow you to adjust the stacking order of existing paths and text blocks.

All the Way Forward or Back

Two commands in the Arrange menu let you send objects to the absolute front or back of an illustration. If you select an object and choose Arrange » Bring To Front, Illustrator moves the object to the front of the stack. The object is treated exactly as if it were the most recently created path in the illustration and will therefore be described last when previewing or printing.

By selecting an object and choosing Arrange » Send To Back, Illustrator treats a selected object as if it were the first path in the layer and describes it first when previewing or printing.

Lots of programs provide Bring To Front and Send To Back commands. But Illustrator offers some weird keyboard equivalents. Rather than ⌘-F and ⌘-B, as in everything from the first MacDraw onward, Illustrator uses ⌘-equal for Bring To Front and ⌘-minus for Send To Back. The equal key also has a plus sign on it, so plus and minus make sense for front and back. It just takes a little thought adjustment (Particularly since these same shortcuts zoom in and out in Photoshop, where most Illustrator artists spend more time).

You can apply both commands to whole objects only. If a path is only partially selected when you choose either command, the entire path is moved to the front or back of the illustration. If you select more than one object when choosing Bring to Front or Send to Back, the relative stacking of each selected object is retained. For example, if you select two objects and press ⌘-equal, the forward of the two objects becomes the frontmost object and the rearward of the two objects becomes the second-to-frontmost object.

Relative Stacking

When creating complicated illustrations, it's not enough to be able to send objects to the absolute front or back of an illustration. Even a simple drawing can contain more than a hundred objects. Adjusting the layering of a single object from, say, 14th-to-front back to 46th-to-front would take days using Bring To Front and Send To Back.

Fortunately, Illustrator allows you to send one object in front of or behind another using Clipboard commands. To change the stacking order of an object, select it and press ⌘-X to jettison it to the Clipboard. Then select the path or text block that the cut object should go behind, and press ⌘-B (Edit » Paste In Back). Or, if you'd rather place the cut object in front of the selection, press ⌘-F (Edit » Paste In Front). In either case, Illustrator restores the object to the exact location from which it was cut. Only the stacking order is changed.

If multiple objects are selected when you press ⌘-B, Illustrator places the contents of the Clipboard in back of the rearmost selected object. Not surprisingly, ⌘-F pastes the cut object in front of the frontmost selected object. If no object is selected, ⌘-B sends the object to the back of the illustration; ⌘-F sends it to the front.

The Effect of Grouping and Combining on Stacking

Combining objects into groups also affects the stacking order of the objects in the illustration. All paths in a group must be stacked consecutively. To accomplish this, Illustrator uses the frontmost selected object as a marker when you choose the Group command. All other selected objects are stacked in order behind the frontmost one.

The same holds true for compound paths, linked text blocks, wrapped objects, joined paths, and paths combined with the Pathfinder filters. Ungrouping or otherwise breaking apart objects does not restore their original stacking order.

You can select an object inside a group with the direct selection tool and change its stacking order using the Bring To Front and Send To Back commands. But Illustrator keeps the selected objects inside its group. So rather than sending an object to the front of the illustration when you press ⌘-equal, Illustrator just sends it to the front of the group, while leaving the stacking order of the overall group unchanged.

You can also cut an object from a group and then paste it inside or outside of the group using the Paste In Front and Paste In Back commands. Since Illustrator automatically deselects everything when you cut an object—because the selection has disappeared—pressing ⌘-B or ⌘-F sends the cut object to the absolute back or front of the illustration.

Working with Independent Drawing Layers

In addition to the stacking functions, Illustrator offers self-contained *drawing layers* (or simply *layers*), an almost essential capability for creating complex illustrations. Illustrator was late to join the layering game—Version 5 was the first to offer this feature, years behind drawing rivals FreeHand and Canvas—but its layers are quite possibly the best of any drawing program.

Layers act like transparent pieces of acetate. You can draw an object on any layer and see clearly through all layers in front of it, down to all layers in back of it. An illustration can contain any number of layers; each layer can contain any number of objects; and you can name layers and alter their order as you see fit. You can even hide layers, lock them, and change their display mode independently of each other.

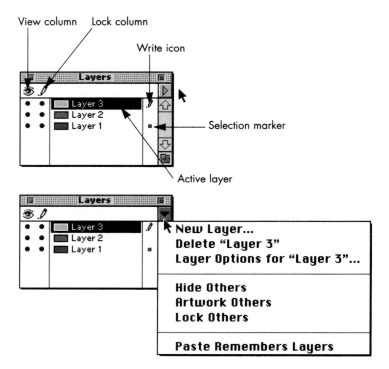

Figure 10-18: Click on the right-pointing arrowhead (top) to display the Layers palette menu (bottom).

To display the Layers palette, choose Window » Show Layers (⌘-Control-L). All existing drawing layers in the illustration are listed as options in a scrolling list inside the Layers palette. The palette includes a menu, which you display by dragging from the right-pointing arrowhead in the upper right corner of the palette. The menu appears unfurled in Figure 10-18.

Adding Layers to an Illustration

Illustrator automatically creates flat illustrations with only one layer. To add a drawing layer to the illustration, choose the New Layer command from the Layer palette menu. The New Layer dialog box displays, as shown in Figure 10-19. Enter a layer name up to 31 characters long into the Name option box.

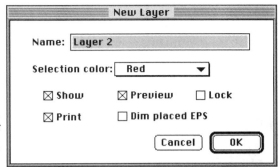

Figure 10-19:
Illustrator lets you name
layers, specify the color of
selections, and modify dis-
play and locking options.

 Note that Illustrator does *not* allow you to replace an existing drawing layer by creating a new layer with the same name. You can have as many layers with the same name as you like (though you probably want to avoid this since it makes for a mighty confusing illustration).

You can specify the color that Illustrator assigns to selection outlines by selecting an option from the Selection Color pop-up menu. If you're new to layers, you may think that Illustrator always shows selected points, segments, and control handles in blue, but this isn't necessarily the case. The program uses different colors to show you what layer you're working on. If you always accept Illustrator's default colors, points on the first layer are blue, those on the second layer are red, followed by bright green, a darker blue, yellow, magenta, cyan, gray, and black. But you can also select from orange, teal, brown, and lots of other colors, or define a custom color by selecting the Other option.

You can also modify a few check-box settings:

- If you want to hide all objects on the layer, turn off the Show check box.

- If you want to view the objects on the new layer in the artwork mode, turn off the Preview check box.

- When the Print check box is selected, all objects on the layer will print. If the option is off, they won't.

- Select the Lock check box to lock objects on the layer so they can't be accidentally altered.

- Select Dim Placed EPS to diffuse imported EPS images so that you can easily distinguish them from graphic objects and text blocks created in Illustrator.

You probably won't want to change any of the check boxes when creating a new layer. They're generally more useful after you've added a few objects to the layer and had a little time to consider how you want the layer to interact with the rest of your illustration.

After you press Return, the new layer name appears at the top of the Layers palette. Illustrator positions the new layer in front of all other layers in the illustration.

 In case you're thinking, "Gosh, I bet I can add layers to the Adobe Illustrator Startup file to make Illustrator give me multiple layers when it creates a new illustration," permit me to dash your hopes right off the bat. You can't. Nor can you drag and drop entire layers between illustrations, the way you can in Photoshop. What a shame.

Moving Objects Between Layers

When you select an object in the illustration window, the corresponding drawing layer becomes highlighted in the scrolling list. You'll also see a tiny colored selection marker along the right edge of the Layers palette. This represents the selected objects. If you select multiple objects on different layers, Illustrator shows multiple selection markers, one for each layer on which the objects sit.

To move the selected objects from one layer to another, drag the colored selection marker up or down the scrolling list. You can drag the marker to any layer that is neither hidden nor locked. You can drag only one marker at a time; so if you have objects selected on two layers, and you want to move them all to a third layer, you have to drag one selection marker to the third layer and then the other.

As you drag the marker, the cursor changes to a finger to indicate that you are moving objects between layers, as in Figure 10-20. Upon releasing the mouse button, Illustrator transfers the selected objects from one layer to the other. The points and segments in the objects appear in the new layer's color to show that the move is complete, as in the second example in Figure 10-20.

 To clone selected objects between layers, Option-drag the selection marker inside the Layers palette. After you release, the selected objects exist independently in both layers, just as though you had copied them from one layer and pasted them into another.

Creating, Combining, and Stacking Objects on Layers

The highlighted name in the Layers palette represents the active drawing layer, on which future objects will be created. To change the active drawing layer, click on a layer name in the scrolling list. Then start drawing to create objects on that layer.

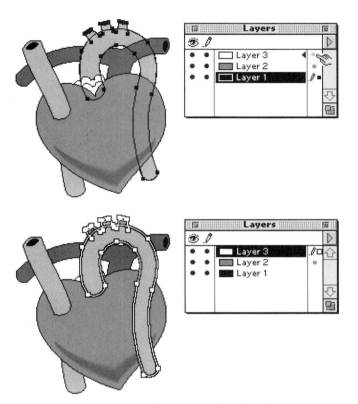

Figure 10-20: Drag a selection marker (top) to move
the marker and all selected objects to a different layers
(bottom).

A group, compound path, or other collective object must exist on a single layer. So if you group or otherwise combine objects from different layers, Illustrator sends all objects in the group to the layer belonging to the frontmost object. You'll notice this right away, because the points and outlines of the selected objects will all change to the same color.

You can change the stacking order of objects within a layer using the Send To Back and Bring To Front commands. For example, if you apply the Bring To Front command to an object on Layer 1, Illustrator brings it to the front of that layer only, not all the way to the front of the illustration.

If you want to also be able to change the stacking order inside layers with the Paste In Front and Paste In Back commands, choose the Paste Remembers Layers option in the Layers palette to turn it on. (Or you can select the Paste Remembers

Layers check box in the General Preferences dialog box.) When on, this option instructs Illustrator to remember which layer an object comes from when you send it to the Clipboard. Illustrator then pastes the object back onto that same layer, regardless of which layer is active. If cut or copied objects come from multiple layers, Illustrator pastes them back onto multiple layers.

 When the Paste Remembers Layers option is turned on, copying and pasting an object from one illustration into another pastes both the objects and the layer. Therefore, to copy an entire layer from one illustration to another, first turn on the Paste Remembers Layers option. Then click on the layer name you want to copy and choose Lock Others from the palette menu (or click on the pencil icon) to lock the other layers so you can't select them. Press ⌘-A and ⌘-C to copy all the objects on the unlocked layer. Now switch to the other illustration and press ⌘-V. Illustrator pastes the objects on a new layer and adds the copied layer name to the Layers palette.

By default, however, the Paste Remembers Layers option is turned off. This allows you to cut and copy objects from various layers and paste them onto the single active layer in the illustration. I'm not crazy about this default setting, since you can already clone objects between layers by Option-dragging the selection marker. Also, it prevents you from using ⌘-B and ⌘-F for inter-layer stacking. But you can easily switch between turning the option on and off, and whatever setting you select will be saved from one session to the next with the other preference settings.

Modifying Your Layers

After you've created a few layers and added some objects to those layers, you can change the way the layers look, protect layers, change their order, and generally monkey around with them. In fact, one of the primary purposes of layers is to permit you to change huge clumps of objects at a time. Illustrator lets you modify layers—and all the objects on those layers—in the following ways:

- To change the order of layers in the illustration, simply drag a layer name up or down in the Layers palette. The top layer is in front, the bottom layer is in back. Illustrator likewise shuffles the objects assigned to that layer behind or in front of objects in other layers.

- To change the name of a layer, double-click on it to display the Layer Options dialog box (which looks just like the New Layer dialog box from Figure 10-19). Enter a new name and press Return.

- The first column in the Layers palette—under the eyeball icon—lets you change the display mode for each layer. A solid or hollow circle in front of a layer name indicates that all objects on that layer appear on screen. A solid circle means that the layer shows up in both the artwork and preview modes, while a hollow circle means that the layer displays in the artwork mode at all times.

Click on the circle to hide it and, by so doing, hide all objects on that layer in the drawing area. Unlike Arrange » Hide, Illustrator saves the state of a hidden layer. It's a wonderful way to hide sensitive drawings from future users. To display objects on a hidden layer, click in front of the layer name in the first column.

Option-click on the circle to switch the layer from the preview mode to perpetual artwork mode. The circle changes to hollow. You can also click on the eyeball icon to hide all but the active layer. Or Option-click on the eyeball to display all layers except the active layer in the preview mode. All of these techniques will speed up screen redraw if Illustrator is chugging along a tad too slowly.

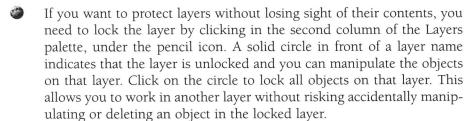

If you want to protect layers without losing sight of their contents, you need to lock the layer by clicking in the second column of the Layers palette, under the pencil icon. A solid circle in front of a layer name indicates that the layer is unlocked and you can manipulate the objects on that layer. Click on the circle to lock all objects on that layer. This allows you to work in another layer without risking accidentally manipulating or deleting an object in the locked layer.

You can protect all layers except the active layer by clicking on the pencil icon at the top of the column. Then, click in front of specific layer names under the pencil to indicate the additional layers you want to unlock.

If you select a locked layer, a little pencil with a line through it appears in the right-hand column of the Layers palette. This shows you that you can't write to this layer unless you first unlock it.

To prevent a layer from printing, double-click on it and turn off the Print check box in the Layer Options dialog box. But remember what you've done! Illustrator doesn't give you any warnings when printing that some layers are turned off. Many an artist has lost his hair trying to figure out why certain objects aren't printing from his illustration while others are printing just fine.

If you want to trace from a color image, import the image in the EPS format, select the Placed EPS radio button when Illustrator presents it to you, and assign the image to its own layer. Then double-click on the layer and select the Dim Placed EPS check box in the Layer Options palette. Illustrator diffuses the colors to about half their original luster, permitting you to clearly distinguish the image from your paths, so you can manually trace the image contours with the pen and freehand tools. (You cannot trace such an image with the autotrace tool; this tool works on black-and-white templates only.)

You can delete a layer—even if it's chock-full of text and paths—by clicking on the layer name and choosing Delete from the Layers palette menu. If the layer contains any objects, an alert box appears, warning you that you are about to delete a layer that contains artwork.

What's the fuss? If you delete a layer by mistake, you can press ⌘-Z to immediately restore it and its objects.

Vacuuming Your Illustration

I've made a lot of noise in this chapter about protecting your illustration from clumsy coworkers, clients, and (gasp!) freelancers who may get your accounts in the future. But what if it's the other way around? What if an incredibly gifted person like you has to muck about inside a cruddy pieces of artwork created by some imbecile from your company's dim past?

Back when I worked in a service bureau, I used to have this problem all the time. We were constantly getting files from folks who didn't quite know what they were doing. As a result, they tended to leave remnants of their previous efforts behind. Stray points, transparent shapes, and empty text blocks littered the virtual landscape like roaches laid waste with a bug bomb.

That's why Illustrator 6 includes the Cleanup filter. You won't need it very often, but when you do, it's great. Just choose Filter » Objects » Cleanup to display the dialog box in Figure 10-21. You can opt to delete single points that have no segments, paths that have no fill or stroke, and text blocks that have no text. All the refugees from the Island of Misfit Objects get whisked clean away.

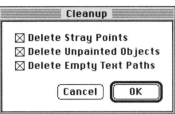

Figure 10-21:
Illustrator 6 now lets you
scrub away random rub-
bish from old illustrations.

Watch out for the Delete Stray Points check box. If you've added your own custom center points (as discussed earlier in the "Adding a Center Point" section of this chapter), then turn the Delete Stray Points option off! Otherwise, Illustrator will delete your center points faster than you can say, "Aaugh, wait, I didn't mean to do that!" Naturally, you can press ⌘-Z to reverse the procedure. But the change is so subtle, you may not notice the loss of your center points for a few minutes, or even longer. And by then, you may be stuck with it.

CHAPTER **11**

TRADITIONAL HOMESPUN TRANSFORMATIONS

Back when Illustrator first came out in 1987, we couldn't believe our luck. Right there in the toolbox were four splendid transformation tools. They allowed us to scale, rotate, flip, and slant absolutely any object we could create in Illustrator, whether path or text. Heck, we could even transform individual points and segments. Wow!

Ah, how easily amused we were back then. To think that we actually put up with a mere four transformation tools when now, in Illustrator 6, we have . . . er, the very same four transformation tools. Okay, sure, they're the same tools, but now you can . . . uh . . . scale, rotate, flip, and slant objects. But you can also . . . transform partial paths.

 If all this sounds familiar, it is. Adobe hasn't done much of anything to Illustrator's transformation tools since the program's inception. Oh, the way you use the tools changed slightly a few versions back, and Illustrator 6 lets you scale and rotate from the Control palette. The new version has also rolled the old Move, Scale, and Rotate Each filters into Arrange » Transform Each. But the basic transformations themselves are identical. Neither Illustrator nor rival FreeHand seems capable of thinking beyond these four basic functions!

Having got that off my chest, Illustrators 5 and 6 have added a series of special effects filters, many of which are very useful (as I explain in the next chapter). But Illustrator hasn't fully promoted any of these filters to the more powerful category of fully functioning transformations. Only one filter—Twirl—can be performed using a tool; you can't modify the appearance of gradients, tile patterns, and other fill effects with a filter; and you can't duplicate the effects of any filter with the Option key or ⌘-D.

So if you're familiar with previous versions of Illustrator, you'll have little problem adjusting to the absolutely unchanged, same-as-ever transformation functions. (Look for the Illustrator 6 icon to read about the slight maintenance adjustments.) But even for you world-weary old timers (and faithful readers from previous editions), this chapter is still worth reading. To help new and experienced users alike, I've added lots of specific techniques for using the tools. Hopefully these will spark your imagination so you can go off in bold, new directions of your own.

Same old transformations, totally new treatment. I suppose that's the best you can expect during an election year.

Making Objects Bigger and Smaller

Let's start things off with a bang by talking about scaling. In case you're unclear, scaling is when you enlarge or reduce something, or make it thinner or fatter, or taller or shorter. Put a fellow on the rack, and you're scaling him. See how it works?

In most programs, you can scale a selected object simply by dragging its corner handle. But not so in Illustrator. In this program, only one tool lets you resize objects, and that's the scale tool.

The Scale Tool and the Origin Point

After selecting one or more objects—paths, text, or imported images (it matters not)—drag with the scale tool in the drawing area. Illustrator enlarges or reduces the selection with respect to its center. If you drag away from the center of the selection, as in Figure 11-1, you enlarge the objects. If you drag toward the center, you reduce them. It's so simple, a child could do it. (And no doubt many have.)

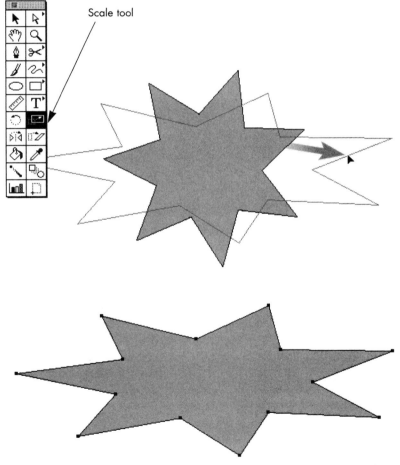

Scale tool

Figure 11-1: Using the scale tool, drag away from the center of a selection (top) to enlarge it (bottom).

The scale tool calculates the center of a selection the same way every other Illustrator function does, based on a rectangular bounding box. Therefore, it may not always suit your needs, especially if you're trying to keep objects aligned as you resize them.

Good thing you don't have to accept the default center. You can scale a selection with respect to any point in the illustration window. This *origin point* (also called a *reference point* or *scale origin*) represents the center of the transformation. To demonstrate how an origin point works, in Figure 11-2 I have enlarged a star several times over with respect to a single origin. All of the white arrows in the figure emanate from the origin, showing how the points move outward uniformly from this one point.

Figure 11-2: A star scaled repeatedly with respect to a single origin point.

Figure 11-2 shows a proportional enlargement. In non-proportional resizings (as in Figure 11-1), you don't get such clean lines from the origin point. But one fact remains: The portions of the selection that are closest to the origin change the least. This is not to say that objects closer to the origin point resize less dramatically than objects farther away. All selected objects scale by the same percentages. But as Figure 11-3 illustrates, objects farther away from the origin *move* more dramatically.

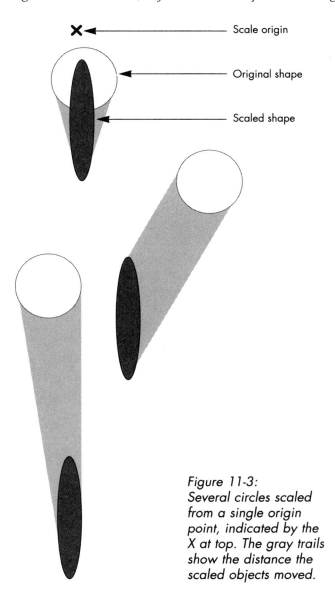

Figure 11-3:
Several circles scaled
from a single origin
point, indicated by the
X at top. The gray trails
show the distance the
scaled objects moved.

In the figure, the X shows the origin point, the white circles represent the original objects, and the dark ovals represent the scaled objects. While the top oval close to the origin point barely moved at all, the bottom oval moved quite a distance. When the origin lies outside the object, the scale tool scales the distance between the selected object and the origin point, as well as the object itself. If this sounds strange, give it a try and see.

Therefore, the origin point impacts the positioning of objects, while the distance you drag with the scale tool determines the extent of the resizing. The following steps explain how to set the origin point and scale from it:

1. Select the objects you want to scale.

2. Click with the scale tool where you want to position the origin. If you click within 2 points of an anchor point or guideline, Illustrator snaps the origin to that point.

3. Drag with the scale tool. Illustrator resizes the objects with respect to the origin. If you drag away from the origin, you enlarge the selection. If you drag toward the origin, the selected objects shrink.

 After clicking to set the origin point, begin dragging about an inch or two away from the origin. This gives you room to move inward, and provides you with more control. If you ignore my advice and start the drag too close to the origin, you have little room to maneuver, making it difficult to reduce the selection and magnifying the effects of your cursor movements.

Likewise, if you don't click to set the origin (and instead accept the default center origin), be sure to start dragging an inch or two away from the center.

 If you drag from one side of the origin point to the other, you flip the selection. Although Illustrator also provides a separate reflect tool, the scale tool is the only one that lets you flip and resize at the same time. (By contrast, the reflect tool lets you flip and rotate simultaneously.)

Scaling with the Shift Key

As when drawing and reshaping paths, you can use the Shift key to constrain a transformation. However, Illustrator goes well beyond the constraints provided in most drawing and layout programs:

● You can Shift-drag to scale a selection proportionally, so the height and width of a selected object are equally affected. Or you can scale the selection exclusively horizontally or vertically when pressing Shift.

For example, if you Shift-drag up and to the right, you scale the selection proportionally, as in the top example of Figure 11-4. But if you Shift-drag to the right—while keeping the up and down movement to a minimum—you scale the width of the selection without changing its height, as in the bottom example.

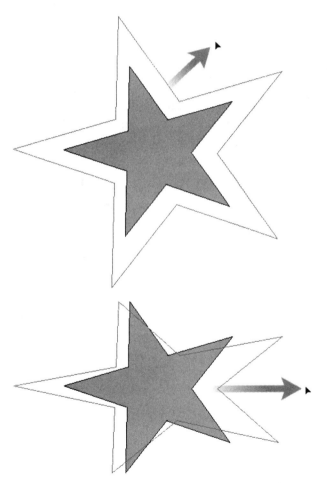

Figure 11-4: Shift-drag diagonally to scale a shape proportionally (top). Shift-drag horizontally to change the width of the shape only (bottom).

If the shape seems to jump around a lot when you have the Shift key pressed, it's because you began your drag in a bad place. Release and press ⌘-Z to put things back where they were. Then click to set the origin, and start your drag in a diagonal direction from the origin. For example, you can start the drag up and to the right from the origin, or down and to the left. It's when you start the drag in horizontal or vertical alignment with the origin that you run into problems. It's particularly limiting when you want to perform a proportional scaling.

● In truth, my advice so far assumes that you haven't rotated the constraint axes from their default 0-degree setting. If you have changed the constraint axes, you can still scale proportionally with the Shift key, but you can no longer scale the selection exactly horizontally or vertically. Instead, you scale in line with the constraint axes angles.

As it turns out, rotating the constraint axes is an essential first step when scaling rotated shapes. For example, suppose you want to lengthen the rotated paths in Figure 11-5. Here's what you'd do:

1. First determine the angle of rotation by dragging across a flat segment with the measure tool. I dragged across the bottom segment in Figure 11-5 to produce the angle value of 16.534 degrees in the Info palette.

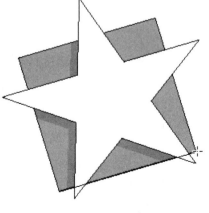

| X: 239.4135 pt | W: 171.1286 pt | D: 178.5102 pt |
| Y: 369.5615 pt | H: 50.8025 pt | ∠ 16.534° |

Figure 11-5:
Drag across a straight segment in a group of rotated paths to discover the angle by which you should rotate the constraint axes.

2. Press ⌘-K to display the General Preferences dialog box, and enter the angle value from the Info palette into the Constrain Angle option box. Naturally, I entered 16.534. Then press Return to apply the rotation.

3. Click with the scale tool to set the origin (or don't click to accept the bounding box center as the origin). Then Shift-drag with the scale tool to change the height or width of the selection.

In Figure 11-6, I Shift-dragged downward to lengthen the selection. Notice how Illustrator exactly stretches the height of the objects without affecting the width in the slightest.

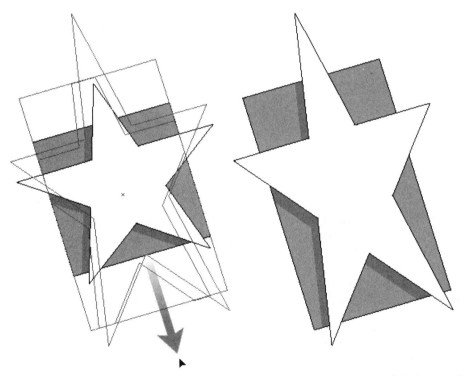

Figure 11-6: After rotating the constraint axes 16.534 degrees, I Shift-dragged with the scale tool (left) to make the shapes taller, but not wider (right).

Is it absolutely necessary to rotate the constraint axes before scaling rotated shapes? Couldn't you just drag with the scale tool at roughly the same angle and produce the same results? Absolutely not! Figure 11-7 shows me dragging at the very same angle as in Figure 11-6 with the constraint axes set to 0 degree. Illustrator scales along the standard axes, and therefore slants the shapes as it

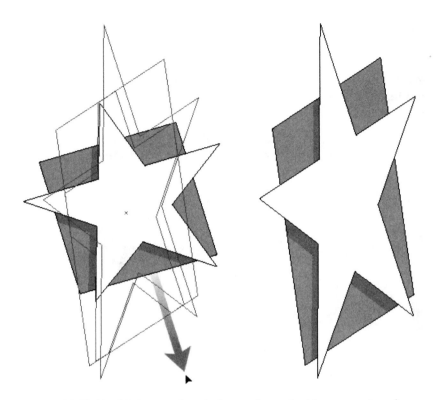

Figure 11-7: Had I dragged with the scale tool without rotating the constraint axes (left), I would have slanted the shapes as well as stretching them (right).

scales them. You can get away with not pressing Shift, but you absolutely *must* rotate the constraint axes if you want to get the effect shown in Figure 11-6.

Duplicating Objects as You Scale Them

The scale tool also lets you clone objects as you scale them. To scale a clone and leave the original unchanged, press the Option key in mid drag and keep the key pressed until after you release the mouse button. If you enlarge the selection, you may cover up the original with the clone, but the original will be there, lurking in the background. (If you're at all concerned, press ⌘-minus to send the clone in back of the original so you can see all shapes.)

After you scale a clone, you can create a series of scaled clones by pressing ⌘-D or choosing Arrange » Repeat Transform. This is a particularly useful technique for creating perspective effects. By reducing a series of clones toward a far off origin, you create the effect of shapes slowly receding into the distance.

For example, I began with three stars and a rectangle, as in Figure 11-8. (The two outside stars are slanted slightly with the shear tool, which I'll explain later in this chapter.) To create the shadow behind the shapes, I selected all shapes, clicked with the scale tool at the X in the figure, and Shift-Option-dragged to proportionally reduce the objects (very slightly) and clone them. Then I sent the shape to back (⌘-minus), chose Filter » Pathfinder » Unite to combine them into a single shape, and filled the shape with black.

×

Figure 11-8: Using the X as the origin point, I cloned and scaled the rectangle and stars to create the black drop shadow.

To create the perspective effect, I selected all the shapes—including the drop shadow—and grouped them (⌘-G). (The grouping was merely a precaution to facilitate future editing.) I clicked again at the origin point with the scale tool and again Shift-Option-dragged toward the origin to create a proportional clone. The clone was in front of the original, so I pressed ⌘-minus to send it to back. Then I pressed ⌘-D to create another reduced clone and ⌘-minus to send it to back. I kept pressing ⌘-D and ⌘-minus—a total of 18 times in a row, in fact—until I arrived at the effect shown in Figure 11-9.

Perspective duplication is an extremely easy effect to perform, and it looks great when applied to simple shapes and large letters converted to paths. Figure 11-10

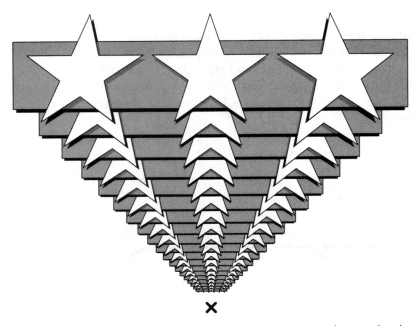

Figure 11-9: I next scaled and cloned all shapes, sent them to back, and duplicated the action several times in a row.

is an example of perspective text. Starting with some converted black text, I reduced a cloned version of the text (using the X as an origin) and filled the clone with white. Then I selected the black text again, and cloned and reduced it very slightly. I repeated the reduced clone by pressing ⌘-D about 12 times in a row to get a perspective effect similar to what you see in the figure.

I could have stopped there, but since all these paths mean a lot of work for the printer, I thought I'd simplify things by selecting all the black paths and choosing Filter » Pathfinder » Unite. This command took about two minutes to complete on my Power Mac (a Radius 81/110). Then I stroked the path with a 6-point outline to get the end result shown in Figure 11-10.

A few of you brainy types are thinking, "But, Deke, can't you just create one reduced version of the paths and blend between the large and small group of letters?" No. Unfortunately, Illustrator lets you blend between no more than two paths at a time. If you try to anticipate this by combining the large and small collections of letters into compound paths, Illustrator recognizes only the subpaths that you click on with the blend tool. Suffice it to say, blending in this particular case involves more work.

×

Figure 11-10: I created this effect by scaling and duplicating a series of black letters behind the white ones.

For those of you who've never heard of the blend tool—and wish I would quit making little inside references to the more experienced half of the class—you can learn all about this special tool in Chapter 17.

Resizing by the Numbers

The scale tool is great—it's one of my favorite tools!—but it's not the only way to resize objects inside Illustrator. You can also enlarge and reduce by entering precise numerical values into two different dialog boxes and one palette.

Scaling from the Control Palette

 Let's start with the least capable (but most convenient) of the three, the Control palette. After selecting an object, you can enter a value into the scale option box, spotlighted in Figure 11-11. The value is measured as a percentage of the object's original size. Values below 100 shrink the selection; values above 100 enlarge it. All resizings are proportional and accurate to 0.01 percent.

After you enter a value, press Return to apply it and deactivate the palette; press Tab to apply the scale value and highlight the rotate value. You can also press Option-Return or Option-Tab to clone the selection and scale the clone. You can even repeat the operation by pressing ⌘-D.

To reposition the origin point, click on one of the nine squares in the reference point icon on the left side of the Control palette. All points are measured with respect to the selection's rectangular bounding box.

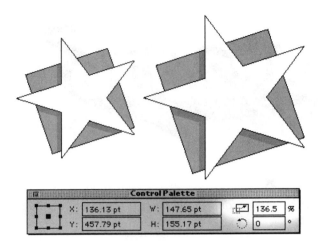

*Figure 11-11:
Enter a value into the
scale option box (spot-
lighted on right) and
press Return to any
selected objects.*

Using the Scale Dialog Box

After selecting a few objects on your Things To Scale list, double-click on the scale tool icon in the toolbox. This brings up the Scale dialog box, captured in all its radiant glory in Figure 11-12. Illustrator automatically positions the origin point in the center of the selection (according to the big, bad, bounding box).

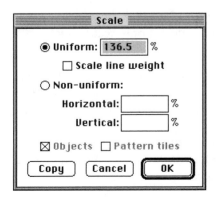

If you want to position the origin point for yourself, Option-click in the illustration window with the scale tool. (When you press the Option key, Illustrator gives you a lot of hints that something's about to happen. You'll see a tiny ellipsis next to the scale tool cursor, and the status bar in the lower left corner of the illustration window reads *Scale: click to choose origin.* What a communicative program.) Option-clicking with any transformation tool simultaneously positions the origin point and displays the appropriate dialog box.

*Figure 11-12:
This dialog box lets
you specify the exact
percentage by which
a selection is enlarged
or reduced.*

To proportionally scale the width and height of the selection, enter a value into the Uniform option box. This value is accurate to 0.001 percent, 10 times more accurate than the scale value in the Control palette.

When the Uniform radio button is selected, you can have Illustrator likewise scale the line weights of all selected objects. When the Scale Line Weight check box is selected, Illustrator scales the line weight by the Uniform value. A 4-point stroke subject to a 125 percent scaling changes to 5 points thick. If the check box is off, the stroke is unaffected.

 Illustrator remembers this setting the next time you Shift-drag with the scale tool. (The option affects proportional scalings only.) So if you find that your line weights are getting thicker and thinner as you scale them, you know the culprit. Double-click on the scale tool icon and turn off the Scale Line Weight check box. (You can also modify this setting inside the General Preferences dialog box.)

To independently scale the width and height of an object—a feat you can't perform from the Control palette—enter values into the Horizontal and Vertical option boxes. A Horizontal value less than 100 percent makes the selection thinner; a value greater than 100 percent makes it wider. These values in the Vertical option box translate to taller and shorter. If you enter negative values, Illustrator flips the selection.

 You can switch from the Uniform to Non-Uniform option boxes by simply pressing the Tab key. Stop all that clicking and try Tab today! (I should write ad copy, don't you think?)

The Objects and Pattern Tiles check boxes are strictly to modify objects with tiled fills. If you want to learn about these options—for all four transformation dialog boxes—read the stirring account in Chapter 15.

To scale the selection, press Return or click on the OK button. Press Option-Return or click on Copy to clone the selection and scale it.

 Oh, and one more thing. All of Illustrator's transformation dialog boxes act as recording devices, keeping track of the last transformation applied, whether using a tool or the dialog box itself. Sadly, the Scale dialog box ignores the results of the Control palette, and it doesn't pay attention to the next command, Transform Each. But it knows what the scale tool is up to.

Scaling from Multiple Origins

Illustrator 5 introduced filters that allowed you to scale from a different origin point for each and every selected object. Illustrator 6 has taken these filters and combined them into a single more functional command known as Arrange » Transform Each.

When you choose the Transform Each command, Illustrator displays the dialog box shown in Figure 11-13. You enter the amounts by which you want to resize the width and height of the selected objects into the first two option boxes. To perform a proportional resizing, enter the same value for both Horizontal and Vertical. Then press Return to apply the changes, or click on the Copy button to clone and scale. (For the present time, Option-Return doesn't work inside this dialog box.)

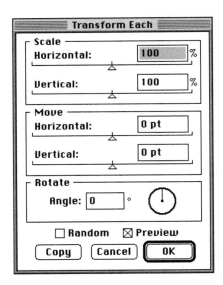

Figure 11-13:
The Transform Each dialog box lets you scale each selected object from its center.

When you apply the Transform Each command, Illustrator scales each selected object with respect to its own center. In the first example of Figure 11-14, for example, I've added festive bobbles to the spikes on the star. But after a few moments of intense scrutiny, I decided the bobbles are uniformly too small. Back in the old days, I would've had two options—scale each bobble one at a time to prevent them

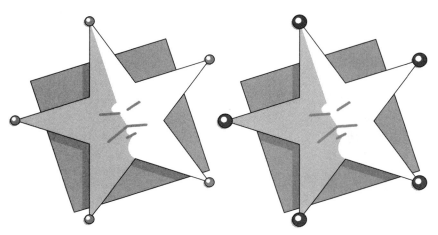

Figure 11-14: After selecting the small bobbles on the spikes of the star (left), I enlarged every one of them using the Transform Each command (right).

from shifting around, or redraw the darn things. But in Illustrator 6, I can simply apply Arrange » Transform Each. By entering 150 percent into both the Horizontal and Vertical option boxes, I achieved the larger bobbles in the second example of Figure 11-14. (I also darkened the circles to make them stand out more.)

Why not just use the scale tool, Control palette, or Scale dialog box? Because all of these functions work from a single origin point, which can shift the objects in different directions. Figure 11-15 shows what happens when I double-click on the scale tool icon, enter a value of 150 percent, and press Return. The bobbles actually move away from their shared center. By contrast, the Transform Each command ensures that the objects scale in place.

 At the bottom of the Transform Each dialog box is a Preview check box that lets you see the effects of your changes without leaving the dialog box. But be careful when Preview is turned on. In the first release of Illustrator 6, this feature has a small bug that may confuse and infuriate. After entering a value into an option box, be sure to press the Tab key before pressing Return to apply your settings. If you don't press Tab—which tells Illustrator to preview the setting you just entered—the command has a habit of duplicating values from other option boxes.

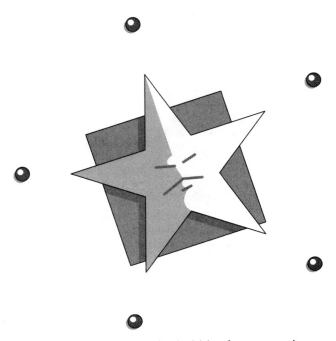

Figure 11-15: Enlarging the bobbles from a single center point with the scale tool sends the circles flying in all directions.

Select the Random check box to apply random resizings to individual selected objects. Illustrator scales each selected path to a different percentage, ranging from 100 percent to the values you enter into the Horizontal and Vertical option boxes. In Figure 11-16, I randomly scaled and nudged the converted letters in the word *wacky*. I entered 150 for Horizontal and 300 for Vertical. I also entered 20 points into the Move Vertical option box. Illustrator randomly scaled and moved the letters within the specified ranges, as shown in the second example in the figure.

Always turn on the Preview check box when using the Random option. This way, you can see Illustrator's random effect before applying it. If you don't like what you see, turn Preview off and then turn it back on again. This forces Illustrator to generate a new random effect. Keep clicking on the Preview check box until you get what you want. Then press Return.

Figure 11-16: Here I used Transform Each to randomly scale and nudge a few letters, created in the wonderfully wacky font Sho.

Scaling Partial Objects

Whether you select just a few points or a whole path, both the Control palette and Arrange » Transform Each affect entire paths at a time. But you can use the scale tool or Scale dialog box to scale partially selected paths and text objects.

For example, you can use the scale tool to enlarge a text block without changing the size of the text inside it. Option-click on the rectangular text container with the direct selection tool, then click with the scale tool to set the origin point and drag away. As long as you haven't selected any text—you don't see any baselines, do you?—Illustrator enlarges or reduces the containers and rewraps the text inside.

You can also scale selected points and segments in a path. The primary advantage of this technique is that you can move points symmetrically. See, Illustrator doesn't provide any specific means for moving points away from or toward an origin point. Moving is the one transformation that has nothing to do with origins (which is why I don't discuss it in this chapter). The closest thing to an origin-based move function is the scale tool.

Consider the sinister Figure 11-17. In the first example, I've selected four points in the star that makes up the outer shape. (I've added halos around the selected points to make them easier to locate.) After setting the origin point at the bottom of the shape—indicated by the cursor in the first example—I dragged up and

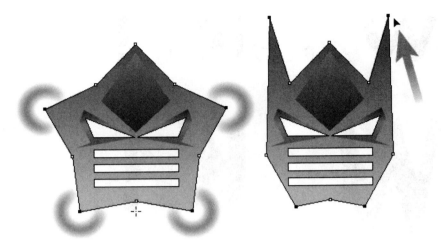

Figure 11-17: After selecting four points (surrounded by halos on left), I dragged with the scale tool to move the points according to their proximity to the origin.

inward on the upper right point. This caused all selected points to move up and in toward the center, based on their proximity to the origin point. Because the two upper points were far away from the origin, they moved up dramatically, forming sharp bat ears. The lower points were closer to the origin, so they moved only slightly to form the chin, as the second example shows.

Whenever you apply the scale tool to a selected point, you stretch the neighboring segments, just as when dragging points with the direct selection tool. You can also apply the scale tool to selected curved segments. In Figure 11-18, I took an everyday average circle and selected each of its segments with the direct selection tool, without selecting any of the points. (I marqueed the two bottom segments and then Shift-marqueed the top two.) Then I dragged with the scale tool to enlarge the selection from the center, as the figure shows. Illustrator stretches the segments an equal distance in four directions.

So in addition to its normal resizing functions, the scale tool does double duty as a symmetrical move tool. It's little surprise, if you think about it. All the scale tool is doing is moving and stretching segments away from and toward a fixed point. Once you understand its geometry, the scale tool becomes a never-ending source of inspiration. (And I'm not just saying that to be poetic.)

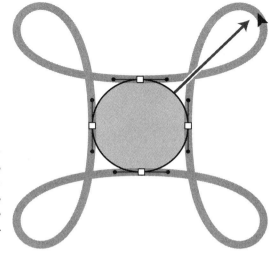

Figure 11-18:
By dragging the
selected segments in
a circle with the scale
tool, I stretched the
segments in perpen-
dicular directions.

Rotating Objects Around the Origin

Once you know how to use one transformation tool, the other three become putty in your capable grasp. The rotate, reflect, and shear tools share many common characteristics with their scale sibling. So rather than laboriously examining every single detail of each tool, as if this is the first word of Chapter 11 you've ever read, I'll make quick work of the familiar stuff and stick in as many tool-specific tips and techniques as these humble pages will permit.

For example, here's a summary of the basic workings of the rotate tool—the left-hand neighbor of the scale tool—with occasional figures:

   Drag with the rotate tool to rotate a selection around its bounding-box center. Or click to set the origin point and then drag to rotate, as in the second example of Figure 11-19. Because rotation is a strictly circular movement—in fact, you *always* rotate in perfect circles—the origin point acts as a true center, as the arrows in the figure demonstrate.

   It doesn't matter where you start dragging when using the rotate tool. At any time, you can gain more precise control over a rotation by moving the cursor farther away from the origin. Slight movements close to the origin can send your objects into exaggerated spins that are difficult to control.

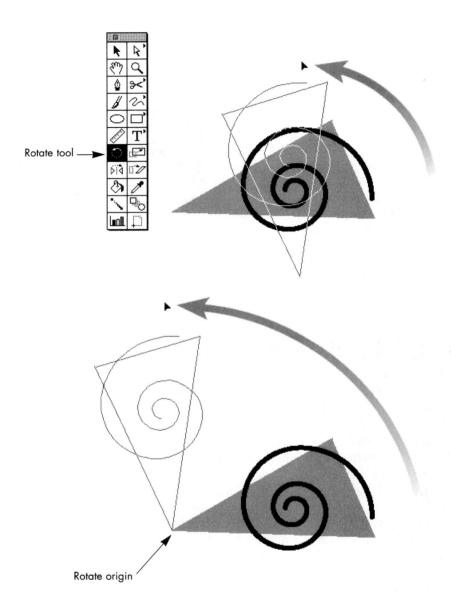

Rotate tool

Rotate origin

Figure 11-19: The difference between merely dragging with the rotate tool (top) and first clicking at the tip of the triangle and then dragging (bottom).

Press the Shift key when dragging to rotate in 45-degree (1/8 turn) increments. (The constraint axes have no influence over Shift-dragging with the rotate tool.)

Press the Option key after you begin dragging and hold it until the drag is finished to rotate a clone of the selection. Then you can repeat a series of rotated clones by pressing ⌘-D or choosing Arrange » Repeat Transform.

In the top example of Figure 11-20, I started with two simple paths: a spiral (black) and a two-point curve (gray). I rotated a clone of the spiral 45 degrees by clicking at the X with the rotate tool and Shift-Option-dragging the spiral. Then I duplicated the spiral clone six more times by mercilessly beating ⌘-D. I only needed to create three duplicates of the two-point curve, since I wanted to connect every other spiral. So I Shift-Option-dragged the curve 90 degrees and pressed ⌘-D twice.

After joining the spirals and curves at their endpoints, I embellished these basic paths with layered stroking effects (as I explore in typically systematic fashion in Chapter 16). Then I added some text and skewed it with the shear tool. The result is a lovely frilly pattern that I plan to market as Deke's Designer Embroidery Coasters. Put in your order today.

Select an origin from the reference point icon on the left side of the Control palette. Then enter a value into the palette's rotate option box (bottom right) and press Return or Tab to rotate the selection. Press Option-Return or Option-Tab to clone and rotate.

 Illustrator interprets rotations in degrees. There are 360 degrees in a full circle, so a 360-degree rotation would return the selection to its starting position, while a 180-degree rotation would turn it upside down. Positive values rotate counterclockwise; negative values rotate clockwise.

Double-click on the rotate tool icon in the toolbox to display the Rotate dialog box. Enter a value into the Angle option box and press Return to rotate the selection, or Option-Return to rotate and clone. Illustrator rotates the selection around its center.

If you want to position the origin point, Option-click with the rotate tool to bring up the Rotate dialog box. The point at which you click becomes the origin.

Figure 11-20: After repeatedly rotating and cloning a spiral and a curved segment (top), I joined a pair of spirals with each curve and duplicated the paths using progressively heavier strokes (bottom).

Choose Arrange » Transform Each and enter a value into the Rotate option box to rotate multiple objects around their individual centers. To demonstrate the principle of individual rotation, I've gone and appended little stars to the big star's spikes in the left example of Figure 11-21. In retrospect, I decided I wanted to have the little stars rotated at the same angle as the larger one. I first used the measure tool to find the angle of the top side of one of the large star's arms. (I dragged from left to right, as labeled in the figure.) This same side is horizontal in each of the little stars, so the measurement tells me the precise amount I need to rotate.

Then I chose Arrange » Transform Each and entered the measured value—18.214 degrees—into the Rotate option box. Illustrator rotated each selected shape around its center to produce the darkened stars on the right side of the figure.

Had I used the Rotate dialog box or Control palette to rotate the little stars, I would have caused the shapes to pivot away from their points, as in Figure 11-22. As when scaling, the Transform Each command rotates selected objects in place.

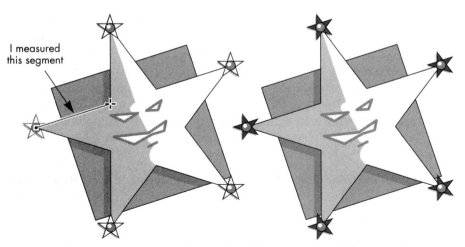

I measured
this segment

Figure 11-21: After measuring the angle of the large star (left), I used the Transform Each command to rotate the little stars 18.214 degrees (right).

Figure 11-22:
Using any of the other
rotate functions moves
the little stars around in
a partial circle.

- Select the Random option inside the Transform Each dialog box to rotate selected objects randomly within the range specified in the Rotate option box. For example, if I enter a Rotate value of 30 degrees, Illustrator rotates each object anywhere from 0 to 30 degrees.

- You can use the rotate tool and Rotate dialog box to move selected points around in a circle. In Figure 11-23, for example, I took a star and added points to it by choosing Filter » Objects » Add Anchor Points. Then I selected the new points only (which appear inside the circular highlight in the figure). I clicked with the rotate tool at the star's exact center—which I determined using Object » Average, naturally—and dragged to move the selected points around in a circle. This allowed me to edit the shape while maintaining radial symmetry—meaning that each spike looks the same as the other spikes.

Stars are wonderful transformation primitives because they have straight sides that jut in and out, and they are born with radial symmetry. In other words, you can have a lot of fun rotating and scaling partial stars. The central shape in Figure 11-24 began life as a five-pointed star. I added points over and over again with Filter » Objects » Add Anchor Points. Then I carefully selected corresponding points on each spike and alternatively scaled and rotated them. That's it; I never drew a line.

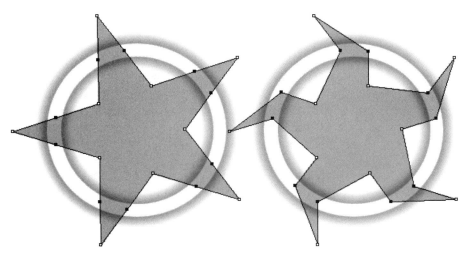

Figure 11-23: After adding points to the star, I selected the new points (left) and rotated them around the shape's center (right).

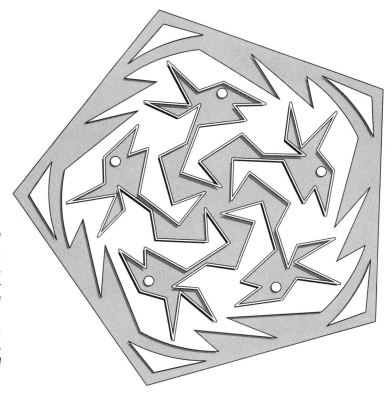

Figure 11-24: The central shape used to be a five-pointed star before I attacked it with the Add Points filter and the scale and rotate tools.

Flipping Objects Back and Forth

Most drawing programs provide Flip Horizontal and Flip Vertical commands so that you can quickly reflect selected objects. But not Illustrator. As far as Illustrator is concerned, those commands might be easy to use, but they don't provide enough control. So in typical Illustrator fashion, the reflect tool is hardly convenient for quick flips, but just the thing when accuracy is paramount.

The following is everything you need to know about flipping in Illustrator:

- The reflect tool works a little differently than its fellow transformation tools. When you drag with the reflect tool, you change the angle of the *reflection axis*. As demonstrated in Figure 11-25, the reflection axis is the mirror that the selection is reflected into. The portions of the object that lie on one side of the axis flip to the other. Because you can tilt the mirror, the reflect tool flips and rotates objects at the same time.

- If you immediately start dragging with the tool, the reflection axis hinges on the center of the selection. But if you first click to set the origin point and then drag with the reflect tool, the axis pivots on the origin. In the top example of Figure 11-25, for instance, I clicked below and to the left of the selection. I then began dragging in a direct line above the selection, which resulted in a vertical axis. As I dragged down and to the right, the axis inclined into the position shown in the second example in the figure.

- Shift-drag with the reflect tool to constrain the axis to a 45-degree angle. When the axis is upright, the selection flips horizontally. When the axis is horizontal, the selection flips vertically.

- Press the Option key when dragging to flip a clone. You can repeat a flipped clone by pressing ⌘-D, but why would you want to?

- Most of the time, it's easier to flip via the Reflect dialog box. To bring up the dialog box, double-click on the reflect tool icon in the toolbox. Or Option-click with the tool in the illustration window to set the origin point.

  The Reflect dialog box contains three options for specifying the angle of the reflection axis around which the flip occurs. Select the Horizontal option to flip the selection vertically, just as a gymnast swinging on a horizontal bar flips vertically. Select the Vertical option to flip the selection horizontally, like a flag flopping back and forth on a vertical flagpole. You can also enter a value into the Angle option box to specify the exact angle of the axis. A value of 0 indicates a horizontal axis; 90 indicates a vertical

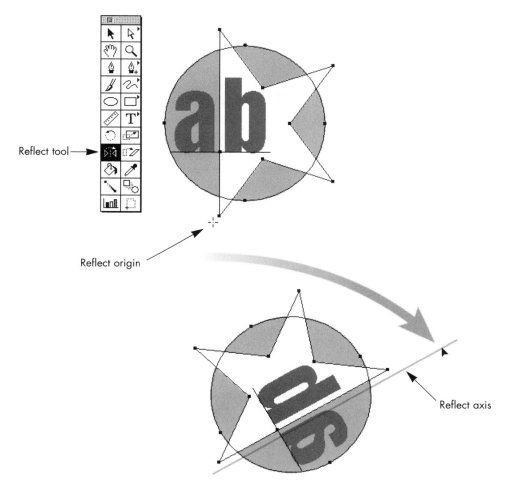

Figure 11-25: Click with the reflect tool to set the origin point (top), then drag to flip and rotate the selection around the reflection axis.

axis. Though you can enter any value you want, everything beyond 0 through 90 is repetitive.

Press Return to flip the selection. Press Option-Return to clone and flip.

By comparison to the scale and rotate tools, the reflect tool is very dull. You can't perform special effects with it. And though you can flip partial paths, there's rarely any reason to do it. Still, it's a very practical tool, and Illustrator would be the worse without it. When you gotta flip, you gotta flip.

Slanting Objects the Weird Way

The final transformation tool is the oddly named shear tool (located just below the scale tool). Rather than removing wool from sheep—as the tool's name implies—the shear tool slants selected objects.

 Now, does "shear" suggest slanting to you? It doesn't to me either. Let's see, hmmm . . . nope, Webster's doesn't say anything about slanting when defining the verb *shear*. Just cutting and cropping. Granted, the noun *shear* can be a force that causes something to slide against itself relative to a parallel plane of contact. But A) most folks don't know what the heck that means; B) it's not the same thing as slanting, now, is it? And C) why name one tool after a noun when the rest are verbs? Here I've been making fun of the name of this tool since the first edition of my book, and Adobe refuses to budge! Doesn't the company even *care* about new users?! FreeHand calls its tool the skew tool, which is a little obscure but, you know, it ultimately makes sense. But shear! What kind of word is shear? Why not sheer? Or how about Cher?! I mean, those makes about as much sense as shear!! I know, let's just give it a little symbol, like the artist formerly known as . . . blaaugh! *(Crash.)*

Oops, sorry. I got so excited I fell out of my chair.

But despite the tool's dopey name, this is an important tool. It slants objects horizontally, vertically, or in any other direction. So don't be put off by the name. This is a tool that deserves to be part of your daily transformation regimen.

Because the shear tool is a little more demanding than the other transformation tools, I devote the entire following section to explaining its basic operation. After that, I cover the Shear dialog box.

Using the Shear Tool

As with the other transformation tools, you can start right in dragging with the shear tool. But I recommend that you don't. Of all the transformation tools, this one is the most difficult to control. So you're best off specifying an origin point to keep things as predictable as possible.

Click to set the origin point. I find it helpful to set the origin in the lower left corner of the selection. Then I move the cursor to the opposite corner of the selection—upper right—and begin dragging. Illustrator slants the selection in the direction of your drag, as demonstrated in Figure 11-26.

Illustrator figures two ingredients into slanting an object: the amount of slant applied and the axis along which the slant occurs. The distance of the drag determines the amount of slanting; the angle of the drag determines the angle of the axis.

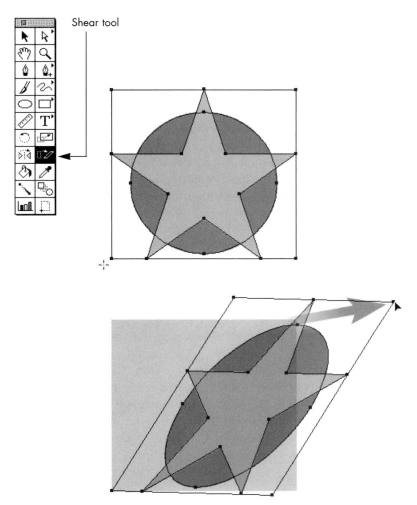

Figure 11-26: Click in a corner with the shear tool (top), then drag from the opposite corner to slant the selection (bottom).

Notice that although I dragged up and to the right in Figure 11-26, the selected objects slanted slightly downward. I dragged up about 10 degrees, so the axis is angled at 10 degrees. The weird thing is, when dragging with the shear tool, all axis angles clockwise from 45 degrees around to –135 degrees (about 1:30 to 7:30 on a clock face) slant objects downward. Axis values from –135 to 45 degrees (7:30 to 1:30) slant objects upward. Mathematically, it doesn't have to be this way, but it is when using the shear tool.

Meanwhile, if you drag in a 45-degree or −135-degree direction, Illustrator stretches the selected objects all the way to Tierra del Fuego. If you notice your objects go haywire, just move your mouse up or down a little to restore the selection to a recognizable state.

Slant Sensibly with Shift

 Because of the odd way Illustrator calculates the effect of dragging with the shear tool, I almost always keep the Shift key down. Shift-dragging with the shear tool constrains the axis to a multiple of 45 degrees. As I've told you, two of these multiples—45 and −135—turn the axis into a force of absolute evil. But if you Shift-drag in a roughly horizontal or vertical direction, you'll achieve very predictable results.

The shear tool is especially useful for slanting type and adding shadows. I've accomplished both of these tasks in Figure 11-27. To create the first shadow at the top of the figure, I clicked with the scale tool along the baseline of the letters. Then I Option-dragged from the top of the letters down past the baseline to flip and scale a clone. I then filled the clone with gray. In the second example, I clicked with the shear tool along the baseline of the letters and Shift-dragged from left to right to slant the shadow horizontally. Finally, I selected all letters, clicked at the base of the first T with the shear tool, and Shift-dragged up on the M. This slanted the letters vertically, as in the last example in the figure.

Defining the Slant and the Axis

Illustrator lets you slant and clone by pressing the Option key when dragging with the shear tool. You can also display a Shear dialog box by double-clicking on the shear tool icon in the toolbox, or by Option-clicking with the tool in the illustration window.

As shown in Figure 11-28, the Shear dialog box offers an Angle option box for specifying the amount that you want your objects to slant, and three Axis options for specifying the axis along which the slant should occur.

Specify the angle of the shear axis exactly as you would the angle of the reflection axis inside the Reflect dialog box. Select the Horizontal option to slant the selected objects to the left or right; select the Vertical option to slant up or down. You can also angle the axis by entering a value into the lower Angle option box. Because the axis extends to either side of the origin point, values over 180 degrees are repetitive. (Values of 45 or −135 degrees don't cause problems in the Shear dialog box; they just mess things up when dragging with the shear tool.)

Figure 11-27: After flipping a clone of the letters with the scale tool (top), I slanted the clone horizontally with the shear tool (middle). I then selected all letters and slanted them vertically (bottom).

Regardless of the selected Axis option, you'll want to enter a value for the Angle option at the top of the dialog box. Here's where things get tricky. Illustrator interprets just about every other value that's measured in degrees in a counterclockwise direction. (It's the standard geometry model that you undoubtedly learned or neglected in an ancient math course.) This is true for rotations, angled axes— including the shear axis—and directional movements. The only exceptions are the

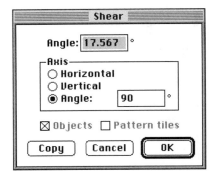

Figure 11-28:
Illustrator measures the highlighted Angle value in a clockwise direction, counter to every other option box in the program.

Angle value at the top of the Shear dialog box and the one in the Twirl dialog box (see Chapter 12), which Illustrator applies in a clockwise direction. Therefore:

- When the Horizontal radio button is active, a positive Angle value slants the selection forward and a negative value slants it backward. Seems sensible.

- But when the Vertical radio button is active, a positive Angle value slants the selection up on the left side of the origin and down on the right, so it looks like it's pointing downward. A negative value slants the selection upward. That's just plain weird.

An Angle value of 30 degrees creates a pretty significant slant. Anything beyond 90 to –90 degrees is repetitive. And you definitely don't want to enter anything from about 80 to 90 degrees (positive or negative) because it pretty well lays the selected objects flat.

Slanting is easily the least predictable of the transformations. I considered including a huge chart showing what happens to an object when you apply all kinds of different Angle and Axis Angle values, but take my word for it, you would've been more confused after looking at this thing than you were before. That's why I recommend sticking with horizontal and vertical slants when possible. If you need to slant objects a little up and a little over, do it in two separate steps. It'll save wear and tear on your brain.

After all, you're going to need every one of the synapses you were born with for the next chapter, which covers Illustrator's exciting and bewildering array of special effects. If you thought the shear tool was a little odd, wait until you get a load of this bunch. Many are good, a few are bad, and the rest are just plain wacky.

HOG-WILD
SPECIAL EFFECTS

Every so often, someone informs me that he or she prefers Photoshop to Illustrator because "I'm just not a vector person." It's not that Illustrator isn't a fine product that permits you to create terrific artwork; it's a matter of feeling comfortable and creative inside the program. In Photoshop, inspiration comes in the form of scanned images, which you can enhance or distort using a mouth-watering collection of special effects filters. But in Illustrator, you have no choice but to draw everything from scratch. Right?

Not exactly. Clearly, Bézier curves are more labor intensive than pixels. (I think anyone who isn't trying to sell you something would admit that.) But you don't have to painstakingly draw each and every curve by hand. You can rough out primitive compositions with ellipses, stars, text characters, and the like, and then embellish these objects using Illustrator's automated functions.

If you read Chapters 9 and 11, you already have a sense of the marvels you can accomplish by combining and transforming shapes. But that's only the proverbial tip of the iceberg. In this chapter, I show you how to apply a wide range of bona fide special effects—functions so radical that they can mutate common shapes into extraordinary forms that would take you minutes or even hours to draw by hand. In Figure 12-1, for example, I started with nothing more than a line of type and a five-pointed star. Three filters later, I arrived at the unqualified masterpiece that you see before you. As you can see, Illustrator lets you run roughshod over objects in the same way

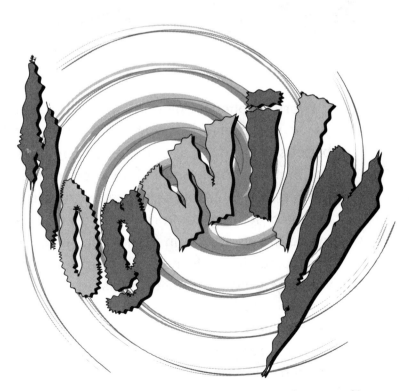

*Figure 12-1: Thanks to the Twirl, Free Distort, and Zig Zag filters,
I was able to convert a humble star and collection of converted
type into some very strange and complicated paths.*

that Photoshop lets you use and abuse images. Both programs are equal parts finely-tuned graphics applications and platforms for fortuitous experimentation.

Throughout the following pages, I look at the special effects functions of Illustrator 6 and explain a little bit about how they work and why they're better than they were in Illustrator 5. I also include some information and opinion about add-on filters from companies like MetaTools and Extensis. Though you have to fork over more cash to purchase these packages—in the $100 to $200 range—they can significantly enhance your ability to create and obliterate objects in Illustrator.

Freelance Features

Most of Illustrator's capabilities are built into the main application. But many tools and commands come from little subprograms called plug-ins. By default, all plug-ins reside in the Plug-ins folder inside the same folder as the Illustrator application. (You can change this using File » Preferences » Plug-ins, as described in Chapter 2, but few folks ever do.) When you launch Illustrator, the program loads all the plug-ins into memory and makes them available as tools, commands, and palettes inside the program.

 You can find out information about any plug-in by choosing the About Plug-ins command from the Apple menu. Then select a filter from the scrolling list and click on the About button to see who wrote it. More interesting, you can click on the Summary button to save a text file to disk listing every single plug-in that Illustrator is running. Okay, so this isn't the sort of revelation that you circle with a highlighter. (Only a couple of you will scurry to your diaries and scribble, "Illustrator suddenly made sense today when I learned how to use the About Plug-in command!") But it's an organizational tool I thought you should know about.

You can add plug-ins from other companies by copying the files into Illustrator's Plug-ins folder. The Plug-ins folder contains several subfolders; you can put the third-party plug-in inside any of these subfolders, or create a new one. As long as the file is somewhere inside the Plug-ins folder, Illustrator loads it during startup.

Some plug-ins manifest themselves as tools and palettes, and a few appear as commands under the Object and Type menus. But most show up as commands in the overflowing Filter menu. Because the commands in the Filter menu vary dramatically in purpose and approach, I discuss them in context throughout this book. But just so we're all on the same wavelength, here is a complete list of the commands in the Filter menu with brief snippets about what they do and where to turn for more information:

- **Filter » Colors (Chapter 14)**: Illustrator lets you modify the colors of many objects simultaneously using the commands in the Filter » Colors submenu. But, of course, you'll need some color theory under your belt to understand these commands, which is why Chapter 14 exists.

- **Filter » Create » Fill & Stroke for Mask (Chapter 17)**: In Illustrator, a path that masks other objects can't have a fill or stroke. So this command clones the path twice and assigns one clone a fill and the other a stroke.

- **Filter » Create » Object Mosaic (Chapter 13)**: Illustrator offers some weird filters, but this one may be the weirdest. It traces a bunch of colored squares around an imported image, to convert the image to an object-oriented mosaic. Now there's something we can all integrate into our artwork!

- **Filter » Distort (Chapter 12)**: These are the special effects filters that I discuss in this very chapter. They muck up objects but good!

 Filter » Ink Pen (Chapter 17): My nomination for the hardest commands to use in all of Illustrator 6 appears in this submenu. But, they're powerful. You can design custom fill patterns, including dots, crosshatches, and squiggles. If you've ever envied FreeHand's PostScript fills patterns, the Ink Pen commands may be the answer.

- **Filter » Objects » Add Points**: This filter doubles the number of anchor points in a selected path by adding a point in the middle of each segment. I alluded to this command in Chapter 11. But thanks to Illustrator's new curve fitting (which I explain in this chapter), the Add Points filter is not very useful anymore.

- **Filter » Objects » Cleanup (Chapter 10)**: This filter vacuums stray points, transparent paths, and empty text blocks from your illustration.

- **Filter » Objects » Offset Path (Chapter 9)**: Choose the command to clone a path and expand it a specified number of pixels. Illustrator places the clone behind the original path.

- **Filter » Objects » Outline Path (Chapter 16)**: This command traces a path around a stroke. You can then fill the path with a gradation, reshape the thickness of the path, and perform other operations that aren't applicable to strokes.

- **Filter » Pathfinder (Chapter 9)**: The Pathfinder filters combine selected paths by tracing around them, retaining their intersections,

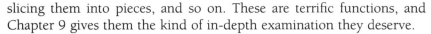

slicing them into pieces, and so on. These are terrific functions, and Chapter 9 gives them the kind of in-depth examination they deserve.

● **Filter » Select (Chapters 5 and 14)**: One of the commands in this submenu—Filter » Select » Inverse—lets you swap the selected and deselected objects in an illustration, as I explained in Chapter 5. The other commands select objects according to their fill and stroke attributes, as covered in Chapter 14. You can also select masks and stray points.

● **Filter » Stylize » Add Arrowheads (Chapter 16)**: This command adds an arrowhead to the end of a line. Illustrator bases the size of the arrowhead on the thickness of the stroke, which is why I discuss the filter in Chapter 16.

● **Filter » Stylize » Calligraphy (Chapter 16)**: This filter is similar to Filter » Objects » Outline Path, except that it traces a variable-width path around a line. It makes any path look like you drew it with the brush tool.

● **Filter » Stylize » Drop Shadow**: Okay, everyone repeat after me: "The Drop Shadow filter is absolutely worthless, devoid of merit, and incapable of producing anything resembling remotely acceptable results." It clones selected paths, sends them to back, and colors them so they don't look anything like drop shadows. I explain more satisfactory shadow techniques in Chapters 9, 11, and 17.

 Filter » Stylize » Path Pattern (Chapter 16): The new Path Pattern filter lets you apply specially constructed tile patterns to the stroke of a path. Illustrator can stretch and bend the tiles so that the tiles follow a path's twists and turns like the diamonds along the back of a rattlesnake.

● **Filter » Stylize » Round Corners**: This last filter rounds off the corners in a selected path. You enter a Radius value—as when specifying the rounded corner of a rectangle—and Illustrator does the rest. In fact, you can use the filter to round off the corners of a rectangle long after you draw the shape. You can also apply it to stars, characters of text, and other shapes that have lots of corners. In Figure 12-2, I've applied a Radius value of 12 points to a star, a rectangle, and some type converted to paths.

Few of the commands from the Filter menu are applicable to text objects. If you want to apply a special effect to text, first convert the text to paths using Type » Create Outlines.

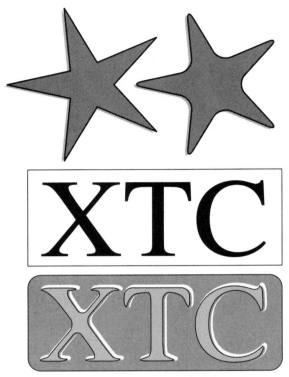

Figure 12-2: Here I've applied the Round Corners filter to a star, a rectangle, and some Times Roman text.

After you choose a command from the Filter menu, it appears at the top of the menu (even if you later undo the command). This allows you to quickly reapply the filter by choosing the first command in the menu, or by pressing the keyboard equivalent ⌘-Shift-E. To reapply the filter with different settings, press the Option key and choose the command, which forces the dialog box to appear. Or, new to Illustrator 6, press ⌘-Shift-Option-E.

The Missing Transformation

Illustrator is missing one basic kind of transformation that's included with just about every drawing program *except* FreeHand, from the ancient MacDraw to the midrange Windows wünderkind CorelDraw. Even image editor Photoshop offers it. I speak, of course, of four-point distortion, which allows you to yank on the corner handles of a selected object to stretch it. Four-point distortion is useful for simulating perspective, or for simply fitting an object into a new space.

Illustrator's four-point distortion surrogate is Filter » Distort » Free Distort. Far from a fully integrated transformation, this command requires you to distort a selection inside a dialog box, as demonstrated in Figure 12-3. As long as the Show Me check box is on, you can see the selected objects inside a dotted bounding box. The objects appear without either fill or stroke—as in the artwork mode—so that you can see all portions of overlapping objects.

 That's nice. But wouldn't it be even better if you could see the deselected objects as well, so that you could distort the selection within its environment? Frankly, this is the most boneheaded implementation of four-point distortion that I've seen inside any piece of software. It's functional, but that's about the nicest thing you can say about it. I mean, the dead-gone-dead SuperPaint did a better job than this!

But whether we like it or not, we might as well make the best of it. Here are some things to keep in mind when dragging corner handles:

- Drag a handle to stretch the selection in that direction. It's as if the image were photocopied onto taffy (except that you don't have to wedge the taffy into the paper tray).

- If you drag in line with the original dotted bounding box, Illustrator snaps your cursor into horizontal or vertical alignment. This is great for creating straight perspectives that don't lean forward or backward.

 To create an extreme effect, you can drag outside the central window, or even outside the dialog box, as in the second example of Figure 12-3. However, if you do so, you won't be able to retrieve the dragged handle except by clicking on the Reset button to restore the selection boundary to a rectangle.

- If after you distort an object, you select a different object and press ⌘-Shift-Option-E to again display the Distort dialog box, Illustrator shows the effects of the previous distortion on the new selection. In other words, the handles go to the position you last set them. This allows you to repeat the distortion or slightly modify it. (The corner handles may not look right if you apply the Free Distort command to an object that's already been distorted.) If you want to create a completely different distortion, click on the Reset button.

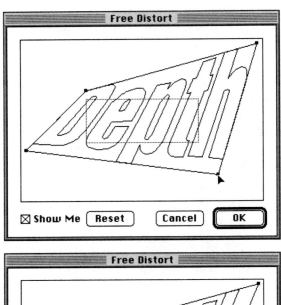

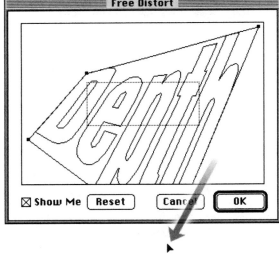

Figure 12-3: In the Distort dialog box, you can drag one of four corner handles to stretch a selection (top). You can even drag outside the dialog box (bottom).

Though a seriously flawed command, a gifted artist like yourself can use Filter » Distort » Free Distort to his or her advantage. I mentioned earlier that you can create perspective effects. In fact, with the help of a few other filters, you can create stuff that looks like it came out of a 3-D program.

In Figure 12-4, I've taken my distorted text from Figure 12-3 and applied Filter » Objects » Offset Path to it (with an Offset value of 3 points) to clone and expand the characters. I removed the overlapping segments by choosing Filter » Pathfinder » Unite. Then I nudged the offset path down and to the right a few points, so they aligned as shown in Figure 12-5. Finally, I filled both sets of paths with different gradations (as I explain in Chapter 15). This results in a surprisingly realistic beveled effect.

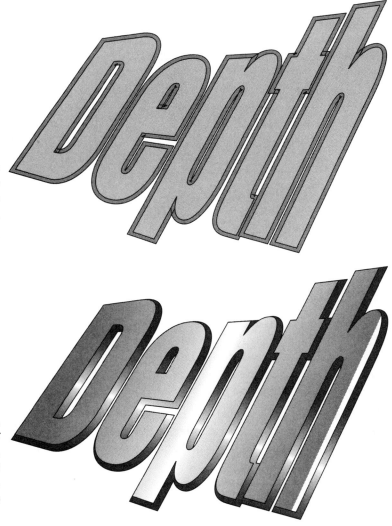

Figure 12-4: After distorting the converted text, I cloned and expanded the text by applying the Offset filter.

Figure 12-5: I nudged the two sets of paths into alignment and filled both with different gradations.

The New Improved Twirl

Illustrator 6 provides two variations on the Twirl filter. One is the command Filter » Distort » Twirl and the other is the twirl tool in the plug-in tools palette. Both twist selected objects around a central point, like spaghetti twirling around a fork.

Having problems visualizing? Well, imagine for a moment that you're in Little Italy, admiring a strand of tacky spaghetti that's slightly stuck to your plate. A man in a striped shirt plays an accordion as you begin to twirl the noodle, coaxing it gingerly from the dish. Maybe it's the music, maybe it's the wine, but you can't help but notice that the part of the noodle that's closest to the fork rotates most dramatically, while the faraway portions stretch to keep up, not yet willing to release their grip on the plate. Now imagine that you can twirl your fork up to 4,000 degrees—more than 11 complete rotations—and you have Illustrator's Twirl filter.

In case you're simply not in the mood for pasty pasta analogies, Figure 12-6 shows the effect of the twirl filter on some virtual spaghetti converted to paths. Each line of type is twirled 60 degrees more than the line above it.

Twirling in Illustrator

To twirl a selection, choose Filter » Distort » Twirl and enter the amount of twirl you want to apply in degrees. A positive value twirls clockwise, a negative value twirls counterclockwise. Figure 12-6 demonstrates the effects of three negative twirls (–60, –120, and –180 degrees).

If you prefer the tangible, real-time feedback of a tool, click on the first icon in the plug-in tools palette to select the twirl tool. Then drag in the illustration window to twirl all selected objects. In Figure 12-7, I've dragged about a quarter turn clockwise. You can drag up to 11 times around a selection to increase the magnitude of the twirl. But more than two revolutions tends to result in a lot of straight edges.

You can also Option-click with the twirl tool to bring up a dialog box and enter a numerical Twirl value. This is the same dialog box that appears when you choose Filter » Distort » Twirl. But what the heck, Option-clicking with a tool is sometimes more convenient than choosing a command.

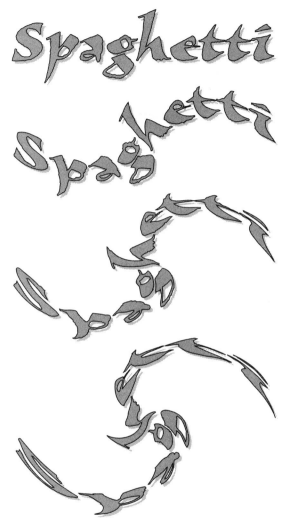

Figure 12-6:
The results of twirling
a line of converted
Visigoth type (top)
–60, –120, and –180
degrees (second through
fourth examples).

Perhaps what you *can't* do with the twirl tool is more important. For example, both the Twirl command and twirl tool spin the selection around its bounding box center. Even if you click with the tool to set an origin point and then drag—as with a transformation tool—Illustrator ignores your origin and twirls around the center, just as if you had never clicked. The program acts like it's paying attention to you—the cursors change and all that—but your actions have no effect on the twirl.

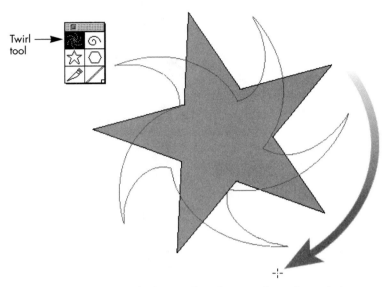

Twirl tool

Figure 12-7: Drag with the twirl tool around a selected shape to twist it by some arbitrary amount.

Hopefully, this is just a problem with the first release of Illustrator 6 that Adobe will soon rectify. In fact, it's possible that Adobe has already fixed the problem and you're sitting there scratching your head thinking, "Gosh, it seems to work fine for me." If so, here's a list of other things that don't work now but ought to one day:

- If this were a typical transformation tool, you'd be able to press the Option key before releasing with the twirl tool to clone the selection. But sadly, this function is absent from the twirl tool in Illustrator 6.0.

- When you display the Twirl dialog box, it should tell you the degree that you last spun an object with the twirl tool. But although this value changes every time you use the tool, there seems to be no correlation. Heck, it'll show you a negative value after a positive twirl.

- The Shift key has no effect on your drag, you can't repeat a twirl by pressing ⌘-D, and you can't twirl partial paths (just whole paths at a time).

Now you know why I didn't discuss the twirl tool with the transformation tools in Chapter 11. Even the modest reflect tool could wipe the floor with this thing.

All Hail Curve Fitting

While still not as sophisticated as it should be, Illustrator 6's twirl functions are significantly better than the old Twirl command in Illustrator 5. In the previous version, the Twirl filter merely shuffled selected points around; it had no effect over control handles or the curvature of segments, nor was it able to introduce anchor points of its own. In order to get halfway decent results, you had to triple or quadruple the number of points in a path using the Add Anchor Points filter.

 But Illustrator 6 includes a little thing called *curve fitting* that makes all the difference in the world. This permits Illustrator to accurately calculate complex distortions when applied to straight and curved segments alike.

Figure 12-8 tells the whole story. I started with the two semicircles shown in the background of the figure. Then I twirled the shapes 300 degrees in both Versions 5 and 6 to produce the foreground shapes.

- In Illustrator 5, I had to choose Add Anchor Points four times in a row to get a halfway decent effect. And even then, the Twirl filter merely moved the points to different position, resulting in a jagged effect composed entirely of straight segments.

- In Illustrator 6, I didn't have to add a single point. Thanks to the new curve fitting, the Twirl filter was able to add its own points and control handles where needed to create curved segments. The effect isn't perfect—the curve still looks a little flat in places—but it's a huge improvement.

Illustrator 6 makes its curve fitting available to all plug-ins. This means MetaTools, Extensis, and other companies can also take advantage of it when they design their filters. It may seem like a small thing—and, I might argue, one that Adobe should have introduced in Illustrator 5—but it will undoubtedly have a big effect on the way that we work inside drawing programs in the next few years. Thanks to curve fitting and the improved special effects filters that go with it, we'll be able to spend less time fastidiously constructing paths and more time exploring areas of personal style and object composition. When Adobe and other vendors make good on the promise of curve fitting, Twirl and other filters will seem less like special effects and more like common transformation tools.

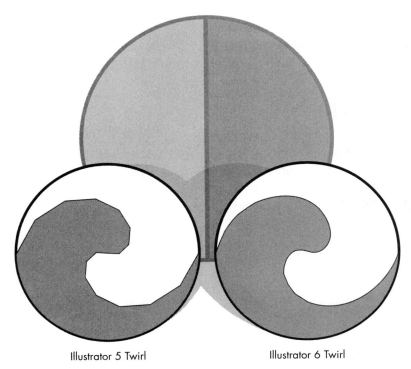

Illustrator 5 Twirl   Illustrator 6 Twirl

Figure 12-8: The results of twirling two semicircles (background)
inside Versions 5 and 6 of Illustrator.

The Scary Path Wigglers

The four remaining commands in the Filter » Distort submenu mess up the outlines of paths without changing the direction or general shape of the path. In other words, the commands shake up a path without steering it completely off course. That's why I call these filters "path wigglers." Of course, you don't have to call them that. In fact, if you said, "Golly, you should see what I can do with a path wiggler!" in public, I'd be surprised if someone didn't slap you. (I wouldn't be surprised if the new telecommunications bill makes it a misdemeanor to say "path wigglers" on the Internet.)

Figure 12-9 demonstrates each of the path wigglers applied to lines of boring old Helvetica Inserat. The word *ghosts* is the product of the Roughen filter, *zombies*

Figure 12-9: The path wiggler filters can turn common, dreary typefaces into something very frightening.

comes from Zig Zag, *monsters* was scrambled by Scribble and Tweak, and *vampires* received the blunt end of Punk and Bloat. (I used Free Distort and Twirl to abuse *Halloween*.) Also worth noting, the frayed outline was a standard rectangle before I subjected it to the Roughen filter.

Figure 12-10 shows the dialog boxes associated with the four path wigglers. I show them all together because they share a few common elements. Depending on the filter, you're permitted to adjust the amount of wiggling, the quantity of wiggles, and just what it is that gets wiggled. You can also view the results of your set-

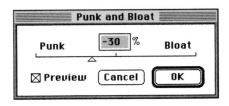

Figure 12-10:
All the path wiggler
dialog boxes offer
Preview check boxes so
you can see the results
of your settings before
pressing Return.

tings in the illustration window by selecting the Preview check box. Each time you press the Tab key, Illustrator updates your paths on screen.

 Two of the filters—Roughen, and Scribble and Tweak—produce random results within a specified range. You can force Illustrator to generate new results without changing the range by turning the Preview check box off and back on.

The following paragraphs explain how each of the path wiggler filters work, in the order their dialog boxes appear in Figure 12-10. I include a figure with each description to give you an idea of how different settings affect a few typical paths.

● **Roughen**: The Roughen filter adds points to selected objects and then moves the points in random directions, giving your paths a serrated, spiky look. The Size value indicates the distance that each point can move, expressed as a percentage of the longest segment in the path. The Detail value determines the number of points that Illustrator adds to each inch of segment. Select the Smooth radio button to convert all points in the paths to smooth points; select Corner to make them all corner points.

Figure 12-11 shows the results of various Size and Detail values applied to some converted text. In fact, the letters themselves tell the settings. For example, *S2D4* means a Size value of 2 percent and a Detail value of 4 points per inch. The shape in the background started off as an eight-pointed star. The Smooth radio button was selected in every case.

 Zig Zag: One of the few new filters included with Illustrator 6, Zig Zag gives your paths an electric jolt by adding a series of zigzags. The Amount value controls the distance that each point can move, which in turn determines the size of the wiggles. Use the Ridges value to specify how many zigzags Illustrator adds per segment. As you can see in Figure 12-12, long segments—like the sides of the As—get long wobbly ridges, while the ridges along short segments—as on the bottoms of the characters—are more tightly packed.

● **Scribble and Tweak**: Unlike Roughen or Zig Zag, the Scribble and Tweak filter does not add points to selected objects. Rather, it moves existing points and control handles in random distances and directions. There are two radio buttons, Scribble and Tweak. Ultimately, they do the same thing; the only difference is that Scribble moves

Figure 12-11: Various Size and Detail values applied to converted text with the Roughen filter.

points and control handles a percentage of the longest segment (just like the Roughen filter), while Tweak measures movements in points.

Use the Horizontal and Vertical values to specify the maximum distance points and control handles can move. Use the check boxes to decide which elements move. If you want to move the points but not the handles, turn off the two Control Points options. (The "In" option controls handles associated with segments entering points; the "Out" option controls handles for outgoing segments.) If you want to make the points stationary and move just the handles, turn off the Anchor Points check box and turn on the other two.

Figure 12-12: A few sample Amount and Ridges values applied to character outlines with the Zig Zag filter.

Figure 12-13 shows the results of moving elements with both the Horizontal and Vertical values set to one of three percentage values. I moved just the points in the left column and just the handles in the second column.

Punk and Bloat: The Punk and Bloat dialog box is the simplest of the bunch, featuring a single slider bar and related option box. Negative values (which tend toward Punk) move points outward from the center of a path and twist segments inward. This creates an angular, almost gothic look. Positive values (on the Bloat side) move segments inward and curve segments outward, turning them into puffballs. The left column of Figure 12-14 demonstrates a few Punk values, while the right column shows off Bloat. Which kind of path would you rather be?

Figure 12-13: With the Scribble and Tweak filter set to Scribble, I adjusted the locations of anchor points (left) and control handles (right).

The So-Called Third-Party Solutions

Folks in the computer biz are forever going on about "third parties." These aren't the sort of drunken revelries that don't get started until midnight, after you've polished off hors d'oeuvres at the Johnson's and Twister at the Green's. It's more in the spirit of legal parties—you know, like when the party of the first part wants to take the party of the second part for every penny the party's worth.

Figure 12-14: A sampling of values applied with the Punk and Bloat filter.

As it just so happens, you're the first party. I bet you didn't even know that you were actually involved in all this, but you're number one. And in this particular case, Adobe is the second party, since Adobe created Illustrator. If some other company comes along to enhance the functions inside Illustrator, that company becomes the eagerly awaited third party.

Presently, several third-parties provide plug-ins for Illustrator. In the next few pages, I'll introduce you to two such parties—MetaTools, makers of KPT Vector

Effects, and Extensis, the folks who sell DrawTools. These aren't the only companies making Illustrator plug-ins—Alien Skin, Cytopia, BeInfinite, and Letraset are other third parties working to bolster Illustrator's core features. But where special effects are concerned, Vector Effects and DrawTools happen to be the most interesting plug-ins around.

Oh, and because FreeHand 5 supports Illustrator filters, you can use any third-party filter collection with FreeHand as well. And you don't even have to copy the filters to two different folders. Just create an alias of the folder that contains the filters inside Illustrator's plug-ins folder (using File » Make Alias at the Finder desktop). Then place the alias inside the Xtras folder which is inside the Macromedia folder inside your System Folder.

KPT Vector Effects

The filter package that I find myself using most often is KPT Vector Effects ($199) from MetaTools (805/566-6200). Though the interface is a tad bit prominent for some folks' tastes, Vector Effects is a truly inspired collection of filters that enhances Illustrator's capabilities more significantly than the upgrade from Version 5.5 to Version 6.

KPT stands for Kai's Power Tools, named after MetaTools' popular and affable evangelist. The strange thing is that Vector Effects was created and programmed by a fellow named Sree Kotay, who had originally called the package Sree's Cool Tools. But when one licenses one's product, one learns servility.

Though Vector Effects works its magic inside dialog boxes, it provides excellent previewing capabilities and permits you to apply several effects at once. In the Vector Distort dialog box, for example, you can view your selection inside a preview window, as shown in Figure 12-15. You can magnify the preview, scroll it with a hand tool, and so on. You then add "influences," which are areas of distortion. In Figure 12-15, I've created three influences, two of which bend the selection outward as if it's projected onto a sphere, and the other of which warps the selection. (The three influences appear as different regions of gray inside the preview area.) Though it takes a little getting used to, Vector Effects provides a very flexible working environment. You can even save your settings for later use, or select from an array of preset distortions.

Altogether, Vector Effects includes 13 filters, which allow you to precisely position points, adjust the colors of selected objects, and apply special effects. Figure 12-16 demonstrates three of the effects. The 3D Transform filter rotates and

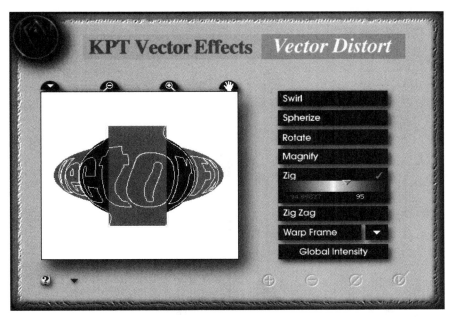

Figure 12-15: Dialog boxes in Vector Effects are like separate programs unto themselves.

extrudes objects in three-dimensional space, as in the first example in the figure. The Warp Frame filter lets you distort a selection by bending its bounding box. The middle example is one possible result. And the ShatterBox filter subdivides objects and nudges them in random directions, as in the last example.

DrawTools

Extensis (503/274-2020) is a Portland-based company that's quickly making a name for itself in the plug-in business. They create extensions for PageMaker, QuarkXPress, and Photoshop, not to mention DrawTools ($149) for Illustrator. Though not quite as versatile as Vector Effects, DrawTools provides many of the same distortion effects without the huge, screen-gobbling interface.

Figure 12-17 shows the dialog box for DrawTools' Free Projection filter, which works very much like Vector Effects' Warp Frame. The dialog box is less distracting, but the preview doesn't allow you to zoom in and out, and you can't select from a menu of presets as in Vector Effects. On the plus side, you can clone the selection as you distort it by turning on the Save Copy of Object check box.

Figure 12-16: Effects created using the 3D Transform (top), Warp Frame (middle), and ShatterBox (bottom) filters included with KPT Vector Effects.

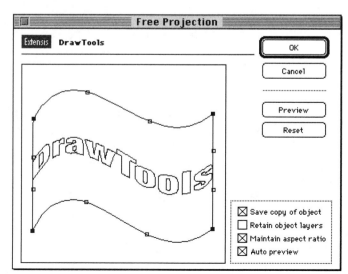

Figure 12-17: You can bend the bounding box around a selection to distort the shapes inside using DrawTools' Free Projection filter.

The obligatory Figure 12-18 shows a few of the kinds of tricks you can pull off with DrawTools. To create the gray sphere in the background, I applied the Globe filter to the word DrawTools in Helvetica Inserat. The filter wrapped the text around a sphere, distorting it almost beyond recognition. I then added the wavy text by applying the Free Projection filter to that very same collection of converted Helvetica Inserat characters. It looks like a line of path text, except that all the letters are positioned upright. Finally, I create the base of the sphere using the Cone filter, which naturally wraps the selection around a cone.

Figure 12-18: Here I modified a line of converted text using the Globe (background), Free Projection (wavy text), and Cone (bottom) filters.

DrawTools needs previews throughout all of its dialog boxes, and some of the options are a teeny bit technical. But, at $50 less expensive than Vector Effects, it provides many of the same distortion effects as well as a few unique tricks of its own. DrawTools also includes a few filters for mixing and replacing colors, including one that converts color illustrations to grayscale (something Illustrator can't do on its own). You can also adjust the stacking order of objects, by switching two selected objects, for example, or simply nudging them a level forward or back.

Probing the Third Dimension

 At this point, you might be thinking, "Gee willickers, I wish I had Vector Effects or DrawTools so that I could create nifty three-dimensional effects in my spare time." Well, the truth is, you can thanks to an addition to Illustrator 6. Few folks seem to realize it, but Illustrator 6 ships with Dimensions 2.0, which is a modest 3-D drawing program that Adobe created a couple of years ago. Dimensions is essentially a 3-D plug-in for Illustrator that runs as a separate application.

Assuming you own a CD-ROM drive, you'll find Dimensions inside the Adobe Products folder on the Adobe Illustrator Deluxe CD. Just double-click on the installer program and away you go. This is not a demonstration of Dimensions, it's the real thing. There's even a serial number and documentation for the program inside the Illustrator box.

The fact that Dimensions is a 3-D drawing program means that you have to spend a fair amount of time navigating 3-D space on your 2-D screen. If you're unfamiliar with drawing in 3-D, you'll undoubtedly find it confusing, bewildering, and nerve-wracking, just as all artists do. But if you're willing to invest a little effort, it makes a nice addition to Illustrator.

I wish I could show you how Dimensions works from start to finish. But that would take me a few hundred pages that are better spent on Illustrator's core features. So instead, I'll walk you through a simple exercise that integrates both Dimensions and Illustrator. If the exercise piques your interest, read the documentation included with your copy of Illustrator. (I know, no one reads the documentation—and if they did, I'd be out of a job—but go ahead and do it this one time.)

One of the things Dimensions excels at is creating three-dimensional type. Figure 12-19 shows a line of type created in the Adobe font Mezz, followed by the same text embellished inside Dimensions. The following steps show you how you can create your own 3-D type:

1. **Create some type in Illustrator, and make it big**.

    You can create the text in Dimensions, but Illustrator is faster and it provides better controls. In fact, it's almost always a good idea to create your base objects in Illustrator and then port them over to Dimensions.

2. **Copy the text to the Clipboard**.

    You don't have to convert the text to paths. Dimensions does this automatically. Just select the text in Illustrator and press ⌘-C. (Unfortunately,

Figure 12-19: A line of type created in the font Mezz in Illustrator (top) and the same text extruded in Dimensions (bottom).

there's no drag-and-drop between Illustrator and Dimensions. Adobe would have had to update Dimensions to pull that off, which would have meant more work. As things stand, Adobe just flung Dimensions in the Illustrator 6 box and said, "Look kids, it's free!")

3. **Launch the Dimensions application**.

   If this is the first time you've launched the program, you'll be asked for a serial number. Look inside your Illustrator box for the registration card, which contains the serial number. I'd love to give you my number, but if I did that, Adobe would hire thugs to rough me up. And none of us wants that, do we?

   If you have a lot of fonts loaded into your system, Dimensions takes approximately three years to boot up. Just wait it out.

4. **Drag inside the Dimensions document window with the 2-D artwork tool**.

   After Dimensions starts up, it displays an empty document window, just like Illustrator. To add free-form objects to the document—as opposed to cubes, spheres, and other primitive shapes—you have to create a two-dimensional canvas. You do this by dragging with the 2-D artwork tool, labeled in Figure 12-20. Drag to create as big a canvas as you can, but don't knock yourself out. Size isn't important. (At least, that's what I keep telling myself.)

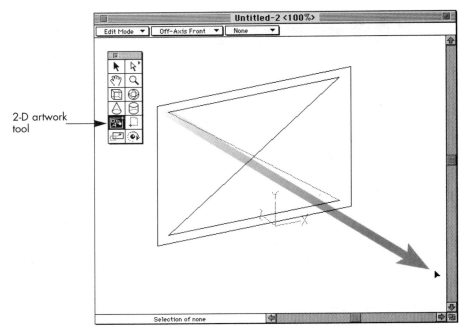

2-D artwork
tool

Figure 12-20: Drag with the 2-D artwork tool to add text to your new
Dimensions document.

When you release the mouse button, Dimensions displays a 2-D
drawing window. The tools in the toolbox also change, as you can see
in Figure 12-21. The 2-D drawing window has a lot in common with
Illustrator's illustration window, including many of the same tools and a
few of the commands in the Artwork menu. But Illustrator is several
times better equipped.

5. Paste the text from the Clipboard.

When you press ⌘-V, Dimensions adds the text to the 2-D drawing
window, as in Figure 12-21. Then click on the close button in the upper
left corner of the window. The program asks you if you want to apply
your changes. Press Return to answer in the affirmative.

6. Choose Operations » Extrude.

Or press ⌘-Shift-E. Dimensions displays the Extrude palette pictured in
Figure 12-22. To extrude an object is to pop it off the screen into the
world of three dimensions. Extruding a shape adds sides to it, giving
the object depth. The letters back in Figure 12-19 were extruded, as
were those way back in Figure 12-16.

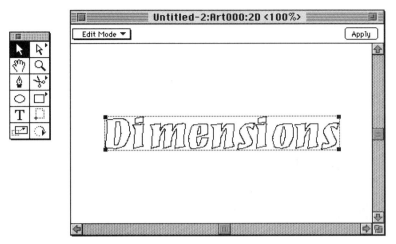

Figure 12-21: Paste the text copied from Illustrator into Dimensions' 2-D drawing window.

The Extrude palette lets you specify the depth of the extrusion. You can also bevel the edges to give the corners a sculpted look.

7. Enter a value into the Depth option box.

I entered 20 points, but you can enter anything you want. To get an idea what the extrusion looks like, click on the Apply button in the palette. It may be hard to make out what's going on with all the anchor points, but you should be able to get a rough idea.

8. Click on the New Bevel button at the bottom of the Extrude palette.

This allows you to add a beveled edge to the text. (This button appears as Edit Bevel in Figure 12-22, because I've already added a bevel.) A dialog box comes up, asking you to find a bevel on disk. Locate the Bevel Library folder inside the same folder that contains the Dimensions application, and open it. Then open any bevel that sounds fun.

9. Close the bevel window, and click on the Apply button in the palette.

Dimensions wants you to see what your bevel looks like so that you can edit it if you like, but you don't have to leave it up on screen. The bevel is now loaded, so you can close the window to get it out of your way. Select a different Extent option if you want to—the bottom option adds a bevel around the edges of the shapes; the top option carves into the shapes. Then click on the Apply button to add the bevel to the selected text.

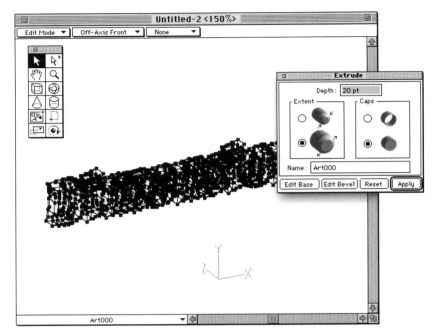

Figure 12-22: Use the options in the Extrude palette to give the letters depth and carve a bevel into the corners.

10. Fill your text with the color of your choice.

Right now the text is probably black. You can change the color by choosing Appearance » Surface Properties or pressing ⌘-I, which is the shortcut for the Paint Style palette in Illustrator. As shown in Figure 12-23, the Surface Properties palette bears a strong resemblance to Illustrator's Paint Style palette, permitting you to fill selected shapes with gray values or colors. In the figure, I merely changed the Tint slider to 25 percent to select a light gray. But you can make the color whatever you want.

11. Choose View » Shaded Render.

Or press ⌘-Shift-Y. This produces a shaded preview of the letters on screen. It may take a minute or more depending on the speed of your computer, but go ahead and let 'er rip. After the command finishes, Dimension beeps at you. If you're having problems seeing the text for all the anchor points, just click on an empty portion of the screen to deselect everything. That's what I did to look at my text in Figure 12-23.

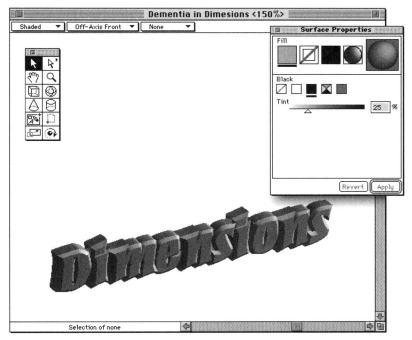

Figure 12-23: Lighten the color of your text so that Dimensions has sufficient color range to create shadows and highlights.

12. Select the text and copy it.

Click on the letters to select them. Then press ⌘-C to send the text to the Clipboard.

13. Go back to Illustrator and paste the 3-D text.

Dimensions creates its 3-D objects and shading as a series of filled paths. You can edit these paths in any way you see fit in Illustrator. But take care—the pasted text is actually one big group.

To create the 3-D text shown in Figure 12-19, I selected all the letters by alternately Option-clicking and Shift-Option-clicking with the direct selection tool. Then I filled the letters with light gray and stroked them with thin black outlines. I also press ⌘-equal to send them to the front of the group, so that the strokes showed clearly.

Believe it or not, that exercise covered about 10 percent of Dimensions. You can create basic objects like cubes, spheres, cones, and cylinders using the drawing tools in the toolbox. You can also rotate objects in 3-D space with the trackball tool (in the lower right corner of the toolbox) and change the position of the light source using Appearance » Lighting (⌘-Shift-L).

Dimensions is not what I'd call a powerful program. And it isn't nearly as convenient for extruding type as Vector Effects' 3D Transform filter. But it shares much of the same "look and feel" as Illustrator—including a few identical keyboard equivalents—and, by golly, it's free. If you're willing to at least give it half a chance, you may discover that's it's a handy little tool.

BECOMING MASTER
OF THE RASTER

Illustrator 6 is the first version of the esteemed illustration program to recognize pixels in all of their splendor. In previous versions, you could import EPS images. But the program merely tagged the file on disk for printing purposes and displayed a low-resolution preview of the image on screen. Not so in Illustrator 6. The new Illustrator converts most kinds of images to its native file format. This means you can view individual pixels on screen, edit pixels using Photoshop filters, convert paths and text objects to pixels, and even trade images with cousin Photoshop.

But this pixel awareness comes at a price. Images take up lots of room in memory and equally large amounts of room on disk. For example, if you import a high-resolution Photo CD image into Illustrator, the illustration file takes up about 35MB on disk. That's right, 35MB, big enough to fill 25 floppy disks!

Why so big? After all, a Photo CD file takes up 5MB on a CD-ROM. Understand, though, that Illustrator expresses each and every illustration file in PostScript code. This is why Illustrator is so good at printing to PostScript printers—it already has the code ready and waiting. Illustrator likewise converts an imported Photo CD image into PostScript, which is an extremely inefficient image-handling format. Also important, Photo CD images are compressed on disk to make them as small as possible, whereas Illustrator offers no image compression whatsoever. So the image grows inside Illustrator's decompressed PostScript tummy from 5MB to seven times that size.

 How does Illustrator handle such enormous files? In the old days, the program kept the illustration in memory at all times, even when saving the file to disk. (In fact, saving is merely the duplication of data from RAM to your hard drive.)
But if you have, say, 12MB of RAM assigned to Illustrator, there's no way it can keep a 35MB image in memory. So Illustrator saves a portion of the illustration to a temporary file on disk called a *scratch file*. The program places the scratch file inside the Preferences folder in the System Folder and names it something like *AITempImageFile#1*. Scratch files slow down Illustrator tremendously, because it takes the program much longer to access data from a disk—which is mechanical—than from RAM circuitry—which is exclusively electronic.

The moral, therefore, is to import small images into Illustrator. This can mean a full-page image containing 72 pixels per inch (ppi), or a quarter-page image at twice that resolution. (Resolution is measured linearly—both tall and wide—so doubling the resolution quadruples the number of pixels.) The important thing it to keep the pixels to a minimum.

If you want to work with a high-resolution image that fills a big portion of the page, first save the image as an EPS file. Then import it into Illustrator using File » Place, as directed in Chapter 3. And be sure to select the Placed EPS (not Parsed EPS) radio button when given the chance to do so. This way, Illustrator merely tags the EPS file on disk and imports the small preview image, just as in the old days.

For more on the differences between EPS and every other file format, read the following section. If you think you already have this confusing bit of theory figured out, skip a couple of pages ahead to the "Trading Graphics with Photoshop" section, in which I impart some actual techniques.

EPS Versus All the Rest

In Illustrator, placed EPS images are unique kinds of objects. If you import an EPS image and select the Placed EPS radio button, Illustrator creates a link to the image file on disk. The image consumes very little room in the illustration—100K tops—regardless of how much space the original EPS image takes up on disk. Therefore, when working with large images, Illustrator is still most comfortable with the EPS format, just as in days gone by.

 You can locate a tagged EPS file on disk by selecting the placed EPS image and choosing Object » Attributes (⌘-Control-A). The Attributes dialog box contains an additional pop-up menu called Location of Placed Art. Click on the pop-up menu to see the folder hierarchy for the tagged image, which tells you where to find the original file on disk.

All other kinds of images work differently. These images may come to Illustrator through a variety of different routes:

- You can import an image saved in TIFF or some other standardized file format, such as JPEG, Photo CD, or PCX.

- Or you can import an EPS image and select the Parsed EPS radio button. This treats the image as if it came from some other file format.

 Well, except for one very odd difference. Illustrator includes a rectangle with the parsed EPS image that acts as a mask. You can change the size of the rectangle with the scale tool to crop the image. But it's very easy to move the rectangle without the image, which ends up hiding a portion of the image. For more information on masks, read the "Filling Objects with Objects" section of Chapter 17. Or just delete the rectangle and avoid the confusion.

- You can drag an image from Photoshop and drop it—*kerplunk*—into an Illustrator window.

- You can also convert objects to pixels directly inside Illustrator using Object » Rasterize.

In any of these cases, Illustrator imports all pixels into the illustration and converts the pixels into PostScript code, an operation known as *parsing*. Illustrator has to save all the pixels to disk, so that the illustration may take up 1MB or more of disk space. But it also means you can take advantage of a whole bunch of special effects options. Here are a few of the things you can do to so-called "parsed" images that you can't do to a placed EPS image:

- Use Object » Rasterize to convert a color image to grayscale. You can also convert an image to black-and-white, or change the number of pixels in an image.

- You can apply Photoshop-compatible plug-ins, such as the Gallery Effects filters included with Illustrator 6.

- Choose Filter » Create » Object Mosaic to convert a parsed image to a bunch of colored squares. You can then edit those squares using any of Illustrator's tools or commands, just as if you had drawn them with the rectangle tool.

- If you convert the image to black-and-white, you can colorize the image from the Paint Style palette.

- You can also colorize grayscale images using Filter » Colors » Adjust Colors, as explained in the "Adjusting CMYK Values" section of Chapter 14.

- The Selection Info command tells you all kinds of information about a parsed image that it refuses to share when a placed EPS image is selected. This is especially useful if you've stretched or shrunk the image with the scale tool.

- When you magnify a parsed image, you see more detail (depending on the resolution of the image). Magnifying a placed EPS image merely causes the pixels to appear larger.

Not all factors favor parsed images. Illustrator lets you move, scale, rotate, flip, or slant any kind of image, whether placed EPS or parsed. You can view black-and-white versions of EPS images in the artwork mode (if the Show Placed EPS check box is turned on in the Document Setup dialog box); whereas parsed images always look like hollow rectangles. And a placed EPS image gets an X through it, making it easier to select and modify when Area Select is turned off in the General Preferences dialog box.

If all this sounds confusing, you're not alone. Frankly, Illustrator's image management is much more convoluted than it ought to be. But while strange, the distinction between placed EPS and parsed images is very important. My advice is to read the remainder of this chapter to get a feel for how images work inside Illustrator. By the end of it, you should understand all of your options, and you'll be equipped to determine whether the benefits of parsed images are truly worth the price.

Hoist that Raster and Rake Those Pixels

You know you've finally reached the enviable status of Hopeless Computer Dweeb when you know the meaning of the word *rasterize*. In regular human terms, it means to convert objects to pixels. You probably aren't aware of it—you're so busy paying attention to things that actually matter—but your computer is constantly rasterizing things. Every time you edit an object, Illustrator and your system software rasterize paths to display them as pixels on screen. With the help of Adobe Type Manager, Illustrator rasterizes characters of type to screen pixels. And when you print your artwork, your printer rasterizes the mathematical path definitions as teeny printer pixels. Rasterizing is as integral to your computer's existence as generating red blood cells is to yours.

 Legend has it that the word "rasterize" was coined during the early days of monitor development. Your monitor displays stuff on screen by projecting pixels in horizontal rows. (It happens so fast—about 60 to 75 times a second—that your gullible eyes interpret the screen image as both continual and stationary.) It's almost as if the monitor were raking pixels across the screen, which is where the word *raster*—Latin for *rake*—comes in. Nowadays, rasterize is the word for any kind of pixel creation, whether on screen, inside a printer, or inside a program like Illustrator.

 Object » Rasterize is merely Illustrator's way of saying, "Here I am making all these pixels. Maybe you'd like to play around with them for a while."

- When applied to paths or text objects, the Rasterize command converts the objects to pixels. The pixels appear inside a rectangular image boundary, just as if you had imported a parsed image from disk.

- When applied to a parsed image, the Rasterize command lets you change the number of colors in the image, or increase or decrease the number of pixels.

The Rasterizing Options

When you choose Object » Rasterize, Illustrator greets you with the dialog box shown in Figure 13-1. The dialog box offers the following options:

● **Color Model**: Use this pop-up menu to specify whether you want to create a color image, a grayscale image, or a black-and-white image. Two options, RGB and CMYK, result in color images. The RGB option results in an image that takes up less room on disk, but may not print exactly as it appears on screen. A CMYK image takes up more space on disk, but prints more accurately. For more information about the amazing world of RGB and CMYK color theory, read Chapter 14.

To convert a selection to a grayscale image, select the Grayscale option. Select Bitmap to if you want the image to contain black pixels only. All other pixels inside the image boundary will be transparent.

Figure 13-1:
The Rasterize dialog box
converts selected objects
into an image. Or you
can change the number
of colors and pixels inside
an image.

● **Resolution**: Select one of the first three radio buttons or enter a value into the Other option box to specify the number of pixels in the image. Select Screen for 72 ppi, Medium for 150 ppi, and High for 300 ppi. Figure 13-2 demonstrates the effect of converting the sea lion from Chapter 1 to an image using the Screen and Medium settings. An image rasterized at the High setting is virtually indistinguishable from the original objects, even when printed from an imagesetter or other high-resolution device.

As you can see in the figure, a high-resolution image looks smoother than a low-resolution one, but it also takes up more space on disk. As a general rule of thumb, an image with twice the resolution takes up four times as much space on disk. In Figure 13-2, for example, the image on left consumes about 100K, while the image on right consumes about 400K.

Screen, 72 ppi   Medium, 150 ppi

Figure 13-2: The sea lion illustration from Chapter 1 rasterized at 72 and 150 ppi.

 After you enter a high resolution value and press Return, you may experience a long initial delay before Illustrator displays a progress bar. The delay can be so long, in fact, that you may think Illustrator has crashed. Before you give up and restart your computer, allow Illustrator a solid couple of minutes to show some sign of life.

Anti-Alias: If you want to soften the transitions between neighboring pixels of different colors, select this option. *Antialiasing* (pronounced *anti-alias-ing*) is an oddly named blurring technique that eliminates jagged edges while only slightly reducing the focus of an image. (The story behind its name is more convoluted than the origin of "rasterize.") If you prefer that Illustrator convert objects to pixels without any blurring, turn the check box off.

Figure 13-3 compares an image created with and without antialiasing. The difference is slight at this medium resolution (150 ppi), but you can still make out subtle differences. The bottom image is more sharply focused, but the edges are sometimes jagged, particularly along the black outline. Antialiasing is much more pronounced at lower resolutions, but you may want to turn it off at higher resolutions to speed up the rasterizing time. This check box has no effect whatsoever on file size, and is dimmed when the Bitmap option is selected from the Color Model pop-up menu.

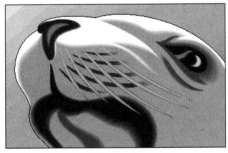

Figure 13-3:
An image rasterized
at 150 ppi with the
Anti-Alias check box
turned on (top) and
off (bottom).

🌑 **Create Mask**: This check box masks away transparent portions of the original objects to keep them transparent. It is only useful when rasterizing objects, not when converting parsed images. Because this option requires a bit of background explanation, I explain it at length in the following section.

Maintaining Transparency

Except when working with black-and-white images, *all* pixels inside an image are opaque. In other words, there is no such thing as a see-through pixel inside a grayscale or color image. So the transparent areas in selected objects become white pixels when rasterized. In Figure 13-4, for example, I've rasterized a line of type at 20 ppi. (Anti-Alias was turned on.) As the second example shows, the areas between letters become white.

Figure 13-4:
If I select some type (top) and
rasterize it without creating a
mask, the transparent areas
between letters turn white
(middle). A mask ensures that
the transparent areas remain
transparent (bottom).

To make these areas transparent, you have to "mask" them away by selecting the Create Mask check box. Illustrator uses the original character outlines to determine which portions of the image are opaque and which are transparent, as in the third example in Figure 13-4. (I added the black outlines around the letters to make the mask more obvious.) The low resolution of the image combined with the smooth outlines of the mask produces the unusual appearance of tiled letters.

 Though indisputably useful, the Create Mask check box can cause problems. As I discuss in Chapters 17 and 18, masks slow down printing time considerably and may even prevent an illustration from printing altogether. And there is no more precarious item you can mask than an image.

Consider Figure 13-4. Character outlines constitute an extremely complex mask because Illustrator has to combine them into a single, elaborate compound path. Only by lowering the rasterizing resolution to 20 ppi was I able to get the illustration to print. (Prior to that, my LaserWriter kept pooping out.) If you want to use a higher resolution image, make sure your original objects are fairly simple. Or just leave the Create Mask check box turned off and live with the white pixels.

Putting Object » Rasterize to Good Use

The Rasterize command is one of Illustrator 6's slyest features. On the surface, it looks rather simple and limited. I mean, how often are you really going to want to convert objects to pixels? But if you're willing to invest a little time and imagination, Object » Rasterize turns out to be a robust feature with a fair number of practical uses.

The following are a handful of techniques designed to expand your raster awareness. Every one of them was impossible prior to Illustrator 6:

● Object » Rasterize is the only command in all of Illustrator that's capable of automatically converting a color illustration to grayscale. Frankly, it's a stupid oversight, but it's true nonetheless. If you're curious how a color illustration looks in grayscale, select and clone all objects in the illustration, then rasterize the objects as a low-resolution grayscale image with Anti-Alias turned off. Because your original objects are still intact, you can then use the grayscale image as an approximate visual model for how you should manually recolor the objects in your illustration. (You can click on the image with the eyedropper tool, but this lifts a CMYK composite of the gray value, which won't help you. Check out Chapter 14 for the whole story.)

 If you find yourself converting to grayscale fairly often, you may want to invest in a third-party package that lets you convert color illustrations to grayscale without resorting to pixels. Examples include Vector Effects from MetaTools (805/566-6200), mentioned in the previous chapter, and Socket Set from Cytopia (415/364-4594).

When you rasterize objects to a black-and-white image using the Bitmap option, the white pixels become transparent. You can then select a Fill color in the Paint Style palette to specify the color of the black pixels. Add in the fact those black-and-white images take up relatively little room on disk, and you have a great means for creating quick texture patterns.

In Figure 13-5, for example, I started out with a compound path in which converted characters of text cut holes into a black rectangle. (This way, I can see through the text in the last example in the figure.) I next drew a rectangle in front of the compound path and filled it with a gradation. To arrive at the third example, I rasterized the gradation using the Bitmap option and a resolution of 72 ppi; then I clicked on the Black icon in the Paint Style palette and changed the Tint value to 50 percent to fill the rasterized image with gray. In the final example, I sent the bitmapped image to back, cloned and nudged it ever so slightly, and filled the clone with white. This way, the white bitmap partially covered the gray one, creating an embossed texture.

I know FreeHand artists who go absolutely nuts with bitmap texture effects. Now that Illustrator 6 supports black-and-white images, you can, too.

*Figure 13-5:
After combining text
with a rectangle (top), I
drew a gradient rect-
angle (second), con-
verted the rectangle to a
bitmap, and filled it with
gray (third). Then I sent
the bitmap to back,
cloned and nudged it,
and filled the clone with
white (bottom).*

You *must* assign a color to the black pixels in a black-and-white image. If you want the pixels to stay black, then click on the Black icon in the Paint Style palette. Otherwise, the fill for the image is set to None. Although the pixels appear black on screen, they print as transparent.

You can confirm the resolution of a selected image, whether rasterized inside Illustrator or imported via File » Place, by choosing File » Selection Info. Inside the Selection Info dialog box, choose the Raster Art option. Illustrator shares with you several tidbits of information about the image, including a Resolution item, spotlighted in Figure 13-6. (In Illustrator, you can disproportionately resize an image—just like any other object—with the scale tool. This squishes or stretches the pixels, which is why the Selection Info dialog box lists two Resolution values, one horizontal and the other vertical. If you haven't scaled the image, the two values are identical.) When you finish noting the Resolution value, press Return or click on the Done button to close the dialog box.

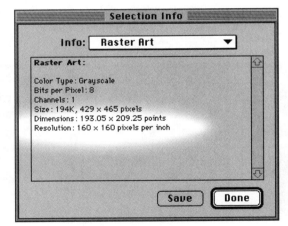

Figure 13-6: Choose File » Selection Info and select the Raster Art option to discover the resolution of a selected image.

If you import a black-and-white TIFF, MacPaint, PCX, or EPS image, Illustrator automatically treats the white pixels as transparent. But if you import a black-and-white PICT image, or drag and drop an image from Photoshop, Illustrator leaves the white pixels opaque. Whatever Illustrator's reasoning behind this weird quirk—can you say "arbitrary distinction"?—you can make the white pixels transparent with the Rasterize command.

 First, check the resolution of the image using File » Selection Info, as directed in the previous item. (This is very important, since the Rasterize command has no inkling of the resolution of a selected image.) Then choose Object » Rasterize, select the Bitmap option, and enter the Resolution value that you noted inside the Selection Info dialog box. This ensures that you don't mess up the image while fixing it. After you press Return, Illustrator makes the white pixels transparent and lets you assign a color to the black pixels.

● This can also be a problem when importing grayscale PICT images or dragging and dropping a grayscale image from Photoshop. If Illustrator complains that an image is RGB during the printing cycle when you know darn well the image is grayscale, convert it to grayscale using Object » Rasterize, taking care to maintain the resolution as directed above.

● If an image is taking up too much room on disk or in memory, you can lower its resolution by selecting a different Resolution option in the Rasterize dialog box. Make sure to keep the Anti-Alias check box turned on to ensure the best transitions. Changing the number of pixels in this way is called *resampling*, because Illustrator has to generate new pixels by averaging the old ones. In technospeak, this averaging is called *interpolating*.

 If you're an experienced Photoshop user, you may be wondering what kind of interpolation Illustrator uses when resampling images. When Anti-Alias is turned on, Illustrator uses *bilinear* interpolation, which means the program averages five pixels at a time. (Photoshop's more sophisticated *bicubic* interpolation factors in nine pixels.) When Anti-Alias is off, Illustrator doesn't average pixels at all; it just throws away the pixels that it deems appropriate. (This is the same as Photoshop's "nearest neighbor" interpolation.)

● Raising the Resolution value is never a good idea; Illustrator isn't smart enough to generate detail out of thin air, so you just increase the number of pixels without providing any benefit.

 You can convert a black-and-white bitmap to a credible grayscale image by lowering the resolution by about half and selecting the Grayscale option. Make sure Anti-Alias is turned on. Illustrator automatically generates five or six levels of gray.

Figure 13-7: Starting with a Digital Stock image (top), I drew an ellipse around it (middle) and rasterized the circle into the image (bottom).

Fusing Objects and Images

 I have one last tip up my sleeve before I move onto bigger and better things, and this one is my favorite: You can fuse objects and imported images into a single image using Object » Rasterize. This allows you to use Illustrator as an object-oriented image editor—kind of like a poor man's Live Picture.

For example, I imported the top image in Figure 13-7 from a Digital Stock Professional CD. But I wasn't happy with the circular strip of neon surrounding the Deli sign. It was too dark; it needed some punching up. So I traced around the outline of the neon with the oval tool and assigned it a thick white stroke and no fill. I had to slant the oval with the shear tool to make it match the image, as in the second example of the figure.

I checked the resolution of the image using File » Selection Info; it turned out to be 160 ppi. Then I selected both image and ellipse and chose Object » Rasterize. I selected the Grayscale option, entered 160 into the Other option box, and turned on Anti-Alias to soften the edges of the oval. When I pressed Return, Illustrator set about rasterizing the ellipse into the image, as you can see in the last example in Figure 13-7.

Though Photoshop offers its own object-oriented tools—including the pen tool and a few others—Illustrator provides a much wider range of drawing options. So if you find that you can't accomplish a certain effect in Photoshop, try turning the job over to Illustrator. After adding objects and rasterizing them into the image, you can save the final effect as a PCX file (as explained back in Chapter 3) and then open it up again in Photoshop.

Trading Artwork with Photoshop

Illustrator and Photoshop have been able to trade paths and pixels back and forth for a few years now. But with Illustrator 6 and Photoshop 3.0.5, the two programs have become closer trading partners than ever before. You can drag and drop artwork or transfer it via the Clipboard. The results vary depending on which direction you drag—from Illustrator into Photoshop or vice versa—and what kind of objects you have selected. The following sections tell all.

Dragging Objects into Photoshop

Just as you can drag selected objects from an illustration window and drop them into the Scrapbook (as I explained in Chapter 9), you can drag objects from Illustrator into Photoshop. Since Photoshop can't accommodate objects—except as selection paths—the program converts the objects into pixels, much like Object » Rasterize.

Because Photoshop is a faster and more efficient image-handler than Illustrator, you may find that dragging and dropping from Illustrator into Photoshop is frequently a preferable alternative to the Rasterize command. But you should keep the following tidbits of information in mind:

- You have to be using System 7.5 and Photoshop 3.0.5 or later. Earlier versions don't support drag and drop.

- You have to have enough RAM to run Illustrator and Photoshop at the same time. I can barely get the two programs to play ball on my 20MB PowerBook—and even then, drag and drop works sporadically—so I'm recommending that you have 32MB of RAM or more.

- Make sure you have an image window open in Photoshop so you have a place to drop the objects from Illustrator.

- You can drag any path or text object from Illustrator into Photoshop. But you can't drag images, whether placed EPS or parsed. If you want to transfer an image from Illustrator to Photoshop, save the image from Illustrator in PCX or one of the other image formats and then open the file inside Photoshop.

- After you drop the objects into the image window, Photoshop sets about rasterizing them in the background. You remain inside Illustrator; the system does not automatically switch you to Photoshop. If you want to see the objects rasterize, you have to switch to Photoshop manually via the Applications menu or by clicking on the image window. A progress bar keeps you apprised as Photoshop churns away.

- The rasterized objects appear inside Photoshop as a floating selection. This permits you to move the objects into place before applying them to the underlying image. Or you can convert the objects to an independent layer by Option-double-clicking on the words *Floating Selection* in the Layers palette.

- When using the Rasterize command, you manually specify the number of colors and resolution. But Photoshop decides these things automatically, according to the color mode and resolution of the image window. The higher the resolution, the more pixels Photoshop assigns to the rasterized objects.

Figure 13-8 shows the difference between dragging a line of type from Illustrator to Photoshop when the image resolution is set to different values, specifically 72 ppi and 180 ppi. In both cases, the type size was 100-point inside Illustrator, but the letters grew in pixels when I raised the resolution inside Photoshop.

Therefore, the image resolution directly affects the size of rasterized objects. If the objects appear too small, delete them, increase the resolution of the Photoshop image using Image » Image Size, and drag the objects from Illustrator again.

Figure 13-8: A line of 100-point text dragged from Illustrator into Photoshop when the image resolution was set to 72 ppi and 180 ppi.

Photoshop likes to generate error messages when rasterizing Illustrator objects. If Photoshop complains that it can't find a font or some other gibberish and it offers you a Continue button, click on that button or press Return. About 50 percent of the time, the program will come through just fine despite its whining.

 If you don't quite know your way around Photoshop, and you've found this book helpful, I encourage you to check out my *Macworld Photoshop Bible* from IDG Books. Not only is it the bestselling guide to Photoshop, it was at last report the number one book on *any* desktop publishing topic. (Thanks to my vast fortunes, I've paid off my K-Mart credit card and instructed my comptroller to redirect my purchasing power to Sam's Membership Warehouse.) *Macworld Photoshop Bible* makes a great gift, so buy several copies. And be sure to ask about the case discount. My wife and cat thank you.

Dragging Images into Illustrator

You can also drag images from Photoshop and drop them into Illustrator. Either select the image you want to drag with one of the selection tools and then drag it over. Or you can drag an entire image or layer with Photoshop's move tool. (If you drag a layer, the previously transparent pixels turn white inside Illustrator.) Illustrator imports the image as a parsed image.

 The important point to remember when dragging from Photoshop into Illustrator is that the image comes over at 72 ppi. So if the image is set to a higher resolution inside Photoshop, Illustrator abandons pixels *without even warning you about it.* Bad Illustrator, bad! To make sure you don't lose (or gain) any pixels in the transition, set the image resolution to 72 ppi inside Photoshop using Image » Image Size. Then drag and drop the image into Illustrator, and resize the image as desired using the scale tool.

 The problem is: What if you want to set the image to a very specific resolution? Well, for those of you who dread math, I have bad news. You have to use division, and on a calculator, no less. Divide 72 by the desired resolution. Then multiply that number by 100. Select the image, double-click on the scale tool icon in the toolbox, and enter your value into the Uniform option box.

For example, say you want to set a drag-and-dropped image to 160 ppi inside Illustrator. You would divide 72 by 160 to get 0.45. Then multiply 0.45 by 100 to get 45 percent. Double-click on the scale tool, enter 45, and press Return. Illustrator shrinks the image down to size. Because the number of pixels remains constant, Illustrator has to squish the pixels into a smaller space, thereby upping the resolution. To confirm that you've got it right, choose File » Selection Info, select the Raster Art option, and take a look at the Resolution value. It should be right on.

Copying and Pasting Paths

For some reason—the ways of Illustrator are forever mysterious—you can't drag paths from Photoshop into Illustrator. Why would you want to? Well, say that you've traced a path around an image inside Photoshop and you want to use that path as a mask inside Illustrator (as I explain in Chapter 17). You need to transfer that mask as an object, not as an image. And drag-and-drop between Photoshop and Illustrator is an image-only experience.

To transfer paths, you have to rely on the Clipboard, just as in previous versions of these two programs. Copy the path in Photoshop (⌘-C), switch to Illustrator, and paste (⌘-V). The path appears selected inside Illustrator, but without either fill or stroke. Be sure to assign a fill or stroke from the Paint Style palette to keep track of the path in the preview mode.

You can likewise use the Clipboard to transfer paths from Illustrator into Photoshop without converting them into pixels. When you paste Illustrator objects into Photoshop, you get a little dialog box asking if you'd like to paste the objects as pixels or as paths, as shown in Figure 13-9. Select the second radio button—Paste As Paths—if you want to use the objects as selection outlines or clipping paths. You can then edit the paths with the five tools in Photoshop's Paths palette, all of which work like their counterparts in Illustrator.

Figure 13-9:
This dialog box allows
you to transfer paths
intact from Illustrator
into Photoshop.

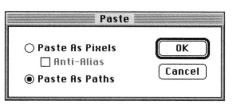

 If the paste command doesn't seem to work inside Photoshop, display the Edit menu to see if the Paste command is dimmed. If it is, Illustrator didn't transfer the Clipboard properly, a common problem. Go back to Illustrator and press ⌘-Option-C to copy a PICT version of the selected objects. Then return to Photoshop and try pasting again to get the Paste dialog box in Figure 13-9.

The Better Autotracing Tool

Remember how enthusiastically I berated Illustrator's wretched autotrace tool in Chapter 4? (If not, you can read the "Tracing a Black-and-White Template" section for my thoroughly indignant appraisal.) To sum up: you can trace only one path at a time, you can trace black-and-white templates only, and the template feature is a major pain in the aft quarters. It's inconvenient, inadequate, and altogether inept.

Illustrator's tracing capabilities are so bad, in fact, that they are outclassed by Photoshop's. That's right, Photoshop is a better tracing tool than Illustrator. You can trace multiple paths at a time, you can trace grayscale and black-and-white images alike, and you don't have to monkey around with a template. It couldn't be more convenient.

The following steps explain how to trace a scan inside Photoshop and transport the paths into Illustrator:

1. Open the scanned image in Photoshop and edit it as desired.

Line drawings and text will trace most successfully. Even Photoshop's tracing function doesn't accommodate photographs and other continuous-tone artwork.

If you don't have a scan, you can create something directly inside Photoshop. In Figure 13-10, I started off with a simple line of American Typewriter text. Then I modified it with the Ripple and Spherize distortion filters, two effects that are not available inside Illustrator.

Figure 13-10: I used Photoshop to embellish some text with a couple of special effects that are beyond Illustrator's capabilities.

2. Convert the artwork to grayscale.

If your artwork is in color, convert it to grayscale by choosing Mode » Grayscale. You don't absolutely have to perform this step, but you'll get the most predictable results if you do.

3. Convert the image into a selection.

You need to convert the image into a selection in order to take advantage of Photoshop's tracing function. And by far the easiest way to do this is to switch to the Channels palette (by choosing Window » Palettes » Show Channels) and Option-click on the word Black. Or just press

⌘-Option-1. This automatically selects all the light areas and deselects the dark areas.

4. Inverse the selection.

However, you want to trace the dark areas, so you need to reverse the selection. To do this, choose Select » Inverse.

5. Choose the Make Path command.

Switch to the Paths palette (Window » Palettes » Show Paths) and choose the Make Path command from the palette menu, as shown in Figure 13-11. Photoshop displays a dialog box that requests a Tolerance value. This option works exactly like the Freehand Tolerance option inside Illustrator's General Preferences dialog box (discussed in Chapter 4). For the best results, enter a value of 1 or 2 and press Return.

 To bypass the dialog box, you can click on the dotted circle icon along the bottom of the Paths palette (labeled *Convert to paths* in Figure 13-11).

In either case, Photoshop converts the selection to a series of paths. Unlike Illustrator's autotrace tool, Photoshop generates multiple paths simultaneously, so you don't have to waste a lot of time clicking.

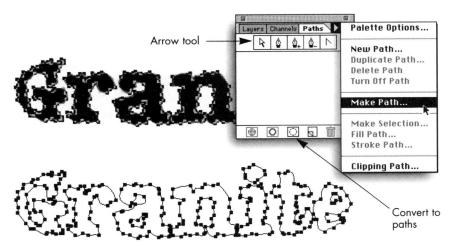

Figure 13-11: Choose the Make Path option to convert the selection to paths. The paths appear by themselves at bottom.

6. Option-drag with the arrow tool to select the paths.

You can select the arrow tool by clicking on its icon along the top of the Paths palette, or just press the T key twice in a row. Then hold down the Option key and marquee around the paths to select them. (The arrow tool works like the direct selection tool in Illustrator, so pressing Option ensures that you select entire paths.)

7. Copy the paths.

If you don't have enough RAM to run Photoshop and Illustrator at the same time, you can choose File » Export » Paths to Illustrator to save the traced paths as an illustration file.

8. Switch to Illustrator, paste the paths, and fill them with black.

When you paste the paths into Illustrator, they appear neither stroked or filled. You'll do well to fill them with black so you can see them in the preview mode.

If you exported the paths to an Illustrator file in the previous step, open them inside Illustrator using File » Open. Then press ⌘-E to switch to the artwork mode so you can see the transparent paths, select them, and fill them with black. You may also want to get rid of the crop marks by choosing Object » Crop Marks » Release and pressing the Delete key.

9. Restore any compound paths.

Photoshop doesn't know a compound path from a pile of compost, so it's little surprise that the holes in the *a* and *e* from *Granite* show up opaque in Illustrator. To create holes, press ⌘-8 (Object » Compound Path » Make) while everything's still selected. You'll probably have to redirect some of the paths by choosing Object » Attributes (⌘-Control-A) and fiddling with the Reverse Path Direction check box.

For example, to create the top example in Figure 13-12, I used the direct selection tool to select all paths except the ones along the insides of the *a* and *e*. Then I pressed ⌘-Control-A and turned off the Reverse Path Direction check box. Next I selected the paths inside the *a* and *e*, pressed ⌘-Control-A, and turned Reverse Path Direction on.

You can then edit the traced paths as you would any other kinds of objects inside Illustrator. To create the second effect in Figure 13-12, I applied Filter » Objects » Offset Path with a value of 3 points, followed by Filter » Pathfinder »

Unite. Then I selected the original paths and repeated the process with an Offset value of 1.5. I filled the back compound path with black, the next with gray, and the front path with white. Then I nudged the white and gray paths with the arrow keys. To create the drop shadow, I again cloned the black path, sent it to back (⌘-minus), filled it with light gray, and nudged it into position.

To create the third example in Figure 13-12, I went a few steps farther. I selected the white path, chose the Offset Path filter yet again, and entered a value of −1.5, which traced along the insides of the letters. I brought this new path to front (⌘-equal) and filled it with gray. To cut away the overlapping salvage generated by the Offset Path command, I chose Filter » Pathfinder » Divide. Then I carefully Shift-clicked with the direct selection tool on each letter to deselect the main

Figure 13-12: After pasting the paths into Illustrator, I combined them into a compound path (top) and used the Offset command along with a few Pathfinder filters to create a series of depth effects (second through last).

characters of text, and pressed Delete to get rid of the salvage. I pressed ⌘-U and ⌘-8 to ungroup the selection and restore the compound path (necessary to counteract the consequences of the Divide filter). And I filled the shapes with gray.

I next copied the new compound path (⌘-C), pasted it in front (⌘-F), and nudged it slightly down and to the right. I Shift-clicked on the first compound path with the arrow tool to select it as well and chose Filter » Pathfinder » Intersect. By finding the intersection of the two compound paths, I was able to create the inset carved shapes. I filled these with light gray, as in the bottom example in Figure 13-12. Then I pasted the original compound path in back (⌘-B) to complete the effect.

Obviously, I did most of the work on these letters after bringing them into Illustrator. But the original shapes came directly from Photoshop. The fact is, Photoshop is a terrific tool for tracing grayscale line drawings and text effects. Simply stated, if you have Photoshop, you never need use Illustrator's sickly autotrace tool again.

Applying Image Filters

There are two kinds of filters that you can apply to parsed images inside Illustrator 6. The first is the entire category of Photoshop-compatible filters, and the second is Filter » Create » Object Mosaic. The irony is the single Object Mosaic filter offers more potential than all the Photoshop-compatible filters put together.

 Both FreeHand 5.5 and Illustrator 6 support Photoshop-compatible filters. But by the admission of folks at both Macromedia and Adobe, this is more of a sales feature than a practical tool. Think about it. If you're like 90 percent of Illustrator users, you already own Photoshop, which is far better at handling Photoshop-compatible filters than any drawing program.

So why in the world would you apply filters inside Illustrator?

- 🌑 If you don't have enough RAM to run Photoshop and Illustrator at the same time, there is a certain convenience factor. You might prefer to use Photoshop filters inside Illustrator rather than quit Illustrator, launch Photoshop, apply a few filters, quit Photoshop, and return to Illustrator. To put it mildly, quitting and restarting programs is no fun.

- 🌑 Photoshop filters can be useful for testing out effects on small or low-resolution images inside Illustrator. Then you can return to Photoshop and apply the filters to a larger, high-resolution image.

Illustrator provides multiple undos, Photoshop currently doesn't (though this is likely to change). So you can apply several filters in a row in Illustrator with the full knowledge that you can always backtrack. In Photoshop, you don't have this luxury.

So that's it. Kind of makes you want to rush out and experiment with those Photoshop-compatible filters as soon as possible, huh? Meanwhile, the Object Mosaic filter converts pixels into object-oriented squares. You can then edit these squares inside Illustrator like any other paths. Suddenly, you have pixel-for-pixel control over an image, directly inside Illustrator. It's not the kind of thing you need to do on a daily or even weekly basis, but it can be helpful.

Photoshop-Compatible Filters

Ever heard of the Gallery Effects filters? These were the first commercially sold filters for Photoshop. Well, whether you've heard of them or not, you might want to know a thing or two about them since you now own them.

Gallery Effects was originally created by some folks at a company called Silicon Beach, the same people who created SuperPaint and now sell SmartSketch (the latter being a wonderful program, by the way). But before Silicon Beach could get the filters to market, Aldus—the creator of PageMaker—bought the company. A few years later, Adobe bought Aldus and got Gallery Effects in the bargain.

Personally, I'm not a big fan of the Gallery Effects collection. These filters invoke a bunch of "gee whiz" effects, many of which you can already apply using Photoshop's native filters (with a heck of a lot more flexibility). Granted, many of the Gallery Effects filters are intriguing, but most are too peculiar to be useful on a regular basis.

Now, I don't know what the folks at Adobe think, but their opinion of Gallery Effects can't be too terrifically high. After all, rather than selling the three collections of filters independently for $100 to $200 apiece—as Aldus did—Adobe tosses the whole kit and caboodle in for free along with Illustrator 6. So, at least from a marketing perspective, these filters have been reduced to a means of promoting one of Illustrator 6's new capabilities.

When you install Illustrator, you also install 12 Gallery Effects filters into the Gallery Effects folder inside the Plug-ins folder. Just so you know what you've got, Figure 13-13 shows all 12 filters applied to a single image. I don't know about you, but it makes me hungry just looking at that figure.

If you decide that I'm nuts and the Gallery Effects filters are great—it's been known to happen—you can find the larger 48-filter collection on the CD-ROM that comes with your Illustrator 6 package. Just look in the Adobe Products folder.

Figure 13-13: The 12 Gallery Effects filters that are installed along with
Illustrator 6 applied with their default settings.

Copy the filters into the Plug-ins folder on your hard drive. They'll be available
inside the Filter menu the next time you start Illustrator.

Better yet, trash the Gallery Effects filters in Illustrator's Plug-in folder, and then
copy all the Gallery Effects filters from the CD-ROM into Photoshop's Plug-ins
folder. These filters aren't great, but they're a heck of a lot more useful inside
Photoshop than they are inside Illustrator. In Photoshop, you can make partial
selections, mix filters images with the underlying original, and perform all kinds
of other tricks that are beyond Illustrator's capabilities.

Then, to access Gallery Effects and other Photoshop filters inside Illustrator, make an alias of the folder that contains the filters and place that alias inside Illustrator's Plug-ins folder. (To make an alias, choose File » Make Alias or press ⌘-M at the Finder desktop.) For example, if you make an alias of the Filter folder from Photoshop's Plug-ins folder, you can make such stalwarts as Radial Blur and Lens Flare available inside Illustrator. You can even run the Filter Factory and filters created with Filter Factory.

Converting an Image to Squares

Select an image and choose Filter » Create » Object Mosaic to convert the image into a series of colored rectangles. The rectangles imitate pixels—and each rectangle takes up the same amount of room on disk and in memory as a similarly-sized pixel would—but you can edit the rectangles just as if you had drawn them with the rectangle tool.

When you choose Filter » Create » Object Mosaic, Illustrator displays the dialog box shown in Figure 13-14. It contains a lot of options, but they're fairly easy to use:

- **New Size**: The Current Size area shows the dimensions of the image in points. You can adjust the size of the mosaic picture by entering new values in the New Size option boxes.

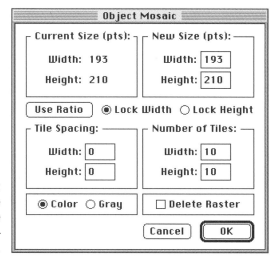

Figure 13-14:
Use this dialog box to
convert a parsed image
into a series of object-
oriented rectangles.

⚫   **Tile Spacing**: Enter the amount of space you want Illustrator to insert between rectangles in the Tile Spacing option boxes. To make the rectangles fit snugly together—usually my preference—leave the values set to 0.

⚫   **Number of Tiles**: Enter the number of rectangles that Illustrator should draw across and up and down into the Number of Tiles option boxes. If you enter a Width value of 40, for example, Illustrator draws 40 rectangles across the width of the image.

⚫   **Use Ratio**: If you want the New Size and the Number of Tiles values to conform to the ratio of the original image, then enter the desired values into either the two Width or the two Height option boxes, and then click on the Use Ratio button. For example, let's say you want the mosaic to be 300 points wide with 30 tiles across. First, enter each value into the appropriate Width option box. Then select the Lock Width radio button to tell Illustrator to change the Height values and leave the Width values intact. And finally, click on the Use Ratio button to automatically adjust the Height values so that you'll get a proportional mosaic made up of perfect squares.

⚫   **Color/Grayscale**: If you want Illustrator to fill the tiles with CMYK colors, select the Color radio button. Select the Gray option to fill the rectangles with shades of black.

⚫   **Delete Raster**: Select this option to delete the image after converting it to a mosaic. To retain the original image, turn the check box off.

After you apply the Object Mosaic command, Illustrator draws the rectangular tiles and combines them into a single group to facilitate editing. One of my favorite ways to edit tiles is to choose Arrange » Transform Each, because it permits you to scale or rotate each tile with respect to its center. You can also introduce some randomness to the tiles to make them appear a little less rigid.

Take a look at Figure 13-15. I start out with a mosaic 40 tiles wide and 21 tiles tall. I've stroked each tile with a thin black outline. To achieve the second example in the figure, I chose the Transform Each command, selected the Random check box, and adjusted the Scale values. I set the Horizontal value to 200 percent and the Vertical value to 150. The third example shows the results of random movements (2 and 3 points), and the fourth shows random rotations (up to 90 degrees).

If you want the mosaic rectangles to look like true mosaic tiles, you need to add highlights, like those shown in Figure 13-16. In the first example, I cloned the mosaic. Then I used the Transform Each command to shrink the tiles to 80 percent horizontally and 20 percent vertically. (Random was turned off.) After nudging the tiles into position, I deleted their strokes and filled them with white.

Figure 13-15:
An image converted to a
mosaic 40 tiles wide and
21 tiles tall (top) followed
by the effects of random
scaling (second), movements
(third), and rotations
(bottom) applied with the
Transform Each command.

To create the second example in Figure 13-16, I again cloned the mosaic. Then I used Arrange » Transform Each to reduce each tile to 60 percent horizontally and vertically. To lighten the tiles, I chose Filter » Colors » Saturate (a command I discuss in the next chapter) and entered a value of –30 percent. And I deleted the strokes. That's it; I didn't even have to move the tiles.

In the final effect, I selected the original mosaic from the previous example and used the Transform Each command to rotate the tiles 30 degrees. This gave the tiles a slightly 3-D effect, as if each tile were a square bead.

Figure 13-6:
Three variations on
highlighted tiles, all
created by cloning the
tiles and scaling or
rotating them with
Transform Each.

Mosaics can slow down Illustrator's redraw speed dramatically, and they can take a very long time to print. If you're not sure what kind of effect you want to apply, try it out on a small mosaic pattern with 10 tiles or fewer. Then after you have the effect figured out, apply it to a larger mosaic. This will save you a considerable amount of time and help to prevent general exasperation.

Adding a Border Around an Image

Before I close the chapter, I want to pass along one last bit of wisdom that'll make you slap yourself on the head. (But don't do it too hard; I don't want some kind of lawsuit over this thing.)

 Every once in a while, I hear someone complain that Illustrator can't automatically draw borders around images the way QuarkXPress and other programs do. If you share this concern, follow these amazingly straightforward steps:

1. **Select the image.**

   It doesn't matter if it's a placed EPS image or a parsed image.

2. **Bring up the Info palette.**

   Press ⌘-Control-I.

3. **Note the W and H values.**

   If they're really long—with four digits after the decimal point—write the values on a Post-it note and stick the note on the wall next to your favorite Dilbert cartoon.

4. **Click on the top left corner of the image with the rectangle tool.**

   Up comes your pal, the Rectangle dialog box.

5. **Enter the values you wrote on the Post-it note.**

   Look for the Dilbert cartoon.

6. **Press Return.**

   Illustrator creates a rectangle the exact size of your image.

7. **Assign a stroke to the rectangle and make the fill transparent.**

   Ooh, get a load of that lovely border.

8. **Select image and border and group them.**

   Press ⌘-G, naturally. Now the border can't get away so easy.

"Cool," I can hear you say, "Now if only Illustrator provided a cropping tool." In fact, Illustrator arguably provides the best cropping capabilities of any program on earth. But it's a big topic that's equally applicable to objects and images, so I don't discuss it in this chapter. Turn to Chapter 17, and keep an eye out for the many appearances of the word *mask*.

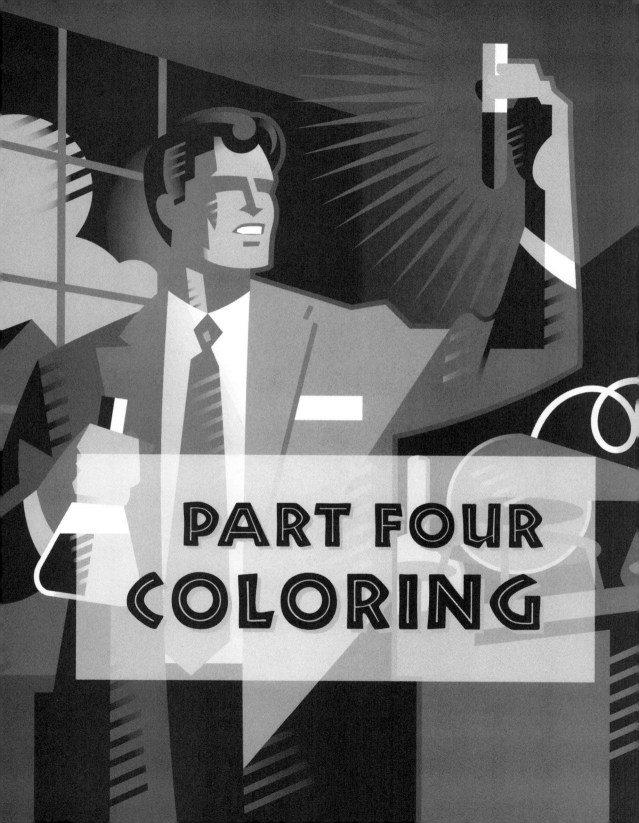

PART FOUR
COLORING

CHAPTER 14

THE SLIPPERY SCIENCE OF COLOR

Back before I immersed myself in computer graphics, I could never understand how companies managed to own colors. In a world where colors are as free and abundant as dirt, color technologies like Technicolor and the Pantone Matching System represent multi-million dollar businesses. Even children's Crayola colors are trademarked. Is no tint of grassy green or hue of rosy red safe from these marauding color pirates?

The fact is, the colors we see in nature are ours to enjoy, free from corporate intrusion. But it takes technology and science to represent colors in film, in photographs, on the printed page, and on your computer screen. For example, to represent a sprig of evergreen on a piece of paper, you can't take the sprig and mush it into the paper fibers. You have to find natural and synthetic colors that blend together to create a reasonable facsimile. This imitation of the real world is what the slippery science of color is all about.

In this chapter, I explain a little bit about color theory and a whole lot about how color works inside Illustrator. I show you how to select colors from predefined, trademarked libraries, or how to define your own colors using combinations of primary printing pigments. I also introduce the Paint Style palette, the Custom Color dialog box, the eyedropper and paint bucket tools, the Color filters, and all the other major points of interest along Illustrator's Great Color Way.

Color technology is one of the most complex areas of computer graphics. But even if you're brand spanking new to the subject, you have reason to rejoice. You use a Macintosh computer (which is currently a few years ahead of Windows in color science), you own Adobe Illustrator (a most capable color editor), and you're armed with this helpful book (need I say more?). How can you possibly go wrong?

The Great White Light and the Breakaway Color Republics

I hate theory, you hate theory—I don't think I've ever met anyone who just loves a good dose of theory. But I'm afraid I have to share a few basic color observations before moving on to the more exciting and practical discussions of how you use color in Illustrator. See, color is a highly misunderstood topic, particularly among the folks who work with it every day. Whether you're a graphics novice or a publishing professional, it pays to arm yourself with as much basic color knowledge as possible. Just as it helps to know a little something about motors when you take your car in for repair, it helps to know the fundamentals of color when you enter a print shop.

The most common misconception is that color exists in the real world. Plants, rocks, and most animals are completely unaware of color as we know it. This is because similarly colored objects share no common chemical or physical properties. And a single chemical—like copper—may change in color dramatically under slightly different conditions.

Color is all in your head. It's based on so-called white light from the sun or some other light source filtering through or bouncing off a surface. The light then passes into your eye and mutates into nerve impulses that shoot into your brain.

Color is a fantastic illusion that humans (and other primates) perceive differently than any other life form, and you and I may even perceive somewhat differently than each other. If you were visited by a being from another planet, chances are very good that you and that person would have no common color vernacular whatsoever. You can't hear, feel, smell, or taste color because color is an inherent ingredient in sight. In fact, you don't see color; your brain makes it up as a means of interpreting the light waves registered by your eye.

The World According to Your Eye

So let's talk about your eye. Inside this amazing orb are a bunch of light-sensitive cells called rods and cones. Rods pick up dim light and are good for detecting brightness and motion. Cones are responsible for color—they react best to strong light. Cones hang out in the central portion of the retina, and rods populate the outer regions. Therefore, you can judge colors most accurately by examining them in daylight and looking directly at them.

There are three kinds of cones. Generally speaking, each is sensitive to red, green or blue light. If all cones are stimulated, you see white. If both the red and green cones get excited but the blue cones shut down, you see yellow. What's important here is that the light coming into your eye may bounce off a yellow object, pass through a yellow filter, or come from a combination of red and green lights shining together. Your eye doesn't know the difference.

Computer screens and televisions fool your eye by speaking directly to your cones. The inside of the monitor is coated with red, green, and blue phosphors that emit light. So a yellow pixel is really a combination of red light shining for the benefit of the red cones and green light going to the green cones. If there's no blue light coming from the pixel, the corresponding blue cones take a nap.

RGB Light

Therefore, red, green, and blue are the *primary colors* of light. In theory, all visible colors can be expressed using a combination of these three basic ingredients. Intense lights, or multiple lights projected together, produce lighter colors. That's why red and green mix to form yellow, which is lighter than either red or green. Similarly, red and blue mix to form a hot pink called magenta, and blue and green make a bright turquoise called cyan. Full intensities of all three primaries form white; equal amounts of each color in lesser quantities make gray; and the absence of red, green, or blue light is black.

This is called the *RGB color model*. You may also hear someone refer to it as the *additive color model*, since increasing the amount of a primary color increases the brightness. Electronic scanners read photographs by shining red, green, and blue lights on them, which is why the RGB color model is a favorite of Photoshop. You can also import RGB images into Illustrator, or rasterize objects using the RGB color model.

CMYK Pigments

Unfortunately, paper is not capable of shining light in your face the way a monitor is. Instead, light reflects off the surface of the page. So it's a lucky thing that white light—whether from the sun or an artificial light source—contains the entire visible spectrum. Just as red, green, and blue light mix to form white, white contains red, green, and blue, as well as all other combinations of those colors. Every single color you and I can see is trapped in a ray of sunlight.

When you draw across a piece of white paper with a highlighter, the ink filters out sunlight. A pink highlighter, for example, filters out all non-pink light and reflects pink. This is the exact same way that professional printing colors work. There are three primary inks—cyan, magenta, and yellow—all of which are translucent pigments that filter out different kinds of light:

- Cyan acts as a red light filter. When white light hits a white page, it passes through the cyan ink and reflects all light that is not red—i.e., green and blue.

- Likewise, magenta ink filters out green light.

- And yellow ink filters out blue light.

So an area that appears red on screen prints in magenta and yellow on paper. The magenta and yellow ink filter out the green and blue light and leave only red to bounce back off the page. Cyan and magenta mix to form blue; cyan and yellow make green. All three inks together ought to make black. (I'll tell you why they don't in a minute.) And a complete absence of ink reveals the white page. Because less ink leads to lighter colors, this is called the *subtractive color model*.

In a perfect world, CMY would be the exact opposites of RGB. But colored inks are not nearly as reliable as colored lights. It's a simple trick to split white light into its pure primary components. You've probably seen it done with prisms. But generating pure inks—such as a cyan that filters all red and no green or blue whatsoever—is practically impossible. Throw in the bleached piece of wood pulp that passes for an absolute white backdrop and you can see how ink purity might prove a real problem. Cyan, magenta, and yellow simply can't manage on their own.

To compensate, color printing throws in one additional ink, black. Black is the *key* color—the one that helps the other inks out—which makes black the K in the *CMYK color model*. Black ensures deep shadows, neutral grays, and—of course—nice, even blacks.

Cyan, magenta, yellow, and black ink are the four printing primaries. Some folks call them *process colors*, which is why CMYK printing is sometimes called *four-color process printing*. (The word *process* is an old printing term, simply meaning that the colors are automatically generated to imitate a wider range of colors.)

Process inks are measured in percentages. The maximum intensity of any ink is 100 percent, and the minimum is naturally 0 percent. For example, 100% black is pitch black, while 75% black is dark gray and 50% black is medium gray. Here are some more recipes to keep in mind:

- 50% cyan plus 50% magenta is a light violet. Increase the cyan to make the color more blue; increase the magenta to make it purple.

- 50% magenta plus 50% yellow is a medium scarlet. Increase the magenta to make the color more red; increase the yellow to make it more orange. 100% yellow by itself is a lemon yellow. To get a cornflower yellow, add about 15% magenta to 100% yellow.

- 50% yellow plus 50% cyan is grass green. Add more yellow to get a bright chartreuse; add more cyan to tend toward teal. To get a sea blue, combine 100% cyan and 20% yellow.

- You can add the *complimentary* ink (the odd CMY ink out) to deepen a color. For example, if you have 50% cyan plus 50% magenta, adding the complimentary ink—yellow—creates mauve. Add the complimentary ink instead of black when you want to darken a color without dulling it.

- Adding black both darkens a color and makes it duller. Just a hint of black—10% to 25%—is great for creating drab colors like olive, steel blue, beige, and brick red.

- Brown is an amalgam of everything, with the emphasis on magenta and yellow. For example, 20% cyan and black with 60% magenta and yellow is a rich sienna.

 All these color combinations assume that you're printing to white paper. Because all inks except black are translucent, any paper color except white will blend in with the colors and change how they look, usually for the worse. When you're new to publishing, it's tempting to experiment with differently colored papers; after all, white is so boring. But about 90 percent of all professional work is printed to white paper because white permits the widest range of colors. Unless you have a specific reason for doing otherwise, stick with white.

But even though you can create a wealth of colors with CMYK, it simply can't measure up to RGB. The CMYK model has a smaller *gamut*—or color range—than its RGB cousin. Vivid colors in particular—including bright reds and oranges, brilliant greens and blues, and eye-popping purples—fall outside the CMYK gamut.

Spot Colors

That's why *spot colors* exist. Spot colors (also known as *solid colors*) are separate inks that you can add to the four basic process colors, or use instead of the process colors. For example, you might print a two-color newsletter using black and a spot color. Or, if you can't match a client's logo using process colors, you can add the proper spot color to your four-color printing job.

Pantone is probably the best known vendor of spot colors, offering a library of several hundred premixed inks that are supported by just about every major commercial print house in the United States. Like many other desktop publishing programs for the Mac, Illustrator provides complete support for the Pantone Color Matching System (or PMS for short).

The problem with adding spot colors is that they increase the cost of your print job. For every spot color that you add, you have to pay for the ink and the printing plate, as well as the time and labor required to feed the paper through another run. (Each color has to be printed in a separate pass.) Even companies with deep pockets rarely print more than six colors per page (CMYK plus two spots). This is also the reason that the Pantone Color Formula Guide 1000—which contains every spot color in the company's library—costs close to $100.

Getting the Right Color

The number one problem with color printing is that what you see on screen may not match what you get back from the printer. As discussed in the "Color Matching" section of Chapter 2, you can use Illustrator's built-in color management command (File » Preferences » Color Matching) to correct the colors on your monitor. But while this command is important when printing imported images (as I discuss in Chapter 18), it isn't particularly adept at making on-screen colors more accurate. You can also experiment with an automated color management tool such as Apple's ColorSync. But ColorSync and other programs are best suited to correcting color images created in Photoshop, and few color management programs provide specific support for Illustrator.

The tried and true system is to arm yourself with swatch books from Trumatch (212/302-9100) and Pantone (201/935-5500). With a swatch book in hand, you don't have to rely exclusively on the colors you see on screen; you can refer to the book to see how the colors look when printed. Trumatch's $85 Colorfinder shows a huge range of process color combinations. Pantone's Color Formula Guide 1000

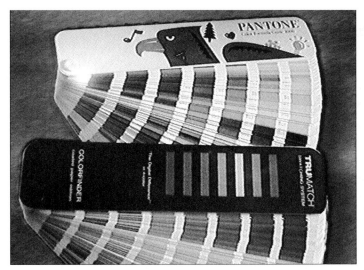

*Figure 14-1: If you're serious about color printing, the
Pantone Color Formula Guide and Trumatch Colorfinder
swatch books are a must.*

is the first and foremost reference for spot colors. Both are pictured in gorgeous
black-and-white in Figure 14-1.

Pantone also provides a $75 CMYK color book called the Process Color System
Guide. It contains more colors than its Trumatch equivalent, and it lists the ingredients in CMYK order (as opposed to Trumatch's initially confusing YMCK). But
the Trumatch numbering system is more logical, and the Colorfinder book has one
major advantage. It was created on a Macintosh computer.

Unfortunately, no color swatch book is 100-percent reliable. The colors age
over time, so that your book and your printer's book may look slightly different.
But if you store the book in sensible location—put it in a drawer, don't leave it sitting on a windowsill—it should remain accurate for a full year or more.

 If you have any concerns about a color, take your swatch
book in with you and tell the guy at the desk that you expect
him to nail Color X on the nose. If the guy says, "Now, lady,
much as I'd like to, it's very difficult to guarantee an *exact*
match," while picking his teeth with some card stock, take
your business elsewhere or expect a big savings. If he shows you his swatch
book and you find that your colors are a bit different, chances are that you
can arrange an equitable compromise. Many printers are even willing to provide swatch books that they print themselves if you're a regular client.

The fact is, predictable color *is* achievable. But the methods for getting good color haven't changed much since the old days.

- Don't believe everything you see on screen.

- Refer to a swatch book when in doubt, and be willing to change your swatch book every year or two.

- Find a good print house. Printers are like car mechanics—some are excellent, and others exploit their customers' inexperience. If you ever for a minute think that you're being fed a line, get a second opinion. Consider it a bad sign if your printer knocks Illustrator's output capabilities. Illustrator is by no means perfect, but when it comes to color printing, there's no better piece of software. This is one case where it's a bad carpenter who blames his tools.

- Develop a close working relationship with your print house. Where color is concerned, you're at the printer's mercy. But most professional printers are willing to help you out and make you happy.

After a full decade of electronic publishing, I manage to get the colors I want—or a reasonable facsimile—about 80 percent of the time. And nearly all of the 20 percent of color problems that I have are image printing inaccuracies that I have to rectify in Photoshop. With a little bit of effort, you can get Illustrator to perform very reliably.

Defining Colors Inside Illustrator

Because Illustrator is first and foremost a printing program, you define all colors by varying the amount of cyan, magenta, yellow, and black. (You can't define RGB colors except from the Color Matching dialog box, and then only for screen display purposes.) You can even define and modify spot colors using the CMYK color model, which gives you the option of later converting the spot colors to process separations.

- You can create process colors in the Paint Style palette. If you want to name a process color so that you can use it over and over again, choose Object » Custom Color.

- You can also use the Custom Color dialog box to define spot colors. Or you can load entire libraries of spot colors using File » Import Styles.

I discuss all of these options—and more—in the next sections.

Editing Colors in the Paint Style Palette

The Paint Style palette is Illustrator's primary color control center. Every Illustrator user that I know quickly learns to bring up the palette and leave it up on screen at all times. It is easily the second most essential palette in Illustrator, second only to the toolbox.

To display the Paint Style palette, press ⌘-I. (Why *I*? I suppose it could stand for *intensity*, *imbue*, or the fact that color is in the *I* of the beholder. But I know for a fact it's because *I* is the third letter in the word *Paint*; ⌘-P, ⌘-A, ⌘-N, and ⌘-T were already taken.) You can also choose Object » Paint Style or Window » Show Paint Style if you have an aversion to shortcuts.

Shown in Figure 14-2, the Paint Style palette lets you change the fill or stroke of a selected object. I cover fill and stroke in great detail in Chapters 15 and 16. But for now, I will say this: You decide whether you want to modify the fill or stroke of a selection by clicking on the Fill or Stroke icon in the upper left corner of the palette. Then you apply a color using one of the following techniques:

- Select a color that looks good from the color swatches along the left side of the palette. Illustrator lists the ingredients in the color beneath the swatches. For example, *F: 30C 60M 30Y* means that the fill is set to 30% cyan, 60% magenta, 30% yellow, and 0% black.

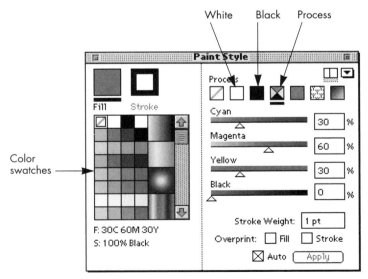

Figure 14-2: The Paint Style palette is a most excellent place for creating and editing process colors.

You can also drag a color swatch and drop it onto the Fill or Stroke icon. For example, if the Stroke icon is underlined, you can change the fill by dragging a color swatch and dropping it onto the Fill icon. Dragging and dropping color swatches allows you to edit the fill or stroke of an object without first activating the Fill and Stroke icon.

- To use white, just click on the White icon in the upper middle portion of the palette. A Tint slider bar appears, set to 0 percent. You can enter a higher value or drag the slider triangle to get gray.

- To color an object black, click on the Black icon (right next door to White). Just as when you click on White, you get a Tint slider bar, but this time it's set to 100 percent. Reduce the Tint value to get gray.

  In fact, you can get white when the Black icon is selected by reducing the Tint to 0 percent; and you can get black when the White icon is selected by upping the Tint to 100 percent. The two icons are merely opposites of each other.

- To create your own CMYK process color, click on the Process icon (immediately right of the Black icon). Then modify the Cyan, Magenta, Yellow, and Black slider bars, or change the values in the option boxes. Remember, higher tints create darker colors, lower tints create lighter shades.

The White and Black icons allow you to vary the amount of black ink in a fill or stroke without adding any cyan, magenta, or yellow. Exclusively black tints are known as *gray values*, because they print to black-and-white printers just as well as color ones.

 A common misconception is that gray values aren't colors because they don't include CMY. But black ink is just as much of a color pigment as CMY or any spot color. The only non-color is white, because white prevents all inks from printing and reveals the paper color (which may or may not be white).

Applying Colors

As long as the Auto check box near the bottom of the Paint Style palette is turned on, Illustrator automatically updates the colors of selected objects every time you drag a slider triangle, or press the Return or Tab key after entering an option box value. If you turn the Auto check box off, you have to click on the Apply button to apply the color.

Because the Apply button has a heavy outline around it, you might think you can activate it by pressing Return. But the Return key merely deactivates the palette without applying the color to the selection. You have to press the Enter key to apply the color, or press ⌘-Return to apply the color and close the Paint Style palette. You can also double-click on the Fill or Stroke icon. Despite all these wonderful techniques, I recommend you just leave the Auto check box on and avoid the Apply button altogether.

Showing and Hiding Panels

You can expand and collapse the Paint Style palette by clicking on the panel icon in the upper right corner of the palette (labeled in Figure 14-3). The panel icon matches the three panels inside the Paint Style palette. The white portions of the panel icon show which panels of are visible; the gray portions of the icon represent hidden panels.

- Click on a tiny panel inside the icon to show that panel in the palette. If you click on the upper left or upper right portion of the icon, you see that single panel in the palette. Click on the lower portion of the icon to see the entire palette.

- Click on the line between the left and right halves of the panel icon to display the top two panels but hide the bottom one.

- You can also display a menu of panel options by dragging from the down-pointing arrow icon, as demonstrated at the bottom of Figure 14-3.

 Click in the zoom box to switch back and forth between the last two palette configurations. For example, I either like to look at the whole palette or just the upper right panel. After specifying those two displays using the panel icon, I can toggle between them with the zoom box without ever referring back to the panel icons again.

A handful of Paint Style options are available no matter which panel is visible. These include the Fill and Stroke icons, the Stroke Weight option box, the Auto check box, and the Apply button.

Playing with the Color Swatches

The color swatches appear only when the upper left panel of the Paint Style palette is visible. By default, Illustrator offers 80 flat colors in the small swatches

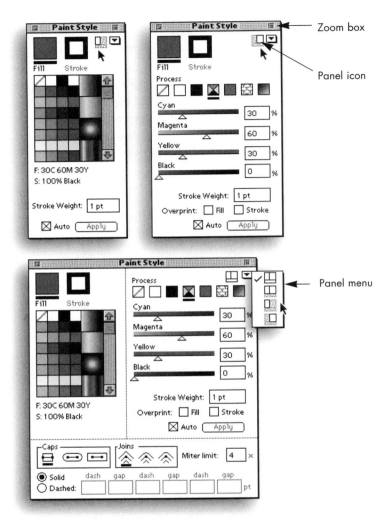

Figure 14-3: Click in the panel icon or select an option from
the panel menu to decide which of the three Paint Style
panels are visible.

and eight gradations in the large swatches. However, you can add and delete
colors in any way you see fit:

● To append a gray value or process color that you've created to the
scrolling list of color swatches, scroll to the end of the list and Option-
click on an empty color swatch. (Technically, these swatches aren't

empty, they're filled with white. But how many white swatches does one really need?)

 You can also drag the color from the Fill or Stroke icon and drop it onto an empty color swatch.

If you don't like a swatch, you can replace it with a new color by Option-clicking on it. Or you can drag the color from the Fill or Stoke icon onto the swatch.

Option-drag a swatch from one position to another to duplicate it.

To delete a color swatch and leave it white, ⌘-click on it. When you press ⌘, Illustrator shows you a little scissors cursor so you know you're about to cut a color. Frankly, I don't see much purpose in this technique, since Illustrator doesn't automatically shift the neighboring colors into new positions; it just leaves a hole. But I couldn't live with myself if I didn't share all of my knowledge, however good-for-nothing it may be.

When you ⌘-click, Illustrator displays an alert box to make sure you want to delete the color. You can't undo the deletion of a color, so Illustrator is merely looking out for your welfare. If you want to avoid this warning in the future, ⌘-Option-click on the swatch. With the Option key, there's no warning; the color just up and disappears.

 To delete many colors at a time, ⌘-drag over them (or ⌘-Option-drag to avoid the warning). This is a useful way to clean out an entire section of swatches and start over on them. But take heed; Illustrator deletes small and large swatches alike.

 If you want to reset the color swatches to their factory defaults, ⌘-Shift-click on any swatch. Funny thing about this shortcut: It only restores the visible swatches in the scrolling list. All swatches toward the bottom of the list turn white, even though they may have had colors to begin with. I recommend you avoid this shortcut, since it doesn't work correctly.

 The color swatches are saved with the illustration. They do not translate from one illustration to the next. If you want to save a set of color swatches that you intend to use again and again, open the Adobe Illustrator Startup file that resides in the Plug-ins folder. Then edit the color swatches inside that illustration and save it to disk. From that point on, all new illustrations will use those same color swatches.

If you have a problem getting Illustrator to use the color swatches from the Adobe Illustrator Startup file in a new illustration, try this: Close the new illustration and open the Adobe Illustrator Startup file. Then press ⌘-N to create another new illustration and close the Startup file. The color swatches should now look hunky dory.

Using the Slider Bars

You wouldn't think something like slider bars would deserve their own section, but Adobe has built a bunch of little convenience features into the slider bars in the upper right panel of the Paint Style palette:

- Notice how the slider bars appear in different colors? This shows you what colors you'll get if you drag the slider triangle to that position. Each time you drag a slider triangle (or enter a value into an option box and press the Tab key), Illustrator updates the colors in the slider bars. This way, you're constantly aware of the effect that modifying a primary pigment will produce.

- If you like a color along the length of a slider bar, just click on it. The slider triangle for that ink will immediately jump to the clicked position.

 To create a lighter or darker tint of a process color, Shift-drag the slider triangle. As you drag, all the slider bars change to demonstrate the tint. To gain the most control, Shift-drag the triangle associated with the highest intensity color. (Any ink set to 0 percent does not move, since adding the ink would change the color rather than the tint.)

- You can also Shift-click on a spot along a slider bar to adjust the tint by leaps and bounds. All inks (not set to 0 percent) change to maintain a constant hue. If the point at which you click is too high to maintain a consistent tint, only that one ink will change. To make certain you change the tint and not the one ink, Shift-click and hold anywhere along the slider bar, then move your mouse until the sliders all move to some legal position.

 Option-click on a slider bar to change an ink intensity in 1-percent increments. Option-click to the right of the slider triangle to increase the intensity by 1 percent; Option-click to the left of the triangle to reduce the intensity.

Shift-Option-click to change the ink in 5-percent increments. If you click very fast, you change just the one ink. But if you click and hold for a half second or more, you can adjust all inks at once, as when changing the tint. This is a very small but useful distinction. It takes some practice to get it exactly right, but it's worth the effort.

 If you want to quickly edit a color value, press ⌘-I to highlight the contents of the first option box. This might be Tint or Cyan, depending on whether the selected object contains a gray value or CMYK color. Then enter a new value and press Return.

- And as inside any palette, you can advance from one option box to the next by pressing the Tab key. Or go in reverse order by pressing Shift-Tab.

If you're an adept Photoshop user, and you're wondering whether you can use the up and down arrow keys to modify option box values as inside the fab image editor, the answer is no. Where slider bars are concerned, the two programs go their own ways.

Creating a Named Color

The Paint Style palette is ideal for applying process colors on the fly and saving colors as swatches. But if you intend to use a color on a regular basis, you'll want to give it a name and save it along with your illustration for quick and easy retrieval. You can use these colors as both process and spot colors. You can even print a named color as a spot color one time, and as a process color the next. (See the section "Process Color or Spot?" later in this chapter.)

You create and modify named colors in the Custom Color dialog box, shown in Figure 14-4. There are four ways to access this dialog box:

- To create a new color, choose Object » Custom Color. The dialog box comes up with the first default named color—Aqua—selected.

- If you like, you can edit a specific named color. First, display the list of named colors in the Paint Style palette by clicking on the Custom icon, which is the green square above the slider bars (labeled in Figure 14-5). Then double-click on the color name that you want to edit.

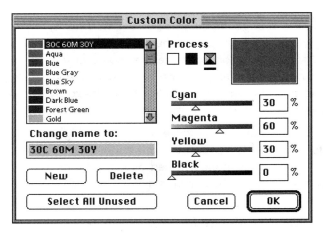

Figure 14-4:
You can create and
edit named colors—
whether process
colors or spot
colors—inside the
Custom Color
dialog box.

 To name the color used to fill or stroke a selected object, drag the color from the Fill or Stroke icon and drop it onto any one of the icons above the slider bars in the Paint Style palette. For example, in Figure 14-5, I dragged the Fill color and dropped it onto the Black icon. It may seem strange, but it works. When the Custom Color dialog box appears, it contains the CMYK ingredients and even offers a name for the color, such as *30C 60M 30Y* in Figure 14-4.

Custom icon

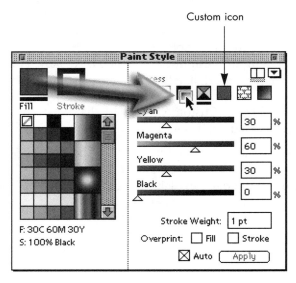

Figure 14-5:
Drag a color from the
Fill or Stroke icon onto
one of the right-panel
icons to name the color
inside the Custom Color
dialog box.

To name one of the swatch colors on the left side of the Paint Style palette, drag the swatch and drop it onto any one of the icons above the slider bars. Again, the Custom Color dialog box shows the ingredients and offers a name.

To edit a color, you can enter values in the option boxes or manipulate the sliders using any of the techniques I described for the Paint Style palette. You can also create a new color by clicking on the New button. Then edit the CMYK values and enter a name for the color into the Change Name To option box.

The Custom Color dialog box permits you to create many colors at a time. When you finish, press the Return key to close the dialog box and accept your changes. (Or press Escape to abandon your new and modified colors.)

Selecting and Organizing Custom Colors

The Custom Color dialog box provides a handful of options for selecting and organizing named colors. For example, you can click on a color name inside the scrolling list. Or you can activate the list by pressing Tab or Shift-Tab until a heavy border surrounds it. Then scroll up and down the list by pressing the up and down arrow keys, or enter a few characters for the color name you want to select.

 Illustrator 6 has a very sophisticated color search system. If you press *Y-E-L*, for example, Illustrator selects the first yellow in the list, which happens to be Orange Yellow. Typing *G-R-E* selects Forest Green before it selects Grass Green or Lime Green. This is a little different than other programs, where pressing a letter takes you to the first item that begins with that letter.

The Custom Color dialog box also offers the Delete and Select All Unused buttons to help you get rid of unwanted colors:

Delete: Click on this button to delete a selected color from the list. Illustrator removes the color from *all* open illustrations. If the color is in use, Illustrator warns you that deleting it will arbitrarily assign black to all objects filled and stroked with the color.

 If you delete a color by mistake, press Escape to cancel the operation. If you realize your mistake after pressing the Return key, you can still restore the color by pressing ⌘-Z.

Select All Unused: This button selects all colors that are not applied to paths or text blocks inside any open illustration. Then you can click on the Delete button to trash them.

Applying Named Colors

As with all colors, you apply a named color to a selected object using the Paint Style palette. Click on the green Custom icon in the upper right portion of the palette, and select a color name from the scrolling list. Figure 14-6 finds me selecting an appropriately named spot color. Illustrator even shows you the name of the color underneath the color swatches on the left side of the palette.

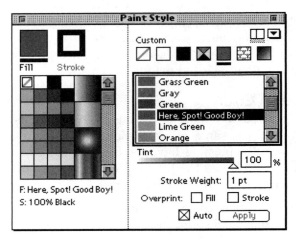

Figure 14-6:
After applying a
named color from the
Paint Style palette, you
can modify the inten-
sity of the color using
the Tint slider bar.

You can modify the intensity of a color by changing the Tint value. Again, all the standard techniques discussed a few pages back in the "Using the Slider Bars" section apply to the Tint slider bar as well.

After you fill or stroke an object with a named color, Illustrator creates a link between the object and its color. This means that if you ever go back to the Custom Color dialog box and modify the named color, you change the colors of all objects filled and stroked with that color as well. If you're familiar with style sheets in Microsoft Word or PageMaker, named colors work the same way. This ability to change a single item and automatically influence several other items at the same time is called *global editing*. If you're sufficiently organized, it saves a ton of time.

Process Color or Spot?

Generally speaking, you decide whether to convert a named color to CMYK separations or use it as a spot color during the printing process. To specify how you want to print a color, choose File » Separation Setup to display the great big Color Separation dialog box.

If this is the first time you've entered this dialog box, most of the options appear dimmed. You have to open a printer description file using the Open PPD button. (Assuming you've installed PSPrinter 8.3, as I urge you to do in Chapter 18, you'll find the printer description files in the Printer Descriptions subfolder inside the Extensions folder in your System Folder.)

The all-important process and spot color options are located in the bottom right corner of the Color Separation dialog box. I've spotlighted these options in Figure 14-7. By default, the Convert to Process check box is turned on, which automatically converts all named colors to their process color ingredients. If that suits you fine, press the Return key and continue illustrating. If you prefer to print one or more named colors as spot colors, turn the check box off, as in the figure.

After you turn off the check box, the color list (labeled in Figure 14-7) comes to life. The list contains the names of the four process colors in italics, plus all named colors used to fill and stroke objects in the illustration. To the left of the color names are three columns with dots, headed up by small icons. Click under an icon to position the dot and specify how the color will print:

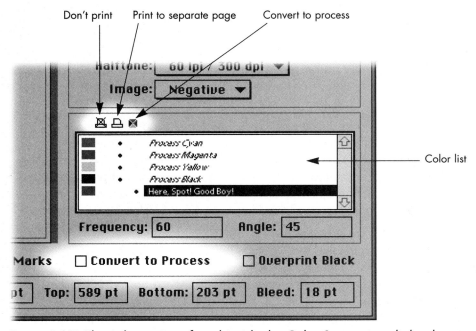

Figure 14-7: The color options found inside the Color Separation dialog box, which you display by choosing File » Separation Setup.

- Click under the first icon (the little printer with an X through it) to tell Illustrator not to print that color. If you only use black and a spot color, for example, Illustrator automatically turns off the Process Cyan, Process Magenta, and Process Yellow items.

- Click under the second icon to turn a named color into a spot color. This icon ensures that Illustrator prints the color to a separate page or sheet or film, which is what spot colors are all about.

- To break down a color into its process ingredients, click under the last icon (which looks like a tiny CMYK target). This column is exclusively for custom colors. You can't convert cyan, magenta, yellow, or black to a process color since it already is one.

Don't fret too much if you don't immediately understand how these options work. This section is meant merely as an introduction to the color printing process, so you understand where custom colors fit in. I explore printing is much more detail in Chapter 18.

Converting Custom to Process on the Fly

If you want to convert a named color assigned to a single object to its process ingredients, select the object and merely click on the Process icon in the Paint Style palette. When you click on the Process icon, Illustrator keeps the color of the object (and the CMYK values) intact, but breaks the link between the named color and the object. Without any more effort, you have an object that will automatically print to process color separations regardless of the settings in the Color Separation dialog box.

 To convert multiple objects filled or stroked with named colors to process colors, select the objects and choose Filter » Colors » Adjust Colors. After the dialog box comes up, select the Custom to Process check box and press Return. That one option is all it takes. For complete information on the Adjust Colors command, read the "Adjusting CMYK Values" section later in this chapter.

 Keep in mind that you can't globally edit the colors of objects filled with process colors. So if you ever go back and modify the CMYK values assigned to the named color, the objects you converted to process colors will remain unchanged.

Using Predefined Color Libraries

Illustrator 6 ships with several libraries filled with predefined colors from Pantone, Trumatch, and others who make their money from this most intangible of all possible intellectual properties. Adobe supplies the libraries as documents in the Color Systems subfolder inside the Utilities folder which lives in the same folder as the Illustrator application.

If you open one of these files using the standard File » Open command, you make the colors available to all other open illustrations. You can also import the entire library into an illustration using File » Import Styles, but it's unlikely you're going to need the hundreds of colors that comes with each file. All those colors can prove a tad overwhelming, and they needlessly increase the size of an illustration on disk.

The following items briefly introduce the color brands in order of their impact on the American market—if you'll pardon me for being so unscrupulously ethnocentric—from smallest impact to greatest:

- **Focoltone and Toyo**: Both Focoltone and Toyo fall into the negligible-impact category. Both are foreign standards with followings abroad. Focoltone is based in England, while Toyo hails from Japan. Neither have many subscribers here in the States, and then the basic purpose is to satisfy foreign clientele.

- **Trumatch**: Designed entirely using a desktop system and with desktop publishers in mind, the Trumatch Colors file contains more than 2,000 process colors, organized according to hue, saturation, and brightness. The colors correspond to the Colorfinder swatch book that I mentioned earlier. Trumatch happens to be my favorite process color collection, and I keep a copy of the Colorfinder close at hands at all times.

- **Pantone**: The largest color vendor in America is Pantone. It provides two files in the Color Systems folder—Pantone Colors (Coated Paper) and Pantone Process Color System. If you're interested in printing Pantone spot colors, the Pantone Colors (Coated Paper) file is for you. These colors correspond to the Color Formula Guide 1000 swatch book. The Pantone Process Color System file contains process colors that match printed colors in the Process Color System Guide swatch book.

 Strictly speaking, it's not a good idea to separate spot colors from the Pantone Colors (Coated Paper) file into their supposed CMYK ingredients. The whole reason Pantone spot colors exist, after all, is to fill in the considerable gaps left by the four basic process colors. That said, some Pantone colors convert to process colors better than others. For example, you can simulate Pantone 129 yellow quite well using 15% magenta and 76% yellow. And 100% cyan plus 9% magenta is a dead ringer for Pantone 2995 blue. (Who can figure this numbering scheme?) But close-by Pantone 2935 blue bears about as much resemblance to 100% cyan 47% magenta as royal blue bears to mud. If you want to see exactly how Pantone spot colors convert to process, you need to purchase yet another swatch book, the Process Color Imaging Guide 1000.

When you open one of the files from the Color Systems folder using File » Open, it doesn't look like much of anything. Just some text explaining the legal gobbledygook, as in Figure 14-8. But if you click on the Custom icon in the Paint Style palette, you'll find a long list of named colors.

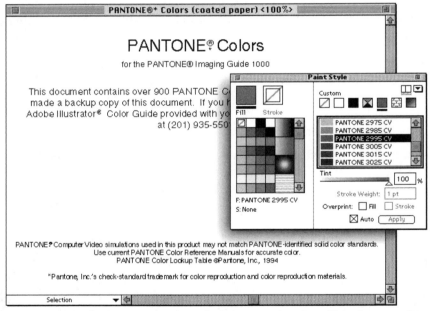

Figure 14-8: The Pantone Colors document with a handful of spot colors displayed inside the Paint Style palette.

Scrolling through hundreds of colors in a tiny list is no picnic. Luckily, you can quickly scroll to a specific color from the keyboard. Click on the scrolling list in the Paint Style palette to activate it (or press Tab when the Tint value is highlighted), then enter a number. If you type *2995* while the Pantone Colors file is open, you'll select Pantone 2995 blue. If you type *31-a*

with the Trumatch Colors file open, you select the similar process color
Trumatch 31-a. Be sure to enter the hyphens when selecting Trumatch colors.

If the Paint Style palette doesn't seem to respond correctly as you type in numbers, it's probably because you're typing too fast. If you slow it down a little, it
should work.

 If you use a small cache of colors on a regular basis, you
can add them to the Adobe Illustrator Startup file. For
example, if one of your clients sells lawn flamingos, you
might want to keep Pantone 225 pink on hands at all times.
Just open the Startup file (in the Plug-ins folder), draw a rectangle, and fill it with the Pantone or Trumatch color that you want to use on a
regular basis. If you want to add more colors, draw more rectangles and fill
them up. After you save the Startup file, those colors will be available to all
illustrations, whether old or new.

Applying the Overprint Options

I have one more set of options from the Paint Style palette to explain before
moving on to Illustrator's other colorful features. These are the Overprint check
boxes, spotlighted in Figure 14-9. These options control whether the color applied
to the fill or stroke of the selected object mixes with the colors of the objects
behind it. When the Fill or Stroke check box is turned on, the fill or stroke color
overprints the colors behind it, provided that the fill or stroke color is printed to a
different separation from the background colors.

*Figure 14-9:
The Overprint check
boxes let you mix
colors in overlap-
ping objects, as long
as the colors print to
different separations.*

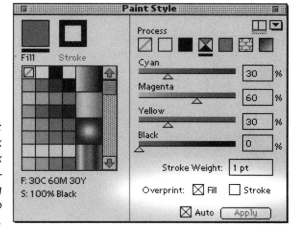

For example, suppose you've created a Mardi Gras illustration consisting of three spot colors, Pantones 2592, 3405, and 1235, which any resident of Louisiana can tell you are purple, green, and gold. Purple can overprint green, green can overprint purple, and either may overprint or be overprinted by gold, because Pantones 2592, 3405, and 1235 print to their own separations. However, a 30% tint of purple cannot overprint a 70% tint of purple, because all purple objects print to the same Pantone 2592 separation.

When one color overprints onto another color, the two colors mix together. You could overprint purple onto gold, for example, to get a deep brown color.

If the Overprint check boxes are turned off, as by default, any portion of an object that is covered by another object is *knocked out*; that is, it doesn't print when the two objects are output to different separations. This ensures that colors from different separations do not mix with each other.

Overprinting Process Colors

The Overprint options have no influence over black-and-white illustrations that don't require separations. If the selected object is filled with one or more process colors, only those colors on different separations overprint. For example, suppose you have two objects, one filled with 30% magenta and 75% yellow (gold) and another filled with 70% cyan and 95% magenta (purple). If you select the gold object and turn on the Overprint Fill check box, the intersection of the two objects is printed with 70% cyan, *30% magenta*, and 75% yellow. The magenta value from the gold object wins out—even though it's lighter than the magenta value in the purple object—because overprinting doesn't affect colors on the same separation.

The downside of overprinting is that it doesn't show up correctly on screen, nor does it proof correctly to color printers. There's no way to tell by looking at an object whether it will overprint or not. So you have to keep an eye on the Overprint check boxes in the Paint Style palette.

If you want to mix the colors in overlapping objects and see the results on screen, choose Filter » Pathfinder » Hard. As explained back in Chapter 9, the Hard filter splits the intersection of two selected objects into a separate path and fills the intersection with a mix of the objects' colors. If I applied the Hard filter to our gold and purple objects, the Hard filter would fill the intersection with 70% cyan, *95% magenta*, and 75% yellow. So it uses the darkest of the two magenta values, which is slightly different from over-printing. But quite frankly, in most cases, the darker value is preferable. And, of course, you can always edit the color of the intersection if you aren't satisfied with the result.

The only problem with the Hard filter is that it always converts spot colors to their process color equivalents. So if you want to mix two spot colors, and you want them to remain spot colors, you have no choice but to use the Overprint check boxes.

Overprinting Black Ink

Though you may find yourself occasionally using the Overprint options to mix spot colors, most professionals apply overprinting primarily to black ink in order to anticipate printing problems. Because black is opaque—and it's typically the last ink applied during the printing process—it covers up all other inks. So it doesn't look much different when printed over, say, cyan than when printed directly onto the white page. But while overprinting has little affect on the appearance of black ink, it prevents gaps between a black object and a differently colored neighbor. Even if the paper shifts on the printing press, the black ink comes out looking fine.

 In addition to the Overprint check boxes in the Paint Style palette, Illustrator 6 provides two means for overprinting black ink— Filter » Colors » Overprint Black and the Overprint Black check box in the Color Separation dialog box. For complete information on both of these time-saving features, read Chapter 18. This is where I discuss the more nitty-gritty sides of overprinting, color separations, and registration problems in their proper context.

Transferring Colors Between Objects and Images

Any illustration program worth its salt permits you to take a color from one object and transfer it to another. This way you don't have to scribble down notes about how different objects are colored when creating new objects that you want to match exactly. In FreeHand, you drag colors from palettes and drop them onto objects. In Illustrator, you lift colors with the eyedropper tool and plunk them down with the paint bucket. I know some folks who wish that Illustrator would adopt FreeHand's drag-and-drop strategy; after all, it involves fewer mouse clicks and you don't have to select any special tools. But Illustrator's approach is equally convenient and more flexible in the long run, as you'll soon see.

Using the Paint Bucket

The paint bucket tool—ninth icon on the left side of the toolbox—applies colors from the Paint Style palette to objects in the illustration window. To use the tool, specify the desired fill and stroke attributes in the palette, then click on the target object that you want to color. If the object has no fill, you'll need to click on the outline, as demonstrated in Figure 14-10. Not only does Illustrator fill and stroke the object, it also selects it.

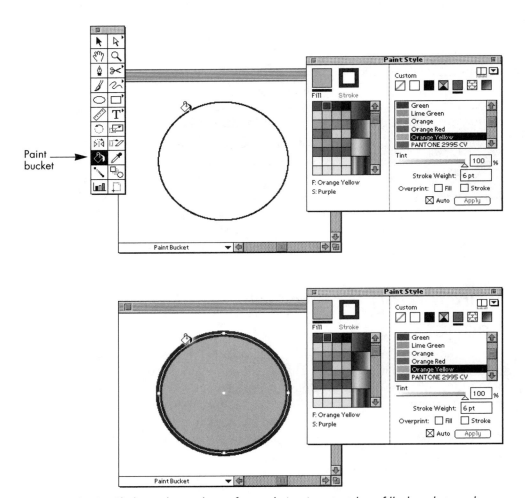

Figure 14-10: Click on the outline of a path (top) or inside a filled path to color the path with the attributes specified in the Paint Style palette (bottom).

You can even Shift-click with the paint bucket to color and select multiple objects at a time. For example, suppose you wanted to assign three objects a green fill, and then move them to a new position. You could specify the green fill in the Paint Style palette, click and Shift-click on the objects with the paint bucket tool, and then ⌘-drag to access the arrow tool and move the objects.

You can also use the paint bucket on text and black-and-white images. But to color type, you have to click on the alignment point, baseline, or text path, just as when selecting text with the arrow tool. You can't click directly on the letters. When you click on a black-and-white image (in which the white pixels are transparent), the paint bucket fills the black pixels with color.

Using the Eyedropper

Next door to the paint bucket in the toolbox, the eyedropper is the paint bucket's opposite. It lifts colors from objects and puts them inside the Paint Style palette. To use the eyedropper, click on a path or on the alignment point, baseline, or path belonging to a text object. The eyedropper cursor becomes partially black to show that you're lifting color.

 One of the best kept secrets of the eyedropper tool is that you can transfer the color of a path's stroke to the Fill icon in the Paint Style palette. Just click on the very edge of the stroke—as in the bottom example of Figure 14-11—where it exceeds the boundary of the path. When successful, the cursor stays white rather than filling partway with black. This technique works best when working with fat strokes.

 Tips abound for using the eyedropper. If you double-click on an object with the eyedropper, you not only lift the colors from the object but you also apply the colors to all selected objects. This enables you to transfer a fill and stroke from one object to multiple selected objects in one fell swoop.

 You can lift colors from any image inside Illustrator, whether placed EPS or parsed, imported or rasterized. The color on which you click becomes the fill color in the Paint Style palette. Unfortunately, Illustrator converts the color to a process color, even if you click on a black-and-white or

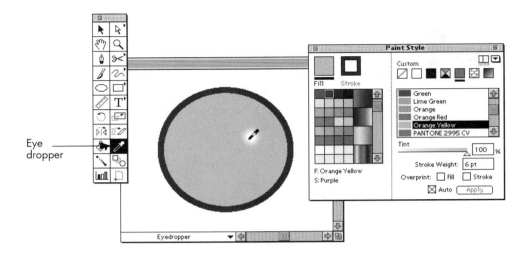

Eye
dropper

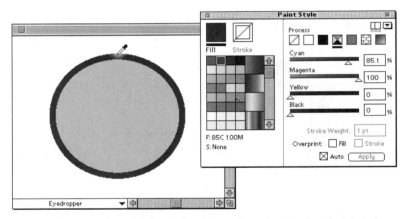

*Figure 14-11: Click inside a path to lift both the fill and stroke (top). Click on the
edge of a stroke to lift the stroke color and use it as a fill (bottom).*

grayscale image. And don't think you can just toss the CMY values and keep
the K, because Illustrator uses more complex algorithms to calculate its
grayscale-to-process conversions. If you click on a 50% black pixel in an
image, for example, you'll get a process color composed of 47% cyan, 35%
magenta, 33% yellow, and 4% black (depending on the settings in the Color
Matching dialog box).

You can even lift colors from background windows, including an open image inside Photoshop, or the Finder desktop. But you can't just click outside the illustration window; that merely switches applications. You have to click and hold inside the illustration window, and then drag outside the window. As you drag, the color of the Fill icon perpetually changes to reflect the color under your cursor. When you get the color you like, release.

More Suck-and-Dump Trivia

Double-click on either the paint bucket or eyedropper icon in the toolbox to display the dialog box full of check boxes shown in Figure 14-12. These options allow you to select the specific attributes that are applied and lifted with the paint bucket and eyedropper. The options are grouped according to fill and stroke attributes. Deselecting the Fill or Stroke check box turns off and dims all corresponding options below it.

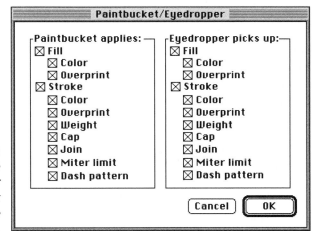

Figure 14-12: Double-click on the bucket or dropper icon in the toolbox to access these check boxes.

And one more thing: You can toggle between the paint bucket and eyedropper by pressing the Option key. If the bucket is selected, pressing Option gets you the dropper. When the dropper is selected, press Option to get the bucket. As a pal of mine from Adobe likes to say, the Option key allows you to alternately "suck and dump" colors without changing tools. (Now if they'd only put that into the manual!)

Applying Automated Color Manipulations

The Filter » Colors submenu contains a total of seven filters that affect the colors of selected objects and imported images. The filters permit you to increase or decrease the intensity of primary inks and, in some cases, spot colors. While the filters aren't nearly as capable or sophisticated as similar color correction commands found inside Photoshop, they do make it possible to edit multiple objects and colors simultaneously, which can save you a significant amount of time.

I already mentioned that I'll be discussing Filter » Colors » Overprint Black in Chapter 18. I discuss the remaining six color correction commands in the following sections.

Adjusting CMYK Values

Filter » Colors » Adjust Colors is Illustrator's most capable color correction command. You can vary the amount of ink assigned to a CMYK object, convert spot colors to process colors, or colorize grayscale objects. You can also modify the colors of parsed RGB and CMYK images.

Choose the Adjust Colors filter to display the Adjust Colors dialog box, as shown in Figure 14-13. Here you can adjust the percentage composition of cyan, magenta, yellow, and black in the selected objects by adjusting the slider bars or entering new values in the option boxes. Enter positive values to add ink, enter negative values to reduce the ink intensity.

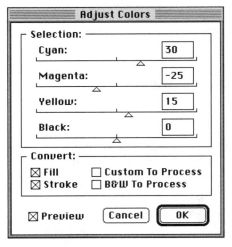

Figure 14-13:
The Adjust Colors
dialog box allows you
to increase or decrease
the percentage of
CMYK inks assigned
to selected objects.

Note that the values in the Adjust Colors dialog box represent absolute values. In other words, each value raises or lower an ink by exactly that percent. For example, if I were to apply the values shown in Figure 14-13 to an object with a 100% magenta fill, Illustrator would change the fill to 30% cyan, 75% magenta, and 15% yellow. This is different—and decidedly less useful—than the way most of Photoshop's color commands work. Photoshop's best color-correction functions—Levels, Curves, and Variations—change the relative coloring of images. For example, they permit you to increase or decrease the intensity of medium cyan values within a selection, without affecting non-cyan colors or full-intensity cyans. Only one command in Illustrator, Filter » Colors » Saturate, permits relative color modifications, but even it doesn't begin to compare to Photoshop's capabilities.

The Adjust Colors dialog box also offers the following check boxes, all of which are new to Illustrator 6:

- **Fill**: Select this option if you want to modify the fills of selected objects. Turn the option off if you only want to change strokes.

- **Stroke**: Same thing, only opposite. Turn the check box on if you want to adjust strokes; turn it off if you only want to affect fills.

- **Custom To Process**: Select this check box to convert named colors to CMYK values and modify those values according the option box values. If you turn this check box off, Illustrator ignores named colors in a selection and leaves them unchanged.

- **B&W To Process**: Select this check box to colorize grayscale objects. For example, if you select the B&W To Process option and enter a Magenta value of 55 and a Yellow value of 100, you colorize the grayscale objects with pumpkin orange. If the check box is turned off, grayscale objects remain unaffected, even by the Black value (which is truly bizarre).

This is a useful option, but why in the world doesn't Illustrator provide a similar check box that converts all colors to grayscale? Most clip-art these days is created in color, while most Illustrator graphics continue to be printed in black-and-white to keep costs down. So converting CMYK to grayscale seems to me at least as important as converting grayscale to CMYK. Where color correction is concerned, it's hard to believe Photoshop and Illustrator actually come from the same company.

- **Preview**: Select this check box to keep apprised of the effects of your color modifications as you work inside the Adjust Colors dialog box. Keep this option on to avoid surprises.

 Illustrator 6 also lets you modify the colors inside parsed images. But with the exception of the Black value, the Adjust Colors options affect only RGB and CMYK images. This is true even if the B&W To Process check box is turned on. The good news is that you can edit grayscale images using the Black slider bar. (Meanwhile, the Black slider bar has no effect on grayscale objects unless you first select the B&W To Process check box. Excuse me, is everybody in the Adobe continuity department on vacation?)

 To colorize a grayscale image, first convert it the RGB or CMYK color model using Object » Rasterize. (Be sure to confirm the resolution of the image using File » Selection Info, as explained in the "Putting Object » Rasterize to Good Use" section of Chapter 13.) Then use the Adjust Colors filter to add cyan, magenta, and yellow ink to the image.

Changing Overall Ink Intensity

 If you want to apply relative adjustments to the colors of selected objects, choose Filter » Colors » Saturate. Once spread out over four commands, the new Saturate command displays a small dialog box with a single slider bar and a corresponding option box:

- Enter a negative value to decrease the intensity of CMYK inks in selected objects filled or stroked with process colors. This also reduces the tints of selected objects filled or stroked with named colors. (The Saturate command does not convert named colors to process, so spot colors remain intact.)

- Enter a positive value to increase the intensity of CMYK inks or the tint of named colors.

Unlike the Adjust Colors command, Saturate makes relative color adjustments. If you apply a Saturate value of 50 percent to an object filled with 20% cyan and

50% magenta, Illustrator changes the fill to 30% cyan and 75% magenta. That's a 50 percent increase in the previous intensities of both inks.

The command isn't entirely consistent. For example, it changes white absolutely; for example, where a 50 percent Saturate increases a 10% black fill to 15% black, it changes a white fill to 50% black. And the Saturate command becomes completely unpredictable when applied to grayscale images.

 Be advised that Illustrator's definition of "saturation" has nothing to do with the *true* definition of saturation. In Photoshop, for example, saturation is the difference between a color picture and a black-and-white picture. The color picture is intensely saturated, the black-and-white picture has no saturation whatsoever. By contrast—no pun intended—Illustrator's strange breed of saturation is the difference between a color picture and a blank page. Since the levels of cyan, magenta, yellow, and black diminish uniformly, no saturation results in white.

Therefore, after everything is said and done, Filter » Colors » Saturate is best suited to lightening or darkening the colors of several objects at once (as I did when lightening the mosaic tiles in the "Converting an Image to Squares" section of Chapter 13). You can use the command to establish highlights or shadows, whether the selected objects are filled and stroked with gray values, CMYK, or named colors.

Inverting Selected Colors

Upon choosing Filter » Colors » Invert Colors, Illustrator changes the CMY values of all selected objects filled with process colors to their opposites. For example, 10% cyan, 20% magenta, 30% yellow, and 40% black inverts to 90% cyan, 80% magenta, 70% yellow, and (still) 40% black. Only the black value remains unchanged.

The Invert command also inverts objects filled and stroked with gray values. Black inverts to white, white inverts to black—it's just like a photographic negative. Only named colors go unaffected (as the command is overly fond of warning you).

Creating Color Blends

The remaining three commands in the Filter » Colors submenu—Blend Front to Back, Blend Horizontally, and Blend Vertically—create continuous color blends between three or more selected objects. Each command uses two extreme objects as base colors and recolors all other selected objects between the extremes.

In the first example in Figure 14-14, I've created a series of circles by Option-dragging a circle with the rotate tool and pressing ⌘-D several times in a row. I filled two of the circles with medium gray. Then I selected all of the circles and applied the various Blend filters to get the results shown in the other examples in the figure.

In each case, Illustrator used different circles for the base colors. (I've stroked the extreme circles with heavy outlines in each Blend example.) When I chose Blend Front to Back, Illustrator used the back and front circles as extremes, and recolored the circles stacked in between. The Blend Horizontally command blended between the left and right extremes, and Blend Vertically blended between the top and bottom circles.

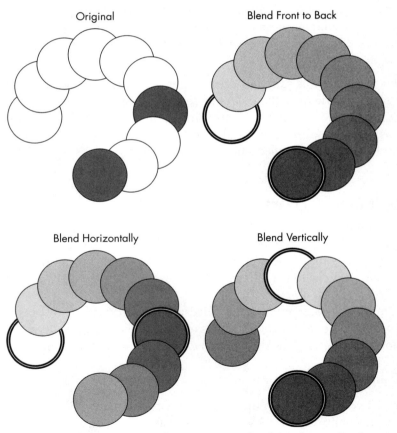

Figure 14-14: The results of applying each of the three Blend filters to the original collection of circles shown at upper left.

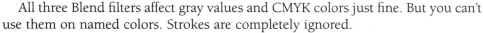

All three Blend filters affect gray values and CMYK colors just fine. But you can't use them on named colors. Strokes are completely ignored.

The Blend filters are great for modifying the colors in a series of objects created with the transformation tools and Arrange » Repeat Transform (as in Figure 14-14). You can also use them to recolor a series of objects created with the blend tool, as I discuss in Chapter 17.

Selecting Objects by Color

The last color filters I cover in this chapter allow you to select objects according to the way that you've colored them. These commands are available from the Filter » Select submenu:

- **Same Fill Color**: This filter selects all paths that are filled with the same color as the selected object. For some reason, the filter refuses to select text objects (as do the other filters I discuss here). However, if you have a text object selected, the filter will select paths that are filled with the same color.

- **Same Paint Style**: Choose this filter to select any paths that share the exact same fill and stroke attributes as a selected object.

- **Same Stroke Color**: This filter selects all paths that are stroked with the same color as the selected object. This filter ignores line weight, caps, joins, and all other stroke attributes except color.

- **Same Stroke Weight**: If you want to select all objects that are stroked with a certain line weight, select an object with that line weight and choose the Same Stroke Weight filter. This filter ignores color, caps, joins, and everything else except line weight. (See Chapter 16 for the lowdown on strokes.)

The color selection filters are essential for making global changes to objects filled or stroked with gray values and CMYK colors. For example, in Figure 14-15, I decided that the two darkest grays in the illustration on the left were interfering with the black of the letter M. I selected one of the objects filled with the darkest gray, chose Filter » Select » Same Fill Color to select the others, and entered a new Tint value in the Paint Style palette. After repeating this process for the objects filled with the next darkest shade of gray, I arrived at the more intelligible illustration on right.

Figure 14-15: Using the Same Fill Color filter, I easily changed all the occurrences of the two darkest gray fills in the left-hand illustration.

None of the color selection filters will work properly if the you have more than one object selected, and those objects have different fill or stroke colors. For the best results, select just one object and then choose a filter. Also, some folks have reported problems using Illustrator 6's Select filters on their Power Macintosh computers. Adobe claims that this problem should be resolved in an upcoming bug-fix release.

GRADATIONS AND OTHER FAB FILLS

In Illustrator, you can fill the interior of any path with a single color, a blend of colors, or a custom pattern. Though it may not sound like much, this is one of Illustrator's most essential capabilities.

If Illustrator couldn't fill objects with opaque colors, your paths and character outlines would be without form or substance. You'd be able to see through each and every path to the path behind it, like some kind of chaotic Miro-inspired scribble art. In fact, fill and stroke are all that separate the preview mode from the wireframe artwork mode. If you ever wonder what the world would be like without fill, just press ⌘-E. (Lordy, imagine presenting *that* to a client! It gives me the willies just thinking about it.)

If push came to shove, you *could* live without stroke. You could draw thin shapes—like those produced by the brush tool—and fill them. In fact, I know many artists who barely use strokes. But there's no getting around fill. It enables you to design complex illustrations, create shadows and highlights, or simply add color to a document. Fill is the skin wrapped around the skeleton of a path, the airbrushing inside the frisket, the drywall over the studs. Fill permits you to show viewers exactly what you want them to see.

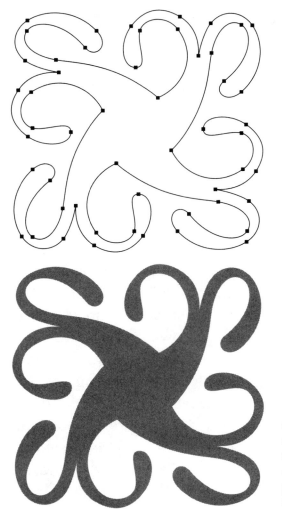

*Figure 15-1:
In the artwork mode, the
fill of a closed path is
invisible (top). But in the
preview mode, the fill per-
meates the shape (bottom).*

Filling Closed and Open Paths

Before I explain how you define and apply cool fills like gradations, there are a few basic principles I'd like to clarify. First of all, you can fill any kind of path, whether open or closed. (This is one fundamental advantage Illustrator has over FreeHand, which lets you fill closed paths only.) When you fill a closed path, the entire interior of the path is affected. Figure 15-1 shows a closed path as it appears selected in the artwork mode, and the same path filled in the preview mode. The shape acts like a malleable water balloon—the fill seeps into every nook and cranny of the outline.

Following that same logic, new users sometimes worry that a fill leaks out an open path and gets all over the page. (Don't laugh—that's exactly what happens in a painting program.) But in Illustrator, the fill is held in check by an imaginary straight segment drawn between the two endpoints. Figure 15-2 shows an open path in the artwork and preview modes. I've added a thick stroke so you can see that the path is open. The straight segment without a stroke is the imaginary segment Illustrator adds to keep the fill from pouring out.

Filled open paths can be very useful for creating indefinite boundaries in a graphic. The paths with the thick outlines in Figure 15-3 demonstrate this technique. For example, because the forward wing is an open path, it is not stroked where it connects with the body of the rocket. And because the wing and body are filled with the same shade of gray, the fill of one path appears to flow into the fill of the other. The path around the body of the rocket is also an open path. It opens at the base, creating another indefinite boundary.

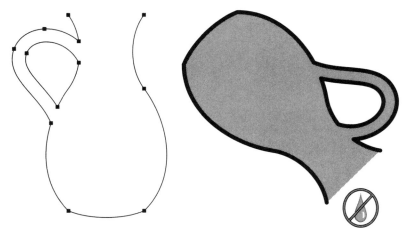

Figure 15-2: After drawing an open path (left), I filled it and tipped it upside down (right). And yet, by the miracle of the imaginary straight segment, not a drop of fill is spilled.

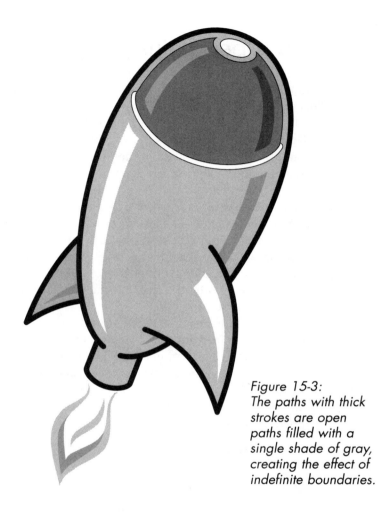

Figure 15-3:
The paths with thick
strokes are open
paths filled with a
single shade of gray,
creating the effect of
indefinite boundaries.

Filling Type and Text Blocks

You can also fill text objects to change the colors of individual characters, or to change the background color of a text block. If you select a text object with the arrow tool and apply a fill, the fill affects all the type in the text object and leaves the associated path unchanged.

For instance, the first example in Figure 15-4 shows a text block selected with the arrow tool. If you fill the object with a light gray, the

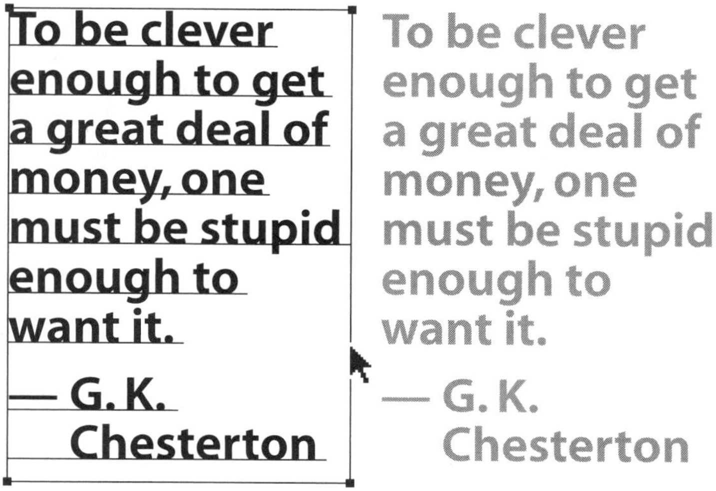

To be clever enough to get a great deal of money, one must be stupid enough to want it. — G. K. Chesterton

To be clever enough to get a great deal of money, one must be stupid enough to want it. — G. K. Chesterton

Figure 15-4:
If you apply a fill
color to a text
block selected with
the arrow tool (left),
Illustrator fills the
text (right).

type becomes filled, as shown in the second example in the figure. The result is gray type against a white background.

But if you select the path around the text block with the direct selection tool and apply a fill, Illustrator fills just the path. The characters inside the text block remain filled as before, as demonstrated in Figure 15-5.

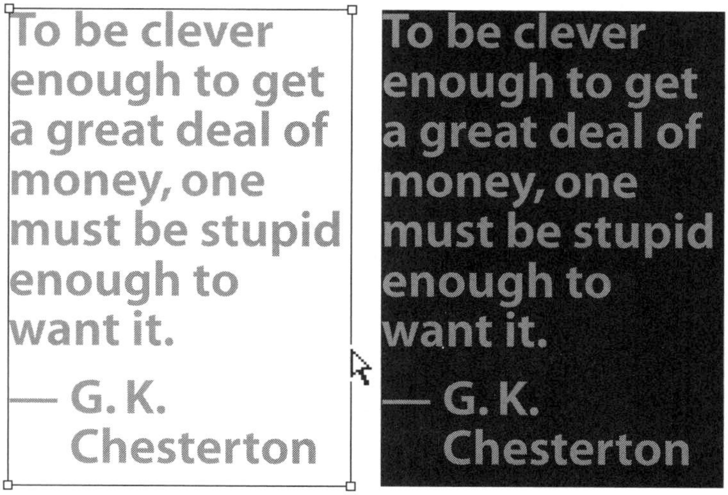

Figure 15-5:
If you select the
path of a text
object with the
direct selection
tool (left) and
then apply a fill,
Illustrator fills the
path only (right).

To be clever enough to get a great deal of money, one must be stupid enough to want it. — G. K. Chesterton

To be clever enough to get a great deal of money, one must be stupid enough to want it. — G. K. Chesterton

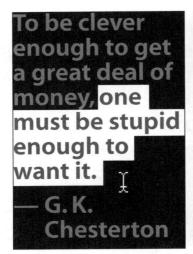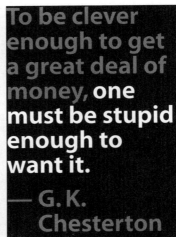

Figure 15-6: By selecting text with the type tool (left), you fill only the highlighted characters (right).

To fill single characters and words, you have to select the text with the type tool. Like any character-level formatting attribute, such as font or type size, fill affects only the highlighted characters, as demonstrated in Figure 15-6. In this way, Illustrator allows you to apply several different fills to a single text object.

Applying a Fill from the Paint Style Palette

The Paint Style palette is Illustrator's central headquarters for filling objects . Whether you're filling paths or text blocks, follow these steps:

1. **Select the path or characters that you want to fill**.

   You can use the arrow, direct selection, or type tool. In fact, you can be in the middle of drawing a path with the pen tool and still fill a path. As long as you can see selection handles or highlighted text in the illustration window, you can apply a fill.

   If no object is selected, modifying the fill changes the default settings.

2. **Display the Paint Style palette**.

   Press ⌘-I. (If pressing ⌘-I hides the palette, press ⌘-I again to bring it back.)

3. Click on the Fill icon.

You'll find that in the upper left corner of the palette. When active, the Fill icon is underlined and the word Fill is black (whereas Stroke is dimmed).

4. Select an icon from the top row of icons on the right side of the palette.

These icons appear labeled in Figure 15-7. I already explained many of these options—White, Black, Process, and Custom—in Chapter 14. I cover the Tile Pattern and Gradient icons later in this chapter. If you want to remove the fill from a path—to make the interior transparent—click on the None button.

 In place of Steps 3 and 4, you can drag a swatch from the scrolling list on the left side of the palette and drop it onto the Fill icon.

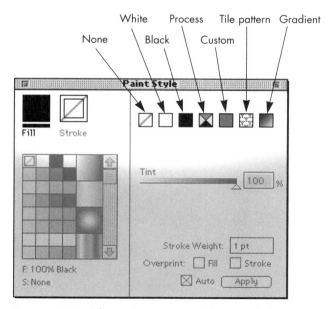

Figure 15-7: After selecting the Fill icon, click on one of the labeled icons to change the color or pattern assigned to selected paths and text.

5. Edit other options in the palette as desired.

For example, you can adjust the slider triangles to change the amount of cyan, magenta, yellow, or black ink in a process color. Or you can select a named color, tile pattern, or gradient from a list.

6. Press the Return key.

This tells Illustrator to return its focus to the illustration window.

 Step 6 is very important. Each and every time you touch an option in the Paint Style palette, you should get in the habit of pressing the Return key. Even if you click on the None icon and there are no other options to adjust, Illustrator thinks the Paint Style palette is active until you press Return.

If you don't believe me, try this. Draw a rectangle. Click on the Fill icon in the Paint Style palette, then click on the White icon to fill it with white. Now press and hold the spacebar to get the hand tool and drag inside the illustration window. Normally, this scrolls the illustration, but because the Tint option box is active, Illustrator displays an error message explaining that you can't enter a bunch of spaces for the Tint value. Not a big deal, but it's distracting nonetheless. If you had pressed Return before pressing the spacebar, the problem would have been averted.

Gradients in the Key of Life

Flat fills such as gray values, process colors, and named colors—all covered in the previous chapter—are very well and good. But if you're serious about imitating real life or giving your illustration a sense of depth, you'll appreciate Illustrator's unparalleled *gradations*. A gradation (or *gradient fill*) is a fill pattern that fades from one color into another. Illustrator lets you assign up to 32 colors to a single gradation. (Arch rival FreeHand 5.5 is technically limited to 2; it fudges extra colors using masks.) You can even fade between spot colors (another something FreeHand 5.5 cannot do).

Figure 15-8 demonstrates the power of gradations. I drew these relatively simple, structured paths to represent RCA cables for the book *Mac Multimedia & CD-ROMs for Dummies* (IDG Books Worldwide). The left pair of cables shows the paths filled with flat gray values; the right pair is filled with gradations. As you can see, the gradations make all the difference in the world, single-handedly transforming the paths from cardboard cutouts into credible representations of three-dimensional objects.

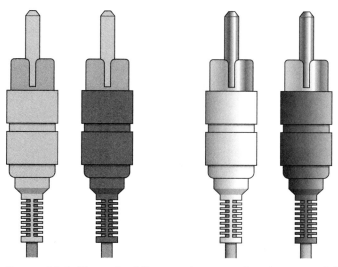

Figure 15-8: The only difference between the objects on left and their counterparts on right is that the latter are filled with gradations, which lends them the air of authenticity.

You can create one of two types of gradient fills:

- A *linear gradation* is one in which the color transition follows a straight line. All of the gradations in Figure 15-8 are linear, flowing horizontally from left to right.

- A *radial gradation* starts with a pinpoint of color and fades outward in concentric circles.

Figure 15-9 shows examples of linear and radial gradations. A linear gradation can flow in any angle, just so long as it flows in a straight line. And a radial gradation can begin at any location inside a shape as long as it flows outward in a circular pattern.

If you want to create a gradation that doesn't quite fall into either of these camps—such as the wavy-line pattern at the bottom of Figure 15-9—you have to create a custom blend using the aptly named blend tool, and then mask the blend inside a shape. Chapter 17 discusses blends, masks, and other extraordinary fill options.

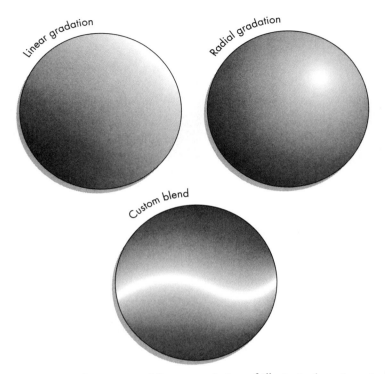

Figure 15-9: The two top fills are varieties of Illustrator's automated gradations. To create the bottom fill, I had to use the blend tool.

Applying and Modifying Gradations

To apply a gradient fill to a selected path, select the Gradient icon in the upper right corner of the Paint Style palette. (To apply a gradation to text, first choose Type » Create Outlines.) Then select one of the named gradations in the scrolling list below the icons. These are the predefined gradients contained in the Adobe Illustrator Startup file (assuming you haven't added any gradations of your own).

The problem with Illustrator's predefined gradations is that you probably won't find much use for them. It's not Adobe's fault; the predefined collection represents a healthy variety. It's just that gradations aren't particularly versatile creatures. A gradation created for one illustration is unlikely to be useful in another. Figure 15-8, for example, contains eight gradations, none of which come from Illustrator's default collection, and none of which I've ever used again.

So you'll spend a lot of time designing new gradations inside Illustrator. To create and edit a gradient fill, choose Object » Gradient or Window » Show Gradient. Better yet, double-click on the name of a gradation listed in the Paint Style palette. Any of these actions displays the Gradient palette, shown in Figure 15-10.

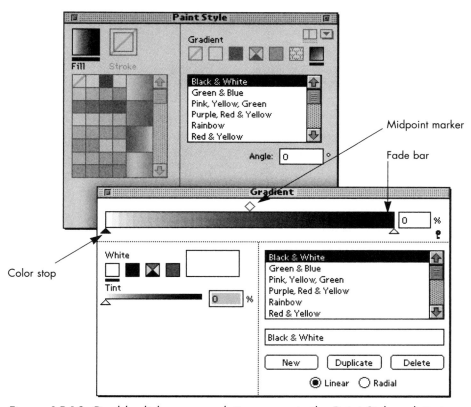

Figure 15-10: Double-click on a gradation name in the Paint Style palette to display the Gradient palette, which lets you design new gradations.

The Gradient Fade Bar

Along the top of the Gradient palette is the *fade bar*. The starting color appears as a triangular *color stop* on the left; the ending color is the triangular stop on the right. The diamond in the middle, called the *midpoint marker*, represents the spot where the two colors mix in exactly equal amounts. You can change the location of any stop or marker by dragging it. Or you can click on a stop or marker to select it and then enter a value into the percentage option box to the right of the fade bar. The selected stop or marker appears black.

- When numerically positioning a selected color stop, a value of 0 percent indicates the left end of the fade bar; 100 percent indicates the right end. Even if you add more color stops to the gradation, the values represent absolute positions along the fade bar.

- When repositioning a midpoint marker, the initial setting of 50 percent is smack dab between the two color stops; 0 percent is all the way over to the left stop, and 100 percent is all the way over to the right. Midpoint values are therefore measured relative to color stop positions. In fact, when you move a color stop, Illustrator moves the midpoint marker along with it to maintain the same relative positioning.

Figure 15-11 shows a gradation from light to dark gray subjected to various color stop and midpoint marker settings. As you can see, moving the color stops compresses the area in which the colors fade. In the second example in the figure, for example, the colors fade exclusively between the 30% and 90% stops. The areas to the left of the 30% stop and right of the 90% stop are filled with flat colors.

Meanwhile, moving the midpoint marker changes the rate at which colors fade. In the third example in Figure 15-11, the colors fade very quickly between the 0% color stop and the 25% marker, but fade more slowly on their way to the 100% stop. The opposite is true in the fourth example; the colors fade slowly at first and then speed up at the end. The last example in the figure shows the result of moving both the color stops and the midpoint marker.

Adjusting the Colors in a Gradation

You can change the colors in a gradation by selecting a color stop and editing the color options in the lower left portion of the palette. These include the White, Black, Process, and Custom icons, along with corresponding slider bars and option boxes, all of which work exactly like their counterparts in the Paint Style palette (as discussed in Chapter 14).

Have you ever wished you could lift a color from an object in the illustration window while working in the Gradient palette? Well, it turns out, you can. First, select the color stop you want to modify. Then select the eyedropper tool and Control-click on an object with a flat fill. Illustrator applies the fill color to the selected color stop.

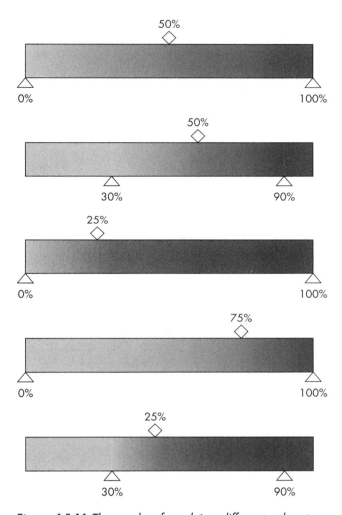

Figure 15-11:The results of applying different color stop and midpoint marker values to a single gradation.

As I mentioned in the previous chapter, Illustrator is one of the few applications that lets you blend between spot colors without converting them to their process ingredients. This can be a real advantage when creating two- and three-color documents. To create a gradation between two spot colors, assign named colors to each of the two color stops using the Custom icon. Then, after applying the gradation to a few shapes, print the illustration to spot-color separations (as detailed in the "Process Color or Spot?" section of Chapter 14). Illustrator will print a black-to-white gradation on one separation and a white-to-black gradation on the other, so that the two spot colors fade into each other in the final color reproduction.

Adding, Deleting, and Swapping Color Stops

Congratulations, you are now three bullet points away from knowing everything there is to know about color stops:

- Two color stops make for a two-color gradation. But you can go as high as 32 colors per gradient fill. To add a color stop, click anywhere along the bottom of the fade bar. A new triangle appears where you click. Illustrator also adds a midpoint marker between the new color stop and its neighbor. You can move the color stop, assign a different color to it, or reposition the midpoint marker, just as before.

- To remove a color stop, drag the triangle down into the lower portion of the Gradient palette. The triangle vanishes and the fade bar automatically adjusts as defined by the remaining color stops.

 To switch the colors of any two color stops, drag one color stop onto the other. Illustrator swaps the colors and automatically updates the gradation. Illustrator automatically shifts the position of the midpoint marker to compensate for the reversed color stops.

The Other Gradient Options

The fade bar is easily the most important part of the Gradient palette. But I would be remiss if I didn't also mention the following:

- If you want to work from an existing gradation, select its name from the scrolling list below the fade bar. When the list is active (with a heavy border around it), you can select a gradation by typing a few letters in its name.

- To create a new gradation based on a selected one, click on the Duplicate button. Illustrator creates a clone of the gradation. You can now edit the clone without affecting any objects filled with the original gradation.

- To create a completely new gradient, click on the New button. Illustrator automatically fills it with white and black.

- Change the name of a selected gradient by replacing the contents of the option box above the New button. If the list is active, you can press the Tab key once to highlight this option box; then enter a new name.

Be sure to change the name of a gradient any time you edit it. Why? Because open illustrations share gradient fills. For example, suppose you modify the definition of Green & Blue, one of Illustrator's predefined fills. As you do so, you change the colors of objects filled with Green & Blue throughout *all* open illustrations. Perhaps more upsetting, if you open an illustration you created last year using Green & Blue, it automatically changes as well. I prefer to use differently named gradients to avoid any confusion.

- Click on the Delete button to delete a gradation from all open illustrations. If you delete a gradient fill that's been assigned to objects inside an open illustration, Illustrator warns you that those objects are about to be filled with black. (Unlike when you modify a gradation, the Delete button does not affect illustrations that you open in the future. If you delete Green & Blue from one illustration, and then open an illustration that uses Green & Blue, then Green & Blue is back in business.)

- At the bottom of the Gradient palette are two radio buttons—Linear and Radial—that let you specify whether you want to create a linear or radial gradation. If this doesn't ring a bell, refer back to Figure 15-9.

When creating a radial gradation, the left color stop represents the center color in the fill; the right color stop represents the outside color. If you want the gradation to produce a highlighting effect, as in the left example in Figure 15-12, make the first color lighter than the last one. If you make the first color darker than the last, the edges of the shape are highlighted, as in the right example in the figure.

Figure 15-12: Two radial gradations, one in which the first color is white and the last color is dark gray (left), and the other in which the colors are reversed (right).

To the right of (and slightly below) the fade bar is a flag icon. Click on the flag to contract the Gradient palette so that just the fade bar is visible. Click again to expand the palette. It's difficult to edit gradations when the palette is collapsed, but you can store the palette collapsed when it's not in use.

Adjusting a Gradient Fill to Fit Its Path

When you first assign a linear gradation to a path, Illustrator orients the gradation horizontally so it fades from left to right. When you assign a radial gradation, the gradation starts in the center of the shape. Neither of these two settings is very interesting, which is why Illustrator lets you change the angle of a linear gradation and reposition colors inside any gradation.

Changing the Angle Value

One way to change the angle of a linear gradation is to enter a value into the Angle option box in the Paint Style palette (just below the scrolling list of gradient fills). This is useful if you want to match the angle of an object ascertained with the measure tool.

For instance, in the top example of Figure 15-13, I've assigned the predefined Steel Bar gradation to a star. To make the angle of the fill match the angle of the shape, I first drag with the measure tool from the base of the star to its tip, as the arrow in the figure shows. The Info palette informs me that the angle is 112.792 degrees. (Oh sure, I could tell it was 112 degrees just by looking at it, but I wasn't sure about that 0.792.)

I then pressed ⌘-I to activate the Paint Style palette and pressed Tab to highlight the Angle value. The bottom example in Figure 15-13 shows the result of entering a new Angle value of 112.792 and pressing Return. (Illustrator rounds off the value to 112.79 because the Angle value is accurate only to 0.01 degree.) The angle of the gradation now matches the angle of the star precisely.

The Angle value is also useful for matching the angles of multiple gradations to each other. Select the object that contains the properly angled gradation and note the Angle value in the Paint Style palette. Then select the objects that you want to match and replace the Angle value with the new one.

Keep an eye on the Angle value, however. Each time you change it, it becomes the default setting for the next object. Even if you select a different gradation, the Angle value remains intact until you manually enter a new value or select an object filled with a different gradation.

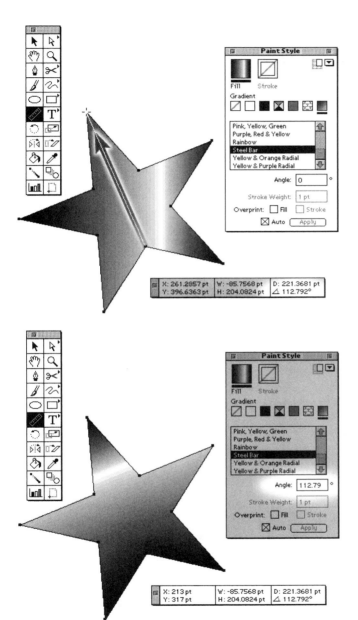

Figure 15-13: After measuring the angle of a shape filled with a gradation (top), I entered the measured value into the Angle option box in the Paint Style palette (bottom).

Using the Gradient Vector Tool

For those times when you want to reposition colors in a gradation, Illustrator offers the gradient vector tool (second-to-last tool on the left side of the toolbox). You can also use the tool to change the angle of a gradation, which is frequently more convenient than entering a numerical Angle value.

Adjusting a Linear Gradation

If a selected object is filled with a linear gradation, drag across the object with the gradient vector tool to change the angle of the gradation. The first color appears at the point where you start your drag and the last color appears where you release the mouse button. The angle of the gradation matches the angle of the drag, as demonstrated in Figure 15-14.

Figure 15-15 shows a single light-to-dark gray gradation set to different angles with the gradient vector tool. The white lines show the direction of the drag for

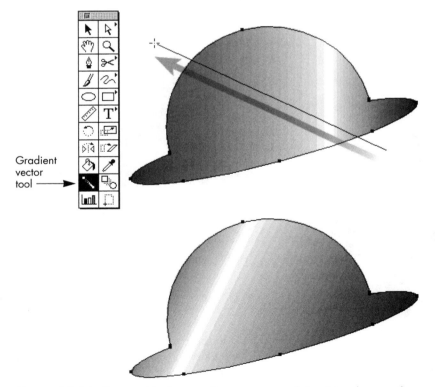

Gradient
vector
tool

Figure 15-14: Drag with the gradient vector tool (top) to change the angle of the gradation inside a selected object (bottom).

each shape. The black dots show where I started dragging, the white dots show where I stopped.

In the first example, the start and stop points lie well outside the shape, so the first and last colors fall outside the shape as well. This draws out the gradation and attenuates the range. Though the gradation runs from 15 to 70 percent black, you can only see 25 to 60 percent black inside the shape.

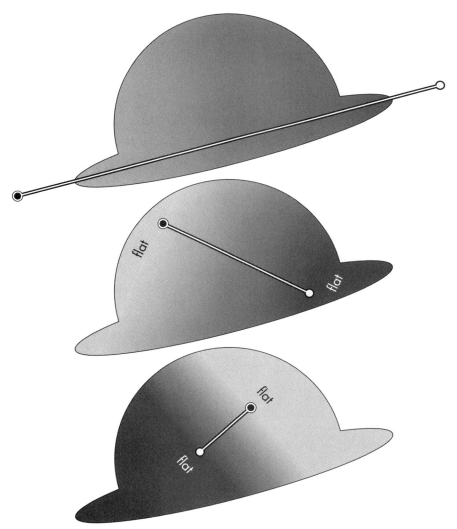

Figure 15-15: Three examples of the effect of the gradient vector tool on a gradation. The black dots show where I started dragging; the white dots show where I released.

● The start and stop points fall inside the second shape. Now we can see the full range of the gradation. But when a gradation doesn't fully traverse a path, you get areas of flat color, as labeled in the figure.

● Too much flat color can interrupt the rhythm of the gradation. In the last example, I dragged across a very short distance with the gradient vector tool. The resulting gradient fill flies by quickly, leaving large areas of flat color inside the shape.

It's especially unwise to leave flat areas of white inside a gradient fill. The transition from printed ink to no ink is harsh enough without accentuating the problem by magnifying the size of the no-ink area. To give you a sense of what I'm talking about, Figure 15-16 shows examples of four black-to-white gradations, each one ending earlier inside its shape. Without much effort, most folks can see a sharp cutoff point where the last shade of gray gives way to white. The funny thing is, the transition frequently appears more abrupt when the illustration is output from a high-resolution imagesetter than when it's output from a laser printer. If in doubt, I suggest you run your own tests.

Figure 15-16: Leaving large flat areas of white can ruin the effect of a gradation and result in a crisp boundary between ink and no ink.

To avoid this effect, substitute 5-percent black (or some other very light shade) in place of white in your linear gradations. This way, you always have a little ink coverage in the gradation, no matter how slight. (This assumes a properly calibrated printer, of course. If the printer is a little off, 5-percent black can turn white. Again, print a few tests to be sure.)

Modifying a Radial Gradation

Using the gradient vector tool on an object filled with a radial gradation changes the balance of the gradation and repositions its center. If you drag across a selected radial gradation, Illustrator repositions the first color to the point at which you start dragging. It extends the outer ring to the point at which you release.

In Figure 15-17, I took the linear gradation from Figure 15-15 and selected the Radial option to convert it into a radial gradation. I also changed the first color to white. As before, the black dot shows where I started dragging and the white dot shows where I stopped. In a radial gradation, the first color is never flat, no matter where you start dragging in an object (which is why white doesn't tend to create problems for radial gradations the way it does for linear ones). But the last color can go flat, because Illustrator fills the area beyond the drag with the last color (as indicated by the words *Flat* in the figure).

 If you click in a radial gradation with the gradient vector tool, Illustrator repositions the first color in the gradation independently of the outer ring formed by the last color. Figure 15-18 shows the result of clicking inside each of the shapes from Figure 15-17. In each case, Illustrator moved the first color, white, to the point where I clicked (as indicated by a sparkle) and offset the gradation to produce a sort of spotlight effect. For those of you keeping score, you cannot do this in FreeHand.

Dragging Through Multiple Paths

Another feature of the gradient tool is that it allows you to apply a single gradation across multiple selected objects. In this way, all objects appear lit by a single light source. To accomplish this effect, select several objects, fill them with a gradation, and drag across them with the gradient vector tool. Illustrator creates one continuous gradation across all selected shapes.

Figure 15-19 shows two lines of text converted to path outlines. In the first line, I selected the characters and filled them with a 5-color gradient. Illustrator filled each letter independently. In the second line, I dragged across the selected characters with the gradient vector tool, resulting in one continuous, angled gradation.

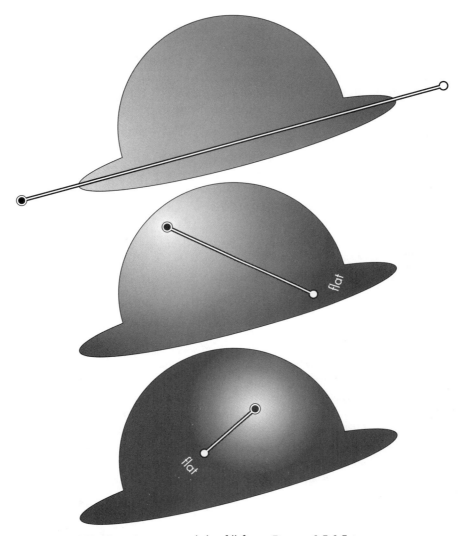

Figure 15-17: Here I converted the fill from Figure 15-15 to a radial gradation. The black and white dots show where I started and stopped dragging with the gradient vector tool.

The background rectangle in Figure 15-19 is filled with a slightly lighter duplicate of the 5-color gradation set to the same angle as the bottom line of text. In fact, if truth be told, both the rectangle and the bottom characters were selected when I dragged with the gradient vector tool. This means

Figure 15-18: I clicked at each of the sparkles to offset the first color in the radial gradation independently of the last color.

you can angle and position multiple gradient fills at the same time, so that the fills lighten and darken at precisely the same points.

More Gradient Vector Trivia

Finally, just for the record, here are a few more tidbits of gradient vector tool information you might want to sock away inside that incredibly full brain of yours:

Figure 15-19: After applying a 5-color gradient fill to a few converted letters (top), I dragged over the letters with the gradient vector tool (bottom).

● Like so many other tools inside Illustrator, you can Shift-drag with the tool to create a gradation that flows horizontally, vertically, or at a 45-degree angle.

● You can modify the angle of a Shift-drag by rotating the constraint axes. For example, back in Figure 15-13, I set the angle of a gradation to 112.79 degrees using the Angle value. But had I wanted to reposition the first and last colors as well as rotate the gradation, I could have entered 112.79 into the Constrain Angle option box in the General Preferences dialog box, and then Shift-dragged with the gradient vector tool. Just remember to set the Constrain Angle value back to 0 when you're done.

● Assuming the Snap to Point check box is on in the General Preferences dialog box, the gradient vector tool snaps to points and guides in the illustration window.

Slanting Gradations

So far I've showed you three ways to transform gradations. You can change the angle of a linear gradation, which is the same thing as rotating the gradation inside its shape. You can move the first and last colors around, which is the same thing as scaling the gradation. (As I explained in Chapter 11, relative movement is what scaling is all about.) And if you reverse the first and last colors in a gradation, you flip the fill. That leaves just one transformation unexplored—slanting.

 Because the rows of color in a linear gradation stretch off into infinity, you can effectively slant a linear gradation by dragging with the gradient vector tool. (Try dragging slightly against the direction of the path and you'll see the rows of color slant. Skip ahead to Figure 15-22 to see an example of this technique.) To slant a radial gradation, however, you have to use the shear tool, as explained below.

As it turns out, every one of the transformation tools transforms the gradient fill inside a path as well as the path itself. Therefore, to slant a radial gradation, you can select the path with the arrow tool and then use the shear tool to slant it. For example, Figure 15-20 begins with a rectangle filled with a radial gradation. After selecting the rectangle, I double-clicked on the shear tool icon in the toolbox to display the Shear dialog box. Then I entered a value of 60 degrees with Horizontal selected from the Axis options. The result is the second example in the figure. As you can see, Illustrator has slanted both the object and the circular rings inside the gradient fill.

Now, at this point, I have two options. I can restore the rectangle to its original orientation and leave the gradation slanted. Or I can apply the slanted gradation to a different sets of paths.

 To restore the rectangle, you could select all of the segments in the shape—without selecting any of the points—by clicking and Shift-clicking on each segment with the direct selection tool. Then double-click again on the shear tool icon and enter an opposite slant value (−60 degrees, in my case) to reverse the transformation. Because the path is only partially selected—all segments but no points—Illustrator slants the object but not the fill. Very cool.

The problem with this technique is that it works properly only if the selected object is made up entirely of straight segments. A single curved segment ruins the effect. Also, it involves an awful lot of clicking and Shift-clicking, which can prove rather monotonous after a while.

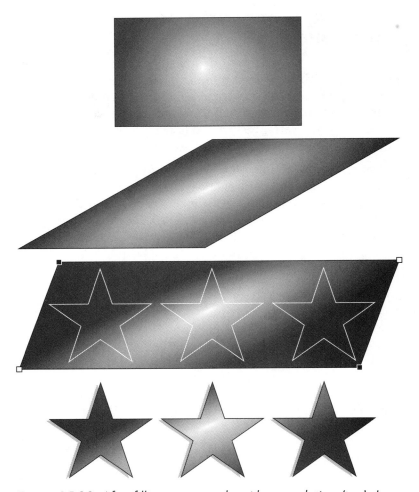

Figure 15-20: After filling a rectangle with a gradation (top), I slanted the shape (second), selected two points and slanted them the opposite direction (third), and intersected the rectangle with some compound stars (bottom).

That's why I prefer to apply the slanted gradation to one or more different paths using the Intersect filter. In the third example of Figure 15-20, I selected the upper left and lower right corner points in the skewed rectangle and slanted them –70 degrees to widen the shape. Then I positioned three stars in front of the rectangle and combined the stars into a single compound path (⌘-8). I next sent the stars to back (⌘-minus), Shift-clicked on the rectangle with the arrow tool to add it to the selection, and chose Filter » Pathfinder » Intersect. Illustrator found the intersection of the compound stars and rectangle and applied the fill from the forward shape, which was the slanted gradation.

Some artists like to use Illustrator's masking function (discussed in Chapter 17) to fill an object with a slanted gradation. But masks can cause printing problems, especially when applied to gradations. And at the very least, they increase the print time. By contrast, the Intersect filter creates a clean, cookie-cutter effect that takes no more time to print than the original slanted object.

 If you know exactly how far you want to slant a gradation, you can engage in a little preemptory slanting. Before applying the gradation, slant the object in the opposite direction of how you'd like to slant the gradient fill. Then apply the gradient fill and slant the object back to its normal orientation.

Figure 15-21: Another way to slant a gradation is to slant the shape in the opposite direction, apply the gradation, and then reverse the slant.

In Figure 15-21, for example, I started with the gray spade (a converted Zapf Dingbats character). Then I double-clicked on the shear tool and entered –60 degrees with a horizontal axis. After applying the radial gradation, I again double-clicked on the shear tool and entered 60 degrees. The result is an upright shape with a slanted fill.

Resetting a Gradation

After transforming a gradation—whether with the transformation tool or the gradient vector tool—you may find that you've modified a fill too much and you're better off restoring the default orientation. To accomplish this, simply fill the object with black and then reapply the gradation. If the gradation remains rotated, enter 0 into the Angle option box in the Paint Style palette and press Return.

Creating Gradient Shadows

Gradations naturally lend themselves to shadows. When you shine a light source on an object in real life, the shadow fades away from the object. This is a function of ambient light, which reflects around the object to progressively lighten the shadow.

Figure 15-22 shows what I mean. Created entirely inside Illustrator—using the transformation tools and the Free Distort filter (on the 8)—this illustration

Figure 15-22: Real-life shadows almost always fade slightly, just as this gradient shadow becomes lighter as it slants away from the 8 ball.

exploits gradations to produce a photo-realistic effect. I filled the 8 ball with a black-to-white radial gradation. I set the midpoint marker for the gradation to 87 percent to exaggerate the black and leave just a slim lining of white. The hint of horizon is a slanted rectangle filled with a very short light gray-to-white linear gradation. The shadow is also filled with a linear gradation. To get the skewed fill effect, I dragged almost straight down with the gradient vector tool. (This is what I meant by dragging against the direction of the path back in the "Slanting Gradations" section.)

Gradient shadows require more work when they cross differently colored shapes. Though the shadow shown in the first example of Figure 15-23 is filled

Figure 15-23: A gradient shadow laid over differently colored background shapes looks nasty (top). But if you mix the shadow and background shapes, you can achieve a highly realistic effect (bottom).

with a gradation, it doesn't look even remotely plausible because it fails to take the background shapes into account. But by defining some additional gradations and taking advantage of the Intersect filter, I'm able to arrive at the top-notch work of *Zot* art shown in the second example.

The following steps tell how to mix a gradient shadow with background objects that contain flat fills:

1. **Create a new gradation for each background shape and add the colors from each object to the shadow.**

   The gradient shadow in the top example in Figure 15-23 ranges from 35% to 15% black. The darker of the two background shapes is filled with flat 40% black and the lighter contains 20% black. Therefore, I created two duplicates of the original gradation (using the Duplicate button in the Gradient palette). Then I colored one gradation with 75% to 55% black (that's 40% + 35% to 40% + 15%); and the other with 55% to 35% black (20% + 35% to 20% + 15%).

   It's even easier if the background shapes contain CMY colors and the shadow is exclusively black. Then you just mix the CMY values with the black; no adding is necessary. For example, suppose the darker of the two shapes in Figure 15-23 is filled with 100% cyan, and the other is filled with 100% yellow. The first of the two new gradations would range from 100%C 35%K to 100%C 15%K; the second would range from 100%Y 35%K to 100%Y 15%K.

2. **If the shadow is made up of many shapes, you need to combine them into a single compound path.**

   The shadow in Figure 15-23 comprises three converted characters, known the world around as *Z*, *O*, and *T*. Since the letters don't overlap, you won't be able to find the intersection of the letters with the background objects in Step 6. By selecting the letters and pressing ⌘-8, I instruct Illustrator to consider these shapes as a single compound path. Now I can apply the Intersect filter with impunity.

3. **Send the shadow behind the background shapes.**

   Press ⌘-minus. The first example in Figure 15-24 shows my progress so far. It doesn't look like much, but it's full of promise.

4. **Select the shadow and one of the background shapes.**

   Since the shadow is already selected, you can just Shift-click on the first shape with the arrow tool.

Figure 15-24:
After sending the original
shadow to back (top), I
found the intersection of
the shadow with the first
shape (middle), and then
found the intersection of
the shadow and the
second shape (bottom).

5. **Copy the selection and paste it in front**.

   That's ⌘-C, ⌘-F. This prevents you from harming your original paths.

6. **Choose Filter >> Pathfinder >> Intersect**.

   Illustrator draws new paths around the regions where the shadow and background shape overlap.

7. **Fill the selected paths with the first gradation**.

   I filled my paths with the 75% to 55% black gradation, as in the second example in Figure 15-24.

8. **Repeat Steps 4 through 7 for each additional background shape**.

   I have only one more background shape, so I selected it and the original shadow, copied them and pasted them in front, applied the Intersect filter, and filled the resulting paths with the 55% to 35% gradation. The last example in Figure 15-24 shows what I got.

9. **Make sure the gradations flow in the same direction**.

   Select all the shadow shapes and drag across them with the gradient vector tool. This ensures that the shadows go in a consistent direction and the colors change at a consistent rate.

You may have noticed that the strokes in Figure 15-24 aren't quite where they ought to be. Because my background shapes had strokes, the Intersect filter assigns strokes to my new shadows as well. To arrive at the finished effect in Figure 15-23, I had to delete these strokes. Then I copied one of the background shapes, selected the corresponding shadow, pasted the shape in front, and made the fill transparent. This restored the stroke around the shape without interfering with the shadow. I then repeated the process on the remaining background shapes. (For complete information on this technique, read the "Stroke on Fill" section of Chapter 16.)

Strictly speaking, it is possible to mix a gradient shadow with a gradient background object, but, personally, I think it's more trouble than it's worth. You have to convert both gradients to blends using Object » Expand, and then mix all the objects together using Filter » Pathfinder » Soft. Illustrator needs a ton of memory to pull this off—calculating tens of thousands of path intersections is nothing to sneeze at. And even if it works, you're left with a sufficient number of objects to clog the mightiest printer. Meanwhile, the simplified approach demonstrated in Figure 15-23 looks great and prints like a dream.

Filling Objects with Tiles

In Illustrator, you can fill both paths and text objects with *tile patterns*, which are rectangular patterns that repeat over and over inside a shape. It's just like the tiles on a kitchen floor, only you don't have to gets your hands all messy when applying the mortar. You can create your own tile patterns, or select from the vast Collector's Edition library included on the Illustrator 6 CD-ROM.

 Tile patterns are perhaps the most difficult kind of object to print from Illustrator. In fact, I can pretty much guarantee that if you use more than three different tile patterns inside a single illustration, it doesn't stand a snowball's chance in the microwave of printing. To prevent heartbreak and frustration, apply tile patterns to simple objects, and don't use more than two or three per illustration. Your nervous system thanks you.

Applying and Modifying Tile Patterns

Apply tile patterns from the Paint Style palette by clicking on the Pattern. Then select one of the named patterns in the scrolling list below the icons. As always, these represent patterns stored the Adobe Illustrator Startup file.

But if Illustrator's default collection of gradations isn't particularly useful, the default patterns are even worse. These are some of the dullest patterns I've ever seen. Heck, I wouldn't allow these tiles in my guest bathroom.

 Incidentally, the pattern names with numbers and periods—like *DbLine1.2.outer* and *Laurel.inner*—aren't meant to be used as tile patterns. Though they show up in the tile pattern list, they're actually path patterns, which are specifically designed to follow the stroke of a path. I examine path patterns in Chapter 16.

To create your own tile pattern or add some pizzazz to one of the dull ones, choose Object » Pattern, or double-click on a pattern name in the Paint Style palette. The Pattern dialog box appears out of the blue, as in Figure 15-25.

You can convert a collection of selected objects to a tile pattern by clicking on the New button. (If you haven't selected anything, the New button is dimmed.) If you want to use one of the predefined patterns as a starting point, select the pattern name and click on the Paste button. Illustrator pastes the tile into the illustration window. Then press the Return key and edit the pattern just as you would any other collection of paths.

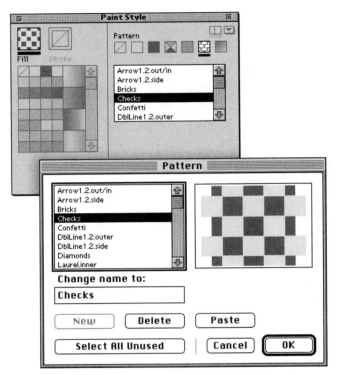

Figure 15-25: Double-click on pattern name in the Paint Style palette to display the Pattern dialog box, which lets you create and edit tile patterns.

Creating a New Tile Pattern

To create a tile pattern in Illustrator, you simply select a bunch of objects, choose Object » Pattern, click on the New button, and press Return. Illustrator automatically incorporates the objects into a rectangular tile. Really, that's it.

Ah, but if you want to create something that looks halfway decent, you have to do a little more work. As with so many other operations inside Illustrator, so many nuances are involved in creating a tile pattern that you can learn only by making one yourself. To this end, the following steps walk you through the task of designing a cool-looking tile pattern:

1. **Create a new illustration**.

   Even if you ultimately intend to apply the tile pattern to an existing object, it's a good idea to start off with a new document. Besides, tile patterns are shared between all open illustrations, so what you create in one window you can apply in another.

2. **Assemble a few objects to create a basic design**.

In the first example in Figure 15-26, I took an airplane character from the Zapf Dingbats font and converted it to path outlines. (If you have Zapf Dingbats—named for influential type designer Hermann Zapf—press Shift-9 to get the plane.) Then I rotated a clone of the plane 90 degrees and pressed ⌘-D twice to create two more rotated clones.

3. **Draw a rectangle around the design with the rectangle tool**.

This rectangle represents a single tile in the tile pattern. The rectangle should cut slightly into the design, as it does in Figure 15-26. Objects that overlap one edge of the rectangle will repeat at the opposite edge. This helps to interrupt the rectangular rhythm of the pattern and create a more free-form appearance.

4. **Copy the rectangle, then convert it to a guide**.

Press ⌘-C, ⌘-5. If you've ever created a tile pattern before, this may sound like an odd step. But it permits you to align portions of the pattern to ensure invisible transitions from one tile to the next.

5. **Paste the rectangle in front, then separate its edges**.

Press ⌘-F, then click on each of the four corners of the pasted rectangle with the scissors tool. You now have four straight segments which you can use to align objects to the tile.

6. **Select the top edge and all objects that overlap the top edge**.

I selected both the top edge and the upward-pointing plane.

7. **Option-drag the selected edge downward until it snaps to the bottom of the rectangle**.

By pressing the Option key, you clone the object; and by dragging the edge instead of the object itself, you ensure a snug fit with the rectangular guide. The second example in Figure 15-26 shows me snapping a clone of the plane along the bottom edge. Just as the nose of the plane extends out of the tile past the top edge, it now extends into the tile from the bottom edge. This ensures that the plane will flow smoothly from one tile into the next.

8. Next select the bottom edge and the objects that overlap that edge, and clone them onto the top edge.

In my case, I selected and cloned the downward-pointing plane.

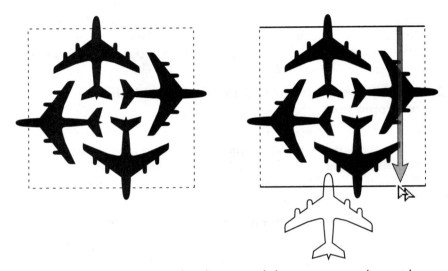

Figure 15-26: First, I created a design and drew a rectangular guide around it (left). Then I Option-dragged the plane that overlaps the top of the rectangle to clone it and snap it into position along the bottom of the rectangle (right).

9. Repeat Step 8 for the objects that overlap the left and right edges as well.

After completing this step, I had a total of eight planes. The nose of each plane overlapped a side of the rectangle. And the same plane that overlapped one side also overlapped the opposite side. As a result, all of the planes will enter and exit the tiles in precise alignment.

10. Edit the objects as needed.

It's unlikely that you'll get your design exactly right on the first try. You may need to tweak it here and there. But pay careful attention to what you do. If you change the way one object overlaps an edge of the rect-angle, you have to modify the matching object along the opposite edge in kind.

For my part, my plane pattern left gaps at each of the four corners of the tile. So I took another Zapf Dingbats character—the one that looks like a steering wheel (which you get by pressing the quote key)—and converted it to outlines. Then I selected the inner circle of the character with the direct selection tool, pressed ⌘-Control-A to get the Attributes dialog box, and selected the Show Center Point check box. I next selected the entire character with the arrow tool and dragged it by the center point so it snapped into alignment with one of the corners of the rectangle. Finally, I Option-dragged the character a total of three times to snap it to the remaining corners. Figure 15-27 shows the objects in my completed design. As you can see, one quarter of each steering wheel lies inside the rectangle, so that a single wheel will appear each time four tiles meet.

11. Select all the straight segments around the edges of the rectangle and delete them.

Their work is done.

Figure 15-27: After cloning and snapping the planes into place, I added steering wheels to fill in the corners of the tile.

12. Unlock the guide and convert it back into a normal object.

Assuming the guide is locked, press ⌘-7 to unlock it. Then Shift-Control-double-click on the guide with the arrow tool to convert it to an object. (Or select the guide and press ⌘-6.)

13. Fill and stroke the objects—including the background rectangle—as desired.

When filling objects, use flat colors only. The Pattern dialog box cannot accommodate objects filled with gradations or tile patterns.

I used a popular embossing technique to create the effect shown in Figure 15-28. First, I selected and grouped all objects except the rectangle to make them easier to edit. Then I filled the rectangle with 30% black and the grouped objects with 25% black, so that the rectangle and group were nearly identical in color. To create the shadow for the embossing effect, I selected the group, copied it, and pasted it in back. Then I nudged it down one point and to the left one point, and filled it with 55% black. To create the highlight, I selected the original group and pressed ⌘-B again. Then I nudged the copy up one point and to the right one point, and filled it with white. The result is what you see in Figure 15-28.

Figure 15-28: I cloned and filled the plane and wheel shapes to create this common embossing effect.

14. Select the rectangle and copy it.

It's now time to get rid of all the junk that's exceeding the boundaries of the rectangle. Illustrator wants a clean, rectangular edge, or it'll make one for you (and you don't want that).

15. Paste the rectangle in front of everything.

The easiest way to do this is to press ⌘-Shift-A to deselect everything, and then press ⌘-F to paste the rectangle at the front of the illustration. If the rectangle is filled, it will cover up some stuff, but don't worry about it. The rectangle dies a fiery death in the next step.

16. Select everything and apply the Crop filter.

Press ⌘-A, then choose Filter » Pathfinder » Crop. After a few moments of intense calculating, Illustrator crops away all portions of the selected objects that lie outside the frontmost rectangle. The rectangle also gets gobbled up, leaving behind a perfect tile.

17. Choose Object » Pattern.

Illustrator displays the Pattern dialog box.

18. Click on the New button.

Illustrator adds an item called *New Pattern* to the scrolling list and shows a preview of the tile, as in Figure 15-29.

19. Name the pattern.

Enter a name into the Change Name To option box, and press Return.

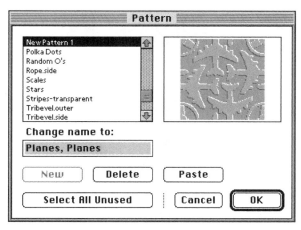

Figure 15-29:
Choose Object » Pattern
and click on the New button
to convert the selected
objects into a tile pattern.

Well done! You have successfully completed a tile pattern that would make your dear mother's heart swell with unmitigated pride. You can now select an object inside any open illustration and apply your new tile pattern from the Paint Style palette.

Just to make more work for myself, I created a couple of variations on my Planes, Planes tile pattern and applied the patterns to the shapes shown in Figure 15-30. The patterns are identical except in color. After creating the first pattern, I cloned the original objects and used Filter » Colors » Saturate to create lighter and darker variations. (I entered a value of 30 percent to darken one set of objects, and −30 percent to lighten the other set.) Then I used the Pattern dialog box to save each of these variations as yet another pattern. In Figure 15-30, I filled the plane with the light pattern, the shadow with the dark pattern, and the background rectangle with the very first pattern. Notice how the objects in all three patterns align precisely, making for seamless transitions.

Figure 15-30: This illustration contains three objects filled with three different tile patterns. The patterns vary only in color.

Figure 15-30 is an example of an illustration that may be too complex to print. After creating the figure, I couldn't get it to print to my LaserWriter IINTX for the life of me. (Granted, the NTX is an aging machine equipped with Level 1 PostScript, but it's a reliable workhorse of a printer.) I converted the tile patterns to elaborate masks using Object » Expand, but the page still wouldn't print. Ultimately, I broke up the masks (by choosing Object » Masks » Release) and used the Crop filter to carve the shapes into the expanded patterns. I had to assign a whopping 30MB of RAM to Illustrator to get the crop filter to work, and even then, it took several minutes per shape. Total time lost: 2 hours.

I keep hoping Illustrator is going to resolve its pattern printing problems once and for all, but my experience suggests that Illustrator 6 still has a ways to go. So let my wasted efforts be a lesson. Filling an intricate outline like the large foreground plane with a relatively complex tile pattern may be enough to break the camel's back. Use tile patterns conservatively, or stay the heck away from them.

Organizing Tile Patterns

If you're still with me after that cheery note, then you're undoubtedly dying to know about the other buttons inside the Pattern dialog box. So here they are:

- **Delete**: Click on this button to delete a selected pattern from the scrolling list. Illustrator removes the pattern from all open illustrations, so exercise caution.

- **Paste**: Ideally, you should save the original objects used to create tile patterns in a separate illustration file. That way, you can always go back and edit them at a later date. But many folks delete the objects the moment they finish establishing the tile in the Pattern dialog box. Luckily, Illustrator is there for you. If you've discarded your original objects, you can always retrieve them by selecting the pattern name and clicking on the Paste button. Illustrator pastes selected versions of the original objects into the illustration window and awaits your next move. Press Return or click on the OK button to confirm the paste.

 After modifying the objects, you can save them as a new pattern. You can also redefine an existing pattern. To accomplish this, select the objects and choose Object » Pattern. Then select the name of the pattern that you want to redefine from the scrolling list and press the Return key. Don't be put off by the fact that Illustrator doesn't show any sign of acknowledging the redefinition. You just have to have faith.

- **Select All Unused**: This button selects all patterns in the scrolling list that are not applied to objects in any open illustration. Since patterns consume space on disk and in RAM, it can be a good idea to delete patterns that you're not using, provided they exist in some other illustration. To delete unused patterns, click on the Select All Unused button, then click on Delete and press Return.

Previewing and Printing Patterns

Tile patterns take a long time to print—when they print at all—so Illustrator permits you to temporarily deactivate them. If you want to proof an illustration without having a tile pattern slow things down, choose File » Document Setup (⌘-Shift-D) and turn off the Preview and Print Patterns check box. From now on, objects filled with tile patterns will print as gray and appear gray on screen.

To reinstate the tile patterns, press ⌘-Shift-D and turn the check box back on. Keep in mind, although you can fill text with a tile pattern and stroke any object with a pattern, filled text and strokes always appear gray on screen, regardless of the Preview and Print Patterns check box. It's Illustrator's way of telling you, "Oh, sure, you *can* apply patterns to text and strokes, but I surely don't recommend it."

Transforming Tiles Inside Objects

I mentioned earlier that Illustrator always transforms a gradient fill along with its object. But things are more flexible where tile patterns are concerned. You can transform an object and its pattern fill together, or transform just the object or just the pattern. Here's how it works:

- To transform tile patterns with their objects, press ⌘-K to display the General Preferences dialog box and turn on the Transform Pattern Tiles check box. This option affects all transformations, including movements made with the arrow tool.

- If you want a tile pattern to remain unmolested no matter how much you may molest the filled object, then leave the Transform Pattern Tiles check box off. Back in Figure 15-30, for example, I was able to freely move the plane, shadow, and background rectangle without jarring the patterns out of perfect alignment.

The Move, Scale, Rotate, Reflect, and Shear dialog boxes are all equipped with two check boxes—Object and Pattern Tiles. By default, just the Object check box is active. This transforms the selected objects without transforming any pattern fills. If you select both Object and Pattern Tiles, Illustrator transforms both items. You can also turn off the Object check box and turn on Pattern Tiles to transform the tiles without affecting the objects at all.

Figure 15-31 shows examples of pattern tiles transformed independently of their objects. Rotating and slanting are particularly useful for camouflaging the linear appearance of a pattern. Scaling is handy for showing off more or less of a pattern at a time. Though I don't show it, you can move a pattern to align tiles with the edges of an object. And flipping . . . well, flipping isn't all that useful, but it's good to have around just in case.

Scaled 50 percent

Rotated 30 degrees

Figure 15-31: You can manipulate a pattern fill independently of its object by turning off the Object option and turning on the Pattern Tiles option inside any transformation dialog box.

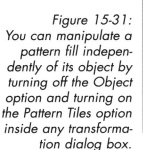

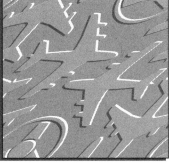
Slanted 40 degrees

Scaled, slanted, and rotated

🔘   If you turn on the Pattern Tiles check box in addition to the Object check box inside *any* dialog box, Illustrator activates the check box in *all* dialog boxes. It also selects the Transform Pattern Tiles option inside the General Preferences dialog box. The arrow tool and all transformation tools will affect both objects and pattern fills until you turn off one of these options.

🔘   On the other hand, if you turn on the Pattern Tiles check box but turn off the Object check box, Illustrator transforms the pattern fill one time only. Adobe was worried that it might be confusing to find yourself transforming only tile patterns—particularly since most objects aren't filled with patterns—so this particular combination of options is not saved as a default.

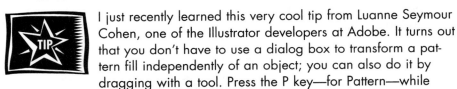

I just recently learned this very cool tip from Luanne Seymour Cohen, one of the Illustrator developers at Adobe. It turns out that you don't have to use a dialog box to transform a pattern fill independently of an object; you can also do it by dragging with a tool. Press the P key—for Pattern—while dragging with the arrow tool or any transformation tool to modify the tile pattern inside a shape and leave the shape unchanged. Just be sure to press the P key *before* you start dragging. (Too bad Adobe didn't implement G-dragging for gradient fills!)

Opening Tile Patterns from the CD-ROM

Before we move out of fills and into the lesser but equally intriguing world of strokes, I should point you to the first-rate library of tile patterns included on the Illustrator 6 CD-ROM. Inside the Illustrator Goodies folder is a folder called Adobe Collector's Edition. Nestled therein are several more folders with folders inside folders. But you can browse them all by simply double-clicking on the ACE Catalog icon. This opens a Fetch file which shows thumbnails of every tile pattern document.

After a few annoying alert boxes, a Find window appears. Click on the Find All button to display a window full of previews, as in Figure 15-32. The first 26 documents contain simple objects, including stars, snowflakes, and arrows. (Though worth checking out, they bear a strong resemblance to Zapf Dingbats characters.) Scroll past these simple objects to get to the tile pattern documents.

Fetch's thumbnails are awfully small, but you can get a remote idea of what's going on. If you see a thumbnail that looks interesting, go back to Illustrator and

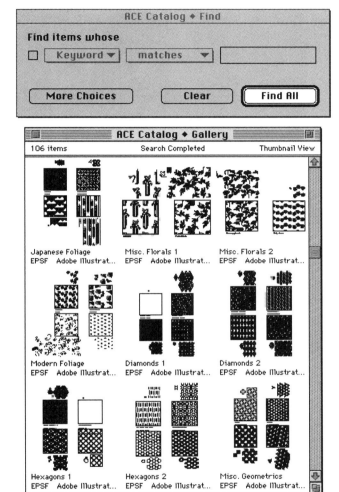

Figure 15-32: Double-click on the ACE Catalog file to browse through a Fetch catalog of thumbnails showing predefined tile patterns.

open the file from the CD. All patterns saved inside that file immediately become available to all open illustrations. The files also include the original objects used to create the tile patterns. All tile patterns are in gray. But the objects are grouped to facilitate the application of different colors.

STROKING

YOUR CURVES

Stroke is a gizmo in the PostScript printing language that controls the appearance of the outline of a path. Strokes share many similarities with fills. A stroke can be any gray value, CMYK color, or named color. A stroke is equally applicable to path and text objects (though you can't stroke imported images). And you apply stroke attributes from the Paint Style palette. But unlike fill, you can't stroke a path with a gradation. Stroked tile patterns don't look right on screen. And stroke includes a handful of unique attributes that fill has no use for (as we will naturally explore in this chapter).

Stroke is a secondary attribute in Illustrator—sort of a Park Place to fill's Boardwalk—for the very same reasons that editable text is sometimes less useful than text converted to paths:

- First, you can't just click any old place on a stroke to select the path. You have to click precisely on the path outline—which runs through the center of the stroke—much like you have to click on the baseline to select type.

- Second, some of Illustrator's functions are downright stroke-unfriendly (as some functions don't work on text). The knife tool destroys strokes, as do many of the Pathfinder filters—namely Divide, Trim, Merge, Crop, Hard, and Soft. You can't find the intersection of two strokes or unite them. The Blend filters ignore strokes and Object » Expand misinterprets them.

- Third, you have to rely on Illustrator to display the stroke properly on screen (the way you rely on Adobe Type Manager to correctly display type). Illustrator is nearly always right on target, but there are times where the onscreen stroke and the printed stroke may not exactly match. Try to make two curves with thick strokes exactly touch each other (without overlapping) and then print the curves to a high-resolution imagesetter to see what I mean. Eyeballing simply isn't as reliable as snapping the points in two unstroked paths, which absolutely guarantees alignment.

And last, the stroke of a path is always uniform in thickness. If you want to create a line of variable thickness, you have to draw it as a filled path, just like "lines" drawn with the brush tool.

Some artists don't use strokes. Or they use strokes as interim measures, ultimately converting the strokes to path outlines using Filter » Objects » Outline Path (as explained later in this chapter). I'm not saying *you* shouldn't use strokes. I use them, most of the illustrations in this book contain strokes—cripes, some of my best friends have strokes! But be aware of their limitations as you are mesmerized by their potential.

Stroking Paths

A stroke strides the outline of a path, just as a monorail strides its electric track. In Figure 16-1, I've applied a couple of different strokes to an open path and a closed path. In each case, I've drawn in the path itself as a thin white line to show how the path always runs through the center of its stroke. This is important to

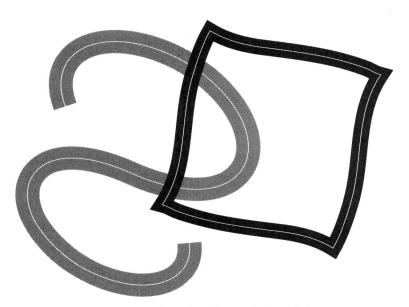

*Figure 16-1: Open and closed paths stroked with heavy outlines.
The paths themselves are shown in white.*

keep in mind when selecting and aligning stroked paths. You can also exploit this feature to create overlay effects, as you will in the "Stacked Stroke and Fill Effects" section later in this chapter.

You can use strokes to exaggerate or mitigate the corners of a path. In Figure 16-2, I applied two different kinds of "joins" to identical starbursts. The black joins look sharp enough to pierce rocks. The gray joins are soft and stubby. You can also create an absolutely inexhaustible supply of dashed strokes, and even round off the dashes if you want.

 Watch out for straight lines that look like they're stroked when they're not. If you draw a straight line by clicking at two points with the pen tool, and Illustrator applies the default settings of a black fill with no stroke, the fill follows the line on screen, creating the appearance of a thin stroke. The problem is, the false stroke won't print accurately, particularly to a high-resolution imagesetter. Be sure to manually assign a stroke using the options in the Paint Style palette, and never accept a thin stroke applied to a straight line at face value.

Figure 16-2: Strokes can be sharp or soft or even dashed. Again, I've drawn the paths in white to show how the strokes build up the corners.

Stroking Type and Text Paths

As with fill, stroke affects type differently depending on how the type is selected:

- If you select a text object with the arrow tool, applying a stroke affects all type along the path. The first example in Figure 16-3 shows selected path text. In the second example, I applied a transparent fill and a thin black stroke. As you can see, Illustrator stroked the type but not the path.

- If you select the path with the direct selection tool, you can apply a stroke to the path only, leaving the text as is. In Figure 16-4, I used the direct selection tool to apply a thick gray stroke to the path. You can also select the rectangle around a text block or the path around area text.

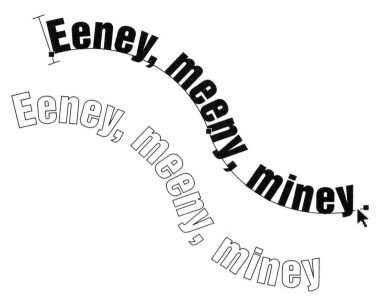

Figure 16-3: If you stroke a text block selected with the arrow tool (top), only the text becomes stroked (bottom).

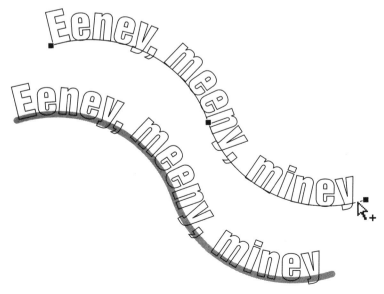

Figure 16-4: Select the path with the direct selection tool (top) to stroke just the path and leave the text unchanged (bottom).

● Select text with the type tool to stroke single characters or words. In this case, stroke is just another character-level formatting attribute that affects selected characters independently of deselected ones, as demonstrated in Figure 16-5. Using the type tool, you can apply several different strokes to a single text object.

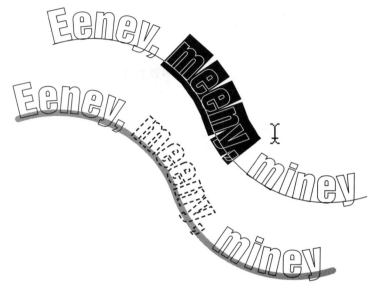

Figure 16-5: By selecting text with the type tool (top), you stroke only the highlighted type (bottom).

Applying a Stroke from the Paint Style Palette

If you were to count all of the options inside the Paint Style palette, you'd find that more are devoted to fill than to stroke. The following steps explain how to use these options to apply a stroke to a selected path or text object:

1. **Select the objects that you want to stroke**.

   If no object is selected, editing the stroke changes the default settings.

2. Expand the Paint Style palette.

If the palette isn't already available, press ⌘-I. Then expand the palette to full size so you can see all three panels, as in Figure 16-6.

3. Click on the Stroke icon.

Figure 16-6 spotlights the selected Stroke icon. A big underline shows that Stroke is active and Fill is not.

4. Specify the color of the stroke by selecting from the row of icons on the right side of the palette.

These icons work just like they do when the Fill icon is selected. From left to right, they are None, White, Black, Process, Custom, and Tile Pattern. (Only Gradient is missing, because you cannot stroke with a gradation.) You can color a stroke with the White, Black, Process, or Custom icon, exactly as described in Chapter 14. Though stroking a path with a tile pattern is just begging for trouble—if it was easy to print, don't you think Illustrator could display it accurately on screen?— you are certainly welcome to apply a pattern as directed in Chapter 15. If you want to remove the outline from a path and leave only the fill, click on the None button.

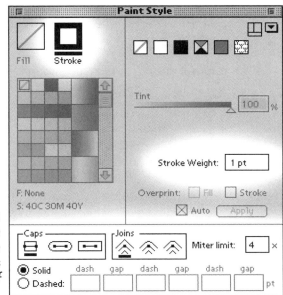

Figure 16-6: Select the Stroke icon and mess around with the spotlighted options to modify the stroke of selected objects.

 You can also drag a swatch from the scrolling list on the left side of the palette and drop it onto the Stroke icon. The Stroke icon doesn't even have to be selected.

5. **Change the Stroke Weight value**.

   This value determines the thickness of the stroke. Illustrator always presents you with a Stroke Weight value of 1 point when you click on the Stroke icon, even if the last objects you stroked had a different thickness.

6. **Select icons from the Caps and Joins options**.

   These options appear in the bottom panel of the Paint Style palette. The Caps icons determine how the stroke wraps around the ends of an open path. The Joins icons control the appearance of the stroke at corner points. The Miter Limit option box appears to the right of the options only when the first Joins icon is selected. Otherwise, it's dimmed. (I'll explain this option in a few moments.)

7. **Select the Dashed radio button to create a dashed outline**.

   Then enter values into the Dash and Gap option boxes to specify the length of each dash and each gap between dashes. (This option, too, will be explained just up ahead, good and trusting reader.) If you don't want a dashed stroke, select the Solid radio button.

8. **Press the Return key**.

   Illustrator returns its focus to the illustration window.

Many options that affect stroke—including the Stroke Weight option box and all the options in the bottom panel of the Paint Style palette—are available anytime a stroke has been assigned, even if the Fill icon is selected. (If the stroke is set to None, all stroke options are dimmed.) This means you can modify these stroke attributes regardless of which icon is active. You only need to select the Stroke icon if you want to change the color of a stroke, and even then you can drag a color swatch and drop it onto the dimmed Stroke icon if you prefer.

Weight, cap, join, and dash pattern are all powerful stroke attributes that bear further explorations. That's why I discuss each one in detail in the following sections.

Line Weight

The Stroke Weight values control the thickness of a stroke. Folks who spent their formative years laying down lines of sticky black ruling tape with X-acto knives prefer the term *line weight*, so that's the term I'll use in my discussions. In Illustrator, line weight is always measured in points, even if the ruler units are set to inches or millimeters. Of course, if you want to create a stroke one inch thick, you can enter *1 in* and press Return. But stroke—like text—is best served by a tiny and precise unit of measurement.

You can enter any number between 0 and 1000 (more than a foot), accurate to 0.001 point. However, I advise against specifying a line weight value smaller than 0.1. A 0.3-point line weight is commonly considered a hairline, so 0.1-point is about as thick as dandruff. Figure 16-7 shows several line weights applied to a frilly path. The 0.1-point line is barely visible. Any thinner simply will not reproduce.

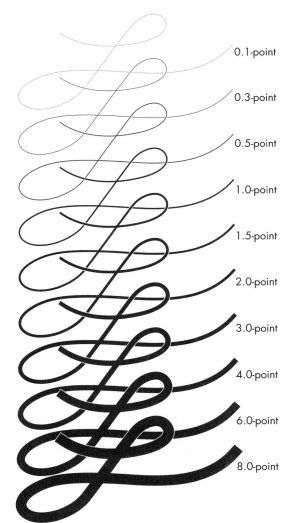

Figure 16-7:
Several examples of
line weights printed
from Illustrator. The top
line is barely visible;
anything thinner is
essentially invisible.

Do *not* enter a line weight of 0. This tells Illustrator to print the thinnest line available from the output device. The thinnest line printable by a 300-dpi laser printer is 0.24-point thick. However, high-resolution imagesetters easily print lines as thin as 0.03-point, or 10 times thinner than a hairline. Such a line cannot possibly survive the reproduction process.

You change line weights a lot in Illustrator, so it's worth knowing how to do so quickly, without using the mouse.

- If a selected line is stroked with white, a shade of black, or a named color, you can press ⌘-I and Tab to activate the Stroke Weight value. Then enter a new value and press the Return key.

- If the line is stroked with a CMYK color, press ⌘-I followed by Shift-Tab twice. (You can also press Tab four times in a row, but pressing Shift-Tab twice seems easier to me.) Then enter a new Stroke Weight value and press Return.

Line Caps

You can select from three *line caps*, which determine the appearance of a stroke at an endpoint. Line caps are generally useful only when stroking an open path. The only exception is when you use line caps in combination with dash patterns, in which case Illustrator applies the cap to each and every dash, as I explain later in this chapter.

The three Caps icons in the Paint Style palette work as follows:

- **Butt cap:** The first icon in the Caps box is the *butt cap* option, the default setting and the most commonly used line cap. (Whether it's fit for polite company I can't say, but *butt* is the official PostScript term for this kind of cap.) Notice the black line that runs through the center of each of the icons in the Caps box. This indicates the position of the path relative to the stroke. When the butt cap option is selected, the stroke ends immediately at an endpoint and is perpendicular to the final course of the path, as in the top diagram in Figure 16-8.

- **Round cap:** The second icon represents a *round cap*, which wraps the stroke around the path to form a circle at the endpoint. The radius of

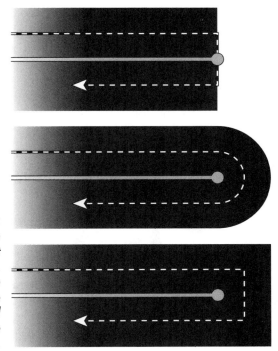

Figure 16-8:
Diagrams of the three
kinds of line caps—butt
(top), round (middle),
and square (bottom). The
gray line indicates the
path, while the dotted
line shows the stroke
moving around the path.

the circle is half the line weight, as demonstrated by the second diagram in Figure 16-8. If you have a 4-point line weight, for example, the round cap extends exactly 2 points out from the endpoint.

The main purpose for using round caps is to soften the appearance of a line. The line appears to taper, rather than abruptly end. I frequently apply round caps, especially when using thick strokes.

Square cap: Last and least is the *square cap* icon. Here, a square is attached to the end of a line; the endpoint is the center of the square. Like the round cap, the square cap sticks out half the line weight from the endpoint, as the bottom diagram in Figure 16-8 shows. The only difference is that the square cap has very definite corners, making it appear to jut out more dramatically.

Use square caps when you want to close a gap. For example, if you want the stroke from an open path to meet with the edge of another stroked path, the square cap gives the open path a little extra length.

Figure 16-9 shows a collection of seven open paths repeated three times, each with different line caps. In the first eye, the lines with butt caps either clear each other or barely touch. In the round cap eye, the caps close many gaps, but you can plainly see that the touching lines are not part of the same path. (See, don't round caps look better? I just love them.) In the third eye, the square caps completely eliminate even the hint of gaps in the corner of the lids and the spot where the top iris path meets the top lid. The square caps give the paths a more substantial appearance all around.

Figure 16-9: I drew each of these eyes using the same collection of open paths. The only difference is the line caps—butt on left, round in the middle, and square on right.

Line Joins

The Paint Style palette offers three *line joins*, which determine the appearance of a stroke at the corners of a path. The stroke always forms a continuous curve at each smooth point in a path, but you can use line joins to clip away the stroke at corner points and cusps. Here's how each of the Joins icons work:

 Miter join: The first Joins icon represents a *miter join*, which is the default setting. If a corner has a miter join, the outside edges of the stroke extend all the way out until they meet to form a crisp corner. The first star in Figure 16-10 is stroked with miter joins. Compare its perfect spikes to the rounded and chopped off corners in the other stars. Watch out, though. Illustrator may cut a miter join short according to the Miter Limit value, explained in the next section.

Figure 16-10: Each of these stars is stroked with a different line join—miter (top), round (middle), and bevel (bottom). Notice that the joins affect all corners in the paths, whether they point out or inward.

 Round join: The second icon is the *round join* option, which is identical in principle to the round cap. Half of the line weight wraps around the corner point to form an arc, as in the second star in Figure 16-10. Round joins and round caps are so similar, in fact, that they are almost exclusively used together. The only time you should avoid round joins is when a dash pattern is involved. Because round joins actually form complete circles around corner points, they can interrupt the flow of the dashes.

 Bevel join: The third and last icon applies a *bevel join*. Very similar to a butt cap, the bevel join shears the stroke off at the corner point. As in the bottom star in Figure 16-10, the bevel join creates a flat edge at each corner point. The length of this flat edge varies depending on the angle of the segments. A gradual angle results in a short bevel; a sharp angle results in a longer one. Figure 16-11 shows a path made up of segments that meet at progressively sharper angles. I've traced the bevels with white lines to demonstrate their increasing lengths. For comparison's sake, the inset shows the five bevels arranged in a row, with the top bevel on left and the bottom bevel on right.

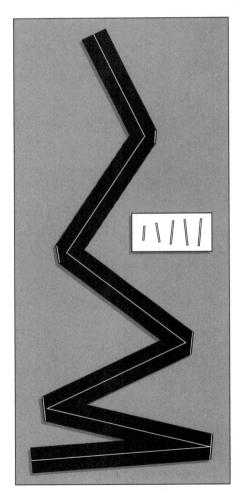

Figure 16-11:
As segments meet at
sharper angles, the bevel
joins lengthen. Each bevel
is repeated in the inset for
side-by-side comparison.

Giving Excessive Miter Joins the Ax

Directly to the left of the Joins icons in the Paint Style palette is the Miter Limit option box. This value tells Illustrator when to chop off excessively long miter joins. The Miter Limit value represents a ratio between the length of the miter—from inside to outside corner—and the line weight, both diagrammed in Figure 16-12. In other words, as long as the miter length is shorter than the line weight multiplied by the Miter Limit value, Illustrator creates a miter join. But if the miter length is longer than the line weight times the Miter Limit value, Illustrator chops off the miter and makes it a bevel join.

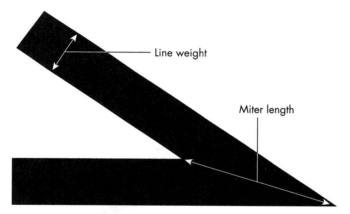

Figure 16-12: The miter length grows as the angle between two segments shrinks.

The length of a miter grows as its segments move closer together. If I had applied miter joins to the path in Figure 16-11, for example, the bottom joins would be more likely to get chopped off than the top joins. A miter can grow especially long when two curved segments meet to form a cusp. As shown in Figure 16-13, two inward-curving segments create a serious Pinocchio effect. What's worse, the join doesn't curve along with the segment; it straightens out after the corner point. The result is an unbecoming spike that looks completely out of place with the rest of the path.

But the solution of hacking away the join (as so painfully illustrated in the second example of Figure 16-13) is a harsh compromise. In fact, it's not a compromise at all. Illustrator either gives you a ridiculously long miter, or it bevels it completely. If you want to preserve the precise quality of a miter join without allowing it to take on a life of its own—and a rather lewd one at that—you should manually

Figure 16-13: It is truly a shame that miter joins lose control when applied to curved segments (top, extending off to the right), but is chopping them clean off (bottom) really the best solution?

adjust your path to increase the angle between segments, which in turn reduces the length of the miter. The Miter Limit option should be considered a last resort.

The Miter Limit value can range from 1 to 500, provided that the value multiplied by the line weight doesn't exceed 1800 points. The default value is 4. A miter limit of 1 tells Illustrator to lop off every join, and is therefore identical to selecting the bevel join icon. If either the round or bevel join icon is selected, the Miter Limit option appears dimmed.

Dash Patterns

The options along the bottom of the Paint Style palette allow you to apply a *dash pattern* of a stroke. Dash patterns are repetitive interruptions in a stroke. For example, a standard coupon border in a newspaper ad is a dash pattern.

The Solid radio button creates a solid stroke with no interruptions. To create a dash pattern, select the Dashed radio button, which brings to life six previously dimmed option boxes. Each option box represents an interval, measured in points, during which the stroke is on or off over the course of the path. The Dash values determine the length of the dashes; the Gap values determine the length of the gaps between the dashes.

You don't have to fill all Dash and Gap options with values. In fact, most folks simply fill in the first pair of option boxes and leave the rest blank. Whatever you do, Illustrator repeats the values you enter and ignores the empty option boxes.

 If you like, you can just enter a value into the first Dash option box and be done with it. Illustrator applies the value to both the dashes and gaps. If you enter a Dash value of 6, for example, the stroke is on for 6 points and then off for 6 points.

The ghost grid in Figure 16-14 shows a sampling of dashes created using only the first pair of Dash and Gap options. These horrifying members of the spirit world are arranged into columns and rows according to their Dash and Gap values.

If you scrutinize the phantoms carefully—a task best left to the stout of heart, I admit—you may notice that the dashes pile up at the point where the path starts and stops. For example, each eerie eye begins at the bottom of the shape, which is why you sometimes see an extra long dash at this point. Each macabre mouth begins at the top, and every spectral shroud starts in the bottom left corner.

When stroking a closed path, you ideally want the sum of the dash and gap to divide evenly into the length of the path outline. This way, you don't have any dash pile-ups. Unfortunately, Illustrator provides no mechanism for telling you how long a path is, so even if math is your friend, you can't figure it out. So your only recourse is trial and error. In the first ghoul in Figure 16-15, I applied a Dash value of 6 and a Gap of 3 to the eyes. But as the white circles show, I ended up with an extra long dash at the bottom of each shape. The solution? I gradually raised the Gap value in 0.01-point increments until the dash shrunk back to the proper size. A Gap value of 3.11 finally did the trick.

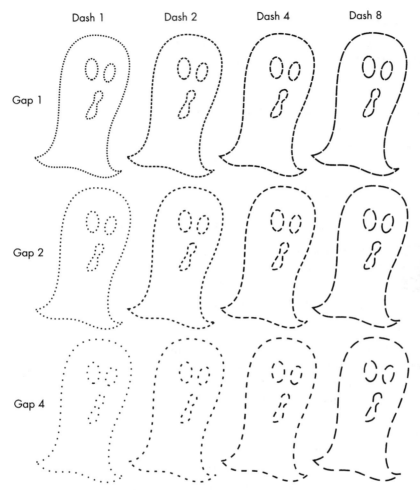

Figure 16-14: A grid of dash patterns demonstrating 12 combinations of Dash and Gap values.

Besides the predictable uses, dash patterns are great for creating sparkles. The sparkles in the hair and on the ear of the woman in Figure 16-16 are actually circles—drawn with the oval tool—stroked with dash patterns. The Dash values range from 1 to 3 points, with Gap values from 2 to 7. The length of the sparkles is a function of the line weights, which run as high as 18 points. As you can see, the dashes actually flair as they go around the circle, thickening up toward the outer edge. It's a simple, elegant effect.

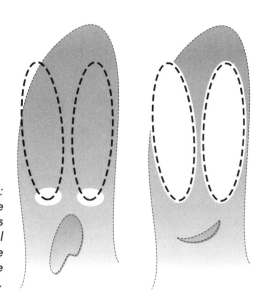

Figure 16-15:
After applying a stroke
with a 6-point dashes
and 3-point gaps (left), I
gradually raised the
gap value to eliminate
any dash pile-ups (right).

Figure 16-16:
Before boarding the Orient
Express, this temptress
adorned herself with several
fetching (but surprisingly
cheap) dash-pattern sparkles.

Using Line Caps with Dash Patterns

Another thing to consider when applying a dash pattern is the effect of the active line cap. This is because Illustrator treats the beginning and ending of each dash in a pattern as a start and stop in the stroke. Therefore, both ends of a dash are affected by the selected line cap, which makes it possible to create round dashes.

I stroked each of the three lines in Figure 16-17 with a 16-point line weight that included a dash pattern and round caps. I entered 0—yes, 0—for the Dash value and 26 for the Gap. When you specify the length of each dash to be 0, you instruct Illustrator to allow no distance between the round cap at the beginning of the dash and the round cap at the end of the dash. The two round caps therefore meet to form a complete circle.

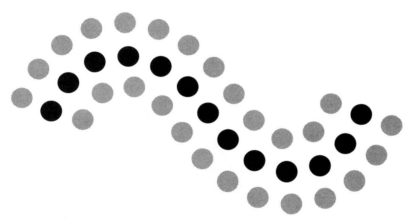

Figure 16-17: Three lines stroked with the same dash pattern in different colors. I selected the round cap icon and set the Dash value to 0, resulting in circular dots.

Figure 16-18 shows a diagram of two dashes set to 0 with round caps. The path appears in gray; the dotted lines show the round cap wrapping around the 0-point dash. Notice that the only thing separating the circles is the Gap value. The Gap value defines the distance from the center of one circle to the center of the next, while the line weight determines the diameter of each circle. Therefore, to prevent one circular dot from touching the next, the Gap value must be larger than the Stroke Weight value. In Figure 16-17, for example, the 26-point gap is greater than the 16-point line weight, creating a 10-point break between each pair of dots.

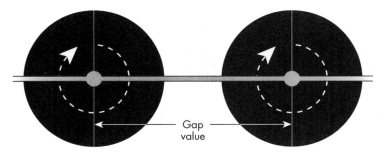

Figure 16-18: A diagram of a dash pattern with a 0-point dash and round caps. The thick gray line represents the path, while the dotted line shows the stroke wrapping around each dash.

If the Gap and Stroke Weight values are equal, the dots just barely touch. And if the gap is smaller than the line weight, the dots overlap.

Raising the Dash value above 0 elongates the dashes so they're no longer circular. The larger the Dash value, the more the dashes look like little submarines.

Stacked Stroke and Fill Effects

You can achieve alternatively practical and remarkable effects by cloning an object in place and varying stroke and fill attributes from one clone to the next. By stacking a series of strokes and fills on top of each other, you cover up some portions of the strokes and fills, and permit other portions to show through. It may sound weird, but it's merely another technique for getting precisely what you want out of this powerful program.

Fill on Stroke

The problem with stroke is that you can't scoot it side to side on a path, the way you can scoot type along the baseline using baseline shift. The stroke always straddles the path, so that one half of the stroke lies on one side and one half lies on the other.

Why is this a problem? Well, suppose you want to draw a thick outline around some important text. In the top example in Figure 16-19, I've applied a 3-point stroke. This means the stroke cuts 1.5 points into the letters, making them illegible and terribly ugly.

Front Page News
Front Page News

Figure 16-19: Type with a 3-point stroke (top), and the same type with a 6-point stroke topped off by a filled clone with no stroke (bottom).

Ideally, you'd simply ask Illustrator to move the stroke to the outside of the path. But, ask though you may, Illustrator will ignore you. The following, nonverbal solution is much more productive:

1. Set the stroke to twice the desired line weight. I set mine to twice 3-point, which makes 6-point.

2. Clone the text. You can either press ⌘-C, ⌘-F or ⌘-Shift-Option-↑, ↓.

3. Remove the stroke by selecting the None icon in the Paint Style palette.

4. If the selected object is not already filled, assign a fill. In my case, I filled the letters with white.

The result is the second example in Figure 16-19. The white clone blocks out the portion of the stroke that intrudes into the letters. Half of the stroke from the original letters appears outside the filled clone. Because I doubled the line weight to 6-point, I'm left with the same 3-point outline as in the previous example. But this time, it looks way the heck better.

 Besides permitting you to scoot the stroke outside your letters, this fill-on-stroke technique increases your range of options. For example, you can offset the filled clone to create a slightly three-dimensional look. In the first example of Figure 16-20, I nudged the clone up and to the right one point. The black stroke is now two points thick above and to the right of the letters, and four points thick below and to the left. In the second example in Figure 16-20, I nudged the clone another point up and to the right. I also selected the original letters and applied round joins to smooth away the corners.

Front Page News

Front Page News

Figure 16-20: The result of nudging the cloned letters one point (top) and two points (bottom) up and to the right. I also rounded off the stroked letters in the second example.

If you want to scoot the stroke to the *inside* of a path—exactly the opposite effect demonstrated in Figure 16-19—you have to use Illustrator's masking function. First stroke the path with twice the desired line weight. Then clone the path, select both the clone and the original, and choose Object » Masks » Make. For more information on using and abusing masks, see Chapter 17.

Stroke on Fill

The opposite of fill-on-stroke is—you guessed it—stroke-on-fill. You clone a path, make the fill transparent, and apply a stroke. The purpose of this technique is to reinstate a stroke that gets covered up or appears partially obscured.

In Figure 16-21, I started with my flashy News logo positioned in front of a stripe (which is actually a slanted rectangle). I wanted to make the logo appear translucent, so that the white of the letters and the gray of the stripe mixed together. After converting the letters to path outlines, I combined them into a single compound path (⌘-8). Then I selected both the letters and the stripe, cloned the shapes, chose Filter » Pathfinder » Intersect to retain the overlap area, and applied a light gray fill. (I could have used the Soft filter instead of Intersect, but that would have destroyed the original letter outlines, which I still need.) I also set the stroke to None, because I only wanted to stroke the letters, not the light gray area.

The problem with the result—shown in the second example in the figure—is that the light gray overlap obscures some of the stroke. So to re-establish the stroke, I applied the stroke-on-fill technique. I selected the white letter outlines,

Figure 16-21:
I created a translucent effect by assembling white letters and a gray stripe (top) and adding a light gray overlap with the Intersect filter (middle). Then I pasted the stroked letters in front with a transparent fill (bottom).

copied them (⌘-C), selected the light gray shapes, and pasted the letters in front (⌘-F). Then I set the fill to None to achieve the effect shown in the bottom example of Figure 16-21. This creates a separate stroke above the fray, making it appear as if the letters have multiple fills. It's a simple but extremely useful effect.

Stroke on Stroke

Now we leave the realm of the practical and ascend to the plane of pure special effects. You can stack differently stroked clones onto each other to create parallel lines, outlined lines, hollow dashes, and lines with depth. These aren't what I would call strictly practical techniques, but they can be a lot of fun. And no matter how many pages I devote to sharing a few of my effects with you, you'll be able to come up with twice as may of your own an hour later.

First, the basics. The top example in Figure 16-22 shows two identical lines, one in front of the other. The first line has a 12-point black stroke, while the clone in front of it has an 8-point white stroke. The white stroke clears a path through the black one, leaving what appear to be two parallel 2-point lines.

Figure 16-22:
Three sets of stacked paths,
each with a 12-point black
stroke in back and an 8-point
white stroke in front. I assigned
butt caps to the top lines,
round caps to the middle, and
square caps to the bottom.

Both of the strokes in the top example include butt caps. But if you want to connect the ends of the paths to create a single, continuous outline, you'd apply a round cap or square cap. In fact, this is precisely how I arrived at the other lines in Figure 16-22. I applied round caps to produce the second example and square caps to get the third.

Figure 16-23 shows the same three sets of lines from Figure 16-22, but this time I've introduced dash patterns. In every case, the Dash value was set to 8 and the Gap to 16. In the butt cap example at top, this resulted in a series of fragmented dashes, almost like a pattern of equal signs. But with round and square caps applied, each dash turns into an identifiable unit with either curved or straight edges.

Figure 16-23:
The same paths from
Figure 16-22, subject
to dash patterns with
a Dash value of 8 and
a Gap of 16.

Now you know everything there is to know. From here on, you can take off in a million different directions. You can add as many clones as you want, stroking each clone with a progressively thinner line weight to reveal portions of lower clones and cover up other portions. You can alternate line caps and experiment with the Dash and Gap values.

Figure 16-24 shows the evolutionary progression of a squad of flying sushi rolls. Starting from the second example in Figure 16-23, I selected the top line and changed the Dash and Gap values to 0 and 24 respectively. This not only resulted in absolutely circular white dollops of rice, but it maintained the rhythm—or *periodicity*—of the pattern. Before, the Dash and Gap values were 6 and 18, which add up to 24. Now, they still add up to 24. As long as I maintain this total, the dashes remain in alignment. Also worth noting, the stroke starts on the left side of the figure. This is why the rice circles appear on the left sides of the black seaweed wrappers. I didn't do anything special to achieve this effect; Illustrator did it for me. What a wonderful sushi chef Illustrator would have been.

To create the bits of avocado in the second line of rolls, I cloned the white path and changed the color to gray and the line weight to 4 points. Finally, I copied the original black path and pasted it in back of the white path. I then set the line weight to 24 points, selected the butt cap, and set the Dash and Gap values to 4 and 20. This created the all-important wings shown in the last row in Figure 16-24. To create the shadows behind the sushi, I selected both the wings and the seaweed wrappers. Then I copied both shapes, pasted them in back, nudged them down and to the right, and colored them with light gray. Sushi squadron, you are ready to fly.

Figure 16-24:
I kept cloning the line and adjusting the line weights, dash patterns, and colors to create the feared flying sushi squadron.

Selecting Stacked Strokes

Selecting from a bunch of identical cloned lines can prove very confusing. You can always select the path on top, but how do you select the others? One way is to periodically lock paths with Arrange » Lock (⌘-1). For example, to select the black path in the second row of sushi in Figure 16-24, you could click on the line with the arrow tool, press ⌘-1, click again, press ⌘-1, and click a third time. This would select the front line of avocado, lock it, select the next line of white rice, lock it, and then select the black seaweed wrappers. When you finish editing the path, unlock everything by pressing ⌘-2.

 Locking requires that you count your way down. To select a path in back of three others, you have to click and lock three times, and then click a fourth. If you need more visual feedback to prevent your brain from inverting, use Arrange » Hide (⌘-3) instead of Lock. Select the front path and then press ⌘-3 to hide it. The path disappears temporarily, showing you that it's now out of your way. When you finish with your edits, press ⌘-4 to bring the hidden paths back.

Making Deep Strokes

I don't know if you remember back this far, but in Figure 11-20—I know, that was several chapters ago—I created an emblem using stacked strokes to produce depth effects. Well no matter, I'm going to show you how to produce similar effects in this section.

After stacking a few strokes on top of each other, all you have to do to produce the effect of depth is nudge the paths slightly. The top pair of shapes in Figure 16-25 originate from a modified letter Z from the Sho font. (There are two Z's in the figure, in case you're having problems focusing.) The letter is repeated a total of four times, stroked from back to front with 16-point black, 8-point gray, 4-point black, and 2-point gray. It just looks like a bunch of strokes on top of each other, moderately interesting if you're a stripe enthusiast, but that's about it.

But look what happens when I nudge the paths. In the second example in Figure 16-25, I have nudged each path up and to the left with respect to the path behind it. In each case, I nudged the path as far as I could without having it go outside the boundaries set by the 16-point black path in back. This way, there's always a hint of black around the edge of each stroke, enough to suggest depth without pushing the illusion too far.

The effect also works with dash patterns. In the first example of Figure 16-26, I took the second Z from Figure 16-25 and applied a dash pattern with a Dash value

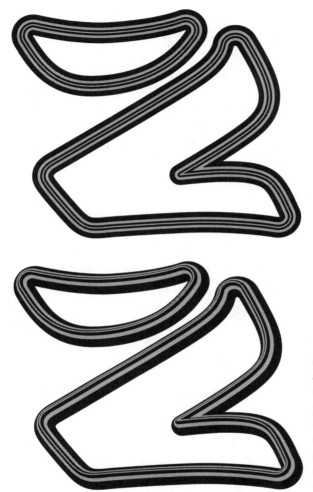

Figure 16-25:
A simple collection of
four identical stacked
paths with progres-
sively thinner strokes
(top) and the same
paths and strokes
slightly offset from
each other (bottom).

of 0 and a Gap of 20. It looks like a bird's-eye view of a bunch of truffles. In the second example, I returned the top two paths to solid lines. Now we have a track mounted on top of a layer of suction feet. If you can dream it up, you can create it.

Now, Sho is a calligraphic, almost primitive looking type-face that lends itself to weird depth effects. Since you prob-ably don't have a copy of Sho lying around, you might be wondering how you come up with a primitive font of your own to experiment with. The answer, of course, is to make one. In Figure 16-27, I took a character set in Helvetica Bold and converted it

Figure 16-26:
Two variations on the Z
from the previous figure,
created using dash
patterns with a Dash value
of 0 and a Gap of 20.

to paths using Type » Create Outlines. Then I used Filter » Distort » Roughen
to pound some bumps and dents into the path. But be sure you apply the
Roughen filter before you start cloning and stroking the path. If you apply
Roughen to several paths at a time, you'll get a random effect like the one
show at the bottom of Figure 16-27.

Figure 16-27:
The result of applying the
Roughen filter and then cloning
the path and stacking the strokes
(top). Compare this to what hap-
pens if you apply Roughen after
you clone and stroke (bottom).

Fashioning Arrowheads without Flint

That's it for the stroke options in the Paint Style palette. From here on out, I'll be discussing a few commands from the Filter menu that specifically affect strokes. First among these is Filter » Stylize » Add Arrowheads, which permits you to add arrowheads to the ends of open paths.

After selecting an open path—the filter doesn't work on closed paths or text objects—choose Filter » Stylize » Add Arrowheads to display the Add Arrowheads

Figure 16-28:
The Add Arrowheads
dialog box lets you
select from 27 different
arrowheads that you can
add to either end of an
open path.

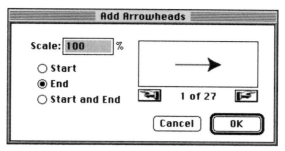

dialog box shown in Figure 16-28. The size of the arrowhead is dependent upon two factors—the line weight of the selected path and the percentage value in the Scale option box. Figure 16-29 shows five paths with different line weights, varying from 0.5 to 6 points, each with the Scale value set to 100 percent. Illustrator's default scaling generally suits 1-point and 2-point lines, but you'll want to raise or lower the Scale value if the line is thinner or thicker, respectively.

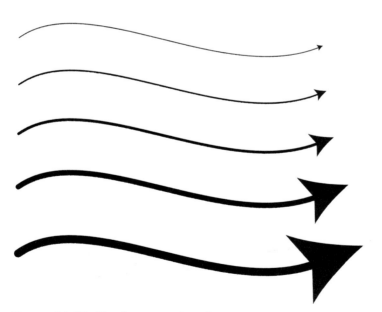

Figure 16-29: The first arrowhead option as it appears when applied to lines 0.5, 1, 2, 4, and 6 points thick. For all lines, the Scale value was set to 100 percent.

Illustrator lets you specify whether you want to apply the arrowhead to one end, the other, or both ends of the open path. Which end is which depends on how you drew the path. Generally, you just want to make a guess and go for it. If it turns out to be the wrong end, press ⌘-Z and ⌘-Shift-Option-E to undo and redisplay the Add Arrowheads dialog box. Then try the other end.

You have 27 arrowheads to choose from. Scroll through the collection by clicking on one of the two hand icons. Figure 16-30 shows 26 of the arrowheads in order—numbers 2 through 14 down the left side and 15 through 27 down the right.

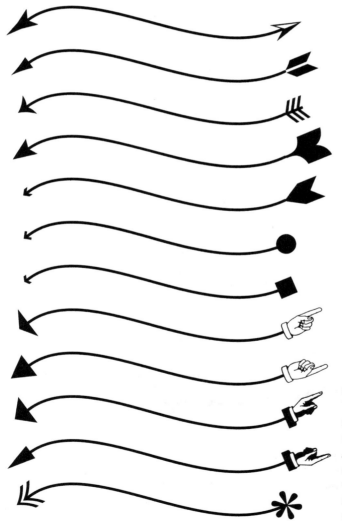

Figure 16-30:
You can apply any of these festive arrowheads using the Add Arrowheads filter. In each case, the line weight is 2 points and the Scale value was set to 100 percent.

(Arrowhead number 1 appears in Figure 16-29.) Note that you can only assign one variety of arrowhead at a time. If you want to assign an arrow to one end of a path and a tail to the other, you have to choose the Add Arrowheads command twice.

After you press the Return key, Illustrator assigns the arrowhead to the path. The arrowhead is a separate path—or in some cases, several paths—that Illustrator groups with the original open path. This is important to keep in mind when transforming the path. If you scale the path disproportionately, for example, you'll squish or stretch the arrowhead. If this happens, select the arrowhead with the direct selection tool, delete it, and then apply a new arrowhead.

If you select the line and arrowhead with the arrow tool, the Paint Style palette displays question marks for both the Fill and Stroke icons. This is because the line is stroked but presumably not filled, while the arrowhead is filled but not stroked. If you want to change the fill or stroke of either portion of the object, use the direct selection tool to select either line or arrowhead independently.

 If you've already positioned the open path exactly where you want it, you'll notice that Illustrator appends the arrowhead to the end of the path, elongating it. To move the arrowhead back into the proper position, try this: Marquee around the entire arrowhead with the direct selection tool. This selects both the arrowhead and the endpoint of the line. Then drag the arrowhead by its tip and snap it onto the previous location of the endpoint. This technique doesn't always do the trick when working with curved lines, but it fixes straight lines without a hitch.

Converting Strokes to Filled Paths

Illustrator provides two filters that convert stroked lines to filled shapes. One is Filter » Objects » Outline Path, and the other is Filter » Stylize » Calligraphy. The latter produces an effect that you could apply manually in about 12 seconds, were there any reason on earth to do so. But the former is as practical as a good pair of shoes.

Choose Filter » Objects » Outline Path to instruct Illustrator to trace around the stroke of a selected object. Figure 16-31 shows a star that used to be stroked with a 6-point outline. Illustrator actually traced two paths around the stroke, one along the inside and the other along the outside, resulting in a compound path.

 As you can see in the first example in the figure, the program has to trace all the way into the miter joins, which makes for quite a few overlapping segments. To remove the overlaps, choose Filter » Pathfinder » Unite. As you can see in the second star in Figure 16-31, the Unite filter removes overlapping segments and simplifies the path in the bargain

Figure 16-31: Starting with a star with no fill and a 6-point stroke, I applied the Outline Path filter (left) followed by the Unite filter (right).

Why is Outline Path so gosh-darn wonderful? Take as examples the arrows in Figure 16-32. I started with a 4-point line with a nondescript arrowhead. Then I selected the line independently of the arrowhead with the direct selection tool, and converted it to a closed path using the Outline Path command. I next selected both the converted path and the arrowhead and combined them into a single shape using Filter » Pathfinder » Unite. To get the result shown in the second example in the figure, I filled the arrow shape with white, stroked it with a thin black outline, and cloned the path to create a light gray drop shadow. Without the Outline Path filter, this would have been very difficult to pull off.

But while the second example in Figure 16-32 would have been difficult without Outline Path, the third example would have been impossible. Here I used our old friend Filter » Objects » Offset Path to create a larger version of the arrow path. (I set the Offset value to 2 and the Line Join option to Round.) Then I nudged the first arrow up and to the right a little and filled both paths with the same gray-to-white gradation. Finally, I used the gradient vector tool to point one gradation one direction and the other in the opposite direction.

Figure 16-33 demonstrates another of Outline Path's miracles—the filter permits you to create variable-width lines. In the top example, I took a converted letter with a 16-point black stroke, abused it with Filter » Distort » Roughen, cloned and nudged the beleaguered path, and applied an 8-point gray stroke to the clone. It's very similar to what I did back in Figure 16-27.

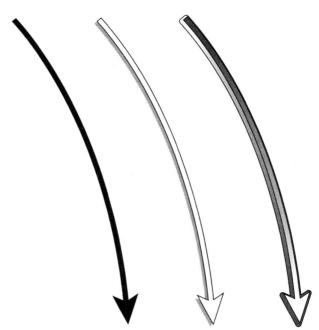

Figure 16-32:
After adding an
arrowhead to a line
(left), I converted the
line to a closed path
and united it with the
arrowhead (middle).
Then I applied the
Offset Path filter and
filled both paths with
gradations (right).

In the second example, I introduced a new element—Outline Path—and arrived at a significantly different result. I started with the same 16-point *Z* but immediately converted the stroke with the Outline Path filter. Then I applied the same settings as before with the Roughen filter. But this time, the Roughen command modified both edges of the compound path around the *Z*, randomly altering the thickness of the outline. (By contrast, the outline of the top *Z*, while random in shape, is uniformly thick.) I could no longer clone the path and change its stroke, so I chose the Offset Path filter and entered a value of −4. This produces a similar effect to reducing the stroke by 8 points since the filter shaves 4 points off either side of the path. The Offset command produced a lot of garbage, so I manually decided what to keep and what to throw away with the direct selection tool and Delete key. Then I nudged the path up and to the left and applied a gray fill. As you can see, Outline Path and Offset Path permitted me to create an effect that's more prehistoric than ever.

Meanwhile, Filter » Stylize » Calligraphy takes a line and makes it look like it was drawn with the brush tool. (Of course, if you're like most folks, you haven't touched the brush tool since I explained it back in Chapter 4, which only enhances your burning interest in the Calligraphy filter.) The Calligraphy filter simply offsets a selected line and joins the offset and original paths into a single

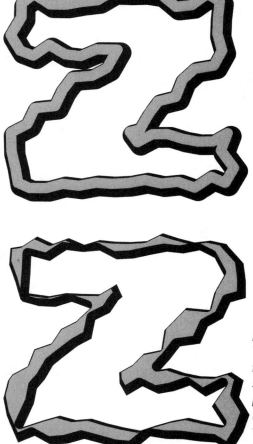

Figure 16-33:
The effect of the Roughen
filter on a couple of
stroked paths (top) com-
pared with its effect on a
few filled shapes created
with the Outline Path
command (bottom).

shape. When you choose the command, Illustrator presents you with a dialog box asking the distance (Pen Width) and direction (Pen Angle) of the offset.

In Figure 16-34, for example, I drew one of those loopy underline things that John Hancock might have used to courteously irritate King George III. Then I applied Filter » Stylize » Calligraphy with a Pen Width value of 4 points and a Pen Angle of 120 degrees. The right example in the figure is the result.

Now, I could have gotten exactly that same effect by cloning my original loopy path and joining the endpoints of the clone and original with straight segments using Object » Join. Because the calligraphic path is a single shape, the overlapping

Figure 16-34: Thanks to the Calligraphy filter, we can all take a ridiculously loopy path (left) and embellish it with revolutionary flare (right).

areas drop out and turn transparent. There's really no way to fix this problem that doesn't involve a lot of manual labor, so what is the point? This is, by all accounts, a very goofy filter.

Twisty-Turny Tile Patterns

 Illustrator 6 offers a new filter that takes up where tile patterns leave off. The Path Pattern filter repeats a tile pattern along the twists and turns in a path, much as if the patterns were characters of text fit to a curve.

Figure 16-35 shows the difference between a path stroked with a tile pattern from the Paint Style palette and the same tile pattern applied with the Path Pattern filter. (In both cases, the line weight was set to 36 points. I added a black drop shadow behind the left path to accent the boundaries of the stroke.) In the left example, the tile pattern looks like it's cut from a sheet of wall paper. But the path pattern in the right example precisely follows the course of the path.

*Figure 16-35: A tile pattern applied to a stroke from
the Paint Style palette (left) compared with the same
tile pattern applied with the Path Pattern filter (right).*

Filter » Stylize » Path Pattern applies a pattern as a series of new paths, which
you can edit just like any other paths inside the program. For this reason, path
patterns don't cause printing problems, as can tile patterns assigned from the Paint
Style palette. So feel free to use path patterns, confident in the knowledge that
your artwork will print like a champ.

 The Adobe Illustrator Startup file includes a few tile patterns
created specially to serve as path patterns. But the CD-ROM
that ships with Illustrator 6 includes way more. Look inside
the Illustrator Goodies folder on the CD to find a folder
called Path Patterns. Open this folder and double-click on the
Path Patterns Catalog file to view a Fetch catalog which shows the contents of
the path pattern files. (For more information on browsing a Fetch catalog,
read the "Opening Tile Patterns from the CD-ROM" section at the end of
Chapter 15.) Open a file in one of the subfolders inside the Path Patterns
folder to make its patterns available to all other open illustrations.

Using the Path Pattern Filter

Before applying a path pattern, select the path you want to stroke and set both the fill and stroke attributes in the Paint Style palette to None. I know this may sound weird, but because the Path Pattern filter converts tile patterns into paths, it leaves your original path behind, completely unharmed. If the original path is filled or stroked, you may be able to see it through any nooks and crannies in the tile pattern. Of course, you can always select the original path and change its fill or stroke later on, but it's a good precaution to eliminate any potential interference up front.

Next, select the path and choose Filter » Stylize » Path Pattern. Illustrator displays the Path Pattern dialog box, shown in Figure 16-36. Because the options in this dialog box are so plentiful and unusual, I describe them individually in the following list:

- **Sides and Corners**: To apply a tile pattern to a path, select it from the scrolling list. You can apply a pattern to each of three icons in the top left corner of the dialog box—Sides, Inner Corner, and Outer Corner. The pattern assigned to the Sides icon affects the majority of the path, including all segments and smooth points. But wherever Illustrator runs into a corner point, it applies the patterns assigned to one of the two Corner icons. The Inner Corner icon affects corners that point outward

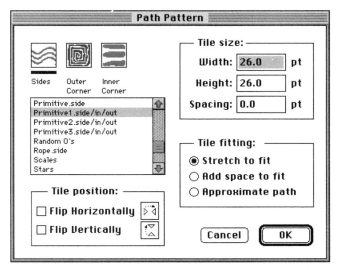

Figure 16-36: Select the tile patterns you want to apply from the scrolling list and enter a line weight into the Width option box.

from the center of the path; the Outer Corner icon affects inward-pointing corners. (If you leave the Inner Corner and Outer Corner icons set to None, Illustrator skips the corner points and does its best to apply the Side pattern to the rest of the path.)

Many of the predefined patterns are specifically designed to serve as side and corner patterns. They end with suffixes like *side* and *inner*. Others can serve in various capacities. The Primitive patterns from the Ancient file off the CD share the suffix *side/in/out*, which means you can use them any way you want to. In Figure 16-37, I applied three Primitive patterns to a primitive shape. Those ancient types would have loved it.

Tile Size: To specify what amounts to the line weight of the stroke, enter a value into the Width option box. The Height value automatically changes to keep the tile proportional. (You can't modify the Width and Height values independently, and there's no reason to do so. Illustrator stretches the tiles to fit automatically, so just let it do its stuff.)

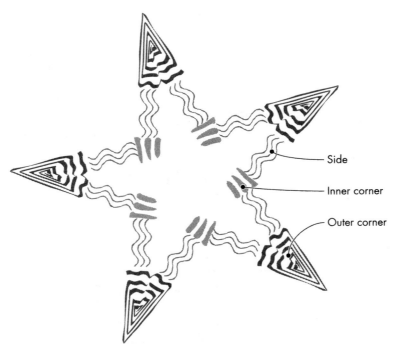

*Figure 16-37: If a path contains corners—like this star—
Illustrator applies different patterns to the sides, inner corners,
and outer corners.*

If you want to insert blank space between individual tiles, enter a value into the Spacing option box. To make the tiles fit together without gaps—usually the better choice—leave the Spacing value set to 0.

Tile Fitting: By default, the Stretch to Fit radio button is selected, which tells Illustrator to stretch the tiles as needed so they exactly fit the segments between corner points. If you want to apply the tiles exactly as they were drawn, with no stretching—what are you, some kind of tile purist?—then select the Add Space to Fit radio button. Figure 16-38 demonstrates how this option changes the way the Primitive patterns fit my star.

The third radio button—Approximate Path—is applicable to rectangles only. When selected, it changes the size of the stroked rectangle to fit the tiles. This option is especially useful when creating a rectangular border around an illustration. If the selected path in the illustration window is not a rectangle, Illustrator ignores this setting and stretches the tiles, as by default.

Figure 16-38: Selecting the Add Space to Fit option prevents Illustrator from stretching tiles and inserts gaps in between tiles instead.

Tile Position: Use these check boxes to flip the individual tiles in a pattern horizontally or vertically. Nothing special. These options are here if you need them, that's all.

Applying Patterns to Open Paths

Back in Figure 16-35, I stroked a couple of open paths. If you look back at the figure, you may notice that I've created special little curlicues that extend off either end of the right path. These are known as *cap tiles*, and you can apply them using a special, undocumented trick.

First select an open path and press the ⌘ key while choosing Filter » Stylize » Path Pattern. This brings up the expanded dialog box shown in Figure 16-39. It contains the same options—though sometimes in different places—plus two additional icons in the upper left corner, Begin Cap and End Cap. The Begin Cap icon applies a tile to the first endpoint in the selected path, and the End Cap icon assigns a tile to the last endpoint.

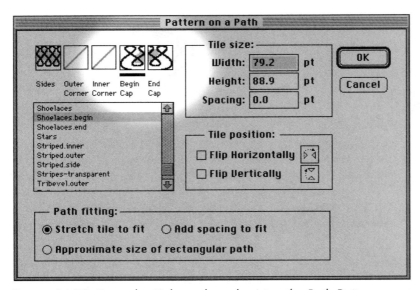

Figure 16-39: Press the ⌘ key when choosing the Path Pattern command to display the Begin Cap and End Cap icons, shown here as spotlighted.

This dialog box has a habit of coming up when you press ⌘-Shift-Option-E to repeat the Path Pattern filter, since the ⌘ key is down. If you don't want to apply cap tiles, or if the selected path is closed, just leave Begin Cap and End Cap set to None.

The Illustrator 6 CD doesn't ship with any patterns specifically designed as cap tiles. But you can use any tile you like as a cap tile. Or if you're feeling ambitious, try designing some cap tiles of your own. Figure 16-40 shows the two cap tiles I designed along with the side tile between them. That little mark below the side tile is a bit of the flourish from the cap tiles. In order to maintain alignment, each tile has to be the same height. So I duplicated this bit of the flourish in the side tile and set its fill and stroke to None to make it invisible.

Figure 16-40: The original objects used to create the beginning cap (left), side tile (middle), and end cap (right). The mark under the side tile is there to ensure proper alignment.

Text Patterns

Earlier, I mentioned that path patterns are like text on a curve. Well, not quite. Though Illustrator can fit characters of type to the dips and bumps in a path, it can't stretch the characters the way the Path Pattern filter stretches tiles.

 If you want to create text that stretches on a path, just convert the text to a tile pattern and apply it to a path using the Side icon in the Path Pattern dialog box. It's really very easy.

In Figure 16-41, I started with a line of type converted to paths. I also added a little rectangle at the end to serve as a spacer; if Illustrator repeated the text more than once, I didn't want the *t* from *Most* running into the *T* from *Those*. I set the fill and stroke of the rectangle to None to make it invisible. Then I selected all the characters and the rectangle, chose Object » Pattern, clicked on the New button inside the Pattern dialog box, and named the tile Dream. Then I selected a large open path and used the Path Pattern filter to apply the Dream tile to it. The result is the second example in Figure 16-41. Notice how Illustrator has stretched the tops of many characters—such as the M's—something it can't do to text on a curve, included for the sake of comparison at the bottom of the figure.

Figure 16-41: After converting a line of text with a spacer rectangle to a tile pattern (top), I used the Path Pattern filter to stretch the text to fit onto a path (middle). By comparison, plain old text on a curve looks pretty clunky (bottom).

CHAPTER **17**

BLENDS, MASKS, AND SPECIAL INKS

Blends and masks continue to be two of Illustrator's most powerful and flexible capabilities. They are truly tools of the advanced user. One permits you to create custom gradations and shape morphings; the other permits you to clip those gradations—or any other collection of objects— inside a path. These are not tools for the timid; the blend tool takes skill, effort, and time to master, and the mask function can choke the printer if used unwisely or in excess. But if you value control and versatility, blends and masks are for you.

This chapter concludes with a feature new to Illustrator 6, termed Ink Pen. This unusual and exceptionally complex feature combines the powers of blending and masking to create cross-hatch, line, and dot patterns. Unlike tile patterns, Ink Pen patterns can change over the course of the shape, becoming progressively lighter and darker like gradations. You need a strong will to put up with the Ink Pen Effects dialog box—easily the most daunting collection of options inside all of Illustrator—but your labor will not go unrewarded.

In other words, welcome to the hard stuff in Illustrator. When you finish with this chapter, you'll fully deserve to stick a gold star on your monitor.

Using the Blend Tool

Blending is one of Illustrator's most exotic and oldest capabilities. Back when every one of its competitors offered automated gradations, Illustrator allowed you to design your own custom gradations. Illustrator's blend tool wasn't easy to use—and it's still something of an inconvenience—but it yielded an unlimited range of results. There wasn't a gradation you couldn't create if you put your mind to it.

Now, Illustrator offers what is undoubtedly the finest automatic gradient fill function of any drawing program (as discussed in Chapter 15). But the blend tool—unchanged in more than six years—remains exceedingly useful. Anytime you want to go beyond linear and radial gradations, the blend tool is at your beck and call.

The job of the blend tool is to create intermediate paths between two selected extremes. Figure 17-1 shows a trio of blends. In each case, the front and back shapes—which have been assigned thick strokes in the figures—are the extreme paths that I drew; the blend tool created the others. Illustrator automatically calculates the shapes, fill and stroke colors, and line weights of the intermediate paths, varying them in gradual increments between one extreme and the other.

To make a blend appear as a gradation, just dispense with the strokes. Figure 17-2 shows the same paths as Figure 17-1, with most of the strokes set to None. To create the outer strokes, I copied the backmost path, pasted it in front, assigned a stroke and made the fill transparent.

To operate the blend tool—second to last icon on the right side of the toolbox—follow these steps:

1. **Specify the fill and stroke of the paths you want to blend**.

   Illustrator can blend between any two flat colors, including gray values, CMYK colors, and named colors. But it cannot blend between gradations. Illustrator can also blend strokes and line weights, but don't expect to be able to blend between two different line caps, joins, or dash patterns.

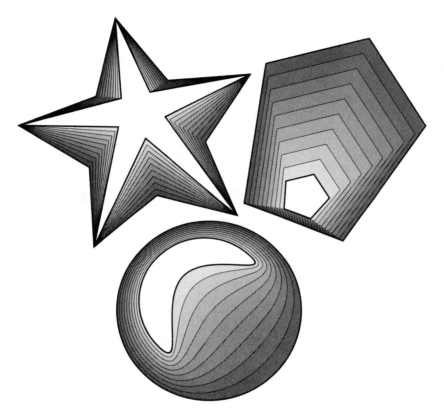

Figure 17-1: Examples of three sets of blends created using the blend tool. The shapes with the heavy strokes represent the original extremes.

2. **Select the two paths**.

Illustrator can blend no more and no less than two paths at a time. Both paths must be open or closed, but not one of each. Text objects are right out, and the blend tool doesn't account accurately for compound paths. If you blend between two compound paths, Illustrator ignores the holes.

 Paths with the same number of points work best. But if one path has more points than the other, you can even things out by selecting all points in one path and the same number of points in the other path. See the upcoming section "Deciding which Points to Select."

Figure 17-2: You can create continuous gradations between two extremes by making the strokes transparent.

3. Click on one point in each selected path with the blend tool.

First click on one point, then click on another. If you miss a point—even slightly—Illustrator produces a very tiresome error message and makes you start over. If the paths are open, you have to click on an endpoint. Click on some other point, and you get another error message. Alert boxes are a familiar part of blend tool territory.

The points on which you click have a big impact on the final blend. If possible, click on similar points in both paths. In Figure 17-3, for example, I clicked on the lower left point in the outside cone, and then on the lower left point on the inside cone. See the section "Deciding Where to Click" for more info.

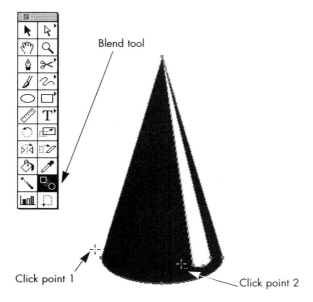

Blend tool

Click point 1

Click point 2

Figure 17-3: After selecting the blend tool, I clicked on the lower left point in each of two selected shapes.

4. Specify the number of steps in the blend.

After the second click with the blend tool, Illustrator displays the Blend dialog box shown in Figure 17-4. Into the Steps option box, enter the number of intermediate paths—or *steps*—you want the blend tool to generate. You can either enter a low value to create an incremental terracing effect, or a high value to produce a smooth gradation. Back in Figure 17-1, I specified 8 steps. But in Figure 17-2, I used 44.

Figure 17-4: The Blend dialog box comes to life after you click a second time with the blend tool.

Deciding how many steps to use is no easy proposition. The default Steps value is Illustrator's recommendation, based on the colors of the selected paths. But it's almost always too high, even for high-resolution printing. For a technical evaluation of steps, with some numerical recommendations, read the "Deciding the Number of Steps" section.

5. **Change the First and Last values (or, better yet, don't).**

   The First and Last values determine how Illustrator positions, shapes, and colors the first and last steps in the blend. In the first example in Figure 17-5, I entered 98 steps and accepted the default First and Last values. The result is a smooth, steady blend. In the second example, I again used 98 steps, but I changed the First and Last values to 40 and 60 percent, respectively. This caused Illustrator to bunch up the steps into the center of the cone. Because I was blending between a black path and a white one, Illustrator colored the first step with 40% black and the last step with 60% black. So the space occupied by the steps is small, and the range is small.

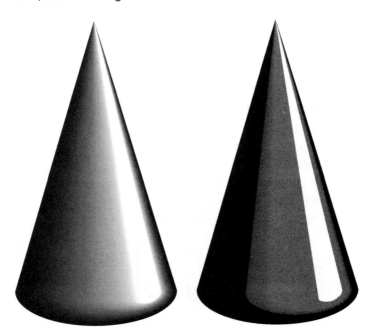

Figure 17-5: Two blends containing 98 steps, one in which I accepted the default First and Last values (left), and the other in which I changed the values to 40 and 60 percent (right).

Frankly, the First and Last values are dumb. What the Blend dialog box really needs is a midpoint control, like the midpoint marker in the Gradient palette. This would allow you to accelerate the blend at a specific point. But as it is, you'll probably just want to ignore the First and Last options and let Illustrator calculate the most satisfactory values on its own.

6. Press the Return key.

This instructs Illustrator to generate the blend. Illustrator creates the number of steps specified, and fills and strokes the steps automatically. It also combines the steps into a single group. Because there are typically so many steps, grouping helps to keep things a little more tidy. The original extreme paths, however, remain ungrouped.

Deciding Which Points to Select

The blend tool always tries to blend between pairs of selected points in opposite paths. This is no problem when both paths contain the same number of points. Illustrator merely takes a point in Path A, finds its buddy in Path B, and blends between them. But if the paths are so much as one point different, Illustrator gets mixed up. It tries to blend between pairs of points at first, but then gives it up about midway through.

Figure 17-6 is a perfect example. Here I've blended between a five-sided polygon and a five-pointed star. You'd think Illustrator would be able to figure out what close cousins these paths are, but all Illustrator knows is that the star contains ten points and the pentagon contains only five. If you look closely, you can

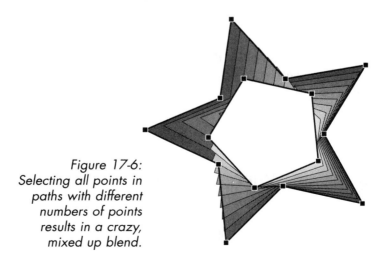

*Figure 17-6:
Selecting all points in
paths with different
numbers of points
results in a crazy,
mixed up blend.*

see a clear progression of steps between the bottom three points in the star and the bottom three points in the pentagon. But the rest of the blend is chaos and confusion. The steps eke outside the star, twist all over the place, and generally make a mockery out of any semblance of an orderly gradation.

The solution to this problem is to carefully select the points you want to blend with the direct selection tool. For example, in this case, I'd select all five points in the pentagon, and then select five corresponding points in the star. The points that make the most sense are the five spike points, selected in the first example of Figure 17-7. This causes the corners of the pentagon to blend into the spikes in the star. But I could also select the five crease points, as in the right example in the figure. This also results in a logical, constant blend, though the effect is somewhat unusual. Either way, I told Illustrator exactly what I wanted, and Illustrator delivered.

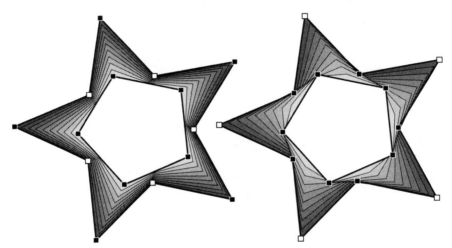

Figure 17-7: If you select the same number of points in each shape—in this case, five points apiece—things become orderly. (The selected points appear black.)

Deciding Where to Click

When clicking with the blend tool, you have to click on a selected point, and if the path is open, you have to click on an endpoint. Those are the only hard-and-fast rules. But merely following the rules doesn't ensure good results. Which points you click can make or break a blend.

The two click points tell Illustrator the locations of the first pair of points it should blend. The program then wanders around the shapes in a clockwise direction and pairs up the other points. Figure 17-8 shows the results of blending two five-pointed stars after clicking on different points in the two shapes. I always clicked on the lower right point in the small star, but I clicked on a total of six different points in the larger star. As you can see, this has a profound effect on how the blend progresses.

Figure 17-8:
The sparkles show
the points where I
clicked on each
pair of shapes with
the blend tool.

Each small star in Figure 17-8 was originally filled with white. I changed the fills to None after blending the shapes to permit you to see the steps in back, some of which would have been covered up if I had left the star white.

Though many of the effects in Figure 17-8 are interesting, only the first three are suitable for creating gradations, as demonstrated in Figure 17-9. And even then, the third example is a mighty unusual gradation with harsh edges. Your safest bet is to click on a matching point in each object, as in the first example. This results in the smoothest possible progression.

Figure 17-9:
Here I used the same click points as in Figure 17-8, but I got rid of the strokes and increased the number of steps to 88 per blend.

Recognizing When You Need More Points

Though it may seem unfair, you can still end up with harsh edges after taking the precautions of selecting an equal number of points in both shapes and clicking on similar points. Consider the first example in Figure 17-10. Both shapes contain four points (all selected) and I clicked on the lowest point in each shape. And yet, as the second example shows, I ended up with harsh edges. The top and bottom of the white shape look like they're thrusting forward from the black ellipse. No, no, no, we simply cannot have this!

The problem is that two of the paired points in the two shapes aren't properly in line with each other. That is, if a crow were to fly from one point to another, it

Figure 17-10:
If you can't draw straight
lines between the paired
points in your shapes
without running over seg-
ments (left), you'll end up
with harsh edges in your
final blend (right).

would smack into a segment. I've drawn dotted lines between the paired points in the first example. The lines between the left and right pair of points are unobstructed, but the lines between the top and bottom pairs intersect the smaller shape. These are precisely the areas in which our problems occur.

The solution is to add more points. If you add a point to every segment in each shape, you can ensure that all points are in line. Use the add point tool, not the automated Add Anchor Points filter. As shown in Figure 17-11, you don't want the points to be spaced consistently. What matters is that you can draw a straight line between every pair of points in the shapes and not come in contact with any segments. As the dotted lines show, this is precisely what

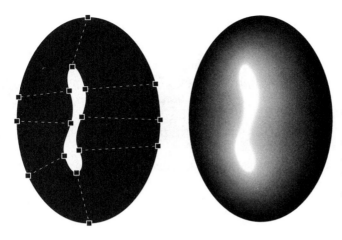

Figure 17-11:
Use the add point tool to
add points to both shapes
so that all straight lines
drawn between the
paired points are unob-
structed (left). This ensures
a fluid gradation (right).

I've accomplished in Figure 17-11. Then I select all points and blend between them, creating the silky smooth gradation shown in the second example.

Deciding the Number of Steps

Another problem that plagues blends is a pesky printing phenomenon called *banding.* Rather than printing as a seamless gradation, the blend exhibits distinct bands of color. When banding occurs, gradient credibility goes out the window. Figure 17-12 offers an exaggerated example. In the first blend, I created 13 steps, hardly enough to produce smooth shading. You can see almost every step in the shape, resulting in lots of bands. The second blend is much smoother, but it also contains 198 steps.

Unfortunately, while using very few steps practically guarantees banding, having lots of steps doesn't necessarily prevent it. You have to print enough steps to take advantage of your printer's ability to generate gray values, but not so many that one or more steps appear out of sync with their neighbors. In an ideal blend, each printed step corresponds to a unique gray value and varies from its neighbors by a consistent amount. Illustrator creates unique, consistent steps automatically, no matter how many steps you assign, but this doesn't mean they'll necessarily print correctly. It all hinges on the answers to two questions:

- Is the printer properly calibrated?
- What is the resolution and screen frequency of the printer?

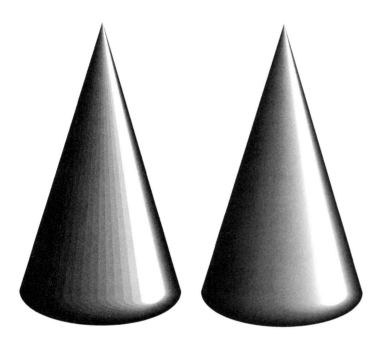

Figure 17-12: A blend with banding (left) and one with seamless color transitions (right).

You can't anticipate bad calibration. You just have to hope that your service bureau or commercial printer has its machinery in top condition. But you can account for resolution and screen frequency. Very briefly—I cover both topics in more detail in Chapter 18—*resolution* is the number of pixels the printer can print per inch (just like screen resolution). And *screen frequency* is the number of halftone dots that print per inch. Printer resolution is measured in dots per inch (dpi), and screen frequency is measured in lines per inch (lpi). The resolution is fixed, but the screen frequency can change. For example, a typical LaserWriter prints at 300 dpi, but the lpi can be set to 60 or 53.

If you print a 60-lpi screen from a 300-dpi LaserWriter, each halftone dot measures 5 pixels wide by 5 pixels tall. (That's because 300 ÷ 60 = 5.) And a 5-by-5 dot contains a total of 25 pixels. If all pixels are turned off, the halftone dot is white. All pixels turned on produces black, and turning on 1 to 24 pixels produces a shade of gray. Including black and white, that's a total of 26 gray values, which is the absolute maximum number of shades a 300 dpi, 60 lpi LaserWriter can print.

That's just one example. Printers vary from model to model. But if you know the dpi and lpi values, you can calculate the number of printable gray values using this formula:

$$(dpi \div lpi)^2 + 1$$

Take a top-of-the-line Linotronic imagesetter, for example. The resolution is 2,540 dpi, and the default screen frequency is 133 lpi. When you divide 2,540 by 133, you get 19.097. Then you multiply 19.097 by itself and add 1 to get 365 gray values, quite a few more than the LaserWriter.

There is one caveat, however. PostScript printers can't generate more than 256 shades of gray, regardless of their resolution or screen frequency. That's why Illustrator automatically suggests 254 steps in the Blend dialog box when blending between a black and white shape—256 minus black and white leaves 254.

I hate to make you do too much math, so here are the maximum number of gray values associated with a few popular resolutions and screen frequencies:

Resolution	Screen frequency	Maximum shades of gray
300	53	33
300	60	26
400	60	45
400	75	29
600	60	101
600	75	65
600	90	45
1200	75	256
1200	90	179
1200	120	101
1200	133	82
1270	75	256
1270	90	200
1270	120	113
1270	133	92
2400	up to 150	256
2540	up to 150	256

After you find the maximum number of gray values, you need to factor in the range of colors in your blend. A black-to-white blend requires all the gray levels your printer can produce. Just take the value in the last column of the table and subtract 2—black and white. For example, if you're creating a black-to-white blend for a 1270 dpi, 90 lpi printer, you want 200 − 2 = 198 steps.

If the color range is smaller, there's no sense in using all those steps because your printer won't be able to print them. So multiply the maximum printable gray values by the percentage change in color and then subtract 2. The range of grays in a blend from 70% black to 20% black is 50 percent. If you plan to print this to our 1270 dpi, 90 lpi printer, you'd multiply 200 by 0.5 (50 percent), which is 100. Then subtract to get 98 steps.

When creating color blends, look for the biggest CMYK difference. For example, let's say you want to blend between a shape filled with 40%C 30%M 20%Y 10%K and one filled with 100%C 40%M 30%Y 20%K. The biggest variation between any of the process colors is 100%C minus 40%C which is 60 percent. So you'd multiply 200 by 0.6 (60 percent) to get 120, and then subtract 2 to calculate 118 steps in the blend.

Lastly, factor in size. If the blend covers the whole page, then you have to use all the steps you can (according to the above calculations). But if it's a small gradation, you may be able to get away with less. For example, a blend one inch wide doesn't merit 118 steps. You can probably get away with half that many, or 59. If you decide to decrease the number of steps, always divide by an even number, like 2, 3, or 4.

After all this, you may be thinking it's just easier to accept the Steps value Illustrator gives you and call it a day. And certainly, you can do that if you like. But if you notice banding inside your printed illustrations, come back to this section and give it another try.

On the other hand, if this brief introduction to banding has only whetted your appetite, check out *Real World Scanning and Halftones* (Peachpit Press) by David Blatner and Steve Roth. Tough topic, smart guys, ideal combination.

Deactivating the Error Message

The blend tool is notorious for generating error messages. If you don't click exactly on a selected point or you click on an interior point in an open path, up comes an alert box, demanding your urgent attention. If you already know all the things that can go wrong when blending and you don't need an alert box in your face every 16 seconds, you can tell Illustrator to stop bugging you.

To get rid of the blend alert boxes, quit Illustrator and open the Adobe Illustrator 6.0 Prefs file in a word processor. (You can find this file in the Preferences folder inside the System Folder.) Look for an item called /blend. It is followed by the line /warning 1. That 1 tells Illustrator you want warnings. To turn off the warning, change the 1 to a 0. Then close and save the Prefs file and launch the Illustrator application. From now on, Illustrator will just beep when you use the blend tool incorrectly. (If you hear a beep after the second click, you have to start over with the first click again.)

Don't worry about editing this file. If something goes wrong, you can always throw away the Prefs file at the Finder level. The next time you start Illustrator, it will automatically create a fresh one.

Cool Blend Tool Tricks

I've droned on about the blend tool for quite a while now, but I haven't even begun to tell you all the great things you can do with it. Though I can't share every blend tool and custom gradation trick I've invented or gleaned over the years, I will suggest a handful of what I consider to be the most interesting tips and tricks in the following sections. With any luck, they'll inspire you to develop more sophisticated techniques of your own.

Morphing Path Outlines

In addition to generating custom gradations, the blend tool is a shape-modification tool. Much like the Pathfinder filters, you can use the tool to take two paths and combine them into a third. This technique is known as *morphing*.

In Figure 17-13, I've taken a series of shapes and morphed between them. Each column in the figure represents a separate morph, with the original shapes in gray at the top and bottom. In each case, I create three steps between the two originals. This way, I have an instant library of intermediate shapes to choose from; no other path-combination feature provides such a range of alternatives.

But I should warn you, it's not quite as easy as it looks. I had to spend a few minutes on each pair of original paths, making sure the two had the same number of points. For example, the pair of stars in the first column each have 20 points, even though the top star has half as many spikes as the bottom. The circle and star in the second column each have 16 points, and so on. I inserted most of the points with Filter » Objects » Add Anchor Points, but I had to add a few manually with the add point tool.

Figure 17-13: A series of morphings, arranged in columns, created between a shape at the top and its counterpart at the bottom.

You can also use the blend tool to morph type converted to path outlines. In Figure 17-14, I started with a line of type in Bookman Light Italic and another in Bookman Bold Italic. (Both are widely available LaserWriter Plus fonts.) I created the three rows of white letters with the blend tool. If you're a type enthusiast, you'll love this technique because it permits you to generate your own custom styles and weights without purchasing more fonts. But it takes some skill and effort. When converted to path outlines, the light and bold characters contain different numbers of points—not wildly different, but enough to keep you on your toes. There's no room for automation here; you have to insert points manually with the add point tool.

There's also the little matter of the compound paths used to create the *B*, *e*, and *d*. You have to blend between each subpath in a separate operation. For example, I had to blend three times to get all of the *B*—once for the outside and twice for the two holes. Then you have to ungroup the steps and combine each set of paths into a compound path by pressing ⌘-8. The results are wonderful, but you'll definitely work up a sweat before you finish.

Figure 17-14:
Three character morphs cre-
ated by blending between
the top row of Bookman
Light Italic and the bottom
row of Bookman Bold Italic.

If you're feeling extra brave, you can even blend between character outlines and standard shapes. In Figure 17-15, I tried my hand at blending between three converted characters of Helvetica and a modified star, figure 8, and spiral. As you can see, I modified the letters slightly before morphing by changing the compound paths of the *A* and *B* into continuous outlines. I also abused the shapes at the bottom of the figure fairly significantly. The shapes in the middle of the figure were culled from a series of eight steps (shown in the background in gray). I can't claim

Figure 17-15:
I blended between three
Helvetica characters
(top) and some basic
shapes (bottom) to create
a series of morphs that
are at once utterly
abstract and recogniz-
able as letters (middle).

that these type/path crossbreeds are in any way beautiful—in fact, they're almost comically ugly—but they possess a certain mutated quality that I wouldn't have achieved without the free-spirited blend tool.

Creating Multi-Color Blends

You know you've earned your blend tool black belt when you successfully tackle multi-color gradations. By creating a series of colored shapes and blending between them in succession, you can create photo-realistic graphics with sharp outlines and exact edges, the Holy Grail of commercial artwork.

Figure 17-16 shows eight shapes I created to represent a cat's eye. All but one of these shapes is designed to function as the beginning or end of a blend. The medium gray path through the middle of the eye served as the end of one blend

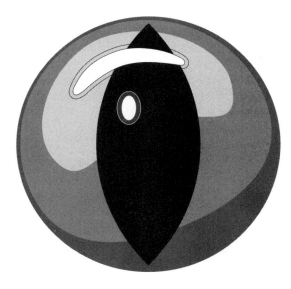

Figure 17-16:
These eight shapes were
the only ones I had to draw
to create a realistic cat's
eye. I generated all others
in Figures 17-17 and 17-18
with the blend tool.

and the beginning of another. Only the lozenge-shaped pupil is not part of a blend, but was instead designed to crop the blend. (If you can't wait to see how the finished cat's eye turned out, sneak a peek at Figures 17-18 and 17-19.)

Notice in Figure 17-16 that other than the pupil, no two paths overlap. This ensures that I don't have to blend a path with the bits and pieces from another blend, which would be a real nightmare.

The white shapes in the figure represent highlights. The rings around the white shapes were created with the Offset Path filter and are both filled with the same colors as the shapes behind them. I used the shapes to soften the highlights. (The strokes in the figure are there just so you can see the shapes. None of the paths were actually stroked when I blended them.)

First, I wanted to emulate the shades of light and dark inside the pupil. So I copied the outer circle, the light gray shape, and the two highlight shapes that intersect the lozenge, and pasted them in back of the shape. I filled the outer circle with black, kept the highlight white, and filled the other two shapes with 70% black. Then I blended between the two large shapes and the two highlight shapes to get the effect shown on the left side of Figure 17-17. I next selected all of my new shapes and the lozenge and chose Filter » Pathfinder » Crop. The command took a minute or so to finish, leaving behind the gradient lozenge that appears on the right side of Figure 17-17.

Figure 17-17: I copied a few shapes, pasted them behind the lozenge, filled them with dark colors, and blended between them (left). Then I used the crop filter to cut away portions of the blend outside the pupil (right).

In the first example of Figure 17-18, I blended between the three eye shapes. First I blended from the dark gray shape to the medium gray shape. Then I blended from the medium gray shape to the light gray one. All that remained was to blend the highlights, which is what I did to get the right example in Figure 17-18. I also added a stroked path behind the large circle of the eye to give it a little more definition.

Figure 17-18: I blended the large gray shapes behind the pupil (left) and then blended the two sets of highlight paths (right).

The hardest part is deciding what kinds of paths to draw in the first place. The trick is to pay careful attention to what you see in the real world, and simplify the forms enough to prevent one gradation from overlapping another. In Figure 17-19, I added a few elements that I saw in my cat's eye, notably the white membrane over the iris and the dark skin around the eye. (I positioned the thin, upper eyelid in front of the eye, and the dark skin blend behind the eye. And I used the Crop filter to slice the shape of the membrane into the blend shapes, just as I did for the pupil.) Multi-color blending demands that you balance realism with stylization in roughly equal portions.

Figure 17-19:
The finished cat's eye
includes five additional
blends, the large one in
back of the eye and the
other four in front.

Blending Strokes

Back when I began this chapter, I mentioned that the blend tool incrementally varies two stroke attributes—color and line weight. This last fact is very important since it means that you can blend a thick stroke with a thin one to create a softened edge.

Figure 17-20 demonstrates one of the common stroke-blending effects, the old neon text trick. I started by converting some text to paths, and splitting and joining the letters with the scissors tool and Join command to combine all letters into a single, open path. (After all, in a real neon sign, one tube forms all the letters.) I assigned the line an 8-point black stroke. Then I cloned the line, nudged it upward a couple of points, and gave it a 0.5-point white stroke. The result appears at the top of Figure 17-20.

 It's important that you nudge one path slightly away from the other before blending. If one path exactly overlaps the other, you can't click on the back path with the blend tool. Even when the paths are a couple of points apart, you'll probably need to zoom in to a very magnified view size (say, 400 percent or more) before you can click on the points without Illustrator complaining.

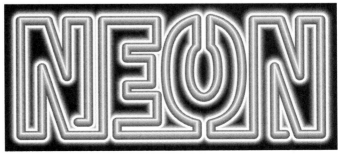

Figure 17-20: Here I've taken two stroked paths (top) and blended between them to create a neon effect (middle). Then I blended between a 12-point white stroke and a 24-point black one to create the glow (bottom).

After setting up my paths, I zoomed in and clicked on an endpoint in each path. (You have to click on an endpoint in an open path, remember.) Then I specified 14 steps, enough to ensure that each step changes by exactly 0.5 point. The second example in Figure 17-20 shows the result.

 You don't need many steps when working with strokes because the distances are so small. A line weight variation of 0.5 point means that you can only see about 0.25 point of color around each side of the stroke. (With the strokes offset, the color bands may be as wide as 0.3 point, but that's about the maximum.) To ensure a 0.5-point line weight variation between your steps, use this simple formula. Of the two strokes you want to blend, subtract the thinner line weight from the thicker one. Then multiply that number by 2 and subtract 1. For example, I subtracted 0.5 from 8 to get 7.5. Multiplying that number by 2 produced 15, and subtracting 1 gave me 14. For the record, the line weight of these 14 steps are 1, 1.5, 2, 2.5, 3, 3.5, 4, 4.5, 5, 5.5, 6, 6.5, 7, and 7.5. You can't go wrong.

To create the glow in the last example in Figure 17-20, I first copied the rear path. Then I hid the neon letters to get them out of my way (⌘-3), pasted the path in back (⌘-B), and changed the stroke to 12-point white. To create the blend-to path, I pasted to back again, nudged the pasted path up two points, and changed its stroke to 24-point black. Then I blended between the two paths with the blend tool. (To calculate the number of steps, I subtracted 12 from 24 to get 12; multiplied that by 2 and subtracted 1 to get 23.) To make the background black, I drew a black rectangle behind the whole thing. And I pressed ⌘-4 to bring the neon letters back from hiding.

 Notice that the strokes in Figure 17-20 have round joins. The same is true for the blended strokes in Figure 17-21. Round joins invariably blend best because they smooth out the transitions at the corner points. Miter and bevel joins result in harsh corners which rarely benefit a gradation.

Neon isn't the only effect you can produce by blending strokes. You can also create soft shadows. In Figure 17-21, I started by converting some letters from the typeface Eras to paths. Then I stroked the letters with 1-point medium gray and made the fill transparent. I cloned the letters, nudged them down and left, and sent them to back. I stroked the clone with 12-point white. Because each letter is an independent path, I had to use the blend tool a total of five times, once for the inside of the O and another for the outside. (The letters have no fill, so I didn't have to worry about recombining each of the 21 O steps into compound paths.)

Figure 17-21: Soft shadows created using blended strokes work only when the shadows are spread apart (top). If the shadows overlap, they develop distinctly un-shadow-like edges (bottom).

Finally, I cloned the letters again, changed the fill to white, and removed the stroke to create the white letters up front.

An important point to remember when creating soft stroke shadows is that each shadow has to completely clear the shadows around it. That's why the letters in the top example of Figure 17-21 are spread far apart from each other. If a stroke from one shadow cuts into a stroke from a neighbor shadow, it ruins the effect, as in the bottom example.

You can even blend between strokes with dash patterns. The blend tool can interpret between different dash patterns, and it can maintain a consistent dash pattern throughout all steps. And by virtue of its ability to incrementally change line weights, it can change the size of dashes with round caps, as demonstrated in Figure 17-22. I started with three copies of my Z paths from Chapter 16, each stroked with the same dash pattern (Dash: 0, Gap: 20), but with different colors and line weights. Blending between these paths results in the luminous beads shown in the second example in the figure. I also added soft drop shadows, again varying the line weight and color but leaving the dash pattern unchanged.

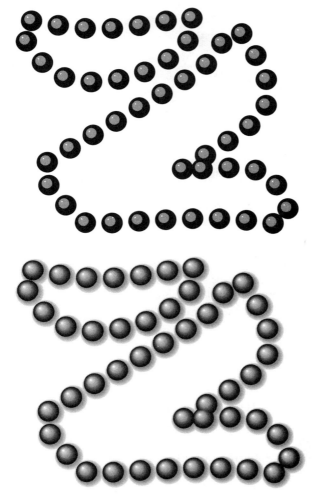

Figure 17-22:
I started with three sets of
paths (top), stroked with
different colors and line
weights, but all having
the same dash pattern.
Blending between these
paths resulted in a series
of three-dimensional
beads (bottom).

Reblending Colors

When it comes to blending, many Illustrator users covet their FreeHand neighbors. In FreeHand, you can edit either of the extreme paths in a blend, and the program will automatically update the steps in between accordingly. No such luck in Illustrator. If you decide to change the shape of one path or the other, you have to delete the blend and recreate it.

But things are not quite so gloomy where colors are concerned. You can change the color of one extreme path or the other and then update the color of the steps using

Filter » Colors » Blend Front to Back. In the top example of Figure 17-23, for instance, I've blended between two stars, the back one filled with black and the front one filled with white. Then I edited the extreme paths, changing the back one to white and the front one to gray (as in the second example). Next I selected all paths in the blend—the two extremes and all steps—and chose the Blend Front to Back filter. Illustrator immediately revised the colors of the steps, as the third example shows.

Figure 17-23: After blending between two stars (top), I changed the colors of the front and back shapes (left) and updated the colors of the steps using the Blend Front to Back filter (right).

     Unfortunately, like many of Illustrator's filters, Blend Front to Back is not perfect. It entirely ignores strokes—both colors and line weights—so you can't use it to update the colors of stroke blends. And it isn't capable of changing the number of steps in a blend, which may be necessary to prevent banding. In Figure 17-23, I changed a white-to-black gradation to a gray-to-white gradation, so if anything, I have too many steps. But if you want to widen the range of colors in your blend, you'll probably want to delete the blend and recreate it using the blend tool.

 If you think the number of steps in your blend may be sufficient, but you can't quite remember how many steps there are, select the steps with the arrow tool and choose File » Selection Info. Then select Objects from the Info pop-up menu. The first item in the list tells you exactly how many paths are selected (which is the number of steps).

Editing a Gradient Fill

Now that I've told you nearly everything there is to know about blends, I'd like to share one more little secret. Every gradation in Illustrator is actually a blend. That's right, Illustrator calculates each color in a gradient fill as a separate step in a blend. It hides the details from you to keep things tidy. But as far as Illustrator and the printer are concerned, gradations and blends are all variations on the same theme.

 Illustrator 6 gives you the power to tear down the walls. At a moment's notice, you can convert any object filled with a gradation to an object filled with a blend. Just select the object and choose Object » Expand. An alert box comes up, asking you how many steps you would like to create. Ignore the nonsense about 40 steps for the screen and 255 for the printer that Illustrator recommends in the alert box. Instead, follow my advice from the "Deciding the Number of Steps" section earlier in this chapter. That is, take the number of gray values your printer can print and multiply it by the percentage color range. Just one difference—don't subtract 2. The first and last colors are part of the gradation, so you don't want to delete them from the Steps value.

When you expand a gradation, Illustrator converts it to steps inside a mask. The shape that was previously filled with the gradation serves as the mask. Illustrator selects the mask and all rectangular steps inside the mask, as shown in the right half of Figure 17-24.

 If you want to simplify the mask into a series of cropped steps, choose Object » Mask » Release, then choose Filter » Pathfinder » Crop. That's all it takes. You lose the flexibility of a mask—which I describe at length in the next section—but cropped steps are tidier on screen and you can be sure the steps will print.

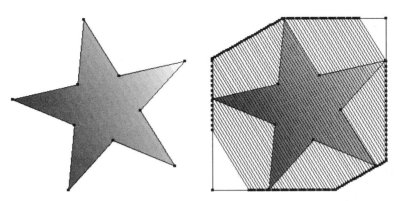

Figure 17-24: Choose Object » Expand to convert a shape filled with a gradient fill (left) to a mask filled with colored steps (right).

One of the best reasons to convert a gradation to steps is to exactly pinpoint the locations of colors inside a shape. For example, in Figure 17-25, I've drawn two intersecting stars, each filled with gradations that converge at a common color. To achieve the effect, I split one star in half using the scissors tool and sent the left half to back. In order to make the transition between the forward half and the full

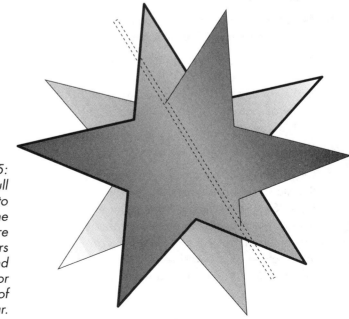

Figure 17-25: After converting the full star (heavy outline) to a blend, I lifted the band of color where the full and half stars meet (dotted line) and used it as the first color in the gradient fill of the half star.

star (with the heavy outline) as seamless as possible, I wanted them both to intersect at precisely the same shade of gray. But there's no way to find the exact color in a gradation at a specific point. So I had to convert the full star to a blend using Object » Expand. Next I opened the Gradient palette and Control-clicked with the eyedropper tool on the band of gray where the stars meet. (I've surrounded this band with a dotted line in Figure 17-25.) This gray value became the first color in the gradient fill assigned to the forward half star.

Filling Objects with Objects

Illustrator's *masking* feature allows you to take one group of objects and put them inside of a selected path. The path becomes the *mask*, and the objects inside the mask are the *content element*. The mask clips away all portions of the content elements that fall outside the boundaries of the mask. Most artists use the masking feature to fill a path with a blend, but content elements can be stroked paths, text, or imported images. The mask itself must be a path.

To create a mask, do the following:

1. **Bring the mask to front**.

   Select the path that you want to fill with other objects, and bring it to front (⌘-minus). A mask must be in front of its content elements.

2. **Select the path and all objects that you want to put inside it, and choose Object » Masks » Make**.

   If you select objects inside different groups, compound paths, or masks, Illustrator will complain. So it's best to select the objects with the arrow tool prior to choosing the command. When successful, Illustrator clips away all portions of the content element that fall outside the frontmost path in the selection.

3. **Choose Arrange » Group**.

   Or press ⌘-G. This groups the mask and its contents together. Though this step is not absolutely necessary, it makes your illustration a little tidier. See, unless you group, you can select the mask and each and every object inside the mask independently of its neighbors using the arrow tool. If you take a moment to group, you can use the arrow tool to select the entire mask—including its contents—and use the direct selection tool to dig around inside the mask.

Figure 17-26 shows an example. Here I've assembled a completely random collection of Zapf Dingbats planes, made even more random using Arrange » Transform Each. (I couldn't have achieved this effect with tile patterns.) Then I positioned a stylized shirt outline in front of the planes, as the top example shows. I next selected all paths and chose Object » Mask » Make. (I also pressed ⌘-G to keep things tidy.) The result is the bottom example in the figure. *Viola*, instant pajama top.

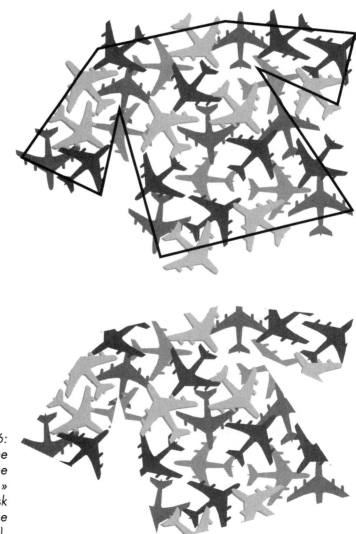

Figure 17-26:
After selecting the
planes and shirt outline
(top), I chose Object »
Mask » Make to mask
the planes inside the
shirt (bottom).

Restoring a Mask's Fill and Stroke

Notice that Illustrator has dispensed with the stroke around my shirt in the bottom example of Figure 17-26. This is because masks cannot include strokes of fills. They are dummy objects used to stencil the content elements, and that's all. If you want to reinstate the fill and stroke of a mask—or add new ones—here's what you do:

1. **Select the mask outline with the direct selection tool**.

   If you ignored my words of wisdom and neglected to group the mask—do I have to come over there and make you to do it?—then you can select the mask outline with the arrow tool.

2. **Assign the desired fill and stroke attributes inside the Paint Style palette**.

   Bizarre as this may sound, your actions won't affect the selected path one iota, but just go ahead and do it. It'll make a difference in a moment.

3. **Choose Filter » Create » Fill & Stroke for Mask**.

   Illustrator displays an unnecessary dialog box, telling you what it's about to do. (Aren't you glad it doesn't explain itself every time you choose a command?) Press Return to tell it to quit mouthing off. Suddenly, the fill and stroke come to life.

Figure 17-27 shows the result of applying the Fill & Stroke for Mask to the shirt outline. I managed to reinstate my stroke and add a gray fill.

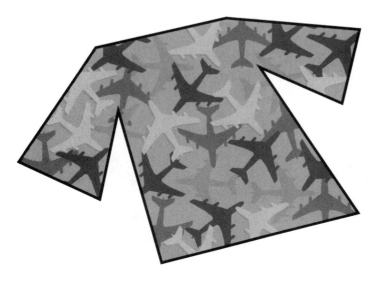

Figure 17-27:
The result of applying
Filter » Create » Fill &
Stroke for Mask to
the shirt outline,
which reinstates my
stroke and adds a fill.

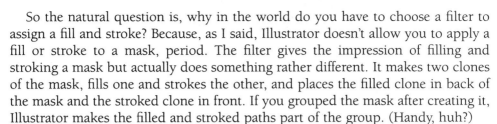

So the natural question is, why in the world do you have to choose a filter to assign a fill and stroke? Because, as I said, Illustrator doesn't allow you to apply a fill or stroke to a mask, period. The filter gives the impression of filling and stroking a mask but actually does something rather different. It makes two clones of the mask, fills one and strokes the other, and places the filled clone in back of the mask and the stroked clone in front. If you grouped the mask after creating it, Illustrator makes the filled and stroked paths part of the group. (Handy, huh?)

This means that if I were to Option-click with the direct selection tool on the shirt outline in Figure 17-27, and then drag it, I would move just the stroked clone. The mask, content elements, and filled clone would stay where they are.

Selecting Inside Grouped Masks

Here's something to keep in mind when editing the mask in the future. In order to access the actual mask outline, you have to select the stroked clone, lock or hide it (⌘-1 or ⌘-3), and then click again to select the mask outline. For the record, here's how to select objects inside a grouped mask with the direct selection tool:

- To select a point or segment inside any content element, just click on it. To select an entire path, Option-click. (No surprises there.)

- To select a point or segment on the stroked outline, click on it, or Option-click to select the entire thing.

- To select the mask outline, Option-click on the outline and press ⌘-1 to lock the stroked outline. Then click to select a point or segment, or Option-click to select the entire path. Press ⌘-2 to unlock the stroked path when you're done.

- To get to the filled outline, Option-click on the path, press ⌘-1, Option-click again, and press ⌘-1. Now the filled path is the only outline left unlocked (other than the content elements). Click or Option-click as desired. Press ⌘-2 to unlock when you're done.

- Marquee a point in the mask outline if you want to move that point in all three outlines (mask, stroke, and fill) simultaneously.

- To select the entire mask—including mask outline, stroked and filled paths, and content elements—Option-click twice on an object in the mask.

When you select the entire mask, you see the outlines of all objects. Many of the outlines extend outside the mask, like the panes in Figure 17-28. This is because every one of these objects is still fully available. If I were to drag one of the clipped

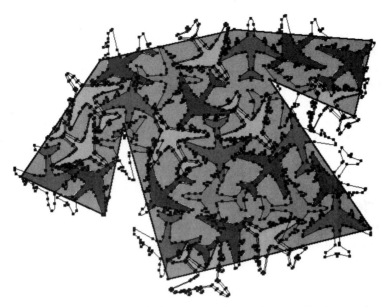

*Figure 17-28: Option-click twice with the direct selection tool
on any object inside a grouped mask to select everything.*

planes back inside the mask, I could again see the whole thing. The mask is a live
stencil that shows you everything inside its perimeter and nothing outside.

Masking Versus Cropping

This live quality is the primary factor that distinguishes Object » Masks » Make
from the somewhat similar Filter » Pathfinder » Crop. The Masks » Make and
Crop commands work similarly—in both cases, the front path clips all selected
paths behind it. If you were to apply the two commands to identical collections of
filled paths, the results would even look the same. But where masking is a live
operation that permits changes, cropping does permanent damage. Masking hides
portions of content elements that extend outside the mask, cropping deletes them.

Also worth noting, the Crop filter deletes strokes and is not applicable to text
or imported images. Masking, meanwhile, can accommodate any kind of object.

But where cropping results in a simple collection of filled objects, masking requires
more work on the part of the printer. Masks take longer to print than cropped
paths—several times longer in some cases—and a sufficiently complicated mask that
contains lots of complex objects can prevent your illustration from printing.

So use masks when you need them and apply the Crop filter when you don't. In Figure 17-29, for example, I used the Crop filter to stencil the shadows out of the arms, neck, face, and ears. But I used masks for the hair and shirt. I retained the mask for the shirt because I wanted to preserve the ability to edit the planes later on down the line. And I used a mask for the hair because of the white stroke from the head that extends up into the hair. The Crop filter would have deleted this stroke. If I had reapplied it, I wouldn't have gotten the white head line to align with the black head line precisely at the hair line.

Figure 17-29: The shirt and hair were created using masking. I created the other stenciled shapes using the Crop filter.

A mask is a special kind of combined object, like a group of compound path. This means you can use the Paste In Front and Paste In Back commands to introduce additional elements to the mask. In Figure 17-29, I create the black line around the hair by cloning the mask outline and applying a 4-point stroke. Then I cut the path, selected the white head line with the direct selection tool, and pressed ⌘-B. Illustrator masked away the half of the stroke that rides along the outside of the path, leaving what looks like a 2-point line weight. And the white line overlaps the black one, giving the head an inverted appearance inside the hair.

Compound Masks

If you want a collection of content elements to continue through multiple masks, you should assemble the mask shapes into a compound path before applying the Masks » Make command. In Figure 17-30, for example, I create two identical star blends, one from white to gray (no strokes), and the other from gray

Figure 17-30: The shapes in this face all are members of a single compound path that I then turned around and used as a mask. His expression arises out of fear that he might not print.

to black (with strokes). Then I drew the paths for the goofy face—the four circles, the eyebrows, and the two mouth shapes—and combined them are into a compound path. (I also had to use Object » Attributes to reverse the direction of one of the pupils to make it transparent.) Then I took the compound path and combined it with the white-to-gray star blend using Object » Masks » Make. The result is a single star blend that progresses uniformly from one path to another.

Though compound masks are very powerful, they demand still more work than regular masks. Figure 17-30 didn't give me any printing problems—it took a while, but that's only to be expected—but you should be aware that you're potentially treading into dangerous territory when you flirt with compound masks.

Disassembling a Mask

You can return a mask into a standard, everyday collection of objects by choosing Object » Masks » Release. If you grouped your mask, you should also ungroup the objects to make them independent. (It doesn't matter whether you release the mask first or ungroup first; either order is okay.) The content elements become entirely visible again. The former mask remains transparent, though you can now assign a fill and stroke from the Paint Style palette.

Designing a Custom Cross-Hatch

 Illustrator 6's new Ink Pen filters let you take a simple object called a *hatch pattern* (or just plain *hatch*) and repeat it over and over inside a path at different sizes, angles, and densities. In principle, it's the same thing as defining a custom halftone pattern. Instead of printing little round halftone dots, you print little crosses, straight lines, or squiggles.

Figure 17-31 shows a big *X* filled with a bunch of tiny *X*'s. The tiny *X*'s are the hatches. Notice how the little *X*'s change in size and angle throughout the big *X*. If you squint your eyes, this produces an effect very much like a gradation, starting off light in the lower left corner and becoming darker toward the upper right.

You define a hatch using Filter » Ink Pen » Edit. Then you fill a path with the hatch pattern using Filter » Ink Pen » Effects. The latter filter converts a selected path into a mask, and fills the mask with several hundred hatches. In Figure 17-31, for example, the big *X* is the mask and the little *X*'s are content elements. This means that after applying the hatch pattern, you can edit the individual hatches as much as you want.

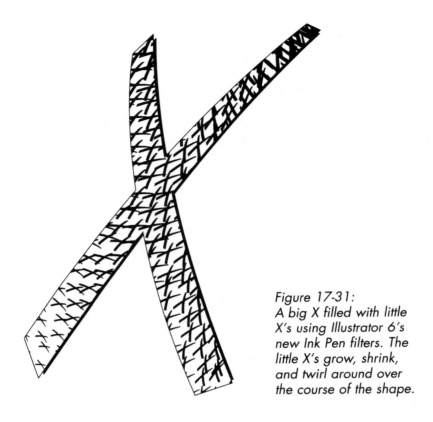

Figure 17-31:
A big X filled with little
X's using Illustrator 6's
new Ink Pen filters. The
little X's grow, shrink,
and twirl around over
the course of the shape.

The following sections explain how the two Ink Pen filters work.

Creating a Custom Hatch Pattern

To create a hatch, follow these steps:

1. Draw a few simple objects.

Keep them very simple. The best hatches contain anywhere from 2 to 20 anchor points, and only one to three paths. After all, simple objects mean faster and more reliable printing. This is one time where you want to leave the razzle-dazzle to Illustrator. In Figure 17-32, I've drawn an X using a minimal 12 points, which is more complicated than any of Illustrator's predefined hatches.

2. Assign fills and strokes to the objects as desired.

Whatever fill color you use will show up when you apply the hatch pattern to a path using Filter » Ink Pen » Effects. But don't get too hung up on it; you can always override the fill color, so you might as well just use black.

 Stroke is more important than fill color. It doesn't matter particularly what color or line weight you use, just whether or not you assign a stroke. If you do, you'll be able to tell Illustrator to vary the thickness of the stroke over the course of the mask. If you set the stroke to None, you won't be able to vary the thickness, but the final effect will print a little faster, too.

3. Choose Filter » Ink Pen » Edit.

The prospective hatch objects should be selected when you choose this filter. The Ink Pen Edit dialog box comes up on screen, looking something like Figure 17-32.

4. Click on the New button.

Illustrator asks you to name the pattern. Enter a name and press Return. In Figure 17-32, I named my pattern *Slim X*. The name appears in the Hatch pop-up menu, and a preview of the hatch appears in the lower left corner of the dialog box.

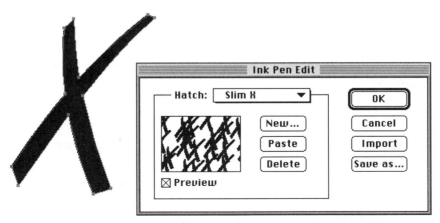

Figure 17-32: I select the X path and choose Filter » Ink Pen » Edit to convert it to a hatch.

5. Click on the OK button or press Return.

Illustrator closes the Ink Pen Edit dialog box and stores the hatch pattern with the foreground illustration.

You can also use the buttons in the Ink Pen Edit dialog box to delete a hatch from the illustration, or paste the selected hatch in the illustration window so you can edit it. You can also import a hatch saved to disk, or save a selected hatch to disk.

Applying a Hatch Pattern to a Path

Creating a hatch is easy. Filling a selected path with a hatch pattern is significantly more complicated. But if you take it slow and give it some time, you can generate some pretty interesting effects. Here's the rub, in step-by-step form:

1. Select the path you want to fill with a hatch pattern.

It has to be a path. No text blocks or imported images allowed.

 If you want the hatches to match a certain color or gradation, assign that color or gradation to the path from the Paint Style palette.

2. Choose Filter » Ink Pen » Effects.

Illustrator displays the massive dialog box shown in Figure 17-33. Isn't that something? When I first saw it, I moaned audibly. But having spent some quality time with it, I now look on it as an old friend. A ridiculously fussy, outrageously inflated, exasperatingly difficult old friend.

3. Select the hatch pattern you want to apply from the Hatch pop-up menu.

The Hatch pop-up menu—the most important option in the dialog box— is hidden away in the lower right corner, at the top of the Style area.

4. Use the Hatch Color, Background, and Fade options to change the color of the hatches.

If you want to change the color of the hatches to match the colors in the selected path in the illustration window, select the Match Object option from the Hatch Color pop-up menu. In the first example in Figure 17-34, I applied the Match Object option to an object filled with a gradation. Illustrator used the colors from the gradation to fill the individual hatches.

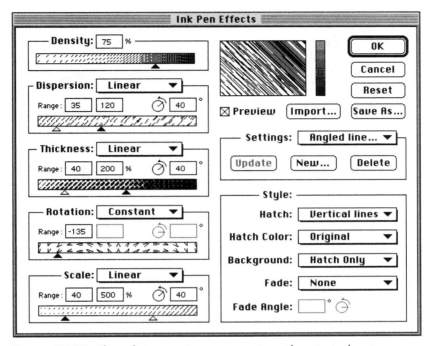

Figure 17-33: Though it contains more options than just about every other dialog box in Illustrator put together, the Ink Pen Effects dialog box is well organized and exceedingly capable.

To place the hatches in front of the fill assigned to the selected path, select the Retain Fill option from the Background pop-up menu. In the second example in Figure 17-34, I set the Hatch Color pop-up menu to Original to leave the hatches black, and selected the Retain Fill option to keep the original gradation in the background.

You can also choose to fade the colors of the hatches to white or to black by selecting options from the Fade pop-up menu. For example, assigning the To White option to a bunch of black hatches creates a black-to-white gradation. You can set the angle of the gradation using the Fade Angle value (or drag inside the tiny icon if you prefer). A fourth option, Use Gradient, matches the colors of the hatches to the gradient fill assigned to the selected path. This option produces the very same effect demonstrated in the first example in Figure 17-34, except that you can modify the angle of the gradation using the Fade Angle option.

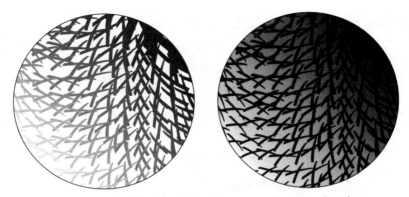

Figure 17-34: Paths filled with hatches using the Match Object (left) and Retain Fill (right) options from the Hatch Color and Background pop-up menus, respectively.

5. Specify the density of the hatch pattern.

The Density slider bar in the upper left corner of the dialog box changes the number of hatches that are packed into the shape. Raise the Density value or drag the slider triangle to the right to increase the hatch population; reduce the value or drag the triangle to the left to nuke those hatches till there are barely any of the suckers left alive.

In the upper right corner of the dialog box, you can keep an eye on the effects of raising or lowering the hatch population in the preview box. To the right of the preview box is a density adjustment bar. Click on a light swatch in the bar to decrease the number of hatches; click on a dark swatch to raise the number. What's the difference between this bar and the Density slider bar? The little density adjustment bar works in big, clunky increments, but otherwise, not a thing. One merely compounds the effects of the other.

6. Modify the Dispersion, Thickness, Rotation, and Scale options until the men in the white suits come to take you away.

These options are at the heart of what makes the Ink Pen feature so cool, but learning how to use them is no small task. Each of these options includes a pop-up menu, a couple of Range option boxes, an angle option box and icon, and a slider bar with one or two triangles.

- **Dispersion**: These options control how far Illustrator is allowed to move hatches up, down, and sideways inside the selected path.

- **Thickness**: The Thickness options let you modify the line weights of stroked hatches. If the selected hatch doesn't include a stroke, the Thickness options are dimmed.

- **Rotation**: Use these options to rotate the hatches inside the selected path.

- **Scale**: These options enlarge and reduce the hatches.

All four sets of options are actually transformations—Dispersion is move, Thickness scales the stroke, and Rotation and Scale are what they say they are. They work much like the options inside the Transform Each dialog box discussed back in Chapter 11, except that they affect hatches instead of selected objects.

All four of these pop-up menus include an identical collection of six options They permit Illustrator to transform the hatches within a set range, or apply constant transformations. Figure 17-35 shows each option as it affects the Scale settings. The hatch pattern used in the figure is a simple black circle.

- **None**: Select this option to prevent the transformation from working at all. Throughout Figure 17-35, Dispersion, Thickness, and Rotation were all set to None. In the first example, Scale is set to None as well.

- **Constant**: This option applies a constant transformation value to all hatches. You are permitted just one option box and one slider triangle. In the Constant example in Figure 17-35, the single Scale value is set to 75 percent.

- **Linear**: Select this option if you want to create a gradation of transformations. You enter two Range values to specify the minimum and maximum transformations, and Illustrator varies between them at a constant rate from one end of the selected path to the other. You also specify the angle of the variation using the option box and icon at the right side of the slider bar. It's like a linear gradation. In the Linear example in the figure, the Range values were 50 and 150 percent, and the angle was set to 45 degrees (as they were for the remaining examples as well).

- **Reflect**: The Reflect option varies the transformation from the center of the shape outward. Therefore, it starts with the second Range value, gradually varies to the first, and then varies back to the second, as the Reflect example in the figure demonstrates.

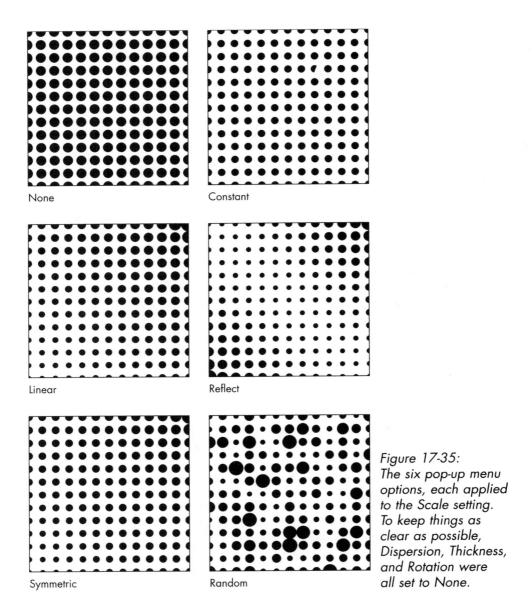

None

Constant

Linear

Reflect

Symmetric

Random

Figure 17-35:
The six pop-up menu
options, each applied
to the Scale setting.
To keep things as
clear as possible,
Dispersion, Thickness,
and Rotation were
all set to None.

Symmetric: At first glance, the Symmetric and Linear examples in Figure 17-35 appear identical. But there is a subtle difference. The hatches in the Linear example increase in size at a constant rate from the lower left corner to the upper right corner of the square. Not so in the Symmetric example. The hatches grow quite a bit at first, flatten out somewhat in the middle, and grow briskly again at the end. The Symmetric option is supposed to simulate shading around a cylinder—changing quickly, flattening out, and changing quickly again. But the effect is so slight, I doubt most viewers will notice. Oh well, at least the Adobe engineers gave it the extra effort.

Random: If you want Illustrator to transform the hatches ad hoc, select the Random option. In the Random example in the figure, for example, Illustrator has randomly scaled the hatches from 50 to 150 percent. The angle options are dimmed when you select Random because, well, an angle would imply order and Random directly opposes order. (You can have a random angle, but you can't have an angled Random.)

If you're interested in producing a gradient effect, set the Thickness and/or Scale settings to Linear, Reflect, or Symmetric. This allows the hatches to grow and shrink, just like the halftone dots in a standard gradation. It doesn't matter how you set the Dispersion or Rotation options. Neither of these options simulates a gradation, although they can be used to enhance the effect.

7. Press the Return key to apply the hatch pattern.

As I said, Illustrator converts the selected path in the illustration window to a mask and fills it with hatch objects. The mask and its contents are automatically grouped. Each hatch is a separate path, so you can edit it with the direct selection tool (among others). And if you prefer to crop the hatches into independent paths that are easier to print, choose Object » Mask » Release followed by Filter » Pathfinder » Crop.

The only Ink Pen Effects options I ignored in the above steps are those in the Settings area in the upper right portion of the dialog box. Because this dialog box contains so many options, Illustrator lets you store settings for later use. To store all settings in the Ink Pen Effects dialog box, click on the New button and enter a name for the settings. You can retrieve a collection of settings by selecting an option from the Settings pop-up menu. If you modify a few settings, you can assign them to the named item in the pop-up menu by clicking on the Update button. And, of course, you can trash a collection of settings by clicking on the Delete button.

That, my friends, is it. I have now told you everything there is to know about using the tools, commands, filters, palettes, dialog boxes, options, and cursors available to Adobe Illustrator 6. The only topic I've omitted is printing. I can't imagine why printing would interest you; the way we go through paper and film in this country is a crime against God and nature. But if life seems senseless without output—I confess that I've managed to waste several million pages creating big fat books like this one over the years—then turn the page and read the final chapter.

PRINTING YOUR ILLUSTRATIONS

There are a lot of programs out there that print high-resolution, object-oriented type and graphics. PageMaker, QuarkXPress, FreeHand, and others describe type and graphics using a series of mathematically positioned points and mathematically defined curves. But if I had to cast a vote for the most reliable printing program of the bunch, it would have to be Illustrator. Although PageMaker, XPress, and FreeHand are all well versed in the art of output, Illustrator outperforms them all, printing objects exactly as you see them on screen with the lowest likelihood of error (though, as I have warned throughout previous chapters, printing errors are possible). Where printing is concerned, Illustrator is the model by which all other programs are judged.

 Illustrator's one nagging printing problem in previous versions was merely a convenience issue. In order to print color separations, you had to run a separate utility called, aptly enough, Separator. Adobe long defended this strange requirement by boasting that the Separator utility, while a bother to use, was the best color separation program out there. But with Illustrator 6, Adobe has finally bit the bullet and integrated all of Separator into the core Illustrator application. To print color separations, you press ⌘-P, just as in every other program for the Mac. And what do you know? There's no loss of functionality whatsoever. We truly live in an age of miracles.

This chapters explains how to print your illustrations to a PostScript-compatible printer (also called an *output device*). Although Illustrator is capable of printing to non-PostScript printers, like StyleWriters and other inexpensive ink-jet devices, this is not its forté. I don't mean to be a PostScript elitist—heck, I own one of those little Hewlett-Packard DeskWriters—but every high-resolution, professional-quality device includes a PostScript interpreter. If you want to proof your artwork to another kind of printer, fine. You'll find the process works very much like I describe it in this chapter. But when it comes time to print the finished artwork, PostScript is the only way to go.

Printing Composite Pages

A *composite* is a one-page representation of an illustration. A black-and-white composite, printed from a standard laser printer or professional imagesetter (which I describe in a few pages), translates all colors in an illustration to gray values. A color composite, printed from a color printer or film recorder, prints the illustration in full color. Composites are useful when you want to reproduce the illustration in black-and-white, proof an illustration, or fire off a few color photocopies. But you can't use them for professional-quality color reproduction. For that, you need to print color separations, which I discuss later in the section "Printing Color Separations."

Printing a composite illustration is a five-step process:

1. If your computer is hooked up to a network, use the Network control panel to select which network connection the printer is connected to.

2. Use the Chooser desk accessory to activate the PSPrinter driver and select the network printer.

3. Choose File » Page Setup to determine the size of the printed page.

4. Position the page-size boundary in the drawing area.

5. Choose File » Print (⌘-P) to print the illustration to the desired output device.

I explain each of these steps in detail in the following sections.

Selecting a Network

Most Macintosh computers sold in the last four years include two kinds of printing ports. One is the serial LocalTalk port, and the other is the EtherTalk port. The LocalTalk port connects directly to a printer or to an AppleTalk network. The EtherTalk port connects to an Ethernet printer or large-scale Ethernet network. If you work in a large office, you're probably connected to other computers over Ethernet, which is the standard networking protocol throughout corporate America. If you work in a small office or at home, you probably print by way of the LocalTalk port.

If you have access to multiple networks, you can switch from one network to another using the Network control panel. Choose Apple » Control Panels » Network to bring up the Network window shown in Figure 18-1. Depending on your model of computer, you'll probably find at least two icons—LocalTalk and EtherTalk. In Figure 18-1, I have a third, Remote Only, which I can use to print through my modem to a remote network. (This is a function of Apple Remote Access, which freelancers like me have to use to communicate with distant editors.) Select the kind of network that contains the printer you want to use, and click in the close box in the upper left corner of the window.

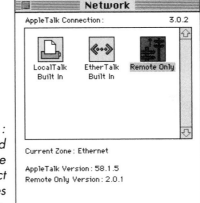

Figure 18-1:
If your computer is hooked up to multiple networks, use this control panel to select the network that includes the printer you want to use.

Your Mac can communicate over several different kinds of networks, but it can only access one at a time. So if you are sharing files, say, over Ethernet, and you switch to a LocalTalk printer, an error message appears, telling you that the Ethernet connection is about to be broken. This is the price one pays for connectivity.

 If you are connected to a single network—or no network at all— you can probably point the Network control panel to the proper network once and ignore it from that point on. But EtherTalk sometimes requires a little extra attention. In order to initialize EtherTalk, your Mac sends out a signal to the network. If it doesn't get a response—whether it's because there's no machine on at the other end of the network or the hub is down—the system automatically switches over to LocalTalk. This is especially a problem for small businesses like mine that rely on EtherWave or a similar transceiver; if you don't have two transceivers or adapters up and running at once, you can't activate EtherTalk. This means every so often, you may have to go back to the Network control panel and turn the darn thing on again.

And if you find yourself schlepping a PowerBook from one client's office to the next and connecting into various company networks to print proofs, you'll have to visit the Network control panel quite frequently. In fact, it's not a bad idea to keep an EtherWave AAUI Transceiver or PowerBook Adapter (both from Farallon, 510/814-5000) in your bag in case you need to connect into a corporate network where the general mood does not run in favor of Macs.

Choosing a PostScript Printer

To select a printer, locate the Chooser desk accessory in the list of items under the Apple menu. The Chooser dialog box comes up, as shown in Figure 18-2. The dialog box is split into two halves, with the left half devoted to a scrolling list of printer driver icons and network zones, and the right half to specific printer options.

Select the PSPrinter icon, spotlighted in Figure 18-2. PSPrinter is the most recent PostScript *printer driver* direct from Adobe, the inventor and custodian of PostScript. It helps Illustrator and the system software translate the contents of an illustration to the output device.

 If PSPrinter is not available in the left-hand list of icons, or if you haven't yet installed the newest version, PSPrinter 8.3, do so now. Insert the CD-ROM that came with your copy of Illustrator and open the Adobe Products folder. Inside, you'll find the PSPrinter 8.3 subfolder. Open it and double-click on the Installer program. This installs the PSPrinter driver as well as lots of PostScript printer description files, which I'll describe in a moment. Together, they make Illustrator 6 print at peak form.

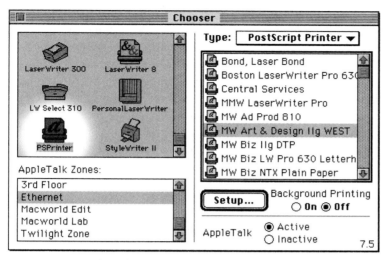

Figure 18-2: Select the PSPrinter icon inside the Chooser window to select and initialize a PostScript printer.

If the network includes multiple zones, you'll see two scrolling lists on the left side of the Chooser dialog box, one with icons and one with text, as in Figure 18-2. Select the zone that contains the desired printer from the lower list. If you don't see any zones, don't worry about it. They only exist to keep us all at the mercy of network administrators who bandy about mystical terms like *bandwidth* and *gateway* to dull our minds and keep us docile.

After you select the required printer driver and, if necessary, gain access to the proper zone, you can select the name of your printer from the scrolling list on the right side of the dialog box. Under the list are two sets of radio buttons, Background Printing and AppleTalk. The latter refers to the communications protocol required to hook your Mac to a network. If you turn it off, you won't be able to access your printer anymore, so by all means leave it turned on.

Background Printing isn't quite so cut and dry. When enabled, this option quickly *spools* an illustration and lets you resume working without a lot of waiting around. Illustrator describes the illustration to a system-level program called PrintMonitor. When it finishes spooling, the software frees up and lets you get back to business while the system software prints the illustration in the background. Unfortunately, spooling can interrupt foreground tasks and increase the likelihood of printing errors. Though it succeeds more often than it fails, PrintMonitor *can* drop code, which may result in some very strange problems. If perfect output is more important than fast output, turn Background Printing off.

The PSPrinter driver supports *PostScript printer description* (PPD) files. PSPrinter can't account for the tiny differences between different models of PostScript printers, so each PPD serves as a little guidance file, customizing the driver to accommodate a specific printer model. After selecting a printer, you can access the proper PPD by clicking on the Setup button. (Or just double-click on the printer name in the list.) A new dialog box claws its way onto your screen, as shown in Figure 18-3. Click on the Auto Setup button to instruct the system software to talk to your printer and automatically determine the proper PPD. If the system fails, or if it selects the dreaded Generic option, click on the Select PPD button and try to locate the proper PPD file inside the Printer Descriptions folder in the Extensions folder in your System Folder. When you finish, click on the OK button or press Return.

Figure 18-3: Use this dialog box to select the proper printer description file for your particular brand of PostScript printer.

At the top of the list of printers is a new pop-up menu labeled Type. By default, it's set to PostScript Printer. But if you prefer, you can select the Virtual Printer option, which lets you prepare an illustration for output to a PostScript printer when no such printer is currently hooked up to your computer. For example, you might select this option prior to submitting an illustration to be printed from an imagesetter at a service bureau. Use the Setup button to select the PPD file for the kind of printer you think the service bureau will be using, and press Return.

When you finish selecting options in the Chooser dialog box, click on the close box in the upper left corner of the title bar. If you've changed the printer, the system delivers an alert box telling you that you have to visit the Page Setup dialog box. Tell it to go away and leave you alone; everything is already in hand.

Setting Up the Page

The next step is to define the size of the page on which you intend to print your illustration. Choose File » Page Setup command to display the PSPrinter Page Setup dialog box in Figure 18-4, which contains the following options:

● **Paper**: Select the size of the paper you want to print on. The specific options available from this pop-up menu depend on which PPD file you selected inside the Chooser. For example, I selected the PPD file for the Linotronic 530 imagesetter using the Virtual Printer option inside the Chooser dialog box. Then when I selected MaxMeasure from the long list of Paper options in the Page Setup dialog box, the page icon on the left side of the dialog box kindly explained the dimensions of this page, as you can see in Figure 18-4. (Most PPDs don't provide this handy feedback; the page icon just contains a big, useless *a*.) The Linotronic 530 can print a page 18 inches wide and more than 3 feet tall, suitable for a small poster. I could also select a Custom option and enter my own page dimensions in the page icon area.

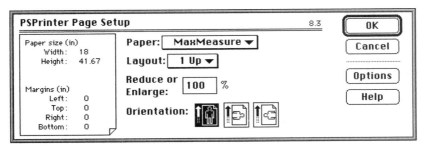

Figure 18-4: Use the Page Setup dialog box to specify the size and orientation of the printed page.

● **Layout**: This option lets you print multiple miniaturized versions of your Illustrator pages per each sheet of paper. You can print 2 or 16 pages at increasingly more drastic reductions. It saves paper and cuts down on print time. But it only makes sense if your illustration contains multiple pages, which most illustrations don't.

Reduce or Enlarge: To scale your illustration as you print it, enter any value from 25 to 400 percent in this option box. Generally, you'll only want to use this option to reduce overly large artwork when proofing it on a laser printer or other device that's limited to letter-sized pages.

Orientation: New to the PSPrinter 8.3 driver, the Page Setup dialog box presents you with three Orientation options. By default, the page is positioned upright, in the portrait position. But if you want to print a wide illustration, you can select one of two landscape options. One rotates the page onto its right side when printing; the other rotates it onto its left side. This permits you to print illustrations onto pages that already have holes punched into them. Depending on how you load the paper into the paper tray, you may prefer one landscape option to the other.

Click on the Options button to bring up the dialog box shown in Figure 18-5. The check boxes in this dialog box allow you to perform a few printing effects that you generally don't need to bother with, but sometimes come in handy. The sample page on the left-hand side of the dialog box demonstrates the effect of the selected options. The big *a* represents the illustration on the page, and the dotted line represents the margin size.

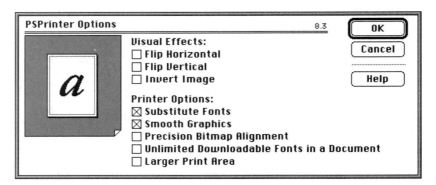

Figure 18-5: The PSPrinter Options dialog box lets you perform certain printing effects, which range from moderately useful to nonfunctioning.

 The options in the PSPrinter Options dialog box are most useful when printing an illustration to a mid-range output device, such as a laser printer. If you're printing to a color thermal-wax or dye-sublimation device or an imagesetter, some of the options—particularly Flip Horizontal, Flip

Vertical, and Invert Image—may duplicate or nullify settings in the more important Print Options dialog box, described in the "Printing the Pages" section. Be sure to read that section to learn more.

The check boxes in the PSPrinter Options dialog box work as follows:

- **Flip Horizontal**: Select this option to flip the objects in an illustration horizontally on the printed page. When printing film negatives, turn on this check box to print the illustration so the emulsion side of the film is away from the viewer, called *emulsion down*. Turn the check box off to face the emulsion side toward the view, called *emulsion up*. I explain film negatives more thoroughly in the "Printing Color Separations" section later in this chapter.

- **Flip Vertical**: This check box flips the illustration vertically on the printed page. You can use this option instead of Flip Horizontal to specify the emulsion side of a film negative. However, if you select both Flip Horizontal and Flip Vertical, you nullify the effect, returning the emulsion side up. Selecting both options also has the effect of printing the illustration upside down.

- **Invert Image**: Select this option to change all blacks to white and all whites to black. This check box prints a photographic negative of the illustration and is used primarily when printing to film. Most commercial printers prefer film negatives when transferring artwork to printing plates.

- **Substitute Fonts**: This check box supposedly substitutes the fonts Geneva, Monaco, and New York with their PostScript equivalents Helvetica, Courier, and Times. But if you try to use it with Illustrator, the program automatically turns the check box off and prints the TrueType versions of Geneva, Monaco, and New York. In other words, ignore this option.

- **Smooth Graphics**: Here's another one to ignore. Back in the old days, when MacPaint was a hot program, folks were bound and determined to get their jagged black-and-white images to print with smooth edges. The Smooth Graphics check box did just that, averaging pixels to give them smooth though gummy edges. Well, it doesn't matter how you have this option set in Illustrator. Imported black-and-white images always have jagged edges, just as the Mother Nature meant them to have.

- **Precision Bitmap Alignment**: This option reduces a typical 72-ppi image dragged over from Photoshop to 96 percent of its original size, making it compatible with a 300-dpi laser printer. This increases the resolution of a 72-ppi image to 75-ppi, which is evenly divisible into 300. Unless the laser printer is your final output device, I recommend that you leave this option alone.

- **Unlimited Downloadable Fonts in a Document**: This check box is designed to help moron applications that don't know how to properly download fonts. Some programs try to download every font in a document at the same time, which can overwhelm the printer's memory. This check box tells the program to wise up. Illustrator manages its fonts just fine without this silly option.

- **Larger Print Area**: When selected, this option enlarges the imageable area of an illustration when output to a laser printer. The margin size displayed in the drawing area becomes larger, showing that you can print a larger portion of the artboard. For example, when printing a letter-sized page, this option increases the size of the imageable area from 7.7 by 10.2 inches to 8.0 by 10.8 inches on most printers. This is a very useful option when proofing an illustration, but it's unnecessary when imagesetting, because imagesetters can print all the way to the edge of both paper and film.

Adjusting the Page Size

You can modify the page boundaries in the artboard by selecting one of the View radio buttons inside the Document Setup dialog box, which I introduced back in Chapter 3. To display the dialog box, choose File » Document Setup or press ⌘-Shift-D. Then select the desired radio button:

- **Tile Imageable Areas**: Select this radio button to subdivide the artboard into multiple partial pages, called tiles. I talk more about tiling large artwork in the "Tiling Oversized Illustrations" section later in this chapter.

- **Tile Full Pages**: Select this radio button to display as many whole pages as will fit inside the artboard. Use this check box to print a multi-paged document like a flier or a two-page ad.

- **Single Full Page**: Select this radio button to display a single page size inside the artboard. This ensures that you will print just one page for the entire illustration.

After selecting one of these options and pressing the Return key, use the page tool to position the page size relative to the objects in your illustration. If the dotted page boundaries are not visible, choose View » Show Page Tiling. If you selected the Tile Imageable Areas option in the Document Setup dialog box, the page number of each tile is listed in the lower left corner of the tile. This way, you can specify the particular pages that you want to print when outputting the illustration.

Printing Pages

To initiate the printing process, choose File » Print or press the trusty keyboard equivalent, ⌘-P. The standard Printer dialog box appears, as shown in Figure 18-6. Most of the options are the same as those you see when printing from any Macintosh application, but a few are unique to Illustrator. Here's how they work:

● **Copies**: Enter the number of copies you want to print in the Copies option box. You can print 999 copies of an illustration, but if you want to print any more than 10, you're better off having them commercially reproduced. Commercial reproduction provides better quality for less money, and it ensures less wear and tear on your printer.

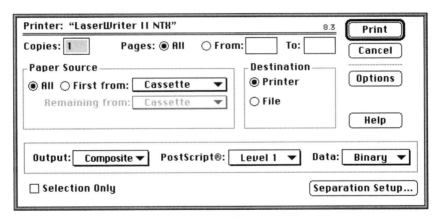

Figure 18-6: The Printer dialog box allows you to print the pages in your illustration to a PostScript-compatible printer.

● **Pages**: Specify a range of pages using the Pages options. By default, the All radio button is selected. If the drawing area displays a single page size, Illustrator will print just that page. If the drawing area contains multiple pages or tiles, Illustrator prints all pages that contain objects. To define a specific range of pages or tiles to be printed, enter the page numbers in the From and To option boxes. These numbers should correspond to the page numbers displayed in the lower left corners of pages in the drawing area.

- **Paper Source**: If you want to print your illustration on a letterhead or other special piece of paper, select the First From radio button, then select Manual Feed from the accompanying pop-up menu. You can then print the remaining pages in the illustration to pages in the paper tray using the Remaining From pop-up menu.

- **Destination**: This option allows you to generate a PostScript-language definition of the file on disk rather than printing it directly to your printer. Select the Printer option to print the image to an output device as usual. Select File to write a PostScript-language version of the image to disk. You can then submit the file to a service bureau and have the printer technician download the file. This way, the technician can't accidentally (or purposely) modify the illustration when he or she opens it inside Illustrator.

If you selected the Virtual Printer option inside the Chooser, the Printer radio button is dimmed, leaving File as your only option. For more information on saving PostScript language files, read to the "Printing to Disk" section later in this chapter.

- **Output**: Select the Composite option from the Output pop-up menu to print a black-and-white or color composite of your illustration. Select the Separate option to print color separations. I explain the latter option in more detail in the next section.

- **PostScript**: Select Level 1 or Level 2 depending on the kind of PostScript that's built into your output device. Most PostScript printers manufactured in the last three years are Level 2, while most older machines are Level 1. (For what it's worth, Adobe introduced Level 2 in 1991, but it took a while to catch on.) Apple's Printer Utility 2.0 will tell you the PostScript capabilities of your printer. If you don't know, leave it set to Level 2 and hope for the best.

- **Data**: If your network doesn't support binary encoding, select the ASCII option to transfer data in the text-only format. The printing process takes much longer to complete, but at least it's possible. When in doubt, however, leave this option set to Binary.

- **Selection Only**: If you just want to print the selected objects in the illustration, select this check box. When the option is turned off—as by default—Illustrator prints all objects, whether selected or not.

Separation Setup: This button displays the Color Separation dialog box, which allows you to specify settings for printing color separations. I explain this humongous dialog box from A to Z in the next section.

The Printer dialog box also includes an Options button that brings up yet another printing dialog box—what would we do without all these piles and piles of printing options?—as shown in Figure 18-7. The Print Options dialog box always contains the first three rows of options shown in the figure, but the options below the dotted line vary depending on which PPD you've selected. The options shown in Figure 18-7 correspond to the Fiery XJ MajestiK (a server for color photocopiers from EFI), but there are roughly a billion other options that could appear in that spot. Or, as in the case of my LaserWriter IINTX, you might not see any options below the dotted line. Here's how the options you do see work:

Cover Page: This option lets you print an extra page that lists your name, the application, the name of the illustration, the date and time, and the printer for the current job. The cover page may precede or follow the rest of the illustration. It's designed to be used in an office setting where lots of folks use the same printer. The idea is the artwork is more likely to get back to you if it has a cover on it. But, come on, you don't need a cover. Everyone recognizes your artwork from a mile off.

Print: These options are designed to translate colors to grayscale or color printing. If you're printing a black-and-white illustration, you

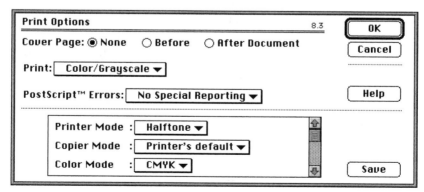

Figure 18-7: The options at the bottom of the Print Options dialog box vary from one PPD to the next. Some PPDs don't offer any options below the dotted line.

don't need to worry about them. The first option, Black and White, is totally irrelevant to Illustrator; the option is provided merely for backwards compatibility with previous PostScript printer drivers. Use the last option, Calibrated Color, when printing a color composite to a Level 2 printer; it helps match the printed colors to those that you see on screen. Otherwise, leave the option set to Color/Grayscale, which is the default setting for printing any composite illustration.

- **PostScript Errors**: This option controls how the system reports PostScript printing errors. The default option, No Special Reporting, just reports errors in passing in the progress window at the top of the screen. If the Background Printing option in the Chooser is turned off, you can select Summarize on Screen to report the error message on screen. (Too bad this isn't the default setting, but too many folks print in the background to make that feasible.) Or you can select Print Detailed Report to print the error message. This last option is generally a waste of paper and only to be used if you can't get a satisfactory response from your printer using any other method.

To discover the meaning and uses for the options below the dotted line, consult the documentation that came with your printer. If you're printing a file to disk with the intention of taking it to a service bureau, consult the service bureau about these options. If you want to lock these settings in as defaults for future illustrations—so you don't have to mess with them every time you print—click on the Save button. (This button is only available when there are additional options below the dotted line.) When you finish, click on the OK button or press Return.

Click on the Print button in the Printer dialog box (or press Return) to initiate the printing process. Two small windows appear, a progress window at the top of the screen and a cancel instruction window slightly lower (both pictured in Figure 18-8).

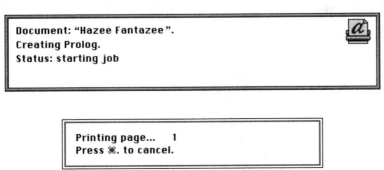

Figure 18-8: The only way to cancel a print job is to repeatedly hit ⌘-period with the persistent fury of a desperate pugilist.

If you want to cancel the print job, you should be able to press ⌘-period, but Illustrator is rarely paying close enough attention to recognize such a subtle gesture. As anyone who prints for a living can tell you, you have to whack ⌘-period 10 to 15 times in a row to gets the program's attention. No joke.

Printing Color Separations

Professional color reproduction requires that you print an illustration to *color separations*. You print a separate sheet of paper or film for each of the process color primaries—cyan, magenta, yellow, and black—or for each spot color in the illustration. You can even add spot colors to the four process primaries to enhance the range of colors in the final document or target the colors in a logo or other color-sensitive element. But keep in mind that every additional separation you print incurs additional cost. For every extra sheet of paper or film, additional ink has to be applied to the pages, and extra labor costs are charged for making the plates and running the plates and paper through the press.

 There is little point in printing color separations from a laser printer, and certainly no reason to print from any kind of color device. The only category of printer up to the job of color separations is an *imagesetter*, which is a typesetter that's equipped with a graphics page-description language like PostScript. An imagesetter prints photosensitive paper or film by exposing it to light, much like a camera. (Some imagesetters output directly to printing plates, eliminating the middle man.) But unlike a camera, an imagesetter knows only two colors, black and white. The colors are applied with inks on the printing press.

You can print color separations of an illustration in one of the following ways:

- Take the Illustrator file to a service bureau or commercial printer and let a qualified technician deal with it.

- Import the illustration as an EPS file into PageMaker or QuarkXPress. Then take the PageMaker or XPress file to a service bureau and let these folks do their jobs.

- Print the separations directly from PageMaker or XPress to an in-house imagesetter.

The last option—printing the color separations directly from Illustrator on your own—either to an in-house imagesetter or to a file that you can later deliver to a service bureau—is perhaps the most unlikely scenario of them all. But it is the reason that Illustrator integrates color separation capabilities, which is why I explain it in great detail in the next few pages.

To print color separations from Illustrator, do the following:

1. Prepare the illustration just as you did when printing the composite, using the Chooser, the Page Setup command, and the page tool.

2. Choose File » Print or press ⌘-P to display the Printer dialog box.

3. Select the Separate option from the Output pop-up menu.

4. Click on the Separation Setup button to display the Color Separation dialog box. Modify the settings as desired and press the Return key to return to the Printer dialog box.

5. Press Return again to start printing.

Step 4 is the only one that requires much effort, and it requires quite a bit. Figure 18-9 shows the Color Separation dialog box in full regalia. The dialog box is divided into two parts—the separation preview on the left side of the window

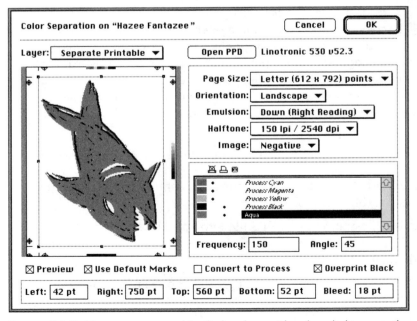

Figure 18-9: You can access this dialog box either by clicking on the Separation Setup button inside the Printer dialog box, or by choosing File » Separation Setup.

and a series of separation options along the right-hand side, as well as a few above and below the preview.

If most of the options are dimmed, you need to select a PPD file. Click on the Open PPD button, then locate the desired PPD file inside the Printer Descriptions folder in the Extensions folder in your System Folder. The PPD file you select will determine which options are available in the pop-up menus throughout the Color Separation dialog box. In Figure 18-9, I've selected the Linotronic 530—a top-of-the-line imagesetter—as listed to the right of the Open PPD button.

The other options in the Color Separation dialog box work as follows:

- **Layer**: Use this pop-up menu to specify which layers you want to print inside your illustration. (If the file contains just one layer, skip this option and move on.) The Separate Printable option prints just those layers that you have set to print; if you turned off the Print check box for a layer in the Layer Options dialog box (as discussed in the "Modifying Your Layers" section of Chapter 10), the layer won't print. Select the Separate Visible option to print all layers that are visible on screen, even if the Print check box is off. And select the Separate All option to print all layers, whether hidden or turned off. The preview shows the results of the option you select.

- **Page Size**: This pop-up menu lists the page sizes available for your output device, based on the active PPD. Next to the common name of each page size is the imageable area of the page, measured in points. Keep an eye on the preview to make sure the illustration and all the printer marks around the illustration fit on the page. In Figure 18-9, for example, the printer marks are getting slightly cut off. If I upgrade my Page Size choice to Letter.Extra (684 x 864) Points, I can avoid this problem.

  Assuming you've selected the PPD file for an imagesetter, you can define your own page size by selecting the Custom option from the Page Size pop-up menu. This displays the dialog box shown in Figure 18-10. The default values for the Width and Height options are the dimensions of the smallest page that will hold all the objects in your illustration. The Offset option allows you to add space between your illustration and the right edge of the paper or film. If the Offset value is left at 0, the output device will automatically center the illustration on the page.

  The Transverse check box controls the orientation of your custom page relative to the paper or film. By default, the printer places the long side of a portrait illustration parallel to the long edge of the film. You can reduce paper or film waste by rotating the illustration so its short side is parallel to the long edge of the film, known as *transverse* orientation. Then use the Offset value to specify the amount of space that lies between your illustration and any printed image that follows it.

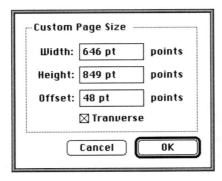

Figure 18-10:
This dialog box allows
you to specify a custom
page size as well as a
distance between pages.

And now back to the Color Separation dialog box:

- **Orientation**: Set this option to Portrait or Landscape, just as you have inside the Page Setup dialog box. This option works independently of the Transverse check box; if the Orientation option is set incorrectly, you'll cut off part of your illustration. In Figure 18-9, for example, I've drawn my fish on a horizontal artboard, so I selected Landscape to make sure every scale on the creature prints.

- **Emulsion**: The Emulsion options control how the illustration prints relative to the emulsion side of photosensitive film. The names given to the options, Up and Down, refer to the sides of the film on which the emulsion is laid. When printing film negatives, you probably want to select Down from the pop-up menu; when printing on paper, Up is usually the correct setting. (Be sure neither Flip Horizontal nor Flip Vertical is selected in the PSPrinter dialog box—shown back in Figure 18-5—since either will nullify the Emulsion setting.) Consult your commercial printer to confirm which option you should select.

- **Halftone**: Weird as it may sound, traditional printing presses aren't capable of applying shades of color to paper. They can apply solid ink or no ink at all. That's it. So to represent different light and dark values, imagesetters generate thousands of little black circles called *halftone dots*, as illustrated in Figure 18-11. The halftone dots grow and shrink to represent respectively darker and lighter shades of color.

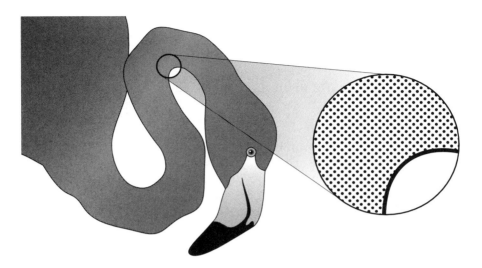

Figure 18-11: A gray value is printed as thousands of little halftone dots. The dots can grow and shrink to imitate different shades.

You can specify the density of the halftone dots by selecting an option from the Halftone pop-up menu in the Color Separation dialog box. The first value before the slash represents the *screen frequency*, which is the number of halftone dots per linear inch. And the second value represents the *printer resolution*, which is the number of tiny printer pixels that print in a linear inch. You can figure out the number of printer pixels that fit inside the largest possible halftone dot by dividing the second number by the first. For example, in this book, all illustrations are printed at a resolution of 2,540 dpi and a screen frequency of 120 lpi. If you divide 2,540 by 120, you get a little more than 21, which means that a halftone dot inside a very dark shade of gray is 21 printer pixels tall and 21 pixels wide.

Fascinating as this may be, the real question is, as always, which option should you use? Unless you have a specific reason for doing otherwise, set the printer resolution (the second value) as high as it will go. If you're printing to paper, you probably don't want to set the screen frequency (the first value) any higher than 120 lpi, since the dots may grow and clog up as the illustration is transferred to film and then to plates. When printing to film, screen frequencies of 133 lpi and higher are acceptable. Consult your commercial printer if you are at all unsure.

● **Image**: The Image option controls whether the illustration prints as a positive or a negative image. If printing to paper, the default Positive is usually the correct setting. However, when printing to film, you'll probably want to select Negative. (The Invert check box in the PSPrinter Options dialog box should be turned off; otherwise, it will interfere with the Image setting.)

● **Color list**: The scrolling list of colors below the Image pop-up menu allows you to specify exactly which colors you want to print to independent separations. The process colors are listed in italics, any named colors appear dimmed. A series of dots appear in front of the colors. The dot for each color falls into one of three columns, headed up by icons that are labeled in Figure 18-12. These icons specify whether the color doesn't get printed at all, whether it gets its own separation, or whether a named color is converted to its process ingredients.

By default, Illustrator is ready to convert all named colors into their process ingredients. If you want to print at least one named color to its own separation, turn off the Convert to Process check box. The named colors in the list immediately change from dimmed to black. Then click in front of the named color under the tiny printer icon in the second column to print that color to its own separation. For all other named colors that you want to convert to CMYK, click in the third column. For example, in Figure 18-12, I've set Aqua to convert to CMYK colors,

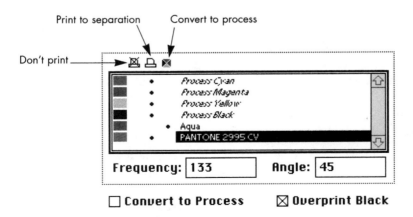

Figure 18-12: To decide which named colors you want to separate and which you want to convert to their CMYK ingredients, turn off the Convert to Process check box.

because no printer in the world stocks an ink called Aqua. But I've set Pantone 2995, an ink readily available at just about every print shop in the country, to print to its own separation.

 Frequency and Angle: In addition to changing the overall screen frequency of the illustration, you can modify the frequency of a single separation. You can also change the angle of the halftone dots. Back in Figure 18-11, for example, you can see that the halftone angle is 45 degrees—that is, each dot is angled 45 degrees from its closest neighbor. To change either the frequency or angle, select a color from the list and enter a new value in the Frequency or Angle option box.

Why would you want to change either of these values? To avoid creating weird patterns between the halftone dots from different separations. See, by default, all process colors are set to the same frequency. Black is angled at 45 degrees, cyan is set to 15 degrees, magenta is 75 degrees, and yellow is 0 degrees. Rotations of 90 degrees or more are repetitive, because the halftone dots extend in all different directions. This means that cyan, magenta, and black are each rotated 30 degrees from each other; only yellow is closer—measuring only 15 degrees from cyan and magenta—but yellow is so light, its halftone dots don't create a patterning effect.

So far, so good. There's no reason to change the process colors. The problem is, how do you prevent a spot color from clashing? Unless you know exactly what you're doing, you shouldn't mess around with the Frequency value. And there aren't really any good angles left. This leaves you with the following frequency and angle options:

If you're printing an illustration that contains one or two spot colors and black—but not cyan, magenta, or yellow—leave black set to 45 degrees, and set the spot colors to 15 and 75 degrees. It doesn't matter which one you set to which. If you only have one spot color, pick an angle—15 or 75—and go with it. When printing a spot color in addition to CMYK, pick a color—black, cyan, or magenta—that the spot color never overlaps. (If the spot color overlaps all three, return to your illustration and modify it so the overlap no longer exists.) Then mimic the angle of that color. For example, if the spot color and cyan never mix—you don't blend between the two colors, mix them together in a gradation, or overprint one on top of the other—then you would set the angle of the spot color to 15 degrees.

 Preview: This check box turns the preview area on and off. Unless you have a slow computer that's not quite keeping up with your actions, leave this check box on. The preview provides important feedback that you don't want to do without.

 Use Default Marks: The old Separator utility used to allow you to specify exactly which kinds of printer marks you wanted to use and even position them on the printed page. But no more. Now you can either print or not print a predefined collection of printer marks. Turn this check box on to print the marks; turn it off to hide them.

The printer marks include star targets and registration marks to aid in *registration*. To register plates is to get them into exact alignment, so one color doesn't appear out of sync with another. Illustrator also prints crop marks around the entire illustration and different types of progressive color bars along the edges. Most importantly, Illustrator labels each separation according to the ink it goes with. There is *no* good reason to turn this option off. But I sure do wish Illustrator still let you customize the marks.

- **Convert to Process**: I already covered this check box in the "Color list" item. When on, it converts all named colors to their process ingredients. When off, you can select which named colors you want to print as spot color and which you want to convert to CMYK.

- **Overprint Black**: Select this check box to overprint all black ink inside the illustration. Overprinting black is a common way of anticipating registration problems. Also, it permits you to create so-called "saturated blacks." Although black is theoretically as dark as dark can be, you can create colors that are visibly darker by adding cyan, magenta, or yellow to solid black. The result is a rich, glossy black. But overprinting every black in your illustration has its drawbacks. If you have a black rectangle positioned on top of a dark CMY object, you can end up applying more ink than the page can absorb. Most paper stocks max out at about 300-percent saturation. If you go over that—for example, 90%C 80%M 70%Y 100%K adds up to 340 percent saturation—the ink can actually puddle or run, creating some messy results. Unless you're sure your illustration is safe from oversaturation, I would avoid the Overprint Black check box and use the more selective Filter » Colors » Overprint Black, as I explain near the end of this chapter.

- **Bounding box**: The bounding box options—Left, Right, Top, and Bottom—allow you to adjust the size of the area Illustrator allots to the illustration. The default values represent the smallest bounding box that can be drawn around the illustration. Printer marks appear in the margins around the bounding box; the bounding box itself appears as a dotted rectangle inside the preview.

You can modify the bounding box either by dragging the corner handles in the preview, or by changing the values in the Left, Right, Bottom, and Top option boxes. These values represent the distance from the edge of the page size (specified with the Page Size pop-up menu) and the edge of the bounding box. Therefore, entering smaller values increases the size of the bounding box; entering larger values shrinks the bounding box. Illustrator automatically moves the printer marks so they stay outside the bounding box.

- **Bleed**: Though this last option may sound like a practice that died with medieval barbers, it actually controls the distance from the edge of the bounding box to the beginning of the crop marks. In printing, a *bleed* is the distance that an image extends off the printed page. For example, a bleed of 18 points ensures that even if the page shifts 1/4 inch on the press or the trim is 1/4 inch off, the illustration still fills the entire page and extends off the sides. How you set the bounding box affects the amount of illustration that is permitted to bleed off the edge. The Bleed value (which can vary from 0 to 18 points) determines how much of this bleed gets printed, and offsets the crop marks and other printer marks so they don't overlap too much of the printed artwork. Unless you're running out of room on the film, you're better off leaving the Bleed value set to its default and highest value, 18 points.

Printing to Disk

When you print an illustration to a PostScript printer, Illustrator *downloads* a PostScript-language version of the file to the printer. The printer reads the file and creates your illustration according to its instructions. Illustrator also allows you to print an illustration to disk; that is, write the PostScript-language file to your hard drive. This way, you can control how an illustration will print, even though you don't have direct access to the output device. You can then send the file off to your service bureau over a modem, or copy the file to disk and drop it off on your way home from work.

Printing to disk is easy. Use the Virtual Printer option in the Chooser to select the PPD file for the printer that you intend to use. Then press ⌘-P, fiddle with the desired options, and hit the Return key, which activates not the OK button but the Save button.

In return, you'll be greeted by the dialog box shown in Figure 18-13. You can name the file and specify its destination, just as in any Save dialog box. You can also select from a few other options:

- **Format**: Select the format that you want to use to save the illustration from this pop-up menu. The pop-up menu offers three EPS options, but there's no reason to select any of them. You can create an editable EPS file from inside Illustrator. To create a file you can download to a printer, select the PostScript Job option, which is the default setting.

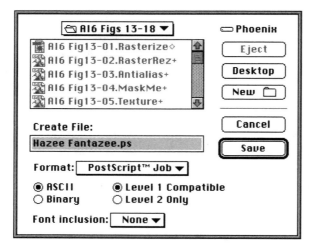

Figure 18-13:
This dialog box
allows you to print an
illustration to disk and
save font definitions
along with the file.

- **ASCII or Binary**: If the folks at the service bureau will be downloading this file from a Mac, select the Binary option. Binary encoding is much faster, much more efficient, and results in smaller files. Only select the ASCII option if you'll be doing something weird and perverse with the file, like giving it to a Windows or DOS user.

- **Level 1 or 2**: You'll have to consult with your service bureau on this one. If the service bureau uses an imagesetter equipped with Level 2 PostScript, by all means select the Level 2 Only option. Otherwise, select Level 1 Compatible.

- **Font inclusion**: If you used any special fonts in your illustration—any-thing besides Times, Helvetica, Courier, and Symbol—select the All But

Standard 13 option. This tells Illustrator to include printer font definitions for every font that you use, except Times and the others. If the intended printer includes the LaserWriter Plus family of fonts—including Palatino, Bookman, Avant Garde Gothic, New Century Schoolbook, Zapf Chancery, and Zapf Dingbats—select the All But Standard 35 option. Adding font definitions to your file greatly increases the size of the illustration on disk, but it also prevents your text from printing incorrectly. If you're sure your service bureau is already equipped with all the fonts you're using, select the None option to minimize the size of the illustration on disk.

Click on the Save button or press Return to save the file. Illustrator will deposit a file on your disk, ready for downloading to the printer of your choosing.

Unusual Printing Considerations

So much for the huge array of printing options that are crammed into the major printing dialog boxes. Though these options are very important—some clearly more important than others—you'll spend most of your time pressing ⌘-P, hitting the Return key, and going off to get some coffee.

Unfortunately, things don't always go according to plan. Sometimes, you have to spend a few minutes massaging your illustration in order to get it ready to deliver the most ideal results in less than ideal conditions. Most problems can be overcome using the options that I've already described, but others can't. Those that can't are the subject of the remaining pages in this chapter.

The following sections explain all the preparatory alternatives that Illustrator permits prior to printing your artwork. Though none of these measures is obligatory—or even customary—they are the sorts of options that you'll want to be at least vaguely familiar with. For example, you can slice and dice large illustrations, insert your own crop marks, overcome printing errors, and anticipate registration problems using tools and commands that are spread out from one end of the illustration window to the other. These are the fringe printing features, out of touch with the common illustration and miles away from the automated worlds of the Page Setup and Print commands. But when things turn slightly uncommon, you may be very glad to have them around.

Tiling an Oversized Illustration

By virtue of the Page Setup dialog box, Illustrator provides access to various common page sizes. But many artists require custom page sizes that mid-range printers can't accommodate. So how do you proof oversized artwork using a typical laser printer?

To proof your artwork to letter sized pages, choose File » Document Setup (⌘-Shift-D) and select the Tile Imageable Areas radio button. Illustrator automatically sections your illustration into separate tiles as indicated by the dotted lines in the drawing area. If these breaks will not permit you to easily reassemble your artwork, use the page tool to manually reposition the dotted lines.

Even after meticulously setting up and printing the tiles, your pages may not fit together properly. Most notably, the tiles may fade toward the outside of the paper, so that the pasted artwork appears to have gutters through it. The only solution is to adjust the tiles with the page tool, print a page, adjust the tiles again, print another page, and so on. Illustrator doesn't provide any automated means for creating an overlap from one tile to the next.

Creating Crop Marks

Crop marks indicate the boundaries of an illustration. Most imagesetters print pages between 12 and 24 inches wide, regardless of the actual size of the illustration. When you have the illustration commercially reproduced, the printer will want to know the dimensions of the final page size and how the illustration should be positioned on the page. Crop marks specify the boundaries of the reproduced page. Properly positioned crop marks help to avoid miscommunication and additional expense.

Illustrator automatically creates crop marks around an entire illustration when you print color separations (as I discussed in the "Printing Color Separations" section). But what if you want to print a grayscale composite? Or perhaps you want to more precisely control the placement of the crop marks in the illustration window. In either case, you can take advantage of Object » Cropmarks » Make, which lets you manually position crop marks inside the illustration window.

To create crop marks, draw a rectangle that represents the size of the final reproduced sheet of paper. Then, with the rectangle selected, choose Object » Cropmarks » Make. Illustrator converts the rectangle into crop marks. For example, in Figure 18-14, I drew a business card. Then I drew a rectangle around the card in the first example and converted the rectangle to crop marks in the second example. Notice that the marks are positioned well outside the rectangular boundary, preventing them from appearing on the final card. The objects that extend outside the crop marks—including the gray bars and my personal insignia, the elegant yet meaningless Smiley Cyclops—will bleed off the edge of the business cards.

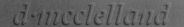

DekeMc@AOL.com

CIS: 70640,670

who needs a business card these days?

DekeMc@AOL.com

CIS: 70640,670

who needs a business card these days?

Figure 18-14: After drawing a rectangle to specify the size of the trimmed illustration (top), choose Object » Cropmarks » Make to convert the rectangle to crop marks (bottom).

If no object is selected and a single page is displayed in the drawing area (i.e., the Single Full Page radio button is active in the Document Setup dialog box), choose Object » Cropmarks » Make to create crop marks around the page. This is an ideal way to add crop marks to a black-and-white illustration.

Unfortunately, only one set of crop marks can exist inside an illustration. When you choose Object » Cropmarks » Make, you delete any previous crop marks while creating new ones. Also, you can move crop marks after you create them. You have to convert the crop marks back to a rectangle by choosing Object » Cropmarks » Release, edit the rectangle as desired, and then choose Object » Cropmarks » Make again.

When you display the Color Separation dialog box—whether by clicking on the Separation Setup button in the Printer dialog box or choosing File » Separation Setup—Illustrator automatically sizes the bounding box in the preview to the exact size of the area surrounded by the crop marks. This is a handy method for sizing the boundary, typically more accurate and easier to manipulate than the bounding box controls inside the Color Separation dialog box.

Flatness and Path Splitting

You can encounter a fair number of errors when printing an illustration, but one of the most common is the *limitcheck* error, which results from a limitation in your printer's PostScript interpreter. If the number of points in the mathematical representation of a path exceeds this limitation, the illustration will not print successfully.

Unfortunately, the "points" used in this mathematical representation are not the anchor points you used to define the object. Instead, they're calculated by the PostScript interpreter during the printing process. When presented with a curve, the interpreter has to plot hundreds of tiny straight lines to create the most accurate possible rendering. So rather than drawing a perfect curve, your printer creates an approximation with hundreds of flat edges. The exact number of edges is determined by a variable known as *flatness*, which is the maximum distance a flat edge can vary from the mathematical curve, as illustrated in Figure 18-15.

The default flatness value for a typical laser printer is 1 pixel, or 1/300 inch. This means the center of any flat edge of the printed curve can be at most 1/300 inch from the closest point along the perfect, mathematical curve. If you were to raise the flatness value, the printer could draw fewer flat edges, which quickens the print time but results in more blocky curves.

Each tiny line in the polygon rendering is joined at a point. If the number of points exceeds your printer's built-in path limit, you'll see the telltale words *limitcheck error* in the progress area on screen, and the illustration will fail to print. The path limit for the original LaserWriter was 1500, seemingly enough flat edges to imitate any curve. But when you factor in such path variations as compound paths and masks, both of which merge shapes with hundreds or thousands of flat edges together, things can get extremely complicated.

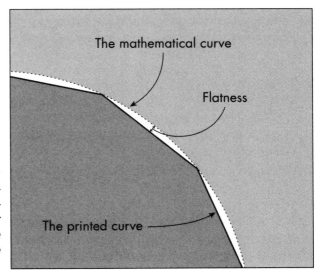

Figure 18-15:
The flatness value deter-
mines the greatest dis-
tance between the center
of a flat edge and the
closest point along the
true mathematical curve.

There are three ways to overcome limitcheck errors:

 The first method is to select the Split Long Paths check box in the Document Setup dialog box (⌘-Shift-D). Then enter the resolution for the final output device into the Output Resolution option box. (Higher resolutions produce less dramatic results.) The next time you save or print the current illustration, Illustrator will automatically break up every path that it considers to be at risk into several smaller paths. In most cases, this won't affect the printed appearance of your illustration.

WARNING Unfortunately, there's no way to automatically reassemble paths that Illustrator splits apart. If you ever need to join them back together, you have to do so manually, which complicates the editing process. So be sure to save your illustration before selecting the Split Long Paths check box, then use File » Save As to save a copy of the split illustration under a different name.

Another problem is that Illustrator's automated path-splitting feature only accounts for the complexity of a single path. It doesn't consider masks, tile patterns, or other factors that are more likely to cause limitcheck errors.

If path splitting doesn't suit your needs, you can change the flatness of individual paths. Select the path that seems responsible for the error—bearing in mind that tile patterns, masks, and compound paths are the most likely culprits—and choose Object » Attributes (⌘-Control-A). Then lower the value in the Output Resolution option box. This raises the flatness value, which equals the resolution of your printer divided by the Output Resolution value. For example, when printing to a 2,540-dpi imagesetter, changing the Output Resolution value to 635 changes the flatness of the selected path to 2540 ÷ 635 = 4. This further flattens out the path and increases its likelihood of printing.

But the best solution is to use masks and tile patterns wisely, as I encouraged you to do in Chapters 15 and 17. If a complex mask isn't printing, for example, choose Object » Mask » Release to release the mask followed by Filter » Pathfinder » Crop to permanently crop the content elements. Though this may necessitate some manual edits on your part, it will almost always solve the printing problem, and it allows you to print smooth curves without worrying about strange printing issues like flatness.

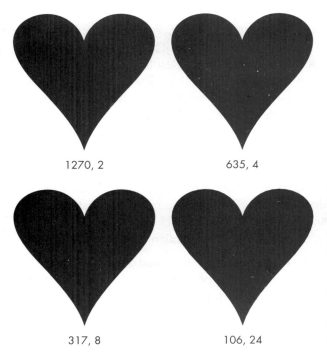

1270, 2   635, 4

317, 8   106, 24

*Figure 18-16:
A single path subjected to different Output Resolution values. (The numbers after the commas are the flatness values, assuming a printer resolution of 2,540 dpi.) Lower values mean more flattened curves.*

Many of the Pathfinder filters have a habit of producing alert boxes when they complete, warning you that they may have generated paths that are too complicated to print. Ignore these messages! They are almost always inaccurate. Wait until you encounter a limitcheck error before you worry about an overly long path.

The default Output Resolution for every illustration you create is 800 dpi. This means that curves printed to a 2,540-dpi imagesetter will be treated to a flatness of approximately 3, while lower resolution printers will use lower flatness values. You can print a test version of an illustration by lowering the Output Resolution in the Document Setup dialog box to, say 300, and leaving the Split Long Paths check box turned off. This will significantly speed up the print time at the expense of the curves.

 All Output Resolution values are saved with an EPS file and included with the illustration even if you import it into another application. So don't expect an illustration to print any better from PageMaker or XPress than it does directly from Illustrator.

Printing Pattern Tiles

As I mentioned more than once in the previous section, tile patterns can cause limitcheck errors. But more commonly, they can cause *out-of-memory* errors by overwhelming the amount of RAM available to your printer. (Yes, like computers, PostScript printers have RAM.) See, Illustrator downloads the tile as if it were a font to your printer's memory. In this way, the printer accesses tile definitions repeatedly throughout the creation of an illustration. So if the illustration contains too many tile patterns or if a single tile is too complex, the printer's memory may fill up, in which case the print job is canceled and you see an out-of-memory error on screen. (If your printer just stops working on a job, even though Illustrator seems to have sent the illustration successfully, this is likewise an indication of an out-of-memory error.)

Out-of-memory errors are less common when printing to modern, high-resolution imagesetters, because these machines tend to include updated PostScript interpreters and have increased memory capacity. Therefore, you will most often encounter an out-of-memory error when proofing an illustration to a mid-range laser printer or other low-memory device. Try one of these techniques to remedy the problem:

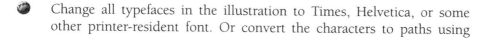 Change all typefaces in the illustration to Times, Helvetica, or some other printer-resident font. Or convert the characters to paths using

Type » Create Outlines. This way, Illustrator won't have to download both tile and font definitions.

- Print objects filled with different tile patterns in separate pages. Then use traditional paste-up techniques to combine the patterns into a composite proof.

- Turn off the Preview and Print Patterns option in the Document Setup dialog box. All tile patterns will print as medium gray. This technique allows you to proof all portions of your illustration except the patterns.

When you print the illustration to an imagesetter, it will probably print successfully because of the imagesetter's increased memory capacity. But if the illustration still encounters an out-of-memory error, you'll have to delete some patterns or resort to traditional paste-up techniques, as suggested in the second item above.

Trapping Selected Paths

Mainstream applications like PageMaker, XPress, FreeHand, and (alas) Illustrator are still in the stone age when it comes to *trapping*, which helps to cover up registration problems that sometimes occur when printing full-color documents. If your commercial printer's plates are slightly out of register—as they frequently are—gaps may form between high-contrast edges. It's always a good idea to employ a professional printing company that has lots of experience in color printing and guarantees its work. But even the most conscientious printers may be off by as little as a half point, enough to cast a shadow of shoddiness across your artwork.

Full-service (read mega-expensive) printers will trap your work for you using dedicated systems from Scitex or Crosfield. Other printers may charge you a little extra to trap your illustration with Macintosh software such as TrapWise or IslandTrapper. If your printer does not provide trapping services, however, you may want to create your own traps inside Illustrator.

Illustrator's Trap filter works by creating a new path of a specified thickness that overprints the neighboring paths below it. The result is a slight darkening of colors where two paths meet, an imperfect solution that is nevertheless much preferable to a white gap.

You can't trap an entire illustration. Instead, you trap two or more neighboring paths at a time. Also, the filter works only on paths with flat fills. It can't handle gradations, tile patterns, strokes, text, or imported images.

 If you want to trap a stroke, first convert it to a filled path by choosing Filter » Path » Outline Path. To trap text, convert the characters to paths with Type » Create Outlines. You'll only want to trap large text, such as headlines or logos. Traps around small letters can make the text gooey and illegible.

The trick when using the Trap filter is to recognize which paths need trapping and which do not. Here are a few instances where trapping may be helpful:

- Two paths filled with different spot colors.
- A path filled with a spot color neighboring a path filled with a process color.
- Two paths filled with process colors that don't share any primary color in common. For example, an 80% cyan path next to a 50% yellow, 40% magenta path needs to be trapped.

If two neighboring paths are both filled with process colors, and they share one or more primary colors in common, trapping is not necessary. For example, if a 50% cyan, 20% magenta path overlaps a 70% cyan, 30% yellow path, a continuous screen of cyan will occur between the two paths even if the magenta and yellow plates are incorrectly registered. Likewise, you don't have to trap between two paths filled with different tints of a spot color. Registration problems have no effect on paths printed from the same plate.

 The Trap filter is pretty smart about telling you when you need and don't need to trap. If the filter refuses to work, it means that the paths are too similar to require trapping. (This assumes that the paths are filled with flat colors; gradations, strokes, and other attributes can trip up the Trap filter as well.)

To trap two or more selected paths, choose Filter » Pathfinder » Trap, which displays the Pathfinder Trap dialog box shown in Figure 18-17. The options in this dialog box work as follows:

- **Thickness**: This is the key option in the dialog box. Here you specify the width of the overprinting path created by the filter. The default value, 0.25 point, is awfully small, only sufficient to remedy extremely slight registration problems. If your commercial printer is a top-of-the-line operation, this is sufficient. If your printer is more the workaday, get-the-job-out variety, a value of 0.5 or 1 might be more appropriate.

- **Height/width**: This value represents the ratio between the vertical and horizontal thickness of the trapping path. A value of 100 percent means that the trap will be the same thickness—as specified in the previous option—throughout its length. Raise the value to increase the vertical thickness of the trap; lower the value to decrease the vertical thickness. The horizontal thickness is always the exact width entered into the Thickness option box. The purpose of this option—in case you're wondering—is to

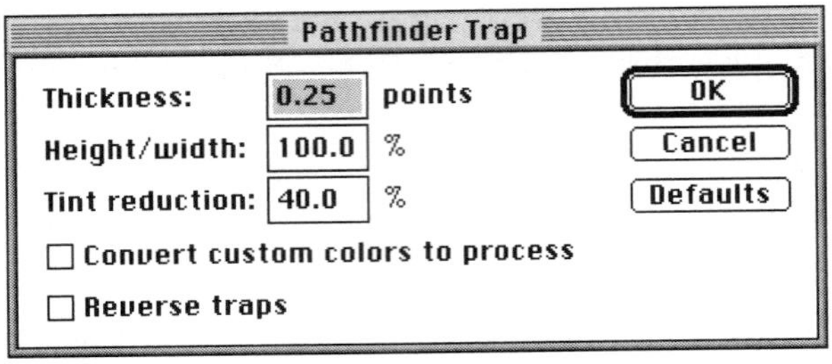

Figure 18-17:
Using this dialog box,
you can create a sliver
of a path that traces
the border between a
pair of selected paths.

account for differences in vertical and horizontal misregistration. Check
with your printer to find out if any compensation is needed.

- **Tint reduction**: When trapping paths filled with spot colors, Illustrator
  fills the trap with a tint of the lightest color. So if a selected yellow path
  neighbors a selected brown path, the trap is filled with a tint of yellow.
  The light yellow trap looks lighter than either of the neighboring paths
  on screen, but because it overprints, the trap leaves the yellow path
  unaffected and slightly darkens the brown path.

  When trapping process-color paths (or if you convert the trap applied
  to spot colors to a process color using the Convert Custom Colors to
  Process check box), Illustrator mixes a 100-percent tint of the darker
  color with a lighter tint of the lighter color.

  Whether you're trapping spot or process colors, the Tint Reduction
  value determines the tint of the lighter color. A light tint appears less
  intrusive than a dark one, so the default 40 percent is a good value for
  most jobs.

- **Convert custom colors to process**: This check box fills the trap with a
  process color regardless of whether the trapped paths are filled with spot
  or process colors. Generally, you'll want to leave this option off. If the
  lighter color is a spot color, it stands to reason that the trap should be a
  tint of that spot color. Only if the darker of two neighboring paths is filled
  with a process color *and* the screen angle of the spot color might interfere
  with those of the process colors should you select this option. *Never* select
  it when trapping two neighboring paths filled with spot colors.

- **Reverse traps**: This option changes the fill of the trap to favor the
  darker color instead of the lighter one. Select this option when you disagree with Illustrator over which of two neighboring colors is lighter.
  For example, when trapping a red path and a blue path, Illustrator will

most likely see the blue path as lighter, where you may see it as darker. If you don't like the way Illustrator fills the trap, undo the operation and reapply it with Reverse Traps selected.

After you press Return, Illustrator creates a trapping path along the border between each pair of neighboring selected shapes. Figure 18-18 shows two trapping scenarios (converted to grayscale for purposes of this book). In each case, just the outlined paths were selected. As you can see, Illustrator only creates traps around the neighboring borders of the selected paths; portions of selected paths that do not neighbor other selected paths are ignored.

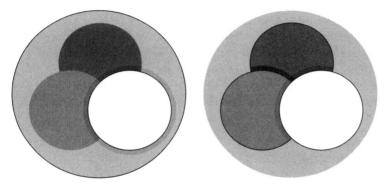

Figure 18-18: The results of two trapping operations. In each case, the outlined paths were selected, paths without outlines were not. The dark strips are the traps.

This system works great when trapping spot colors, but it gets a little weird when trapping process colors. For example, suppose in the first example in Figure 18-18, the small selected circle is yellow, and the large selected circle is deep purple. The overprinting trap will have hints of both yellow and purple, even when it overlaps the deselected circles, which may be green, orange, or any other color. The fact is, the purple of the background circle has no business being there.

 To avoid this problem, remove the tint of the background path from the trap. In the case of my example, I would simply remove the purple from the trap and leave the yellow intact. A yellow trap surrounding a yellow path is always acceptable, regardless of the paths it overprints.

Note that if you try to reapply the Trap command with different settings by pressing ⌘-Shift-E, Illustrator displays the Pathfinder Options dialog box (discussed briefly in Chapter 9). Just press the Return key to exit this dialog box and continue on to the Pathfinder Trap dialog box.

Overprinting Black Paths

Another way to trap two objects is to overprint one on top of the other. If you have a text block full of small type, and the type is black, you'll probably want to select the Overprint Fill check box in the Paint Style palette. This way, Illustrator prints the text on top of any background colors, ensuring no gaps between characters' outlines and neighboring colors.

 Overprinting black is such a common practice that Illustrator 6 provides a filter to automate the process. It allows you to overprint a specific percentage of black through the fills and strokes of all selected objects. To use the filter, select all the objects you might want to overprint, and choose Filter » Colors » Overprint Black. Illustrator displays the Overprint Black dialog box shown in Figure 18-19.

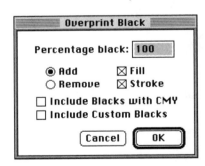

Figure 18-19:
Use the Overprint Black filter to overprint all selected objects that contain a specific percentage of black.

The options in this dialog box work as follows:

- **Percentage Black**: Enter the intensity of black ink that you want to overprint. All objects with that exact percentage of black will overprint. (The documentation says that colors with *at least* this much black will overprint, but this is not how the filter works in Illustrator 6.0. The filter affects a specific percentage, not a range.)

- **Add and Remove**: If you want to overprint colors, select the Add radio button. If you want to remove overprinting from selected objects—so that they knock out the colors behind them—select Remove.

- **Fill and Stroke**: Use these check boxes to overprint—or remove the overprinting from—fills, strokes, or both fills and strokes. By default, both check boxes are selected.

- **Include Blacks with CMY**: To overprint CMYK objects that contain a specific percentage of black, select this check box. For example, if you set the Percentage Black value to 40 percent, and a selected object is filled with 30%C 20%M 10%Y 40%K, this check box must be turned on for the filter to affect the object.

- **Include Custom Blacks**: When this check box is on, the Overprint Black check box will overprint named colors that contain a specific percentage of black. If you intend for your objects to print as spot colors, then you should leave this option off. (Since the CMYK values are for screen display purposes only, the Black value in a spot color has nothing to do with the printed ink.) But if you plan on converting all named colors to CMYK, go ahead and select this option as the mood hits you.

This filter would be better if you could change a range of blacks at a time (an oversight that Adobe might fix in the future). And it'd be nice if the filter could automatically detect oversaturations and make sure that overprinted blacks don't smudge on the printed page. But it's a decent first attempt, and it's safer than simply selecting the Overprint Black check box in the Color Separation dialog box.

INDEX

F

H

Halftone dots, 705
  custom, 77
  optimized, 64
Halftone pop-up menu, 704–705
Hand cursor, 26, 88
Hand icons, 628
Hand scrolling the artboard, 46, 88
Hand tool, 22, 50. *See also* Fist cursor
Handles. *See* Bézier control handles
Hanging indent to paragraphs, 204–205
Hanging Punctuation check box, 206
Hard filter (in Pathfinder), 371, 373, 538–539
Hatch Color pop-up menu, 681
Hatch pop-up menu, 680
Headline text, converting to paths, 271
Height/Width option box, 719–720
Help menu icon, 17
Hide Character palette command, 48, 191
Hide (deselected objects) command, 48
Hide Edges (of selections) command, 48, 142
Hide Info palette command, 48
Hide Layers palette command, 48
Hide page tiling, 65
Hide Paint Style palette command, 48
Hide Paragraph palette command, 48
Hide Rulers command, 48, 378
Hide (selected objects) command, 48, 402–403
Hide Tab Ruler command, 48
Hide Template command, 48, 132
Hide Toolbox command, 48
High pass filter, 66–67
High-contrast artwork, 6
Highlight Font option, 52
Highlight Kerning option, 52
Highlight Size option, 52
Highlight Tracking option, 53
Highlighting text characters. *See* Type tool, selecting with
Holes inside a path. *See* Compound Paths command
Hollow arrow. *See* Direct Selection tool

Horizontal
  color transitions, 24
  flipping/slanting of object, 24
Horizontal Only radio button, 388, 390
Horizontal Scale option, 196–198
Hyphenation. *See* Auto Hyphenate check box; Discretionary hyphen
Hyphenation Options preferences, 43–44, 208

I

Icons in dialog boxes, 31, 33
IFF (Interchange File Format), 76, 93
Ignore button, 70
Illustration windows, 17–18
  multiple, 69
  sizing, 46
Illustrations, 7
  magnifying, 8, 22
  with multiple views, 91
Illustrator 4.0 (for Windows), 74
Illustrator (graphics workshop program)
  compared with CorelDraw, 375
  compared with FreeHand, 69, 218, 375–376
  compared with PageMaker, 218
  compared with Photoshop, 5–9, 449
  compared with QuarkXPress, 218
  complemented by Photoshop, 9, 69. *See also* Photoshop (image-editing program)
  document-producing capability, 59
  EPS format. *See* EPS (Encapsulated PostScript) format
  history of, 4–5
  logicality of, 11, 13
  RAM required, 15
  Version 7, predictions regarding, 69
Image options, 706
Imageable area, 17–18
  moving within artboard, 25
Imagesetters, printing to, 694, 701, 717–718
Import File dialog box, 251

X

Z